THE GEBUSI

Lives Transformed in a Rainforest World

THE GEBUSI

Lives Transformed in a Rainforest World

Bruce Knauft
Emory University

Boston Burr Ridge, IL Dubuque, IA Madison, WI New York
San Francisco St. Louis Bangkok Bogotá Caracas Kuala Lumpur
Lisbon London Madrid Mexico City Milan Montreal New Delhi
Santiago Seoul Singapore Sydney Taipei Toronto

The McGraw·Hill Companies

Mc Graw Hill **Higher Education**

The Gebusi: Lives Transformed in a Rainforest World

Published by McGraw-Hill, a business unit of The McGraw-Hill Companies, Inc., 1221 Avenue of the Americas, New York, NY 10020.

ISBN 0-07-297263-7

1 2 3 4 5 6 7 8 9 0 DOC/DOC 0 9 8 7 6 5 4

Vice president and Editor-in-chief: *Emily Barrosse*
Publisher: *Phil Butcher*
Sponsoring editor: *Kevin Witt*
Marketing manager: *Dan Loch*
Project manager: *Mel Valentin*
Manuscript editor: *Thomas Briggs*
Art director: *Jeanne M. Schreiber*
Design manager: *Preston Thomas*
Cover designer: *Preston Thomas*
Interior designer: *Adriane Bosworth*
Art manager: *Robin Mouat*
Illustrator: *Mapping Specialists*
Production supervisor: *Randy Hurst*

The text was set in 10/12 Janson Text by TBH Typecast, Inc. and printed on acid-free, 45# New Era Matte by RR Donnelley, Crawfordsville.

Cover image: Courtesy of Bruce Knauft.

Library of Congress Cataloging-in-Publication Data

Knauft, Bruce M.

The Gebusi : lives transformed in a rainforest world / Bruce M. Knauft.

p. cm.

Includes bibliographical references and index.

ISBN 0-07-297263-7 (softcover)

1. Gebusi (Papua New Guinea people)—Social conditions. 2. Gebusi (Papua New Guinea people)—Cultural assimilation. 3. Gebusi (Papua New Guinea people)—Social life and customs. 4. Social change—Papua New Guinea. 5. Acculturation—Papua New Guinea. 6. Papua New Guinea—Social life and customs. I. Title.

DU740.42.K524 2005

305.89'912—dc22

2004053887

www.mhhe.com

For Eileen
Without whose help this book could not have been written

About the Author

Bruce Knauft is Samuel C. Dobbs Professor of Anthropology and Executive Director of the Institute for Comparative and International Studies at Emory University in Atlanta. He has taught a broad range of students, including many who have gone on to conduct anthropological fieldwork in diverse world areas. Author of six previous books and numerous journal articles and chapters, Professor Knauft has written extensively on topics and issues in cultural anthropology. He has been interested in the Gebusi people of Papua New Guinea since his first fieldwork among them in 1980–82.

Contents

List of Map, Figures, and Photographs

Map

Figures

Photographs

Web Site Categories

Note: A range of color photographs and captions for each of the following topics can be viewed on the Web site for this book at www.mhhe.com/knauft1.

Entry

- Geographic location of the Gebusi
- Lowland rainforest of interior New Guinea
- Landing at the Nomad Station

Introduction: In Search of Surprise

- Living with the Gebusi—1980 versus 1998

Chapter 1: Friends in the Forest

- First patrol in the rainforest
- The village of Yibihilu
- Typical villagers
- Good company among the Gebusi
- Our house in the village

Chapter 2: Rhythms of Survival

- The Gebusi longhouse
- Foraging and hunting
- Leisure time
- Making sago palm starch
- Forest lands and streams
- Gardening—horticulture
- Women's "carrying capacity"
- Health and disease
- Pigs
- Fieldwork

Chapter 3: Lives of Death

- Sickness, death, and mourning
- Central actors in a village crisis
- Burials and funerals
- Hosting angry visitors
- Central actors revisited

Chapter 4: Getting Along with Kin and Killers

- A married couple
- Sorcery inquest and kinship: a case study

Chapter 5: Spirits, Sex, and Celebration

- Male joking and cavorting
- The Gebusi dance costume
- A village affair
- Female joking and beauty

Chapter 6: Ultimate Splendor

- Preparing to be initiated
- Trials of manhood
- Initiates as red birds-of-paradise

- The biggest "attack"
- The dance of seduction
- Costumes on display
- The biggest feast
- Young women and men

Chapter 7: Reentry

- Arriving once more
- Individuals, before and after
- A new village, a new house
- Fieldwork revisited
- Moods of scenic color
- The Catholic Church
- Economy and time in transition
- School and church

Chapter 8: Yuway's Sacred Decision

- Yuway—1981 versus 1998
- The path of Christian conversion
- Experiencing church
- Modiay's sin and redemption
- A new kind of funeral

Chapter 9: Pennies and Peanuts, Rugby and Radios

- Women as market sellers
- Schooling for children
- Sports for men and boys
- Boys' drawings: "What I want to be in the future"
- Girls' drawings: "What I want to be in the future"

Chapter 10: Mysterious Romance, Marital Choice

- A traditional man in search of a wife
- Attempting a marriage by sister-exchange
- A modern married family

Chapter 11: Sayu's Dance and After

- Sayu—young child, adult man
- Sayu's traditional dance
- Economic change: the town of Kiunga
- Friends at home
- Rituals revisited
- Modern performance and body art
- National Independence Day: costume as diversity
- Dancing to a new beat

Chapter 12: Toward the End

- Remembering the place of the past
- Bruce's final feast
- Neo-traditions and modern festivity
- The ghost of the past in the present
- Friends I will miss

Preface

BACKGROUND

Anthropology is little without powerful portrayals of foreign peoples and cultures. For beginning students, the wonder of learning about different ways of life can be both thrilling and provocative. The range of human diversity both stretches our envelope of understanding and prods us to reconsider our own beliefs and practices. Over the years, a number of short books have filled this role in anthropology by exposing students to potent examples of cultural variety. Often, these works take the form of an ethnographic case study—a book-length description of a group of people who live in a foreign country or in underappreciated circumstances closer to home. For teaching purposes, these condensed ethnographies form useful complements and counterpoints to the textbooks that are commonly used in anthropology courses. By nature, textbooks tend to be expansive in scope but less nuanced in portraying individual societies or cultures. By contrast, this is just what a short ethnography is designed to do. But even short ethnographies can be densely detailed. In part, this is because authors want to impart as much information as possible. And in part, it's because an anthropologist's scholarly reputation can suffer if his or her work is not packed with description.

In the present book, I consider myself fortunate to swim against this tide. First, I have already had the opportunity to lay a scholarly foundation by writing a number of academic books and articles about both the Gebusi and their culture area in Melanesia, which lies to the north and northeast of Australia in the Pacific Ocean. Second, I have accumulated many experiences and documented many stories among the Gebusi that have not yet been published. Finally, I am fortunate that the Gebusi are—as I hope you will agree—an amazing, intriguing, fascinating, difficult, and quite wonderful people. As such, I feel privileged to write a book designed to capture poignant and sometimes dramatic aspects of Gebusi lives as well as of my own experiences when I lived among them.

Over time, I have come to believe that Gebusi experiences and my own provide insight into issues addressed in undergraduate anthropology courses. In addition to general topics such as subsistence, kinship, economics, politics, religion, and art, these include the aims and methods of anthropological fieldwork, the personal challenges and moral dilemmas of conducting ethnography, and the ways in which local people become enmeshed with wider influences and larger regions. Finally, and perhaps most importantly, because my experiences with the Gebusi have spanned a large arc of social and cultural transformation—from their remote isolation in the early 1980s to their active engagement with national and global lifestyles in the late 1990s—their development illustrates key issues in the study of social and cultural change.

During my adult life, this book has grown up with me, both personally and professionally. Over the past several years, it has been a pleasure for me to write it. I hope you will find it at turns both informative and enjoyable—and in the best of all worlds, both of these at once.

KEY FEATURES

This book contains a wide range of reference materials, instructional information, and links to Web-based photographs and text entries that have been specially designed for use by students and instructors.

Notes and References

For those who wish to check or remind themselves about the identity of an individual mentioned in the book, an alphabetical List of Persons in the endmatter provides this information. Further information about topics and issues discussed in the book can be found in the Notes section that follows the main text. For easy reference, main topics are **boldfaced** in the Notes. Readers can skim these boldface entries to find specific topics of interest and may also find information concerning a specific reference or passage in the main text by consulting the "Notes to pages X–Y" indicators at the top of each page of the Notes section. In addition to providing contextual information, the Notes contain wide-ranging citations concerning broader topics and issues in the comparative study of societies and cultures. These sources are compiled and listed in the References section at the end of the book. Taken together, the endnotes and their references can guide students and teachers who wish to use this book for developing paper topics or completing course assignments—as well as for conducting independent investigations or simply to satisfy the reader's curiosity regarding practices or beliefs described in the main text.

For those who wish to pursue deeper investigation concerning the Gebusi specifically, principal publications concerning them are summarized toward the beginning of the notes and are listed with full citations in the References. These works contain detailed accounts of many aspects of Gebusi society and culture as well as comparative and theoretical assessments of their broader significance.

Topical Guide for Instructors

For teachers, a Topical Guide for Instructors is included in the endmatter of this book. This provides a topical teaching outline of the book's chapters plus a correspondence list between the chapters of this book and the chapters of five commonly used anthropology textbooks. As the guide suggests, *The Gebusi* can be read in chapter-by-chapter conjunction with major textbooks. The book can also be read as a whole and then referred to by topic in conjunction with lectures or assignments that pertain to a specific chapter or section of a given textbook. The page edges of the Topical Guide for Instructors have been shaded to facilitate easy reference.

Web Site Image Library

Of special note is the Web Site Image Library that has been configured for students and instructors who use this book. More than three hundred quality photographs of the Gebusi that my wife and I took are posted in thumbnail and in enlarged format in the book's Web pages, along with contextualizing descriptions and further ethnographic information. Organized by chapter for easy reference, the photos and descriptive information allow readers to undertake a visual journey into the lives and practices of the Gebusi. The photographs follow the development of individuals, events, and practices as they emerge within and between sections of the book. A categorical table of contents for the Gebusi Web pages can be found following this book's own table of contents. The corpus of Gebusi photos and descriptions is also indexed by both topic and name. As such, the student or instructor can easily locate images that pertain to a specific anthropological topic or to follow the moods and changes of a specific individual over time.

Together, the combination of photos and related textual information provides what we hope will be a new avenue for Web-based ethnographic instruction and student interest. The McGraw-Hill Web pages for *The Gebusi* are viewable with unrestricted access at http://www.mhhe.com/knauft1.

Sound Clips

Selected sound clips of Gebusi music can be found under "Gebusi Research" on the author's home page (type "Bruce Knauft" in <http://www.google.com>).

ACKNOWLEDGMENTS

It is hard to express the personal and professional debt that I feel toward my many Gebusi friends and acquaintances. Deepest thanks go to Sayu Silap, Didiga Imbo, and Yuway Wapsiayk, and to Gwabi Gigi, who in 1998 lent me his new house to live in. I also acknowledge aid and support in both 1980–82 and 1998 from officials and staff at the Nomad Station and the Catholic Church; my fieldwork among Gebusi would have been much more arduous without their help. In 1998, I was aided in many ways by the local constables, teachers, pastors and the Acting Area Administrator, Sam Gaiworo.

As anthropologists are aware, field research, especially in remote locations, is difficult if not impossible to complete without financial assistance from funding and granting agencies. I gratefully acknowledge funding for my field research among the Gebusi in 1980–82 from the U.S. National Science Foundation, the U.S. National Institutes of Mental Health, and the Rackham Graduate School at the University of Michigan, Ann Arbor. In 1998, my fieldwork and its write-up were funded by a U.S. Department of Education Fulbright Faculty Research Grant, the Wenner-Gren Foundation, the Harry Frank Guggenheim Foundation, the U.S. National Science Foundation, and the University Research Committee of Emory University. Final revisions to the book manuscript were completed in 2003 during my initial months as an National Endowment for the Humanities Fellow at The School of American Research, Santa Fe, New Mexico—an organization that has provided me generous support and a wonderful working environment.

Numerous persons have read and commented on drafts of this book, and I owe them all great thanks. Of particular note are Joanna Davidson, Edward (Ted) Fischer, Carla Jones, Stuart Kirsch, Burt and Ruth Knauft, Eileen Marie Knauft, Donna Murdock, Ana Schaller de la Cova, Holly Wardlow, and Paige West. The anthropology editor at McGraw-Hill, Kevin Witt, has been wonderfully supportive during all phases of this project, and the comments of five reviewers whom he enlisted were a great help to me in revising the manuscript. Thanks are due Shannon Gattens for her work on the Gebusi Web pages. Thomas Briggs merits special recognition for his work as a superior copy editor. All shortcomings remain my own. Small portions of this book overlap in substance though not in exact wording with one of my previous works, *Exchanging the Past*, published by the University of Chicago Press in 2002.

I owe a special debt to my undergraduate and graduate students at Emory University. They have given me the courage not simply to teach anthropology from the heart but to go back to the field and learn it all over again.

This book is dedicated to my wife and colleague of twenty-five years, Eileen Marie Knauft. Eileen has been my constant partner and spiritual companion, including during the six months of 1998 when I was in Papua New Guinea and she could not be physically with me. To this is added the substantive ethnographic information that she collected exclusively with Gebusi women during 1980–82. Some of this information has been published under her maiden name, Eileen Cantrell, as listed in the References at the end of this book. Virtually all the photographs of the Gebusi from 1980–82 were taken by Eileen—both those published in this book and those posted on the book's Web pages. As a complement to the photos of Gebusi that I myself took in 1998, hers constitute about one-half of the total images both in this book and on the Web site. Her permission to publish these remarkable early-period photographs of the Gebusi is gratefully acknowledged.

Without Eileen's help, insight, support, and continuing cooperation, this work could not have been completed.

Entry

IT LOOKS SO GRAND from a thousand feet up, the forest glowing deep, green, and vast. The broccoli-tops of the trees form a huge and endless carpet, an emerald skin guarding worlds of life within. You look down to see two blue-brown ribbons of water etching through the forest. You follow them through the window of your tiny plane as they snake toward each other and merge in gentle delight. Below, in the nestled crook of these two rivers, you look closer, to where the green shifts from dark to bright, from old forest to new growth that is repeatedly cut down but always sprouting anew. Inside this lime-green patch, you see a score of white squares arranged neatly in two rows. Ten line evenly on one side while their partners face them across a broad lawn, metal roofs glinting in the strong sun. You recall how these structures were built as homes by early Australian patrol officers, so colonial and rugged, trekking in across the swamps and rivers. Adjacent to the houses is the rectangle they laid out, flat and long, its grass kept short and trim. Your plane will swoop down on it now, the gilded spine of that book you have come so far to read. But its content is not what you thought it would be, it is not a text at all. As you descend, its meaning becomes the faces that line the airstrip, bright and eager as their skin is dark. They watch expectantly as you land. You open the door to a searing blast of heat and humanity. Welcome to the Nomad Station.

Introduction
In Search of Surprise

Like most anthropologists, I was unprepared for what I would find. In 1980, Eileen and I had been married for just a few months when we flew from Michigan across the Pacific. We were going to live for two years in a remote area of the rainforest north of Australia, in the small nation of Papua New Guinea. I was twenty-six years old and had never been west of Oregon. I had no idea what changes lay in store either for us or for the people we were going to live with.

Well into the twentieth century, the large and rugged tropical island of New Guinea harbored people who had had little, if any, contact with outsiders. In the area where we were going, initial contact between some groups and Westerners had not occurred until the 1960s. The four hundred and fifty people whom we encountered had a name and a language that were not yet known to anthropologists. As individuals, the Gebusi (geh-BOO-see) were amazing—at turns regal, funny, infuriating, entrancing, romantic, violent, and immersed in a world of towering trees and foliage, heat and rain, and mosquitoes and illness. Their lives were as different from ours as they could be. Practices and beliefs that were practically lore in anthropology were alive and well: ritual dancers in eye-popping costumes, entranced spirit mediums, all-night song-fests and divinations, rigid separation between men and women, and striking sexual practices. A mere shadow to us at first, the dark side of Gebusi lives also became real: death inquests, sorcery accusations, village fights, and wife-beating. In the past, cannibalism had been common, and we later discovered that a woman from our village had been eaten a year and a half prior to our arrival. As I gradually realized, the killing of sorcery suspects had produced one of the highest rates of homicide in the cross-cultural record.

The challenge of living and working with the Gebusi turned our own lives into something of an extreme sport. But in the crucible of personal experience, the Gebusi became not only human to us but also, despite their tragic violence, wonderful people. With wit and passion, they lived rich and festive lives. Vibrant and friendly, they turned life's cruelest ironies into their best jokes, and its biggest tensions into their most elaborate fantasies. Their humor, spirituality, deep togetherness, and raw pragmatism made them, for the most part, great fun to be with. I have never felt more included in a social world. And what personalities! To lump them together as simply "Gebusi" is as bland as it would be to describe David Letterman, Michael Jordan, Arnold Schwarzenegger, and Hillary Rodham Clinton as simply "American." The Gebusi were not simply "a society" or "a culture"; they were an incredible group of unique individuals.

Anthropology is little if not the discovery of the human unexpected. I had gone to the Gebusi's part of the rainforest to study political decision making. Armed with a tape recorder and a typewriter, I planned to document how communications with spirits during all-night séances produced concrete results—the decision to launch a hunting expedition, conduct a ritual, fight an enemy, or accuse a sorcerer. But spirit séances more closely resembled an MTV soundtrack than a political council. The spirit medium sang of spirit women who flew about seductively and teased men in the audience. The male listeners joked back and also bantered loudly with one another. In the bargain, their own social relations were intensified, patched up, and cemented. That community decisions could actually emerge during the night-long séance seemed almost beside the point. And yet, the results were sometimes really important, including one spiritual pronouncement that ended up forcing some villagers to leave and form a new settlement. Sorcerers could be scapegoated and threatened with death; people could be accused or found innocent of crimes. Politics, friendship, and side-splitting humor combined with sexual teasing, spirituality, and conflict in ways that made my head spin.

You might imagine the first time I tried to translate a Gebusi spirit séance from one of my tape recordings. I sat with male informants in all seriousness as the recorder played. At first, they were astonished to hear their own voices. But they quickly shifted from amazement to howling laughter. Then they attempted, image by laborious image, line by laborious line, to explain the humor that I had committed to tape. With no reliable interpreters, I was learning their language "monolingually." As it turned out, the spiritual poetry of Gebusi séance songs bore as little relation to their normal speech as rock lyrics do to the sentences of an anthropology textbook. The Gebusi responded to my confusion by gleefully repeating the jokes that I had recorded. Although I was unable to turn nighttime humor into daytime clarity, I certainly gave the men a good laugh—and fueled my own uncertainty. Seeing our strange interaction, Eileen asked the women what was going on. She was told that many of the songs I was trying to write down were "no good" or "rotten."

For the most part, Gebusi were not only jovial but considerate, quick to apologize, and adept at making the best of difficult situations. I ended up liking most of them a lot. But floundering in their culture, what was I do with my own sense of morality, ethics, gender, and justice?

Cultural anthropology has often been driven by competing desires. Anthropologists have long been dedicated to appreciating the diverse customs and beliefs of the world's peoples. In the Western tradition, this goal was emphasized during the eighteenth and nineteenth centuries by European scholars such as Giambattista Vico and Johannes Herder. Later, it was emphasized by the "founding father" of American anthropology, Franz Boas. A similar theme runs through one of the oldest books in the Western world—Herodotus's *History.* Writing in the early fifth century B.C.E. for a Greek audience, Herodotus described in largely appreciative terms the different customs of foreign peoples, such as the Persians and Egyptians.

In modern times, cultural anthropologists have been passionate to understand foreign peoples through the lens of their own customs and beliefs. Why should Western ways of life be considered superior? Anthropologists are mindful of many injustices caused by Western societies when they historically "discovered" and then exploited or enslaved people from other parts of the world. Many regions—North and South America, Oceania, most of Africa, and large parts of Asia—were conquered militarily and then exploited politically or economically by Western nations, companies, or corporations. These incursions have deeply influenced social relations within foreign societies as well as between them. Although subordination and stigma based on gender, age, race, ethnic identity, and religion have long existed in many parts of the world, these have often been fueled or supported—wittingly or unwittingly—by Western influence.

Much as anthropologists appreciate cultural diversity, then, we also see life in the crosshairs of inequality and domination. And though inequities can be linked to outside forces, they do not always depend on them. Among Gebusi, the domination of women and the scapegoating of sorcerers grate roughly against the splendor of Gebusi ritual performance, spirit belief, and communal festivity. These paradoxes cannot be explained away by the impact of colonialism or Western intrusion. It is often hard for anthropologists to reconcile the wonder of cultural diversity with the problems caused by inequity and subjugation. Our mission is not to resolve these tensions so much as to expose and understand them.

Ultimately, the Gebusi presented surprises beyond the good company of their social life or the violence of their sorcery beliefs and gender practices. It was only later, after returning from the field, that I realized how rare it was even in New Guinea for indigenous customs to flourish with so little inhibition. But my biggest surprise came in 1998, when I returned to live and work with the Gebusi. I suspected that many new influences had swept through their lives during the sixteen years that I had been gone. I readied myself to document these changes and to take them at face value. But how could I have known what lay in store?

By choice, my old community had picked up and moved from the deep forest to the outskirts of the Nomad Station, which boasts an airstrip and a government post. Previously isolated in their rainforest settlements, the Gebusi were now part of a multiethnic community in and around the station at Nomad, which includes more than a thousand persons speaking five different languages. In their new setting, my Gebusi friends were now stalwart Christians worshipping at one of three local churches—Catholic, Evangelical Protestant, or Seventh Day Adventist. Their children learned to read and write at the Nomad Community School for seven hours a day, five days a week. Gebusi men and boys organized their own rugby and soccer team, the "Gasumi Youths," which played supervised matches against rival groups each weekend on the government ballfield. On Tuesdays and Fridays, Gebusi women lugged heavy net bags of food from the forest and from their gardens to the Nomad Station market in hopes of earning a few coins. New crops such as manioc, peanuts, and pineapples sprouted in their gardens. Sweet potatoes were now a starch staple, and tubers were also grown for sale at the market.

Gebusi entertainment had also changed. On Friday and Saturday nights, young people tried to find a "party," "video night," or "disco" in the general area of the Nomad Station. Fast dancing to cassette tapes of rock music was now the rage. Traditional spirit séances had been replaced by modern music sung to the accompaniment of guitars and ukeleles. When children drew pictures of what they wanted to be when they grew up, their pages filled with colorful portraits of pilots, policemen, soldiers, heavy machine operators, nurses, teachers, rock singers, and Christians in heaven. Though traditional dances still represented a kind of history or folklore, indigenous rituals were rarely staged in the villages. Given the decline of spirit mediumship, the Gebusi had no effective way to communicate with their traditional spirits. Death inquests and sorcery practices had been replaced by Christian funerals and burials. Violence against sorcery suspects was practically nonexistent. The Gebusi themselves said that they had exchanged their old spirits for new ones associated with Christianity and with a more developed way of life. In the process, however, they had become subordinate to outsiders who were in charge of activities and institutions associated with the Nomad Station.

If Gebusi were uncommonly traditional in 1980–82, they have since, in their own distinct way, become surprisingly modern and acculturated. Not all peoples change so quickly, of course. In fact, Gebusi may now be almost as unusual in their openness to outside influences as they were previously for being beyond their direct reach. These changes seem all the more striking given that the Nomad Station is still inaccessible by road; outsiders and goods can reach it only via expensive airplane flights. From above, the Nomad Station looks largely the way it did in 1980. The region has no local resources to spur economic growth or a cash economy, and out-migration is still negligible.

Why, then, have many Gebusi moved near the Nomad Station and altered their way of life? Beyond relatively small changes in local government and the regional economy, their transformation stems in significant part from new aspirations and beliefs. These fuel Gebusi desire to participate in church, school, market, and government initiatives—and to subordinate themselves to the outsiders who control these local activities and institutions.

My fortune has been to live with a remote people who maintained amazingly rich traditions but then sought out and developed a locally modern way of life. The experiences of Gebusi can't, and don't, reflect those of other peoples around the world. But they do illustrate how people develop their own forms of contemporary life even in remote areas. The process of being or becoming modern is a global phenomenon, but it is neither simple nor singular. Cultural change in the contemporary world is as diverse as the colors that refract through a prism. By seeing these refractions, we can understand how people in various regions share increasingly modern experiences but develop in unique ways. Some peoples resist outside influences more than Gebusi have done. Others blend old customs with new ones more readily than Gebusi have seemed to do. Some peoples or regions agitate for their own autonomy while others accept national or international authority. Through these alternative processes, people respond to the economic, political, military, and religious influences that affect their local area. To study these developments is to engage an anthropology of cultural change and social transformation.

Given their distinctive path of tradition and change, the Gebusi provide an intriguing framework for viewing topics commonly covered in anthropology courses. These include the growing or gathering of food; the ways in which kinship organizes people into groups; patterns of social and economic exchange; features of leadership, politics, and dispute; religious beliefs and spiritual practices; issues of sex and gender; the construction of ethnicity; the impact of colonialism and nationalism; and, through it all, the dynamics of sociocultural change. The first part of this book portrays these developments among the Gebusi in 1980–82; the second part examines them in 1998. Rather then describing the Gebusi in general terms, I present them as individuals whose lives have unfolded along with my own over the course of eighteen years.

My purpose in writing this book has been both simpler and more difficult than providing a general account of Gebusi culture. Rather, my goal has been to let the Gebusi as people come alive to the reader, to portray their past and their present, and to connect the dramatic changes they have undergone with those in my own life and in contemporary anthropology.

PART ONE

1980–82

CHAPTER 1

The author snaps fingers in a welcoming line of adult Gebusi men. (PHOTO: Eileen Marie Knauft)

Friends in the Forest

THE BANANAS WERE ALL piled up, hot and grimy. Steam floated up from the pile—as if the air around us could have gotten any hotter. Some were stout as well as long, but most were slender, and a few were quite tiny. But their variety in dozens was a mystery to us then. All of them had been carefully scraped, but long strands of soot and globs of charcoal remained from their time in the fire.

What to do with this mound of starchy bananas, presented to us so formally in that first village? Kukudobi villagers had probably not seen a white person since 1975, five years before our arrival. At that time, the Australian patrol officers who had tramped to major settlements once a year and counted the local inhabitants suddenly left for good—along with the other Australians. Like a tempest in the forest, our arrival had certainly caused a hubbub. Children fled and men gulped with curious excitement. Emerging from under the trees, the four local men who were carrying our supplies took the lead, and we followed them ("When in Rome . . .") to the central longhouse. We sat down cross-legged, and a flood of villagers did likewise around us.

They must have done the cooking quickly or known about our arrival in advance, because it wasn't long before the smoldering stack of starch was brought in on a palm leaf platter and laid down with gusto in front of us. I was suddenly the focus of intense public silence. Short men with bamboo tubes through their noses looked on from all around. I was too embarrassed to check with our carriers or even with Eileen about what I should do next. Everything was heat and stickiness. I took one of the sooty plantains and began to munch on it, trying to show appreciation, and Eileen did the same. The bananas were dry, but we forced ourselves to chew through one and pick up another. The people around us started to grin as we swallowed their food. Our progress was slow, however, and, judging from the size of the platter, our task was ultimately hopeless. Using my hands, I signaled that the pile of food was large, my stomach was small, and many people could certainly be fed. What a relief when they broke into pleasant conversation and stretched out their arms, sharing the bananas throughout the longhouse. We had apparently passed our first test.

Anthropologists often talk about "the gift," especially in Melanesia. How people put hard work and sweat, good intentions and hopes into tangible things that they give to one another speaks volumes about human connection. Gifts are at once a social economy and a materialized emotion. As Marcel Mauss suggested, gifts reflect and reinforce social bonds between givers and recipients. In American society, gifts at Christmastime are loaded with meanings that are reflected in whom we give presents to, how much thought and investment we put into each gift, and what reactions or returns we get in response.

As in many parts of New Guinea, Gebusi believed that gifts should be given to visitors who were peaceful. Their most basic gift was the fruit of their most regular work, as well as their primary source of nutrition: starchy cooked bananas. Well beyond the giving of basic food, however, material exchange was linked to human connection. Gebusi relationships were defined by the things that one gave or did not give to others. Later on, I established an "exchange name" with each man in our village—based on something that one of us had given to or shared with the other. Gusiayn was my "bird-egg," and Iwayb was my "Tahitian chestnut." Based on my own gifts, Yuway became my "fishing line," and Halowa my "salt." Whenever we saw each other, we called each other by these names, and our relationship was referred to similarly by others: "Here comes your 'bird egg'; there goes your 'salt'." To have a social identity and to have given and shared something that was memorable were one and the same.

In that first village of Kokudobi, Eileen and I were fortunate to have accepted those starchy bananas; we ate some and shared the rest with others. It was a simple act, but symbolic in ways we could not have anticipated. The patrol officers before us had also come to forest villages—once a year, to count heads for the colonial census. But they had brought along their servants or "houseboys" to cook the tins of meat and bags of rice they had hauled in. In our case, word had already spread that we were husband and wife looking for a rainforest village to live in, and that we ate local food. So we received a hopeful reception of cooked bananas. The other features of traditional welcome were not yet on our horizon—the calling out of gift and kin names, the hearty snapping of fingers with each host, the dramatic sharing of smoke-filled tobacco pipes among men, the drinking of water from twelve-foot-long bamboo tubes, and the palaver that lasted until the hosts arrived with great whoops to present more food. But even in that first village, the lead card of social life, the giving of food, had been extended, and we had accepted. It was a good start.

As we soon found out, all the villages we visited wanted us to live with them. Though bossy, the Australians had provided a trickle of outside goods, and when they left, the trickle had dried up. Local people craved the trade items they now associated with us as white-skinned outsiders: cloth, salt, beads, fishing hooks, soap, and, especially, metal tools. When contrasted to a blunt stone adze, a steel ax goes through a rainforest tree like a knife through butter. Metal axes made it easy for people to clear bigger garden plots, grow more food, and build stronger houses. Metal knives and machetes found many further uses, from skinning animals to clearing weeds.

Besides stoking a passion for trade goods, the Australians left a political legacy that the Gebusi roundly appreciated: they pacified the Bedamini. More numerous and aggressive than the Gebusi or their other neighbors, the Bedamini people had traditionally sent war parties deep into neighboring areas. Their tactics were brutally efficient: surround an enemy longhouse at dawn, set it ablaze, and slaughter the inhabitants as they fled. Gebusi had been repeatedly victimized by these raids; in some cases, whole villages had been wiped out. Not infrequently, the Bedamini would cut up the bodies of those they had slain and carry them home for feasting. It is important to distinguish rumors of cannibalism from the actual practice. But its occurrence has been well documented and admitted among Bedamini—and by Gebusi themselves following the killing of sorcery suspects.

Being but 450 people against the Bedamini's 3,000, and with fewer residents in most of their settlements, Gebusi were no match for Bedamini warriors. If Australian patrol officers had not stepped in and stopped Bedamini raids, the Gebusi might have been only a remnant people by the time we arrived. As it was, thirteen years of colonial influence had gradually curtailed Bedamini expansion. In 1980, Gebusi were still visibly scared of the Bedamini, but they were seldom killed and no longer massacred by them. Despite, or perhaps because of, colonial intervention against their enemies, Gebusi themselves had rarely felt the boot of colonial domination. Australian patrol officers had been rough and bossy, but the benefits of their military intervention far outweighed the costs of their brief annual visits. Among Gebusi, the officers' main objectives were to update the local census and to lecture the villagers, via interpreters, about keeping the village clean and living in harmony with one another. The Australians viewed the Gebusi as victims rather than aggressors and as "quiet tractable people"; they seldom intervened in Gebusi affairs. Hence the irony that, even as the Bedamini were being pacified by armed patrols, the Gebusi were left alone to continue sorcery inquests, executions, and even cannibalism within their own communities. Living deep and scattered in the rainforest, they concealed their own actions from colonial interference.

Though the Gebusi in 1980 appeared to be a pristine people, in fact they were not. What we took to be "traditional" had flourished in the wake of the Australian pacification of the Bedamini and in the larger clearings, gardens, and villages that the Gebusi had produced with steel tools. Because Gebusi associated physical growth and social development with spiritual regeneration, the benefits of Bedamini pacification and of steel implements affirmed their religious values as well as their social life. Like streams that converge in the forest, material production and spiritual reproduction came increasingly together in major rituals, especially during the initiation of young people into adulthood. Gebusi lives swelled with the combined power of religious, sexual, and social force. Ironically, then, colonial intrusion gave the Gebusi the freedom to develop many of their own customs and beliefs. In some ways, Gebusi had become even more "Gebusi-like" than they had been before! Although the Gebusi seemed unacculturated, their traditions underscored the importance of changes all around them. A tribal powerhouse had been laid low while the neighboring Gebusi had been left to cultivate their own customs. By the 1980s, Gebusi resented Bedamini not so much for their former raids as for being recipients of government development projects that the Gebusi wanted for themselves.

That the Gebusi combined an exuberant tradition with a desire for outsiders made them a perfect fit for Eileen and me. Little wonder that we were enamored of them or that they wanted us for themselves. At first, however, we weren't interested.

Our journey had begun with a blank spot on a map. That was where my graduate advisor and I had thought, back at the University of Michigan, that I would find the most fascinating people. The largest scale maps then available were produced by the U.S. Army—in case even the remotest parts of the globe needed military intervention. The map of Papua New Guinea's Western Province showed an unknown space that stretched across a swampy rainforest north of the Tomu River. The two of us thought that the culture of the people who lived there could be roughly triangulated on the basis of what was known about groups that lived twenty-five to forty miles away in different directions. There was no name for the peoples of the Tomu River, but I talked by phone to a missionary who had completed some aerial survey work in the area. He thought that the closest people were probably the "Kramo." Armed with this information, I obtained funding from the U.S. National Science Foundation and the U.S. National Institutes of Health to study political consensus formation led by spirit mediums among people called the Kramo in a remote rainforest in Papua New Guinea's Western Province.

But there was a good reason for the blank spot on the map: no one lived there. Eileen and I finally accepted this fact after leaving Kukudobi and trudging for what seemed like forever to the distant village of Honabi, at the extreme edge of the settlements of the Honibo ethnic group. There, the inhabitants told us consistently, and in as many ways as our inadequate language would allow, that there was nothing farther ahead of us but swamp and mosquitoes, both of which we had already endured to our limit. They also informed us that the few people, called the Kabasi, who had previously lived in this area had deserted it and gone to live near a crocodile skin trading post well to the east. Even if we had wanted to continue our trek into their erstwhile territory, our four carriers would not have gone with us. Our trail had ended. In professional terms, we had traveled to Papua New Guinea on doctoral research grants to study people whom we couldn't find or who didn't exist (see map 1).

Sensing our uncertainty and perhaps our fear, the Honibo people brightly insisted that we stay and live with them instead. Though they claimed that they had a tradition of entranced spirit singing, their assertions were hedged with ambivalence. When we probed deeper, they also admitted that they typically abandoned their village for several months during the dry season, split into tiny groups, and foraged for food even deeper in the rainforest. As the evening grew longer and the mosquitoes bit harder, the prospect of adopting their lifestyle for two years seemed more dreadful than admitting failure. Not knowing what else to do, we opted to trudge back to the Nomad Station via the village that our carriers lived in, which was not altogether out of the way. The more we found out about this impending stop, the more interested we became. By this time, our carriers had become real

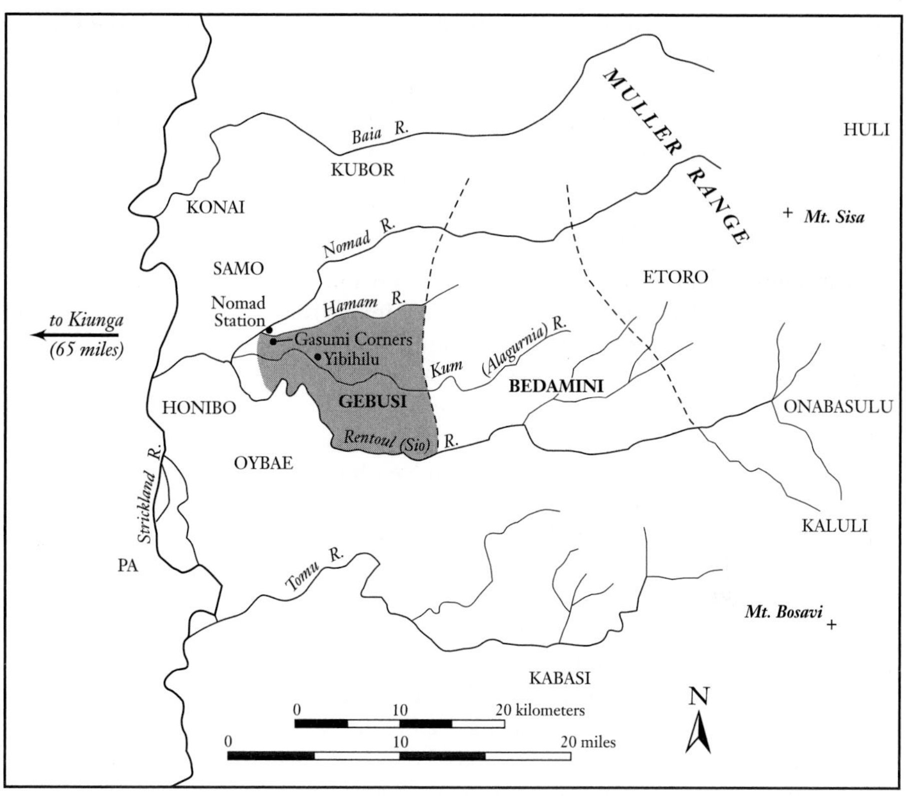

people to us. Yuway was a wonderfully decent young man, as sensitive as he was tall and strong for a Gebusi. He had a spontaneous sense of concern, interest, and patience even though we couldn't yet communicate verbally. He would wait to help Eileen and me over slippery log bridges, and he usually volunteered to shoulder the heaviest load. Nogo never said much, but he was as sinewy and dependable as a tree, and he was always alert. Wahi was our nominal interpreter, and though his translations ultimately proved more troublesome than helpful, he was socially and physically agile. Finally there was Swiman, older than his unmarried companions by half a generation but more muscled than they. He would flash a captivating smile under his impish hooked nose and pepper his remarks with articulate bursts that, given the reactions he got from the other three, convinced us that he was both very funny and very smart. As Wahi informed us, Swiman was also a spirit medium who held communal séances on a regular basis.

When we finally reached their village of Yibihilu, the "place of the deep waters," we thought we had reached the local version of paradise. We had stumbled for days through a sea of foliage, mud, and vines under a closed rainforest canopy. We felt like the miniature children in *Honey, I Shrunk the Kids!* as they navigated enormous obstacles in a galactic backyard of foliage. I yearned to look up and out, to see more than the next hidden root that could send us sprawling. The "place of the deep waters," by contrast, was perched on a forty-foot bluff overlooking a serpentine bend in the Kum River. The porch of the longhouse extended out over a canyon through which the river rushed before pooling in a serene basin some hundred yards wide and across which we could see a crocodile lazing in the sun. Farther downstream, the watercourse was calm enough to be traveled by canoe—which was far preferable to tromping through the muddy forest. At dusk, the sky above the river became a breathtaking sunset. The villagers would stop and stare. *Bubia maysum*—"The crimson is being laid down."

If the village seemed majestic, the people were even better. Having learned more about us from our four carriers in five minutes that the other villages had in five days, their kin and friends gave us the kind of warm welcome, especially in such a remote place, that made us feel on top of the world rather than at its end. As the traumas and troubles of our journey were discussed to the tiniest detail, the villagers laughed good-naturedly. That we were already trying to speak their language—however haltingly—was widely and enthusiastically noted. That we ate local food and that I had somehow carried my own backpack, which the men enjoyed trying on, were also taken as positive signs. But the greatest bonus was that Eileen was present. White women had rarely been seen by the Gebusi, and probably never in Yibihilu. Eileen shared food and laughter with the women and played with the children. They were ecstatic and responded in kind. If the men "had" me, the women took Eileen into their own world.

In remarkably short stead, our physical presence, our possessions, and our desire to speak the local tongue seemed to paint us as paragons of goodness, a gold mine of goods, and a three-ringed circus of entertainment rolled into one. Our hands were shaken, fingers snapped, and bellies gorged with countless gifts of food. Everyone seemed quite genuinely to want our friendship. And if our reception was anything less than overwhelming, we were too euphoric to notice. As if we needed further encouragement, Swiman held an all-night spirit séance. Word of our presence had drawn villagers from surrounding hamlets. Given the convergence of so many people and the surge of good feelings, a songfest of celebration was almost inevitable. The stars shone as they do only when there is no competing light for hundreds of miles. The songs of the men swelled as the silhouette of the forest canopy loomed over us in the moonlight. Beneath the glow, the men's deep harmonies echoed through the village as if in a wild cathedral. The music was different from and more amazing than any I had ever heard. I knew that the Gebusi believed in a whole realm of forest spirits and unseen places that come alive through the songs of the spirit medium. But as the sound washed over me, I knew almost nothing of its meaning. In the moment, this only added to the mystery and splendor of the Gebusi cosmos—a world of wonder I had come to explore.

There was so much that we didn't know about the Gebusi at first—including their name. Our ethnographic maps and the missionary who had told us about the "Kramo" had placed a group called the "Bibo" at our present location. But the people of Yibihilu found this terrifically funny. They brought us a large starchy banana and indicated that this was the only "bibo" in their territory—one of their three dozen varieties of plantains. There were no people called "Bibo." They said in no uncertain terms that their own identity, and also their language, was "Gebusi."

The discoveries of fieldwork had already brought us full circle. Eileen and I had gone halfway around the world to study a Kramo people who didn't exist. We had projected their presence based on our incomplete maps and our imaginations. But the people we did find—and came to like so quickly—were, at least in academic name, an undiscovered group. As green and insecure as we were at the time, this was a comfort. In retrospect, though, our nominal "discovery" exposed as much about ourselves as it did about the people we were living with: it revealed our Western drive to label other peoples and to project onto them our own sense of discovery. Like many anthropologists, we were starting to learn new things about our own way of life at the same time, and in many respects for the very reason that we were trying to reach out and understand the life of others.

Beyond the Gebusi's name, we also quickly encountered one of their central concepts—one that took much longer to understand. With predictable difficulty, we had been trying to explain exactly why we had come to the rainforest. Villagers were especially curious about this because we didn't fit the mold of whites they had previously encountered or heard about. Were we patrol officers who ordered people around and then disappeared for another year? No. Were we those white people they had heard about but never seen who held up black books and exhorted villagers not to dance or be initiated but to sing to a new spirit instead? No, not that either. Then why had we come? We tried to communicate that we wanted to learn and speak their language, to understand their songs, to watch their dances, to join them at their feasts—in short, to be with them as they lived and learn what they were like. In a flash, they seemed to grasp our meaning: we wanted to learn their *kogwayay*. They appeared so certain of this that we had no choice or desire but to agree with them. Of course, we had no idea what *kogwayay* referred to. In truth, though, they were entirely correct.

Kogwayay is—or at least was in 1980–82—the single word that best describes the heart of Gebusi culture. In a way, the term even represents their concept of culture itself—their notion of beliefs, practices, and styles of living that are unique to them as a people. At one level, *kogwayay* refers to customs and beliefs that make the Gebusi different from other people. As Gebusi themselves use the term, it refers especially to their distinctive traditions of dancing, singing, and body decoration. But what is the term's deeper meaning? The Gebusi themselves were not much help here. For them, *kogwayay* was a catchall marker of cultural distinction rather than a tool for dissecting it.

When you think about it, it's not surprising that people have a hard time explaining concepts that are central to their culture. Such meanings are often seen as "beyond words." How easy would it be for your average American, Canadian, or Englishman to define and explain what "love" is to someone who had never heard of this term? In the case of *kogwayay*, we were fortunate that the word breaks down into three distinct units of meaning, what linguists call morphemes: *kog*, *wa*, and *yay*. *Kog* conveys "togetherness," "friendship," and "similarity." These meanings reflected the collective and communal nature of Gebusi life. Gebusi almost always preferred to do things with as many other people as possible, and they hated being alone; they were the opposite of loners. The *wa* component of the word is the Gebusi root of *wa-la*, "to talk." It refers to pleasant dialogues and conversations that are roundly shared. This is what the men did in the longhouse at night—they "*wa*-lad" by sharing news and gossip, joking, fantasizing, and telling stories around the small yellow glow of the resin lantern. It was the Gebusi equivalent of the late-night talk that echoes through the halls of a college dorm. Hour after hour and evening after evening, I came to realize how rare it was for the Gebusi to get angry with one another in these gabfests. Disagreements were tempered by friendly smiles; embarrassments were covered by jokes and shifts of conversation.

Yay supplied the exuberant conclusion to *kog-wa-yay*, its exclamation point. Particularly for males, to *yay* or to *kay* is to cheer, yell, joke, and cry out as loudly and happily as possible—and preferably in unison with other men. These yells have bodily meaning as well. When a Gebusi called out in concert with those around him, his "breath-heart" *(solof)* pushed out and mingled with that of others. To *yay* or *kay* is to send forth and unite human spiritual energy; it is a vital assertion of collective life.

Taken together, what do *kog*, *wa*, and *yay* mean? And why should we care? No single English word captures their essence—and this fact is important. As anthropologists, we were charged with learning and conveying concepts that are important to other people even when they exceed our initial understanding. *Kogwayay* clearly was important to the Gebusi. The word was frequently used and talked about, it evoked strong feelings, and it was highly elaborated in central rituals and ceremonies. In Gebusi culture, *kogwayay* was what anthropologist Sherry Ortner has more generally called a "key symbol." Collectively, the three meanings of the word—togetherness, talk, and cheering—conveyed core Gebusi values of happy social unity, of living in good company with one another. And *kogwayay* permeated Gebusi social life. It was evident on a daily basis and reached a climax at important events such as feasts, dances, spirit séances, and the initiation of teenagers into adulthood.

Although *kogwayay* was a powerful and deeply held concept, it did not stand alone. It highlighted the positive side of Gebusi culture, the bright side of their moon. Most peoples try to depict themselves in a good and favorable light, and the Gebusi were no exception. If you were asked to name central values in American and other Western societies, you might mention concepts such as "freedom," "individuality," "love of country," "economic success," "love," and "family values." Of course, we all know that these are sometimes ideals more than realities. Many marriages end in divorce; families can be shackled by poverty; and discrimination based on race, ethnicity, sex, or age can be as deeply ingrained as it is illegal. A critic from another culture might argue that American society is cutthroat, egotistical, hedonistic, imperialistic, and much less equal or free than we like to believe. If culture is an assertion of ideals and values, these can sometimes serve to cover up problems or difficulties. In this sense, culture is a double-edged sword of beliefs and representations. On the one hand, it emphasizes values and ideals that are often, if not typically, good and healthy. On the other hand, by trumpeting these values, it can also downplay or deny less pleasant realities. Certainly, it would be short-sighted to dismiss the importance of cultural values. Where would we be without them? So, too, it is good to appreciate the values of other people, including the Gebusi. But it's also important to recognize the underside of culture—realities that are neglected by cultural ideals. Both sides of this coin are important.

Where do we draw the line between an appreciative and a critical view of cultural values? Do we emphasize the fight to free the slaves during the American Civil War? Or the history of slavery that made that war necessary? Do we emphasize the human benefit of toppling a dictator like Saddam Hussein? Or the many lives that have been lost along the way? Such questions have few simple answers. But asking them makes us more aware of both the positive power of culture and the problems it can hide.

Gebusi culture can be viewed in this same light. The good company of *kogwayay* was a strong practice as well as a wonderful ideal. But *kogwayay* was also controlled and dominated by men. It was men rather than women who collectively cheered and publicly yelled. Men were the ones who gathered for public talk each evening on the large porch that overlooked the river. During this same time, women were largely confined to whispered conversations in a cramped female sleeping room along one wall of the longhouse, away from the men and older boys. In terms of decision making, it was typically men who determined which settlement their respective families would live in—who would have togetherness and with whom. Men took definitive charge of the events most strongly associated with *kogwayay*—ritual feasts, dances, spirit séances, and initiations. At feasts, men from the host village would proudly present visitors with piles of cooked sago starch—though this food was produced by women's back-breaking labor. In the evenings, it was men who dressed up in stunning costumes to dance. At initiations, young men were the main focus and were decorated most elaborately. As if to deny the notion of motherhood, boys were nurtured to manhood not by females but, as described in Chapter 5, by the men themselves—through the transmission of male life force from one generation to the next.

Male control was even more pronounced at spirit séances. Late in the evening, men would gather in the dark longhouse and arrange themselves around the spirit medium while he sat, smoked tobacco, and slowly went into a controlled trance. The medium's own spirit would then leave his body and be replaced by a soul from the spirit world. After a while, the new spirit's voice would start chanting through the spirit medium, first whispering and then singing in soft but audible falsetto tones. As the words of the spirit became clearer, the men clustered around the medium and formed a chorus to echo his words. Their singing encouraged his spirit to sing louder and with greater confidence. Gradually, the spirit's chants became full songs, each line of which was repeated in full harmony and top voice—often repeated in several refrains—by a robust male chorus.

Gebusi women, however, were rigidly excluded from the séance, although they were exposed to its constant presence while they sat or tried to sleep in their cramped quarters. Meanwhile, the men shouted, joked, and laughed; the occasion was an all-night song-fest of male bravado. Perhaps most strikingly, the primary spirits who sang were young women. And not just any women—these were gorgeous young spirit women who ached to joke and have sex with Gebusi men. In effect, the men's séance singing created, voiced, projected, and received back their sexual fantasies of women—at the same time that real Gebusi women could be beaten by their husbands or brothers for being flirtatious. In contrast, the spirit women were literally embodied by the men themselves, first in the voice of the male spirit medium (through his female spirits) and then in the men's collective chorus. It was hard to avoid the conclusion that spirit séances were, in significant part, a male fantasy in which masculine sexual desire was celebrated at the same time that Gebusi women themselves were excluded, controlled, and sometimes disparaged.

Given this masculine bias, what were we to make of Gebusi "good company"? Was *kogwayay* merely a male cultural value that disguised men's dominance over women? This question puts us at the crux of anthropology's appreciation of cultural difference, on the one hand, and its critique of inequality, on the other. For the most part, Gebusi women accepted and appreciated the culture they lived in. At spirit séances, they sometimes took offense at male joking, but more often they indulged and even enjoyed it. The women were excited and galvanized by ritual feasts and initiations, and they actively played their own roles at these events. On these and other occasions, they enjoyed interacting with women who visited from other settlements—even though their etiquette, attire, and hospitality were much more subdued than that of the men. It was true, at least in part, that Gebusi women lived willingly in the cultural shadow of Gebusi men. Sometimes they resisted their second-class status, but for the most part, they accepted and even embraced it. As Eileen found out, the women swelled with pride at their own and the men's accomplishments, even when men presented the fruits of women's work as their own. So, too, women tended to accept men's collective prerogative to take violent action against sorcery suspects and also (though not in all cases) the right of a man to beat his wife.

Just as Gebusi women reached a basic if occasionally ambivalent accommodation with Gebusi men, the same was true for Eileen and me. Anthropologists are not immune to the ethical tensions of the communities they study. Indeed, it seems impossible during the course of fieldwork *not* to be influenced by moral and ethical tensions. Admitting these tensions is important; they form part of our work and part of who we are. For our part, Eileen and I had encountered strong debates about gender relations and women's rights when we were students at The University of Michigan. Women I knew and respected, including Eileen, identified strongly with the cause of women's rights. So did I. Gender and sex were also becoming central issues of anthropological study. Hard as it may be to imagine now, the activities and opinions of women in foreign cultures had often been neglected in earlier anthropology research. To remedy this bias, it was important to actively study both women's experiences and their relations with men in ethnographic fieldwork.

In many if not most regions of the world, the activities and experiences of men and women differ significantly. Among the peoples and cultures of New Guinea, the division between male and female realms has often been especially marked. Given this, Eileen and I figured that I would study men's lives and that she would study women's. But the Gebusi were more complicated than that. It was obvious from the start that notions of femaleness and fantasies about women were central to the ceremonial life of men. Conversely, the discrepancy between men's fantasies and the actual role of women was substantial. But when Eileen tried to investigate these issues, she was largely blocked. Men would not talk about the role of women in the spirit world with Eileen, but only with me. When she tried to attend a spirit séance or even pass a message to me, a Gebusi man would block her entry or tell her angrily to go away. By contrast, the men absorbed me into their culture with gusto, including in their all-night songfests, ritual joking and smoking, feast preparations, and initiation secrets. Though women worked to enable many of these events, they stayed on the sidelines and often had little to say about the proceedings. By contrast, men had an elaborate verbal culture and talked energetically with visiting outsiders. Extending this pattern, they actively cultivated my ability to speak Gebusi so that they could share information with me.

All in all, it was hard to fight the impression that I was "getting" Gebusi culture—its rich and dominant masculine side—while Eileen was left with the women in the shadows. Moreover, the social life of Gebusi men was, simply put, a lot of fun. I enjoyed their banter and horseplay, smoked their tobacco through big bamboo tubes, joked with them, and participated in community feasts. It was easy to whoop it up. To her deep credit, Eileen held her ground and gathered an amazing wealth of information about Gebusi women. Some of this is already published; the rest will inform her own book-in-the-making. As is common in communal but sex-segregated societies, Gebusi women had their own female-centered interactions. Their more muted style of socializing is easier to appreciate in hindsight, however, than it was for either of us at the time. The children, though, were a source of joy for us both. Eileen took a particular liking to an impish little boy named Sayu. He was four or five years old and simply the most charismatic child either of us had ever known. His mother, Boyl, was an attractive woman with a broad smile and, we thought, the strongest intellect in the village. This sealed her friendship with Eileen; theirs was a special relationship. For a while, we had Boyl cook and share food with us, with Sayu never far away. However, her husband became jealous, and this ended the arrangement.

My relationship with Eileen was, of course, quite different from that of Gebusi husbands and wives, and this influenced our relationship with our neighbors. Early on in our fieldwork, we would wake up in the morning to see the amazed eyes of children staring through the floorboards of our bedroom. They had gathered under our stilted house to see how a man and a woman actually slept together. Perhaps they wondered if we even had sex in a shared bed—because Gebusi men and women always slept in separate parts of the longhouse and had intimate relations only when away from others in the forest. Notwithstanding our active and willing involvement with Gebusi, we asserted our privacy at these and other times. We fashioned doors from sheets of plywood that we had carried in, and we attached these to the walls of our house with stretch cords. But the idea of marital privacy within a closed house made little sense to the Gebusi. Their own houses were communal; anyone in the community was welcome to come in. Men and women had the privacy of their gardens in the forest—not the public space of a domestic residence. So, if villagers wanted to visit us when our "doors" were closed, they would sometimes climb in through windows that we had cut in the walls to let in more light.

In the beginning, we didn't know what would happen next. We knew that the people of Yibihilu were vibrant and welcoming and that their culture was alive with song and celebration. We had naiveté, energy, and trust in our purpose. And these were indispensable for fieldwork that was both frighteningly difficult and ultimately limitless. After several weeks of visiting, it was time for us and for the people of Yibihilu to decide if a house should be built for us at "the place of the deep waters." The villagers continued to be friendly, and some of them were becoming our personal friends. But they were also incredibly unlike us, and we felt the powerful force of this difference.

One night, the conversation finally turned—uncertainly, via Wahi—to how long we would stay in Yibihilu. Dusk was turning into night, and the men and boys around me became silhouettes with bones in their noses and feathers in their hair. Trophy skulls of pigs and cassowaries swayed from the rafters. A chunk of resin sizzled on the stone lamp. I looked up and saw people and personalities I was beginning to know. But they also appeared alien. Some were covered head to foot with the scaly skin of ringworm. Others had streaks of soot or caked ulcers on their skin or large cracks in the thick callouses that lined their feet. Their toes splayed, as if they had been born to stride along mossy log bridges that Eileen and I inched across timidly. Even when sitting down, I towered over them. My gawky white six-foot-plus frame stood out against their dark bodies, which averaged just five feet four inches at full height. But their skill and prowess in the forest dwarfed my own. How quickly and silently they could climb a tree, club a lizard, shoot a fish, or ford a stream. I knew that until recently they had eaten the flesh of persons killed as sorcerers. Their polished arrows were propped in the corner. Many layers of their culture remained obscure to me. The joy of our beginning made me question whether my giddiness would change to disillusionment when the novelty of our warm welcome wore off. But the dice, it seemed, had already been rolled. After undergoing years of scholarly training, getting married, journeying halfway around the world, and enduring mosquitoes and leeches, and with my personal and professional identity on the line, how could I turn back? They asked, "How long do you think you will stay?" I heard myself say, "Two years." My head swam as I heard the hubbub around me. But in the best Gebusi tradition of "everything is going to be fine," the discussion quickly turned to where the thatched house for Eileen and me should be built. On this side of the village? Or on that one? The following morning, we laid strings on the ground to mark where the walls would be. Eileen made sure they weren't too close to the edge of the cliff. And the villagers built our home above them.

Web site images of events and topics described in this chapter can be found at http://www.mhhe.com/knauft1.

CHAPTER 2

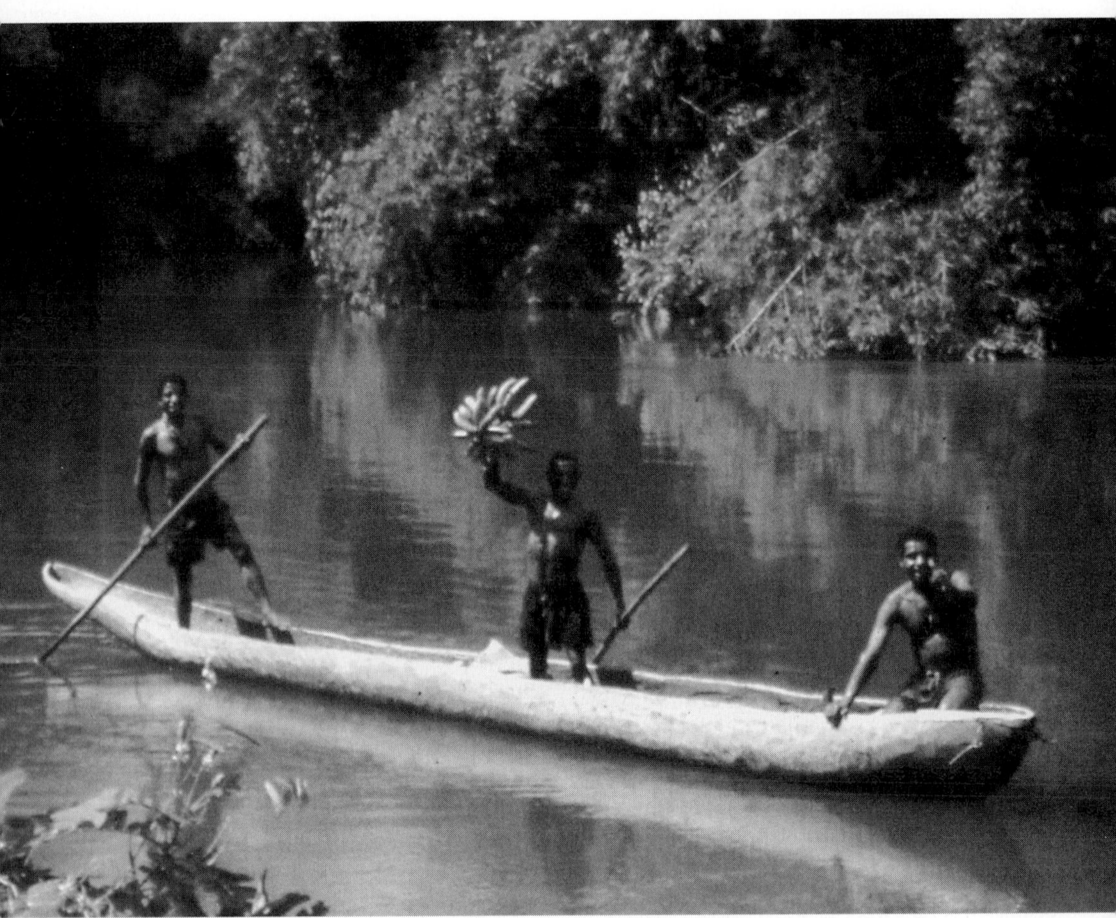

Men bring back bananas from gardens along the Kum River. (PHOTO: Bruce Knauft)

Rhythms of Survival

Boyl slung her load of leaves to the ground as the other women staggered into the village and followed suit. The foliage had been stripped from sago palms, folded, and then loaded onto their backs in net bags that were supported by tumplines across their foreheads. These leaves would form the bulk of our house, as they do all Gebusi dwellings. We hardly guessed that a house made mostly of leaves could provide shelter against up to fourteen feet of rainfall each year and in temperatures that regularly top one hundred degrees. But they do. The leaves are carefully pinned to wooden strips about five feet long, from which they extend by almost a yard. Hundreds of these leaf strips are then lashed like shingles to the roof beams of the house, with just an inch or so overlap between each strip and the one above it. For the village longhouse, which measured 74 by 34 feet, the tens of thousands of leaves needed for the structure easily weighed several tons. The bulk of the dwelling was the massive roof, which peaked almost 25 feet high in the air and sloped over the house's windowless walls until it almost touched the ground.

We were intrigued to see our own house take shape. Yuway and the other men scampered over the frame like skilled acrobats, hoisting log supports and the heavy ridgepole. Without measuring tape, plumb line, or any materials other than wood, leaves, and vines, they built the roof and then the rest of the house with all the confidence of a first-rate construction crew. The Gebusi overcame a lack of formal training with practical ingenuity and intimate knowledge of forest materials. Their indigenous numbers are just three: "one" (*hele*), "two" (*bena*), and "two plus one" (*bene bwar hele bwar*). Anything greater than that is simply "many" (*bihina*). Counting was as irrelevant to the Gebusi as their physical skills were finely honed. As ad hoc engineers, they were astounding. This is not to say that arithmetic has been undeveloped in the history of other non-Western cultures. Western counting systems are themselves based on Arabic numerals that are mid-Eastern in origin. In New Guinea itself, some societies have developed elaborate numerologies. Like the ancient Babylonians, the Kapauku people of West New Guinea developed a base-sixty number system, which they used to count items into the thousands just for fun. But one group's chosen passion is another's source of apathy. Although the Gebusi shortchanged their numerals, they had a rich vocabulary for a seemingly endless variety of plants, vines, and trees, each of which had special properties and uses.

If culture humanizes the environment, the Gebusi longhouse was their biggest accomplishment of material culture. Being the main gathering place for the fifty-two residents of Yibihilu, the "house long" (*masam sak*) was their tangible sign of village cooperation, physical prowess, and collective labor. Materially minded anthropologists describe culture as "adaptive" because its creative diversity has allowed humans to survive in so many different physical environments—from the Arctic to the tropics and practically everywhere in between, for tens of thousands of years. Whereas other animals are limited largely by genetically determined or "instinctual" paths of behavior, we humans add an enormous capacity for learning and for organizing our efforts through language. As Leslie White put it, culture gives us an "extra-somatic" way to adapt to the world around us.

Given the prominence of the Gebusi longhouse, it surprised us that it was often almost empty. Although humming with energy when the village was full of people, the central dwelling gave way to the surrounding forest as a focus of activity during the bulk of most days. Wahi goes off with a group of young men to spear fish. Boyl and her husband depart to collect bananas from a distant garden and to see if tubers are ready to harvest. Two young girls leave with their adult sisters to forage for fresh bamboo shoots, to rummage in the nest of a wild bush hen for eggs, or to scoop freshwater prawns from beneath rocks in the stream. Along the way, they keep their eyes open for a stray bush rat or snake that could be clubbed with a stick or sliced with a knife. Men carry bows and arrows and keep a keen eye out for signs of a wild pig, a sleeping lizard, a possum on a low-lying branch, or a large, flightless cassowary bird scavenging in the brush. Even a good-sized tarantula can be seized for the cooking fire. The Gebusi eat practically anything that moves.

By late afternoon, those within a reasonable distance return to the village for an evening meal and general conversation. The atmosphere is languid as families congregate. Men sit together and share large bamboo tube pipes filled with powerful home-grown tobacco. Women chat as they stoke the hearth and cook the bananas. Back in the forest, some families find themselves too deep in the bush to return for the night; they make a temporary camp and sleep in a makeshift shelter or lean-to. Imba and his wife, Walab, walk for a day to distant clan land, accompanied by their siblings and children. The men in the group chop down and split open a stately sago palm; then the women pound the soft interior of the tree into pith. Deep in the forest, it can take women two weeks or more to process the pith and leach its pulpy fiber into heavy bundles of caked sago flour. In the meantime, the whole group lives in the forest. Imba and his male kin hunt and forage; the children play together or set off with a group of adults to gather breadfruit or Tahitian chestnuts from stands of trees. The minicommunity sleeps in a temporary shelter of poles and sticks covered with sago leaf thatch to keep out the rain. When the sago palm is completely processed, the fruits of the women's labor are bundled in bark, wrapped in leaves, slung on their backs in big net bags, and hauled to the river, where the sago can be taken back to the settlement by canoe. For weeks on end, the heavy parcels will supply starchy flour that can be easily stored and then wrapped in fresh leaves and cooked directly on the fire.

Beyond its food, the rainforest is ripe with meaning. Hogayo lingers by an old settlement where his father was born; Walab stops to drink from a stream that belongs to her mother's family line. Memories are associated with each stand of trees, creek, small hillock, or patch of old garden land that has since been overgrown. For the Gebusi, to walk through the forest is to relive past experiences and to remember what the forest has provided their kin, their ancestors, and themselves. They rediscover how the trees have grown, when their fruits will be ripe, what animals have left traces nearby, and when the area can be revisited to reap one or another natural harvest. The forest is not simply "land," it is a living tableau with meaning and nuance in each nook and wrinkle. Gebusi describe their lands with fondness and nostalgia. They name individual places and luxuriate in their tranquil distinctions. When the Gebusi sing at dances and séances, many of their most haunting songs recall places in the forest.

Between daily trips and more extended ones, the residents of Yibihilu spent almost half their nights—45 percent, to be more precise—in the forest or at another settlement. In earlier days, they could easily scatter to the bush if they knew or thought that enemies or foreigners were coming. It is no surprise, then, that the early Australian patrol officers struggled to locate groups of Gebusi in the forest. Partly out of frustration, they labeled the local population as "nomads." Indeed, they designated the whole region as the Nomad Sub-District and named their government station the Nomad Patrol Post. In essence, though, they were mistaken. Anthropologists define nomads as people who have no permanent residence—people who shift their settlement every few weeks to hunt and or to tend their livestock. Sedentary peoples, by contrast, build durable houses and live in long-lasting settlements. Certainly, the Gebusi longhouse qualifies as a durable residence, and even in pre-colonial times, Gebusi villages lasted for at least several years. Though the Gebusi travel extensively across their lands, they identify themselves as members of a specific settlement and spend over half of their nights in their principal residence.

If the Gebusi lifestyle sometimes flirts with being seminomadic, it is tempered by the benefits of growing food in gardens that can be reached by an hour or two of walking from the main settlement. Notwithstanding festive attractions of communal village living, Gebusi survival depends on growing crops, especially bananas, in cleared gardens. In their part of the lowland rainforest, large game animals aren't plentiful. These are mostly wild pigs or flightless cassowaries, which look like strange, small ostriches. Though the Gebusi eat and enjoy the smaller creatures of the forest, these don't supply many calories on a daily basis. It is doubtful whether the Gebusi could survive on the basis of hunting, fishing, and gathering alone.

In a very few areas of the world, including along the coast of the northwestern United States and southwestern Canada, wild resources such as fish and nuts were plentiful enough so that indigenous peoples could form large and complex societies even without growing their own food. Along parts of the south coast of New

Guinea, where the swamp is flush with both fish and sago palms, native peoples flourished and could maintain quite large villages while foraging for these wild foods. But in the rainforest where the Gebusi live, which is two hundred miles inland, fish and sago aren't plentiful enough to provide for a steady diet. So the Gebusi plant gardens—even if they do this as simply and with as little work as possible.

The biggest task, at least for the men, is the felling of trees. Though most families maintain individual gardens, large ones also may be cleared as a communal project. After several weeks at Yibihilu, we went with some villagers to see how this was done. We left in high spirits, the men whooping and the children frolicking. It was going to be a big garden. As we walked twenty minutes to the site, it felt more like a festive occasion than a work brigade.

Along with the rest of the men, I took turns chopping trees and resting by the makeshift cooking fires while chatting, munching bananas, and smoking Gebusi tobacco. To my surprise, Yuway told me not to chop any of the trees all the way through—each time I was stopped when I was only about halfway done. The other men were doing the same. Perplexed, I asked why. I became only more confused when Yuway and the other men made dramatic pantomimes of noise and crashing. After two more hours of "half-work," hardly a single tree had been felled. My companions seemed quite content and even expectant while I remained baffled. Our work pace dwindled until only a handful of men were left at one end of the large plot. There, they attacked a particularly large and majestic piece of timber—while the rest of us were waved off to the far margins of the area. Everyone took great pains to tell Eileen and me that we should not, under any circumstances, wander back into the garden area. Knowing that the Gebusi had deep spiritual ties to their land—and that many of their spirits lived in large trees—I thought that the land might now be under a spiritual taboo. Perhaps special rites or spells would be performed by the senior men to supplicate the spirits of the largest tree before it fell, so they wouldn't be angry about the destruction of their "home." Maybe after that, I thought, we would finish chopping the biggest tree's smaller cousins. But I was wrong.

A few minutes later, the enormous tree began to creak and groan in response to the continuing blows of the senior men's axes. Though towering above the lesser trees, a thick skein of vines and foliage knitted it to its neighbors. Finally, it tottered, leaned, and fell with an amazing crash. With equal speed, its force spread to the other trees in domino fashion—through the entire acre of half-cut timber. In a flash, hefty trunks were toppled and flung in all directions—like telephone poles ripped up by a falling master pylon. It was frightful, wonderful, and awe-ful—an arboreal tornado. Then, as quickly as it started, it was over. All that remained were the whoops of the men, the blizzard of leaves that filled the sky on their way to the ground, and a garden plot strewn with fallen trees. In shock, I had to sit down.

As I regained my bearings, my confusion persisted. The trees had been felled with remarkably little effort, to be sure. But now their massive trunks and branches smothered the garden land beneath. How could the plot be planted, much less cultivated? Yuway and the others were unconcerned. They pointed out that banana suckers and root crop seedlings had already been stuck in the ground, several days before. When I had arrived at the site and the trees had still been standing, I had not even noticed them. Although a few of these plantings were now crushed by the fallen limbs, most of them were merely sheltered from the blaze of the sun and the pelting of future rains by the branches that now hovered just over them. Without this covering, the new seedlings would have wilted in the tropical rays or been washed away by torrential storms. As the foliage of the fallen trees decomposed above them, however, the crops beneath would sprout through these fertilizing remains and would then be strong enough to grow unshielded from sun and rain. Though the garden now looked like a chaos of fallen limbs, it was, in fact, a finely honed and ingenious means of cultivation. Anthropologist Edward Schieffelin gave the practice a fitting name: "felling the trees on top of the crop."

The main food planted in Gebusi gardens is, of course, plantains—starchy bananas. These require almost no weeding, grow quickly, and don't bear fruit until the plants have hoisted their caloric pods beyond the reach of wild pigs. As a result, the Gebusi dispense with having to building fences to keep animals such as pigs away from their crops. Theoretically, the bananas could be eaten by birds and fruit bats when they ripen, but most of the plantains are of the starchy variety rather than the sweet one that attract flying freeloaders. In any event, villagers usually harvest the fruit before it is ripe enough for birds and bats to eat. By simply throwing them on the fire, they make the hard plantains edible: as the thick banana skin is charred, the fruit inside softens and cooks. Retrieved with wooden cooking tongs, the bananas can then be scraped of their charcoal and eaten straightaway.

The Gebusi grow crops without laboring heavily on their land. Because they let the land lie fallow and regenerate for many years, if not for a generation, before recutting and replanting it, their food raising qualifies as "horticulture." By contrast, anthropologists usually define "agriculture" as cultivation that requires greater effort—practices such as irrigating, fertilizing, plowing, fencing, and/or terracing. These techniques increase the quantity of crops that can be raised on a given piece of land, but they exact a heavy toll in physical labor or mechanized intervention. The Gebusi stay happily on the other end of this continuum. Because they have plenty of land, they have little need to invest great effort in any one plot. Even the best garden plots are abandoned after one or two plantings. Weeds, shrubs, and then trees emerge as the rainforest reclaims its terrain. A new layer of nutrients enriches the poor clay soil. Ideally, the grandson of the man who planted the initial garden comes back to reclaim and recultivate it. In so doing, he draws upon the ancestral substance of the regenerated land as he augments his own essence and the growth of his family. The resulting cycle of reproduction is hence spiritual and cultural as well as caloric and demographic—the rejuvenation of land, food, people, and spiritual bonds. Given that land is plentiful, it is easily lent to friends and kin. As such, the land and the energy of the spirits are a collective rather than an individual resource.

Across generations, Gebusi have maintained an ample supply of food in a part of the rainforest that is not particularly bountiful. And in the process, they don't seem to have strained themselves unduly. Certainly, they endure stints of intense labor. Women carry more than their share of heavy loads through the rainforest, and they transport firewood, food, and even their babies in net bags slung on their backs. Although men can also bear such burdens, it is women who give the Gebusi their ultimate "carrying capacity." Even for women, however, many hours on most days drift by in relaxation—conversing, eating, and playing with children. And the men have even more time for social pursuits than the women. Their palavers extend for long hours into the evening, by which time most women are asleep. Every week and a half or so, the men gather for an all-night spirit séance. After this extended songfest, they typically sleep for a good part of the following day. In addition, there are all-night ritual feasts and dances that energize the entire settlement; these occurred about once a month during 1980–82.

Marshall Sahlins has called simple human cultures "original affluent societies." Although the technology and material culture may be rudimentary, people in such societies typically are able to spend hours each day socializing or lazing around. Although obtaining food and shelter require work, this effort ebbs and flows not so much as a struggle against nature but in relaxed harmony with the environment. From the icy Arctic to the dry deserts of central Australia, simple human societies have survived with plenty of time to spare. Against this standard, the growing complexity and advanced technology of modern societies reduces rather than increases our leisure time. On most nights, the Gebusi get a good nine hours or more of sleep. Here in the United States, I am lucky to get seven. Each of our so-called labor-saving devices brings new demands for productive work.

If Gebusi lives throw the frenzied pace of modern society into relief, they also possess their own afflictions. Their deeper struggle has not been so much to acquire food as to fight off illness and, as discussed in the next chapter, to endure the human violence that is fueled by untimely sickness and death. The Gebusi's biggest enemies have ultimately been very small. Mosquitoes bring the scourge of malaria. Parasitic worms with tiny larvae invade their bodies and cause chronic and draining illnesses. Communicable diseases such as tuberculosis and introduced influenza wreak havoc. In the hot, humid climate, cuts and scrapes can easily fester and develop into skin ulcers. All these ailments sap energy and could be combated by better nutrition. But Gebusi are at pains to improve their diet. Though their staples of plantains and sago brim with starch, they provide little protein. Forest animals can be hunted, but they are hard to catch in large numbers or on a regular basis. Hunting more frequently deep in the forest would also expose Gebusi to yet more mosquitoes and malaria and would put them at greater risk of accident and injury. Malnutrition is hence a problem; young children often have the tiny limbs and distended "sago belly" of a diet that is high in starch but low in protein. Ultimately, the "affluence" of Gebusi leisure is itself an adaptation to their environment: it is more efficient to conserve energy and relax than to work harder while only minimally improving their nutrition.

The Gebusi version of the German fairy tale of Hänsel and Gretel may provide the best example of how they balance energy lost against the effort to obtain food. The Gebusi raise only a few pigs, but their desire for pork is as strong as it is rarely satisfied. Though they would love to raise and eat more pigs, to do this, they would have to remain close to the village, feed the pigs every day, and build fences to either confine the animals or protect their gardens from being uprooted by them. In some parts of the world, including the broad, temperate valleys of highland New Guinea, people do fence their gardens and raise domestic pigs in large numbers in order to provide themselves with a major source of protein. By combining labor-intensive gardening and pig raising, some groups of the New Guinea highlands boast population densities of more than four hundred persons per square mile. As a whole, the indigenous groups of the New Guinea highlands exceeded a whopping one million people. But the lowland rainforest where the Gebusi live tell a very different story. Their land and climate do not favor intensive gardening or the growing of a large surplus of crops to feed many pigs. So they opt for a flexible, mobile, and relaxed mode of subsistence. In 1980–82, the tiny society of four hundred and fifty Gebusi was scattered thinly over extensive lands; their population density was just 6.9 persons per square mile. Even within New Guinea, then, differences in environment and ecology have had a huge impact on the size and scale of societies.

These differences lead us back to Gebusi pig raising—and to how they take the easiest way out. When the opportunity arises, Gebusi capture wild piglets in the forest and bring them back to the village. There, they feed the piglets leftover food, carry them around in little net bags, and, to an extent, tame them. As the pigs get larger, however, it becomes impossible to carry them around and hard to regularly feed them. So Gebusi turn them loose. The critters live in the forest on their own but are individually recognized by their Gebusi owners. Reciprocally, the pigs recognize their owners and return the village on occasion to be fed by them. Usually, they stay in the village for just a few days—until they become enough of a nuisance that food is withheld and they are urged to go back to the forest, where they can grow large on their own. As a novel result, the pigs are neither wild nor domestic but somewhere in between.

When the time arrives for a major feast, the ploy that is found in the Hänsel and Gretel fairy tale is used with a special twist. To kill and distribute their pigs, the Gebusi first must entice them back to the village. In the weeks prior to the feast, Gebusi who are traveling in the forest keep a lookout for the animals. Back in the village, men may hold a séance to ask the spirits where one or another pig has wandered off to. When those in the forest find one of the pigs' tracks, they leave pieces of banana or sago for it to eat. By leaving scraps of food on the trail as they return home—like Hänsel and Gretel in reverse—they lure the pig right into the village, where the beast can be tethered and held for slaughter. It's an ingenious system. Keeping their pigs semidomesticated doesn't allow Gebusi to raise very many of them—barely one for each extended family. But it does provide a reliable source of meat for their most special occasions while avoiding the heavy work of having to feed, tend, and restrain pigs on a regular basis.

This leads to a larger point. Though anthropologists use concepts and categories to classify societies, people like the Gebusi defy easy classification. The Gebusi are "sedentary," but their lifestyle is mobile and almost "seminomadic." They raise crops and are "horticulturalists," but they also hunt and forage. They are efficient at raising pigs, but the animals are only "semidomesticated" and are few in number. Even in terms of New Guinea, the Gebusi have neither the high-intensity food production and population density of highlands dwellers nor the sago-and-fish foraging lifestyle of their lowland neighbors. Personally, I like the fact that the Gebusi are "in-betweeners." Like many peoples when considered closely, they combine or hybridize our own categories of analysis. The many ways that people accommodate their local ecologies are a testament to human creativity and to the power of culture as a means of adaptation. I am continually fascinated by how people not only survive but find meaning and purpose across different parts of the globe. This human capacity seems, if anything, increasingly important today, as we struggle with problems of pollution, global warming, depletion of fossil fuels, malnutrition, and disease in so many parts of the world. As ecological threats grow ever more ominous, humans need to be increasingly resilient and creative in implementing long-term solutions.

Human diversity sparks our appreciation of alternative ways of living. But how do we keep track of this variety? It is useful to have concepts and categories that organize this diversity. For instance, we may classify human subsistence patterns by distinguishing people who rely on wild plant and animal resources ("foragers" or "hunters and gatherers") from those who produce or grow their own food ("horticulturalists" or, more intensively, "agriculturalists") and from those who depend primarily on herds of domesticated animals ("pastoralists"). Or we can designate modern or "capitalist" strategies in which people compete for wage labor and earn money, some of which is used to buy food in stores. So, too, we can distinguish nomadic from sedentary forms of residence, rural from urban forms of living, and nonindustrial from industrial forms of production. However, the exceptions to these categories push us to new levels of understanding. People like the Gebusi, who are in between some of these categories, help us appreciate their intersections as well as their limits. As we will see in Part Two of this book, understanding these combinations becomes increasingly important as we consider patterns of contemporary change and transformation.

If the Gebusi are hard to pigeonhole, so, too, are most other peoples. Even the small region of the South Pacific called Melanesia harbors a huge diversity of different peoples and cultures. And countries that we may think of as single units—such as China, India, Indonesia, Russia, and certainly the United States—house a complex and fascinating range of peoples, cultures, and blendings. This diversity is not only interesting but central to the problems, challenges, and opportunities of the contemporary world.

Within Gebusi society itself, one thing that categories and concepts don't reveal is how much they enjoy their land and how much their lives flow with its moods and nuances. A storm blows in suddenly and doesn't let up for hours. Rain pelts and pockmarks the village; it carves gullies and then little canyons in the central clearing. The streams swell and the rivers roil and flood. Bluffs of clay become slides of slippery mud, and traveling anywhere becomes a wet and sloppy process. All plans are cancelled. But rather than curse the weather, Gebusi simply take the day off. Toasty in their houses, men light up their pipes and chat while women play with children, put some plantains on the fire, or thread more inches on the large net bags they are making. Someone tells a story or a myth. Plans unfold for a coming feast. Those returning in the downpour make fun of how they slipped and how wet and muddy they got. Sometimes, as if to defy the rain, they whoop loudly and march through it proudly.

When a dry spell descends and the rivers shrink, men make plans for spearing or poisoning fish. The low, clear water exposes their prey and makes them easier to catch. Wahi was one of the best fishermen. His favorite stalking place was above the rapids in a quiet pool of the Kum River. He would swim underwater and jab at his targets with a pronged spike. One day, he speared the biggest fish of all—it must have weighed more than twenty pounds. To the people of Yibihilu, landing this giant prize was akin to winning the Super Bowl. Cries of joy and amazement filled the air. As word spread, a feast became inevitable. More than good fortune or skill, the taking of the huge fish affirmed the goodness of the village, the beneficence of the river, and the harmony of the villagers with their forest spirits. Portions of the fish were shared among each and every inhabitant of Yibihilu, the "place of the deep waters." To this day, Wahi is my "fish," my *dio*, based on the piece of fish that he shared with me that afternoon. In the evening, Swiman held one of his biggest and most dramatic séances. In song after song, his spirits described how the big fish had given itself up to Wahi's skill and the strength of his village. The lives of the fish people, their comings and goings in the river, came alive in vivid detail. The other fish were ripe for the taking, the spirits said. The men in the audience went wild.

Although the Gebusi basked in their environment, Eileen and I were hard-pressed to follow their lead. For us, daily physical maintenance was a major challenge. During the course of two years, ailments and illnesses became inevitable: the headaches and chills of malaria; digestive disorders; intestinal worms; skin lesions, boils, and rashes; and jungle rot that thrives in the body's most private parts. Our lives were made bearable by a small arsenal of medications, both for ourselves and the Gebusi. Not being doctors, it was often hard to know how we could or should try to help the Gebusi with our medicines. But the people of Yibihilu were good role models for us: they accepted infirmity when it came and made the best of life while it lasted. Tabway was afflicted with a putrefying ulcer on her thigh. Her leg would be shuddering in torment, but her face would stay calm or even have a soft smile. Sefomay's foot was permanently and painfully swollen to twice its normal size. She would joke that her "leg was rotting"—but her spirit was not.

Sickness and death visited Gebusi at every season of life. Malaria, pneumonia, filariasis or "elephantiasis," tuberculosis, influenza, and diarrhea were both causal and contributing factors. Gebusi were distressed by microbes, parasites, clogged lungs, contaminated blood, and swollen spleens. By the time they reached what we would call middle age, most of them were physically wizened. Almost all adults had had at least one bout of a near-death illness. Sickness dovetailed with poor nutrition, because weaker bodies have a harder time fighting infection. Of girls who lived to be five, only one in three survived to age forty. For boys of similar age, only about one in six lived to into their fifth decade.

The Gebusi could not cheat death, but they enjoyed life while it lasted. They savored simple pleasures, smiled easily, laughed often, and celebrated when they could. Notwithstanding their crusades against sorcery, there was little they could do to reduce their physical risk—either from disease or from one another. The deaths that we witnessed were met with quietude and acceptance. The warm hands of friends gave way to piercing wails only at the end.

Gebusi ailments put our own in perspective. On a daily basis, our two biggest challenges were heat and insects. Such "little" things are almost embarrassing to admit, but chronic discomforts loom as large in fieldwork as they are typically neglected in published accounts. If heat and humidity turned our papers limp and our shoes green with mold, we easily felt the same way. The following extract is from my field notes:

> You can't be cool when the humidity and temperature both exceed 98.6. I sit in the shade of my house and calm myself inside and out. Mental strain fuels sweat and throbs my head. I stay absolutely still, motionless, relaxing, eyes closed. The sweat beads, then dribbles from my brow, chest, and thighs. I splash with water from my basin, but more sweat replaces it. I go to my sleeping room, a bit darker, and take off all my clothes, every stitch. I kneel on the floor beside my sleeping net. Fractions of confinement make a difference. The mesh of my sleeping net holds extra heat that radiates from my body, so I do not go inside it.
>
> The three-point stance is my naked attempt to relax in the heat. I can't lie down, since this creates hot contact between my side and whatever I am laying on; a pool of sweat quickly appears. My best posture keeps an illusion of repose for ten minutes or so with the smallest possible part of my body touching the floor, as much as possible languid in air. The three points of contact are the tip of my big toes, kneecaps, and elbows. This reduces my surface area of contact to a few scant inches. If I get it right, I can hang my head without having to support it with my fingers (since sweat erupts wherever skin touches skin). So my head hangs limp an inch or two off the floor. My mind calms, so does my skin. The sweat still collects across my cheeks and drips from my nose. It splats onto the floor, but softly, slowly.
>
> After ten minutes, I am as serene as I can be. Relaxation is key, since fighting heat makes it worse; heat makes friends with anxiety and stress. Yesterday I misplaced my notebook and my frustration quickly steamed my glasses. My three-point stance won't cure the heat. But it makes it easier to live with.

For their part, the Gebusi hardly minded the temperature or the humidity. They often kept cooking fires smoldering in their houses, which have no chimneys. The added heat and smoke dispersed the mosquitoes and drove away insects that would otherwise infest the thatch and wood of their houses. But for us, the story was different. Eileen and I were raised in northern states—she in Michigan, I in

Connecticut. We couldn't tolerate the added heat and smoke of a continual fire in our home. So we opted for less fire—and got more bugs. Insects were a whole separate dimension of fieldwork. I couldn't ignore them:

> They are everywhere. Even sitting in a canoe in the middle of the Kum River, the creepies and crawlies land on you. Some of them are really strange looking. They sport weird colors and wild-flight torsos and ways of moving that come from another world. Magnified a thousand times, they would be perfect for the next alien thriller from Hollywood. But most of them are innocuous. You just pick or brush them off and move on.
>
> There are several exceptions. The grasshoppers are annoyingly large when they land on you suddenly. The five-inch spiders raise my adrenaline when I find them sharing my room. The cockroaches are everywhere. Hundreds of the big ones live in our cardboard cartons and eat the labels off our precious tins of food. But the mosquitoes I hardly even count as insects because they are so pernicious. Not just because there are so many of them, nor because they fly into our bush house without pause or restriction. It's the malaria and elephantiasis they bring. They wait like cowards until dusk before taunting you with their mock fragility. They lilt in squadrons on low power but somehow float just outside your grasp, waiting like lunar modules to hit your pay dirt. Your swatting hand only flits them away to a yet choicer landing place. "One small bite for one mosquito, one giant risk for mankind."
>
> There is a special insult to getting several bites. How many did you really receive in the dimness? Was it only two? Or four or six? Is that another new one now again, just beside the others? Did you *really* take your antimalarial pill (none of which are one hundred percent effective)? The best thing is for us to go inside our mosquito net—and that very quickly, because *nothing* is worse than having mosquitoes get *inside* the net. But we can't live under a net from six at night until six in the morning. We have to eat and wash, write our notes, and we want to talk with each other and socialize with villagers. The evening should be one of the most enjoyable parts of the day. Wearing heavy clothes or lathering our bodies with high concentrations of DEET isn't feasible night after night. So we have no real solution; we take our hits and do the best we can. But going to the bathroom remains the worst. Mosquitoes love the bottom of our latrine pit, and they fly up in droves whenever something goes down the hole. So they attack our most vulnerable parts when we are most exposed. Talk about a bite in the butt!

If heat and insects were our daily scourge, the Gebusi helped us keep our irritations in perspective. Despite their own much graver ailments, their lives remained rich and fascinating. This is what pulled us beyond the orbit of our own concerns. Call it cultural gravity—the ability of others' lives to sweep you up and draw you in to your own surprise and against all challenges. This is the deepest part of fieldwork, the part that makes you grow. We joked with the Gebusi, shared with them, took part in their activities, and became part of their world. Reciprocally, they seemed to enjoy us, accepted our idiosyncrasies, and included us in their activities as much as they could. In professional terms, this is with what is often described as the primary fieldwork method in cultural anthropology: "participant observation."

Professionally, I think our biggest challenge was to learn the Gebusi language. Given their remoteness, there was no way we could have done this ahead of time. But we had received training in how to learn an unwritten language without the help of translators. In the field, bit by slow, painful bit, we learned to recognize and make sounds that do not exist in English. We compiled lists of Gebusi words and phrases, and we puzzled over their meanings. In all of these tasks, Yuway was my most patient, insightful, and pleasant helper. Increasingly over the course of weeks and months, he and I became special friends. He even helped me tackle the complexities of Gebusi tense and grammar, and these were the worst. The Gebusi like to pile meanings into verbs while leaving out nouns and other phrases. For instance, the question "Would he have killed me?" is spoken in Gebusi as a single verb, "kill" (*golo*), which is then modified by a string of suffixes to indicate a presumed subject, a presumed object, conditional tense, causative action, and interrogative aspect. The whole sentence is one word: *golo-hi-lay-ba*. Fortunately, we knew from the start that learning the language would be our most difficult task. After a few weeks, we could make simple communications in broken Gebusi. After a few months, we began to figure out what the Gebusi were saying to one another (not in the simple, slowed-down language that they used with us, but in the idioms, quick pacing, and assumptions that they used with one another.) My advisor wrote and told us not to get too discouraged. He suggested that if we focused on language learning for the first six months, we would be okay. He also said that our language abilities would continue to improve and that two-thirds or more of our understanding would likely emerge during the last third of our fieldwork. So we would have to be patient. He was right.

Along the way, we developed our own rhythms of daily adaptation. Fieldwork is at heart its own brand of optimal foraging. As the Gebusi shifted their activities to gain the most from their surroundings, we tried to do the same. For us, however, our desire to participate, to observe, and to record our experiences became a dance between "living with" and "writing up." Our days blended language learning, observation, note taking, interviews, writing, and reflection—amid the constant intensity of public social living. I was continually surprised at how long it took me to type up my notes and organize them into topics and larger files. Even when not much was going on in the village, I seemed to be behind in my work. It became painfully obvious that fieldwork was not a process of quickly discovering "the truth." My learning about Gebusi emerged gradually through a blur of confusing experiences and competing interpretations. We repeatedly found that our language skills were deficient, our interpretations misleading, and our assumptions simply wrong. Gaining understanding was an endless process of learning from our own mistakes. We began at the lowest rung, including our language skills. Initially, we asked nonsensical questions like "Is your son a girl?" But just as quickly, we learned to laugh at our foibles. It helped a lot that Gebusi laughed so good-naturedly along with us, just as they did at their own mistakes and problems.

As time went on and our comprehension improved, we came to see cultural anthropology as a kind of dialogue—a conversation between Gebusi meanings and our own understandings. The trick was to have each side of this cultural equation make sense in terms of the other. This task was rooted in participation and observation, but it continued afterward in writing and reflection. Writing ethnography is almost invariably a process of trying to clearly explain events and actions that were, in fact, confusing and opaque when first observed and experienced to begin with. The living and the writing of ethnography both entail a back-and-forth between trial and error, assertion, and reflection.

During fieldwork, this process linked us directly back to our relationship with the Gebusi. In our lives and our work, a balance between give-and-take was key: the ability to admit error and try yet again, to receive as well as give, to be acted upon as well as acting. In this, Gebusi were wonderful teachers. Reciprocity was at the heart of their social life: they maintained a vigilant balance between giving and getting, between acting and being acted upon. As we increasingly came to realize, balanced reciprocity pervaded many if not most aspects of Gebusi culture, including their relation to their physical environment, their distribution of food, their ritual celebrations, their marriage patterns, their connections with the spirit world, and even their patterns of death and killing. The ideal of balanced reciprocity was one of the most personally and professionally important things that we learned from the Gebusi. Within their gendered divisions, they were egalitarian to a fault—loathe for anyone to put him- or herself above someone else in their cohort. They reinforced this norm by constantly striving to maintain a balance between receiving and giving.

> The big feast was yesterday. Today, our friends are happily eating food that the visitors brought and gave them in exchange for the lavish meal our settlement hosted. Since we ourselves contributed fish and rice to the communal effort, people now want to repay us.
>
> This morning, a member of each major family in the village came and presented me with a bird egg. I was deeply touched. Most memorable was five-year-old Kawe, who has become my "biscuit" exchange-name friend. I saw him coming from across the village. With the confident stride and smile of a grown-up, he looked at me from twenty yards away and walked over directly, never shifting his gaze. Stopping in front of me, he flashed his cutest tooth-missing grin and extended his little hand that held his egg. He placed the egg in my palm, turned around, and walked back proudly, never uttering a word or looking back. I will never forget it.

Web site images of events and topics described in this chapter can be found at http://www.mhhe.com/knauft1.

CHAPTER 3

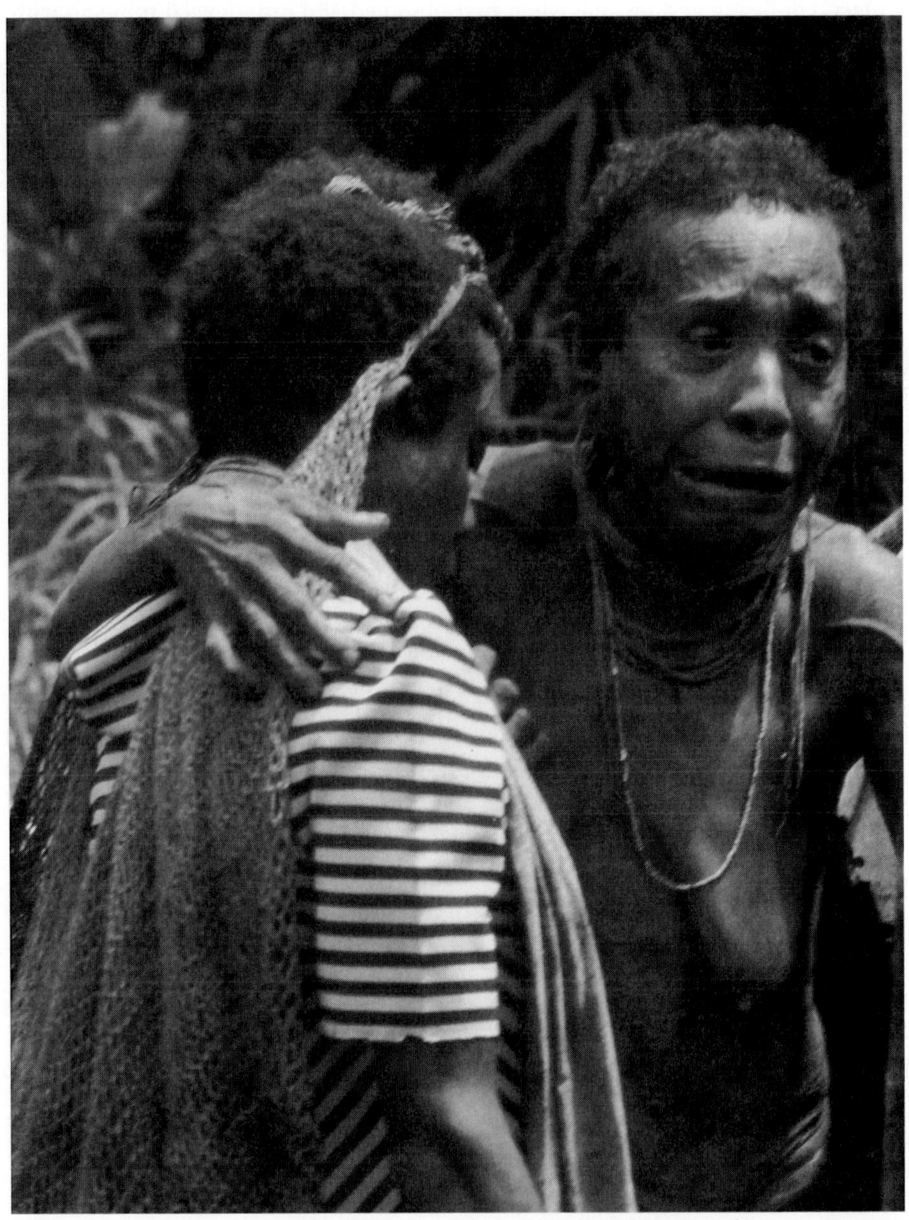

A woman mourns the death of her husband. (PHOTO: Eileen Marie Knauft)

Lives of Death

It is hard to watch a baby die. Its scrawny body cries until its wails lose force and leave a ghostly little corpse. It was also hard on us that Gebusi men didn't seem to mind. During our first five weeks in the field, we saw first one baby die and then another. As the mother wailed with grief, her women-kin gathered in support. But the men continued to joke and smoke in the longhouse, and the boys played gaily in the village clearing. Only the baby's father stayed close by, and even this was with an air of detached waiting—until the small body could be summarily buried. Managing babies and managing death were both women's work; if women bore the day-to-day challenge and joy of caring for new life, they also bore the sting of its death. Along with Eileen, I visited the mother in each case to lend support. But both times I felt, as a man, that the most courteous thing I could do was to leave. As the second infant was dying, I talked with Owaya, its father. He said that the baby was dying "just because." But then he wondered whether a woman from Wasobi might have sent sorcery to kill it. As I later found out, the Gebusi attributed all natural deaths to sorcery. But they really investigated the deaths only of adults and older children.

The Gebusi don't think of infants as fully human until they are about seven months old, when their first teeth emerge. Until then, a human spirit is not thought to be fully rooted in their bodies, and they aren't even given a name. Many infants only flirt with life; a third of them die during their first year. The community in general and men in particular seem to protect themselves from identifying too closely with so many young lives that end so quickly. But this distance is not shared by the mother, red-eyed and weeping, nor by her female kin. The father, for his part, seems awkwardly in the middle, experiencing neither the women's emotion nor the other men's distance. As for us, Eileen cried with the women and deeply felt their pain. I commiserated with her in private. But the men treated me jovially, as if nothing had happened. At heart, I was confused. It was my first real lesson in the contours and confinements of Gebusi emotion.

Just three weeks after the second infant died, a third death hit the village: Daguwa killed himself. Unlike the infant deaths, which were taken as "normal," this one shocked the community. No one could remember a man having killed himself. As I was later to learn, no man, and just one woman, had committed suicide in all the remembered circumstances of almost four hundred adult deaths. Although we didn't foresee it at the time, Daguwa's death drew us into a whirling cultural vortex. Events and experiences that we could hardly understand flew by; we struggled to piece them together. People we knew and liked suddenly did things we could not believe. In retracing this path—with its twists and turns, and my own confusions—I came to know much about the Gebusi, about the culture of life and death, and about the challenges of anthropological understanding.

At first, I didn't believe Yuway and Salip (Boyl's husband) when they came to tell me the news; they seemed so matter-of-fact. But within minutes, we rushed off to the forest so they could retrieve Daguwa's body. When we arrived, the dead man's wife and two other women were already weeping by the corpse. Salip brushed them aside and wailed loudly in front of the body. Daguwa had been Salip's classificatory "brother-in-law" (*gol*) and "initiation-mate" (*sam*). Gebusi settlements coalesce by bringing men—and women—together from different family lines. Relations within the village reflect a rich and tangled web of kinship and friendship based on a wide range of family, marital, and friendly but nonkin connections. Salip and Daguwa had not been members of the same male line, but they had long lived in the same village, had become friends, had been initiated together, and were distantly related through intermarriage.

After Salip finished wailing, the women came back to resume their crying. They called to Daguwa and told him how sorry they were about his death and how much they wanted him back. Their raw emotion was thought to soothe Daguwa's lingering soul and ease its gradual passage to the land of the dead. Meanwhile, Salip smoked tobacco with Yuway and waited until other men from Yibihilu arrived. None of them seemed particularly upset as they discussed how to take Daguwa's body back to the village. Wondering why he had killed himself, I went with others to inspect his body. Daguwa had been a strong, handsome man, but now his face was pale and slack, already beginning to swell in the tropical heat. I looked for signs of foul play. Perhaps his death was a murder disguised as a suicide. But the only sign of struggle was a mark on the front of his faded T-shirt. Something had poked and scratched the fabric for a couple of inches, but the shirt was not punctured, and nothing had pierced Daguwa's skin. To the men, however, the tiny scratch revealed a larger canvas of anger and shame. Before committing suicide, Daguwa had fought with his wife, Saliam. During the scuffle, she had held an arrow, thrust it toward him, and scratched his shirt. Their fight had been about a sexual affair that was generally acknowledged between Saliam and a young man, Sasaga. Publicly cuckolded, Daguwa had been furious; he had wanted to hunt and kill his wayward wife, her lover, or both of them. But Salip and others had discouraged him from doing this. Incensed but lacking other recourse, Daguwa had fought with his wife. But he was further shamed by her scratching his shirt, his prized possession. When she went off to fetch water, the men said, he had taken tubes of poison concocted for killing fish in the stream and, in a fit of rage, had drunk them all. Empty tubes with the smell of the potent toxin were found nearby. Daguwa had died a writhing death after poisoning himself in anger against his wife. But he was so much bigger and stronger than she. Why was his anger so self-directed?

For the moment, all I could do was try to keep up with events as the men lashed Daguwa's body to a stretcher and marched it briskly back through the forest toward Yibihilu. After a while, they stopped for a smoke and a rest. They joked about the upcoming feast and ribbed me good-naturedly about how I would look if I wore a traditional Gebusi male skirt of "ass grass" for the occasion. Though we had outpaced the women, their wailing could now be heard. The men hurried to reshoulder the corpse, but the women were already arriving, including Saliam. By chance, two more women came through the forest from another direction and converged on us at the same moment. They were fictive "mothers" of Daguwa from an adjacent community who had come to view his body. Upon seeing his corpse, and also his wayward wife, they virtually exploded. Screaming, the two of them tore straight into Saliam. She turned to avoid them, but the lead woman walloped her on the back with a steel ax she was wielding, blunt side forward. She followed this with another heavy blow. Then she turned and threw herself on Daguwa's corpse, pawing and crying in great screaming sobs, as if her emotion could wake it up. Simultaneously, the second woman resumed the first one's attack, screeching at full pitch and poking and shoving Saliam with a pointed stick as if she were going to drive it right through her. Two men rushed in to hold her back while others wrestled Daguwa's closest "mother" away from his corpse. The remainder abruptly picked up the body and raced off with it down the trail. Yuway, Salip, and I followed in close pursuit while the women trailed behind.

When we finally arrived at Yibihilu, Daguwa's body was laid in state in his family house, a scant twenty-five yards from our own. A crowd of women screeched and wailed while others arrived in short order. Many of them pummeled and berated Saliam, who hunched and whimpered but could not run away without neglecting her duty to mourn her dead husband. Our neighbor, Owaya, came up and waved a firebrand in Saliam's face. He let forth with a withering diatribe, which he punctuated with shouts of "*Si-nay!*" As I later learned, this translates roughly as "Burn! Cook! We'll eat!" This was what the Gebusi traditionally did to persons executed as sorcerers. Owaya whacked Saliam with his burning stick and then shoved it into the net bag on her back. She gasped, whimpered, and shuffled several feet farther away.

Inside the house, we gathered with the women who had come to weep over the corpse. Like Daguwa's "mother," some of them flailed hysterically when they first arrived. After a few minutes, the atmosphere slowly calmed. But then a man painted in black suddenly lunged through the doorway. With a loud cry, he drew an arrow back in his bow and then released the bowstring with a loud snap. In my shock, I didn't realize at first that he still held the arrow with the other fingers of his shooting hand—he had snapped his bowstring without releasing the arrow. Yelling, he repeated his action and plucked his bow indiscriminately at all of us sitting in the house. In response, Salip rushed in and interposed himself. With calming words, outstretched hands, and a wan smile, he gradually placated the intruder. As Salip and the attacker moved outside, I went with them and saw that more than twenty warriors from other settlements were now massing. Almost as quickly, however, the men of Yibihilu were also gathering, not as antagonists, but as peacemakers. Armed with stoked tobacco pipes, they snapped fingers and shared smokes with each of the visitors in turn. Their action seemed to melt the tension, like cooling rain in the heat of the day. In short order, the visitors retired to the longhouse, where they were provided with resting mats and began to relax. Those of us from Yibihilu scurried to find and cook bananas to give them by way of hospitality.

An hour or so later, a government constable arrived from the Nomad Station. Salip and some other men had taken the rare step of sending him word about Daguwa's death—and inviting him to come to Yibihilu to investigate. Why? Apparently they were worried that the authorities might receive a different tale of Daguwa's death from some other source. After a long conversation through several interpreters, the constable finally wrote a brief entry in his police book: "Reason of death: Suicide caused by his wife fooling around." The constable's mission completed, discussion about Saliam continued. Eileen suggested that there was so much anger toward her that it might be safer if Saliam went back with the officer and stayed temporarily at the Nomad Station. This proposal dovetailed with the opinions of the men and the constable. Saliam was summoned and left with the officer, who departed as quickly and as quietly as he had arrived. Though the main events of the day were finally over, the piercing wails of the women continued through the night.

The following morning, Daguwa's body had become something else. His face had bloated grotesquely. His swollen limbs oozed corpse fluid, and his skin had peeled to expose putrefying red and yellow-green flesh. His belly and even his genitals had swelled with the gases of decomposition. We will never forget the stench. It burned its way up our noses, down our throats, and seemingly into our brains. Equally powerful was the response of Daguwa's female relatives. With unearthly sobs, they draped themselves physically over the corpse, lovingly massaged its slime, and peeled its skin. Then they rubbed their own arms and legs with the ooze that they had obtained from the body. Corpse fluid on their bodies was taken as a tangible sign of their grief, of their physical as well as emotional connection with Daguwa's death. Their bodies had become like his body. Seeing this, it was said, Daguwa's departing soul would know how much they cared for him. Just a little, this would ease his pain and anger at having died. Later, Eileen offered the women soap to wash themselves off. In their grief, they declined.

The men of Yibihilu dug Daguwa's grave right next to his family house. Salip then went into the house, and the women rolled his corpse onto his back. As Salip strained and stood to stand up with the weight of the corpse, its arms flung out dramatically to both sides. The women shrieked. Men rushed to steady the body and then to help Salip place it in the grave. Daguwa's traditional possessions—his bamboo pipe, bow and arrows, and so on—were quickly arranged in the grave by his female kin. Bark was placed over the corpse, and then the hole was filled in. Just as directly, the men retired to the longhouse to rest. The closest female relatives flung themselves on the mounded grave and continued to wail.

Prior to fieldwork, the only dead body I had seen was the sedate face of a friend of my parents during an open-casket funeral. Now I was shocked and repulsed by the events surrounding Daguwa's death. It seemed hideous that his corpse was allowed to decay and that our women friends wallowed in its stench before it was buried. But I also began to realize that this raw transformation—of a human being into a decomposing natural object—was more emotionally and ecologically honest than my own view of death. The reality of Daguwa's disfigurement showed us the fact of his death as nothing else could do. His passing was not hidden, not made pretty, not covered up in a pallid attempt to "spare grief." I remember having read in a psychology text that widows, widowers, and family members in Western societies often had difficulty accepting the death of a loved one. Even in the United States, a grieving wife or husband might "see" or "hear" a dead spouse during the weeks after his or her death. Were Gebusi customs improper? Or was my own culture's attempt to gloss over and downplay the physical nature of death off kilter?

Among the Gebusi, it was ultimately not the extreme actions of the women that puzzled me, but rather the tamer conduct of the men. As they went to the longhouse to smoke, joke, and drink bowls of local root intoxicant, they acted as if nothing was awry. When I heard that a visiting spirit medium would hold a public séance, I thought he would commune with Daguwa's spirit and inquire about his death. Instead, the séance was a songfest of ribald entertainment. When I asked why, the men said that Daguwa's spirit was as yet too angry to talk about his death. In the meantime, because they were all together, they thought it best to relax and have a good time.

It was all rather bewildering. Which details surrounding Daguwa's death were relevant, and which were superficial? How did Gebusi funeral practices and sorcery beliefs influence their social relationships and their emotional lives? I tried to connect the dots by writing descriptions and reflections. Eileen and I talked and talked. But even as the picture stayed fuzzy, additional questions arose. What did Daguwa's sexual and marital problems with Saliam reveal about Gebusi gender relations? Was Daguwa's death exceptional or anomalous in Gebusi society? Or were the events surrounding it typical of Gebusi beliefs and practices? As I struggled for answers, further events both sharpened my questions and reframed them. Gradually, the events following Daguwa's death unfolded into a sorcery investigation—an inquiry into who had "killed" him. Its twists and turns helped me answer each of the questions I had, but not in the ways I expected. In retrospect, I realized that this trail of discovery revealed much about the practice of ethnography, as well as about the customs and beliefs of the Gebusi.

Although the big funeral feast for Daguwa took place just two days after his burial, it ended as a sideshow to events that occurred weeks later. By the time the sorcery investigation resumed, my opinion of Saliam had changed. At first, I thought she had acted immorally and irresponsibly. She had carried on a sexual affair with a young man named Sasaga, and she had apparently shamed her husband into killing himself. But then new facts emerged to paint a different picture. As Eileen found out from the women, Daguwa had years earlier killed not only his first wife but also her small child, Daguwa's own son. These murders had been so awful that villagers had informed the police. Daguwa ultimately had been sentenced to serve a five-year prison term outside the Nomad Station area. He was the only Gebusi we knew of who had been incarcerated.

His prison term over, Daguwa had returned to the area and married Saliam, who had recently been widowed by the death of Daguwa's "brother." Gebusi widows often end up marrying a male family relative of their dead husband. Anthropologists term this "marriage by levirate." Such unions have the effect of keeping the widow's labor and children within the family line of her original husband. Knowing Daguwa's history, however, Saliam did not want to marry him. As newlyweds, they fought, and he frequently beat her. On one occasion, she finally sought recourse from the patrol officers at the Nomad Station. Given her bruises and Daguwa's violent past, the police arrested him again and held him at the local jail. It was while he was in jail that Saliam took up with Sasaga, her young lover. Perhaps she hoped that her relationship with Sasaga would become a de facto marriage before Daguwa was released from jail. But Daguwa was discharged earlier than expected. Enraged, he wanted to kill Saliam and her partner. But Silap and the other men of Yibihilu persuaded him that he would then receive an even longer prison term than the one he had already endured. In the midst of this tense situation, Daguwa took up again with Saliam. But after their fight in the forest, he committed suicide.

From her own perspective, as Eileen reminded me, Saliam could hardly be blamed. She had been saddled with an abusive marriage and a murderous spouse. She had tried to find refuge, sought solace with another partner, and then stood up for herself when Daguwa fought with her. What villagers took as a sign of further travesty—her fighting with her husband and scratching his shirt with an arrow—could easily have been a desperate attempt at self-defense. But Saliam was rebuked not only by the men of Yibihilu but also by the women, and especially by Daguwa's female kin. Sialim had gone outside the community, gotten her husband jailed, and cheated on him. To make matters worse, her romantic affair had been with a young man who had not yet been initiated.

What was I to think? I could criticize Gebusi values as condoning violent sexism. But Saliam had violated standards of marital fidelity that were deeply held by the Gebusi. I felt stuck in the middle between these viewpoints. Most importantly, however, Eileen and I were concerned that Saliam might be seriously injured or even killed. Fortunately, Eileen's timely suggestion that Saliam be protected by the police until tempers in the village cooled dovetailed with the men's desire to forestall yet more government interference—which would surely have followed if she had been severely injured or killed.

As we slowly came to realize, however, Gebusi inquests into and retributions for sorcery did not generally take place until well after the funeral of the person who had died. The main exception was if the corpse itself "signaled" while lying in state that a given sorcery suspect had "killed" him or her. A sorcery suspect might be told that he or she had to vehemently shake the rotting corpse while wailing his or her grief. If the corpse at that moment gave a "sign"—spilling cadaveric fluid, "moaning" due to gases in its lungs, or bulging its eyes out or even opening or bursting them as a result of gas pressure from decomposition within the braincase—then the suspect could be axed to death on the spot. If the "verdict" of the corpse was clear, there would be little protest over the killing from even the closest relatives of the person who was executed. But this had not happened while Daguwa's corpse was starting to decompose. So the men of Yibihilu had soothed the anger of visitors by extending hospitality—snapping fingers, sharing tobacco, giving food, and holding a séance. The villagers felt that further inquiry should not take place in the heat of the moment but should be conducted more objectively over a longer time, somewhat like a murder investigation in Western societies. For the Gebusi, however, the purpose of the inquest was to ferret out the sorcerers who had killed Daguwa through spiritual means. In their belief, all human deaths were caused by people—either through sorcery or through violence. Even a man who had fallen out of a coconut tree and broken his back had been killed by a sorcerer: because the man had successfully climbed many coconut trees in the past, a sorcerer must have made him lose his grip. Deaths from sickness were likewise attributed to sorcery—the sorcerer had caused the lethal illness. In the case of Daguwa's death, the Gebusi took it as self-evident that sorcerers either had driven Daguwa crazy enough to kill himself or had killed him and then tampered with the evidence to make it look like suicide.

Five weeks after his funeral feast, the real investigation into Daguwa's death began. In a nod to neutrality, the inquest séances were conducted by a spirit medium who had had little personal connection with Daguwa. However, these séances were inconclusive. So further investigation was led by our clever friend Swiman, the main spirit medium of the Yibihilu community. By this time, I had discovered that Gebusi sorcery had two main types. In one type, called *bogay*, the sorcerer was believed to secretly tie up the feces or other bodily leavings of the victim—causing a long, painful illness. The sorcerer then "killed" the victim by burning the fecal matter or other leavings. Anthropologists sometimes call this "imitative magic"—magical use of supernatural powers based on the principle that "like produces like." In the other variety of Gebusi sorcery, called *ogowili*, sorcerers were believed to take the form of magical warriors who attacked the victim in the forest, usually when he or she was alone. The sorcerer-warriors then killed the victim with arrows and clubs, ate out his or her insides, magically sewed him or her up, and finally cast a spell to give the person amnesia. Although the victim might amble uncertainly back to the village, he or she would die a sudden death shortly thereafter.

Bogay comes under the heading of what ethnographers call "parcel sorcery," that is, sickness sent by manipulating a parcel of the victim's leavings. By contrast, *ogowili* qualifies as "assault sorcery," a cannibal attack by magical warriors. For the Gebusi, *bogay* explained the torment of a long, lethal illness, while *ogowili* explained deaths that were relatively quick and sudden, as well as those caused by accident—and suicide. In these cases, assault sorcerers were believed to force their victims to put themselves in precarious danger. One way or the other, Gebusi believed that all deaths from sickness, accident, or suicide were caused by sorcery.

In reality, we found no evidence that Gebusi actually practiced either type of sorcery—and we found much evidence that they did not. Assault sorcery—that is, the eating and then magical sewing up of a victim to disguise a lethal attack—is simply impossible from our point of view. Although parcel sorcery is attempted quite genuinely by various peoples, including some in Melanesia, among the Gebusi it was far more a projection than an actual practice. Our detailed observations and investigations suggested consistently that accusations of parcel sorcery represented trumped-up charges against unfortunate suspects. But Gebusi *belief* in the practice of lethal sorcery was unshakable. So, too, Gebusi men were urgently committed to expose sorcerers and take action against them, including within their own community. The result was scapegoating of and violence against persons accused of sorcery.

In Daguwa's case, the death was believed to be caused by assault sorcery (*ogowili*). Although the *ogowili* is thought to be a man who takes the form of a magical warrior, he can sometimes be manipulated to do this by a malicious woman. In principle, then, Saliam could have been found guilty of Daguwa's death, for instance, if she had been shown to have had sex with an *ogowili* and then induced him to drive her husband crazy. For the Gebusi, this was a plausible possibility, especially because she was known to have had a sexual affair with Sasaga.

In his séances, however, Swiman's spirits avoided this path of inquiry and suggested a different scenario. Rather than excoriate Saliam, the spirits described how *ogowili* warriors had descended on Daguwa from a distant settlement while Saliam was away fetching water. Though the assault sorcerers had disguised the evidence and covered their tracks, Swiman's spirits assured the assembled men that signs of their attack could still be found in the forest near where Daguwa's death had occurred. Further, the *ogowili* might then be tracked back to their own settlement, where they could, at least in principle, be attacked in their human form to avenge the killing of Daguwa. To track assault sorcerers through the forest, however, the Gebusi needed the help of the spirits to guide them.

As Swiman's séance ended, at about five o'clock in the morning, the men of Yibihilu got ready to search out the assault sorcerers responsible for Daguwa's death. Uncertain what was going to happen next, I shoved on my boots and grabbed my flashlight in the predawn darkness. The men were carrying bows and arrows, and some had painted their faces black, like warriors. Eventually, we approached Abwiswimaym, the forest plot where Daguwa had drunk poison. The mood became tense as we started to anticipate the ghostly form of an assault sorcerer ahead. Quietly and anxiously, the men sought cover, pointed their arrows, then advanced warily on their spectral enemy. I pinched my arm to remind myself that we were not likely to find an actual person but rather the evidence of a magical attack by spiritual warriors who might still be lurking nearby. After a while, the area was declared safe.

Next, Swiman and Wahi beckoned us to search upstream for the *buluf*—the magically transformed remains of Daguwa after his insides had ostensibly been eaten by the sorcerers. Swiman's spirits helped guide us. Within a few minutes, he called excitedly, and we rushed to see the evidence of the sorcery attack. An odd-looking stick was said to be the "knife" that the sorcerers had used to cut Daguwa open. An indentation in the ground was the "footprint" of an *ogowili.* A discolored patch of dirt was Daguwa's "blood," which they said had poured out during the attack. My companions were as convinced of these associations as I was incredulous; the "evidence" seemed perfectly natural to me. But then again, the very power of assault sorcerers rests in their ability to disguise their attacks and make the results look almost normal. We then searched a nearby stream for Daguwa's "skin" and "bones." We followed the water upstream for a short way in the general direction of a distant community. But at this point, Swiman's spirits lost the trail of the assault sorcerers and could not find it again. Ultimately, then, we could not track the assault sorcerers to their homes or identify them by name. To the men, however, the investigation had generally validated the information given by Swiman's spirits during his séance. With this partial result, we returned to Yibihilu.

Although somewhat satisfied, the villagers wanted to make a final attempt to find exactly who the assault sorcerers were and whether they could track them to their settlement. This was important not only to ensure safety from death-dealing assault in the community but also to assuage Daguwa's spirit, which would be angry if the investigation into his "murder" was not carried out completely. In particular, the men noted that several of their recent fish-poisoning attempts had failed to yield any fish. Perhaps Daguwa's angry spirit was sabotaging their efforts. So, a few days after Swiman's investigation, two more séances were held by another spirit medium at a forest settlement near where Daguwa had died. As it turned out, these inquiries were even less revealing than the previous ones. The trail of the assault sorcerers had grown cold, the spirits asserted, and no attempt to follow it would be successful. In the bargain, they said, Daguwa's spirit had finally been appeased by their efforts. As if to punctuate the spirits' conclusion, the very next day Wahi, our initial guide through the forest, caught the enormous fish that he had long been stalking in the river above the village. That night, Swiman's spirits celebrated in a wild séance. They confirmed that the fish were both plentiful and ripe for the catching by the Gebusi—with the help of fish poison that had now been spiritually restrengthened. Daguwa's spirit would not interfere. Our worries were over.

Although I thought this would be the end of Daguwa's story, its final surprising twists did not unfold for another seven months. During this time, Saliam began to spend more and more time with Swiman's household. Eventually, she willingly consented to marry him—over the entreaties and objections of her young lover, Sasaga. Strong and robust for a middle-aged man, Swiman had been a widower. During our final year of fieldwork, he and Saliam seemed to be happily married.

This would have been a good Hollywood ending, but it was ultimately not the one we came away with. During the months following Swiman's marriage to Saliam, we discovered a startling new fact: three years previously, Swiman had killed Saliam's own true mother. The old woman, named Mokoyl, had been named as the parcel sorcerer responsible for the death of Swiman's first wife. Mokoyl had tried to prove her innocence by conducting a bird egg divination—cooking eggs that were placed inside a mound of damp and uncooked sago starch. Unfortunately, the eggs had been badly undercooked. When Mokoyl had given Swiman one of the eggs to eat—as she was expected to do as part of the divination—he had promptly vomited. This had been taken as a sign that Swiman's dead wife was clutching his throat, refusing Mokoyl's food, and confirming Mokoyl's guilt. A few weeks later (about a year before we arrived in New Guinea), Swiman had attacked Mokoyl while she was alone in the forest with Boyl (the woman who ended up being Eileen's best friend). As Boyl later told Eileen, she herself had tried to run away when Swiman approached. But he had demanded that she stay as a witness, lest he chase her down as well. Petrified, Boyl had watched as Swiman extracted an ostensible confession from Mokoyl and then spilt her skull with his bush knife. He left her dead in the forest as Boyl ran off. Given the spiritual evidence that had seemed to confirm Mokoyl's guilt, most community members had agreed that Mokoyl was guilty and deserved to die. Her body had been summarily buried in the forest. But villagers from an adjacent settlement, knowing that Mokoyl had been a robust older woman with ample flesh, had dug up her body and eaten parts of it before it decomposed. In so doing, they had also indicated their support for the killing. Government officers never found out about the incident.

If we add this last episode to the chain of events surrounding Daguwa's death, what conclusions can we draw? With the benefit of hindsight, reflection, and analysis, anthropologists are charged with making sense of foreign societies and cultures—and with alternative parts of their own. Experience becomes fieldwork, and fieldwork becomes ethnographic writing. But how does this occur? For Eileen and me in the field, it was hard. No one Gebusi sat down and told us the full story of Daguwa's death, its aftermath, and the events that preceded it. Rather, the story emerged from our observations over time, casual conversations, transcriptions of spirit séances, event calendars, and structured interviews with individual Gebusi concerning life history, kinship, and mortality. Also important were oral accounts that we cross-checked concerning events that predated our arrival, such as the killing of Daguwa's first wife and of Saliam's mother. This information was variously written up in our daily entries and in reflections on what we thought was happening. Within a few days (while the information was still fresh), we typed these up as field notes and analyzed them in relation to other information we were gathering. Even with events that we witnessed and experienced ourselves, our awareness was often dim and partial at first—strong in emotion but weak in understanding. An initial event like Daguwa's death, dramatic as it was, became but one end of a tangled web. It sucked us into a thicket of criss-crossed meanings and histories. Village life was a continuing stream of dramas, small and big, that linked people together while exposing their differences. Even in the few weeks between Daguwa's burial and the inquest séances for his death, the villagers undertook spiritual investigations for seven other sicknesses, including my own, when I was stricken with my first serious bout of malaria. Eileen and I found ourselves in an intricate soap opera—truth more surprising than fiction. Lovers, killers, spouses, co-residents, friends, and relatives all played parts in a strong and changing brew. No wonder that coming together in collective good company was so important to Gebusi—or that it was such an accomplishment!

What is "participant observation" in such a world? In the present case, I observed and to some extent participated in the retrieval of Daguwa's body, his funeral and burial, and the spirit séances and sorcery investigations that followed. However, I did not want to participate in any attack on a suspected sorcerer. Eileen helped us facilitate Saliam's departure to a safer place when sentiments against her were highest. This said, we worried that more severe violence might occur. Later in our fieldwork, when our understanding was better, an older woman in the village was accused of being a parcel sorcerer. In this case, we were able to act like kin and side with the woman's supporters when she was forced to test her innocence by cooking a divination sago with a large raw fish placed inside. Fortunately, no violent action was taken against her, but she was nonetheless forced to move out of the village with her closest kin a short while later. Cultural anthropologists often court risk and uncertainty in deciding what to observe and how and when to participate in "participant observation" of fieldwork.

Between events we observed, those we were able to reliably reconstruct, and those we were able to participate in with good conscience, what larger patterns emerge concerning Daguwa's death, its precedents, and its legacy? We can review. My account began with a description of Daguwa's suicide, the attacks on Saliam, and the mourning and burial of Daguwa's body. Then came the surprisingly festive events of the funeral feast held to commemorate him. These were followed by a month of waiting. Then, after other aborted attempts, Swiman, the community's principal spirit medium, conducted a death inquest séance for Daguwa. Surprisingly, his spirits recast the death as an attack by male assault sorcerers from a distant settlement. A hunt in the forest for the sorcerers was suggestive but inconclusive. After two more séances, Daguwa's spirit was declared appeased—and his widow, Saliam, was exonerated. Several months later, in a further surprise, Swiman and Saliam were married. Rounding out this history were events that had occurred before any of those just mentioned. These included, first, Daguwa's killing of his first wife and son; second, Swiman's killing of Saliam's mother, Mokoyl, for the sickness and death of his first wife; third, the jailing of Daguwa for having beaten Saliam; and fourth, Saliam's sexual affair with the young Sasaga during her husband's absence.

This web of events shows how major incidents like Daguwa's death link backward and forward through time. In the process, they connect topics that might seem disparate—sickness and death, marriage, sex, sorcery, homicide, and suicide. In addition, they expose emotional dynamics among Gebusi, relations between men and women, the importance of spirits and spirit mediums, the influence of government incarceration, and even the role of subsistence practices such as fishing and fish poisoning. Far from being separate, these features resonate and twine together.

So what does Daguwa's story tell us, more broadly, about the Gebusi? Here, we can revisit the questions raised previously. Concerning Gebusi sorcery and gender relations, the events surrounding Daguwa's death illustrate the following—all of which were confirmed by many other experiences during our fieldwork:

1. Gebusi women take primary responsibility for mourning and for emotionally identifying with the person who has died. Men investigate the death and take action against those deemed responsible as sorcerers.
2. Gebusi visitors express antagonism at burials and funeral feasts, but this aggression is undercut by the hosts' hospitality. Deeper anger is usually not expressed until proper inquests and divinations have been arranged.
3. The Gebusi believe that all adult deaths from sickness, accident, or suicide are caused by either male assault sorcerers (*ogowili*) or by male or female parcel sorcerers (*bogay*). Of the two, suspects for parcel sorcery (such as Saliam's mother) are more likely to be executed.
4. There is virtually no objective evidence that the Gebusi actually practice sorcery, but they firmly believe in its existence. In this sense, Gebusi sorcery is a form of scapegoating. The Gebusi "confirm" the identity of sorcerers through an elaborate variety of spiritual inquests and divinations.
5. Male spirit mediums play a key role in Gebusi sorcery accusations. The opinion of their spirits during all-night séances is highly influential, and they can direct the finding and interpretation of "evidence" that is used to validate an accusation.
6. Though spirit mediums should be neutral parties, the outcome of the sorcery inquest may end up benefiting the spirit medium who conducts them. In Daguwa's case, Swiman's spirits directed antagonism away from Saliam, whom he ended up marrying a few months later.
7. After sorcery inquests are completed, social relations are often re-established between the families involved—even if an accused sorcerer has been attacked or killed. After Saliam's mother was executed, her relatives made peace with the killers. Saliam herself continued to live in the Yibihilu community after both her mother's killing and her husband's suicide. Indeed, she ended up marrying her mother's killer.
8. Sickness, death, sorcery, and marriage often link in a cycle of reciprocity or balance over time. Events that seem spontaneous, idiosyncratic, or even bizarre may end up illustrating deeper cultural continuities. In Daguwa's case, Saliam was attacked in reciprocity for his suicide. The earlier death of Swiman's wife was balanced by Swiman's killing of Mokoyl and then by the "replacing" of his deceased wife by his marriage to Mokoly's daughter, Saliam.

In all, the events surrounding Daguwa's death revealed practices and beliefs that were distinctive in Gebusi religion, politics, and social relations. What is the role of such characterizations? In writings by anthropologists, one often finds remarks to the effect that "People X believe or do Y under condition Z." On the one hand, these statements are generalizations; they compress or bleach out the complexities of human experience, and they imply that customs repeat themselves rather than changing over time. Neither of these assumptions is correct. On the other hand, if their limitations are admitted, such thumbnail statements can serve as useful guides—general summaries of complicated beliefs or practices.

Generalizations can also be useful for making cross-cultural comparisons. For instance, we can consider the significance of the Gebusi spirit world and their spirit mediums, who orchestrated sorcery inquests and accusations. Gebusi have a pantheon of animal and other spirits that are contacted by these mediums during spirit séances. Such shamanistic practices have been common among decentralized human societies of foragers and rudimentary horticulturalists all around the world. In the anthropological literature, this applies to well-known simple societies such as the !Kung hunter-gatherers of desert South Africa, the Inuit, or Eskimos, of the North American Arctic, the Yanomamo hunter-horticulturalists of the Amazonian rainforest, and the Navajo Native American farmers and pastoralists of the U.S. southwest. In all these societies, spirit mediums, shamans, diviners, or magical specialists harness cosmic or animal spirits to intervene in and help manage human affairs. In most or all of these cases, the shaman or spirit medium who talks with or invokes the spirits is not a full-time specialist but a part-time practitioner who is otherwise a normal adult with no special rights or abilities. Among the Gebusi, spirit mediums like Swiman are indistinguishable from other persons except in the context of spirit séances and divinations. It is even said that the Gebusi spirit medium, sitting in his trance, is unaware of what the spirits are saying through his voice—because his own spirit has temporarily gone off elsewhere in the spirit world. Consistent with the religions of many foraging and so-called tribal peoples, the Gebusi spirit world associates closely with their encompassing physical environment, including the lingering spirits of the deceased. Their notions of spiritual causation are not linked to a higher or all-encompassing god or deity, as is often true in complex state societies, that is, societies with a centralized government that rules over a large population. Instead, the spiritual world among more decentralized peoples, including those who live within contemporary state societies, is often linked to the unseen actions of people. It is consistent with this worldview that the Gebusi attribute all sickness and death to human agency—including the ability of people to harm one another through spiritual means.

During our fieldwork, features of Gebusi life gradually became more meaningful to Eileen and me—and more comparable to customs in other societies. They also sharpened the question of what was "normal" in Gebusi society and what was "anomalous." This links back to our final lingering question concerning the events surrounding Daguwa's death: How typical was it of Gebusi culture? Such questions loom large for anthropology. How do we know if we are observing events that are widespread or "normal" in a given society? Are we paying too much attention to some practices or beliefs at the expense of others? And what patterns of change have emerged to change this balance over time?

In some ways, the events surrounding Daguwa's death were both normal *and* exceptional, both traditional *and* new for the Gebusi. On the one hand, the burial practices, antagonistic displays, sorcery inquests, and spiritual divinations that surrounded his death were "typical" for many Gebusi during the 1970s and 1980s. On the other hand, certain features of Daguwa's case were exceptional, even unique. His was the only male suicide in almost four hundred adult Gebusi deaths that I was able to document and cross-check through genealogical investigation. He was also the only Gebusi who had killed his wife or his child. Not coincidentally, he was the only Gebusi we knew of at the time whose killing of others had been brought to government attention and resulted in long-term incarceration. Quite possibly, Daguwa's experiences, first in prison and then in the Nomad jail, intensified his dilemma upon being released. That is, his unique experience of confinement and stigmatization may have contributed to his ultimate suicide.

Saliam's actions were also unique; we know of no Gebusi, before or since, who has managed to have her husband jailed for wife-beating. She was also exceptional in conducting an open sexual affair while her husband was still alive. These features—Daguwa's unusual violence and Saliam's forceful response—heightened or exaggerated features of male-female opposition in Gebusi culture. Their particular result also relates to the legacy of Australian colonialism and the presence of Papua New Guinean constables at the Nomad Station. Without these influences, Daguwa would not have been imprisoned for the killing of his first wife or jailed for beating Saliam. And yet, these new developments blended almost seamlessly with general patterns in Gebusi culture. The funeral and inquest procedures for Daguwa were quite typical for the Gebusi. The subsequent marriage of Saliam to Swiman completed a cycle of balanced exchange both in death and in life: the death of Swiman's first wife was avenged by the killing of Saliam's mother and then structurally "replaced" by Swiman's marriage to Saliam herself. Saliam willingly accepted, if not actively pursued, this last resolution. Did she really care for Swiman? Was she grateful to his spirits for their help in saving her, or was he simply a convenient protector? Did Saliam dispute the execution of her own mother, or did she accept this killing as legitimate—as some Gebusi do when their relatives are killed as sorcerers? It was hard for us to tell. Perhaps all of these were true for Saliam to some extent. Though it may seem odd or even shocking that a woman could marry her mother's killer, it is not uncommon in cultures around the world for people to live with those who have harmed them or their close relatives. In Western countries, including the United States, this pattern is common in cases of child abuse or wife-battering: the victim may accept and even actively defend the family member who perpetrates domestic violence and suffering.

Events such as Daguwa's death and its aftermath challenged us to the hilt. They also yielded insights that were crucial to our understanding of death and dying, gender relations, scapegoating, women's resistance and accommodation, and the power of human affiliation in the face of violence and suffering. Most ethnographers strive to find generalities while valuing the uniqueness of people and events. They seek to appreciate cultures while exposing their ideologies and inequities. And they try to balance participant observation with the importance of their own feelings and values. Like most ethnographers, we both succeeded and failed in all these respects. But the attempt was well worth the effort.

Web site images of events and topics described in this chapter can be found at http://www.mhhe.com/knauft1.

CHAPTER 4

Antagonists make peace by sharing a tobacco pipe over the grave of the deceased.
(PHOTO: Eileen Marie Knauft)

Getting Along with Kin and Killers

To FOLLOW THE PLAY, you have to know the characters. If the play is in sports, you need to know what team the players are on, what sport they are playing, and what the rules are. For Eileen and me, lives in Yibihilu seemed halfway between a dramatic play and an intense sport. The sport analogy may be stretching things, because the "game" was to manage one's relationship to others in the community, not to defeat a rival team. Indeed, when men and boys in the village played soccer (which government officers had introduced), they preferred the game to end in a tie rather than having one team win and the other lose. But in daily life, people *were* organized into groups. And we had to know the groups and their rules of relationship to know what was going on. Suddenly, a dispute would break out. All at once, one group would be swinging clubs against another, which retaliated in like fashion—while a third group stood as peacekeepers in the middle, trying to break things up. It all happened spontaneously, and we couldn't tell why people divided as they did. The same was true more generally—groups of people would casually depart to forage in the forest, give and receive gifts of food at feasts, or present costume decorations to initiates. Why did some people act together as a group as opposed to others? And why had some people been killed within the community while most others remained friends?

In societies like that of the Gebusi, principles of cooperation and division stem from patterns of kinship and marriage. Anthropologists have long emphasized the importance of kinship, especially in non-Western cultures. In fact, if there is one topic that is specific to anthropology but largely unconsidered by the other social sciences, it is the social organization of kin and relatives. On the surface, kinship is a simple concept. Each of us has a family and relatives, and it seems natural to think that we know about relations between kin. We know about parenthood and about our brothers and sisters; we know what marriage is, who our cousins are, and so on. But things are less obvious when we consider other cultures—or even when we consider our own more closely.

In Gebusi society and many other societies, if you ask someone what group he or she belongs to, the person will tell you the name of his or her clan. A clan is a permanent social group whose members pass down membership through descent from one generation to the next. Members of a clan generally believe that they should not marry one another and that they derive from a common ancestor. We say "believe" because all members of a clan may not, in fact, be able to actually trace links through a male or female line to an ancestor whom they think they have in common. Among the Gebusi, clan membership is passed down through the male line—a bit like the way last names in most Western societies have historically been passed down. So we can call the Gebusi descent groups "patriclans." By contrast, however, most people in countries like the United States do not belong to clans—or even to any descent group at all. They typically belong to "families" but not to larger, permanent named groups defined through descent and possessing special rights and duties. But among Gebusi, all members of a named patriclan call one another "brother," "sister," "father," "father's sister," "grandparent," and so on—even though most of them are what Americans and other Westerners would call "cousins," "uncles," "aunts," and "grand-aunts and -uncles."

Sometimes, the extended ties of descent groups can be quite strong. Take an example relating to marriage. When Saliam's first husband died, she was expected to marry the deceased man's patriclan "brother," Daguwa, who was a widower at the time. This "marriage by levirate" had the effect of keeping Saliam—and her daughter from this previous marriage—within a close branch of her dead husband's patriclan. This was true even through Daguwa was not the true brother but rather what we would call a cousin of Saliam's first husband. In fact, the two men couldn't trace an actual clan relation to each other through their relatives, but both considered themselves to be members of the upper branch of the Yugul clan, *Yugul tabul bwi.* We can graphically show the family relationship that emerged between Saliam and her two husbands, in turn, by the standard symbols that anthropologists use to show kinship: a triangle for a man, a circle for a woman, an equal sign for marriage, a slash to indicate someone who has died, a vertical line for descent, a horizontal line for siblingship, and a slash across a horizontal line to indicate that descent or clanship cannot be demonstrated by actual kinship (see figures 4.1 and 4.2).

If we want to be yet more complete, we can add in Daguwa's first marriage and the children of the two marriages. Because this involves persons who died from homicide, we can indicate these persons with an "X" rather than a slash. Likewise, we can indicate the order of each person's marriages with numerals in boxes (see figure 4.3).

Though kinship diagrams take a bit of getting used to, they are important ways for anthropologists to keep track of social relations among people in small-scale communities. And they can alert us to things we might otherwise miss. For instance, figure 4.3 reminds us that the marriage between Saliam and Daguwa was actually the second one for each of them. It also shows that Saliam had a surviving daughter from her first marriage, that Daguwa's first wife and son were killed and that Saliam and Daguwa's own marriage did not produce any children. Finally, it shows that, despite Daguwa's violence, the clanship between Daguwa and Saliam's first husband helped him maintain his claim to her.

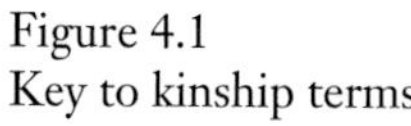

Figure 4.1
Key to kinship terms

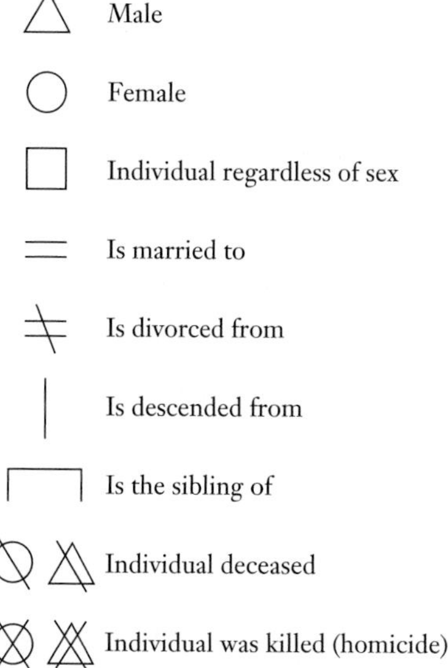

Figure 4.2
Marriage by levirate

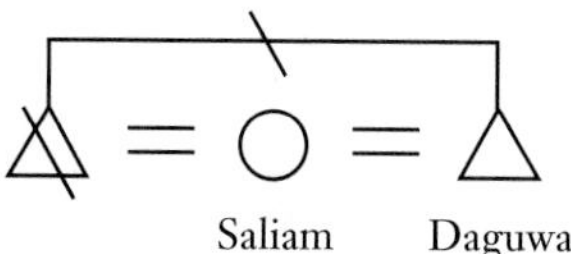

Figure 4.3
Families from leviratic marriage

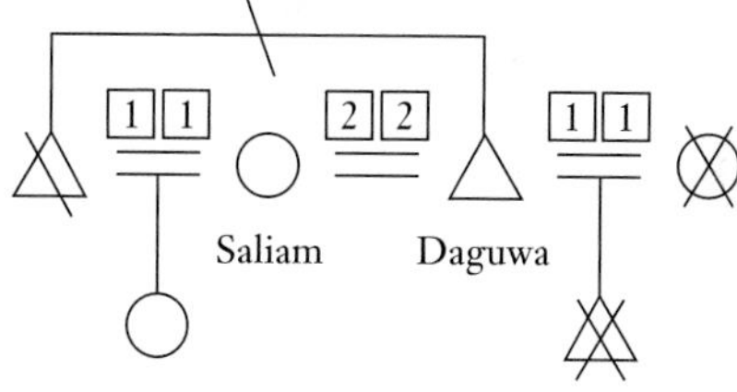

What about the power of "sisterhood" between women as opposed to the bond of "brotherhood" between men? Because the Gebusi trace descent through the male line, broadening "brotherhood" and "sisterhood" works only as long as the links between generations go through fathers; generational ties don't turn the Gebusi into members of the same clan if they are traced through mothers (see figure 4.4). For many of us born and raised in Western countries, the people we consider "cousins" can be related to us on either our mother's or our father's side. But for the Gebusi, a first cousin on the father's side is either a "brother" or a "sister," whereas a first cousin on the mother's side is almost never a member of one's clan at all.

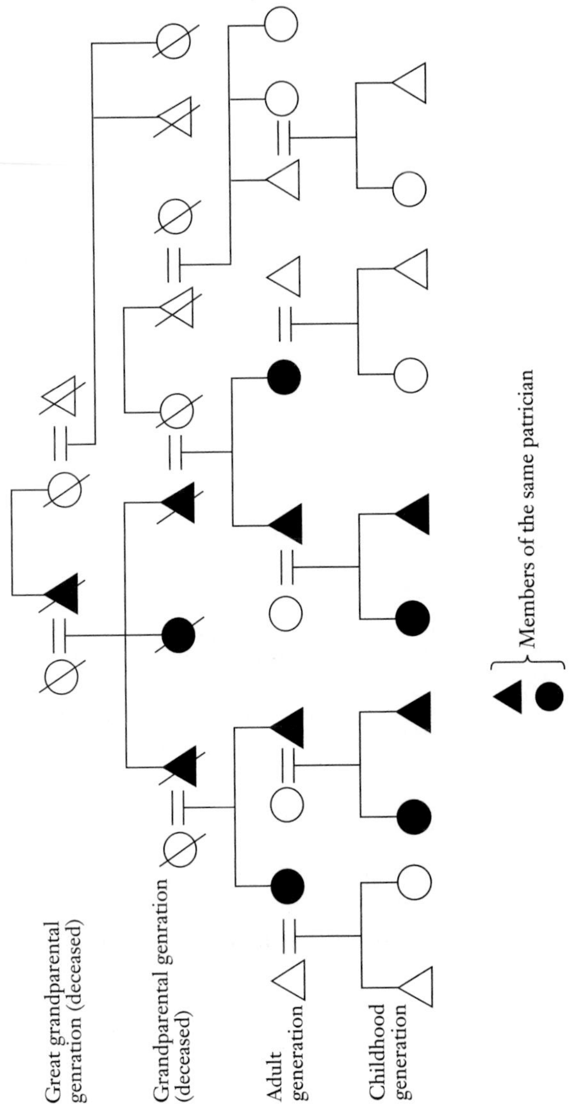

Figure 4.4
Gebusi clanship

In a further twist, Gebusi extend the terms for "mother," "child," and "mother's brother" selectively across generations. In particular, they call the daughter of a maternal uncle their own "mother" (*wi*), and they call the boy or girl born to a paternal aunt their own "child" (see figure 4.5). Strange as it may seem, this kinship system is found in several different parts of the world and is called Omaha kinship (after the Omaha Native Americans, who also refer to these relatives in this way). What this terminology reflects is that you cannot marry into a descent line that your father or father's sister married into, because this would mean you were

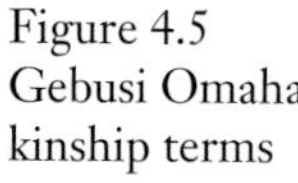

Figure 4.5
Gebusi Omaha kinship terms

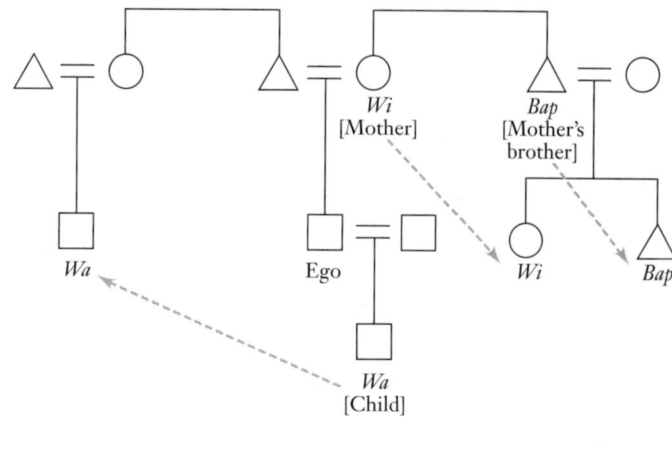

Figure 4.6
Gebusi sister-exchange marriage

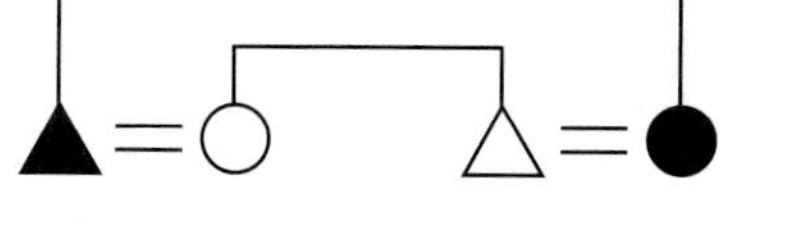

marrying someone you called your "mother" or "child." Instead, your clan branch should wait another generation before remarrying someone in these descent lines. This has the net effect of extending a clan's network of marital alliances to a wider and more diverse range of other clans.

Does this all seem complicated? It certainly was for me. But because my advisor was really into kinship, I had to tackle it. Truth be told, kinship is just about the driest and most boring part of cultural anthropology, at least for most students. When I was in college, I felt about kinship the way I felt about calculus: I knew it must be important, but I really couldn't see the point—and I didn't seem to be very good at it. And Omaha kinship was the tip of the iceberg. There are hundreds of ways that cultures group relatives together, decide who is "really" related to whom, establish rules and patterns of intermarriage, structure alliances and divisions between groups of kin, and so on. To start figuring this out before I entered graduate school, I tried to read Claude Lévi-Strauss's classic *The Elementary Structures of Kinship*. I thought I would go crazy! But then I started doing fieldwork. Learning kinship in the abstract is, well, abstract. But when your friends are dating, marrying, fighting, giving gifts to one another, and all the rest, you often can't figure out who is doing what to whom and why *except* through kinship. And then kinship becomes not just important but a fascinating human puzzle.

In addition to kinship, marriage among the Gebusi is also really important, as it is for most Westerners. But Gebusi practice "preferential sister-exchange." When a woman marries into a given clan, a "sister" of the husband should also marry a "brother" of the bride (see figure 4.6). As such, the marriage of a woman into her husband's clan should be matched by a balancing marriage of a woman from this second clan into her own—so neither side "loses" a woman without gaining one back. It may sound like a strange way of getting married, as if women were pawns exchanged between groups of men. We may like to think that women and men should get married because they want to, not because they feel obligated. But among groups like the Gebusi, sister-exchange is more interesting and surprising than either of these alternatives.

First, the Gebusi ideal of marital balance is taken loosely and can be extended. Because Gebusi have complicated ways of extending "siblingship" beyond even the patriclan, they can sometimes find creative ways to "define" a woman as a kind of "sister." Second, the bride-to-be has a degree of veto power in marriage. If a woman really objects to marrying a given man, her wishes may hold sway. As Eileen discovered, this was also true in the distant past. Some of the oldest Gebusi women told her they had bluntly refused a proposed marriage and hence had thwarted a sister-exchange. Their ability to resist depended on several things. One was how strong-minded and forceful they were. Another was their age at the time. Before government contact, Gebusi women were sometimes "married" when they were as young as ten or twelve years old. I put "married" in quotes because the young woman didn't have sex with her husband until she was older. But she could be physically transferred to the husband's settlement and live with him and his relatives until she reached puberty and the marriage could be consummated. When a woman was given in marriage at a young age, it was harder for her to resist the union. But others might resist on her behalf. If they were alive, a girl's close "mothers," especially her true mother, would vehemently object to marrying off a young daughter. As a result, the marriage of not-yet-adolescent girls in sister-exchange doesn't appear to have been common among the Gebusi.

Alternatively, a teenage girl and a young man could become romantically attracted even though there was little chance that a "sister" of the young man would marry a "brother" of the young woman. Such "unreciprocated" marriages almost always drew vehement objections from the young woman's fathers and brothers. But the young couple could prevail if the woman was strong-willed or ran away with her new husband. Though the parents or brothers of the woman could object mightily, and though they could beat her if they found her, many of these romantic unions persisted and were ultimately accepted as marriages.

Marriage between certain kinds of Gebusi relatives was considered impossible and was completely prohibited. All human cultures put a taboo on some kinds of marriages, such as that between a woman and her own true son. But other rules concerning who can or cannot marry vary widely from one society to another. In some cultures, a person is restricted to finding a partner in one-half, one-quarter, or even only one-eighth of the available descent groups. Western societies tend toward the other extreme: the only marriages that are completely prohibited are usually those within the nuclear family and sometimes between very close cousins. This leaves almost the whole rest of society as an open field in which you can find a marriage partner.

The Gebusi stay somewhere between these extremes. They generally prohibit marriage within the clan, which averages eighteen persons in size. In anthropological terms, this means that Gebusi clans are "exogamous"—their members have to marry outside the clan. For any individual, one or two additional clans may be considered a "brother" clan, based on vague ancestral ties. Marriage between such "brother clans" is frowned upon but not completely prohibited. Other restrictions are less widespread. A Gebusi shouldn't marry the child of a paternal aunt or a maternal uncle. (After all, these persons are "mothers" and "children" to each other!) But more distant relatives on the mother's side are permissible marriage partners. Gebusi like to repeat marriages between clan branches after skipping a generation—so finding a partner from the clan of the father's mother is particularly desirable. Beyond this, however, the field of marriage is largely open; anyone who is not closely related is an eligible spouse. In a village like Yibihilu, an unmarried young person finds that about two-thirds of the appropriately aged persons of the opposite sex are marriageable. Most Gebusi find their marriage partners within their village or among those who live in smaller hamlets within an hour's walk of the main settlement. As such, we can say that Gebusi communities are largely endogamous.

On some occasions, a Gebusi woman actively wants to complete a sister-exchange. If a young woman likes her own brother and his new wife—not to mention the new wife's brother, her own potential spouse—then she looks forward to completing the matrimonial exchange. The two couples will typically live together as a joint family, and such family units tend to be strong and cooperative, both structurally and emotionally.

Ultimately, then, the notion that Gebusi sister-exchange is "preferential" means just that: sister-exchange is preferred "if possible." But if not, that's life. In actuality, just over half of all first Gebusi marriages (52 percent) were sister-exchanges. Most of the remainder were what we liked to call "romantic unions" that did not follow the rules of sister-exchange. Despite the pronouncements of Gebusi men that "we exchange women" (*ulia sesam degra*), women and men who wanted to marry without exchange often found a way to do so. Various features of Gebusi social organization helped them out. Within each Gebusi patriclan are smaller subgroups whose members *can* trace an actual linkage to one another via male descent. In anthropological terms, these small groups are "lineages." More specifically, because Gebusi lineages are traced through the male line, we call them "patrilineages."

The Gebusi don't keep track of their ancestors for more than a generation or two. As a result, Gebusi patrilineages usually include only three or four adults; they are an extended family that typically comprises an adult male, his adult siblings, plus his own children and those of his brothers. Given their small size, a patrilineage at any given time may include only one young unmarried woman—or maybe none at all. Yet it is within the patrilineage rather than the larger clan that a young man's claim to use his "sister" for exchange in marriage remains strong. In essence, then, Gebusi patrilineages represent very tight and very small atoms of kinship defined through male descent. Overwhelmingly, their members live together in the same settlement. Members of the larger patriclan, by contrast, do not necessarily live together; most patriclans are spread out over several settlements.

If Gebusi patrilineages are small, and if members of the larger clan often do not live with one another, then who else do people live with? Typically, they live with other close kin who are related to them by marriage or with close relatives traced through their mothers. For instance, more than 80 percent of men who have a living mother's brother live in the same settlement as this man. Seventy percent of men who have a true brother-in-law reside in the same village as him. From a woman's point of view, this is good: it means that residing with her husband does not generally distance her from her own brother. And when she gets older, she is apt to live in the same village as both her son and her brother. In the mix, she usually resides as well with a range of close female kin on whom she can rely and with whom she can perform collective tasks.

Taken as a whole, Gebusi villages bubble with kinship relations that are variously traced through mothers, fathers, classificatory brother- and sisterhood, and intermarriage. The fifty-two residents of Yibihilu identified with thirteen different clans. The men of the village belonged to seven different clans and eleven different patrilineages. As many as a third of them were totally unrelated to one another. As such, Gebusi villages are multiclan settlements, rather than clusters of people around the men of a single patriclan. This helps explain why Gebusi place such a high value on collective good company and why they are so proud of their ability to cohere their settlement across diverse ties of kinship and friendship. Social ties are made stronger and more enjoyable by the emphasis on being together, talking congenially, and joking and cheering in collective camaraderie.

Having reviewed Gebusi social organization, we can now put the pieces together. In particular, we can ask what portrait emerges from Gebusi patterns of kinship and residence that combine very small lineages, sister-exchange marriage, and village residence based on diverse ties of kinship, marriage, and friendship. As we have seen, only about half of first Gebusi marriages are balanced through sister-exchange. And this creates a problem, because the Gebusi lack any effective way to recompense an extended family or patrilineage that loses a sister or daughter in marriage. In some parts of Melanesia, Africa, and Asia, a woman's marriage can be "paid for" by valuable gifts given by the groom and his kin group to the bride's relatives. These payments are sometimes called "bride-price." Many anthropologists prefer the term "bride-wealth," however, because the transaction is not a human purchase per se but the opening round of wealth exchanges that may last for years between the closest kin of the groom and the bride.

Among the Gebusi, however, bride-wealth or bride-price is rudimentary at best. A groom might give a few small gifts to the mother or brothers of his bride, but these presents typically are small and are not considered an exchange for the woman herself. Instead of material compensation, the Gebusi have practiced a direct or person-for-person form of reciprocity. The ideal, of course, is sister-exchange marriage. But when there is no return marriage, there is also no payment to mollify the bride's kin for the loss of her services. So what happens? Although this causes resentment, the Gebusi tend to sweep it under their cultural rug. Most in-laws claim that they accept marital imbalance and get along well. Indeed, in-laws co-reside just as often when the marriage that links them is unreciprocated as when it is balanced through sister-exchange. Given their strong cultural emphasis on good company, it is not easy for Gebusi to admit or address tensions between in-laws.

Here is where issues of kinship, residence, and social etiquette link to Gebusi politics and disputes. And at least to me, this is where the discussion gets really interesting. It's one thing to know about the kinship and residential makeup of a society. But it's more significant to use this knowledge to understand important and otherwise hard-to-explain trends. For the Gebusi, these have included a very high rate of violence and killing associated with sorcery accusations. Why has the Gebusi rate of killing been so high, and who stands the greatest chance of being killed?

One of the most important facts here is that Gebusi sorcery accusations are especially likely between members of patrilineages that are linked by a marriage that has not been reciprocated. At this point, I should emphasize that the Gebusi themselves do not say this. As we have seen, Gebusi men have a profound ability to emphasize good company and to suppress or dissociate from their anger. Even during a spirit séance when a community member is accused of being a sorcerer, the clan and lineage relatives of the accused usually say nothing at all. They may even continue joking so as not to lose public face. Gebusi believe that sorcery accusations should be proved by tangible evidence. As described in Chapter 3, these clues take a variety of forms, including a "sign" by the corpse, a packet of "skin and blood" identified by a spirit medium, leavings from the victim that have been "burned" by the sorcerer, or divination food that has been undercooked by an accused sorcerer. To Gebusi, these findings represent tangible physical evidence—as real as fingerprints on a smoking gun. Why was the sorcerer accused or attacked? Because, Gebusi say, the objective evidence shows him or her to be guilty! This evidence typically is convincing to a wide range of people and tends to be supported rather than opposed by men from the many clans in the settlement.

Given this context, how can I suggest that unacknowledged tensions related to marriage and sister-exchange inform sorcery accusations between Gebusi patrilineages? Here, we must shift gears. Gebusi's own explanations are crucial, but they do not tell the whole story. Beyond what people think and say, it's important to focus on what they actually do. And especially in small-scale societies, these actions often link to their patterns of kinship and residence.

We all know that people often say one thing and do another. In American society, we may promise to marry someone "until death do us part." But about half of all marriages in the United States end in divorce. As an anthropologist, it is important—indeed, key—to consider the gap between ideals and actions. Among other things, such gaps are crucial if we are to understand patterns of violence or inequality that are minimized or downplayed by people's own perceptions and values. In making this move, however, we create more distance between our perspective and those of the people we are studying. To say that half of Americans who marry get divorced captures neither the joy of a good marriage nor the pain of a bad one. It is a statistical assessment, not an emotional or humanistic one; it pulls us back from understanding human lives.

Anthropologists have often debated which is better—a close-up portrait that is rich with people's experiences, or a more detached view that is systematic and encompassing. Is a statistical depiction more scientific or more dehumanizing? My own opinion is that both views are needed—and that they need to be combined. Like a photographer with a zoom lens, the anthropologist should focus on the details of individual lives and experiences. But she or he should also draw back occasionally—as in the present chapter—and look more dispassionately at the larger picture, statistics and all.

For the Gebusi, Eileen and I tried to gain a societywide view by collecting census material, residence histories, and kinship information. By charting the genealogies of eighteen clans—as far back as Gebusi could remember—I documented the cause and circumstances of death for each deceased person. Then I double-checked each account with someone from a different clan, to make sure the information was accurate. This was a tedious task, as you might imagine. But the Gebusi were interested in the details, and I think they were proud to present them correctly. And when they didn't, they quickly realized that I would uncover their "embellishments" by obtaining a more accurate story from someone else.

To make a long process short, we can return to the question raised previously: How do we know that Gebusi related via unreciprocated marriage accuse one another of sorcery even though the Gebusi don't make this statement themselves—any more than Americans announce at weddings that the marriage is likely to fail? Within the community, statistics reveal that persons related by marriage are more than three times more likely to accuse one another of sorcery than would be expected by chance. In terms of father-in-law/son-in-law relations, the rate of sorcery accusations is a whopping fifteen times greater than would be expected by chance. In more than 70 percent of cases in which a relative via marriage is accused, the marriage that links the patrilineages of the accuser and the victim has not been reciprocated. Viewed broadly, this makes sense. Gebusi marriage is based on "person-for-person" exchange. So is Gebusi killing: the life of the sorcerer is taken "in exchange" for the death of the person who died of sickness. These aspects of positive and negative exchange link together. If there is no exchange for a woman in life, it increases the chances of violent revenge between the two patrilineages when a person in one of them dies from an illness.

Killings of the Gebusi were remarkably frequent. Of all adult deaths, almost one-third were homicides (129 of 394, or 32.7 percent). This rate of violence is even greater than that of the Yanomami, the so-called fierce people of the Amazon rainforest. Per person, this rate of killing equals the carnage of the bloodiest war in world history, World War II in Europe—including the Holocaust. Not all Gebusi killings were individual executions of sorcery suspects, but the majority were—61 percent. Another 21 percent were the result of Bedamini raids, in which large numbers of Gebusi could be killed simultaneously. (These raids were also linked to sorcery in that most of them were instigated by disgruntled Gebusi who contracted Bedamini to venture into Gebusi territory and attack one of their villages that was thought to be harboring sorcerers.) Only 5.5 percent of violent Gebusi deaths resulted from battles or fights between massed groups of Gebusi warriors.

Gebusi adults of both sexes and almost all age categories could be killed as sorcerers. In relative terms, however, the persons most likely to be accused and executed were senior adults—which for the Gebusi means anyone in their thirties or older. Although I don't have the numbers to prove it, I think there are several reasons for this. As they live longer, the Gebusi accumulate more disputes and resentments, including via nonreciprocal marriages. When someone dies of sickness, there is a greater chance that one of these past disputes may consciously or unconsciously inform an inquest that finds the other party guilty of sorcery. In addition, older persons can become increasingly concerned with and angry about their own growing list of friends and relatives who have died. They can also be thought to be angry enough over these deaths to themselves direct spiritual malevolence against others. By contrast, children are never accused of sorcery; in Gebusi belief, they are not old enough to know how to perform it.

Between the extremes of older persons and children, young men may sometimes be accused of sorcery and executed. In the more distant past (the 1950s and 1960s), late adolescent males were commonly targeted as sorcerers. But one category of adults has been almost completely immune from Gebusi sorcery accusation: young women. In their midteens and into their twenties, Gebusi women were virtually never accused or attacked as sorcerers. From a societywide standpoint, this is significant. Young women are crucial to a society's reproductive and demographic survival. As unconscionable as it is in moral and ethical terms, the killing of older persons has less impact on reproduction. Few Gebusi women seem to give birth beyond their early thirties. Men are even more "dispensable" in demographic terms because a relatively small number of men may impregnate a larger number of women to repopulate the society. Enormous numbers of European men were killed during World War I, but the population replenished itself quickly because so many young women were available for childbearing. In the case of the Gebusi, the relative immunity of young women from sorcery execution meant that the internal homicide rate, high as it was, did not preclude their collective survival. People lived in good company even as they killed those they suspected of breaking this rule, especially as they got older. A greater survival threat was posed by the Gebusi's neighbors, the Bedamini, who would indiscriminately kill Gebusi women and children as well as men during their fearsome raids.

What has happened to the Gebusi rate of violent death over time? As Australian colonial officers suppressed Bedamini raiding, from 1963 to 1975, the Gebusi who died of homicide declined from a whopping 39.0 percent of all adult deaths (97 killings out of 249 deaths) to 23.3 percent (24 killings out of 103 deaths). This decline continued during the first seven years of national independence: from 1975 until our departure in 1982, 19 percent of adults died from homicide (8 of 42 deaths). Despite this general improvement, those killings that did occur were targeted increasingly against women. Prior to pacification, the rate of homicide had been 26.4 percent higher for men than that for women. This balance then shifted: between 1975 and 1982, women were killed more than twice as often as men. Why? There are several reasons. First, the Gebusi became increasingly reluctant to kill people whose murder might come to the attention of police at the Nomad Station. Although officers seldom knew what went on in the villages, they might have learned about a killing from angry relatives of the slain person. In practical fact, the killing of a woman—particularly if she was an elderly widow—was not as likely to generate an outpouring of anger as when violence was directed against an adult male. Old widows are sometimes perceived as a drain on the community because they have a declining ability to work, and their childbearing years are over. They may be seen as irritable, uncooperative, and apt to use spiritual power to compensate for their own physical decline. Reciprocally, if older widows do not have grown sons to support them, they can be relatively easy targets of sorcery accusation. And if they are killed in the forest, away from the main settlement, as was the case with Saliam's mother, chances are good that their deaths will not be reported to the authorities.

In some ways, Gebusi violence against sorcerers has gradually become more similar to that in Western history. From the late fifteenth through the late eighteenth centuries, some historians estimate that the Christian church killed approximately 300,000 women as witches. Fear of largely female witchcraft was found in significant parts of Europe and America during the 1600s and early 1700s, including in the famous witch trials at Salem in 1692. Among the Gebusi, however, sorcery is tied less to waves of community hysteria than to resentment over high rates of death due to sickness and to marital imbalances that simmer and fester between in-laws. These tensions ultimately find expression in sorcery inquests, divinations, and accusations.

How have the Gebusi themselves viewed their killing? This question has a certain poignancy because their violence has so frequently been directed against those who are supposed to be friendly acquaintances within the community. To a surprising degree, the Gebusi have rationalized these discrepancies away. For them, it is not murder to kill a sorcerer. Rather, it is a legitimate and proper way to dispense with someone who has him- or herself committed a terrible killing. In Gebusi belief, these persons must be eliminated to keep the death toll due to sickness from climbing even higher. It may be hard for us to appreciate the degree to which the Gebusi believe in their sorcery divinations and inquests. Outside the narrow context of sorcery inquests, most Gebusi were good-natured and friendly, not angry or violent. In contrast to males in some other parts of Melanesia, Gebusi men were self-effacing in public and more likely to minimize than to magnify their aggression. When the death of a close relative or spouse was followed by a verified sorcery accusation, however, even the most mild-mannered man could become a killer. When an ambush and a killing were finally arranged, the accuser was often aided by others who wanted to rid the community of someone considered to be a public menace.

In the aftermath of a sorcery execution, the killer and his supporters were rarely attacked. Instead, the community tended to close ranks behind them. In the same way that accusations needed to have "objective" confirmation and support from different clans in the village, so, too, the person who killed a publicly accused sorcerer could generally count on the support of the community to protect him. Faced with this reality, the relatives of the person who had been killed typically had little choice but to accept the death and either stay in the community or move on to another settlement. Even when they wanted revenge, the men of the sorcerer's patrilineage were few in number—not numerous enough to prevail against the rest of the community.

Beyond our concern for the people who were themselves attacked or killed, why should we care about Gebusi sorcery and violence? One reason is that their accusations reveal the influence of culture in promoting stigmatization. Cultural beliefs can powerfully validate discrimination—as if discrimination was "objective" and "true." Scapegoating of innocent people can be abetted by structural tensions of social organization, kinship, and demography that may lay outside the daily awareness of the actors involved. Given this, a scientific understanding of social organization is particularly important to complement our awareness of people's stated motives and lived experiences. In American society, for example, tensions in family structure that result from class inequality, unemployment, racism, and gendered inequality clearly inform patterns of violence and domestic abuse.

By understanding how inequality works among peoples such as the Gebusi, we may see more clearly how larger patterns of discrimination operate in other societies. For instance, Western cultural values of equality concerning race, gender, ethnicity, nationality, and religion are strongly assumed in discourses of human rights, freedom, and democracy. Amid this positive emphasis, however, it would be easy to overlook patterns of inequality and discrimination that persist in fact. As with the Gebusi, we may confuse how we would *like* society to function with how it actually operates. Just as we may believe in marriage despite a high rate of divorce, we may believe in sexual, racial, and cultural equality and yet find that women are not paid as much as men for doing similar work or that foreigners or racial or ethnic minorities are relegated disproportionately to low levels of income and status. In this regard, it is also easy to neglect patterns of kinship and social organization that are very important to ethnic or foreign-born minorities even though their networks of affiliation often remain outside legal recognition or mainstream cultural understanding. This is not to say that social inequities are necessarily due to willful malevolence. It is rather to underscore how culturally constructed beliefs—and their discrepancy from actual behavior—can be as strong in our own society as we may discover them to be in others. Cultural anthropology often looks to other cultures to rediscover our own beliefs and actions. Beyond their intrinsic value, features of social structure, kinship, and community organization help us understand much about the human condition at home as well as abroad.

Web site images of events and topics described in this chapter can be found at http://www.mhhe.com/knauft1.

CHAPTER 5

A Gebusi dancer embodies spirits at a ritual feast. (PHOTO: Bruce Knauft)

Spirits, Sex, and Celebration

GEBUSI GENDER, SEX, AND spirituality differ greatly from Western practices; they stretch our envelope of understanding. Among these differences, Gebusi admit alternative expressions of sexuality, particularly for men. This is not to suggest that Gebusi practices are a model of sexual tolerance much less of gendered equality. But neither is it to say that they have nothing to teach us. Notwithstanding its tensions and challenges, exposure to Gebusi sexual culture was a rich part of my fieldwork. Although I thought I was tolerant to begin with, I came away with a greater understanding of and respect for sexual diversity than I could ever have imagined. I also became more aware of gendered discrimination than I had been previously. I am grateful that my Gebusi friends let me know about the sexual side of their culture. If sex is often a sensitive topic, it is also an important one, and one that needs to be studied with special sensitivity.

My awareness of Gebusi sexual culture began with the male joking that laced events such as ritual feasts and dances, storytelling, and spirit séances. Here is an example of Gebusi male joking:

YABA [TO DOGON]: *Go over there and sleep with the women. Build your "fire" over there.* [Go over and have sex with them.]

SWIMAN [TO YABA]: *If he goes over there and lies down, where are* you [Yaba] *going to put your "forehead"* [phallus] *to sleep?! You'll just have to go over and lay your "forehead" on* his [Dogon's] *grass skirt!!*

YABA [TO DOGON]: *You're wearing a big grass skirt* [for me to lie on].

DOGON [TO YABA]: [You do and] I'll pull off your loincloth!!

YABA [TO DOGON]: *And you'll sleep there* [in my crotch]*!!*

[Whooping and laughter from the other men.]

DOGON [TO YABA]: *No! I'll give your loincloth to the women and take off their clothes for you* [so you can take the female role]*!!*

[More laughter from the men.]

SWIMAN: *The younger men must be getting tired from ladling out all their "kava" [semen]! I'll ladle out mine with a thrust!!* [Kicks out his foot.]

[General laughter.]

DOGON [TO YABA]: *Can you give some to me??*

YABA [TO DOGON]: *We'll have to lay down "forehead"* [phallus] *as a gift-exchange name!*

YABA AND DOGON [LEANING THEIR HEADS TOGETHER]: *YAY!!*

[Laughter and yelling.]

Simmering in everyday life, male joking found its greatest outlet on festive occasions and during celebrations. Jokesters didn't have to be related to each other; in fact, it was best if they were not. Dogon and Yaba were unrelated and didn't live in the same community; not being otherwise connected, they were all the more in "good company" for being able to joke together. These connections were made easier by men who were related to both jokesters. In the present case, this role was taken by Swiman, who was a community co-resident and distant in-law of Yaba's and a maternal relative of but not co-resident with Dogon. At the time, all three men were widowers in their early thirties. What about the content of their bawdy jibes? Were Yaba and Dogon really apt to have sexual relations or to use "phallus" as a gift-exchange name between them? No; their joking signaled nonsexual friendship. Much sexual joking, some of it quite physical, flirts with possibilities that aren't consummated. Thinking back, the same was true of the locker-room pranks played by members of my high school soccer team in Connecticut. In a similar way, much Gebusi horseplay is what could be called "homosocial" rather than "homosexual." Its humor derives from threatening but not actually engaging in sex.

At first, I wasn't sure if Gebusi males engaged each other sexually at all. Groups to the east of the Gebusi were known to practice male-male sexuality, but peoples farther to their west did not. I thought that my Gebusi friends were more likely to be in the former camp than the latter, but how could I know? Their interactions were certainly full of suggestive jokes. A young man might shout in jest, "Friend, your phallus was stroked, and it came up!" But beneath the surface, how much was orgasmic fire and how much was playful smoke? I suspected that male trysts took place near the outhouse at night during séances and festive dances. To find out if this was true, I found myself sitting near the appropriate longhouse exit during these events so I could see who went out and if they "hooked up." But I felt vulgar as I did so—as if I was snooping around or being a voyeur. Yet I didn't want to "project" sex between men onto the Gebusi if it wasn't documented—and other anthropologists would want to know one way or the other. Imagine how bad it would be to write about Gebusi "homosexuality" only to find, as the missionary who lived north of the Gebusi insisted, that the practice was rare or absent in fact. Unfortunately, my Gebusi friends seemed unable to talk about the subject in a serious way. Any sober query was quickly turned into a joke. At several feasts, I ultimately did see pairs of males slip out toward the outhouse, cavort with each other

to me. This underscores the degree to which sexual diversity can be both personal and collective; if cultural proclivities are variable, individual ones can be even more so. This applies as well to Western sexual identities of being "straight" or "gay"; these can house great diversity in individual practice, including abstinence.

Similar diversity applies in the realm of sexual tolerance. Some societies are more accepting of sexual diversity; others are less so. Despite their other inequalities and constraints, the Gebusi are surprisingly understanding of sexual relations among teenage boys and of bisexuality among young married men. In this respect, the Gebusi are more tolerant than many people in Western societies, in which teenagers who have homosexual or lesbian partners can be highly stigmatized by their families and peers. In one study in the United States, 29 percent of teenagers who identified themselves as gay or lesbian had attempted suicide. Of course, the Gebusi are subject to their own sexual and gender constraints. Even if one takes sexual diversity as a desired goal or value, Gebusi society is hardly a panacea. But the way that cultures differently emphasize and tolerate sexual and gendered diversity underscores the degree to which our own practices are influenced by both cultural orientations and personal choices. This awareness gives us a broader perspective on and a greater understanding of alternative gendered and sexual practices, both in our own society and in others.

Web site images of events and topics described in this chapter can be found at http://www.mhhe.com/knauft1.

CHAPTER 6

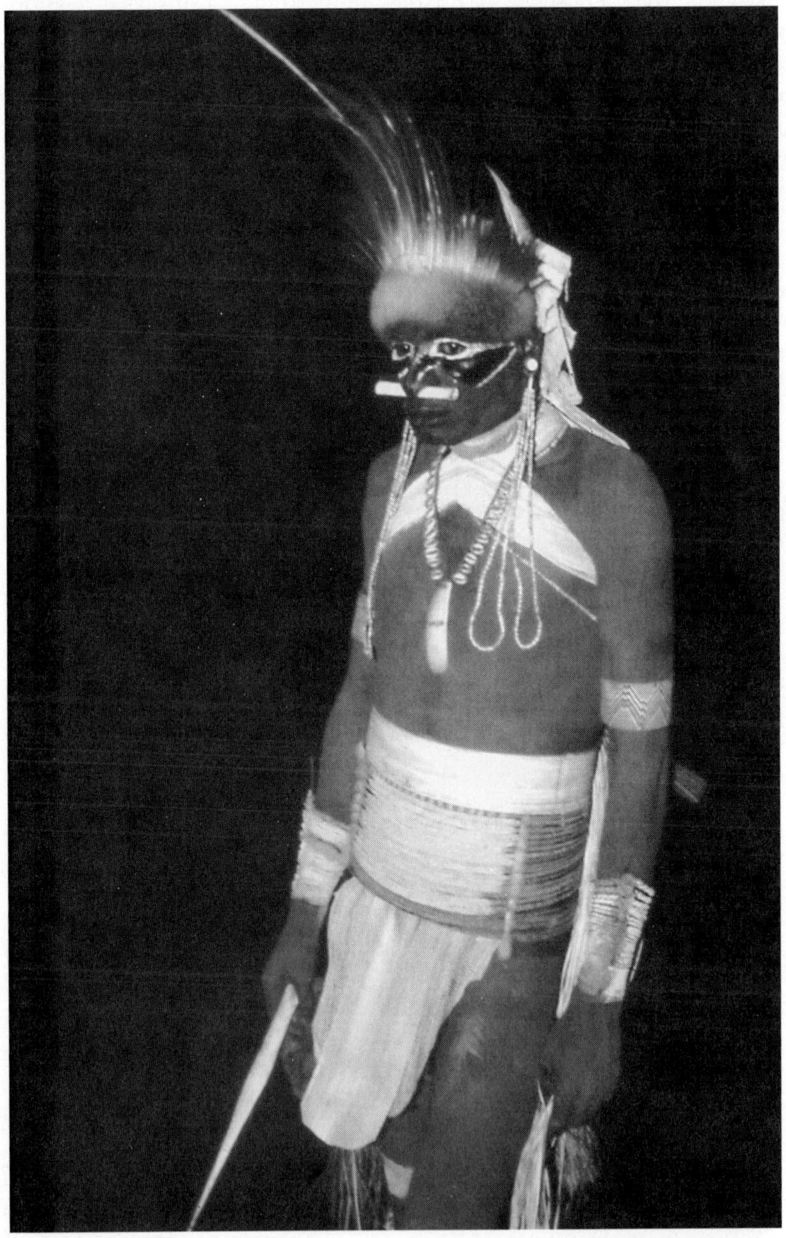

A male initiate (Yuway) in full costume. (PHOTO: Eileen Marie Knauft)

Ultimate Splendor

GEBUSI CELEBRATION OF LIFE, spirituality, and sexuality came together most fully and completely in the climactic events of the male initiation—the biggest and most elaborate spectacle in Gebusi society. Typically occurring just once in the lifetime of each major settlement, the initiation cycle began, in a sense, with the building of the village's central longhouse. The dwelling provided enough space to house relatives, friends, and visitors from the surrounding settlements during the initiation itself. At Yibihilu, the longhouse was built by six extended families from four different clans whose young men lived in the village and were initiated there. These six young men, one from each family group, ranged from about sixteen to twenty years of age. Their names were Wahi, Modiay, Yuway, Haymp, Momiay, and Halia (who was the younger brother of Salip).

After the investigation into Daguwa's death was finally put to rest in the fall of 1980, our friends in Yibihilu began to prepare in earnest for their initiation. During the next six months, much and then almost all activity in the village—and in surrounding settlements—focused on the upcoming initiation. Beyond representing a passage to manhood, the initiation brought together the grandest features of Gebusi society and culture. For such a small and isolated group, the scale, effort, and energy that informed these events were amazing. In October and November, villagers spent several weeks amassing huge piles of firewood to be used to cook immense quantities of feast food. In December, January, and part of February, families went deep into the forest to cut and process sago palms. After the sago was pounded and processed into sago flour by the women, families put the heavy starch into large net bags and hefted them in human caravans back to the village. In late February and early March, the men of Yibihilu dispersed into the forest to hunt and then smoke game, especially wild pigs and cassowaries. At the same time, women went off separately to process yet more sago.

Finally, it was time for everyone to reassemble in the village. The large pigs of the settlement—one for each of the six initiates—were tracked down, lured back to the village, penned in wooden cages, and fed to fatten them further. By mid-to-late March, the village was again a beehive of activity. Enormous piles of leaves and cooking stones were stacked next to the firewood. Food piles grew larger, including coconuts, greens, nuts, bamboo shoots, pit-pit, kava roots, and dried tobacco leaves. By the end of March, when everything was finally ready, the people of Yibihilu had worked and prepared for half a year. During this time, they had amassed enough food to feed virtually all of the more than four hundred Gebusi.

If food represented the initiation's material foundation, the costumes of the initiates were its artistic centerpiece. As previously mentioned, the overall term for initiation is *wa kawala*, "child become big." This refers simultaneously to the growth of the initiates and the process of getting dressed up in their elaborate costumes at the initiation itself. The costumes accrued from a far-flung network that spanned the entire tribe. People were mobilized from diverse settlements to obtain materials and construct the twenty different costume elements that made up each initiate's final outfit. The individuals who constructed these articles were linked to the initiates in a variety of ways—as a lineage or clan brother, a maternal relative, an in-law by virtue of previous marriage, or simply an unrelated friend. During the months and weeks leading up to the initiation, these many sponsors of the young men painstakingly constructed armbands, leg bands, waist bands, chest bands, feathered headdresses, shell necklaces, looped earrings, and other body decorations—all for the particular young man whom they had agreed to help initiate. In addition, each initiate ultimately received approximately a half dozen carved hardwood bows. Each bow was accompanied by a large sheaf of exquisitely carved arrows, and each arrow sported a decorated bamboo shaft and an intricately carved and painted tip of bone or hardwood. Some of the arrowheads had holes bored all the way through them; others were carved with delicate frets along the tip. Rounding out the initiation gifts were spare costume decorations and even newly made household items such as large woven net bags and woven sago pouches for the initiates. But none of the items could be publicly displayed or brought together until the final celebration.

During the weeks and months leading up to the initiation, all this effort grew toward its final climax. But how? The Gebusi have little in the way of leadership. Part of the answer lies in tradition. Based on past experience, families and household heads knew the sequence of preparations and the time needed for each. Just as importantly, they also knew how other families and even those in other settlements would respond to the delays and complications that invariably arose during the months of preparation. Collective planning increased when people came back from the forest and met each other in Yibihilu. Although each extended family was ultimately autonomous, they were eager to trade information, strategize plans and contingencies, and keep intimate track of each other's progress. The people of Yibihilu had already worked together to build their big longhouse. Now their task was to bring their human and spiritual vitality to fruition.

For purposes of organization as well as encouragement, the spirits of the Gebusi world proved enormously helpful. At each stage of planning, Swiman or another spirit medium held a lively séance. The hurdles of preparation were addressed, and positive resolutions charted. As Swiman described it, the spirits were planning to hold their own initiation at the same time that villagers would be holding theirs. Predictably, then, the spirits were generous with advice and support. Armed with otherwordly confidence, our friends at Yibihilu found a full complement of sponsors for each of the six initiates. During the months of preparation, the villagers overcame periods of poor hunting, cured persons who were sick, endured two additional deaths and their associated funerals and sorcery inquests, and managed to find and retrieve their semidomesticated pigs, which had wandered deep into the forest. Despite these obstacles, the villagers' enthusiasm stoked a rising tide of good company. I had never experienced such a frenzy of friendship, laughter, and enjoyment along with plain old hard work. Everyone—women, children, men, and, of course, the initiates themselves—were swept up in the happy maelstrom. And just when we thought the level of camaraderie was about to level off, it would ratchet up to yet a higher level. The Gebusi continued to surprise us.

As we gradually came to realize, the festivities that led up to the initiation mirrored the basic structure of hosting and celebrating that we had already become familiar with. Elaborately decorated visitors would descend on the village in a show of force or aggression. They would then be appeased by gifts from the hosts—the smoking of tobacco, the drinking of water and kava, and the consumption of large quantities of food. Hosts and visitors alike would stay awake through the night while eating, talking, and generally having a good time. If the occasion was particularly festive, one or more of the visiting men would dance in costume as women sang and men joked lustily. At dawn, when everyone was tired and happy, outstanding issues of political contention or dispute would finally be addressed. With so many people from so many kin groups feeling so good, amicable resolutions were all but assured. The visitors would then return home, weary but happy, while the hosts retired for a daytime sleep. In the months prior to the initiation, this same basic pattern of hosting and feasting was used to dedicate floorboards that extended and finished the longhouse, to commemorate a cohort of younger boys who got their ears pierced, and to observe other celebratory occasions.

By mid-March, preparations for the initiation reached fever pitch. Strangely enough, the feast that inaugurated the initiation per se centered on a thin forest vine named *siay*. The name of the feast was *siay sagra*—literally, to "straighten the *siay*." Hundreds of strips of the sturdy fiber would later be wrapped around the wide bark waistbands that the initiates wore as part of their final costumes. In olden days, this strong waistband was like a piece of midriff armor that protected them from enemy arrows. The presentation of the *siay* by their primary sponsors to the initiates marked a formal announcement of the initiation to come. It also established quite clearly which young men would be initiated and who from other settlements would be primarily responsible for supplying their costume parts, bows and arrows, and other gifts.

In planning for the *siay sagra*, for almost a month ahead of time, the men and boys of Yibihilu accumulated dried meat from hunted animals to give to the initiates' primary sponsors. Meanwhile, the women and older girls processed yet more sago. To only a slightly lesser extent, the sponsors also had been occupied with these same tasks—the hunting of game and the processing of sago—to give to the initiate they were sponsoring. When all was ready, each initiate traveled to the settlement of his preeminent sponsor, his *tor*, and invited him to the *siay sagra* feast at Yibihilu the following evening. In response, the young man's *tor* gifted him with a large roll of cooked sago, which the initiate carried back to Yibihilu. Shortly thereafter, the *tor* and his relatives themselves arrived at the feast. After the usual displays and welcoming etiquette, the visitors and hosts exchanged their respective stocks of dried meat. In addition, the *tors* presented each initiate with piles of *siay* that would later be carefully wrapped around his wide waistband. At dawn, after a festive night of eating, singing, and male dancing, the major sponsors received in reciprocity a large roll of cooked sago, greens, and coconut to carry back to their settlements from their respective initiates. In a special twist, the initiates also gave each sponsor an additional stock of dried meat that came from *another* of the sponsors. The sponsor would then respond, "I can't take all this meat! It's too much!!" But the initiate would counter, "It's not meat I hunted myself. It was hunted by X, the sponsor of Y [one of the other initiates]. So please take it!" Following such assurances of mutual humility, the meat was in each case given away to a different one of the initiates' sponsors.

What lay behind this transfer? In terms of Gebusi exchange, it was a brilliant move. The initiates had taken the stocks of meat they had received and traded them among themselves. Then each had taken his new share and given it back to his primary sponsor. In this simple act, the gifts between the initiates, their various sponsors, and their distant settlements were all reciprocated and linked together. What at one level seemed pointless—giving food away and then traveling elsewhere to receive similar items in return—created a framework of trust and connection among many settlements. The gifts also provided a solid down payment related to larger obligations yet to come. In economic and political terms, the *siay sagra* "sealed the deal in advance of the show." In social and emotional terms, it created a sense of good company among the wide range of settlements that would celebrate the forthcoming initiation.

❧ ❧ ❧

Two weeks later came the ultimate festivities. These began with what anthropologists call a transitional or "liminal" period for the initiates. As proposed by sociologist Arnold van Genep and later by anthropologist Victor Turner, major life cycle rituals are in many societies preceded by an "in-between" period that registers ambiguity between the person's previous position and the new one he or she will occupy. For instance, rituals of status elevation are often prefaced by rites of humility, submission, or teasing before the aspirant assumes his or her new role. For the prospective Gebusi initiates, their in-between status was indicated by bold stripes of yellow ocher, painted on them from head to foot. The Gebusi word for yellow, *bebagum*, itself means "in the middle of" or "wedged in between." Along with the stripes of yellow paint, each of the initiates was festooned with a fringed headband, yellow forearm bands, a yellow-painted waist band, a nose plug, a woven throat band, and a single long egret feather, which was stuck in his hair. Perhaps most striking, apart from the initiates' yellow body paint, was a broad white leaf that was attached to the inside front of their waistbands so that it hung down almost to their knees like a large penis. A topic of lewd joking and teasing by the men, the phallic leaf was a public and obvious symbol of the initiates' pent-up sexuality. Each of them was costumed identically, down to the smallest detail. As they lined up and stood with proper humility, it seemed as though their individual identities had been merged into a beautiful and yet humble collective whole.

The initiates' biggest trial was to wear the new wigs that their sponsors now came to give them. The climactic festivities would shortly follow this ritual of "tying the bark wigs" (*uga togra*). But first, its painful prologue had to be endured. Wig wearing may not sound traumatic, but the adornment was made from large wads of sodden yellow bark. Tied in bulky bundles to narrow strands of each initiate's hair, the wig pulled down mightily on the initiate's scalp. In fact, the wet bark was so heavy—I estimated eighty pounds for each initiate—that after it was tied to the initiates' hair it had to be supported with a pole by two helpers, who strained to raise it as each of the young victims, in turn, was ordered to stand up. All the while, the surrounding men crowded around the poor initiates, whooping and joking with abandon. The prime sponsor of each young man then trimmed off the wig's long trailing streamers, which reduced its weight to perhaps "only" twenty-five pounds.

Fighting back tears, the silent initiates were ordered to line up and listen to their elders. The senior sponsor of each initiate then came forward and lectured him on Gebusi values of generosity and virtue: "Always be generous with your kinsmen and in-laws, however long they live." "Don't be stingy with your food. Always give yourself the least." "When you come across your uncle's garden and see he has some nice food, never just take it." "If you ever steal, you will be rotten and no one will like you." "Whenever guests come, you must always snap their fingers firmly and warmly." "Never hide your tobacco away, always share your smoke with anyone who visits." Predictably, the greatest admonitions concerned sex: "You can never, ever chase after another man's wife." "Never flirt with your uncle's woman." "When you see a female 'bird' alone in the forest, you can't just go and 'shoot' it because you think you are 'hungry.'" "Don't you ever pry open the 'cooking tongs' [legs] of a village woman."

Although the sponsors started out serious, their diatribes quickly lost steam; after a few minutes, their speeches labored to maintain an air of stern invective. As the sponsors finally got to their warnings about sex, the men and even the uninitiated boys could barely suppress their smiles and chuckles. Then, with loud cries of "SUI-SUI-SUI," the sponsors shooed the initiates outside to fetch water from the spring, a ten-minute walk away. Amid whoops and hollers, the men and even the boys accompanied the initiates, who carried water tubes and labored to walk while burdened with their wigs.

The initiates' trip to the watering hole turned out to be the prime occasion for revealing male secrets. In some New Guinea societies, elaborate restrictions surround the transmission of sacred male knowledge. In some cases, this information is doled out piecemeal over months or even years. Measured against such standards, the Gebusi were amazingly carefree. As we approached the spring, the men spoke in only slightly lowered tones about the various foods that the new men, once initiated, would not be allowed to eat. Red pandanus could not be eaten because it formed a red paste, like menstrual blood. Slimy forest greens could not be eaten because, when they were cooked, they oozed like a woman's genitalia. River lobsters couldn't be eaten because they once pinched a woman in her upper thigh, which made them turn red. On and on went the list—until I tallied twenty-three food items that would now be taboo to the initiates. In each case, the "rationale" for the prohibition was the same: the food had some association, however circuitous, with women's primary sexual organs. As I later found out, initiated men were not supposed to eat these foods until their first or second child was born. But most of the taboos were observed only loosely in practice. I was told that a hungry man might easily break his food taboos when out in the forest, especially if experience had taught him that there was little harm in doing so. And although the list of dietary proscriptions seemed long, almost none of the items were frequent sources of protein.

As for additional male knowledge, there seemed to be none. For a while, I thought that Gebusi men simply had to have deeper mysteries for me to discover. But I gradually came to recognize that the best-kept secret was the one I had overlooked: Gebusi men had few initiation secrets to reveal. Male sexual encounters with other men had not been hidden from women, and even the initiates had taken no pains to hide their trysts. As for the telling of food taboos at the watering hole, the reactions of the younger boys were quite revealing. Although the men urged the boys to stay away and to cover their ears—lest premature knowledge stunt their growth—most of them edged closer. Some even cupped their hands behind their ears rather than over them, the better to hear the secrets. The men seemed unconcerned. In actuality, the telling of "secrets" was mostly an occasion of laughter and male bravado. Some of the men proclaimed that they would gladly die from breaking food taboos and by exposing themselves more fully to women's sexuality. Like their myths and séances, Gebusi male secrets were at least as much a source of ribaldry as they were sober declarations. Ultimately, the same was also true of the initiates' biggest trauma—the wearing of their bark wigs. Although the wigs were painful, the initiates quickly learned to manage them by hunching forward and shifting the weight onto their shoulders. By two o'clock in the afternoon, Wahi had cut off his own wig entirely. When I asked him why, he claimed that it prevented him from preparing sago for the upcoming feast. By evening, only Yuway and Modiay still wore their wigs, and both of these were gone by the following morning.

In some Melanesian societies, traditional rites of manhood were genuinely brutal. And they sometimes began when boys were only six or seven years of age. Ordeals sometimes included nose bleeding, penis bleeding, tongue bleeding, cane swallowing and vomiting, body scarification, and being beaten, berated, rubbed with stinging nettles, and forced to live in seclusion, in their own excrement, without food or water. In some societies, new initiates were threatened with violent punishment, including death, if they violated male taboos or revealed men's secrets to women. In contrast to these extremes, the Gebusi initiation was thankfully tame. Older men said that their rites of manhood had always been this way—more a celebration than a trial of pain or suffering. The same was true of some other groups in Papua New Guinea, including the Purari peoples of the south coast who, as it happened, were also vigilant headhunters. Again, the diversity of cultures in Melanesia, as in other regions of the world, was remarkable.

After wearing their bark wigs, our young friends enjoyed one last night of sleep—as much as they could get, amid their excitement—for several days to come. The following morning, after being repainted in yellow ocher (but without their bark wigs), they left to revisit their main sponsors in their respective villages. I decided to go with Wahi to Swiman's little hamlet at Sowabihilu. We found ourselves crammed into a mini-longhouse with fifty other people who had come there from settlements farther afield. A similar gathering was held simultaneously at the settlement of each initiate's primary sponsor. In the process, people coalesced at a variety of staging points before coming together at Yibihilu for the climactic festivities.

Once again, each initiate received a thick roll of cooked sago from his primary sponsor. This time, however, the expectant young men and those of us who had accompanied them carried the food directly back to Yibihilu—in the middle of the night. Villagers take pride in navigating the twisted trails of the forest even after sunset, but this time I thought we were pushing our luck. Most in our group staggered not just from the weight of the sago but from the effects of the local root intoxicant of kava, called *gowi*, that Swiman had liberally pressed upon us. As it happened, it was the night of a new moon, so the sky was black. Dim resin torches and my flashlight were our only source of light, but my companions only joked rather than curse the darkness. Somehow, we managed to navigate the trail without falling and to ferry ourselves back across the dark Kum River and on to home. In short order, an impromptu dance sprang up and continued until dawn.

As the sun rose, smoke from a score of blazing cook fires fingered up to greet the morning and shred the fog. The whoops of those stoking the fires and cooking the food soon mingled with the squeals of dying pigs, which stood in their cages as they were shot full of arrows by gleeful men. Singed and splayed to cook on top of the sago, the six large pigs—one for each initiate—would provide the most lavish meal since the last initiation, which had taken place in a neighboring community several years before. By mid-afternoon, the six initiates were finally ready to become truly "big"—to don their crowning costumes. We thronged around them and escorted them from the village a short way into the forest, where they could be dressed. The atmosphere was too festive to be exclusive, and in addition to the young boys who joined us, Eileen was welcomed to come and take photos. Some of the women who had woven parts of the initiation costumes also came along.

Thoroughly cleansed of the lingering yellow paint, each initiate stood up to be painstakingly dressed as an electrifying red bird of paradise. The sponsors and helpers of each initiate took primary charge. They painted with meticulous precision. Then they took the ever-so-carefully-made gifts of feathered headdresses, waist bands, shells, armbands, leg bands, woven chest bands, nose plugs, looped earrings, and more from net bags. All were scrupulously arranged and adjusted on the initiates' bodies. The closest parallel, it seemed to me, although I had never actually witnessed it, involved the careful dressing of a traditional American bride prior to her wedding. The analogy wasn't completely far-fetched, in that the initiation served, in its way, as a kind of male wedding. Each young man would now be suddenly and imminently marriageable. All but one of the initiates would, in fact, be married within a few months. Some of the initiation gifts they received were practically a trousseau to begin domestic life. In contrast to the initiation itself, the marriages that would follow—to women whose identity was not yet known—were strikingly unceremonial. As we later discovered, these unions were tense affairs characterized by worried courtship and adult irritation, and they were devoid of festive gift giving, costumed dancing, or public celebration. It was initiation, not marriage, that involved the cooking and distribution of the village pigs, on the one hand, and the public celebration of virile adulthood, on the other.

If the initiation was like a marriage without women, the initiates themselves were almost like brides. The bright red paint that graced them from head to toe was the ultimate feminine color. Its association with crimson menstrual blood grew deeper as the many food taboos were retold to the initiates while they were being painted and decorated. In the process, a large new phallic leaf was attached to hang down between their legs. Even more than the standard dance outfit (which also included images of other spirits), the initiation costume was a pure expression of the beauty, allure, and sexuality of the red bird of paradise. But before they could be formally displayed and celebrated, the initiates had to be completely costumed and publicly paraded back to the village. Given the importance of this task, the initiates' sponsors refused to hurry despite the beginnings of an afternoon drizzle. Huddled under trees and with bystanders holding palm fronds and our umbrellas overhead to protect them, the initiates gradually emerged in final splendor. Each painted stripe, leg band, armband, and headdress feather was perfectly aligned and exactly identical on each of the initiates. I was deeply moved to see my young friends—Yuway, Wahi, Modiay, and the rest, whom I had come to know so well—so wonderfully transformed. Their beauty was truly awesome.

Against this aesthetic aura, the rain fell harder. The costuming was now complete, but a grand procession back to the village had become impossible. So we retired with the initiates to their family houses on the periphery of the village and waited for the storm to pass. Unfortunately, it did not. Instead, the rain grew stronger and stronger. We sat and sat as minutes became hours, from late afternoon into evening, and from evening into the night. It was an incredible, pelting rain, and it was completely unpredicted. Even as dawn broke, the water continued to thunder. The smooth village clearing had become a torrent of gullies.

There were plenty of ironies. If the storm had held off for just another fifteen minutes (or if the sponsors had been a touch quicker with their decorations), the triumphant procession could have quickly taken place. Then we all would have been happily under the roof of the main longhouse. The visitors would have come with great cries to "confront" the initiates and have had their "anger" dispelled by the silent beauty of their immovable presence. The food would then have been served and eaten, and dances by the visiting men would have continued until morning. In short, everything would have gone according to plan. Now, however, the initiates, their sponsors, and the rest of us had stayed up all night waiting for the rain to stop. Things were even worse for the throngs of visitors. Festooned for their own grand entrances, they had been forced to retreat to the forest and huddle in makeshift lean-tos in a futile attempt to keep dry. Neither they nor we had had anything to eat. Everyone was very tired and very hungry.

Why couldn't the initiates simply be led under cover to the longhouse so the visitors could enter and the food be served? The answer was consistent: "Because the initiates' red paint would run down their bodies." Beyond the importance of having a triumphant procession, it was unthinkable to the men that the beautiful red of the initiates, the congealed symbol of femininity that framed their masculinity, could be at risk of dissolving in the pouring rain. Against the proud and fixed control of the feminine represented on their skin, the specter of red liquid oozing down their carefully appointed bodies was tantamount to male menstruation—the destruction of masculinity rather than its crowning achievement. Although Gebusi gender was amazingly flexible in some ways, it was rigidly fixed in others. So we continued to wait for the rain to end.

To my amazement, almost no one got visibly upset. The principal exception was Salip, who cursed angrily and chastised whatever ghost was raining so literally on his parade. Almost everyone else eased into a kind of meditative doze, neither anxious nor despondent, but serene and trusting that all would work out. Despite the months of preparation and the sheer scale of the event—its social, spiritual, and material significance—the response to the storm was vintage Gebusi: quiet acceptance in the face of frustration. When the rain finally broke, in midmorning, my compatriots managed a few whoops of relief and anticipation. Cooking fires were now restoked and foods reheated. I went to check our rain gauge. It was filled to ninety-three millimeters—a bit shy of four inches of rain. This ended up being the fourth-biggest rainfall during our entire two-year stay—and the biggest within a month on either side of the initiation. Villagers shrugged it off as part of their unpredictable weather: "That's just the way it is" ("*mo ene dasum*").

The six initiates finally lined up by the central longhouse. Standing shoulder to shoulder, they were individually brilliant but yet more spellbinding as a collective whole. Uniting the aesthetic and the material, they literally embodied the full power of Gebusi kinship and friendship, the breadth of their social connections across space, and the fullness of their spiritual identifications over time. Together, the initiates crystalized the beauty, growth, gift giving, and forbearance of the Gebusi as a whole. Into this electrifying vista, visiting men now rushed with abandon—a human stampede of celebratory aggression. Painted warriors bellowed, screamed, and sprinted through the mud as they plucked their bows. Their spiraling circle closed ever more tightly around the initiates in happy displays of mock antagonism—wave after wave, group after group. One man was carried in naked and covered head to foot in mud. His tongue hung out, and a huge mock phallus was tied to his waist. At least for the moment, he was a bloated corpse covered in cadaveric fluid—and indicting everyone around him as a sorcerer. But as might have been guessed, even this gruesome display did not unsettle the initiates, who stood their ground with serenity. Meanwhile, children scattered with ambivalent screams while adults said through their broad smiles that they, too, were scared of the "corpse."

Eventually, the attacks subsided, and the feasting and celebration began in earnest. Predictably, the festivities started with seemingly endless rounds of finger snapping, smoke sharing, kava drinking, and, especially, food giving. With thunderous whoops and hollers, the identity of an initiate's sponsor or other recipient was shouted. A representative from each of the six initiates' families then rushed to press a mound of food upon the pleased but besieged recipient. Special pleasure was taken in "force feeding" the important visitors with great gobs of dripping pig fat—pushing it in their faces until they had taken at least one or two gooey bites.

By midafternoon, it was time for the visitors to reciprocate and give additional gifts to the initiates—especially the prized hardwood bows and sheaves of elaborate arrows. Many of the men plucked the bows dramatically before handing them to the initiates—to show how strong the weapons were. Previously allowed to use only unpainted arrows for hunting, the initiates could now use painted and people-killing arrows in ritual display and, as need be, in warfare. Exhausted as they were, however, the initiates could hardly do more than stand. Even that became difficult, and by evening, they resorted to propping themselves up while sitting lest they topple over in sleep and smear their costumes. As part of their proud ordeal, they had not talked, eaten, or slept for two days.

Seemingly oblivious to their plight, everyone else was now revved up for a full night of partying—eating additional food, smoking more tobacco, and drinking numerous bowls of kava root liquor. Jokes flew as thick and fast as rain had fallen the previous night. By now, the longhouse was packed with people wall to wall, leaving just a small space in the center for the dancers. The yellow light of resin lanterns and bamboo torches cast a golden glow across each face and costume. The outfits of the male visitors were as spectacular and creative as they were plentiful. They included large headdresses of bird-of-paradise and cassowary feathers; red, black, and white face and body painting in innumerable patterns and combinations; bone and bamboo nose plugs and beads; leaf wreathes; and woven chest bands and armbands. Women were festooned as well: almost all of them had fresh grass skirts, bead or seed necklaces, and woven chest bands and armbands. Many also wore headdresses of fringed fiber strips and long egret feathers in their hair.

In addition to the usual male dancing, there was a special dance involving a few young women with their own red body paint, black eye banding, and red bird-of-paradise headdresses. During the plaintive songs of the women's chorus, the female dancers bounced up and down directly across from their male counterparts. Each of the young women held a long, thin rattle that she thrust up and down in front of her as she hopped opposite a male dancer—who was also pulsing up and down to the pounding beat of his drum. The sexual charge of this arrangement was impossible to miss. The men in the audience went wild, and the women also joked and laughed from their sitting places along the side of the dancing area. To cap it off, a few women could be seen joking and flirting directly with men. It was as if, for a single night, the erotic mirth of the spirit woman had become acceptable for Gebusi women as well as for men, at least in the realm of public joking. The night swept up everyone in joyful abandon. We will always remember its intensity.

The morning after was just that. As the visitors left, those from the host village crashed and slept, and so did we. While Gebusi had been busy partying, we had undergone our own initiation. Pumped by adrenalin and coffee, we had primed ourselves to observe and record what we had waited for months to see—and what we knew we might not see again. Unlike the Gebusi, we didn't know what was going to happen next or when or how it would unfold. We worried that we would miss important events. I remembered the story of a well-known anthropologist who, working alone, fell asleep from fatigue at the height of a male initiation rite and missed a key sequence of color-coded costumes that he could never reconstruct. But we were lucky because we had each other. And we had become an integral part of the action. When men gave the initiates bows and arrows, we gave each of them several shotgun cartridges—"Western arrows," as they called them—for hunting with the shotgun we had given the people of Yibihilu. When initiates received their costume elements, we gave them each a pair of bright blue satin gym trunks that we had bought for them during a field break. These gifts were wildly popular and widely talked about, the more so because it was so difficult for the Gebusi to obtain such items deep in the rainforest. In return, the families of the initiates gave us pork and sago. To this day, the surviving initiates still address us as "initiate sponsor" (*tor*).

That morning, however, all we could think of was sleep. But just when we thought the initiation was over, an additional climax occurred. In early afternoon, we awoke to a loud commotion and stumbled out of bed to see what was going on. The initiates had been herded out of the village, their costumes retouched, and then paraded back in. This time, though, they were joined by two unmarried women who stood alongside them in costumes that were, in body paint and feathers, virtually identical to their own. Together, the six young men and two young women linked fingers and stood in a single line. They bobbed up and down in unison as Tosipi, the senior woman of the community, came forth to address them. Going down their line, she gently hit each of them with a sheaf of special leaves and chanted that they would henceforth be strong in heart, in breath, and in spirit. She said to each that he or she would have the inner energy of a buzzing hornet. Then she told them to be kind to and protective of others in the village. Finally, she declared for each of them the name of a young child to whom they were unrelated but whom they were charged to help and protect. With that, she turned and walked away. The initiation was over.

Thinking that we had seen everything the night before, we wrestled anew to make sense of this wonderful ending. Although women had been off-stage for many of the initiation's formal events, a senior woman had now become the center of the final ceremony. Young women had dressed up and danced as part of the previous night's festivities. Now, two women, dressed similarly to the initiates, linked themselves physically to the initiates. The male bird of paradise—the woman who had ultimately been a man—had finally expanded to include real Gebusi women. This was implicit in the night of dancing and joking, but now it was formally proclaimed in a beautiful display of true womanhood—in costumes like those of the young men. Among the Gebusi themselves, the ideal of the beautiful spirit woman had finally and truly embraced women as well as men.

This theme grew deeper that same night. Although the initiation was over, the young men and women were now adults—and free to dance on their own. Still dressed in their red initiation costumes, the male initiates added the feathered halo of the standard dance costume and danced for the first time with drums. Moreover, they danced in pairs with the young women who had stood alongside them at the initiation's benediction. Like their linkage earlier in the day, their ritual union encompassed the male-female beauty of the Gebusi as a whole.

Given these final images, how much did we need to rethink our initial understanding of the whole celebration? Was this a male initiation? Or was it a collective celebration of male *and* female fertility? As was often the case, the intricacies of Gebusi culture made our simple question deliciously difficult. On the one hand, young Gebusi women were painted up similarly to the young men, lined up with them, danced with them, and were charged along with them during the final ceremony to protect a young child. The maturity and sexuality of the young women were obviously on display alongside the young men. In social terms, their costume elements, though not as elaborate or copious as the young men's, linked the young women to those in the community who had given or loaned these items.

On the other hand, in contrast to their male counterparts, the young women were not inseminated or otherwise sexually initiated. They were not subject to painful trials testing their stamina and did not receive bows and arrows or other stocks of possessions and costume elements. They did not have pigs killed for them, did not have important gifts of food given in their name, and were not enjoined to observe special food taboos. They did not establish lifelong relations of initiation-mate and initiate-sponsor with others in the community. In contrast to the young men, the question of whether a given young woman would get dressed up in a red bird-of-paradise costume had been uncertain; it was answered only at the last minute by the young women themselves. Some of them had been shy and decided against it. As opposed to this, the planning and gift giving of the occasion had been orchestrated around the known identity of the male initiates, and this had been central to the scale and scope of the festivities.

In some ways, then, the inclusion of women as active but secondary actors paralleled other aspects of Gebusi ceremonial life. However, the presence of the young women in the final ceremony did underscore the symbolic importance of female as well as male fertility. If the initiation presented the acme of the Gebusi male culture, it also extolled women and Gebusi as a whole. Spirituality, sexuality, materiality, kinship, friendship, and gender: they all came together in joy and happiness. Against all odds and impediments, against all sicknesses, deaths, and frustrations, the Gebusi somehow came together to celebrate their collective good company. It was a unity I had never seen or felt. If the avenues of modern life easily disperse into separate domains—the economic, the political, the professional, the domestic, the religious, and so on—here was a so-called simple society that brought these aspects of life together in full celebration. To me, it was a testament to the human spirit that the Gebusi could create so much that was positive, beautiful, fun, and meaningful amid lives that were so difficult and tenuous. This is the way I like to remember them from that period: triumphantly asserting the richness and joyfulness of their humanity.

Web site images of events and topics described in this chapter can be found at http://www.mhhe.com/knauft1.

PART TWO

1998

CHAPTER 7

People of Gasumi Corners with the author after a Sunday church service. (PHOTO: Bruce Knauft [self-timed])

Reentry

> I feel like a neophyte all over again. Though at best not humiliating, fieldwork is always a humbling experience, and in a good sort of way. Arrows recently barbed at anthropology cast its knowledge as imperialist, gained at the expense rather than for the benefit of other people. But the gawky interloper is usually cut well down to size by the time he or she gets beyond the confines of the hotels, the taxis, and the urban elite to the place in question. Human leveling is ethnography's strength.
>
> —Field notes, June 1998

Leave in 1982, come back in 1998—experience culture as a time machine in reverse. Sixteen years is a long time for the Gebusi. So, too, for me, and also for cultural anthropology. While a whole generation of Gebusi were getting older and producing children, Eileen and I went from young adulthood to middle age in Atlanta. Our son, Eric, went from conception to high school. During the 1980s and 1990s, the world also changed. Market economies, transnational influences, and national agendas spread to the farthest nooks of the globe. Cultural anthropology changed as well. If the late 1970s represented the tail end of anthropology's original interest in remote and so-called primitive societies, the 1980s and 1990s represented the head of its mushrooming interest in social change and transformation. During this time, the field's traditional interest in kinship, social organization, ritual, and exchange broadened to include a full range of contemporary practices and institutions—markets, churches, schools, governments, nongovernmental organizations, and the whole mosaic of social and cultural influences that tie people to their region, to their nation, and to the world at large. More than ever, the diversity of the contemporary world is anthropology's concern.

As anthropologists appreciate new worlds of experience, they also find troubling inequalities. These include the unequal distribution of wealth brought by national and international influence, by the global market economy, and by powerful institutions that interact with local types of domination. These patterns are hardly new. State empires, commercial entities, and other wielders of power have criss-crossed the world for millennia. For more than five centuries, commerce has girded the globe. But in recent years, these linkages have intensified. Now they are not merely present but increasingly central in places like the New Guinea rainforest.

Although my first fieldwork was guided by a search for the culturally remote, I hardly regret its results. Ethnography is as real and important as the lives it encounters, regardless of where these are found. Anthropology will be poorer if it gives up on the full range of human culture—from the remotest outpost to the most cosmopolitan city. By the mid-1990s, however, I felt that my initial work with the Gebusi needed to be updated. Along with the remoteness of the Gebusi, my university and family commitments had kept me from returning. But I missed my Gebusi friends and wondered what had happened to them; a reunion was long overdue. I suspected that their previous customs were in tension with their present conditions. Such tension is an increasingly important topic for anthropologists. Based on what I already knew about them, I was excited at the prospect of reengaging Gebusi lives.

During our first fieldwork, Eileen and I found that external changes had already come to the Gebusi: steel knives and axes, cloth and occasional clothing, the yearly patrols of government officials, the pacification of tribal enemies, and the presence of the Nomad police when the Gebusi themselves called them. Subtler changes had also taken place in terms of physical appearance and personal style. Even by 1980, most Gebusi had given up the traditional custom of tying their hair in dreadlocks in favor of cutting it short. A few men had even sported carefully shaved sideburns—reminiscent of the facial hair the Australian patrol officers wore in the 1970s.

At the same time, much of Gebusi culture was not merely persistent during the early 1980s but in some ways even more viable than it had been during the precolonial era. Courtesy of the Australian patrols, the Gebusi were free of tribal enemies while themselves experiencing little direct intrusion from white people. It was only as I published the results of my first fieldwork and compared my findings with those of other anthropologists that I realized how unusual it was for so many Gebusi practices to have continued so strongly for so long. But what had happened between the early 1980s and the late 1990s? What had become of my Gebusi friends and confidants? Only snippets of information had reached me, and none of it was very revealing. Some colleagues suggested that modern developments—Christianization, education, out-migration, and economic development—would have brought major changes to the Gebusi. But others emphasized that cultural values would keep many things the same.

Even concerning violence, alternative outcomes were possible. By 1982, I knew that violent death among Gebusi had declined to about half of its precolonial level. But Gebusi continued to scapegoat and sometimes to kill one another as sorcerers without much government awareness or intervention. What had happened since 1982 remained a mystery to me. Given the continuing absence of Australian officers—and the reluctance of national police to patrol the rainforest—some colleagues thought that armed conflict among Gebusi would have increased. Violence had reemerged dramatically in many parts of Papua New Guinea, including in highland areas just seventy-five miles to the northeast of the Gebusi. The missionary who lived among the neighboring Bedamini people in 1980–82 said that tribal violence had increased and would continue to do so. But the increasing association of the Gebusi with activities in and around the Nomad Station, where the police were quartered, could offset this trend. So I was uncertain what I would find.

Added to my empirical uncertainties were personal ones. In 1980, I was a fledgling twenty-six-year-old anthropologist. Being a researcher-on-a-shoestring, I had little to lose and everything to prove. I still wonder at the gap between my book learning about Melanesia, which was sizable, and my personal experience in the non-Western world, which in the early spring of 1980 was nonexistent. I had the hubris borne of ignorance and lots of energy, plus an unbridled faith in intercultural understanding. These had galvanized the optimism that is essential not only to succeed but also to keep one from considering too concretely the true difficulty of the task ahead!

Against this background, my motives for fieldwork were different in 1998. I was both more knowledgeable and more worried than before. I was going back to be with people I had known and liked. But I also knew how tough it was to live in the rainforest. In the United States, I had become a professor and author of several books; I busied myself with the life of being an academic. But I had a nagging sense that my work was becoming removed from the people I had known. I needed to get back in the field. I also knew that fieldwork would again be a humbling experience. I wondered if my sense of being a successful anthropologist would fall like a house of cards. And the rainforest knows that a body at age forty-four is not what it was at twenty-six. I was concerned about the burden of my absence on Eileen and Eric, who were busy with work and school in Atlanta; they could not come with me. I worried about the impact on them if anything should happen to me. In fact, I did end up getting bitten by a death adder, and I feared at first that the bite might be fatal. (See the description in the endnotes.)

My uncertainty was also intellectual. A middle-aged outlook often lacks the openness of a younger mind. How would I reconcile my expectation of change among the Gebusi with my appreciation of their cultural past? Anthropology crackles with debates between researchers who focus on global change and those who stress cultural continuity. Are societies more strongly informed by historical values or by recent transformations? Amid such questions, my desire to return to the Gebusi grew stronger. Their very remoteness became a reason to return—to study changes that impact people in so many parts of the world.

As I prepared to leave, I tried (even though I knew it was impossible in fact) to wipe my slate clean of expectations. I told myself to take whatever I found among the Gebusi at face value. I was going back after sixteen years, and I was going solo. After months spent navigating the bureaucracy of research grants, obtaining visa permits, buying equipment, reviewing old field notes, and shedding tears of goodbye, I left for Papua New Guinea. After two weeks in the capital of Port Moresby and several days in the district capital of Kiunga, I finally took the small plane to the Nomad Station. I landed for a half-year of fieldwork on June 25, 1998. That night, I wrote the following:

Tonight, this first evening back, I sit here with Sayu and Howe, who smile brightly as I type on this keyboard. We have just looked at the screen saver, which has amazed them totally. I am caught in a time-warp between the pidgin English called *tok pisin,* Gebusi language, heat, fatigue, and my wonder and amazement.

First touchdown was a rush. Wahi—with a gaunt face and a much receding hairline but still strong and energetic—was the airline agent who met me at the airstrip!! We hugged, shook hands, and snapped fingers about a dozen times. He told me he lives right at the Nomad Station—and that he has three sons and a baby daughter! Then he had to give his attention to the paperwork of the flight while my things were unloaded. When I turned around, I had the wonder of seeing age jump right before my eyes. One after another Gebusi whom I had known came up to greet me. The grown children were the most incredible. There was Sayu, our little friend about whom Eileen had joked that she would adopt and bring back to the States. He is strong, handsome, and smart! He has already become my closest companion and helper among the younger men. He combines his father's quickness and his mother's intelligence, perceptiveness, and friendship—or at least so it seems on my first impression.

Most striking among my adult friends are their hollow faces, withered bodies, and wrinkled skin that I remember as smooth. But my happiness in human connection transcends space and time. We embraced and snapped fingers mightily, including the women. Gazing into the eyes of those whom you know with fond memories from sixteen years ago, and who suddenly live again in the present, is totally thrilling and completely unforgettable. In Gebusi legends, reunions and welcomes are so warm and numerous that people's hands are worn bare by snapping fingers heartily and repeatedly. Today, I allowed myself the hubris of feeling the same way. My middle fingers are really sore from the finger-snapping that I could not keep myself from continuing even if I had wanted to stop. It is like on my wedding day, when the joy of the event caused an actual soreness of smile muscles that were so irrepressibly stretched that they could not help but turn anything in the world to their overpowering good feeling.

Feelings notwithstanding, the day has been hot, and I have a mountain of decisions to make quickly. How many nights will I stay in this unpleasant little house at the Nomad Station? Where will I live after that? How can I build on today's rush of positive feeling? How should I reestablish reciprocity with my Gebusi friends? How will I cook? How many boxes should I unpack? Where are the specific parcels of utensils, sleeping equipment, cloths, toiletries, and so on that I need for this first night? (As expected, there are no real stores at Nomad, so I am glad that I have brought everything with me.) And yet, I simply must take time tonight to write the events of this astonishing day.

Amid the constant stream of visitors whom I did not want to stop, I somehow greeted everyone and found that virtually the entire generation of surviving Gebusi from Yibihilu now live in a "corner" of Nomad just across the Hamam River, about 20 or 25 minutes' walk from the Nomad Station. This is absolutely perfect, my ideal residential scenario! I should have easy access to the Nomad Station and its nationalizing influence while also being able to go with Gebusi back to the forest. Having stowed my things in the government house by about one o'clock, I couldn't resist the temptation to go to this corner settlement and see for myself the lovely place where I will likely be living. It is all simply wonderful.

Within minutes, the Gebusi astounded me. Meeting me at the Nomad Station airstrip, the descendants of Yibihilu boasted a new flock of youngsters and of children-become-adults. Within a few days, however, I found that few men of my own age or older were still alive. Most of those whom I had known as adults had died, including Salip, Boyl, Swiman, Saliam, Sasaga, Tosipi, Wosop, and Imba. Of the six young men we helped initiate, only three—Wahi, Modiay, and Yuway—were still living. I mourned the passing of many friends even as I saw their personalities, amazingly, in their children, now pushing toward their own adulthood. In demographic terms, Gebusi were a new people and more numerous than before—up from 450 individuals to about 615.

Change and turnover notwithstanding, and despite the heat and mosquitoes, it felt wonderful to be back. I was remembered fondly and welcomed joyously. Two children had been named after me during my absence. Once worn, the glove of friendship always seems to fit. Within one day of my arrival, Gwabi, who had been about twelve years old in 1982, insisted that I occupy the new thatched house that he had just happened to finish building beside his older dwelling in Gasumi Corners. With this as my base of operations, I quickly found myself immersed in Gebusi life, going both to Nomad and to the forest, and rediscovering the joys and trials of life in the field. I had worried about my ability to speak Gebusi after so many years, but this came back to me faster than I expected.

My physical setup was largely as it had been in 1980–82 except that now I lived nominally alone—with Gwabi's family in their weathered house just eight feet away. Logistically, the biggest change involved my laptop and micro computers, which greatly enhanced my work. Now I could easily write up, revise, and organize my notes—and even make entries on my microcomputer while interviewing people in their homes. No more spiral notebooks, typewriter, or carbon copies laced with correction fluid! Instead of columned paper, I used my spreadsheet programs to enter and update census, kinship, and other tables of information. But my computers also posed a constant complication: having to fiddle with the solar panels and manage my battery power, on which they were totally dependent. When a pig tore off the wires running from my battery to the solar panels, I almost blew a fuse of my own in frustration and anxiety. Fortunately, I found a way to splice the ends that were left.

In short order, I discovered that the 122 descendants of Yibihilu and its surrounding hamlets had fashioned not just a new settlement but a new way of life. Now they were living on the outskirts of the Nomad Station, just a short walk from its airstrip, school, churches, market, ball field, and government offices. In Gasumi Corners, Gebusi family houses were scattered like islands in an archipelago across three hillocks and a stream. No longer was there a central longhouse to serve as a focus of activity. And the settlement was no longer nestled in the full rainforest. Rather, it was sandwiched between the cleared areas that fanned out from the Nomad Station and the primary timberland that the Gebusi used to inhabit.

From their vantage point at Gasumi Corners, my friends could still walk to their traditional lands in the deep forest, but their lives increasingly revolved around the institutions and activities of the Nomad Station. The result was what might be called a new structure of feeling in Gebusi culture. Within this new world, the social life of the primary forest, including our previous settlement of Yibihilu, was gone. Internally, the new community still retained its kinship connections, including its links via marriage and maternal ties, as well as through clanship. But extended families and even nuclear families now lived separately in small individual houses; there was no central dwelling place to bring people together. As a consequence, the traditional sense of good company—the togetherness, talk, and whooping/joking of Gebusi *kogwayay*—was greatly muted. In terms of material goods, life was much as it had been before. Families had only a few more manufactured items than they did in 1980–82—perhaps an extra knife, a larger metal pot, or a shovel. The biggest visible change was the increased wearing of Western clothes. Unlike before, village women never walked around bare-breasted; they always covered themselves, if only with a ripped blouse. Even the men invariably wore a shirt with their shorts (however stained or torn) when they went to Nomad. Unlike other items, used clothes were occasionally flown in by the baleful and quickly sold at low prices for a profit by an itinerant trader or local official.

With their new interest in activities and organizations at Nomad, Gebusi seemed more punctual and disciplined than previously. The Sunday after my arrival, I got my first taste of what this meant. Sayu had said that the church service would begin when the sun was "so much above the treetops." Gebusi sense of daily time had always been as vague as the morning mists, and events invariably began later than anticipated. Mornings for Gebusi had been a relaxed time, with important affairs left to the late afternoon or evening—when the day was cooling off and people were well fed. That Sunday morning, I left a little ahead of time and figured I would arrive before most of the others. But the houses along the way were curiously empty. What was up? When I got close enough to hear hymn singing, I realized I was late. Late! The very concept had once seemed alien to the Gebusi. But the clock-watching pastor had rung the metal chime first in warning and then five minutes before the service was to start. Though I had missed the signals in the distance, everyone else was on time. On time—another new idea for the Gebusi. In the relaxed world of the rainforest, the rhythms of life had their own languid pace. People could simply not have been hurried. There had been little attempt to mark specific times of day, and there were no words for the days of the week, the months, or even the seasons; activities blended seamlessly from one day to the next. We had easily lost track of the days if we forgot to tick them off on our calendar. Now, however, Gebusi days and even minutes were marked and measured.

Beyond church services on Sunday morning, the new weekly schedule included schooling for local children from Monday through Friday. Classes at the Nomad Community School began promptly at 8:00 A.M. and lasted until 3:30 P.M. Mindful of the time, the children of Gasumi Corners usually left for school before 7:00 A.M.—and got home after 4:00 in the afternoon. The school day itself was divided into sixteen periods, some as short as fifteen minutes. These transitions were frequently marked by the ringing of the school bell. For adults, and especially for women, Tuesdays and Fridays from 8:00–10:00 A.M. were market days. Weekend afternoons were slated for rugby and soccer on the government ball field, particularly for the men and older boys. They arrived early so they wouldn't miss their starting time. The matches were refereed by government timekeepers who sounded a large horn to mark the end of the half and the end of the game. Though most Gebusi could not tell time, all the men seemed to want wristwatches—so they could ask someone else the time or at least appear to be acting based on knowledge of the hour.

If time for the Gebusi was increasingly marked against a daily and hourly clock, its passage now reflected Gebusi hopes for—and failures of—progress and improvement. Tests on Fridays gauged the learning that students had accomplished each week. Unfortunately, few children from Gasumi Corners were on track to finish elementary school—and none were slated to go on to the secondary school in Kiunga. In church, villagers were told that Judgment Day could come at any time—maybe tomorrow, maybe next week, maybe next month. If they waited to repent their sins, it might be too late—they could burn in hell. At the twice-weekly Nomad market, if food wasn't sold by the end of the session, it had to be taken home or given away. In sports, the Gebusi traditionally had played until the score was tied or until everyone had lost track. Now, by contrast, they played on the government ballfield, kept careful track of the score, and played to win by the final horn. In short, the strivings and shortcomings of the Gebusi's lifestyle were now measured against a timeline of hoped-for success.

Running out of time had not been a problem in 1980–82; the past and the future simply cycled into each other. The Gebusi word for "tomorrow," *oil*, was the same as the word for "yesterday." The word for "day after tomorrow" was the same as the one for "day before yesterday" (*bihar*). And the same was true of the word for "three days after" and "three days before" the present (*ehwar*). In terms of generations, Gebusi had used the same word for both their grandparents and their grandchildren (*owa*). And an adult man often referred to his own son as his "father" (*mam*). In the cycling of gardens and fallow land, a boy would ideally grow up to cultivate the lands of his father or grandfather and to eat of the sago palms and nuts trees planted for him there. Life had represented a spiritual and social circle. Even male life force had been physically recycled from one generation to the next. The ideal had been for things to repeat over time rather than to change. Against this background, it was hard to avoid the sense that time for the Gebusi had shifted from a circle of repetition to an arrow of anticipated progress, aimed toward a different and, they hoped, better future.

That our lives should get better over time—and that there is something wrong or unfortunate if they do not—may seem second nature in Western cultures. But for many non-Western peoples, including the Gebusi, this was a new and foreign notion. The mythic past rather than the present or the future had been viewed as the guiding light of success and accomplishment. But now, the Gebusi nursed a budding hope for economic, social, and moral improvement—at the market, at school, and in church. These aspirations were marked by desires we can identify with. The people of Gasumi Corners wanted bigger and better houses, more clothes and commodities, better education, increased opportunities to work for wages, and, generally, more money.

Realities, however, lag far behind. The Nomad Sub-District where the Gebusi live still has no roads to any other part of the country. Supplies must be flown in, which is very expensive. In their remote corner of the rainforest, the Gebusi have no resources or commodities of value to outsiders. Even their hardwood trees are not plentiful enough to attract logging companies. (From an environmental perspective, however, this is extremely fortunate!) The nearest town, Kiunga, lies eighty miles away, across foreign territory, swampland, and rivers. The trek there is dangerous and has been completed by only a few of the most intrepid young men. By air, the trip takes only an hour from Nomad. But the airfare is far too expensive for Gebusi to afford. As a result, the Gebusi have nowhere near the opportunities they would like for jobs, money, commodities, and travel. The little local economy of the Nomad Station depends primarily on the modest salaries of the few government workers who come from other parts of the country to live there. Villagers rarely gain access to regular earnings.

None of this has stemmed a tide of Gebusi hopes. Sayu wants a new boombox and the batteries to power it. Didiga wants a new shotgun—to replace the one I gave his father in 1981. Everyone wants more frequent meals of store-bought food, especially tinned fish and rice, plus new sets of clothes to wear to church and school and around the village. The sports team wants uniforms and sports shoes. But to little avail.

In such an out-of-the-way place, where do these desires come from? Since the 1960s, the Gebusi have known about airplanes, metal tools, clothes, Western-style houses, and commodities like lanterns, shoes, pots and pans, sheets, radios, and boxes with locks—and the money that buys things to put in them. Until 1975, however, these goods were associated with Australian patrol officers, whose way of life was separate, removed, and almost mystically different from their own. During the subsequent years of postcolonial government, however, Papua New Guineans who are recognizably similar to Gebusi have come to live and take charge at the Nomad Station. Like the patrol officers before them, they have conveniences, commodities, and appliances like refrigerators and VCRs that run off the station's power generator. Government officials earn money, wear nice clothes, travel by air to towns and cities, and bring back new goods plus wonderful and sometimes fantastic stories about modern ways of life.

As an anthropologist in the field, it is hard to live outside these changes. Though we lived as simply as we could, Eileen and I were certainly magnets of material curiosity for the Gebusi in 1980–82. Villagers had been fascinated and sometimes amazed by our metal boxes, tape recorder, camera, Western clothes, and supplies, and even the color of our skin and the texture of our hair. Although our purpose was to live with Gebusi rather than to change their lives, we also wanted to help them in any way we could. So our gifts provided a steady stream of coveted goods to them—fishing hooks, salt, soap, matches, medicine, clothes, metal knives, and axes.

In 1998, I developed a similar pattern of material exchange in Gasumi Corners. But the scale of goods and desires had become greater. Villagers wanted flashlights and batteries, cassette players, wristwatches, colorful shirts, and sunglasses. To help satisfy these and other desires on a larger scale, Gwabi and the other villagers decided that, instead of my paying rent for my house, I should visit Kiunga and bring back a planeload of goods that they could collectively own and sell for profit from a little house that they had built as a community store. With the proceeds, they reasoned, they could buy more supplies to restock the store, use some of the profits to buy what they wanted, and draw in increasing numbers of buyers from surrounding areas. At least during the time that I lived in Gasumi Corners, we were all pleased at how well this arrangement developed. When I completed my fieldwork, I paid for plane tickets for Sayu and Didiga to fly back with me to Kiunga. I showed them how to purchase goods and fly with them back to Nomad themselves—that is, how to resupply the community store on their own. (There is no way to order items at Kiunga except in person.) Such small commercial outlets are common in countries like Papua New Guinea. Over time, however, they rarely increase the overall level of village income. Especially in rural areas, such enterprises frequently fail due to problems of transportation and supply, unanticipated costs, and disputes over money.

Notwithstanding difficulties, lack of opportunity, and the bitterness of failure, the allure of material goods and of a more modern way of life act like tidal forces on places like Nomad. By the late 1980s, the attractions of the Nomad Station had become strong enough that virtually the entire community of Yibihilu had picked up and moved—lock, stock, and barrel—to the small portion of Gebusi land that abuts the government station and its airstrip. Back in the rainforest, the village of Yibihilu had been completely abandoned.

Modern wants are hardly unique to the Gebusi; if anything, they are global. Not just tiny stations like Nomad but towns and cities the world over attract people who hope for economic gain and a more modern way of life. But for many migrants, as well as for the Gebusi, the road to economic development is very difficult if not effectively blocked—no matter how hard or creatively people try. So what happens? The Gebusi have developed a lifestyle that seems more modern socially and culturally even if it is not much different from what it was previously in economic terms. At Nomad, these changes include regular participation in the local churches, school, market, sports leagues, and government-sponsored events and programs. These may not yield much in the way of money. Indeed, they can be costly. School requires an annual supply fee for each student, the churches collect weekly offerings, and the sports league requires dues paid to the officials who organize the games. The market can generate income for sellers, but, as we shall see, the proceeds are few. Nonetheless, these activities afford a strong sense of participating in and being part of a lifestyle associated with outside success—as government officials often note. In the Nomad area, being on time, waiting patiently for instruction, and being respectful of outsiders who are in charge—at school, in church, at the market, in government projects, and on the ball field—are all part of this package.

Given all this, I should not have been surprised on that first Sunday. Neither at the fact that everyone was on time nor, more amazing to me, that they sat so quietly and listened so patiently as the service dragged on and the day grew hotter. In 1980–82, the Gebusi had been like branches in the wind—jostling, joking, palavering, going this way and that to their heart's content. Even senior men had rarely tried to give orders. And when they did, it was as difficult to get people to comply as it would have been to herd a bunch of cats. But here was the Christian pastor, a man from a different part of the country. He spoke *tok pisin*, the national language. He harangued parishioners at length, preaching that they must try harder to be good, that it was difficult to get into heaven, and that those who continued in sin would be rejected by God. The people of Gasumi Corners stayed, remained still, and listened. They followed the pastor as he sang hymns and worshiped this stern God. And they did this every week.

When I went to the Nomad Community School, I was struck by a similar dynamic. Rows upon rows of students listened patiently to the provincial instructor, hour after hour. As in church, participation was "call and response" in form. The instructor would read a line or give an answer, and his students would repeat in unison what he had said. The day was long, but the students persisted. In the first grade alone, forty-nine pupils sat cross-legged on the hardwood floor.

There are many other sides to Gebusi lives, of course. And during my new time in the field, I richly experienced and enjoyed these. In their new setting at Gasumi Corners, though, the questions of change that struck me during the first days of my return became increasingly important as the months rolled on. How was it that the Gebusi had adopted hopes, values, and activities associated with a new way of life? How did their present practices relate to their previous ones—and why did Gebusi persist in their efforts despite economic and material frustration? What explanation did the Gebusi themselves offer for why they had given up their old lives in exchange for new ones? More generally, why do some people accept, and even willingly submit to, the authority of national or other outsiders? This last question was especially relevant in the case of the Gebusi. The historical spread of so-called modern influences often has been associated with military, economic, or political force, including through colonialism, trade, and capitalism. This was true in some ways for Gebusi as well: Australian patrol officers introduced clothes, steel axes, and other commodities, and they pacified the neighboring Bedamini. But the Gebusi had continued to live on their own. Their way of life had been mostly on their own terms after the period of colonialism had ended. With the departure of the Australians, even the annual government patrol to the bush had ceased. The Gebusi had been safe in the rainforest. Yet, some six years after Eileen and I left, the people of Yibihilu moved to the outskirts of the Nomad Station. They moved of their own choice; no one coerced them. Even today, it would be feasible for them to go back and live on their own in the rainforest.

In moving to the outskirts of Nomad, Gebusi responded to the gap between life in the rainforest and attractions they saw in a more modern way of life. People in different cultures respond differently to the gap between their aspirations and the realities they find. Some people, like the Gebusi, strongly embrace changes—they actively and fervently seek them out. Others come to accept new influences or ways of life only ambivalently or grudgingly. Still others actively oppose or resist external influences; they prefer to emphasize the value and the integrity of their customs. In actuality, however, these three alternatives are not mutually exclusive. In the crucible of today's world, many if not most non-Western peoples adopt all three of these responses to various degrees, in various ways, and in different parts of their lives. Given this, what has made the Gebusi of Gasumi Corners and surrounding communities so seemingly prominent at the "change" end of the continuum? What informs their willingness to give up relative autonomy and embrace alterations that do not, in fact, afford much chance of material success?

On important answer lies in history. Different cultures have had different relationships with—and degrees of subordination to—Western-style colonialism, trade, and capitalism. In the current era, they also have different relationships with their own national governments. In interior New Guinea, colonialism came very late. Even then, the Gebusi were fortunate to be spared the brunt of colonial "pacification"—and they benefited enormously when the raids of the Bedamini were stopped. As far as I knew, no Gebusi had ever been wounded or killed by a bullet. In economic terms, their primary complaint was not that they had been subject to outside intrusion, but that they hadn't received enough. Given this history, it is little wonder that Gebusi have welcomed rather than rejected powerful outsiders—first the Australians and then the national officials of Papua New Guinea.

Notwithstanding their history, the Gebusi's new lives still left me feeling as if I was in the midst of a split-brain experiment. On the one hand, my friends still pursued their activities in the forest—gardening, hunting, fishing, foraging, and cutting down and processing sago palms. They had their own houses in the dispersed settlement of Gasumi Corners. On the other hand, they were now willing and largely passive subjects—parishioners, pupils, sellers in the market, and participants in government initiatives. These institutions and activities were not merely tolerated but were actively sought out, day after day, week after week. Life in Gasumi Corners and in the rainforest was correspondingly affected. People participated not collectively but individually or as small families in activities at Nomad; each household made its own choices and commitments. Collective life in the settlement declined. In terms of subsistence, Gebusi increasingly grew foods preferred by government officers—so they would have a chance to sell them at the Nomad market. They also hauled provisions from the rainforest to the market in hopes of making a sale. These initiatives continued week after week even though market prices were very low and most of their food did not sell.

Although the Gebusi seemed to pass easily between their old and new worlds, my own experience was disconnected. One day, I would bask in the timeless wonder of the rainforest. The next, I would sit through a two-hour church service, a long government meeting, a desultory market session, an extended lesson in arithmetic at school, or multiple games of rugby and soccer on the Nomad ball field. These newfangled institutions and activities were not, somehow, what I had thought I would be studying. But for the Gebusi, these were important activities—the cutting edge of a vibrant, modern style of life. If I was going to really take their lives at current face value, to appreciate the Gebusi in their own present, I had to both hunker down and lighten up. I needed to experience the Gebusi more fully and genuinely in their new world. I remembered how difficult and confusing my first experiences with them had been in 1980–82. And I realized that the same kind of challenge—and the same potential for discovery—awaited me again.

Web site images of events and topics described in this chapter can be found at http://www.mhhe.com/knauft1.

CHAPTER 8

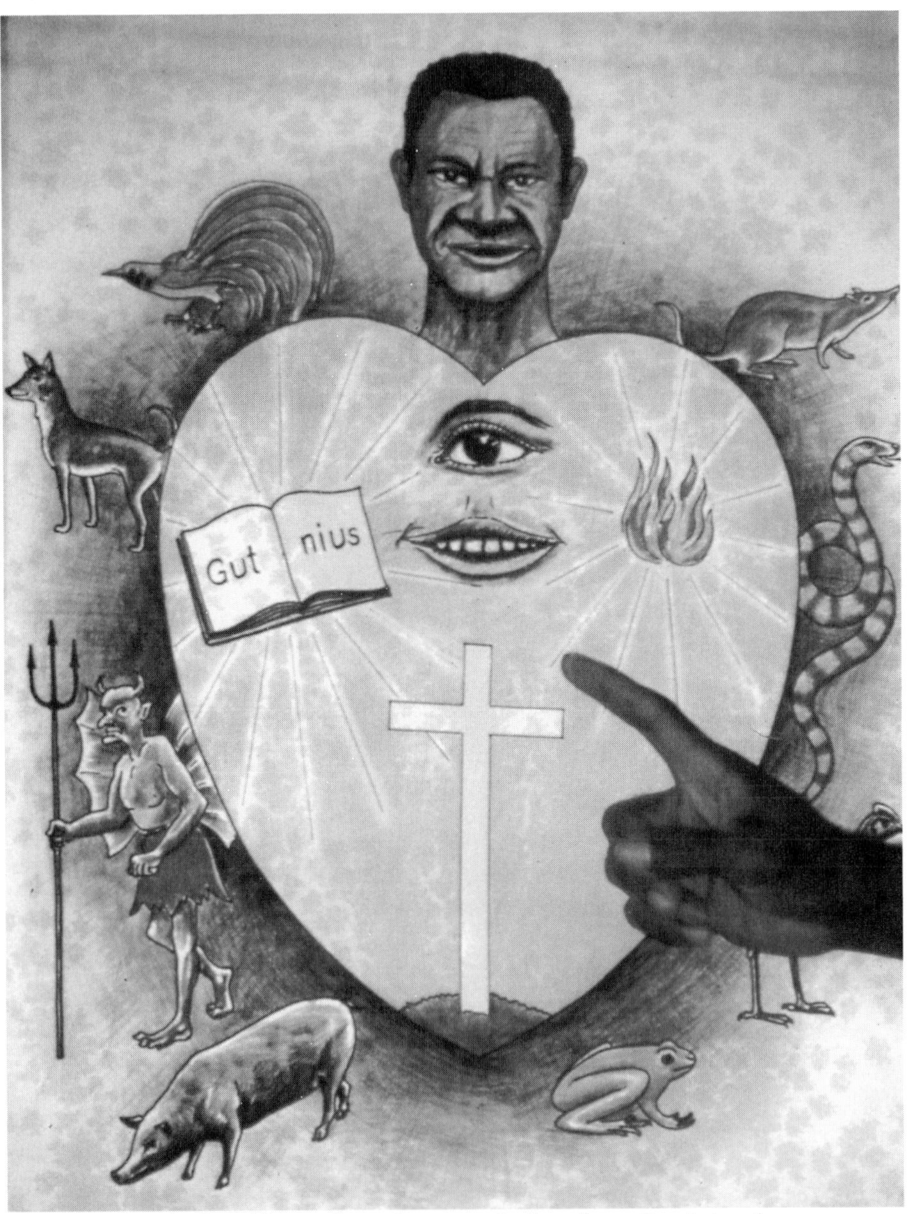

Church poster: the "good heart of man," open to the "good news" and closed to pagan spirits. (PHOTO: Bruce Knauft)

Yuway's Sacred Decision

YUWAY'S EYES SIMPLY SPARKLED. "*Koya, koya!*"—"Friend, friend!" We must have gazed into each other's eyes, snapped fingers, and joked heartily at least a dozen times. I came to his house, a mere five-minute walk from my own, having heard that he had been in the forest a few days earlier, when I first arrived. Yuway had been my most helpful friend in 1980–82. He was an all-around good person and the tallest of the young men we had helped initiate. Shortly after the initiation, he had become a moon-eyed romantic with his fetching wife-to-be, Warbwi, and we had given him gifts to help with his marriage. That had been seventeen years ago. And here he was again, in the flesh! It was so good to see him. Every few sentences, we would smile and clasp each other again, as if to reassure ourselves that our reunion was real. We quickly brought each other up to date. He was touched to hear that Eileen and I now had a son who was full grown and even taller than I. With subdued pride, Yuway told me that he and Warbwi now had four children: an adolescent boy and girl plus two younger sons. I joked with him that he must have been "busier" than I had been; we both broke into laughter.

As a few minutes passed, word spread that we two senior men were having a good jokefest together, and we ended up attracting a score of jovial spectators from surrounding houses. Good-natured as he was, I realized that Yuway was slowly getting embarrassed by our traditional joking. Although I had taken our jests for granted, he started to suppress his grins. From the reactions of others around us, I could sense that old-time joking, though tolerated from me as a middle-aged man who knew their traditions, was funny in part because it was now a bit anachronistic, a touch out of place.

As if to punctuate my perception, Yuway finally told me with a smile that he was an SDA—a member of the Seventh Day Adventist Church. This was the most severe Christian denomination in the Nomad area. I was naturally intrigued, and this led us to a thoughtful discussion of changes in Gebusi religion. Yuway said that he had come to Gasumi Corners from Yibihilu with the others some ten years earlier. Like most of them, he had also joined the Catholic Church soon after. The Catholic pastor had been solicitous of the Gebusi and had even visited some of their settlements in the bush. Because the church he built was between their new settlement near Nomad and the Nomad Station itself, the villagers thought that joining it would be a good way to help establish their new lives. As the people of Gasumi Corners got used to singing in church, Yuway said, they sang less with their own spirit mediums. The community's major shaman, Swiman, himself started going to church and then stopped singing to the traditional spirits entirely. So, too, with the other spirit mediums; they found themselves part of a community that was now singing to a new spirit, to a singular God. When the Gebusi go to church, they say literally, "We go to sing" ("*gio dula*"). Within a few years, the spirit séances that had galvanized Gebusi social life—and that had been such a large focus of my own work—had become history, a thing of the past.

Without spirit mediums, as Yuway explained, people in Gasumi Corners had no real way to communicate with their traditional spirits; their path of connection was "cut" (*gisaym-da*). No longer could they joke with the spirits, ask their advice about sickness or sorcery, or enlist their support for or opinions about fish poisoning and other activities. To my great surprise, the traditional world of Gebusi spirits had withered away. And with their departure, Gebusi social life also had changed. No longer was male sexual joking and camaraderie a focal point or a source of excitement. The people of Gasumi Corners sang to their new God not in the dead of night but in the brightness of the morning, not with humor but with sternness, not in conversation with the spirits but in strict admonishment by a petulant outsider about a supreme spirit. Apparently the preacher and his God had simply been more powerful than the old ones. They had the prestige and wonder of coming from afar, of being associated with the wealth, success, and accomplishments of a wider world. Although the lay pastor lived not far from Gasumi Corners, he was supported by the Catholic Church and flew regularly back to Kiunga and occasionally to his own home in one of the country's mountain districts. He was literate and well educated, wore nice clothes, had a house stocked with supplies, was able to call Kiunga on his own two-way radio, and was bent on presenting his way of life and his God as a model for the Gebusi to follow. They willingly agreed.

Yuway told me that he himself had been one of the Gasumi leaders in the Nomad Catholic Church from 1992 to 1995. (I pinched myself to note how the Gebusi now keep track of years.) But after that, he felt more distant from the parish.

"Why did you join the Seventh Day Adventists?" I asked.

"Well, the Catholic Church is kind of 'soft'; I wanted a church that was 'hard.'"

"How's that?" By this point, I was remembering that the Gebusi word for "hard" (*gof*) also means "strong," "righteous," "angry," and "potentially violent"—as well as "difficult."

"If you are really going to worship God, it shouldn't be a small thing. It should be a big thing. You should really work hard to please God. The Catholics make you work only a little hard. They let people keep lots of customs that God doesn't like—like dancing and smoking tobacco. The SDA Church knows that God doesn't like these and that they are wrong. They make their religion really hard by telling us we can't eat certain things that we like. They make us work a lot in the church yard, and they make us come for Bible learning as well as going to the long service on Saturday morning. They have pictures that show exactly what will happen to you if you have sin—you will burn in hell. With SDA, I know I am really a Christian and that I can go to heaven."

I paused to collect my thoughts. Yuway and my other friends had been so thoroughly "Gebusi" in spiritual outlook back in 1982. Yet his answer revealed not just the onus but the attraction of a fundamentalist Christian faith. Yuway's comment also pointed up the key distinction that the Gebusi make between the three local churches. Catholicism was seen as the "easiest" faith because it had the fewest taboos. Catholics were told to attend church regularly, to worship God rather than other spirits, to avoid fighting, and to not drink kava—their lightly intoxicating drink made from roots. As long as these criteria were followed for a year or two—with some allowance made for backsliding—a Gebusi could be baptized as a Catholic by the priest or bishop on one of his sporadic visits to Catholic parishes in the province.

Although about sixty percent of those in Gasumi Corners ended up becoming members of the Catholic Church, approximately one-fifth (22 percent) belonged to the Evangelical Church of Papua New Guinea. In addition to the Catholics' strictures, Evangelicals had a strong taboo against smoking tobacco and restrictions on participating in pagan rituals. The SDA rules were even stricter. In fact, Yuway's family was the only one in Gasumi Corners to have joined their church. In addition to bans on smoking, drinking, dancing, and observing traditional rituals, the SDAs prohibited the eating of smooth-skinned fish and any kind of pork. This last was particularly significant, because eating pigs was still a prime feature of Gebusi festivities on special occasions. SDA adherents were told that each Saturday was a day for worshiping God in church; all other work or gardening, as well as forms of public entertainment—playing ball, attending feasts, or going to disco—were condemned as irreligious.

Because I knew Yuway to be a caring person, I wondered how his personal beliefs meshed with the SDA reputation for intolerance. He said with all earnestness that he had no anger against those who went to other churches or even those who went to none at all—which included a few in Gasumi Corners. I decided to push him a little: "If someone who is a good person goes to the Catholic Church or to the Evangelical Church instead of SDA, do you think that person can go to heaven when he or she dies? Or not?"

Yuway thought for a minute, but not too long: "I don't know. Only God knows these things. But for me, I think that someone who is good inside can go to heaven, and it shouldn't matter if they go to one church or another."

"What if they don't go to any church at all?"

"Well, if they are given the chance to believe in Father God but still don't do it, it might be hard for God to see them as a good person and let them into heaven. But it's not for me to say."

I was impressed with his answer. It was then that I remembered the arrows that Yuway had been fashioning when I had come up to greet him. Now they were lying next to him, elaborately carved and ready for painting with bright red ochre.

"Those are really nice arrows. Aren't they the kind used to sponsor a young man at an initiation?"

"Yes, I'm sponsoring a young Wapsiayk [a young man from his clan] at Taylmi in probably a month or two."

"Can you still do that and be an SDA?"

"Well, I won't get baptized into SDA myself until after the initiation. It will be the last time for me to eat pork in my life. And if I go just to see the initiation and not because I believe in its spirits, it's okay."

As I mulled over this last response, the sky opened up as if by divine intervention. Suddenly, rain came pelting down. Realizing that it was almost dark—and that the fire for supper was yet to be started at my own house—I smiled and snapped fingers quickly with Yuway and the others before whooping loudly as I raced up the trail. I was thoroughly drenched by the time I reached home.

Reflecting that evening on the day's events, I was struck by Yuway's remarks in relation to what I was finding from the Gebusi who were Catholics or Evangelicals. At Nomad, all three churches featured a fierce God of fire and brimstone—a God who threatened hell and demanded compliance. And all of them held that Judgment Day could come at any time—and that continuing repentance was the only key to salvation. All three churches were "hard," though some were "harder" than others. How was it that different Gebusi belonged to these three different churches—each of which drew members from diverse communities? While I had been visiting with Yuway that afternoon, his two married brothers, Keda and Halowa, had shown up. Keda was a lay leader in the Catholic Church; the previous Sunday, he had been asked to translate parts of the pastor's sermon for the congregation. Halowa, by contrast, was an Evangelical. Each of the three brothers, I realized, belonged to a different church! I increasingly found that Yuway was right: the Gebusi accepted each other's right to choose a religious denomination that suited him best. The "him" is significant here, because most wives attended the church that their husbands had chosen. If Christianity saved the soul of the individual rather than the group, so, too, each individual man, at least, could choose what church to belong to—and whether to believe in God at all. The Gebusi world of moral choices and consequences was no longer governed so strongly by kinship or clanship, but increasingly by a man's choice.

The second thing that struck me involved Yuway's plan to give initiation gifts to a young man while he was also completing the arduous requirements for SDA baptism. How was this possible? Was Yuway being hypocritical? Or was this a classic case of "syncretism," in which two religions are blended together? Or was something else going? The first two of these possibilities didn't seem likely to me; I suspected that something else was at issue. It turned out that Gebusi distinguish between witnessing a traditional ritual and actually hosting or performing in one. At a remote settlement like Taylmi—the last big Gebusi village that had not yet become Christian—one could attend an initiation the same way that Americans can watch an action movie or a historical epic without being considered a violent person or a creature of the past; they can view it as an entertaining drama or spectacle without adopting its values or lifestyle. Indeed, being exposed to "pagan ways" without succumbing to them can itself indicate commitment to Christianity.

It has often been noted that the process of Christian redemption is frequently punctuated by trials and temptations. Preachers at Nomad repeatedly emphasized the danger of "backsliding" into sin and vice associated with tradition. Although the Gebusi willingly submitted themselves to the harangues of the pastor, it was their deviation from Christian thoughts or interests that spurred their sense of needing atonement—the pang of conscience that begs for moral cleansing. Exposure to and ambivalence about traditional customs was integral to the jawboning process of Gebusi conversion to Christianity. Hopes of salvation seemed directly linked to threats of sin.

Three weeks later, I experienced this dynamic by going with Yuway's family to an SDA service at a small nearby hamlet. The pastor's message was bleak. And it became something of a marathon, in that he exhorted the small congregation for a full two hours. Increasingly, they simply hung their heads. That evening, I wrote the following:

> The patience and passivity demanded in church—which I noted immediately among the Catholics—is brought to a firmer and sterner level among the Seventh Day Adventists. Today, the long sermon by the SDA preacher was a case in point. He placed great emphasis on the trials of Jesus: his forty days in the wilderness in the hot sun without food or water, his agonizing death on the cross, his suffering for us all. "Our own hardships are small; we should bear them easily and ask for nothing. We should think of Christ—be grateful that He suffered and died for us." The preacher's concluding harangue, which repeated itself for a good forty minutes, was similarly somber. Saturday should be a day only for SDA worship. Food and market and other work activities should be finished Friday night. Saturday should be sober and worshipful, both morning and night, with no entertainment or even cooking of food. This was the true way to worship God.

Where is the payoff in this scheme? It is deferred. Set against the austere trials of the present is the glorious image of life after death. Heaven was described as a place full of *bip*, or "cargo," a place where people are endlessly happy, without suffering or sickness. I was reminded of the dramatic cults that some Melanesians developed when they first encountered Western goods. These so-called cargo cults arose as local people attempted to obtain or "produce" European goods by conducting magical rites or by mimicking Western behavior. In their conversion to Christianity, however, the Gebusi had bypassed such attempts, accepting that wealth and salvation would come only in an afterlife and not right away. To attain this bliss, they could not ask for much during life here on earth. But on the day of reckoning, God would give his ultimate reward to those few who had truly followed the path of Jesus. My field entry concluded as follows:

> Now I can see, at least dimly, Yuway's attraction to this church. It is severe; it stresses the need to be hard and disciplined for God. This is the modern path

> of dignified compliance in and around the Nomad Station as well as a path for everlasting life. It measures the present not against a happy standard of current success but against trials, and rewards, that were infinitely greater for Jesus.

Yuway's choice foregrounds the path that the Gebusi increasingly take not only in church but also at school, in the market, and even on the ball field: to wait patiently for future success. Across these contexts spreads an ethic of acting with discipline, of listening to outsiders, and of accepting the authority of superiors.

The most dramatic case of religious transformation was undoubtedly that of Modiay. Modiay was the youngest and smallest of the six young men whom we had helped initiate in 1981. In the late 1980s, he married Boyl, Sayu's widowed mother. However, Boyl died shortly thereafter. Following the death inquest, Modiay confronted the person accused of causing Boyl's death through sorcery—a man named Sabowey. Modiay told me that his anger toward Sabowey had come to dominate his thoughts and actions. As he described it, his plan for revenge took on a surgical and almost Zen-like focus. Although Sabowey was almost a foot taller than he was, Modiay sought him out and confronted him alone in the forest. He dodged Sabowey's arrows and split his head with a bush knife. When Sabowey was dead, Modiay cut off his head and left it next to his body in the forest. Then he went to the Catholic compound, told the pastor what he had done, handed him his bush knife, and turned himself in to the Nomad police.

Modiay's killing of Sabowey in 1988 was a watershed. He was sentenced to six years at the national prison in the capital city of Port Moresby. No Gebusi had ever traveled so far. But Modiay hardly saw the city. While in prison, he became exceedingly self-disciplined. He learned to speak *tok pisin*, the national language, converted to Christianity, became a model prisoner, and even became head cook for the warden, who entrusted him with the key to the compound's storehouse of food. To this day, Modiay proudly keeps the letter of reference and commendation that the warden gave him upon his release from prison. He remembers his jailers fondly and with great affection. He still wears the shirt that one of them gave him, and he named his first son Billy, after a prison guard who became his good friend.

Now back in Gasumi Corners, Modiay has become something of a model Christian. Unlike those who hung around the pastor's compound in hopes of wheedling a favor or gaining a benefit, Modiay worked for him out of a sense of personal commitment. He told me that he waited to be baptized until coming back to Nomad because he wanted to be sure—really sure—that his bad ways were completely gone, that he felt no more hate in his heart. He felt grateful that God could forgive even as great a sin as his killing of Sabowey. And he said that he would wait with a Christian heart until Judgment Day to see if God would accept him into heaven. I asked Modiay if he wouldn't be tempted to kill another person for sorcery, especially if one of his own children were to die of sickness. His answer was immediate: "No. No way."

"Why not?"

"It's not for me to take revenge. That's something for the 'Big Fellow' [God] to decide. Besides, the people of Gasumi Corners don't practice sorcery anymore. Even if they wanted to, they would be too scared of what I did to Sabowey to send sorcery again. If my son died, it wouldn't be from sorcery."

Against traditional beliefs, Modiay's view was revolutionary. The Gebusi had once universally attributed fatal illnesses to sorcery. And a man's demand for revenge was greatest when it was a member of his own immediate family who had died from sickness.

While Modiay was in prison, his community had changed. Incited by the pastors, the villagers' redoubled their rejection of violence against suspected sorcerers. The penalty Modiay had been forced to pay—six years in prison, away from his kin—reinforced the reluctance of other Gebusi to follow in his footsteps. The killing of Sabowey became renowned as the last execution of a sorcerer, the end of an era. In the wake of this act, conversion to Christianity swelled rather than diminished. Since then, as far as I know, no Gebusi has been killed or even attacked as a sorcerer. This is fairly amazing: a society with one of the highest rates of homicide known has seen it drop to zero. To me, this underscores the degree to which human violence is not an ingrained or inevitable outcome, but one that is strongly shaped by attitudes and beliefs. I confirmed this lack of violence by detailing and then cross-checking the cause and circumstances of each of the deaths that had occurred during my absence. And yet, I remained somewhat skeptical of this good-news story. The Gebusi belief in sorcery had been so strong, and their desire to seek vengeance so high, that I remained a doubting Thomas—I needed to see in order to believe. Then Uwano died.

A certain depth emerges from the eyes of a man who knows his death throes are starting. Uwano was not old by our standards, probably in his late forties. Perceptive and a convivial joker, he had been my *arga*, my "breadfruit" gift partner, since 1981. We had always greeted each other heartily. But by the fall of 1998, he was a shell of his former self, having only a tiny reserve of strength to fight his death. When I went to visit him at the Nomad Aid Post on his last night, the swelling that would soon take his body had already taken his right arm and back. He gazed upward with a mixture of knowledge and confusion. Then he turned and seemed to recognize me, and a shadow of a smile flickered across his face.

I knew better than to tell him he would get better. I could only kneel down with a helpless smile, look softly into his eyes, and say "*Koya, koya,*" ("friend, friend") as tenderly as I could. I took his hand in mine and stroked it. It was cold, already dead. He looked at me with that slight shake of head that is the Gebusi expression for, "There's no way; it's impossible." Then he was gone from me, eyes drifting into space. His little frame shook with a small spasm, which was all his ravaged body could muster. He did not look back at me as I waited there. After a while, I crept out to the next room to talk with his relatives. The stark glow of the fluoresent bulb in that room with no furnishings cast them all in ghostly stillness.

We always project at death, I think—the Gebusi with their beliefs and me with my thoughts of final human connection. And hopefully Uwano, too, reaching out from his doorway on death's divide. He died a few hours later on October 9, 1998.

I waited instinctively for the sorcery inquests to start. Back in 1980–82, it would have been unthinkable for a prominent man in the community to die without a full-blown inquest to find the sorcerer responsible. But Uwano's body was carried back to Gasumi Corners for a simple Christian funeral. He was dressed in his best Sunday shirt, his head was wreathed with leaves, and he was buried during a graveside service led by a Catholic catechist who read from the Bible.

A few of Uwano's closest relatives grumbled that someone must have killed him. Men voiced vague fears that an assault sorcerer could be on the prowl. But there was no spirit séance, no accusation, no attempt to identify a suspect, and no attempt to take revenge. As if to satisfy themselves, the men walked off to one of Uwano's gardens. They pawed around aimlessly in case an obvious sign of a sorcery attack could be found. But their search was half-hearted, and they quickly lost interest. As one man said with a shrug, "If a spirit medium were around, we might have a chance of finding something. But there isn't." In effect, they were simply paying their respects to Uwano by visiting the place where they thought he might have become sick. Not wanting to waste their trip to the forest, the men gathered weathered logs near his garden and shouldered them back to the village for firewood.

In the wake of this experience, the descriptions of Gebusi deaths between 1982 and 1998 finally made real sense to me. Friends had earnestly told me, in case after case, "So-and-so simply died of sickness. We just don't know why. Only God can know. Maybe she was killed by sorcery. Or maybe by some other kind of spirit. Maybe Satan was trying to fool us into thinking that it was sorcery. Not knowing, we just buried the body and had the pastor read from the Bible." Although the dead person's closest relatives might suspect someone of sorcery, there was little they could do. Without firm spiritual evidence, other people in the community would not support their claim. And if they did try to launch an accusation, it could backfire. The person accused of sorcery could now turn the tables and charge the accuser with making a slanderous accusation without evidence, even bringing the case to the Nomad police.

As I thought about all this, my views of Gebusi Christianity were ambivalent. On the one hand, I felt that much of value in Gebusi culture had been lost. The vibrant wonder of their traditional beliefs had faded, and the poetry, symbolism, music, and awe of their spirit world were almost dead. In their place was a harsh new religion, trumpeted from elsewhere. In adopting their new beliefs, the Gebusi had become passive recipients of outside authority—spiritual, social, and political. On the other hand, Christian teaching and a new way of life had reduced the Gebusi's extraordinary rate of violence. Indeed, their sorcery killings had stopped altogether. Social life was more peaceful than before, and men, women, and even children could walk to Nomad or in the nearby forest without fear of attack. Although the intense camaraderie of earlier days was gone, so, too, was the threat of lethal violence. Life was tamer in many ways.

What about the experience of Gebusi women? Previously, they had enjoyed the energy and splendor of the spirit world, but from the sidelines, as it were. Although spirit women were key figures in the traditional cosmos, Gebusi women themselves had been excluded from séances and had little influence in sorcery inquests; men controlled the spirit world and the use of violence. Now, however, women were Christian along with the men. The responsibility and the reward of being Christian—of repenting sins and gaining salvation—was individual for both sexes. In the church itself, pews were divided evenly, with women on the left side and men on the right. At the Catholic services, men and women attended in roughly equal numbers, but in SDA and Evangelical services, a decided majority were women. Of course, the church pastors and the primary lay leaders in the community were invariably men. And the authority of "Papa God," as he was called, was both stronger and more patriarchal than that of traditional Gebusi spirits. Sporadically but notably, men in Gasumi Corners would echo the tone of the preachers or government officials, adopting a lecturing and authoritative tone in their own community. Finally, the number of Gebusi marriages that were acrimonious as opposed to harmonious was about the same as before.

Adding to my ambivalence about Christianity was another uncertainty: To what extent were the Gebusi's previous beliefs really dead? If only vestigially, the Gebusi still worry about sorcery. In many parts of Melanesia—and in parts of Africa, Asia, Latin America, and even Western countries—belief in sorcery or magic has persisted or reasserted itself. Such beliefs have sometimes melded with Christianity or other world religions such as Islam, Buddhism, or Hinduism. In significant areas of Melanesia and Africa, sorcery beliefs play a major role in disputes and rivalries, including between political leaders. If these customs can continue in modern forms, couldn't Gebusi beliefs come back in new ways? Vengeance against suspected sorcerers certainly seems to be a thing of the past for the Gebusi. But just as their religion has changed radically since 1982, perhaps it will take another new turn in the future.

No matter what happens, however, further changes will occur through the lens of Christian conversions that have already taken place. Even if Christianity is later rejected or disavowed, its present influence will have a significant legacy. In this sense, the hands of time cannot be turned back. And there is every indication that Christian influence among Gebusi is growing ever stronger.

Ultimately, how can we explain Gebusi religion—the complexity of its past, its present, and its indeterminate future? As with many topics that anthropologists study—subsistence, kinship, economics, and politics—the complexities of the present play havoc with the categories of the past. The traditional Gebusi cosmos was full of spirits in the form of humans, birds, fish, lizards, and even trees. Contact with these spirits was made by spirit mediums—spiritual practitioners who had direct, if sporadic, access to the spirit world. As mentioned in chapter 3, Gebusi religion reflected dimensions of animism and shamanism, which have sometimes been suggested as the oldest forms of human spiritual belief. However, Gebusi religion is now clearly, if not predominantly, influenced by Christianity, one of the major world religions. Historically, world religions such as Islam, Buddhism, Judaism, Hinduism, and Confucianism, like Christianity, have been associated with kingdoms or state empires. The spiritual pantheon of most of these religions is centralized or monotheistic, often focusing on a single God or creative force. In recent years, major world religions have spread yet further and become more influential, including in remote areas such as the New Guinea rainforest. Although it once was thought that religion would decline as cultures became more modern, just the reverse may be increasingly true. And in the process, world religions are themselves shaped by the history and beliefs of many different cultures. Global religions meet local persuasions, conversions, and sometimes resistances. At Nomad, the practice of Catholicism, Protestantism, or Seventh Day Adventism is significantly different from what they are in the United States. But they remain strongly Christian nonetheless.

The interaction between global and local religions illuminates the contemporary sweep of spiritual life as it changes over time. Complementing this wider view is the need to appreciate personal experiences that are deeply meaningful and "efferverscent" even though they may not be religious in formal or institutional terms. Although these experiences may surpass the strictures of organized religion altogether, they can increase our awareness of human meanings that are sublime or ineffable. Such awareness can be personal as well as professional. One day, I found it myself in Gasumi Corners. This is what I wrote in my field notes:

> Today by my house, I had little idea what hit me. The breeze sent a faint melody, beautiful and haunting, apparently from afar. I had never heard anything like it. I went magnetically toward the music, but I found no houses in its direction. "You want to hear the singing," Kilasui said, and he pointed me to the path. It led from the village to seemingly nowhere, but the sound grew louder. The sound was as stunning as and yet different from the séance songs of old. I wound through the brush to a small fire that had breadfruit warming next to it. No one was there, but the music was now full all around me. I looked up. Smiling down like nymphs on high were seven radiant boys smothering each other in soft harmony.
>
> I drew irresistibly up into their tree, its white branches grown as if they knew where each step would need to be placed. It swayed slightly with my weight and shook with gentle laughs that echoed the boys themselves. They squealed in delight to have a gawky grown companion, white as their tree, take interest in their singing. This soon brought the attention of other children, some of whom also clambered into the tree and distributed themselves carefully, as if to steady a wobbly ship. Even without their hubbub, my juvenile action could not have gone unnoticed. Now I could see a gathered crowd of women, yet more children, and even Sayu, who grinned at me through the foliage below. Their happiness, mine, and that of the boys made its own harmony, suspended in air with their song.

I had several of those indescribable minutes in that tree—the kind that convince you to the bone that you've done the right thing to go so far, that you have reached an enjoyment and bonding that transcends culture and that words cannot express. The sky was bluest blue, a cool breeze laced their melody, and I looked out thinking I had captured the innocence and joy of forest peoples that Colin Turnbull wrote about so nostalgically decades ago in central Africa. I cannot fully share or reproduce his nostalgia; there are too many complexities, uncertainties, and problems for that. But those stolen moments of innocence, total and beautiful, when one finds oneself inexplicably a young boy again drawn up in a tree, caressed in a sea of angelic smiles, tender harmony, and rainforest awe, can be neither denied nor suppressed. These are the moments that make life not just worth living, but a thousand times over. If music marks the sound of the soul and the wheels of time, the songs of the Gebusi present can be as rich as their spiritual past.

Web site images of events and topics described in this chapter can be found at http://www.mhhe.com/knauft1.

CHAPTER 9

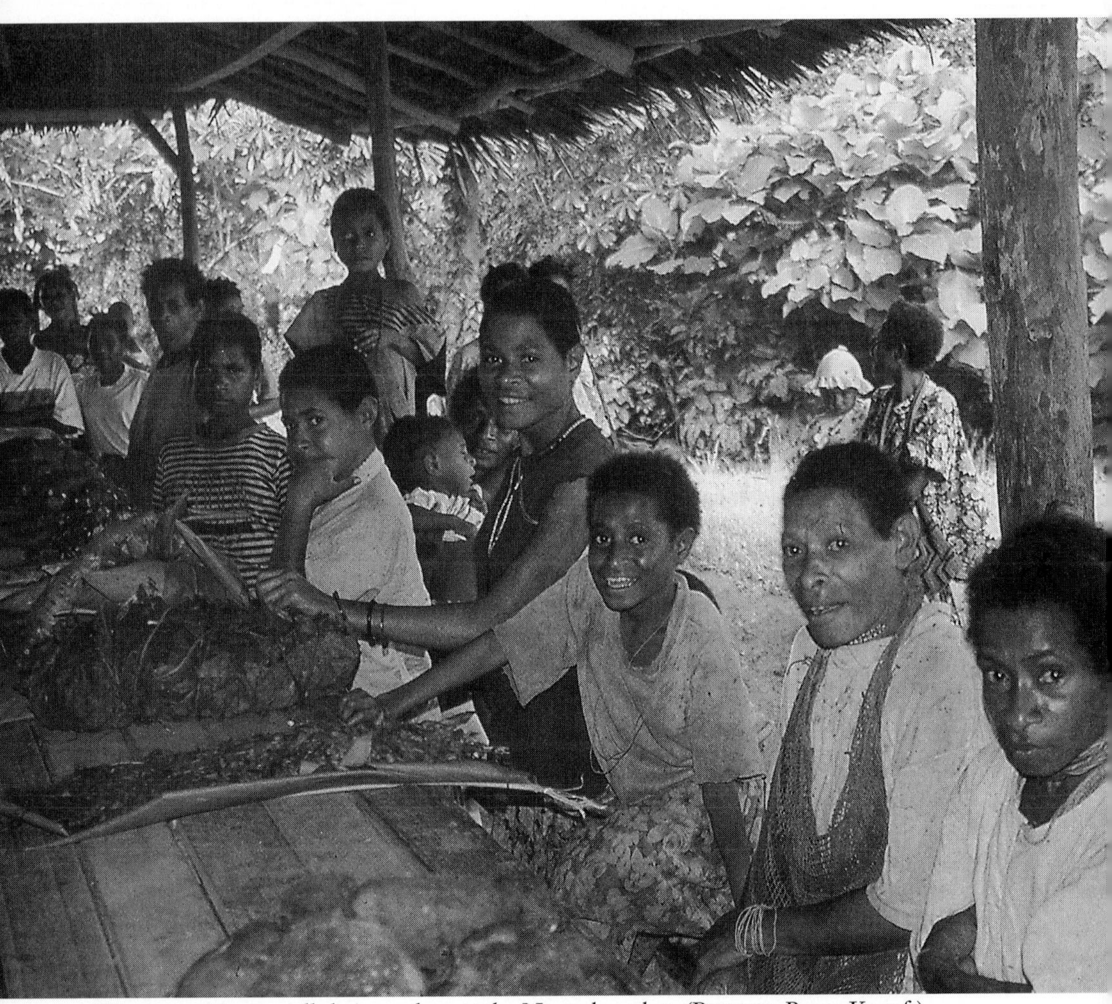

Women waiting to sell their produce at the Nomad market. (PHOTO: Bruce Knauft)

Pennies and Peanuts, Rugby and Radios

Bosap was not happy. The market was winding down, and her piles of bananas and sweet potatoes lay primped for sale like wallflowers that everyone saw but nobody wanted. The other women were similarly forlorn; their produce was still competing with Bosap's on the sellers' tables. Thinking to make light of the situation, as well as to collect more information, I tried to view her glass as half full: "You sold at least a little, right? Maybe two or three sales at 10 cents each?" Bad questions, bad timing. Bosap's normally congenial features, already sober, flashed to a scowl. "Not interested," she said, and turned away. She had sold nothing.

So, too, in her life, Bosap had been passed over, though she usually took everything in stride. As she had laughingly said when I talked to her before, "No man wanted to marry me. But then, I didn't want to marry any of them, either!" Among the Gebusi, Bosap had the rare distinction of becoming an older woman, now in her mid-fifties, without ever having married. When she had been in her thirties, this hadn't stopped her from having a sexual affair with a young man in his late teens. It had created a scandal when Bosap became pregnant, but she had carried on with determination. She did not marry her young lover, who had not yet been initiated, nor any of his older clan-mates, who might have been willing to claim the infant boy and take Bosap as a second wife and domestic helper. Despite the anomaly, Bosap had raised Kuma by herself, with the help of her own kin. It was now the pride of her life that Kuma had become a strong and decent young man who was now almost ready himself to be married. As long as I had known her, Bosap had maintained both her pleasant disposition and her ultimate determination to go her own way. Her good-spiritedness was attested by the fact that, even as an "old woman," she had never been suspected of sorcery in previous years, in contrast to many other older women in Gasumi Corners.

Because Bosap was usually friendly, I was caught off guard by her reply to my query at the market. Bad sales were obviously a touchy personal issue, and there were few buyers—mostly government officials and their wives from the Nomad Station. Nevertheless, women from Gasumi Corners and other communities continued to invest effort in taking their best produce to market in hopes of selling it. At dawn on Tuesdays and

Fridays, they packed their foodstuffs in cavernous net bags and hauled them across the Hamam River and down the muddy path to the Nomad market. Even on a "good day," many women came back loaded down with the same food they had brought. And prices were low. For the equivalent of 60 cents, a buyer could purchase a large bunch of ripe bananas, a pile of shelled Tahitian chestnuts, and a bundle of cooked bamboo shoots. Even at that, few people aside from government workers and pastors had money to spend on food, and their own wages were small, erratic, and undependably paid. But local women kept bringing food to sell, twice every week. The market was their way to have at least some small place in a cash-based economy.

Wanting some insight into this dynamic, I determined to find out exactly how much food the women brought to market, how much they took back or gave away, how much they sold, and how much money they earned. As I realized from my encounter with Bosap, however, this was going to be tricky. Women were eager to hide their many failures and even their few successes—for fear of jealousy. Only a very few of them could actually add up the value of the coins they received in any event, and they quickly shoved their proceeds into tightly wadded bundles. When they did occur, transactions were downplayed or shielded from public view. A purchaser would have the exact change ready and pay it in a lump sum rather than publicly counting coins. Sometimes, he or she would saunter behind the table, privately make the purchase, and furtively sweep the food into a net bag before walking away. Because prices for each pile of food were standardized, there was no need for bargaining or even, in most cases, any conversation at all.

In typical fieldwork fashion, I discovered this etiquette by seriously violating it. I had been pleased to see so many new foods for sale at the first market I attended. Wanting to stimulate the local economy and to obtain some different foods for my own supper, I approached a woman who had bamboo shoots for sale. Lacking pocket change, I pawed clumsily through my various pockets, only to find that the smallest currency I had was a 2-kina bill. As I extended this to her across the table, I could see the color drain from her face. Though worth only one U.S. dollar, the bill was ten times the price of the shoots I was buying. The poor woman had neither the arithmetic nor the coins to make change, so she was forced to initiate a confusing chain of inquiries that rippled in domino effect through all the people around her. Ten-cent loans and other transfers of coins ricocheted through the crowd. After several long and awkward minutes, my requisite 90 cents in change was amassed and dutifully counted for me—as everyone looked on. By this time, I had half a mind to let the unfortunate women simply keep the change. Except for two things. First, I would be wildly undermining the standards of the market, which were predicated on fixed and standardized prices for each pile of food. Second, my transaction had attracted the attention of perhaps half of the two hundred or so people at the market. Setting a precedent of overpayment could have jacked up the cost of my future purchases by as much as 900 percent! So I smiled gamely and apologized pleasantly, trying not to call yet more attention to my gaffe.

How much is a dime worth in Gasumi Corners? The episode reminded me of how cultural meanings, rules, and assumptions—whole worlds of understanding—

underlie the smallest of material exchanges. Back in the United States, I walk into a store and don't give it a second thought. The impersonality of buying an item from someone I don't know, of handing over money in public, of receiving change, and of having other people witness it—all this presumes a series of market assumptions that the Gebusi and their neighbors are just beginning to engage. But—and this is the more important point—Gebusi seem more rather than less motivated to engage this market world at the same time and in some ways for the very reason that they are marginal and awkward with respect to it. Notwithstanding the embarrassment of my conduct at the market, the woman I bought produce from had earned not just my 10 cents but the prestige of selling to an outsider who had money. Of all the sellers with bundles of bamboo shoots, I happened to have chosen hers. She and her kin now had the ownership, presumably collective, of not just some coins but a 2-kina bill that was received very publicly. Notwithstanding its awkwardness, the transaction also conveyed value, which I judged from the grinning palaver of the woman's kin as I walked away. If I had unwittingly trampled on local etiquette, I had also unwittingly reinforced larger assumptions of a market economy: that monetary exchange is at once public, impersonal, and prestigious.

Being either a good or a bad ethnographer (sometimes, it is hard to know which is which), I became more interested than ever in finding what market women at Nomad actually accomplished. Like the churches, the Nomad school, and the local sports league, the market is an interethnic affair—people come to it from various sides or "corners" of Nomad. These corners are inhabited by persons with different ethnic or tribal affiliations. As such, women from Gasumi Corners form only a small fraction of those at the market. But because they were from my own core community, I decided to keep them as my focus.

The first and easiest thing to discern was that most of the sellers were, in fact, women. By counting the sellers from Gasumi Corners on twenty-five different market days, I found that over 91 percent of them (285 of 313) were female. This paralleled my rough sense of the percentage of female sellers attending from other communities and ethnic groups. Although men and boys also came to the market, they seldom sold anything; they tended instead to converse with one another around the periphery of the selling area. Occasionally, they would saunter down the aisle of selling tables under the market's large thatched roof. And once in a while, they would buy a pile of peanuts for a dime. But the center of action—or lack thereof—was the women and their sales. All the women from Gasumi Corners participated; each would gather her best foodstuffs and bring them to market an average of once every ten days. All in all, the market was the prime place for village women to be "modern." Gebusi women also went to church, of course. And in recent years, girls had increasingly become students along with boys at the Nomad Community School. Only at the market, however, were women not merely present but the dominant and central focus of attention. Although they tended to be quiet and retiring rather than talkative or aggressive, they did visit casually with their female kin and relatives, including women from other villages or communities.

How much money did women actually make at the Nomad market? I couldn't easily ask them, but I found that I could count the piles of food that they initially placed on the selling tables. As the market progressed, I strolled casually up and down the aisles, chatting with the women and noting which piles of food had been reduced by sales and in what amounts. Because prices were standardized, it wasn't hard to figure how much the women had sold by the end of the market. Women who were lucky enough to have sold several items were willing to clarify, if I was unsure, how many units they had sold.

Over the course of twenty-five market days, I calculated that the women sold less than half the food that they had brought to the market for sale. The rest was carried back home or given away. A woman's average total earnings per market day were 20 cents—for selling food weighing several pounds or more. More than 20 percent of the women who brought food to market on a given day sold nothing at all.

The inflated price of the few things that could be bought with money at Nomad's tiny home-front stores underscored the difficulty of the women's enterprise. The benchmark goods bought at these stores were one-kilo bags of rice and twelve-ounce tins of low-grade mackerel. Each of these items cost the equivalent of $1.50. This meant that the average woman's sales from almost an entire month of marketing were wiped out when she purchased a single bag of rice or a single tin of fish. In assessing the nutritional value of the rice or fish against the many hours and calories involved in raising surplus food and hauling it back and forth to market, it became obvious that the energy cost of women's marketing far outweighed the benefits they gained from it. In these terms, the market activities of Gebusi women seemed irrational.

Why would someone put more time and effort into an enterprise than they get out of it? This question grew increasingly poignant as I saw women from Gasumi Corners processing and carrying food and then waiting aimlessly at the market, week after week.

The onus seemed greatest for two young adolescent girls, Danksop and Waygo, who would sit wooden or sighing behind their piles of food for hour after hour. But the answer to my question was one that I should have realized all along. In a word: culture. As we know from the things we ourselves buy, there is much more to a purchase—and more to the work that pays for it—than the trade-off between the dollars we spend and the functional use of the things we buy. Why do we prefer a Ferrari to a Ford, Godiva chocolate to Hershey's, or a gold ring to one made of tin? Similarly, why do the Gebusi prefer a single bag of rice to a dozen pounds of potatoes? The answer is the same in both cases: items of value afford prestige and cultural status. If Gebusi marketing seems "irrational," it carries the value and prestige of earning money, of being modern. And it does this for those who are otherwise most shut out of the local cash economy: village women. If men obtain occasional paid work—cutting the grass on the airstrip, doing odd jobs for government officials, or acting as carriers for visitors on a trek—women earn coins at the market.

I realized the larger economic as well as cultural importance of women's marketing when I found my "banker" in Gasumi Corners. Nolop was the cleverest old woman in the settlement. On the way back from the market one day, I joked that though I had money, it was difficult to buy things—I had enough bills but not enough coins. At the next turn in the path, Nolop quietly motioned me away from the others. "I've got coins," she said. "Come to my house." We then continued to our respective homes. After stowing my things, I walked back to her little dwelling. As I did so, I remembered her personal history. This was as colorful as it was fascinating—and it helped explain her initiative in exchanging coins for my bills. I knew Nolop well from 1980–82; she had lived in the house that was second closest to our own at Yibihilu. At that time, she had been married to the easy-going Wosip and raising two boys. She had also been a bold character. Not only had Nolop been caught having a sexual affair with the uninitiated Modiay, but she was the only Gebusi woman we ever knew or heard about who had dabbled in the otherwise all-male art of spirit mediumship. On one occasion in 1981, Eileen had tried to arrange for Nolop to sing a full séance at our own house—with other village women serving as her chorus. However, the men of the village came by so frequently and intruded so petulantly that the women's singing was quickly terminated and not repeated.

Since we had left in 1982, Nolop had endured much. The cyst on her right wrist had grown larger, and it became hard for her to use her hand. About 1990, her oldest, cherished son had been gored to death by a wild pig. Almost immediately afterward, her gentle husband had also died; villagers said that after his son's demise he had lost all appetite and virtually grieved himself to death. Nolop had been left with her remaining son plus a younger daughter, Kwelam. Shortly thereafter Kwelam had become seriously ill from a bone deformity in her hip. But Nolop was as tough as she was smart—always ready with both a witty smirk and an astute way to solve a problem. She had somehow finagled the medical officer at the Nomad Aid Post to have Kwelam flown out for an operation to the Kiunga Hospital—along with Nolop herself. While in Kiunga, without money or kin, Nolop had had to rummage in garbage heaps for daily scraps of food. Lacking a blouse or bra, she had felt the powerful stigma of going bare-breasted in town and had scrounged for rags to cover herself. Despite these abasements, Nolop had cared for Kwelam until she recovered and they could both be flown back to Nomad, at government expense. Today, Kwelam walks with a limp but is otherwise healthy, and she seems to be one of the happiest girls in the village. Nolop's surviving son, Damya, is now married and has an infant daughter of his own. He is one of the most decent lay leaders in the Nomad Catholic Church and also the lead singer in the community's string band chorus.

As Nolop saw her children grow up successfully, she was pressured into marrying a widower named Nogo—the silent, wiry man who had been one of our carriers during our first foray into Gebusi territory. Perhaps she had found him a useful partner at the time. As he aged, however, Nogo became crotchety, and he resented his wife's feisty wit and lack of deference. On more than one occasion in 1998, he beat Nolop. As an unusual stigma, Nogo was criticized for his actions by both the men and the women of Gasumi Corners.

Quite her own person, Nolop went her own way; though she still lived in Nogo's small house, she kept her affairs to herself. These included her earnings from the market, which she squirreled away without telling him. Although most wives try to keep their market money at least nominally to themselves, it tends to become part of the household economy and subject to the decisions of their husbands, especially if the proceeds accrue over time. Women earn money with painful slowness, but men typically decide how any larger sum will be spent. That said, women take pride in the knowledge that their hard-earned funds pay for prestigious tins of fish and bags of rice at community feasts—though their husbands present these gifts and take the credit for them. Even if they keep their own money, many Gebusi women are uncomfortable or embarrassed to make significant purchases by themselves at one of the Nomad stores.

By dint of personal will, however, Nolop had kept her small earnings to herself and for her own children. And she had wisely focused on raising and marketing the one crop that sold most widely and regularly at the market, even though it was not the splashiest or most prestigious: peanuts. Week after week, Nolop sold little piles of peanuts from her big bag. And over time, her 10-cent sales added up. After we were safely in her house, Nolop smiled wryly and carefully unwrapped several unobtrusive bundles. To my amazement, pile upon pile of coins poured out. She didn't know how much she had earned. When I counted up her earnings, they totaled more than 40 kina, or 20 dollars. This was equivalent to two hundred sales of 10 cents apiece at the market—approximately two years of market sales for the average woman of Gasumi Corners.

With easy trust, Nolop was delighted to give me the bulk of her coins in exchange for two of my crisp 20-kina bills. Everyone knew that the bright red "pigs head money," as it was called, was the biggest and most important currency that circulated at Nomad. That Nolop now had two of these bills seemed to give her a profound sense of satisfaction. As she carefully tucked them away, we both knew that she could use them however she wished. And they would be easier to conceal from others' prying eyes than her piles of coins had been. Perhaps Nolop would contribute unexpectedly to a major feast. Or give a gift to her children. Or buy something extraordinary at a special time. As for me, I now had all the coins I needed. As I walked home, I tried to carry my stash in my own net bag as unobtrusively as possible. I smiled at the thought that an economy of new money could, at least on rare occasions, benefit both a Gebusi woman and an outsider without compromising the integrity of either.

My experience with Nolop got me thinking about how women's relations with men were changing. Certainly, church had given women a new sense of spiritual participation—even though men were ultimately very much in charge. So, too, the market at Nomad afforded women a small measure of earning power and economic influence—though men usually controlled any significant sum of money. Other institutions and activities at Nomad also reflected gendered change while simultaneously providing new forms of male dominance. These trends were particularly notable in education, in sports, and, perhaps surprisingly, in theft.

It was difficult for me to talk with women about these and related matters. For an unrelated man to talk with a Gebusi women invariably implies sexual interest. Older women like Nolop and Bosap were easier for me to approach because they were no longer considered desirable as sexual partners or wives. But younger women were a different story. Even for married women in their thirties and forties, a personal interview was difficult to arrange and even more difficult to carry out. I could talk to a woman if her husband or brother was present. But then the man would reinterpret my questions and answer many of them himself.

The same was true of my attempt to talk to schoolgirls at the Nomad Community School; the boys took charge in responding. To be fair, part of the problem involved all the students. Repetitive drills and copying from the board took a toll on the class of forty, sixty, or even eighty pupils who sat cross-legged on the floor or on hardwood benches for hour upon hour. Students were not just Gebusi but came from several different language groups. Their language of instruction was that peculiar dialect of my own native tongue that I like to call "Papua New Guinea English." After a year or two in school, students could understand this form of English fairly well. But the process of learning it left them collectively passive and reluctant to speak up. As in church, powerful outsiders controlled the expression of important knowledge. Villagers were generally too shy or embarrassed to voice an understanding or express a point of view in a language that was not their native tongue. So, like members of the congregation, students from Gasumi Corners and the surrounding communities rarely spoke up. This problem was by far the worst for the girls. To the teachers, however, the students were like the school's leaky water tank: when something new and good was imparted to them, they couldn't retain it but let it seep away.

I got my chance to break this mold when the teachers welcomed me to give guest presentations in each of their classes. My idea was to explore a more interactive form of teaching. Being demonstrative and something of a ham, I showed the students glossy photo essays that my parents had sent me from *National Geographic.* Using the pictures as props, I talked about what it might be like to be a Tibetan pastoralist, sell crafts in Oaxaca, be a Navajo dancer, or raise ponies in the Shetland Islands. I showed them pictures of Atlanta and explained features of living in the United States. Closer to their own homes, I described my early experiences among the Gebusi, showed them photos from my first Gebusi ethnography, and tried to get their views about what had changed at Nomad in recent years. The kids seemed to love my presentations. But when it came to saying much about themselves—indeed, when it came to saying much of anything that wasn't a collective repetition—they were tongue-tied.

At first, I thought they might be reluctant because of my status as a tall white American. Or maybe my words and intonation didn't make full sense to them. However, I took pains to reexpress myself in *tok pisin* and in the Gebusi vernacular, as well as in Papua New Guinea English. Given the amazement many of them had shown when I spoke in Gebusi, I knew they understood. It was only after conducting repeated sessions with all the grades and listening to the teachers lead their own classes that I realized how completely the students had internalized a sense of "active passivity," of listening or parroting without individually speaking. I remember asking a fifth-grade class to name pictures of things without my saying the names first. Although they knew all the words, this simple task was painfully difficult, especially for the girls. I gave one group of girls three photos of pretty flowers. I knew that they knew what they were. I coaxed them with antics and pleasantries to say the word "flowers." They wanted to say the name in the worst way; they beamed as they squirmed. But none of them could speak. Finally, I gently leaned close so one of them could whisper very faintly in my ear, "Flowers."

Although girls from Gasumi Corners and other communities increasingly go to school, the gender gap between them and the boys is as strong as the heat of the midday sun. Girls drop out of school much more frequently than boys. In Gasumi Corners, only 12 percent of the women know *tok pisin*, the national language, as opposed to 60 percent of the men. And unlike a significant number of boys and young men, no girls from Gasumi Corners have completed elementary school.

Outside school, boys dominate in physical activity through sports. Although sports were hardly important to Gebusi in 1980–82—as opposed to ritual fighting and even warfare—competition on the ballfield has since become a more modern, more organized, more disciplined, and less violent arena of collective male rivalry. Schoolboys from Gasumi Corners avidly play rugby and soccer. As they get older, they join community teams that play on the Nomad ball field for much of each weekend afternoon. The games are interethnic occasions at which several hundred spectators ring the field. But (as was also the case in ritual fighting and warfare display) women can rarely be found on the field. Indeed, they can seldom be found even on the sidelines. In contrast to the dozen or so men's matches each weekend, there is a single game of women's soccer—and this is played almost entirely by the wives and elder daughters of government officials. Women from Gasumi Corners told me quite earnestly that they would be glad for their daughters to learn how to play soccer. And they added that they would themselves be glad to go as spectators to see their daughters play. But athletic field sports have become a de facto male province, beginning at school during recess. Few girls feel comfortable learning how to play or joining a team.

Ironically, men's dedication to sports was the ultimate solution to my difficulties in trying to talk freely with Gebusi women. After several sun-bleached weekends of watching one game after another of rugby and soccer, I got bored. It wasn't that I disliked sports. When I had been younger, I enjoyed playing and watching a wide range of sports, and I had even been a starter for my high school soccer team in the Connecticut state finals. But I never enjoyed life as a couch potato. And this certainly didn't fit my expectation of fieldwork with Gebusi. To some extent, I had to look beyond my own resistance. Because watching and playing sports were important to Gebusi men and boys, my hours of watching yielded insights. These concerned not just their style of gentlemanly competition on the field and the caliber of their play (which was surprisingly good, even in bare feet) but the dynamics of their spectatorship. Men in the crowd could interact across community and ethnic lines without the demands of hospitality, etiquette, or reciprocity that accompanied formal visits between settlements or communities. Having uncovered these dynamics, however, I still felt apathetic. So one fine Sunday afternoon, I simply stayed home.

Predictably, the men and boys were all at the Nomad ballgames. But as I quickly realized, this left the village an entirely female place for a few precious hours. Away from their husbands, brothers, and older male children, women's talk became freer and more relaxed. I found that I could interview women fairly easily as long as some of their female relatives were also present. It turned out that most of the women were eager to participate in my "talk-work" sessions. It helped that I had brought special trade goods for women that were otherwise hard to get—

including dresses, bras, and costume jewelry. I had known that the bras and jewelry would be hard to find in bulk in Papua New Guinea, so I brought stocks of these with me from the United States. I can still remember the look on the saleswoman's face in the Dollar Store in Atlanta when I heaped fifteen inexpensive bras into my shopping basket along with mounds of cheap costume jewelry. Sensing that I should somehow "explain myself," I had said to her, without thinking carefully, that I was buying gifts for my many female friends in the rainforest. Aghast at the implications of my statement, I gulped as I guessed what she must be thinking. But it all turned out fine. The sales clerk was Malaysian, and she knew a good bit about rainforest peoples, the difficulty of obtaining trade goods in remote areas, and the politics of gift giving. In fact, she ended up advising me which bras were most likely to fit the short but sometimes well-endowed women of Gasumi Corners. I came away with a fresh understanding about crossing cultural boundaries with women—in Atlanta as well as in New Guinea.

Back in Gasumi Corners, the women greatly appreciated the goods I had brought. I talked with each of them individually as primary interviewees—listening to the woman's life history and getting her opinions and reflections on various subjects. Particularly with less articulate women, their female kin and friends chimed in with helpful promptings, clarifications, and elaborations. Young women and adolescent girls remained the most difficult to talk with. Even when asked by a not-so-young and weirdly acceptable male such as myself, and even with other women supporting them, their responses were often only shuffling feet, embarrassment, and blank looks. I tried to ask what kind of man would make a good husband. Or if they would like to see their own future daughters-to-be go to school. But their charged status as eligible young women overwhelmed their responses. Discussing positive husbandly characteristics implied a young woman's embarrassing preference for one or another young man in the village. Talking about unborn children awkwardly implied that she herself was almost mature enough to be a mother. Nonetheless, all the women, even the younger ones, maintained their desire to work with me. This was partly because the other women were also doing it, and perhaps partly because my interest and history in their community provoked a sense of obligation on their part. But mostly, I think, they wanted the trade goods that I gave them at the end of the sessions.

The final link in my investigation of gendered change—across developments in church, the market, school, sports, and domestic relations—concerned the heightened but different yearnings of women and men for modern goods. Back at Yibihilu in 1980–82, people had been highly desirous of our Western commodities. But we had never feared theft though we kept a wide range of coveted items and trade goods in our house. Living so communally, Gebusi had long since made a virtue of necessity: they maintained a deep respect for other people's property—in a collective world in which stealing was just about impossible to conceal in any event. In 1980–82, even paperclips that we accidentally dropped through the floorboards of our house were dutifully returned to us by children or their parents. By 1998, however, things had changed. Money had become an increasingly important and anonymous commodity. And villagers had become more possessive of Western goods and other property that others in the community did not also own. Nolop's cache of coins was just one example. Families living in separate houses had become more concerned about theft. Desire mounted for metal boxes, chains, and locks.

The potential for theft was greatest between persons who shared neither kinship nor residence. On the one hand, institutions and activities at Nomad—at the ball field, market, aid post, school, and church—extended an individual's network of acquaintances. On the other hand, the limited nature of these interactions created a greater sense of anonymity and risk. In the Nomad police register, theft was the most frequently reported offense—almost twice as common as any other crime. And the vast majority of these accusations were both made by and targeted against men. This pattern was especially well documented in and around the station itself. Although theft in Nomad was only a small problem when compared with the robbery, theft, and violent crime in Papua New Guinea's larger towns and cities, it was still a focus of moral concern. During the months I was there, the biggest case involved the theft of two radios from the Nomad Community School.

Boom boxes are a major icon of modern identity at Nomad, especially for young men. They reference a prestigious world of commodities and accomplishment, of fluent speech in *tok pisin* or English, of rock music, and of sexual allure. The radios in question were also an important sign of modernity for the school. In addition to playing music and tapes, the boom boxes broadcast national education programs in classrooms each morning. Students throughout the country were presumed to listen to the same broadcast for their grade level at a specific time. This larger mission of radio education was reflected in Papua New Guinea's national song, which was sung simultaneously on the radio and in the classrooms:

> In our land of a thousand tongues,
> Brothers and sisters old and young,
> Unite our spirits so we speak as one.
> We have to learn to live together side by side.
> We have to learn to give each other dignity and pride.
> We have the strength to be one people, one nation, one country: P.N.G.!!

Given their significance, the theft of the school radios was a blow to the modern dignity and prestige of the Nomad community—and it raised a great furor. A large public meeting at which officials harangued villagers was held at the station. In particular, they criticized the villagers for letting local boys (it was assumed) carry out such an awful crime and then letting the young rascals get away with it. If the radios were not returned, they claimed, the schoolteachers might not want to live and work in Nomad. They even said that the school might have to be shut down. Given a general shortage of teachers and funds, this was a very real threat—many village schools in the Nomad Sub-District are shut down due to a lack of instructors or of money to pay them. If the central station at Nomad itself was going to be a "bad" place, a place of theft and "backsliding," officials continued, then airplanes bringing supplies might stop landing at Nomad Station altogether.

As the cause of this potential development, villagers were disparaged as sinful and un-Christian, untrustworthy and deceitful. They would face the onus of living in a remote rural area in a state of moral, religious, and economic backwardness. As in church, some villagers hung their heads.

Eventually, the radios were returned—anonymously. But as might have been guessed, they were no longer in working order. For many people, the loss of the radios reflected the difficulty of becoming modern in a place like Nomad. Institutions such as the churches, market, and school have brought people together in new ways and in the service of new endeavors. But they have also created an increasingly impersonal world. This world is marked by new inequalities and resentments, for instance, between government workers who can afford boom boxes and villagers who cannot. For those who are unable to earn a living and learn a modern way of life, pressure mounts to simply take what they can—to resort to crime and reject the slow, frustrating process of becoming modern through tedious and often fruitless discipline. The problem of crime has become a major blight in the larger towns and cities of Papua New Guinea, as it has in urban areas of many other countries. The problem is as yet small but increasing at Nomad. Underlying tensions are particularly pronounced for young men—and they relate to larger patterns of gendered change. If local modern institutions afford women the potential for greater and more active participation than they had in the past, they also threaten masculinity and increase the tensions that young men face as they strive to find modern ways of attaining prestige and success. Under conditions of economic difficulty and minimal opportunity, gendered tensions and preemptive male actions can both easily escalate.

Late in my fieldwork, I sponsored a contest in which Nomad schoolchildren drew what they wanted to be in the future. I was surprised to find that almost half the boys (31 of 64) drew pictures of themselves as forceful, gun-wielding members of the army or the police force. Girls, by contrast, typically depicted their future selves as nurses, teachers, or wives, or "in heaven." In terms of gainful employment, very few of these children will be able to fulfill their aspirations. And yet, their desires remain strong, especially among the young men. At Nomad, men's preeminence and growing impatience—in school, athletic, church, and government activities—seem to contrast with the activities of Gebusi market women. In this regard, the patient but productive labors of Nolop represent a counterpoint to younger and more restless desires, particularly among men, for quicker and more forceful routes to modern success.

Web site images of events and topics described in this chapter can be found at http://www.mhhe.com/knauft1.

CHAPTER 10

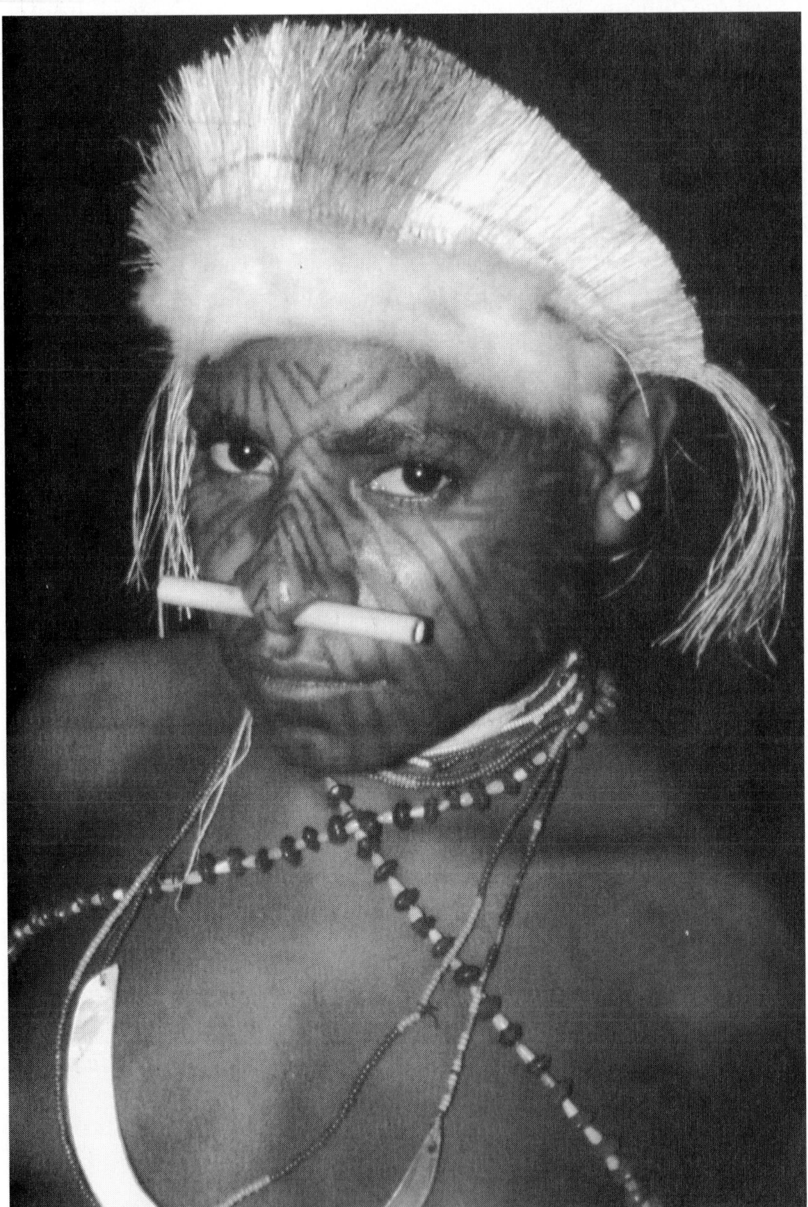

A Gebusi young woman, Toym, whose name also means "taboo." (PHOTO: Eileen Marie Knauft)

Mysterious Romance, Marital Choice

It was one of those ten-minute conversations that starts innocently enough but jerks you through the cultural wringer and spits you out on the other side. It began with a knock on the door. It was Wayabay, and I was surprised to see him. He rarely stopped by, and never unless something significant was up. He always seemed to me as spare with his words as he was decent and direct in his actions. He was clearly troubled, so I asked him in. He came inside and hesitated, strong young man that he was, until the urgency of his inquiry overcame his embarrassment. "Do you have any *adameni?* I would really like some." I had no idea what he was talking about, so I asked him what *adameni* was. He stammered and continued on: "*Adameni* is something special. It has to do with an unmarried woman and an unmarried man. When they really like each other and think of coming together." I still had no idea. Whatever *adameni* was, it related to sexual desire between young people. Wayabay was the oldest of the bachelors, and he was actively trying to find a wife. But what was *adameni?* I wracked my brain. Whatever *adameni* was, it was important to Wayabay. I was as concerned as I was curious and uncertain.

Could Wayabay be asking me for a condom? I knew that he had worked for a trail-clearing crew a few years back and that he had been out to the town of Kiunga. He had a wider scope of knowledge and experience than many of the young men. Perhaps he was now in a romantic liaison and wanted to protect either himself or the girl. This would explain his embarrassment. Although Wayabay seemed too proper a young man to be involved in a casual sexual affair, I had certainly been surprised in the past by the public revelation of Gebusi sexual trysts. So I tried, gently, to describe a condom in the Gebusi vernacular: "There is this thing that men wear when they have sex. Is this like *adameni?*" Wayabay replied, "Well, maybe. I'm not sure." My unease was mounting, but I forged ahead: "This is something that a man puts over his 'thing,' his phallus. It stretches like rubber. He puts this rubber thing over his phallus before he has sex. He has sex with the woman but his 'thing' doesn't touch the woman's 'thing.'"

Now it was Wayabay's turn to be uncomprehending—and mine to be embarrassed. I tried to explain that men can use these rubber coverings when they don't want the woman to get pregnant or when they worry about getting sick from having sex. All of which sounded no better and, indeed, much worse when spoken in Gebusi. Wayabay shook his head vehemently; this was definitely NOT *adameni.*

In despair, we invited Sayu and Didiga into our conversation. Both of them spoke a smattering of English, and both had had more schooling than Wayabay. I mentally cursed myself for not knowing what *adameni* was—this term that was obviously so important in Gebusi sexual culture and that I hadn't uncovered during all my time with them. But Sayu and Didiga had no better luck finding a translation or an explanation. Yes, they said, *adameni* was something for a man. And, yes, it had to do with sex. It also had something do to with *oop,* the generic Gebusi word for "slippery, milky substance" that was especially associated with semen.

Sex. Men. Semen. I was stymied. Could they be referring to some custom or substance having to do with traditional practices of sex between men? This would certainly explain Wayabay's embarrassment. Perhaps he was having sexual relations with one or another young man before finding a wife. I took another deep breath. "Does this *adameni* have to do with Gebusi sex customs between men?" They looked puzzled, so I persisted: "Does it have to do with traditional Gebusi customs? You know, the sex custom in your initiations in which the adolescent boy sucks the phallus and swallows the semen of the man—so he can grow big and achieve more manhood."

Culturally speaking, I had dropped a bomb. Their mouths hung open in disbelief, and their faces grew ashen. Sayu finally broke their silence: "Did our fathers and boys really do that? In the olden times? Did they? Really?!"

Double ouch. I had been terribly rash. Although the three of them had all grown up in a world of male banter and horseplay, none of them, I now realized, had been initiated; the final initiation ceremony had been held before they would have been old enough. They had never been indoctrinated into sexual relations with other men. And given the community's conversion to Christianity, it was quite possible that they had never been told about the practice. Perhaps my three companions had suspected or wondered about men's sexual customs. But perhaps not. Against their willful ignorance, I had asserted the reality of a strange sexual practice, a custom that was hard to believe and that was highly distasteful to them. I had divulged a secret of my own generation and had shocked them. I felt awful. But I also felt that I had to answer them truthfully: "Yes, that is the custom that the men and initiated teenagers followed at Yibihilu when I was here before."

After shaking their heads in disbelief, they stressed, as if it needed emphasis, that *adameni* had nothing whatsoever to do with sex between one man and another. *Adameni* was for use between men and women. This was the only sex that the three of them knew or cared about. What about *oop?* This wasn't semen. The *adameni* liquid was thick and viscous, but it smelled sweet and tasted good. It was something that a man would dab about his eyes, and when a woman looked at him, she would find him irresistible. *Adameni* was evidently some kind of love potion. White people knew all about *adameni,* they continued. In fact, they said, it came from whites and not from Papua New Guineans. Wayabay had heard about *adameni* from men who had been with white people at a logging camp in the southern part of the province. The potion came in a bottle and was quite expensive. But the whites reportedly said that it really worked to attract women. The bottles of *adameni* had a picture of a naked man and woman on the label—just as described in the Bible.

White people. Nakedness. Bible. Irresistible sexual attraction. Eureka! *Adameni* wasn't a Gebusi word after all; no wonder I hadn't known it. Their accent and intonation had completely thrown me off. It was a Western sexual idea. *Adameni* was "Adam and Eve." It was a love potion that unscrupulous traders to the south had peddled at inflated prices in bottles featuring pictures of biblical sex and lovely sin. Wayabay wanted *adameni* to attract a woman. As a quiet and hard-working but traditional young man, he felt that he needed a modern potion to gain a wife.

My companions persisted. Did I have any *adameni?* And if not, could I get any for them? Though I now understood their question, it still wasn't easy to answer. The three of them believed in this love magic, almost desperately in Wayabay's case. I had already deeply embarrassed both them and myself. I recalled the anthropological theory that holds magic to be an exercise in spiritual confidence boosting. The idea is that magic reduces uncertainty and instills faith in one's actions, as in baseball when a batter fingers a lucky charm before stepping to the plate. For a moment, I debated enhancing Wayabay's confidence with women by giving him some of the scented cream I had brought for my skin rashes and telling him to dab some on his cheekbones. But I quickly dismissed this as a bad idea. I had already caused enough cultural confusion for one day. After all these years of knowing about the Gebusi, I thought, I was still challenged, surprised, and sometimes at sea. Learning culture is indeed a lifelong experience.

I showed them my skin cream, which they smelled carefully. I said that it wasn't really *adameni* but that they were still welcome to try some if they wanted to. As for real *adameni*, I said, I didn't know how to get it and thought it might be a waste of good money in any event. They declined my skin cream. Disappointed but at least in mutual comprehension, we finished our conversation, and the three of them departed.

I was left with much to think about. If Gebusi culture had been hard for me to learn in 1980, its changes were now chewing up all my seasoned understandings—with plenty of spit left over. Over the course of sixteen years, cohorts of young Gebusi men had gone from actively and proudly having sex with one another to apparently not even knowing about the practice. Could this really be? Maybe my young friends had suspected or been vaguely aware of the custom from their boyhood years. But if they hadn't been directly exposed to or told about it, their knowledge would have been hazy. Compare it with our own knowledge of sexual practices among those who preceded us—for instance, our often vague knowledge of the different types of private intimacy that our own parents may have had with each other, much less with other partners, at earlier times in their lives. Like many peoples, the Gebusi distinguish carefully between things that are possible but unsubstantiated and those that they have either seen with their own eyes or heard with their own ears from a reliable witness. In this sense of knowing, Wayabay, Sayu, and Didiga had probably not known about sex between Gebusi men. Until I had told them.

Although some cultures have a strong and deep sense of their past, the historical concern of other peoples can be shallow and weak—and Gebusi are decidedly in the latter camp. Gebusi life cycles are short. And as a forty-four-year-old adult man, I was one of the oldest males in the community. The Gebusi do not revere, maintain, or recount historical knowledge in a systematic way. In fact, many of them do not even know the names of their own grandparents. It was not uncommon for me to know more about Gebusi family ancestries, based on the genealogies and life histories that I collected in 1980–82, than it was for younger and middle-aged Gebusi. In retrospect, the gap between my young companions' knowledge of traditional sex practices and my own was not so surprising. In my description, however, I had unwittingly bleached out the rich meaning of and personal variations in Gebusi same-sex practices. These came across to my young friends as a generic custom that was as out of context as it was distasteful.

Beyond the shock, the apparent unawareness, and the possible collusion of ignorance among my three companions, the fact remained that their present desire to attract women was much more important than their concern with sexual behavior between men in the past. That their fathers had inseminated teenage boys may have been offensive, but it didn't change Wayabay's need or desire to find a wife. In the past, insemination had itself been an asset for marriage; a young man who "became big" in his beautiful initiation costume attracted women by his very presence. Initiation had been a natural conduit to marriage; within a few months, all the initiates had been married. Ideally, a woman came to a new initiate of her own accord—or at least allowed herself to be "claimed" for him by his initiate sponsors. The months leading up to the initiation had provided both a special opportunity and a special mandate for sexual trysts among young men themselves. But now, with the demise of initiations, this custom was gone, along with much of men's collective camaraderie.

As I was finding out, the same was also true of women's obligations to marry through sister-exchange. Whereas more than half of women's first marriages had previously satisfied the demands of marital reciprocity, not one of the sixteen marriages in the community between 1982 and 1998 had been a sister-exchange. Although men still insisted rhetorically that their daughters and younger sisters would marry only if the groom supplied a "sister" in return, the practice was moribund in fact. Correspondingly, men could no longer count on obligations of kinship and reciprocity to obtain a wife—any more than they could count on the splendor of ritual attraction. Increasingly, young men were on their own and had to attract a wife through modern forms of courtship.

Wayabay had not been successful in these pursuits. He was several years past the age of normal marriage and was increasingly concerned to find a wife. He was also among the small minority of young men who had not developed a keen interest in activities associated with life at the Nomad Station. He had not been baptized and did not go to church. He played soccer and rugby only intermittently and awkwardly, he would not dance to Papua New Guinea "disco music," and he did not sing in the community's contemporary string band. Instead, Wayabay honed his traditional skills and spent many days hunting in the forest and many hours house building in the village. He was unusually devoted to indigenous dancing and was proud of his ability to travel to feasts and initiations in remote Gebusi villages and dance in traditional costume. In a sense, Wayabay was a good traditionalist born a generation too late. In this context, *adameni* had become a hopeful substitute for the allure of the male initiation costume that Wayabay would never be able to wear.

By contrast, the young Gebusi men who were most successful in attracting girlfriends and brides were those who were, for lack of a better word, more modern. They could joke with some facility in English or *tok pisin*, had been to school for at least a few years, and were more comfortable with the lifestyle associated with the Nomad Station. They managed to finagle a little money, which they used to obtain a jaunty baseball cap, sunglasses, or a colorful shirt. Perhaps they even had a boom box on which they could play cassettes of rock music. They enjoyed playing rugby and soccer if not also dancing to disco (rock) music, and they appeared more at ease outside their own settlement. For Wayabay, however, being locally modern was difficult if not impossible. He could kill a wild boar in the forest but he could not shoot the modern breeze.

Even for bachelors who were relatively self-assured, modern courtship could be a stressful experience. On one occasion, Wayabay's two comrades worked up the courage to go to a disco dance on the far edge of the Nomad Station. (Wayabay himself was too reserved to go.) It was an alluring adventure that held out the prospect of not just seeing but possibly dancing to disco music with marriageable women from another community. This hoped-for attraction paralleled the modern romance that was sung about in cassettes and in the Gebusi's new guitar-and-ukelele bands. The goal was to captivate a woman not by a display of traditional splendor but with modern confidence, skill, and aplomb—to look in her eyes, talk to her directly, and gyrate publicly with her in contemporary dance.

The risks of this endeavor fueled avoidance as well as desire. In fact, we never got to the disco. We approached it at night, stealthfully, as if stalking a wild animal. We crept slowly and noiselessly down the path, the boldest in the lead. Whispered discussion ensued every few yards as to whether we should go through with this chance for public display and humiliation. Flashlights were turned off so no one would know we were there. We strained to hear if there was any music in the distance. Eventually, however, we turned back, too nervous to proceed. During six months and despite several concerted attempts, I never did manage to attend a disco in a community on the far side of the Nomad Station.

The awkwardness of contemporary romance reflects not just new standards of courtship but new material demands—for colorful clothes, sunglasses, shoes, and boom boxes with cassettes. Failing to obtain these, young men may crave a manufactured elixir with a naked man and woman on the bottle, a potion that, with just a magical splash about the eyes, can attract women. In many rural parts of the world, there is great demand for goods that convey a locally modern sense of sexual attraction. New commodities, clothes, cosmetics, and styles of using them frequently combine the allure of a modern way of life with emerging types of romantic desire. I remembered a story on National Public Radio about a Brazilian woman who canoed into the upper reaches of the Amazon and made quite a profit by selling Avon products like deodorant and makeup to Indians in the rainforest.

For young Gebusi men, the desire for modern commodities is further complicated by economic pressures to pay bride-price or bride-wealth. In the absence of sister-exchange, the brothers or fathers of young women often say that they will be satisfied only with a large cash payment from the would-be groom. In some parts of the world—including regions of Africa and south Asia as well as the South Pacific—inflated demands for bride-wealth or dowry cause major problems for young people who want to get married. Fortunately for young Gebusi men, the amount of money they actually pay in bride-wealth is quite low, at least in comparative terms. Of the first marriages in Gasumi Corners between 1982 and 1998, the average bride payment was only 56 kina, 28 dollars. Even this small amount, however, can be difficult for many young men to amass. And the demands of a prospective father-in-law or brother-in-law can easily fuel the groom's sense of inadequacy.

In all, Gebusi courtship is now sandwiched between a rhetorical mandate for sister-exchange, inflated claims for bride-wealth, the desire for commodities, and the demands of modern styles of social interaction. Bachelors in Gasumi Corners often told me that they would never get married. So how do young men find wives? In large part through the idiosyncrasies of contemporary romantic attraction. In the present as in the past, a young woman and a man who are strongly attracted to each other may get married despite the objections of her father or her brothers. If romantic marriage had previously been a "minority option," it had now become the principal, if ever more stressful, way of establishing matrimony. Especially for a man, being locally modern had become an important part of this mix.

❧ ❧ ❧

In Gasumi Corners, an aborted attempt to forge a sister-exchange revealed both the growing importance and the growing stress of young people's choices in marriage. The plan was for an equal marital exchange between two sets of "siblings." Guyul was a cheerful, strapping bachelor about twenty-one years old; his true sister was the comely and straightforward Kubwam, a mature fifteen- or sixteen-year-old ready for marriage. On the other side was Mako, a slight young man about nineteen and his adopted "sister," the vivacious Gami, who was only sixteen but full-bodied and, if anything, readier for marriage than her elder "brother." Gami was to marry Guyul while her "brother," Mako, was to marry Guyul's true sister, Kubwam.

Following spicy rumors that spread throughout the village, the courtship of the two young couples started off well enough. On the way back from one of the markets, each young woman was "seized" by the wrist and led away by a male kinsman of her husband-to-be. Although the show of force conformed to the dictates of public display, neither woman resisted or tried to get away—which they could easily have done. Kubwam appeared forlorn, which is the proper etiquette for a woman taken in marriage. But Gami could hardly keep from smiling despite her presumed sobriety. The four new spouses were told to sit down together and exhorted to attend to their duties as husbands and wives. Much was made of the fact that the brother of Guyul's new wife was also the husband of his sister, and vice versa. It was not simply a double marriage but a linkage among the four of them. Everything was going according to plan.

The two women, Gami and Kubwam, proceeded to trade residences across the four-minute walk that separated their husbands' respective households in Gasumi Corners. Each extended family simultaneously gained a daughter-in-law while losing a daughter. The two mothers-in-law made special efforts to ensure that the incoming brides felt welcome and at home. I paid visits to both households and gave small gifts. With her typical pleasant reserve, Kubwam seemed comfortably ensconced in Mako's household. For her part, Gami was practically ebullient in Guyul's family house; she smiled broadly and engaged eagerly with Guyul's female kin.

The first crack in the arrangement appeared after only a day and a half. Mako started spending time away from his household and away from his new wife, going off with the remaining bachelors. Not yet twenty years old, Mako was still "young" to be a Gebusi husband. In sister-exchange marriages, the younger husbands sometimes took a while to settle fully into the new arrangement. In the present case, Mako's marriage was not yet consummated. But his new wife, Kubwam, continued in the interim to live with Mako's female kin. By themselves Mako's actions represented only a small wrinkle and not a major cause for concern. On the other side of Gasumi Corners, Gami's relationship with Guyul got off to a good start. She had been the village belle—friendly, easy-going, buxom, and with a bright, quick smile. In the preceding months, I had been surprised that the community had allowed her and some of the other young women to joke directly with eligible young men. Outside of special occasions, public joking between men and women had been strongly discouraged in 1980–82.

Within a few days, Gami and her new husband "went off together" to the gardens. When they came back with moony dispositions and euphoric smiles, village gossip was as ribald as it was irrepressible. Guyul and Gami had consummated their marriage, and everyone knew it. But this happiness did not last. Exactly what went wrong I never learned, least of all from Guyul or Gami themselves. But all signals pointed to an abrupt U-turn in their sexual compatibility. Gami's disposition turned suddenly from sweetness to sourness. She wouldn't look at her husband, wouldn't work in his household, and wouldn't eat. She tried to go back to her adopted mother's home but was forced back to her husband's house. She tried again and was again forced back. She refused to cooperate and returned yet again to her own family home. No entreaty made headway; no inquiry bore fruit. "Who knows what goes on in a young woman's heart or mind?!" "Gami is just stubborn and big-headed." "She just won't be married." "But why?" I would ask. "Just because," I was told repeatedly. "That's just the way she is."

As the hours passed, Gami's recalcitrance fueled increasing anger against her in the village. It is a very serious matter for a Gebusi woman to consummate her marriage and then to repudiate it. That a woman could have sex with a husband she had publicly accepted and then reject him after several days of romance struck at the heart of Gebusi morality. Not only was Gami's virtue on the line but also the manhood and self-esteem of her husband, Guyul. The stakes were also higher because the marriage was a sister-exchange. Gami's rejection of Guyul also compromised the union between her "brother," Mako, and Guyul's sister, Kubwam; if her marriage dissolved, her brother's would also be forfeited.

In short order, everyone in Gasumi Corners turned against Gami. Her new husband disdained her, and her mother-in-law was incensed. Her adopted mother was even more furious, as was Mako. Her "mother" slapped her, her "brother" beat her, and she endured a barrage of verbal abuse. "What is WRONG with you?!" "You good for nothing!" "Guyul is a fine man!" "You think you can 'open your skirt' to your husband and then just turn around and say you won't be married?! Huh? HUH?" "Don't you care about your 'brother'?" Don't you care about your 'mother'? No one in this village is going to protect you." "Where are you going to find a new husband? Do you think any man would want you now? Huh? HUH?" "You are alone, no one cares about you." "You can't stay here. You have no home here. Your life here is finished."

Gami never once explained and never argued back. But she wouldn't budge, wouldn't go back to Guyul's household. As the hours mounted into a second day, the tension worsened. Women from other households took up the banner of village honor. Senior women tore into Gami, badgering her in every way they could think of. Finally, Mako had had enough. He grabbed Gami and dragged her bodily out the door. She shrieked and screamed, refusing to leave. Heavier and just as strong as he was, she briefly held her ground. But as Mako again grabbed one of her arms, his mother and another man took hold of the other. Gami was dragged screaming and crying, feet trailing and flailing. By the time they had hauled her fifteen feet from her house, she was covered in mud and bloody scrapes. Still she refused to cooperate. They pulled her by the hair, but she would not give in. Panting and screaming, they told her she could lie there and rot.

Then one of the senior women came over. She was a woman, here nameless, whom I otherwise liked and admired, but whom to this very day I cannot forgive. She silently walked up to Gami, leaned down, and talked to her in low tones. Watching from my doorstep, some forty feet away, I had a sinking feeling that I knew what she was saying, and my suspicion was soon verified. It was terrible to have seen Gami being hit and dragged. But it is almost unimaginable for a young woman to be threatened with a public stripping. For Gebusi, this idea is so deeply shameful as to be a form of death—never forgotten, never expunged. And it is triply so for a nubile young woman. It was true that Gami had badly misjudged the game and the stakes of her marriage. Her girlish fancy, flirtatious behavior, and mature body had led her to the four-sided vise of a sister-exchange. At first, she had complied willingly, even enthusiastically. But then she had come to realize that her actions were an appalling mistake that she would risk her reputation and even her life to repudiate. This new threat, however, made it too costly for her to resist any longer. A minute or two later, Gami calmly got up and walked lifelessly back to Guyul's household.

I assumed that that would be the end of the story, that both unhappy marriages would remain intact. I was wrong. Over the next few days, Gami stayed in Guyul's household, but she would not respond or cooperate in any meaningful way. She remained defiant, a living dead person. In exasperation, her relatives took the matter to a higher authority, the Nomad police. As chance would have it, I was in the police station studying official documents when they trooped in. The village men and a Nomad police officer sat Gami down in a chair, surrounded her, and began their inquisition. A uniformed constable took the lead: "Why won't you marry this man?" "Why did you have sex with him and then refuse him?" "Do you really want to reject your own family?" "What are you going to do if you don't stay married to Guyul?" "We can start charges to put you in jail for immoral conduct." I thought for sure that Gami would crack. Alone, she faced the most powerful men not just in the village but at the Nomad Station. But she refused, not just to comply but to speak. Her only words were "I don't know" and "I don't want to," as she hung her head and sobbed. Fortunately, the men did not touch or strike her. I don't know if my presence deterred them. But I was knotted up inside, frustrated at not being able to intervene. Ultimately, they gave up in desperation and returned Gami to our settlement. A public meeting was then held in Gasumi Corners. Again the invective started as people debated what steps to take next. They also aired their opinions of women's morality in the village more generally—how shameless and loose young women had become.

I had never made a formal speech at a public Gebusi meeting; I had never felt that it was my place to do so. And my mastery of Gebusi was never good enough that I could wrap myself in their oratory. But this time I felt I had no choice. I knew I couldn't change Gebusi customs, alter Gami's predicament, or impose my will on theirs. Still, these were people I had lived with, and they were my friends. I thought what they were doing to Gami was very wrong. As I got up to speak, I started to tremble. It was like that first speech you make to your junior high school class, when you can't remember the words and you know your voice and your bearing betray that everything about you is awkward. But I had to continue. What I said, or at least what I tried to say, was that my Gebusi friends had to respect their own custom—the custom that no one can ultimately force a woman to be married. Even in the old days, I said, some women had refused to be married. No matter what anyone had done, and no matter even what the women themselves had done, they had simply refused. I alluded to some of the failed first marriages of the people sitting around me, including some of the older women who had berated Gami. They, too, I reminded them, ultimately had refused the men they had been pressured to stay with in marriage. The police, I said, respected the same custom, following the law of Papua New Guinea. People could try to persuade a woman to marry, but they simply could not force her to do so. That was all.

I don't know if my words had any effect. I was too nervous to judge people's reactions or to recall things clearly afterwards. I wasn't saying anything revolutionary but merely putting words to the reality that I hoped they would accept—and that they were grudgingly beginning to accept anyway. Then I did something else that I had never done before. After the meeting was over, I asked to talk with Gami. Alone. Of all the things I have intentionally done with the Gebusi before or since, this was the most awkward. An unrelated man simply does not talk with an unmarried woman alone—especially one like Gami, who bore the stigma of sexual immorality. I had to be very clear about my motives. Gami had been a flirtatious and endearing young woman. And anthropology is littered with tales of well-meaning white men who scheme to help attractive women of color, only to unwittingly leave them worse off in their own culture than they had been before.

My request related to Gami's family situation—in particular, to her status as an adopted child. Gami's father had died at Yibihilu shortly after we left in 1982. Her mother, a pretty woman named Tewo, had then remarried a worker at the Nomad Station. Of all the Gebusi women, Tewo was the only one who had moved away from the Nomad area entirely; she had gone with her husband to live with his kin outside Kiunga. When Tewo had left Nomad, her new husband did not have the money to buy a plane ticket for both Gami and her older sister, Mai. Faced with a terrible choice, Tewo had taken Mai with her to Kiunga but left Gami, her younger daughter, behind at Gasumi Corners in the care of her sister and her father's sister. Tewo had hoped to come back or at least to send money for Gami to join her later in Kiunga. This had never happened. But she was still alive and living outside Kiunga. She was the one person in the world who might have cared enough about Gami to take her in.

I knew Tewo from 1982 and thought she was a good person. Because Gami could not read or write, I thought she might like me to write a letter to her mother—to communicate with her and solicit help. Maybe her husband's relatives would help Gami reunite with her mother and allow her, as a young woman, to pursue a life in their community. In many parts of Papua New Guinea, letter writing on behalf of friends is an important means by which people who are separated keep in touch. When I had visited male inmates at the national prison in Port Moresby on entering the country, many of them had immediately accepted my offer to write letters on their behalf and to send them to their families back home. In some ways, I thought, Gami was now a prisoner in Gasumi Corners.

Apart from this, there was something else I wanted to tell Gami. I wanted to tell her that I didn't think she was a bad or wicked person. I wanted to tell her that I thought many young women have to struggle to find a man they can live with. And I wanted to tell her that I thought she was very brave. I knew I was on cultural thin ice. I had no idea if these words would make sense or if they would backfire. But I had to try. And there was no way I could make this attempt with other villagers intervening.

In the village clearing, I told Gami's adopted mother and the others gathered there that I needed to talk to Gami, alone. They looked at me, and I looked at them back. I told them not to worry, that I was only an "old man" and that we wouldn't be long. My excuse was that Gami had never shown me the abandoned spur settlement, just two hundred yards away, where her true mother had previously lived with her. (I also thought that this might be a good place for her to think of her mother and to tell me anything she wanted me to write in a letter.) I was touched that the villagers trusted me enough to let Gami go off with me. Gami herself had been through the wringer already, and who knows what she thought now. She had every reason to be scared of any new development, and she was, in culturally appropriate fashion, reluctant to go with me. To my distress, her relatives now ordered her to accompany me to her mother's old settlement. As I walked slowly out of our hamlet, Gami trailed a good fifteen feet behind. My first thought was to wait for her and say something innocuous. But when I slowed, so did she. It got worse when a twelve-year-old boy crossed paths with us. Gami and I were the spitting image of a married couple—adult man up front and younger wife coming behind. The boy was incredulous; I mumbled that Gami was going to show me her mother's house and that her "mother" had said it was okay. As we neared the site, a second boy, fourteen, appeared. I repeated the story. But he was too captivated by the remarkable sight of Gami with me to be easily deterred. Even as I told him to move along, I could see him scurry away only to hide and watch from the bushes.

My conversation with Gami took place close to the main path and was very short. We stood about a dozen feet apart—as close as we ever got. Both of us looked at the ground or anywhere except at each other. I said that I was sorry for her. I said that I thought she was not a bad person, but a person who had much inside that was good. I said, without repeating the obvious, that I knew she had "worries." Then I said that I had known her mother and that I had been told that she was now living outside Kiunga along with Gami's elder sister. And I asked her if she wanted me to write a letter to her mother to see if there was any way she or other members of her family could help. Nervously, Gami said simply, "No." I continued, "Is there anything else you would like to say? Is there anything that you would like to talk about or that I might do?" She replied again, "No." I responded, "That's fine. I just wanted to ask. We'll leave it go." Then we walked directly back to the village. Gami took the lead, walking much faster than she had before.

I will never know if my awkward attempt to help Gami was an abject failure or merely a nominal one. Perhaps the thought of her mother finding out about Gami's predicament only added salt to her wounds. Perhaps the idea of telling one's long-lost mother about one's indiscretions wasn't that appealing. Perhaps I was guilty of cultural insensitivity or of taking license with Gebusi rules of gendered interaction. I could not know and could hope only that some part of Gami sensed, amid my ineptitude, that I was trying to help rather than hurt her. I know that the best intentions can sometimes have the worst results. But I had to try.

What conclusions can we draw? On a personal level, my experience illustrates the uncertainties of cultural intervention. Although researchers, we are also people, and sometimes we feel compelled to act. But we can't know the consequences of our actions or even if our good intentions will be recognized. Balancing our good intentions against our awareness of their unpredictable results seems at least as important as it is difficult. The interventions of Westerners among foreign peoples often have led to unfortunate consequences even when the intent was noble. To correct for this, a sense of humility and an awareness of our own limitations—as researchers, as advocates, and as human beings—is often called for.

In topical terms, Gami's was a case of thwarted sister-exchange. As we know, this is not a new development among the Gebusi. Strong-willed women have long been able to resist marriages that they truly disliked. But this is not an easy process. It takes courage, and it comes with a cost. This cost goes up substantially when, as for Gami, the thrill of new possibilities turns into a nightmare. For young Gebusi women as well as men, personal choices now seem, if anything, more powerful, and also potentially more painful than they were in the past, when the security and the constraints of kinship were greater. This trend is underscored by the fact that there has not been a sister-exchange in Gasumi Corners for more than fifteen years.

In many areas of the world, an increase in personal options, including for women, is often noted to be a modern phenomenon. In the mix, both the potential and the tribulations of marriage by "love" are on the rise in many countries. Such unions build on the spine and determination that many women have always had while also ratcheting up the stakes of personal choice in marriage. The same can be true for men, who grapple with new forms and expectations of courtship, commodity acquisition, marital payment, and romantic attraction. Who can say if women or men lead happier lives as a result? But in a world of escalating alternatives, the lives of many young men and women are increasingly shaped by the intended or unintended consequences of their own choices.

Amid the clash of choice and constraint, some predicaments work out better than one might possibly have guessed. This was ultimately the case for Gami and also for her male counterpart, the strong, silent, and dependable Wayabay. Despite their respective trials, each of them ended up finding an acceptable spouse after I left the field. In each case, their partner carried a history of difficult choices that complemented their own. And in each case, their partner had been living in the house next door. In December 2001, I received the following in a letter written on behalf of Sayu from Gasumi Corners: "Wayabay got married already to Gami. And ready to deliver baby."

Long live their lives together. Long live their resilience.

Web site images of events and topics described in this chapter can be found at http://www.mhhe.com/knauft1.

CHAPTER 11

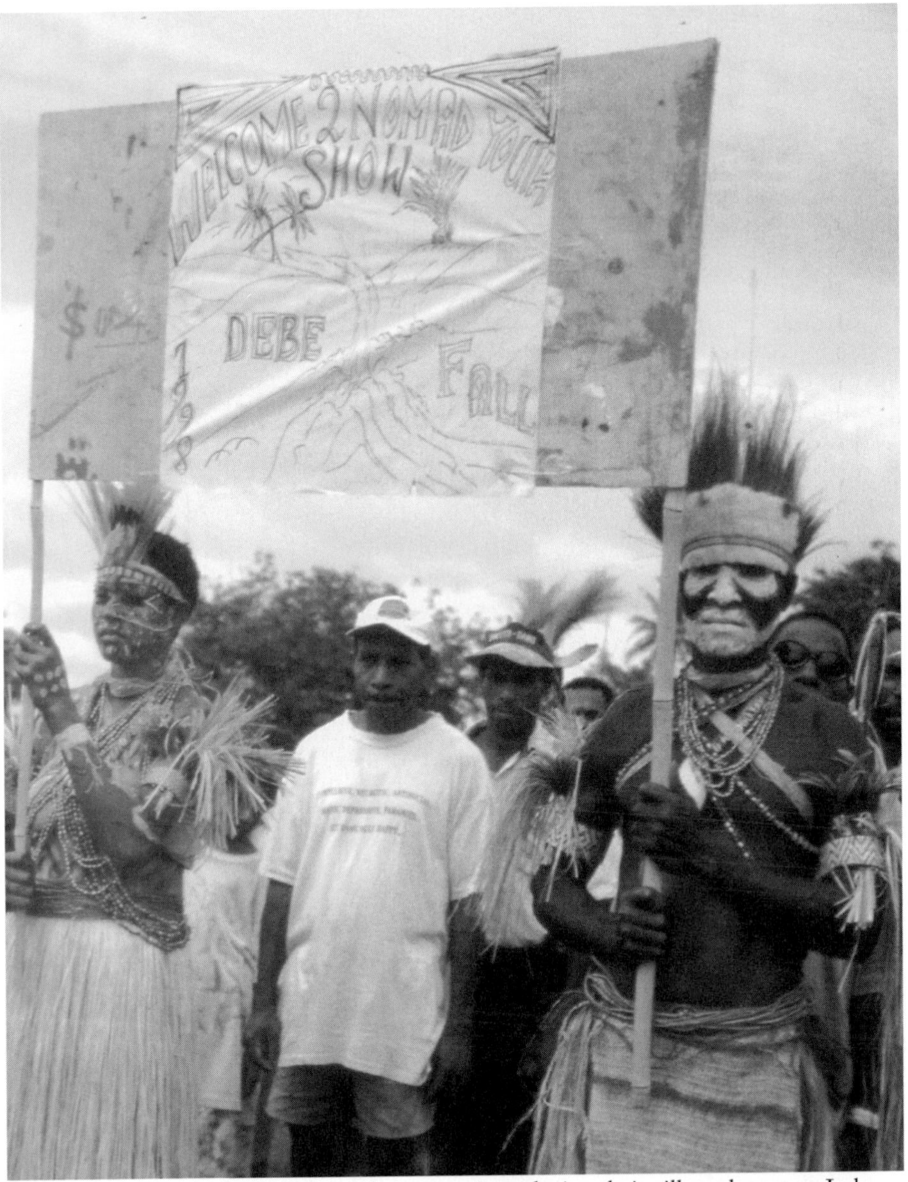

A man and woman in semi-traditional costumes introducing their village dances on Independence Day. (Note: The T-shirt of the man standing in the middle reads, "Compulsive, Antisocial, Manic Depressive, Paranoid, but Basically Happy.") (PHOTO: Bruce Knauft)

Sayu's Dance and After

SAYU SIDLED AHEAD OF me, down the trail and into the dawn. Daybreak bathed us in its softest light as we returned from our all-night ceremony. The previous evening, in a rare expression of a fading custom, Sayu had been the visiting dancer at the village of Kotiey-masam. In the traditional costume, painted and plumed, he had enacted the spirits of old in their full splendor to the beat of his crocodile-skin drum. His jaw had been as firm as the pearl shell just beneath it, his eyes as bright as the red bird of paradise he had become. With a magnetic aura, he had been wonderfully transformed.

As we walked back to Gasumi Corners, I remembered Sayu from sixteen years before, when he had been five years old. His impish smile had lit his face like sunlight streaming through a break in the forest canopy. His play had been as full of Gebusi tradition as it could be. He would wrap his small body in leaves, smear soot on his face, and put a feather in his hair. With supreme whimsy, he would take a length of bamboo as a make-believe drum and dance resplendently at an imaginary feast. He would lisp a fetching echo to the men's songs at night. Or pretend to marry a little girl in sister-exchange. Or cook some sago to divine and accuse a make-believe sorcerer. More than any other child, Sayu had been in our house and in our lives at Yibihilu. Women had said that Eileen was his *wi-helof*, his "side-mother." Now, this dancer of childhood returned home with me at a new dawn in this rainforest of memories.

Since we had left in 1982, Sayu's life had not been at all as I had thought it would have been. In 1985, his young father, Salip, had died. Sayu's mother, the fun-loving Boyl, had perished suddenly just two years after that. Recently remarried, she had been foraging for sago grubs deep in the forest with Sayu and his younger brother, Huwa. Far from the settlement, and before they could return, she had fallen suddenly and fatally ill. The two boys had cried and clutched at their mother as she writhed in agony in the forest at night. A search party later found them and carried Boyl's body back to the village. Sayu was eleven or twelve years old, Huwa was about five. Sayu's new father-in-law, Modiay, was enraged by the death and pursued the sorcery inquest for Boyl with great intensity.

Shortly afterward, as previously described, Modiay, avenged her death by killing Sabowey and beheading him.

When Modiay departed to serve his six-year term in prison, Sayu and Huwa were left behind at Gasumi Corners. Five years later, following a dispute in the village, Sayu decided to leave the community and embark on a young man's adventure. At age seventeen, he and a friend walked eighty miles to the town of Kiunga—through lands he had never seen and groups he had never encountered before. Kiunga was the district capital of three thousand people, muddy gateway to the modern world, and emerald city to those in the forest for hundreds of miles around. Quick and smart, Sayu finagled work in Kiunga as a domestic helper and "houseboy." He lived the life of a successful teenager in town: washing dishes, doing laundry, running errands—and learning to live in his employer's house, ride a bike, watch satellite TV, and dance disco. Two years later, he returned home to the outskirts of Nomad, where his treasured boom box broadcast music to everyone's delight. He had become a dandy, but he remained thoughtful and worked hard.

When I came back to the Gebusi, two years after his own return, Sayu quickly became my companion, helper, and confidant, along with Didiga, who was a good friend to both of us. I helped support them, and we shared many good times. On one occasion, Sayu delicately withdrew from a budding relationship with a flirtatious young woman in a neighboring hamlet. Although things had not turned serious or physical, the woman's father and brother suspected otherwise. The next day, while Sayu and I were doing chores, her male relatives charged out of nowhere, brandishing their bows and arrows. Sayu and I stood side by side as we turned to face them. I told myself to remain appropriately passive but defiant. Livid, the young woman's brother came at us in a dead run. As he closed to about twenty feet, he cocked his bow, drew back his arrow, and snapped his bowstring at us. Then he veered away. I knew well enough from my days at Yibihilu that this was merely a display of aggression, and I bore him no anger. We all laughed about it days later. But my spine had stiffened at the time. At a public meeting, the village councillor concluded that the woman's brother and father had been wrong to intimidate us; they had to pay a fine to Sayu for falsely accusing him of impropriety.

My many memories of Sayu linked back to the present as I walked with him back from his all-night dance at Kotiey-masam. He had danced until dawn for the first time, not to disco, as he had before, but in stately traditional costume. He had become an impressive and handsome young man, both indigenous and modern. As his friend and part-parent, I felt a surge of pride in and affection for him. I thought how deeply pleased Sayu's true parents and his side-mother, Eileen, would have been to see him now. I told him what I felt: my eyes had seen his traditional dancing with the happy heart-spirit of his dead father, his dead mother, and Eileen, back in the United States. Suddenly, my eyes got misty. His lip quivered. I turned away so as not to cry.

The drama of the night receded with the dark as the trail took us back to Gasumi Corners, where traditional dancing is all but dead. The light was brighter now. We finally walked by the Nomad Station, winding our way past its airstrip. Sayu's pearl shell was now crooked, his feathers skewed, and his red-ocher paint smudged on his taut skin. Even on Saturday morning, he was concerned that someone from Nomad might see him in the grass skirts of a traditional dancer. Although he had been the center of ceremonial attention all night long, this had occurred in an old forest village. Slipping behind a shrub, Sayu exchanged his skirts for a pair of shorts. Now hybrid, he left the signs of his dancing above his waist but kept the security of Western clothes below. Around his neck, he now hung the blue beads and cross from his Catholic baptism.

As Sayu had anticipated, we met others along the way. We snapped fingers firmly with them before continuing on and finally reaching Gasumi Corners. There we were greeted by those who did not make the trek—which was most of the village. They asked whether they could hear the tape-recordings I had made the previous night. As the cassette played, we listened to the men's joking, Sayu's drumming and dance rattles, and the women's traditional singing. But there were other sounds that I had barely heard amid my focus on Sayu: the guitar and ukelele of the evening's string band, and the rock 'n' roll of a Papua New Guinean band that one of the visitors played on a boom box. The clash of musical styles had mirrored the mix of celebrants in that old longhouse. Some had adorned themselves in leaves, body paint, and beautiful bird feathers. Others had sported a colorful shirt or hat, or even worn sunglasses in the night. Still others had mixed and matched cheerfully—a collage of body paint here, Western clothing there, a headdress on a hat. They had drifted through shadows thrown alternately by traditional resin torches and modern wick lanterns. All of them had paused appreciatively and even gratefully to pose for my flashing camera—as if the prize of my modern photography would validate their hybrid tradition.

In Gasumi Corners, the men listened to my tape-recording and talked of getting dressed up themselves in traditional costumes—but not for a traditional ritual. Instead, they wondered if they could scrape together enough decorations to perform in traditional costume for the government-sponsored contest that was going to be held at the Nomad Station on Independence Day. Competing communities would stage reenactments of their indigenous dances. Officials would judge the performances and award a pittance of prize money to those whom they thought were best. The men of Gasumi Corners wanted to have at least some chance to be among the winners. They mused that maybe they would dress up Wayabay or one of their other bachelors in the full regalia of initiation—even though none of these men had been initiated nor ever would be.

Listening to the tape-recording and then to the men, I felt I was in a time warp between the past and the present. This was partly from a lack of sleep. All-night feasts invariably give me vertigo the day after—as they seem to do for most Gebusi. By traditional design, staying up all night mixes things up and turns them back to front; the spirits of the dark meld with the humans of the day; the performance of the present enacts the cosmos of the past. But now the spirits had not just vanished with the morning mist; they seemed to be gone forever from Gasumi Corners. It was now midday on Saturday. Only a few men from our village had gone to the feast; most of the men and boys were now preparing to leave for the ballgames at Nomad. Tomorrow, we would sing praises to God in the hot Sunday sun. Then there would be more rugby and soccer. When the men returned from the ball field on Sunday evening, their children would be going to bed—so they could get up and be off first thing Monday morning for a full day of school. As I drifted to sleep, I wondered if my memory of Sayu's dance was already fading.

The following day, my schedule got back to normal. But I didn't know what to expect over the next few weeks. Independence Day was coming up, and ceremonial life would be taking another turn. Would the festivities be traditional, modern, or somewhere in between? Everything now seemed geared to this next celebration. This was true even at Yulabi, a remote Gebusi settlement where a large initiation was being held. I decided to attend as a visitor. To my amazement, most of the rituals were dead ringers for those I had seen in Yibihilu seventeen years before. But many other activities now resembled a Western "party" (*fati*), with music by a string band, snappy Western dress, and the presence of government workers. In some respects, even the initiation at Yulabi represented a preparation for Independence Day. The arrangements were timed so that their ceremonies would take place just one week before the national holiday. This would allow the new initiates to get dressed up again and parade in full regalia before officials at the Nomad Station. Presaging this, the Yulabi villagers held their rites on a sequence of Friday nights so that many people, including government officials, could observe them without compromising either their weekday schedules or their church attendance on Sunday morning. The people of Yulabi were widely expected to convert to Christianity after their initiation was over. This was probably going to be their last full enactment of tradition.

In Gasumi Corners, preparations for Independence Day also intensified. Young men talked excitedly about their local genre of so-called string band singing. I became curious. A quartet of young men from Gasumi Corners had formed a singing group that featured two guitars and a medley of original songs. The leader was Damya, Nolop's son, and one of the singers was Huwa, Sayu's brother. I went one night to hear them perform. And I was blown away. The songs were as stunning and soulful as those of the young boys I had heard earlier singing up in the tree. And their tone was even crisper. The music soared with rich melodies, undulating rhythms, and resonating harmonies. Hard as it was for me to admit it, their new genre was more beautiful than the séance singing of old. How to describe it? The songs were both indigenous and original. They drew important threads from séance singing, including haunting nasal tones, falsetto harmonies, and surging refrains. But their quickened tempo, lighter lilt, and instrumental accompaniment rang clearly modern. The lyrics of the songs borrowed variously from Gebusi, English, *tok pisin*, the vernaculars of neighboring ethnic groups, and even phrases that had somehow been transmitted from distant New Guinean languages and that very few Gebusi could translate. As in séance singing, the songs compressed poetic images that were evocative, longing, and nostalgic; they were short on content but lovingly repeated. Most of them involved contemporary contexts such as school, work, and romance. The following song was especially popular:

I go to school.
I look at my friend from before.
She looks at me and I look at her.
Her eyes fill with tears.
Why did you come to tease me?

Unlike séance singing, which had been spontaneous, string band songs were carefully rehearsed. When the people of Gasumi Corners gathered late in the evening to hear their singers, they were not communing with the spirits but listening to a musical performance. Men in the audience did not chime in with their own singing. There was no spirit medium, no dialogue with spirit women, and no divination for sickness or sorcery. Although some senior men might call out in emotional response, this was the exception rather than the rule. The audience was attentive and respectful, not ribald or raucous.

In a way, string band music had the same relation to séance songs that black American jazz had to the Negro spirituals and folk songs that preceded them. In both cases, a deep cultural tradition of singing gave rise to a modern form of music that was strongly instrumental, had a quicker pace and livelier tone, and carried a more nuanced and playful sense of rhythm. In both cases, the new music spoke to current social conditions in ways that were powerfully evocative and soulful but without being directly religious, spiritual, or excessively emotional. In the United States, my favorite music has long been cool jazz. In Gasumi Corners, it was string band singing. To hear how Gebusi music had evolved was a wonderful surprise.

What about the costuming that the men of Gasumi Corners had talked about? As Independence Day loomed closer, they scurried to locate or trade for items of traditional costuming. How would they use them? Judging from their winks, nods, and smiles, it almost seemed as if each man had his own plan. As I slowly came to realize, there was going to be more to Independence Day planning than either the rehearsal of songs or the presentation of dances. Sports practices also increased based on talk of fierce competition on the ball field. So, too, there was talk of other contests and displays, including disco dancing, "dramas," and a host of humorous as well as serious games.

If initiations had previously been the biggest and grandest spectacles of Gebusi culture, the celebrations of National Independence Day had since been geared to supplant them. But the festivities at the Nomad Station would include more people than the Gebusi. Certainly, Gebusi dancing, athleticism, music, and who knew what else would be on display. But so would those of other ethnic groups that ringed the Nomad Station: Bedamini, Kubor, Samo, Oybae, Honibo, and even distant peoples such as the Pa and the Kabasi. Nomad is the administrative center for a subdistrict that includes some nine thousand people scattered across 3,500 square miles of rainforest. During the week prior to Independence Day, visitors and families from many settlements within several days' walk arrived and stayed in the "corner" of Nomad to which they were most closely affiliated. Gebusi culture was going to be presented as part of an interethnic and even regional festival that was linked, in turn, to celebrations of the independence of the nation as a whole held each year on September 16.

Anthropologists often look to rituals of display and tradition as key expressions of a culture's symbolism and meaning. But as cultures interconnect, their associations increase, and the lines that distinguish them blur. Meanings and identities cut across local boundaries and become regional, national, or even international in scale. Independence Day was simultaneously a Gebusi celebration, a celebration of the Nomad Sub-District, and a celebration of the country of Papua New Guinea. Correspondingly, so-called Gebusi culture has become entangled with the activities and institutions of the Nomad Sub-District and the national and provincial governments, which control the schools, police, and local administration. In the realm of religion, the Gebusi now identified with Christian denominations that are global in scope. Although these influences are external, they interconnect with Gebusi culture. So, too, on Independence Day, Gebusi culture was laced with symbols and meanings associated with other ethnic groups, the Nomad Station, the country of Papua New Guinea, and various forms of Christianity. I realized that my conception of Gebusi culture was expanding to include a much broader range of identifications, meanings, and institutions.

Independence Day at Nomad ended up featuring almost a week of festivities and celebrations. More than a thousand people attended. The ceremonies began with two days of team sports on the Nomad ball field. These competitions escalated through several rounds and climaxed with all-star games that pitted the best players from different ethnic groups against each other. For the Gebusi, their key matches were against the Bedamini. Of course, the Bedamini had raided and sometimes decimated Gebusi villages in the past. Numerically, the Bedamini population remained seven or eight times larger than that of the Gebusi, and they retained a reputation for aggressiveness. On the ballfield, however, the Gebusi had important advantages. Whereas most Bedamini settlements were distant from Nomad, the people of Gasumi Corners and neighboring communities lived in close proximity to the government ballfield. It was difficult for the Bedamini to hone their athletic skills without regular practice and league competition. And Bedamini fighting tactics didn't work as well on the playing field. The matches were closely and vigorously officiated by government referees. And the Gebusi—especially those from Gasumi Corners itself—also had a home field advantage; the matches were played on the same pitch, with the same referees, and with much of the same crowd that they encountered every weekend.

At the end of the competition, the headline could have read, "David beats Goliath!" In an amazing coup, the Gebusi won all except one of their matches against the Bedamini. Their defeated rivals were so frustrated and angry that they accused the Gebusi of using magic to sabotage them. But government officials upheld the Gebusi victories. What was the Gebusi response? From an American perspective, I expected a wild celebration and at least a little gloating. But the Gebusi were more circumspect than that. They knew that the Bedamini were still a numerous and aggressive people. They worried that their enemies might take revenge by breaking into the little store that we had started in Gasumi Corners or even that they would break into my house and steal my things while I was attending the festivities at Nomad. Boastful or gleeful behavior was nixed. This fit with Gebusi reactions after their victories during the regular season; they were remarkably even-keeled and sportsmanlike.

On the eve of Independence Day, the festivities switched gears, and I struggled to keep up. There was excited talk of "dramas." But I had little idea what this meant. As dusk turned into night, a large performance area was roped off next to the government station. At first slowly and then more rapidly, hundreds of people gathered to watch the performances. Finally, they started. What a shock! The bulk of them were spoofs, farces, and parodies of local traditions. And these were acted out by villagers dressed in elaborate indigenous costumes. In one skit, for instance, a man in black paint, wearing a cassowary headdress and an old loincloth, groaned buffoonishly as he tried with clumsy and exaggerated effort to hack down a tiny tree using a traditional stone ax. After every few swings, the stone would fall from the ax handle, and the man would stumble and grunt stupidly while looking for it in the grass. Then he would try to sharpen his ax with a traditional grinding stone—all the while cursing in the coarsest traditional manner. His slapstick antics and rudeness were really quite funny, and the audience laughed loudly. Meanwhile, the man's sardonic companion smoked a traditional pipe and refused to help cut the tree until they almost got into a fight. Again, the audience erupted in laughter. At the end of the skit, the performers explained its "meaning" to the audience in *tok pisin* over a battery-operated bullhorn: "In the old days, we were ignorant. We didn't know about steel axes, and we tried to chop down trees using stone axes. This didn't work, and we got angry and fought with each other."

In skit after skit, one or another traditional practice or belief was skewered to the audience's delight. Many of the customs were ones that I had seen practiced quite genuinely back in 1980–82. Rites that had once been performed with dignity and grace—including magic spells, origin myths, fish poisoning rituals, spirit séances, divinations, and dances—were turned into farce. What bittersweet comedy! As an anthropologist, it was very sad to see such a mockery of rich local traditions—and by the very people who used to practice them. And yet, the skits *were* very funny, sometimes uproariously so. I fought back tears of laughter even as I felt pangs of nostalgia for customs that I had seen very much "for real" just sixteen years before.

For me, the most dramatic skit was performed by some of my friends from Gasumi Corners. It was a spoof of sickness, death, and sorcery divination. The opening performer was Mata—the teenager who had sought to be my romantic partner in 1981 and who was now a senior man with several children. He was caked with mud and wore a large fake phallus strapped around his waist. Smoking continually from a traditional tobacco pipe, he wheezed and coughed in exaggerated fashion until, in a spasm of sickness, he toppled over with a loud thud. This attracted the attention of a spirit medium, played by Damya, the son of Nolop. Damya's costume was absurdly traditional, including an upside-down cassowary headdress and a bark belt that was so oversized that it slid down whenever he got up. Mata proceeded to cry that he was going to die. This prompted Damya to lean over him and screech directly into his ear. This parodied the traditional Gebusi custom of yelling to keep a person's spirit from leaving his body when he or she was near death. Damya's efforts were ineffectual, and Mata rapidly "died." After energetic but farcical wailing, a sorcery suspect was paraded up to Mata's corpse. The suspect was Kawuk, a senior man of Gasumi Corners and staunch supporter of the Catholic Church. (During the early years of colonial influence, Kawuk had, in fact, killed a family of three—a husband and wife accused of sorcery plus their son.) In the skit, Kawuk was brilliantly made up with black paint, white body markings, leaf strips, and feathers. Now it was his turn to be the "victim." He was forced to wail over Mata's corpse in an attempt to prove his innocence. As he did so, the corpse gave a dramatic "sign." A fishing line that had been tied to the tip of Mata's fake phallus was surreptitiously pulled. As the corpse dramatically arched its back and moaned, this large organ raised up suddenly in a monumental erection. Audience members could scarcely contain themselves in laughter. Needless to say, the corpse had indicated that Kawuk was "guilty"—the sorcerer responsible.

Next, Kawuk was taken by Damya and farcically interrogated by him and by the kin of the dead man. Kawuk cried like a baby as they hit him. He initially denied but finally admitted that he had killed Mata with sorcery, whereupon his captors untied him and beat him until he fell down. Then Bulobey—who is Mata's real-life cousin and a former spirit medium who was himself implicated in sorcery killings—took up a large piece of wood. Winding up with histrionic ferocity, he finished Kawuk off with a great wallop (striking the ground right next to where he lay). With Kawuk now "dead," his kin in the skit became incensed and took up their bows and arrows. With great buffoonery, the two sides squared off for a mock bow-and-arrow fight—until they all ran off. That was the end of the skit. To conclude the act, however, the performers now distanced themselves even more clearly from the roles they had been playing. They marched solemnly back into the performance area, lined up in a neat row, and stood at attention in front of the judges. Formally and soberly, they bowed in unison to each side of the audience that encircled them—to the left, to the right, to the rear, and to the front. Finally, with military precision, they marched out, to the cheers of the crowd.

What was I to think? On the one hand, the rich wonder of Gebusi spirit beliefs, the poetry and aesthetics of their spirit mediumship, their cosmology, and even their concern for the sick and dying had been turned, as it were, into mincemeat. On the other hand, the skit represented a stinging critique of the sorcery beliefs, inquests, and fights that had killed many Gebusi in the past. That persons such as Kawuk and Bulobey could play lead characters in this mocking retort—having themselves participated in sorcery violence in years gone by—underscored this rejection. The skit was very well performed. It left me with much to ponder.

In all, over two nights, a total of forty-two dramas were performed. The majority, like the one just described, were spoofs of tradition. But these were thrown into relief by the remaining acts. Some of these were Christian morality plays, with large posters upon which verses from the Bible were written. Others were skits of first contact. In these, local villagers were portrayed as stupid, violent, and clumsy until they were shown the fruits of modern civilization—peace, trade goods, and store-bought food—by benevolent Australian patrol officers (played by villagers). It was hard to watch these acts without thinking that a core insight of anthropology—that indigenous ways of life should be respected—was here being turned upside down by local people themselves. Certainly, there were features of Gebusi tradition that I was glad to see disappear. But much of beauty had been lost in the bargain. And the new inequalities that Gebusi were now experiencing—in church, in school, and at the market—were not always preferable to the social relations they replaced.

The final skits, though few in number, suggested a more sensitive view. These enacted traumas and foibles of trying to live a modern life. The skits portrayed the problems of trying to earn a living in Kiunga, of scrounging medicine for a sick child from a pompous official, and of coping with children who drift into trouble after school. In one poignant little play, an impoverished city youth stole and ran off with a suitcase full of money. When the owner in the skit returned, he pulled out a gun, and shot dead the two security guards he had employed to guard his wealth. Here, the hungry boy had turned into a criminal, but even worse, the powerful boss had become a murderer. Obviously, modern life was not all that it was cracked up to be. Indeed, the skit echoed the life of the provincial premier, who had recently been charged with attempted murder. Despite the seriousness of such themes, the skits maintained a humorous tone. In this way, they promoted a sense of alternative outcomes rather than foregone conclusions.

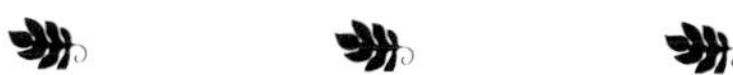

Taken together, the dramas were so rich and varied that I could probably write a whole book about them. But even so, they represented only one slice of the larger festivities surrounding Independence Day—and these continued day and night for several more days! The remaining events supplied yet more missing pieces to the puzzle of contemporary culture in and around Nomad. It was all coming together in my awareness, but only gradually.

Although local traditions had been lampooned at night, they were honored the following day. Troops of performers in gorgeous, meticulously arrayed costumes danced in full customary fashion. The throngs of people who watched the performances were even larger than they had been at the evening "dramas"—more than a thousand strong. A whole range of ethnic groups displayed their dance and initiation rites: Bedamini, Kubor, Samo, and even the Pa from across the Strickland River. Their costumes were spectacular, a photographer's dream. Gasumi Corners was represented by Halowa, Yuway's brother and an Evangelical Christian, who drum-danced in stately costume accompanied by a traditionally dressed Gebusi woman from another settlement. But the performance that stole the heart of the audience—and the judges—was by a group of dancers from the distant Kabasi peoples, who lived three days' hard walk southeast of Nomad. Dancing in a slow and dignified manner while singing haunting songs, they performed both sitting and standing for over half an hour. Many in the audience were visibly enthralled and appeared to never have seen their style of performance.

I couldn't help but think that Independence Day was expanding on traditional practices at the same time that it transformed them. The Gebusi and neighboring groups had always enjoyed the songs and dances of the peoples on their peripheries. In 1981, the Gebusi had invited Samo visitors to dance at their feasts and had themselves traveled to distant settlements to see and appreciate Bedamini dancing. That dancers or visitors risked coming from afar enhanced rather than detracted from the artistic power of their performances. Now, on Independence Day, the Gebusi watched with wonder the dances and initiation costumes of the Bedamini people, the Pa, and, especially, the distant Kabasi.

At the same time, these dances had changed greatly in their meaning and significance. Rather than being performed at night in the darkened longhouse for kin and friends, they were re-created on the official grounds of the Nomad Station for a thousand strangers in the harsh light of day. Even a member of the national parliament was present. The instrumental purpose of the performances was not to initiate a young man, cure a sick person, celebrate a local accomplishment, or reenact the spirits. Rather, it was to celebrate the nation of Papua New Guinea and to provide a secular display of body art and dancing. This was underscored by the rating and judging of the performances by officials. As the men of Gasumi Corners had emphasized, the small amount of prize money given to winning performers was a major motivation for many of the dancers. Some men performed in pseudo-traditional costumes designed to be strange or bizarre enough to attract attention—a papier mâché mask, an immense strap-on phallus, an enormous plastic noseplug, or a towering headdress of feathers and wire. In some of the displays, communities presented boys as young as six or seven years old in the yellow costumes of first-stage initiation. In reality, boys would not have been admitted to this initiation grade until they were at least in their mid teens. As the earlier comments of the men at Gasumi Corners had foreshadowed, some villages were dressing up practically anyone they could, regardless of whether the person was qualified to wear the costume. For many and perhaps most of the performers, the displays did not reflect current practices, beliefs, or rituals in their own villages. Indigenous culture was increasingly enacted as historical folklore for broader consumption.

The following day seemed to confirm this interpretation. I saw the lead dancer of the Kabasi dance troop once again. This time he was dressed in a clean white shirt and was standing with his snappily dressed son watching yet another game of rugby on the Nomad field. That Sunday, I saw him in the congregation at the Nomad Evangelical Church. As Scripture was read, he pulled out his Bible and put on his glasses so he could read the passage for himself. Here was a man who seemed to have been enacting a pristine tradition from a remote settlement. But he was a literate evangelical Christian whose God held traditional beliefs to be satanic. Although some religions develop into hybrid religions, my own sense at Nomad was that many of the performances—as visually spectacular as they were—were motivated by aesthetic and economic reasons and not by the spiritual allegiances of the performers.

If the Independence Day festivities alternately spoofed and then celebrated traditional dances as a kind of secular folklore, they also recast selected features of modern life. Toward the end of the week, a wide range of additional contests were held. These included such playful competitions as drinking quantities of hot tea, pillow fighting while sitting on a beam, having blindfolded women try to split papayas with bush knives, and climbing a greased pole. The atmosphere was similar to that of a country fair. Hundreds of people milled about. Scattered along the walkways were stalls with blaring boom boxes where villagers sold cooked food. Tables of ring toss and even rudimentary gambling were set up for those willing to risk 5 or 10 cents in a game of skill or chance. In the afternoon, an avidly attended "disco contest" was held. The dance ground was thronged with bodies gyrating to the throb of Papua New Guinea rock music broadcast over speakers. Although a few brave girls were there—and even mothers dancing with their daughters—the dance ground was dominated by the older boys. As far as I could tell, all dancing was same-sex: guys paired with guys, and girls with girls. The dancers' outfits represented a mélange of styles ranging from spiffy modern shirts and jeans to slovenly jive-type clothes or traditional costumes. Some young men even dressed up and danced buffoonishly as women.

What sense could be made of this hodgepodge? If local traditions were parodied, the same was also true, at least to some extent, of modern customs themselves. Ultimately, the festivities were an anything-goes celebration in which diverse cultural practices—traditional and modern, nearby and distant—were all put on display for performance, reflection, and playful combination. Within this potpourri, traditional customs were strongly if not radically transformed. Although traditions were highlighted on Independence Day itself, these displays were either divorced from traditional meanings or explicitly debunked, as in the evening "dramas." By contrast, what we might call the rituals and rites of modernity were rooted in the very fact that they were diverse and fragmented. This reflected social life itself in and around the Nomad Station. As opposed to stable and long-term relations among kin and co-residents, life in Nomad has become an increasingly disjunctive, multifaceted, and impersonal affair. Dependable communities characterized by face-to-face interaction have been supplanted by institutions that change under the direction of outsiders. In this hopeful but anxious context, the desire for betterment and progress was now accompanied by a fear that customary practices, however quaint or pretty, were obsolete.

For the people of Gasumi Corners, the festivities of Independence Day ultimately symbolized the hybrid mix-and-match that more generally characterizes their locally modern lifestyle. It was a lifestyle that Gebusi themselves willingly embraced when they moved from the deep rainforest to the edge of the Nomad Station. In reciprocal fashion, the multifaceted culture that was expressed in the Independence Day festivities had become a principal part of their own culture as well.

Web site images of events and topics described in this chapter can be found at http://www.mhhe.com/knauft1.

CHAPTER 12

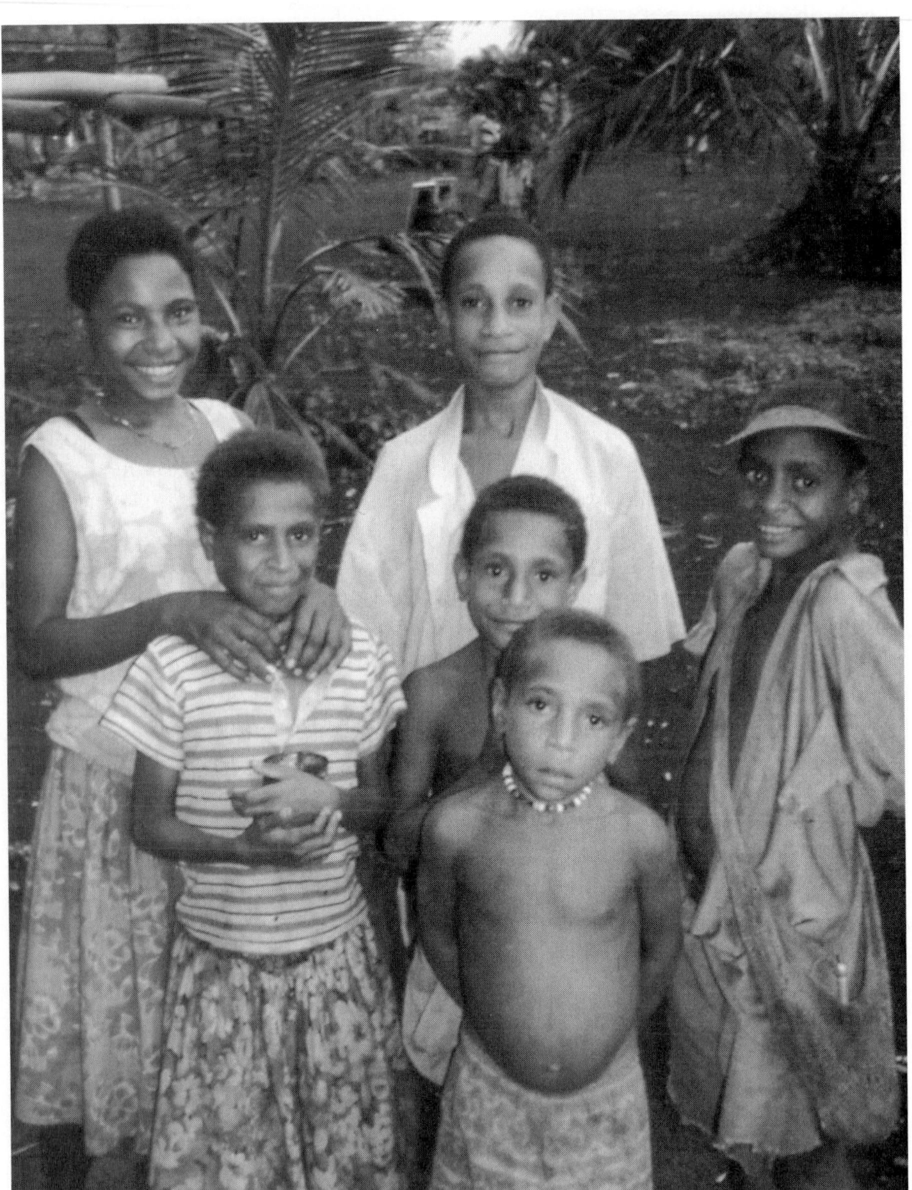

Young people of Gasumi Corners, whom the author will miss. (PHOTO: Bruce Knauft)

Toward the End

In the aftermath of Independence Day, the Nomad area seemed to relax. Having worked and played so hard, people unwound in a kind of collective morning after. A few settlements held subsidiary feasts and celebrations, like a series of happy aftershocks following a marvelous large quake. In Gasumi Corners, the period of respite lasted several weeks before gradually giving way to planning for another festivity. This next occasion would be especially poignant for me—the feast to commemorate my own departure. As my time to leave inched gradually closer, my days became increasingly bittersweet. My friendships had been so deeply rekindled, and new ones had taken root. How could I go?

It ended up being an incredible finale, and I can't claim to be the only reason for its success. Village celebrations have always served multiple purposes. And the Gebusi are the first to keep anyone from getting a big head. But it was hard not to cry when I first heard the song that the Gasumi string band composed to thank me for having come back to them.

With their typical casual gusto, the village started to buzz with preparations. Firewood and cooking leaves were stockpiled, sago was processed, and game was hunted deep in the forest. As a contemporary twist, profits were pooled from our local store to buy a large stock of tinned fish and rice. Added to these were my own gifts to the community, both to individuals and for our collective feast. The latter included additional cartons of store-bought food and a score of coveted shotgun cartridges, which Wayabay and the other young men used to hunt a stunning array of wild pigs and cassowaries.

During the numerous weeks of preparation, everyone was so busy gathering food and materials in the forest that I started to feel lonely in the village. I longed to be with them in their timbered hideaways, and I was nostalgic for the rainforest. So Sayu, Didiga, and I set off to visit those from my immediate hamlet in their makeshift forest camp at Harfolobi. On the way, we traveled the Kum River, under the stately canopy of the towering trees that lined the banks. We climbed up the bluff at Yibihilu. My lip quivered to see our former village and even the site of my first house with Eileen. It was all overgrown, not just with weeds but with good-sized trees turning into forest. Gone as well were so many of my friends from the early 1980s, reclaimed by nature in graves that dotted the former settlement. Up at Harfolobi, I visited the grave of Sayu's wondrous mother, Boyl, and it was hard not to weep. I sat in the crystal waters of the little waterfall where Eileen and I had frolicked as newlyweds. And I enjoyed for the last time the easy rhythm of rainforest living—husbands, wives, and children relaxed and peaceful, and I at home among them.

After several days, obligations drew us reluctantly back to Gasumi Corners, where the buildup for the celebration continued. Although I knew the general contours of the event to come, both from planning and from precedent, what my friends were devising by way of entertainment remained a mystery. I sensed that it would be a vintage Gebusi mix of joy, sadness, and bittersweet remembrance of the past.

On the day of reckoning, visitors came from near and far—all of those still living whom I had known so well, many others whom I had seen occasionally, and a few who knew of me only by reputation. For several days ahead of time, the piles of coconuts, a ton or more of sago starch, mounds of dried game, and stashes of rice and fish spawned a veritable village industry of cutting, cleaning, wrapping, and cooking. Now it was time to pull it all from the cooking fires, divide it up, and give it away. Hundreds of visitors had come. Amid our shouts of laughter and whoops of celebration, the gift giving continued long after dusk turned into night. I was no longer a bystander but a primary host, and I tried to make sure that my friends and acquaintances, the government officials, and even the hangers-on each got an appropriate share.

Then came the entertainment. Would this be a traditional dance, linked to my appreciation of historical customs? Or would it be modern? Instead of choosing a single course, my friends had opted, as it were, to let all the flowers bloom. On one side of my hamlet, in the dim light of a darkened house, a visiting performer danced in the full dignity of traditional costuming. Older men and women were especially drawn to this proud display of days gone by. Mothers held their smallest children, some of whom were possibly seeing a fully traditional Gebusi dance for the first time.

From the other side of the village came the strains of a visiting string band, replete with guitar and ukelele, playing wonderful songs that I had never heard. I flocked with others to bask in the rhythms and harmonies of the string band.

In the middle of the hamlet, in the central clearing, was the festive pièce de résistance: a modern disco. My friends had finagled one of the really nice boom boxes and a set of speakers from workers at the Nomad station and had lugged them all the way to Gasumi Corners. A bright lantern illuminated the area, and the music poured forth. As older folks looked on, youngsters picked up the beat. Within minutes, they were moving and grooving in ways that would have passed quite tolerably in most dance clubs in the United States. In the moonlight and gentle breeze, the joy and sadness of nostalgia blurred together. For me, it was the modern Gebusi equivalent of old *fafadagim-da*—the wistful enjoyment of intense and indescribable longing, of being together while thinking of loneliness and loss.

Swaying to different beats from one end to the other, the village became a three-ring circus of bittersweet pleasure. I shuttled back and forth between the traditional dance, the string band, and the disco in the middle, delighting in each for their part. Together, they formed a fugue of contemporary cadences that were at once discordant and yet strangely harmonious. No one seemed to mind this disjuncture, and neither did I. Perhaps I had learned something new after all—not just to accept this fragmentary experience but to enjoy and be part of it.

I thought back to Sayu's dance and all the years of ritual splendor that had preceded it. Were these now a vestige of fading tradition, or were they a spirit of things to come? I finally realized that the answer could not be one or the other; it was both at the same time. I had long grown partial to many indigenous Gebusi customs. But now I genuinely appreciated their current expression as well. Outpacing my understanding, the people of Gasumi Corners had become modern in their own unique way, and they had reinvented their past in the bargain. What had they given me? Their truest gift had gone beyond the present or the past of their culture. It was something more. They had shown me the surprise of discovery in the unfolding path of human connection.

I had thought that the final feast was over. But I didn't doubt Sayu when he told me they might mount another disco in the clearing the following night. The "day after" is a time for the host settlement to relax and savor the afterglow. Now that all the hard work was done, and everyone had stayed up all night and had had a good time and the visitors had finally gone, the villagers wanted to enjoy things for themselves. So only part of the day was spent sleeping; everyone was too eager to eat leftovers and reminisce about the previous evening.

As for another disco, my feelings were mixed. I was deeply touched that my friends wanted to extend the festivities. But I was also exhausted. So I told Sayu during supper that I'd probably crash for a couple of hours and wake up when things got cranked up—probably around ten or eleven at night. He said that he thought this was a good idea and that he might do the same himself. As my head hit the soggy pillow at 7:30 P.M., the rain had already started. One shower, then another. I was too groggy to really care. If no disco were held, I would get a full night's sleep. And if the rain subsided, well, the music would wake me up.

The next thing I remember was a dream. Or at least I thought it was, as I began to stir. I vaguely heard disco music from a boom box. But I also sensed weird voices and bizarre, off-key singing. As if this wasn't strange enough, it was still raining, not just in showers but in torrents. I was almost too convinced that it *was* a dream to get up. But I finally rolled over and checked my clock. Sure enough, 10:30 P.M., just about the time a disco would be starting. But what was all that odd commotion? I wondered if I should go out and investigate.

I couldn't tell from my door exactly who was dancing or how big the gathering was. But it seemed important enough, or at least unusual enough, to investigate despite the rain. So on with the rest of my clothes and out into the deluge. Under a borrowed canvas that had been propped up into a rough canopy, the young school children of Gasumi Corners werer dancing. Not just dancing, but laughing and whooping with abandon at the top of their lungs, running and gyrating all around, prancing into and out of the rain. One girl, Marbwi, whose portrait graces the cover of this book, was dancing spellbound in the pouring rain—as if the gods had given her divine bliss. They sang to string band disco music with a crazy-fun mix of mock old-fashioned and mock new-fangled bravado.

It was as wonderful as it was weird in that dim lamplight. No adults were awake, none. Even Sayu was slumped dead asleep, his head a scant foot from the blaring boom box. The kids beckoned me. Their mood was much too infectious for me not to join in. Swept up in the wonder of unself-consciousness, ridiculousness, and joy, there I was, dancing wildly in the rain, singing crazily, bounding around with eight- and ten- and twelve-year-old boys and girls. Their infectious happiness and now my own could not be denied by the rain or the lateness of hour or the adults who supervised the children—as if they would have minded.

Those kids and the wild dancing were more refreshing than even the cool night rain. What magic to be reminded that young is a state of mind. That there are ultimately no rules. That joy is boundless, rediscovered every time as if for the first. And that fun can be both unrestrained and good. When I finally danced through the flickering rain back to my house, I fell into a deep, deep slumber, as if all the world was content with my enjoyment to be with the Gebusi.

Web site images of events and topics described in this chapter can be found at http://www.mhhe.com/knauft1.

Conclusion

Sixteen Years and a World of Change

AROUND THE WORLD, TRADITIONS fade and die. But pieces of them are also rediscovered, reinvented in new guises, and expressed in new ways. The paths of the past continue to cross those of the present, even if the latter are increasingly large and well-trodden. Perhaps most importantly, people like the Gebusi continue to experiment with this mix. As an ethnographer and as a person, confronting this process has been important both as an intellectual challenge and as an emotional one. Although the two sides of this coin are often written about separately, I think not only that they are connected in fact but that they mutually determine each other. Where would we be without a healthy tension, a reciprocating balance, between the reflections of our minds and the feelings in our hearts?

In the former vein, I found by the time I was leaving the Gebusi that I was developing a new view of cultural change. I began to move beyond the schism I had been wrestling with—between a view of the Gebusi as orphaned from their rich past and a view of them as vibrant in their present. I started to realize that Gebusi themselves had negotiated these tensions better than I had been able to do in my reflections and analyses. I think they were able to do this in part because of their abiding sense of playfulness and flexibility. My friends might embrace new events and activities as if they were cut off from the past. But they would also voice realizations—through humor and irony, play and performance—that these developments were neither as fixed nor as somber as they seemed to be. So, too, customs of the past could be abandoned, condemned, or even viewed as shocking. But strands of their deeper influence were constantly revived, retooled, and made newly vibrant in the present.

The 122 people of Gebusi Corners have certainly become modern and have given up many of their traditions. The degree of change over a few scant years has been truly remarkable. My Gebusi friends now go to Christian churches, their children attend school, their men play soccer and rugby in the Nomad sports leagues, and their women sell food for cash at the regional market. Villagers pulse to the beat of string bands and disco music even as they enjoy the sights and sounds of traditional dances. The Gebusi have given up active sorcery investigations and are essentially cut off from their rich indigenous cosmos. In the mix, however, their once-elevated rate of violence and killing has continued to plummet; their lives are much more peaceful than they used to be.

In the present, Gebusi crave money, modern goods, and more contemporary styles of life. In part because of this, they have become surprisingly subordinate to outside authority figures—pastors, teachers, referees, buyers at market, and government officials. In the process, their lives embrace an increasingly large and complicated social universe. Although tiny by global and even national standards, the Nomad Station presents a world of difference from life in the full rainforest. It affords contact with new people and new institutions, the challenge and the threat of anonymity, and relations between men and women that go beyond the bounds of arranged marriage or traditional propriety. This life provides new opportunities for the Gebusi while posing new challenges, including gender relations in which young people grapple with issues of romantic attachment, sexuality, and marriage.

In 1998, the institutions of Gebusi social life were more diversified than in 1980–82. In the past, an initiation in the community was at once an economic, political, religious, artistic, and even a sexual undertaking. Sorcery inquests reflected issues of spiritual connection, gendered dominance, moral propriety, social control or violence, residential integrity, negative social exchange, and cosmological balance. Although some of these aspects of Gebusi social life still inform each other, they are increasingly divided into separate "institutions:" the church for religion, the market for economic transactions, the ball field for sports, the aid post for health, government offices for politics, the police station for social control, and Independence Day for bodily art and folkloric performance. In this sense, Gebusi social life now combines more diverse roles and statuses and an increasing range of impersonal relationships. This is a common pattern as societies become enmeshed in a larger and more complex world. It is one of the diagnostic features of becoming modern to encounter an increasing range of people in increasingly diverse contexts and activities.

Gebusi cultural and symbolic developments illustrate this process. Gebusi cultural identifications now embrace a wider web of meanings than they had in the past. These include larger ethnic, interethnic, regional, and national affiliations as well as identification with Christian denominations that are international in scope. Closer to home, personal identity for Gebusi is now variously conferred by being a member of a sports team, a student at school, a member of a church, a seller at the market—or a traditional gardener, hunter, house builder, or dancer. These roles may seem discordant or competing when viewed individually, but Gebusi weave them together in a rich mosaic of contemporary living.

Like other peoples in the contemporary world, Gebusi are becoming modern in their own distinct way. They still value quiet moments in the rainforest, the bonds between clans and other kin, the aesthetic splendor of their traditional costuming, and new forms of music. So, too, the very trappings of their modern life—church, school, market, sports, and the rest—are hardly the same in Nomad as in other countries or even in other parts of Papua New Guinea. Like the new vocabularies that pervade their string band songs, modern life for Gebusi cannot be framed solely in terms of outside influences even though modern life is strongly influenced by them.

The Gebusi are fortunate to have the continuing bounty of their land. They own not only their own settlement sites but also the gardens and pristine forests that provide them with their food and a surplus to boot. Many peoples who experience so-called modernization are not so lucky. The inhabitants of Gasumi Corners are additionally fortunate that part of their land is within a few minutes walk of the largest outpost for many miles in any direction—the Nomad Station. As was evident at the Independence Day festivities, Nomad has become a strong if small magnet in its own sea of rainforest peoples.

Like the Gebusi, I have been fortunate. I have had the rare opportunity to know the Gebusi, to be part of their lives, and to share in their customs. That these have crossed such broad cultural distance during eighteen short years makes my fortune all the greater. The Gebusi in 1980 were neither pristine nor fully "traditional." They had already been influenced by steel tools, by pacification of tribal enemies, and by the yearly patrols of the Australian colonial officers. But the particular constellation of these influences in their local area gave the Gebusi a rare opportunity to develop their culture, in significant part, on their own terms.

Since the mid-1980s, the Gebusi's path of cultural change has not just taken off but practically run circles around its previous scope and scale. This is indexed not only by weekly activities and an altered sense of time and progress but in larger patterns of subsistence, economy, religion, marriage, politics, and aesthetic life. Although the Gebusi past will certainly be revisited in new guises, Gebusi will never be as independent or as remote from outside influence as they once were. Not all peoples embrace outside change as quickly or as readily as the Gebusi. Distinctive patterns of history and culture determine the tracks that different peoples follow. These tracks can be highly diverse even within a small country like Papua New Guinea. But the Gebusi of Gasumi Corners do give us a special window not only on important patterns of culture change but on how these patterns braid richly through the threads of lived experience.

A special good fortune is that the people of Yibihilu and now Gasumi Corners have to a large extent engaged the outside world through their own choices. They have not been subject to the worst excesses of colonialism or modern development. They have not had to endure slavery, violent subjugation, land alienation, heavy taxation, exploitative wage labor, depletion of natural resources, or degradation of their natural environment. In all these respects, they have been very lucky indeed, notwithstanding their isolation or their sense of lagging behind on a modern path of progress. It has been their own desire to leave the full rainforest and pursue activities associated with a more locally modern style of life.

The final fortune is my own. As part of their openness, the Gebusi warmly welcomed me, first with Eileen in 1980–82, and then on my own in 1998. And they gave me the greatest gift that people can give and that we can all appreciate: to share life across differences of culture.

Farewell

ON THE DAY OF departure, I had no shame. The morning started rainy, and I hoped it would continue so the plane wouldn't come. I didn't care that my few boxes were already sealed up and that everything else had been given away. Eventually, however, the rain lessened, and I trudged in sorrow with everyone else to the airstrip. Although Sayu, Didiga, and I were flying off to Kiunga, I was leaving all my other friends behind.

I started choking up well before the plane emerged on the horizon. I knew it would happen, just as it had for the past three days as I gave things away to so many good people. I fought back the tears, but they kept coming. I had known the people of Yibihilu and of Gasumi Corners so well before and now again at the end of eighteen years—first when they were children or young adults and now, a generation later, with their own children in their place. We all knew it would be years before I could return again. Nomad is so very remote. The logistics of living there are difficult, the tropics grind hard on my middle-aged body. My obligations back home remained packed in a whole other life that included my wife, son, and parents, who would all miss me. My Gebusi friends knew this. Those who were middle-aged or older knew as well that I would probably never see them again; they would be dead by the time I was able to return. Despite other changes, their lives remain all too short.

I couldn't think of my camera that last day but took pictures that were more indelible. As I moved down the sorrowful line of those gathered to say their good-byes, I forced myself to peer in the face and gaze into the eyes of each man and woman, each boy and girl from Gasumi Corners. Snapping their fingers in my best and most forthright manner, I burned into my mind the living image of each of these unique persons, so as never to forget their exquisite humanity. Their tear-streaked faces mirrored my own as they fought the impulse to turn away. I sobbed along with them, oblivious to onlookers and people from the Nomad Station—a six-foot, bald-shaven white guy crying with a crowd of villagers.

I lost it when I came to Yuway. Along with Swiman, Wahi, and Nogo, Yuway had led us on our very first patrol in 1980. He had been my most sensitive and caring helper when I was first learning the Gebusi language. He had been my best friend during my initial fieldwork and remains one of the nicest and most decent people I have ever known. As a Seventh Day Adventist, Yuway was now a forward-looking older man, with two of his four children already pushing toward their own adulthood. I looked into his eyes and suddenly blurted out, "Oh friend, friend, when will I ever see you again?!" His wisdom was greater than mine. With a weepy and yet dignified smile, he told me, "I'll see you later, in heaven."

I don't remember much after that. The plane taxied and took me away in the dampness. My last sight at the end of the airstrip was Yuway. He had walked all the way down the path, waiting to catch my last wave through the airplane window as he waved to me one final time. Then I sailed away toward the heavens of Kiunga, while Yuway awaited his own.

Who can deny the world of change in cultures? Or that richness of humanity that persists despite all that would repress it?

Notes

GENERAL

Personal names used in the book are sometimes pseudonyms and sometimes actual names. Actual names are used for persons who have given permission for their real names to be used and for persons whose depiction in the text is nonproblematic and/or if they have been deceased for a number of years. This reflects the fact that the Gebusi generally are pleased to have their real identities represented to the larger world. Pseudonyms have been used in cases in which personal information could be perceived or interpreted as embarrassing, immoral, criminal, or otherwise unflattering, regardless of whether the person is now alive or deceased.

Quotations in the main text that been taken from field notes and from Gebusi have been edited to make them more direct and succinct. I have attempted to retain the spirit and meaning of original remarks. My occasional resort to quoted paraphrase is designed to make the material more understandable to a general audience.

INTRODUCTION

How to appreciate cultural diversity while criticizing inequality and domination. These complementary themes and their historical relationship in anthropology are discussed in greater detail in *Genealogies for the Present in Cultural Anthropology* (Knauft 1996, pp. 48–57).

The Gebusi in 1998 versus 1980–82. An extended scholarly description of Gebusi society in 1980–82 is *Good Company and Violence: Sorcery and Social Action in a Lowland New Guinea Society* (Knauft 1985a). A more detailed account of Gebusi changes in 1998 can be found in *Exchanging the Past: A Rainforest World of Before and After* (Knauft 2002a).

The Nomad Station as a local place of influence and power. See the discussion in "How the World Turns Upside Down: Changing Geographies of Power and Spiritual Influence among the Gebusi" (Knauft 1998a).

Becoming modern—a process that is both culturally diverse and global in scope. See the collected essays on this topic in *Critically Modern* (Knauft 2002c). A fascinating case study of a rural people who are becoming alternatively modern in Togo, West Africa, can be found in Charles Piot's *Remotely Global: Village Modernity in West Africa* (1999). For an urban example that focuses on women in China, see Lisa Rofel's monograph *Other Modernities: Gendered Yearnings in China After Socialism* (1999).

In-depth accounts of specific Gebusi practices. Beyond the present book, information about specific Gebusi practices and beliefs can be found as follows:

Concerning Gebusi in 1980–82:

- colonial history (Knauft 1985a, pp. 12–16)
- emotion concepts and orientations (Knauft 1985a, chapter 3)
- gender relations (Cantrell 1998; Knauft 2004a)
- killing and homicide rates (Knauft 1985a, chapter 5; Knauft 1987c)
- kinship and marital relations (Knauft 1985a, chapter 5)
- myths and folktales (Knauft 1985a, chapter 10; Knauft 1986)
- ritual feasts and dancing (Knauft 1985a, chapter 9; Knauft 1985b)
- sexual relations between males (Knauft 1986; Knauft 1987a)
- sorcery beliefs, inquests, and attributions (Knauft 1985a, chapters 2, 4–5, 7–8)
- spirit séances (Knauft 1985a, chapter 11; Knauft 1989; Knauft 1996, pp. 209–217; Knauft 1998b)
- subsistence and health (Knauft 1985a, pp. 16–21)
- tobacco, drugs, and the use of them to quell rather than to promote violence (Knauft 1987b)

Concerning the Gebusi in 1998:

- Christianity and church (Knauft 2002a, chapters 5–6)
- gender relations (Knauft 2002a, pp. 27–29; see more generally Knauft 1997)
- history of events and changes between 1982 and 1998 (Knauft 2002a, chapter 3)
- market activity (Knauft 2002a, pp. 207–211)
- music (Knauft 2002a, pp. 217–220)
- police and government (Knauft 2002a, chapter 4)
- public culture and Independence Day celebrations (Knauft 2002a, pp. 226–231; Knauft 2002b)
- schooling (Knauft 2002a, chapter 7)
- sexuality between men (Knauft 2004b)

- sorcery beliefs and their decline (Knauft 2002a, chapter 5)
- sports (Knauft 2002a, pp. 211–213)

CHAPTER 1

Gift exchange in Melanesia and elsewhere. The most influential and classic description of gift exchange is *The Gift* (Mauss 1967). This short book uses ethnographic examples from a range of societies—particularly in the Pacific Islands and indigenous North America—to illustrate the social importance of giving and receiving gifts. The account includes a discussion of gift-exchange that is competitive or aggressive in nature—a pattern that occurs in some Melanesian societies (Strathern 1971; Young 1971; see Weiner 1976 concerning exchanges organized by women). Marshall Sahlins (1972a) describes three types of reciprocal exchange—"generalized," "balanced," and "negative"—that inform social relations in many societies. A large literature has developed concerning gift exchange and its ramifications.

The impact of steel tools in preindustrial societies. For a dramatic case example based on ethnographic documentation, see *From Stone to Steel* (Salisbury 1962).

The Bedamini people, adjacent to the Gebusi. Information concerning the Bedamini can be found in Knauft (1985a, chapters 1 and 8; Knauft 1998a) and Sørum (1980, 1982, 1993).

The Western projection of discovery onto non-Western peoples. As "life explorers," cultural anthropologists have often tried to discover things about peoples who are little known or not well understood. In the process, it is easy for them to project their own desires and assumptions onto those they study—including the assumption they have discovered something "new." Even the notion that Columbus "discovered" America in 1492 belies the fact that Native Americans populated and developed trade links throughout the New World thousands of years before this event. Books that document the projections that Western explorers or early anthropologists have made onto non-Western peoples include Todorov (1999), Hodgen (1964), Pagden (1986), and Kuper (1988). Concerning contemporary anthropology, see Stuart Kirsch's article "Lost Tribes: Indigenous People and the Social Imaginary" (1997).

Gebusi *kogwayay* as "good company." A fuller discussion of Gebusi *kogwayay* and its implications can be found in Knauft (1985a, chapter 3).

Cultural "key symbols." Anthropologists have often discussed and debated how to identify and document which concepts, symbols, and metaphors are most crucial in a given culture. The clearest and most influential statement on this issue is Sherry Ortner's short article "On Key Symbols" (1973). In this paper, Ortner defines the characteristics of key symbols and describes how they can be recognized in different cultures.

How to combine cultural appreciation with a critical view of social and cultural inequality. This issue is discussed in Knauft (1996, pp. 48–61).

The anthropology of women and the cross-cultural study of gender relations. These topics have generated a large literature in anthropology since the 1970s. Selected works include *Women, Culture, and Society* (Rosaldo and Lamphere 1974), *Toward an Anthropology of Women* (Reiter 1975), *Sexual Meanings* (Ortner and Whitehead 1981), *Gender at the Crossroads of Knowledge* (di Leonardo 1991), and *Making Gender* (Ortner 1996). Extensive case studies of gender relations are now available for all major world areas. A selective review of recent trends in gendered ethnography and associated theory can be found in Knauft (1996, chapter 7). General books include two different works titled *Gender and Anthropology* (Mascia-Lees 2000; Morgen 1989), and an introduction to women's studies that considers gender from a cross-cultural and cross-national perspective (Grewal and Caplan 2001). The relation of anthropology to feminism is considered in books by Moore (1988, 1994) and Sanday and Goodenough (1990).

The experience of women as ethnographers. This issue has been widely explored in recent years. Representative works include *Women in the Field* (Golde 1986), *Women Writing Culture* (Behar and Gordon 1995), *Self, Sex, and Gender in Cross-Cultural Fieldwork* (Whitehead and Conaway 1986), *First in Their Field* (Marcus 1993), *Feminist Dilemmas in Fieldwork* (Wolf 1996), and *Women and the Invention of American Anthropology* (Lurie 1999). Concerning the sexual orientations of ethnographers themselves, see *Taboo* (Kulick and Willson 1995).

CHAPTER 2

Kapauku base-sixty counting system. This is described in *The Kapauku Papuans of West New Guinea* (Pospisil 1963).

Culture as adaptation. This issue has been extensively studied by materialist anthropologists and those interested in human ecology. Leading proponents of this perspective in the history of American anthropology include Leslie White, Julian Steward, Marvin Harris, Roy Rappaport, and Robert Netting, each of whom wrote many books and articles concerning it.

"Felling the trees on top of the crop." This phrase is taken from the title of an article about this topic by Edward Schieffelin (1975).

Simple humans groups as "original affluent societies." This notion is developed and documented by Marshall Sahlins in his paper "The Original Affluent Society" (1972b).

Agricultural intensification and the evolution of complex human societies. See a general overview of this issue in *The Evolution of Human Societies* (Johnson and Earle 1987). Concerning densely populated areas of the New Guinea highlands in particular, see Feil (1987), Brown (1978), and Watson (1977).

Semidomesticated pigs. Detailed studies of this practice among the Etoro or Etolo peoples, who live northeast of the Gebusi on the other side of the Bedamini, have been published in Kelly (1988) and Dwyer (1989).

Cultural diversity in Melanesia. Although Melanesia contains less than 10 million people, it includes an amazing one quarter of the entire world's languages and associated cultures—approximately 1150 of the roughly 4000 languages estimated to be spoken in the world today (see Wurm 1982a, b; Finegan and Besnier 1989, p. 296). The astounding diversity of customs and beliefs in Melanesia is reviewed in *From Primitive to Postcolonial in Melanesia and Anthropology* (Knauft 1999).

Learning a language in the field. See *Learning a Field Language* (Burling 1984) and *Language Learning in Intercultural Perspective* (Byram and Fleming 1998).

The experience of ethnographic fieldwork. Evocative accounts of fieldwork include *The High Valley* (Read 1965), *The Headman and I* (Dumont 1978), and *Reflections on Fieldwork in Morocco* (Rabinow 1977). Newer and more reflexive accounts by female anthropologists include *Return to Nisa* (Shostak 2000; see also Shostak 1981), *Translated Woman* (Behar 1993), and *Fictions of Feminist Ethnography* (Visweswaran 1994). The process of ethnographic fieldwork is described and analyzed more generally in Watson (1999), Laine (2000), Amit-Talai (1999), Coffey (1999), Jackson and Ives (1996), Lareau and Shultz (1996), and Dresch, James, and Parkin (2000).

CHAPTER 3

The anthropology of sorcery and witchcraft. Gebusi beliefs are technically "sorcery" rather than "witchcraft" because they involve the reported manipulation of physical objects to make individuals deathly ill. By contrast, witchcraft entails the belief in an intrinsic capacity to cause sickness either by an act of mental will, by being possessed by an intrinsically evil spirit, or by having an inherently diseased or corrupted soul.

Concerning sorcery and witchcraft in general, see Marwick (1982). For sorcery and witchcraft in Melanesia, see especially Fortune (1932) and Stephen (1987, 1994). For Africa, see especially Stoller (1987), Evans-Pritchard (1937), and collections by Middleton and Winter (1963) and Douglas (1970). African witchcraft under conditions of contemporary change is discussed by Comaroff and Comaroff (1999) and Geschiere (1997). Concerning witchcraft accusations in Puritan America, see Erikson (1966); regarding magic and witchcraft in contemporary England, see Luhrmann (1989).

Animism and shamanism. It has long been thought that human spirituality originated in "animism," that is, the belief that spirits beings animate the natural environment. Such beliefs have been common among foraging peoples and hunter-gatherers, whose livelihood depends on wild species of animals and plants. Such foraging adaptations have characterized the bulk of our evolutionary history as a species. Among foragers and other highly decentralized peoples, spirits typically communicate with humans through the body of spirit mediums or shamans, who become temporarily possessed or entranced. Concerning the evolution of human spiritual beliefs, see especially Wallace (1966).

Concerning shamanism in simple human societies, see Eliade (1964). For Melanesia, see Knauft (1989), Schieffelin (1977), and Fortune (1935). A dramatic case study of spirit possession among the !Kung San of South Africa is *Boiling Energy* (Katz 1982).

Michael Taussig (1987) has shown how shamanism and spirit mediumship among native peoples of South America have resisted outside influences and promoted healing with respect to suffering caused by colonial subjugation or state oppression. Similar patterns have been documented in southern Africa, for instance, by Peter Fry in his book *Spirits of Protest* (1976). I found a subtler permutation of similar themes in the spirit séances of a particularly creative Gebusi spirit medium from a remote settlement (see Knauft 1998b).

Female spirit possession has sometimes been interpreted as a protest against or resistance to patriarchy (Lewis 2003). A rich case study of female spirit possession in the Sudan has been published by Janice Boddy (1989). See also case examples of female and male spirit possession in Mayotte (north of Madagascar) by Lambek (1981) and a fascinating contemporary account of a Vodou priestess in Brooklyn by Brown (2001).

CHAPTER 4

Kinship and marriage in human societies. For background on kinship, see the classic short book *Kinship and Marriage* by Fox (1967), a reader by Goody (1971), and a more recent volume by Parkin (1997). A massive classic study of alliance and exchange systems of marriage is Claude Lévi-Strauss's *The Elementary Structures of Kinship* (1969). Concerning contemporary uses of kinship in anthropology, see Stone (2001), Schweitzer (2000), and Carsten (2000). For an account of cultural rules in American kinship, see Schneider (1980). Concerning the relationship of kinship to gender, power, and social inequality, see Collier and Yanagisako (1987) and Yanagisako and Delaney (1995).

Killing and homicide across human societies. Comparative rates of homicide in different societies are tabulated in Knauft (1985a, p. 379) and Knauft (1987c). Ethnographic studies of societies with high rates of killing have been published for the Yanomamo of the Amazon (Chagnon 1997) and, in New Guinea, for the Mae Enga (Meggitt 1977), the Jalemo (Koch 1974), the Grand Valley Dani (Heider 1979), and the Tuade (Hallpike 1977), in addition to my initial book on the Gebusi

(Knauft 1985a). Theories of prestate warfare and killing are reviewed based on considerable evidence from Melanesia in Knauft (1999, chapter 3). Display warfare in Melanesia is discussed in Knauft (2002d).

In recent years, the anthropology of violence has expanded to consider the suffering and disruption associated with civil or international war, terrorism, and ethnic strife. Prominent examples include Kleinman, Das, and Lock (1997), Das and associates (2000, 2001), Nordstrom (1997), Nordstrom and Robben (1995), and Nordstrom and Martin (1992). A powerful account of the genocide in Rwanda in 1994 has been written by Gourevitch (1998); see also Mamdani (2001). See Hinton (2002) for an edited collection of papers on the anthropology of genocide.

Persecution of witches in Western countries. Concerning witch persecutions in European history, see Kors and Peters (2001), Ankarloo and Clark (1999, 2002), Scarre (1987), and a dramatic case study by Kunze (1987). Concerning the Salem witch trials in Puritan America, see Erikson (1966), Norton (2002), and Hoffer (1996). Concerning contemporary witchcraft in England, see Luhrmann (1989).

CHAPTER 5

Cross-cultural variation in sexual orientation. This topic has spawned much research in recent years. A general and readable overview of alternative sexual practices in different regions of the world is *Same Sex, Different Cultures* (Herdt 1997). A more scholarly compendium of historical and cross-cultural examples is *Third Sex, Third Gender* (Herdt 1994). Collected editions that consider the contemporary relationship among sexuality, gender, and culture include Lancaster and di Leonardo (1997) and Parker and Aggleton (1999). Ethnographic case studies of alternative sexual orientations from different world areas are available, including for Brazil (Parker 1991, 1999), Mexico (Carrier 1995), New Guinea (Herdt 1981, 1987, 1993; Ernst 1991; Kelly 1976; Knauft 1986, 1987a, 1993: chapter 3 and appendix 1), Native America (Williams 1986), India (Nanda 1990; Reddy 2001), and the United States (Herdt 1992; Herdt and Boxer 1996; d'Emilio 1983, Weston 1991). An influential review of lesbian and gay studies in anthropology has been published by Weston (1993). Sexual orientation in relation to the ethics of fieldwork is considered in edited collections by Kulick and Willson (1995) and Whitehead and Conaway (1986).

New Guinea highlands beliefs concerning female sexual pollution, loss of masculinity, and male "pregnancy." Concerning Hua beliefs in male pregnancy, see Meigs (1976); concerning sexual beliefs and practices among the Mae Enga, see Meggitt (1964). Concerning sexual pollution and gender hostility in the New Guinea highlands more generally, see Langness (1974, 1999) and a rich contrasting view by Strathern (1988).

Sexual orientation among Gebusi women. See documentation and discussion of this issue by Eileen Cantrell (Knauft) (1998).

Sexual relations between women among the Kamula. Evidence on this topic was obtained by Michael Wood (1982).

"Gebusi women regard sexuality as a positive force . . ." This quotation is taken from Eileen Cantrell (Knauft) (1998, p. 99).

Gebusi spirit mediumship. Fuller accounts on this topic can be found in Knauft (1985a, chapter 11; 1989; 1998b).

Gebusi ritual dance costuming. Gebusi dance costuming and symbolism are analyzed in Knauft (1985a, pp. 257–261). An evocative and influential book about ritual dances and emotional dynamics among the Kaluli people, twenty-five miles southeast of the Gebusi, was published by Edward Schieffelin (1976).

Religion as the projection of human society into a spiritual world. This idea was formulated by Emile Durkheim and developed in his book *The Elementary Forms of the Religious Life* (1965 [original in French, 1912]).

Sexual imagery in Gebusi dances and folktales. More information about these topics can be found in Knauft (1985a, chapters 9–10; 1986).

Gender and sexuality diversity in Melanesia. These issues are reviewed and discussed more systematically in Knauft (1999, chapters 2 and 4).

In one study, 29 percent of gay/lesbian teenagers in the United States had attempted suicide. This information is taken from Herdt and Boxer (1996, p. 207).

CHAPTER 6

Male initiations and fertility cults in Melanesia. A review of Melanesian initiation and ritual customs can be found in Knauft (1999, pp. 66–84); see also Whitehead (1986) and Herdt (1982).

The "liminal" stage in rites of passage. The concept of a liminal or "in-between" stage in rites of passage was first developed by the French sociologist Arnold van Gennep (1960 [original in French, 1908]). The notion was expanded and developed by the British and American anthropologist Victor Turner (1969, 1972).

Secrecy in male initiations. Secrecy is strongly evident in studies of male initiation from various world areas, including Melanesia (Herdt 1982, 1993, 2003; Allen 1967) and Africa (Turner 1969).

Harshness of male initiation in some Melanesian societies. Harsh or traumatizing male initiation customs and beliefs are described for Melanesian societies in

Rites of Manhood (Herdt 1982; see also Herdt 1993) and by Langness (1967) and Barth (1975). Concerning male initiations more generally, see Turner (1969).

Benign initiation in some Melanesian societies. The Purari peoples of the New Guinea southern lowlands, who were inveterate headhunters, are particularly striking in this respect; see Williams (1923) and Knauft (1993, pp. 173–178).

Color-coded costumes at the height of a male initiation. See the remarkable account of the rest of the initiation mentioned—among the Umeda people of Papua New Guinea—in Alfred Gell's book *Metamorphosis of the Cassowaries* (1975).

Female initiations and the ritual role of women. A fuller account of women's role in Gebusi initiations can be found in Knauft (2004a). Concerning female initiates and the role of women in initiations and fertility cults in Melanesia more generally, see Lutkehaus and Roscoe (1995), Whitehead (1986), and Bonnemère (2004). An exemplary ethnography of female initiation among the Okiek of Kenya has been published by Corinne Kratz (1994).

CHAPTER 7

The anthropology of global influences. Summary articles by well-known anthropologists about a wide range of global influences and problems can be found in MacClancy's edited collection *Exotic No More* (2002). A reader on globalization by Inda and Rosaldo (2001; see also Trouillot 2003) documents the history and challenge of global influences from an anthropological perspective. The relationship of global problems and culture to capitalism and the history of colonialism has been configured for students by Robbins (2002). See also Bodley (1999). A wide-ranging set of political and internationalist perspectives on the future of globalization has been compiled by O'Meara, Mehlinger, and Krain (2000).

The reemergence of violence in Papua New Guinea. Some parts of Papua New Guinea —especially highlands areas, towns, and cities—have seen a marked rise of violence in recent years (see Strathern 1993; Dinnen 1991).

On getting bitten by a death adder. The following passages are from my field notes.

> September 8, 1998. Field entry: Death Adder
>
> It seemed so innocuous, earlier tonight. I was briskly walking down the trail that I've taken almost every day to the Nomad Station. True, it was dark, but the moon was peeking through the clouds and I had a flashlight to lead the collective way. A troop of seven younger and not so younger guys, aged 12 to 20, were going with me to "video night" at the Nomad Station. I had tried to go to the video before, but it had been rained out. Tonight had seemed a better bet.

Going down the hill to the river, all I felt was a prick in my left foot. Shining the light on the offending object, it was already curled in a tight ball. Must be some kind of really large caterpillar, I thought at first. My young companions knew better. "*Sayamp. Sayamp,*" they intoned. They quickly chopped off its head with a long knife and threw it in the bush. To confirm, I asked Didiga if he knew the English term. "Poison snake," was his answer. I asked in Gebusi, "Is this the same kind of snake that bit and killed my friend Sasaga?" "Yes." My heart started to race.

I looked at my left foot but I couldn't see anything dramatic. All I felt was a kind of mosquito bite sensation in my second toe. But my friends examined it closely. *Moliar galaym:* teeth bite marks. Then followed a period of uncertainty. "Do you feel any really big pain?" "It just feels like a strong mosquito bite." Trying to listen more closely to my own body, I did sense some lightheadedness, sweat, and clammy skin. But I also thought this might be a shock response to the news that I had just been bitten by a death adder. My foot really didn't hurt that much yet—just a dull ache that was easing its way up my foot. "It hurts some, but not a lot."

They examined my toe more closely. Only a little bit of blood and two small scratches. Sebety was the first to venture an opinion: *moliar, warsok mwi*—the teeth had bitten me, but the "death dealing arrow" hadn't. It didn't take me long to figure this out: the snake had bitten me with its small teeth, but I had not gotten a full bite from its fangs. My friends told me that I was unlikely to die even though I might get really sick. If my stride had been a hair less forceful or the snake a millisecond faster . . .

As I sit here typing and trying to distract myself this same night, I reflect on my brush with possible death. I am trying to relax and accept the pain. I don't want to linger on the event or make it too prominent, since this just makes me more conscious of my growing discomfort. So I imagine that my encounter with the snake was like a car accident that could have been fatal but wasn't and won't be. Is there anything I could have done differently, or will now? Yes, of course: wear shoes when going on trails at night. Death adders aren't very long snakes, and they don't strike more than an inch or two above the ground. Keda said that they sometimes come out in the evening, "The death adder was going along the trail at night, just like you!" But I have been on that trail so many times, and so have Gebusi, including at night. We've never seen a snake there before. My friends told me that if they had been going first, it would have been they who would have been bitten. It was just bad luck, a risk of the road, as it were. Other than the pain, my main aftershock seems to be a bad case of indigestion. Which is peaking right now, in fact . . .

Sorry for that break, but I just upchucked my supper. At least I have a conveniently high open porch to heave from. I suppose it is possible that vomiting could be a side effect of death adder toxin. But my foot, though paining me, remains tolerable. Perhaps my stomach upset is a combination of wolfing down dinner prior to leaving for the video, subsequent stress, and taking an excess of Ibuprofen. [Note inserted on October 24, 1998: Actually, this is wrong. I have since learned that a common effect of death adder toxin is digestive upset a few hours after having been bitten. But I am glad I didn't know this at the time!] I feel better having gotten rid of my bile, and am also gratified that my friend Hogayo next door heard my heaves and called over to ask if everything was all right. I told him that I was OK and that I would call out for him if I felt worse.

Strange to say it right now, but I still have to trust in the Gebusi ability to assess the odds of danger and in my own ability to make decisions based on their advice. As such, I don't think you have to worry about me too much as you read this back home. But if your heart races just a little at the outset, that's OK. The experience has made me appreciate my life here and even more so the one with you I have left temporarily behind. If the experience makes you reappppreciate your life, too, or my love for you, so much the better.

September 9, 1998 [the following day]. Field entry: Snake bite update

I am still alive and kicking, though not quite as quickly out of the woods as I had hoped. The second toe on my left foot has become really red, swollen, and painful—like someone has taken a big whack at it with a good-sized hammer. No less, but thankfully no more than this. I do have tenderness on the inside of my thigh and groin on that side—probably from the work my body has been doing to absorb the snake toxin—but I have no radiating nerve pain or other effects. My other toes seem OK, and the rest of my foot is only slightly tender and swollen. I can hobble around and hope to try getting out and about in the next day or two. Everyone in Gasumi Corners is enormously solicitous and sympathetic. So I feel warmly attended to.

September 19, 1998 [ten days later]. Field entry: Snake bite update

I have been going out and about, gingerly at first, since a couple of days after my encounter with the death adder. Today I am tending to inflammation in the toe that was bitten; it has blistered and is threatening to ulcerate. I must take care to keep it bandaged and to wash, disinfect, and redress it frequently. I think all will be fine if I follow this regimen dutifully.

September 25, 1998 [six days later]. Field entry: The second snake!

It was about the thickness of a small death adder. And it stung just a little. And it was shedding its skin. But it was part of me: my own toe. As the skin sloughs off and the new toe emerges, I am reminded of skin changing and snakes. My toe is its own snake. Perhaps it has some sympathy now, venomously injected, for that poor reptile who got its head cut off for biting my appendage so slightly.

I do feel, somehow, that the force of this snake, if not its spirit, has affected me. We slough our skin and moan our lost innocence and look anew at the older and only marginally wiser person we have become. Being bitten and being changed and coming out of a naive chrysalis; these are all part of life. Another spin on the circle of life's wheel. I will never again be the same, trotting so innocently down nighttime trails. (And neither will the snake, being dead.) But as the skin sloughs off and we come up new, I realize there must be new innocence as well. Were we to crush all innocence in safe reflection, we would be living behind the thick glass, believing too much in the poison of the world around us and perhaps in our own.

So once burned and twice learned, but let us hope that a spark of wonder escapes the pulp, as we slough the old to find the new.

October 24, 1998 [one month later]. Field entry: Snake bite update

Just for the record, my foot has now healed completely, and I have been easily hiking about. As if to remind me, however, the toe that was bitten still turns red when it is exposed to the sun. So I keep it covered. As long as I am good to it, it seems to be good to me in return. In the bargain, the spirit of the snake seems finally to have departed for good.

Changes in temporality—in the meaning and sense of time. In recent years, cultural anthropologists have become increasingly aware of different senses of time in different cultures—see collections of essays on this topic edited by Carol Greenhouse (1996) and Diane Hughes and Thomas Trautmann (1995). The German historian Reinhardt Kosellek (1985) found that even in European societies the notion that time unfolds as a linear and nonrepeating path of development was largely absent prior to the latter part of the eighteenth century. But beginning in this period, belief in human improvement and in the ideal of progress became more pervasive in Europe. Although this more modern sense of time is widely distributed and influential today, it contrasts with notions of time in many other societies—as well as those in earlier periods of Western history. In a number of earlier and non-Western instances, the unfolding of time was believed to mark either the eventual or hopeful return to a previous state or the gradual decline from a preceding period of goodness or beneficence. That time is not a circle of repetition or a path of decline but an arrow of newness and expected improvement is not a cultural universal but a distinctively modern idea.

Rainforest logging. Farther to the south of the Gebusi, hardwood timber is a prime resource for lumber companies that practice clear-cut logging. This destroys the rainforest and the livelihood of local people. In many cases, local people don't realize how much devastation logging will cause; they may be persuaded by the lure of money, goods, and trips outside the area to sign away their land in contracts with logging companies (see Brunois 1999; Barlow and Winduo 1997; Wood 1996, 1999). Deforestation from logging is a colossal problem in Melanesia, in the Amazon, in Southeast Asia, and in other rainforest areas. A wide array of resources and activist initiatives concerning rainforest destruction can be found on the Internet.

Modern material aspirations in out-of-the-way places. The Gebusi are not alone in their great desire for increased wealth and more commodities—despite, and even because of, the fact that they live in a remote location. For poignant examples from other parts of Papua New Guinea, see Gewertz and Errington (1996) and Errington and Gewertz (1998); for Amazonia, see Hugh-Jones (1992).

Resistance versus accommodation to social change and "modernization." Non-Western societies that harbored either valuable resources or sizable populations have often been subject to domination or oppression by colonial powers. This has occurred through warfare, slavery or forced labor, land alienation, taxation, removal of resources, and forced acculturation, particularly of indigenous elites. In many if not most cases, indigenous populations have resisted these depredations insofar as they have been able to do so. Domination and resistance as historical precursors to contemporary "globalization" or "modernization" have been foregrounded by anthropological scholars such as Eric Wolf (1969, 1982), James Scott (1998), Michel-Rolf Trouillot (2003), Peter Worsley (1984), and John Bodley (1999). The Gebusi have been fortunate, indeed, to have had a less difficult historical engagement with outside influences than many other societies. Against this background, the special circumstances of Gebusi history highlight the cultural significance of modern material aspirations even when external oppression has not been that great in relative terms.

Decline of communal life. The decentralization of larger and more communal living arrangements—and a corresponding increase in individual family houses or compounds—is a common aspect of change among people who previously lived in collective longhouses. This pattern has been documented in the Amazon and among Canadian Indians (Murphy and Steward 1956) and in much of lowland northern and southern New Guinea. It has also been documented among the Samo people just northwest of the Gebusi (see Shaw 1996).

CHAPTER 8

Fundamentalist conversion and the cross-cultural study of religion. The strength and popularity of fundamentalist Christianity have grown dramatically in recent decades. In addition to the United States, this pattern is highly evident in Latin America, the Pacific Islands, and parts of Africa and Asia (see Hefner 1993; van der Veer 1996; Vasquez 1998; Robbins, Stewart, and Strathern 2001; Schmid 1999). As documented by Philip Jenkins in his book *The Next Christendom* (2002), many converts in non-Western countries are adopting Christian beliefs that are not considered "mainstream" in North America or Europe. By contrast, many mainstream denominations of Christianity have been experiencing a decline in membership, including in the United States. The current spread of Christianity often involves evangelical, Pentecostal, or "fire-and-brimstone" beliefs and practices that appear illiberal or absolutist to many Westerners. At the Nomad Station, the doctrines of all three Christian churches seemed to fit this pattern.

Some scholars suggest that other world religions have also become more fundamentalist in recent decades. This reasoning applies to the attraction of conservative Islam in the mid-East, northern Africa, and Southeast Asia. Islamic fundamentalism has arguably been both reflected in and fueled by the events that led up to September 11, 2001 and the subsequent U.S. invasions of Afghanistan and Iraq.

In India, increasing fundamentalism may also characterize the intensification of Hindu beliefs and practices such as "Hindutva," including strong opposition to Islamic religious practices within the country (see Hansen 1999, 2001). Analogous arguments have been made concerning the influence of conservative Judaism and fundamentalist Zionism in Israel.

It remains to be seen whether these combined patterns are part of a longer-term trend in which "globalization" and "secularization" will be undercut by disputes fueled by religious antagonism and strife. Alternatively, it is possible that current tensions and conflicts are more principally caused by disputes that are ultimately political in nature and that can be managed through diplomacy and negotiation.

Religious conversion versus syncretism (mixing). People exposed to new religious influences have often melded or blended older beliefs with new ones. This pattern has been especially well documented in Latin American varieties of Catholicism (which often mixed with Native American beliefs) and in the proliferation of local Hindu deities and avatars in South Asia. As Robbins (2001) notes, however, fundamentalist sects retard this process by asserting a clear break or rupture between their doctrine and previous beliefs and practices. In future decades, it will be important to investigate how religious fundamentalism attenuates or remains resistant to blending with other practices and beliefs.

Modern progress and religious belief in "deferred gratification." It has often been suggested that an ethic of personal discipline, financial investment, and faith in the longer future are characteristic of both Protestant doctrine and the development and spread of Western capitalism. This idea was first raised by the German sociologist Max Weber (1958, original in German, 1904–05). More recently, scholars have seen striking parallels between the desire to become "modern" and conversion to highly disciplined forms of Christianity in different world areas (see van der Veer 1996; Hefner 1993; Knauft 2002a, pp. 172–173). How these developments will unfold over time and in alternate cultures remains an open question.

"Cargo cults." The attempt by Melanesians to access Western goods through magical or spiritual means has long been of interest to anthropologists. In many cases, the beliefs and practices of cargo cults have blended over time with Christian doctrines, including belief in the Second Coming of Christ and the Apocalypse (at which time God may be believed to bring both wealth and eternal life to those who have been faithful). Studies of Melanesian cargo cults include books by Worsley (1968), Burridge (1960), Schwartz (1962), and Lawrence (1964), and my first published journal article (Knauft 1978). Recent trajectories of millennial or apocalyptic belief in Melanesia have been examined by Robbins (2004; Robbins, Stewart, and Strathern 2001), Schmid (1999), and Stewart and Strathern (2000). An important critique of the Western fascination with cargo cults has been authored by Lindstrom (1993).

Decline of Gebusi sorcery accusations. The demise of Gebusi inquests—including statistics concerning the decrease in divinations, spirit séances, and accusations—is described and discussed in Knauft (2002a, chapter 5).

Christianity and gender. In the combined course of Christianization and "modernization," it is common for women to feel empowered by their new religious affiliation while ultimately being subordinated to and dominated by male religious and other institutional leaders (see Brown 1994; cf. Knauft 1997).

Revival or reemergence of indigenous religious beliefs. Anthropologists have documented the persistence of occult beliefs such as sorcery in a wide range of world regions, including in Africa, South and Southeast Asia, and Latin America, as well as the South Pacific and Melanesia. Older practices and beliefs often combine with new orientations, circumstances, and aspirations. For instance, belief in sorcery may dovetail with belief in magical retribution by or against persons who have gained modern wealth and power at the expense of others (see Comaroff and Comaroff 1999; Geschiere 1997). Although such beliefs have not developed among the Gebusi, they might arise in the future insofar as disparities in wealth grow and solidify within villages. When traditional beliefs reemerge, they are almost invariably shaped by social and cultural changes that have transpired in the interim.

Forest peoples in Africa. My textual reference is to the account of Mbuti Pygmies in the central African rainforest by Colin Turnbull in his popular book *The Forest People* (1961).

CHAPTER 9

Women and marketing in cross-cultural perspective. In many world areas, women are important or primary market sellers of food and domestically made goods. This pattern has been especially well documented in Africa (see Clark 1994; House-Midamba and Ekechi 1995; Kapchan 1996). The role of Caribbean women marketers in the global economy has been effectively discussed by Freeman (2001). Her article also recasts common assumptions about the role of men in understanding globalization.

The social significance of money. Gift-exchange economies based on personal relations can be complicated or supplanted by the impersonal use of money to buy goods. Although gift exchange and the use of money often intertwine in fact, the difference between them has been documented and discussed in two books, both titled *Gifts and Commodities.* The first of these (Gregory 1982) discusses gifts and commodities in the context of Papua New Guinea. The second (James G. Carrier 1995) considers the same issues in the history of Western societies—namely, the rise of consumer society in the United States and Britain, and the ways in which social relations were correspondingly altered during the nineteenth and twentieth centuries. A contemporary account of commodities and consumption in Papua New Guinea has been authored by Foster (2002). Concerning European history, nineteenth-century scholars such as Karl Marx (1988, original 1844) and Georg Simmel (1990, chapter 5; original 1899) gave powerful accounts of how money can make people feel divorced or alienated from one another and from the fruits of their labor.

Commodities and prestige consumption. In many world areas, numerous manufactured goods have become more prestigious than the local goods they replaced. Important studies of modern commodity consumption have been published by Daniel Miller (2001). The relationship between status, material acquisition, and lifestyle has been critically documented for contemporary French society by Pierre Bourdieu (1984). For a colonial example from Zimbabwe in southern Africa, see Timothy Burke's book *Lifebouy Men, Lux Women* (1996). The contemporary study of luxury commodities and social status has important roots in the classic 1899 study by Thorstein Veblen, *The Theory of the Leisure Class* (1965).

The anthropology of schooling and education. Given the importance of schooling for socialization and for wage employment in many world areas, a host of new ethnographic work on these issues is now being conducted or written up. Among existing monographs, that of Stambach (2000), on schooling in the Mount Kilimanjaro area of Kenya, is particularly significant. The research now emerging often reveals that for many students in developing countries, primary and secondary education does not lead in a predictable way to regular employment or economic satisfaction. Concerning Gebusi, see Knauft 2002a, chapter 7.

Theft and the desire for modern gratification, especially for men. An interesting case study of this issue has been supplied in a book chapter by Holly Wardlow (2002). In many countries of the world, and especially in major towns and cities, high rates of crime are associated with unsatisfied desires for commodities and for a modern means of earning a livelihood. This problem is especially acute among unemployed young men. Concerning Papua New Guinea (see Hart Nibbrig 1992; Goddard 1992, 1995; and Dinnen 1991).

Radio, mass media, popular culture, and nationalism. Recent years have seen an explosion of anthropological interest in the local, national, and international impact of mass media. An important collection of current studies, edited by Ginsburg, Abu-Lughod, and Larkin, is *Media Worlds: Anthropology on New Terrain* (2002). Anthropologists are increasingly aware of how local ideals are dynamically related to the influence of radio; TV; the printed media of newspapers, books, magazines, and comic books; and the "small media" of video and tape-recorded cassettes and circulated brochures, photocopies, and letters—as well as cell phones. "Large" media are particularly susceptible to control by state or international institutions, but audience responses to mass media, as well as local control of "small media," often provide a rich interplay between what is broadcast and what is locally accepted or interpreted.

Schoolchild aspirations easily disappointed. The graduation of children who have little chance of employment has sometimes been termed a "diploma disease" that is especially pronounced in developing countries (Gould 1993, pp. 152–154). At the same time, a lack of education can easily make the situation of young people worse rather than better.

CHAPTER 10

Magic and self-confidence. The anthropologist Bronislaw Malinowski (1954) theorized that magical potions and spells have the effect of giving people more confidence in undertaking activities that are otherwise difficult or dangerous.

Contemporary bride-wealth, bride-price, and/or dowry. Young people in societies from a range of world areas, including Africa, the Pacific Islands, and South and Southeast Asia, are increasingly faced with the tension between a growing desire for personal choice in marriage, family expectations, and inflated demands for bride payment or dowry. These tensions are poignantly depicted in the popular movie *Monsoon Wedding*, by Mira Nair, filmed in 2000 in New Delhi, India. Although the tensions surrounding marriage are for the most part reconciled in this film, their resolution is often compromised or conflicted in reality. Among the Gebusi, the tension between personal choice and family expectation is reflected in the case of the thwarted sister-exchange and its effect on the young woman, Gami, described in chapter 10.

The difficulties and dangers of well-intended intervention by outsiders. The subjugation, suffering, or domination of some members of a society has long been a concern to many if not most anthropologists. But what kind of intervention is best or most appropriate? This question is hard to answer in general; it depends on the specifics of the culture, the personalities of the people involved, and the capacities of the ethnographer. As the scope of proposed interventions gets larger in scale, it is unfortunately true that the possibility of unintended and even disastrous consequences also increases—notwithstanding the good intentions of those involved (see Escobar 1995). Feeling compelled to act, anthropologists increasingly recognize the importance of maintaining active dialogue with local people. It is important that the desires of an ethnographer not override the goals and opinions of those specific people on whose behalf he or she hopes to intervene.

Modern lifestyle, romantic attraction, and stigma. Although marriage choices continue to be strongly influenced by family considerations in many societies, young men and women in a wide range of world areas do have increased personal choice in marriage relative to their parents and grandparents. Increasing choice dovetails with new and locally modern forms of romance associated with the acquisition and use of commodities, mass media images, schooling, and the desire for self-actualization or -advancement, including among women. Recent cases studies concerning this pattern include *Invitations to Love*, a book about love letters and modern romance in Nepal by Laura Ahearn (2001), and *Courtship After Marriage*, a study of love and sexuality in Mexican transnational families by Jennifer Hirsch (2003). As these books and other studies reveal, issues of moral impropriety and stigma can nonetheless remain strong, especially for women. Beyond the case of Gami described in the present chapter, for Melanesia see more generally "Gender Identity, Political Economy, and Modernity in Melanesia and Amazonia" (Knauft 1997). A poignant case study of women's sexual choice and also stigma associated with sex and disease is Jessica Gregg's monograph *Virtually Virgins* (2003), which concerns women in the city of Recife, Brazil.

CHAPTER 11

Ritual change and hybrid performance. Anthropologists have long been aware of mixing or "syncretism" between alternative forms of religious orientation and belief. So, too, diverse economic and social influences impact how rituals and other public enactments are materially performed. For instance, African and Roman Catholic religious images are brought together in Haitian Voodoo. (The name Voodoo itself derives from terms in West African languages for "god," "spirit," or "sacred object.") In addition to documenting the combined significance of newer and older influences on ritual performance, anthropologists strive to understand what they mean for ritual practitioners and their audiences—how significant and personally important these combinations are. Trying to unravel and reflect on this issue was one of my challenges in considering Sayu's dance and its aftermath.

Contemporary vis-à-vis traditional music. Sound clips and associated lyrics of Gebusi string band music, as well as traditional sèance singing, are available under "Gebusi research" on my Web site (type "Bruce Knauft" into www.google.com to get the address). Steven Feld (1982, 1995) has analyzed traditional and contemporary musical forms among the Kaluli, who live twenty-five miles southeast of the Gebusi. He has also produced CD recordings of Kaluli music in relation to sounds of the rainforest environment, including *Voices of the Rainforest* (1991) and *Bosavi: Rainforest Music from Papua New Guinea* (2001).

Concerning global musical influences, see especially Timothy Taylor's book *Global Pop: World Music, World Markets* (1997).

Expressions of local, regional, and national public culture. In many world areas, local rituals are now influenced by, if not directly combined with, displays of regional or national culture (see Hobsbawm and Ranger 1992; Anderson 1991).

These, in turn, are influenced by governments and mass media, including radio, TV, posters, advertisements, and music. The broader study of public culture within nations, regions, and locales has become increasingly important to cultural anthropologists. These interests are reflected in the contemporary journal *Public Culture*, including its special issues on globalization (Appadurai 2001), cosmopolitanism (Breckenridge 2002), and alternative modernities (Gaonkar 2001).

Making fun of tradition. Especially where people have difficulty considering themselves respectably modern on the basis of economic development or material acquisition, cultural assertions of progress may be configured through complementary assertions in which older practices or beliefs are held to be backward, ignorant, or uncivilized. In insular Melanesia, a poignant case in point of this described by Frederick Errington and Deborah Gewertz (1994).

Performing and playing with rules of modern decorum. One of the great and seemingly irrepressible features of human symbolic expression is its ability to play with, reinterpret, and make fun of dominant assertions and doctrines. This capacity was described and analyzed in depth by the Russian literary scholar Mikhail Bakhtin (1968) and the anthropologist Victor Turner (1972). This propensity is evident in displays and festivals such as Mardi Gras, Carnival, and Halloween. Such occasions can include what anthropologists have called "rites of reversal," that is, rituals in which normal social relations or rules of etiquette are playfully disrupted or turned upside-down (see Turner 1972).

The cultural enactment of fragmented social relations. It has often been asserted that social relationships become increasingly fragmented as societies modernize and become more complex and larger in scale. In contrast to social life in a small community such as Yibihilu, where people know and relate to one another in many different ways, social life in towns or cities—and even in a small outpost like the Nomad Station—brings together many people who may know little about one another and interact only fleetingly. This tendency was emphasized and scrutinized by classic European social theorists such as Karl Marx, Ferdinand Tönnies, and Max Weber, and by recent scholars such as Anthony Giddens. It is consistent with this trend that rituals and other major expressions of public culture become increasingly complex, fragmented, and disjunctive as they evoke and symbolize social roles and practices that are increasingly diverse.

CHAPTER 12

No notes.

CONCLUSION

Culture and the proliferation of locally modern institutions. As social life becomes locally modern, it reflects ideals of development and aspirations for progress, however these are locally defined. Given the increasing diversity of contemporary social roles and specializations, it is common for activities to be increasingly compartmentalized or "differentiated" into different institutions—such as churches, markets, businesses, schools, sports leagues, community organizations, and political groups.

Cultures becoming modern in their own distinct ways. Although people in virtually all world areas are subject to modern influences, what it means to be developed or to have progress is locally defined and interpreted (see Knauft 2002c). For anthropologists, this means both that societies share increasingly large patterns of social change and that cultural diversity remains powerful and important. In a contemporary world, cultural diversity is in some ways greater, more complex, and more self-conscious than ever.

List of Persons

Bosap: 1998 — older woman, never married, mother of Kuma, regular market seller

Boyl: 1982 — mother of Sayu, wife of Salip; friend of Eileen; **1998** — deceased

Bulobey: 1982 — active spirit medium, newly married; **1998** — Evangelical Church member, married with five children

Daguwa: 1980 — husband of Saliam, committed suicide by drinking fish poison, died childless

Damya: 1982 — young boy, son of Nolop and Wosip; **1998** — married with one daughter, lead Gasumi string band singer, devoted member of the Catholic Church

Didiga: 1982 — young boy, son of Imba; **1998** — grade six graduate and bachelor, good friend and helper of Bruce

Gami: 1982 — born in Yibihilu very shortly after Bruce and Eileen's departure; **1998** — temporary wife of Guyul; **2001** — wife of Wayabay, mother of one child

Guyul: 1982 — young boy; **1998** — temporary husband of Gami

Gwabi: 1982 — young boy; **1998** — builder and owner of Bruce's house, married with one son

Halia: 1981 — younger brother of Salip, died of sickness eleven days after being initiated

Halowa: 1982 — young boy, younger brother of Yuway; **1998** — member of Evangelical Church, married with four children

Haymp: 1982 — initiate, incipient father of Kubwam; **1998** — deceased

Howe: 1982 — young boy, son of Kawuk; **1998** — young man; member of Catholic Church, singer in the Gasumi Corners string band

Huwa: 1998 — orphaned teenage younger brother of Sayu, Gasumi string band singer

Imba: 1982 — senior man of Yibihilu, father of Didiga; **1998** — deceased

Kawuk: 1982 — cofounder of Yibihilu longhouse, married man with two small children; **1998** — senior man of Gasumi Corners, devoted member of the Catholic Church, married with five children

Keda: 1982 — teenage younger brother of Yuway; **1998** — married with one son, active Catholic Church member

Kubwam: 1982 — born in Yibihilu shortly after Bruce and Eileen's departure; **1998** — temporary wife of Mako

Kuma: 1982 — young boy, son of Bosap; **1998** — marriageable bachelor

Kwelam: 1998 — teenage daughter of Nolop

Mai: 1982 — young daughter of Tewo; **1998** — adult woman, lives with Tewo outside of Kiunga

Mako: 1982 — young boy; **1998** — young man, temporary husband of Kubwam

Marbwi: 1998 — young girl, adopted daughter of Gwabi

Mata: 1982 — teenage boy, solicitor of Bruce; **1998** — married with three children

Modiay: 1982 — initiate, friend of Wahi, transient tryst partner of Nolop; **1989** — widower of Boyl, killer of Sabowey, begins prison term in Port Moresby; **1998** — married with three children, devoted member of the Catholic Church

Mokoyl: 1979 — mother of Saliam, killed by Swiman for the sickness death of his wife

Momiay: 1982 — initiate; **1998** — deceased

Nogo: 1980 — carrier for Bruce and Eileen on first expedition, forewent initiation to marry early; **1998** — husband of Nolop, father of teenage girl

Nolop: 1982 — mother of Damya and Korlis, incipient mother of Kwelam, wife of Wosip, transient tryst partner of Modiay; **1998** — older woman, market seller, wife of Nogo

Sabowey: 1989 — adult man, killed by Modiay for the sickness death of Boyl

Saliam: 1982 — widow of Daguwa, mother of one daughter, wife of Swiman; **1998** — deceased

Salip: 1982 — cofounder of Yibihilu longhouse, husband of Boyl, father of Sayu; **1998** — deceased

Sasaga: 1982 — forewent initiation to establish a temporary relationship with Saliam; **1998** — deceased (from a death adder bite)

Sayu: 1982 — young boy, son of Boyl and Salip, friend of Bruce and Eileen; **c. 1994** — lived in Kiunga; **1998** — bachelor, friend, helper, and confidant of Bruce

Swiman: 1980–82 — carrier for Bruce and Eileen on first expedition, main spirit medium of Yibihilu community, widowered father of Wayabay, married Saliam; **1998** — deceased

Tewo: 1982 — incipient mother of Gami; **1998** — living with husband and family outside Kiunga

Uwano: 1982 — Young adult man, "breadfruit" exchange partner of Bruce; **1998** — deceased October 9

Wahi: 1980–82 — carrier for Bruce and Eileen on first expedition, initiate, friend of Modiay; **1998** — married with four children, lives at Nomad Station, devoted member of the Evangelical Church, helps keep track of aircraft cargo

Warbwi: 1982 — new wife of Yuway; **1998** — wife of Yuway and mother of four children

Wayabay: 1982 — young boy, son of Swiman; **1998** — bachelor, hunter and house builder; **2001** — husband of Gami, father of one child

Willy: 1998 — boy, son of Modiay

Wosip: 1982 — husband of Nolop, father of Damya and Korlis; **1998** — deceased

Yaba: 1982 — widowered jokester in Yibihilu; **1998** — deceased

Yuway: 1980–82 — initiate, carrier for Bruce and Eileen on first expedition, language helper and friend of Bruce; **1998** — husband of Warbwi, father of four children, member of the Seventh Day Adventist Church

Topical Guide for Instructors

List of Topics and Textbook Correspondences

GEBUSI CHAPTER	**Kottak, *Cultural Anthropology, 10th ed.***
Introduction: In Search of Surprise	
Main teaching topics: culture and cultural relativism	Chs. 1, 4
Specific topics: • anthropology and culture • appreciating cultural diversity • problems of human inequality • cultural traditions and cultural change • remote cultures and the modern world	
Chapter 1: Friends in the Forest	
Main teaching topics: ethnographic fieldwork, language, and communication	Chs. 2–3, 7
Specific topics: • colonial history and the ethnographic present • choosing a field site and beginning fieldwork • learning a new language • language and key cultural concepts • exchange and reciprocity with informants • gender relations in the field • ethics and cultural values	

TOPICAL CORRESPONDENCE WITH CHAPTERS OF MAJOR TEXTBOOKS

Kottak, ***Mirror for Humanity, 4th ed.***	**Haviland,** ***Cultural Anthropology, 10th ed.***	**Ember/Ember,** ***Cultural Anthropology, 11th ed.***	**Nanda/Warms,** ***Cultural Anthropology, 7th ed.***
Chs. 1, 3	Ch. 1	Chs. 1–2	Chs. 1, 4
Chs. 2, 5	Chs. 2, 4	Chs. 3–4	Chs. 3, 5

(Continued on next page)

GEBUSI CHAPTER	**Kottak, *Cultural Anthropology, 10th ed.***
Chapter 2: Rhythms of Survival *Main teaching topics:* subsistence and adaptation *Specific topics:* • culture as environmental adaptation • house building in the tropics • nomadism versus sedentism • horticulture versus agricultural intensification • mixed subsistence strategies • subsistence, reciprocity, and exchange • tropical health and disease	Ch. 8
Chapter 3: Lives of Death *Main teaching topics:* life cycle, cosmology, and politics *Specific topics:* • sorcery beliefs and investigations • death and funerals • shamanism and spirit mediumship • sexual antagonism • reciprocity through revenge • ethics and reflexivity in fieldwork	Chs. 3, 9, 13
Chapter 4: Getting Along with Kin and Killers *Main teaching topics:* kinship, marriage, and descent *Specific topics:* • kinship and descent • clans and lineages • marriage, bride-wealth, and exchange • demography and gender • social organization, conflict, and violence • structural inequality and discrimination	Chs. 10–11

TOPICAL CORRESPONDENCE WITH CHAPTERS OF MAJOR TEXTBOOKS

Kottak, ***Mirror for Humanity, 4th ed.***	**Haviland,** ***Cultural Anthropology, 10th ed.***	**Ember/Ember,** ***Cultural Anthropology, 11th ed.***	**Nanda/Warms,** ***Cultural Anthropology, 7th ed.***
Ch. 6	Chs. 6–7	Chs. 5–6	Chs. 7–8
Chs. 7, 9–10	Chs. 8, 12–13	Chs. 12–14	Chs. 6, 12, 15
Ch. 8	Chs. 8–10	Chs. 9–10	Chs. 9–10

GEBUSI CHAPTER	**Kottak, *Cultural Anthropology, 10th ed.***
Chapter 5: Spirits, Sex, and Celebration	
Main teaching topics: sex, gender, and spirituality	Ch. 12
Specific topics: • gender and sexuality • studying sexual culture • gendered symbolism in ritual, song, and myth • male-male sexuality • heterosexual desire and marriage • tolerance of gendered and sexual diversity	
Chapter 6: Ultimate Splendor	
Main teaching topics: religion, ritual, and exchange	Ch. 13
Specific topics: • fertility rites and initiation • costume symbolism and display • rites of passage and liminality • displays of aggression and reconciliation • large-scale food exchange • societal growth and collective celebration	
Chapter 7: Reentry	
Main teaching topic: cultural change	Chs. 15–16
Specific topics: • culture change • ethnographic restudy • technology and fieldwork • colonial history • modern life in remote areas • globalization and migration • ethnography of contemporary institutions	

TOPICAL CORRESPONDENCE WITH CHAPTERS OF MAJOR TEXTBOOKS

Kottak, ***Mirror for Humanity,*** ***4th ed.***	**Haviland,** ***Cultural Anthropology,*** ***10th ed.***	**Ember/Ember,** ***Cultural Anthropology,*** ***11th ed.***	**Nanda/Warms,** ***Cultural Anthropology,*** ***7th ed.***
Ch. 9	Chs. 5, 11	Ch. 8	Ch. 11
Ch. 10	Ch. 13	Ch. 14	Chs. 6, 15
Ch. 11	Ch. 15	Chs. 7, 16	Chs. 13, 17

GEBUSI CHAPTER	**Kottak, *Cultural Anthropology, 10th ed.***
Chapter 8: Yuway's Sacred Decision *Main teaching topics:* religious change and world religions *Specific topics:* • religious conversion and change • global Christianity • world religions vis-à-vis local religions • spiritual belief in a modern world • religious experience and personal choice	Ch. 13
Chapter 9: Pennies and Peanuts, Rugby and Radios *Main teaching topics:* market economy, schools, and sports *Specific topics:* • money versus gift-exchange • local markets • women as marketsellers • schooling and sports: gendered differences • radio and mass media in rural areas • desire for commodities and problems of modern crime	Ch. 16
Chapter 10: Mysterious Romance, Marital Choice *Main teaching topics:* changes in sex, romance, and marriage *Specific topics:* • male and female agency in romance • commodities and modern love magic • decline of prescribed marriage • marital choice and moral constraint • decline of ritual homosexuality	Chs. 2, 11–12

TOPICAL CORRESPONDENCE WITH CHAPTERS OF MAJOR TEXTBOOKS

Kottak, ***Mirror for Humanity, 4th ed.***	**Haviland,** ***Cultural Anthropology, 10th ed.***	**Ember/Ember,** ***Cultural Anthropology, 11th ed.***	**Nanda/Warms,** ***Cultural Anthropology, 7th ed.***
Ch. 10	Ch. 13	Ch. 14	Ch. 15
Ch. 12	Chs. 7, 16	Chs. 6, 11	Ch. 8
Ch. 8	Ch. 8	Chs. 8–9	Chs. 9, 11

GEBUSI CHAPTER	**Kottak, *Cultural Anthropology, 10th ed.***
Chapter 11: Sayu's Dance and After *Main teaching topics:* public culture, ethnicity, and nation making *Specific topics:* • regional and national culture • national rites and celebrations • ethnic identity and display • reinventing traditions • history and folklore • uses of the cultural past	Chs. 6, 14, 17
Chapter 12: Toward the End *Main teaching topics:* revisiting culture: humanity and fieldwork in the contemporary world *Specific topics:* • concluding fieldwork • reappreciating cultural diversity • reappreciating cultural change • the power of continuing human connections	Chs. 3–4
Conclusion: Sixteen Years and a World of Change *Main teaching topic:* global trends of cultural change *Specific topics:* • culture change in the contemporary world • local ways of becoming modern • ongoing role of cultural diversity • global change • the importance of communication across cultures	Chs. 15–17

TOPICAL CORRESPONDENCE WITH CHAPTERS OF MAJOR TEXTBOOKS

Kottak, ***Mirror for Humanity, 4th ed.***	**Haviland,** ***Cultural Anthropology, 10th ed.***	**Ember/Ember,** ***Cultural Anthropology, 11th ed.***	**Nanda/Warms,** ***Cultural Anthropology, 7th ed.***
Chs. 4, 13	Ch. 14	Ch. 15	Chs. 14, 16
Chs. 2–3	Ch. 2	Ch. 2	Chs. 1, 3
Chs. 11–13	Chs. 15–16	Ch. 16	Ch. 17

References

Ahearn, Laura. 2001. *Invitations to Love: Literacy, Love Letters, and Social Change in Nepal.* Ann Arbor: University of Michigan Press.

Allen, Michael R. 1967. *Male Cults and Secret Initiations in Melanesia.* Melbourne: Melbourne University Press.

Amit-Talai, Vered (Ed.). 1999. *Constructing the Field: Ethnographic Fieldwork in the Contemporary World.* New York: Routledge.

Anderson, Benedict. 1991. *Imagined Communities: Reflections on the Origin and Spread of Nationalism,* rev. ed. London: Verso.

Ankarloo, Bengt, and Stuart Clark. 1999. *Witchcraft and Magic in Europe: The Eighteenth and Nineteenth Centuries.* Philadelphia: University of Pennsylvania Press.

———. 2002. *The Period of the Witch Trials.* Philadelphia: University of Pennsylvania Press.

Appadurai, Arjun (Ed.). 2001. *Globalization.* Durham, NC: Duke University Press.

Bakhtin, Mikhail M. 1968. *Rabelais and His World.* Cambridge, MA: MIT Press.

Barlow, Kathleen, and Steven Winduo (Eds.). 1997. Logging the Southwest Pacific: Perspectives from Papua New Guinea, Solomon Islands, and Vanuatu. *The Contemporary Pacific* 19 (1) (special issue).

Barth, Fredrik. 1975. *Ritual and Knowledge Among the Baktaman of New Guinea.* New Haven, CT: Yale University Press.

Behar, Ruth. 1993. *Translated Woman: Crossing the Border with Esperanza's Story.* Boston: Beacon Press.

Behar, Ruth, and Deborah A. Gordon (Eds.). 1995. *Women Writing Culture.* Berkeley: University of California Press.

Boddy, Janice P. 1989. *Wombs and Alien Spirits: Women, Men, and the Zar Cult in Northern Sudan.* Madison: University of Wisconsin Press.

Bodley, John H. 1999. *Victims of Progress,* 4th ed. Mountain View, CA: Mayfield.

Bonnemère, Pascale (Ed.) 2004. *Women as Unseen Characters: Male Ritual in Papua New Guinea.* Philadelphia: University of Pennsylvania Press.

Bourdieu, Pierre. 1984. *Distinction: A Social Critique of the Judgment of Taste.* Cambridge, MA: Harvard University Press.

Breckenridge, Carol A. (Ed.). 2002. *Cosmopolitanism.* Durham, NC: Duke University Press.

Brown, Karen McCarthy. 1994. Fundamentalism and the Control of Women. In *Fundamentalism and Gender.* Edited by John S. Hawley, pp. 175–201. New York: Oxford University Press.

———. 2001. *Mama Lola: A Vodou Priestess in Brooklyn* (updated and expanded ed.). Berkeley: University of California Press.

Brown, Paula. 1978. *Highland Peoples of New Guinea.* Cambridge: Cambridge University Press.

Brunois, Florence. 1999. In Paradise, the Forest is Open and Covered in Flowers. In *Expecting the Day of Wrath: Versions of the Millennium in Papua New Guinea.* Edited by Christin Kocher Schmid, pp. 111–130. Boroko, NCD, Papua New Guinea: National Research Institute, Monograph #36.

Burke, Timothy. 1996. *Lifebuoy Men, Lux Women: Commodification, Consumption, and Cleanliness in Modern Zimbabwe.* Durham, NC: Duke University Press.

Burling, Robbins. 1984. *Learning a Field Language.* Ann Arbor: University of Michigan Press.

Burridge, Kenelm O. L. 1960. *Mambu: A Melanesian Millennium.* London: Methuen.

Byram, Michael and Michael Fleming (Eds.). 1998. *Language Learning in Intercultural Perspective: Approaches Through Drama and Ethnography.* New York: Cambridge University Press.

Cantrell, Eileen M. (Knauft). 1998. Woman the Sexual, a Question of When: A Study of Gebusi Adolescence. In *Adolescence in Pacific Island Societies.* Edited by Gilbert H. Herdt and Stephen C. Leavitt, pp. 92–120. Pittsburgh: University of Pittsburgh Press.

Carrier, James G. 1995. *Gifts and Commodities: Exchange and Western Capitalism Since 1700.* London: Routledge.

Carrier, Joseph. 1995. *De los Otros: Intimacy and Homosexuality Among Mexican Men.* New York: Columbia University Press.

Carsten, Janet. 2000. *Cultures of Relatedness: New Approaches to the Study of Kinship.* New York: Cambridge University Press.

Chagnon, Napoleon A. 1997. *Yanomamo.* 5th ed. Fort Worth, TX: Harcourt Brace.

Clark, Gracia. 1994. *Onions Are My Husband: Survival and Accumulation by West African Market Women.* Chicago: University of Chicago Press.

Coffey, Amanda. 1999. *The Ethnographic Self: Fieldwork and the Representation of Identity.* Thousand Oaks, CA: Sage.

Collier, Jane Fishburne and Sylvia Junko Yanagisako (Eds.). 1987. *Gender and Kinship: Essays Toward a Unified Analysis.* Stanford, CA: Stanford University Press.

Comaroff, Jean and John L. Comaroff. 1999. Occult Economies and the Violence of Abstraction: Notes from the South African Postcolony. *American Ethnologist* 26:279–303.

Das, Veena et al. (Eds.). 2000. *Violence and Subjectivity.* Berkeley: University of California Press.

———. (Eds.). 2001. *Remaking a World: Violence, Social Suffering, and Recovery.* Berkeley: University of California Press.

d'Emilio, John D. 1983. *Sexual Identities, Sexual Communities.* Chicago: University of Chicago Press.

di Leonardo, Micaela (Ed.). 1991. *Gender at the Crossroads of Knowledge: Feminist Anthropology in the Postmodern Era.* Berkeley: University of California Press.

Dinnen, Sinclair. 1991. *Law and Order in a Weak State: Crime and Politics in Papua New Guinea.* Honolulu: University of Hawaii Press.

Douglas, Mary (Ed.). 1970. *Witchcraft Confessions and Accusations.* London: Tavistock.

Dresch, Paul, Wendy James, and David Parkin (Eds.). 2000. *Anthropologists in a Wider World: Essays on Field Research.* New York: Berghahn.

Dumont, Jean-Paul. 1978. *The Headman and I: Ambiguity and Ambivalence in the Fieldworking Experience.* Austin: University of Texas Press.

Durkheim, Émile. 1965. *The Elementary Forms of the Religious Life.* New York: Free Press.

Dwyer, Peter D. 1989. *The Pigs That Ate the Garden: A Human Ecology from Papua New Guinea.* Ann Arbor: University of Michigan Press.

Eliade, Mircea. 1964. *Shamanism: Archaic Techniques of Ecstasy.* New York: Bollingen.

Erikson, Kai T. 1966 *Wayward Puritans: A Study in the Sociology of Deviance.* New York: Wiley.

Ernst, Thomas M. 1991. Onabasulu Male Homosexuality: Cosmology, Affect, and Prescribed Male Homosexual Activity Among the Onabasulu of the Great Papuan Plateau. *Oceania* 62:1–11.

Errington, Frederick, and Deborah Gewertz. 1994. From Darkness to Light in the George Brown Jubilee: The Invention of Non-Tradition and the Inscription of a National History in East New Britain. *American Ethnologist* 21:102–122.

Escobar, Arturo. 1995. *Encountering Development: The Making and Unmaking of the Third World.* Princeton, NJ: Princeton University Press.

Evans-Pritchard, E. E. 1937. *Witchcraft, Oracles, and Magic Among the Azande.* Oxford: Clarendon Press.

Feil, Daryl K. 1987. *The Evolution of Highland Papua New Guinea Societies.* Cambridge: Cambridge University Press.

Feld, Steven. 1982. *Sound and Sentiment: Birds, Weeping, Poetics, and Song in Kaluli Expression.* Philadelphia: University of Pennsylvania Press.

———. 1991. *Voices of the Rainforest* (CD sound recording). Salem, MA: Rykodisc.

———. 1995. From Schizophonia to Schismogenesis: The Discourses and Practices of World Music and World Beat. In *The Traffic in Culture: Refiguring Art and Anthropology.* Edited by George E. Marcus and Fred R. Myers, pp. 196–226. Berkeley: University of California Press.

———. 2001. *Bosavi: Rainforest Music from Papua New Guinea* (sound recording, 3 CDs). Washington, DC: Smithsonian Folkways Recordings.

Finegan, Edward, and Niko Besnier. 1989. *Language: Its Structure and Use.* San Diego: Harcourt Brace Jovanovich.

Fortune, Reo F. 1932. *Sorcerers of Dobu: The Social Anthropology of the Dobu Islanders.* London: Dutton.

———. 1935. *Manus Religion.* Philadelphia: American Philosophical Society.

Foster, Robert J. 2002. *Materializing the Nation: Commodities, Consumption, and Media in Papua New Guinea.* Bloomington: Indiana University Press.

Fox, Robin. 1967. *Kinship and Marriage: An Anthropological Perspective.* Harmondsworth, England: Penguin.

Freeman, Carla S. 2001. Is Local : Global as Feminine : Masculine? Rethinking the Gender of Globalization. *Signs* 21:1007–1037.

Fry, Peter. 1976. *Spirits of Protest.* Cambridge: Cambridge University Press.

Gaonkar, Dilip Parameshwar (Ed.). 2001. *Alter/Native Modernities.* Durham, NC: Duke University Press.

Gell, Alfred. 1975. *Metamorphosis of the Cassowaries: Umeda Society, Language, and Ritual.* London: Athlone.

Geschiere, Peter. 1997. *The Modernity of Witchcraft: Politics and the Occult in Postcolonial Africa.* Charlottesville: University of Virginia Press.

Gewertz, Deborah, and Frederick Errington. 1996. On PepsiCo and Piety in a Papua New Guinea Modernity. *American Ethnologist* 23:476–493.

———. 1998. Sleights of Hand in the Construction of Desire in Papua New Guinea Modernity. *Contemporary Pacific* 10(2): 345–368.

Ginsburg, Faye D., Lila Abu-Lughod, and Brian Larkin (Eds.). 2002. *Media Worlds: Anthropology on New Terrain.* Berkeley: University of California Press.

Goddard, Michael. 1992. Big-Men, Thief: The Social Organization of Gangs in Port Moresby. *Canberra Anthropology* 15:20–34.

———. 1995. The Rascal Road: Crime, Prestige, and Development in Papua New Guinea. *Contemporary Pacific* 7:55–80.

Golde, Peggy (Ed.). 1986. *Women in the Field: Anthropological Experiences.* Berkeley: University of California Press.

Goody, Jack. 1971. *Kinship: Selected Readings.* Harmondsworth, England: Penguin.

Gould, W. T. S. 1993. *People and Education in the Third World.* Harlow, Essex, UK: Longman.

Gourevitch, Philip. 1998. *We Wish to Inform You That Tomorrow We Will Be Killed with Our Families: Stories from Rwanda.* New York: Farrar, Straus & Giroux.

Greenhouse, Carol J. (Ed.). 1996. *A Moment's Notice: Time Politics Across Cultures.* Ithaca, NY: Cornell University Press.

Gregg, Jessica L. 2003. *Virtually Virgins: Sexual Strategies and Cervical Cancer in Recife, Brazil.* Stanford, CA: Stanford University Press.

Gregory, Chris. A. 1982. *Gifts and Commodities.* London: Academic Press.

Grewal, Inderpal, and Caren Kaplan. 2001. *An Introduction to Women's Studies: Gender in a Transnational World.* New York: McGraw-Hill.

Hallpike, Christopher R. 1977. *Bloodshed and Vengeance in the Papuan Mountains: The Generation of Conflict in Tuade Society.* Oxford: Clarendon Press.

Hansen, Thomas Blom. 1999, *The Saffron Wave: Democracy and Hindu Nationalism in Modern India.* Princeton, NJ: Princeton University Press.

———. 2001. Wages of Violence: Naming and Identity in Postcolonial Bombay. Princeton, NJ: Princeton University Press.

Hart Nibbrig, Nand E. 1992. Rascals in Paradise: Urban Gangs in Papua New Guinea. *Pacific Studies* 15:115–34.

Hefner, Robert W. (Ed.). 1993. *Conversion to Christianity: Historical and Anthropological Perspectives on a Great Transformation.* Berkeley: University of California Press.

Heider, Karl G. 1979. *Grand Valley Dani: Peaceful Warriors.* New York: Holt, Rinehart and Winston.

Herdt, Gilbert H. 1981. *Guardians of the Flutes: Idioms of Masculinity.* New York: McGraw-Hill.

——— (Ed.). 1982. *Rituals of Manhood: Male Initiation in Papua New Guinea.* Berkeley: University of California Press.

———. 1987. *The Sambia: Ritual and Gender in New Guinea.* New York: Holt, Rinehart & Winston.

——— (Ed.). 1992. *Gay Culture in America.* Boston: Beacon.

——— (Ed.). 1993. *Ritualized Homosexuality in Melanesia*, rev. ed. Berkeley: University of California Press.

——— (Ed.). 1994. *Third Sex, Third Gender.* New York: Zone Books.

———. 1997. *Same Sex, Different Cultures.* Boulder, CO: Westview Press.

———. 1999. *Sambia Sexual Culture: Essays from the Field.* Chicago: University of Chicago Press.

———. 2003. *Secrecy and Cultural Reality: Utopian Ideologies of the New Guinea Men's House.* Ann Arbor: University of Michigan Press.

Herdt, Gilbert H., and Andrew Boxer. 1996. *Children of Horizons: How Gay and Lesbian Youth Are Forging a New Way Out of the Closet.* Boston: Beacon Press.

Hinton, Alexander Laban (Ed.). 2002. *Annihilating Difference: The Anthropology of Genocide.* Berkeley: University of California Press.

Hirsch, Jennifer S. 2003. *A Courtship After Marriage: Sexuality and Love in Mexican Transnational Families.* Berkeley: University of California Press.

Hobsbawm, Eric J., and Terence O. Ranger (Eds.). 1992. *The Invention of Tradition.* Cambridge: Cambridge University Press.

Hodgen, Margaret T. 1964. *Early Anthropology in the Sixteenth and Seventeenth Centuries.* Philadelphia: University of Pennsylvania Press.

Hoffer, Peter Charles. 1996. *The Devil's Disciples: Makers of the Salem Witchcraft Trials.* Baltimore: Johns Hopkins University Press.

House-Midamba, Bessie, and Felix K. Ekechi (Eds.). 1995. *African Market Women and Economic Power: The Role of Women in African Economic Development.* Westport, CT: Greenwood Press.

Hughes, Diane O., and Thomas R. Trautmann (Eds.). 1995. *Time: Histories and Ethnologies.* Ann Arbor: University of Michigan Press.

Hugh-Jones, Stephen. 1992. Yesterday's Luxuries, Tomorrow's Necessities: Business and Barter in Northwest Amazonia. In *Barter, Exchange, and Value: An Anthropological Perspective.* Edited by Caroline Humphrey and Stephen Hugh-Jones, pp. 42–74. Cambridge: Cambridge University Press.

Inda, Jonathan Xavier, and Renato Rosaldo (Eds.). 2001. *The Anthropology of Globalization: A Reader.* Malden, MA: Blackwell.

Jackson, Bruce, and Edward D. Ives (Eds.). 1996. *The World Observed: Reflections on the Fieldwork Process.* Urbana: University of Illinois Press.

Jenkins, Philip. 2002. *The Next Christendom: The Coming of Global Christianity.* Oxford: Oxford University Press.

Johnson, Allen W., and Timothy Earle. 1987. *The Evolution of Human Societies: From Foraging Group to Agrarian State.* Stanford, CA: Stanford University Press.

Kapchan, Deborah A. 1996. *Gender on the Market: Moroccan Women and the Revoicing of Tradition.* Philadelphia: University of Pennsylvania Press.

Katz, Richard. 1982. *Boiling Energy: Community Healing Among the Kalahari !Kung.* Cambridge, MA: Harvard University Press.

Kelly, Raymond C. 1976. Witchcraft and Sexual Relations: An Exploration in the Social and Semantic Implications of the Structure of Belief. In *Man and Woman in the New Guinea Highlands.* Edited by Paula Brown and Georgeda Buchbinder, pp. 36–53. Washington, DC: American Anthropological Association.

———. 1988. Etoro Suidology: A Reassessment of the Pig's Role in the Prehistory and Comparative Ethnology of New Guinea. In *Mountain Papuans: Historical and Comparative Perspectives from New Guinea Fringe Highlands Societies.* Edited by James F. Weiner, pp. 111–186. Ann Arbor: University of Michigan Press.

Kirsch, Stuart. 1997. Lost Tribes: Indigenous People and the Social Imaginary. *Anthropological Quarterly* 70:58–67.

Kleinman, Arthur, Veena Das, and Margaret Lock (Eds.). 1997. *Social Suffering.* Berkeley: University of California Press.

Knauft, Bruce M. 1978. Cargo Cults and Relational Separation. *Behavior Science Research* 13:185–240.

———. 1985a. *Good Company and Violence: Sorcery and Social Action in a Lowland New Guinea Society.* Berkeley: University of California Press.

———. 1985b. Ritual Form and Permutation in New Guinea: Implications of Symbolic Process for Sociopolitical Evolution. *American Ethnologist* 21: 321–340

———. 1986. Text and Social Practice: Narrative "Longing" and Bisexuality Among the Gebusi of New Guinea. *Ethos* 14:252–281.

———. 1987a. Homosexuality in Melanesia. *Journal of Psychoanalytic Anthropology* 10:155–191.

———. 1987b. Managing Sex and Anger: Tobacco and Kava Use Among the Gebusi of Papua New Guinea. In *Drugs in Western Pacific Societies: Relations of Substance.* Edited by Lamont Lindstrom, pp. 73–98. Lanham, MD: University Press of America.

———. 1987c. Reconsidering Violence in Simple Human Societies: Homicide Among the Gebusi of New Guinea. *Current Anthropology* 28:457–500.

———. 1989. Imagery, Pronouncement, and the Aesthetics of Reception in Gebusi Spirit Mediumship. In *The Religious Imagination in New Guinea.* Edited by Gilbert H. Herdt and Michele Stephen, pp. 67–98. New Brunswick, NJ: Rutgers University Press.

———. 1993. *South Coast New Guinea Cultures: History, Comparison, Dialectic.* Cambridge: Cambridge University Press.

———. 1996. *Genealogies for the Present in Cultural Anthropology*. New York: Routledge.

———. 1997. Gender Identity, Political Economy, and Modernity in Melanesia and Amazonia. *Journal of the Royal Anthropological Institute* 3:233–259.

———. 1998a. How the World Turns Upside Down: Changing Geographies of Power and Spiritual Influence Among the Gebusi. In *Fluid Ontologies: Myth, Ritual, and Philosophy in the Highlands of Papua New Guinea*. Edited by Laurence R. Goldman and Chris Ballard, pp. 143–161. Westport, CT: Bergin & Garvey.

———. 1998b. Creative Possessions: Spirit Mediumship and Millennial Economy Among Gebusi of Papua New Guinea. In *Bodies and Persons in Africa and Melanesia*. Edited by Michael Lambek and Andrew Strathern, pp. 197–209. Cambridge University Press.

———. 1999. *From Primitive to Postcolonial in Melanesia and Anthropology*. Ann Arbor: University of Michigan Press.

———. 2002a. *Exchanging the Past: A Rainforest World of Before and After*. Chicago: University of Chicago Press.

———. 2002b. Trials of the Oxymodern: Public Practice at Nomad Station. In *Critically Modern*. Edited by Bruce M. Knauft, pp. 105–143. Bloomington: Indiana University Press.

——— (Ed.). 2002c. *Critically Modern: Alternatives, Alterities, Anthropologies*. Bloomington, IN: Indiana University Press.

———. 2002d. Not Just for Fun: Formalized Conflict and Games of War in Melanesia. In *War and Games (Studies on the Nature of War*, Vol. 3). T. J. Cornell and T. B. Allen (Eds.). San Marino: Boydell Press/Center for Interdisciplinary Research on Social Stress.

———. 2004a. Relating to Women: Female Presence in Melanesian Male Cults. In *Women as Unseen Characters: Male Ritual in Papua New Guinea*. Pascale Bonnemère (Ed.). Philadelphia: University of Pennsylvania Press.

———. 2004b. What Ever Happened to Ritual Homosexuality? *Annual Review of Sex Research* (forthcoming).

Koch, Klaus-Friedrich. 1974. *War and Peace in Jalemo: The Management of Conflict in Highland New Guinea*. Cambridge, MA: Harvard University Press.

Kors, Alan Charles and Edward Peters (Eds.). 2001. *Witchcraft in Europe, 400–1700: A Documentary History*, 2nd ed. Philadelphia: University of Pennsylvania Press.

Kosellek, Reinhart. 1985. *Futures Past: On the Semantics of Historical Time*. Cambridge, MA: MIT Press.

Kratz, Corinne A. 1994. *Affecting Performance: Meaning, Movement, and Experience in Okiek Women's Initiation*. Washington, DC: Smithsonian Institution Press.

Kulick, Don, and Margaret Willson (Eds.). 1995. *Taboo: Sex, Identity, and Erotic Subjectivity in Anthropological Fieldwork*. New York: Routledge.

Kunze Michael. 1987. *Highroad to the Stake: A Tale of Witchcraft*. Chicago: University of Chicago Press.

Kuper, Adam. 1988. *The Invention of Primitive Society: Transformations of an Illusion.* London: Routledge.

Laine, Marlene de. 2000. *Fieldwork, Participation, and Practice: Ethics and Dilemmas in Qualitative Research.* Thousand Oaks, CA: Sage.

Lambek, Michael. 1981. *Human Spirits: A Cultural Account of Trance in Mayotte.* New York: Cambridge University Press.

Lancaster, Roger N., and Micaela di Leonardo (Eds.). 1997. *The Gender/Sexuality Reader: Culture, History, Political Economy.* New York: Routledge.

Langness, Lewis L. 1967. Sexual Antagonism in the New Guinea Highlands: A Bena Bena Example. *Oceania* 37:161–177.

———. 1974. Ritual Power and Male Domination in the New Guinea Highlands. *Ethos* 2:189–212.

———. 1999. *Men and "Woman" in New Guinea.* Novato, CA: Chandler & Sharp.

Lareau, Annette and Jeffrey Shult (Eds.). 1996. *Journeys Through Ethnography: Realistic Accounts of Fieldwork.* Boulder, CO: Westview Press.

Lawrence, Peter. 1964. *Road Belong Cargo: A Study of Cargo Cults in the Southern Madang District, New Guinea.* New York: Humanities Press.

Lévi-Strauss, Claude. 1969. *The Elementary Structures of Kinship.* Boston: Beacon Press.

Lewis, Ioan M. 2003. *Ecstatic Religion: A Study of Shamanism and Spirit Possession,* 3rd ed. New York: Routledge.

Lindstrom, Lamont. 1993. *Cargo Cult: Strange Stories of Desire from Melanesia and Beyond.* Honolulu: University of Hawaii Press.

Luhrmann, Tanya M. 1989. *Persuasions of the Witch's Craft: Ritual Magic in Contemporary England.* Cambridge, MA: Harvard University Press.

Lurie, Nancy Oestreich. 1999. *Women and the Invention of American Anthropology.* Prospect Heights, IL: Waveland Press.

Lutkehaus, Nancy C., and Paul B. Roscoe (Eds.). 1995. *Gender Rituals: Female Initiation in Melanesia.* New York: Routledge.

MacClancy, Jeremy (Ed.). 2002. *Exotic No More: Anthropology on the Front Lines.* Chicago: University of Chicago Press.

Malinowski, Bronislaw. 1954. *Magic, Science, and Religion, and Other Essays.* Garden City, NY: Doubleday.

Mamdani, Mahmood. 2001. *When Victims Become Killers: Colonialism, Nativism, and the Genocide in Rwanda.* Princeton, NJ: Princeton University Press.

Marcus, Julie (Ed.). 1993. *First in Their Field: Women and Australian Anthropology.* Melbourne: Melbourne University Press.

Marwick, Max (Ed.). 1982. *Witchcraft and Sorcery: Selected Readings,* 2nd ed. New York: Penguin.

Marx, Karl. 1988. The Power of Money in Bourgeois Society. In *The Economic and Philosophical Manuscripts of 1844.* By Karl Marx, pp. 135–140. New York: Prometheus Books.

Mascia-Lees, Frances E. 2000. *Gender and Anthropology.* Prospect Heights, IL: Waveland Press.

Mauss, Marcel. 1967. *The Gift.* New York: Norton. (Original, French, 1925.)

Index

GOVERNMENT AND LABOR

The Role of Government in
Union-Management Relations

GOVERNMENT AND LABOR

The Role of Government in Union-Management Relations

HERBERT R. NORTHRUP, Ph.D.

Professor of Industry
Wharton School of Finance and Commerce
University of Pennsylvania

GORDON F. BLOOM, Ph.D., LL.B.

President, Elm Farm Foods Company

1963

RICHARD D. IRWIN, INC.

HOMEWOOD, ILLINOIS

First Printing, May, 1963

Second Printing, July, 1964

Library of Congress Catalog Card No. 63–16885

PRINTED IN THE UNITED STATES OF AMERICA

To Eleanor *and* Marjorie

PREFACE

Government intervention in and control of the union-management relationship has become of increasing importance during the twenty years in which the authors have been researching, teaching, and practicing in the industrial relations field. The authors have attempted to convey to the reader the enormous and pervasive effects of federal and state legislation in guiding, determining, or otherwise affecting decision making by unions and management. Throughout the book, the material is carefully cross-referenced so that chapters dealing with one aspect of government intervention, or with a particular law, are treated in perspective with reference to the total framework of the role of government.

A major objective of this book has been the integration of economic facts, economic analysis, law, and practical behavior in labor-management relations so that the student may acquire not only an awareness of the subject, but also an understanding of conflicting views as to the repercussions certain legislative or administrative acts have had on industrial relations in particular areas or industries.

In this controversial field, the authors have made every attempt to present conflicting views and ideas objectively and thoroughly. Where opinions or ideas are expressed, or proposals made for change, the supporting evidence is presented and the opinions and proposals are clearly set forth as such.

The main interest throughout has been in making available to the student, teacher, and practitioner a book which discusses the role of government in industrial relations in a clear, comprehensive, and interesting fashion. The material has been organized in a manner designed to make the study of this field both enjoyable and understandable. Part I contains a general introduction and background to the field of study. Part II deals with the role of government as a supporter of collective bargaining, a controller of tactics, and a policeman of rights. Part III deals with the role of government as an inducing or compelling agent to obtain peaceful settlement. Part IV discusses the government as an employer. Part V is devoted to concluding remarks and observations.

Many persons have been most helpful in the development of this book. Mr. John Litwack read and commented upon Chapters 2–7. The material in many other chapters was significantly improved by provocative discussions with Professors George W. Taylor, William Gomberg, and John Perry Horlacher of the Wharton School. The materials in Chapters 9, 11, and 14 are based upon a series of studies financed by the Committee on Faculty Projects of the Wharton School with funds provided by the Ford Foundation. The authors are grateful to Dr. Willis J. Winn, Dean of the Wharton School, for this assistance, and to Dr. Richard L. Rowan, Assistant Professor of Industry, at Wharton, who also worked on this project, for aid in research and development of the material. Mrs. Margaret E. Doyle and Mrs. Mary Ross typed the manuscript and performed other valuable clerical duties.

Among the many persons who were most helpful in supplying information to the authors were Messrs. William Simkin, Director, Federal Mediation and Conciliation Service; Eric Schmertz, Member, New York State Board of Mediation; Hyman Parker, Hearings Officer, Michigan Labor Mediation Board; Allan Weisenfeld, Executive Secretary, New Jersey Board of Mediation; A. M. Goldberg, Executive Secretary, New York State Labor Relations Board; Charles Douds, Director, Pennsylvania State Mediation Service; Paul Tinning, Oregon State Conciliator; and members of the staffs of the National Labor Relations Board, National Mediation Board, Wisconsin Employment Relations Board, and the Minnesota Division of Conciliation, among others.

The authors are grateful to the following organizations, publishers, and journals for permission to quote or to utilize copyrighted material: National Industrial Conference Board, McGraw-Hill Book Company, *Journal of Business, Industrial and Labor Relations Review, Labor Law Journal,* The American Academy of Political and Social Science, Committee for Economic Development, American Economic Association, *Journal of Political Economy,* the Industrial Relations Section of Princeton University, and the Bureau of National Affairs, Inc. In the interests of uniformity, NLRB cases in footnotes to the text are cited in the Bureau of National Affairs, Inc. compilation, referred to as LRRM; footnotes citing LRR refer to the Labor Relations Reporter published by the same organization.

This book represents a joint undertaking for which joint responsibility is shared. The authors hope that their combination of academic, government, legal, and business experience in the field of labor economics, labor law, and labor relations has enabled them to integrate into this book facts and ideas which will make this field of public policy as vital and interesting to the reader and student as it is to them.

The opinions expressed herein are the responsibilities solely of the authors and are not to be attributed to any company, institution, or organization with which either author is now, or ever has been in the past, associated.

The dedication is a tribute to our respective wives who have done so much to make this book possible by, among many other things, taking charge of the household while allowing us to disappear into third-floor studies.

HERBERT R. NORTHRUP

GORDON F. BLOOM

March 1, 1963

CONTENTS

PART III. INTERVENTION IN LABOR DISPUTES

PART I

Introduction

In Part I the scope of the problem which will be the subject of our investigation in the balance of this book is defined.

We shall see that relationships between government and labor are many and complex, and that labor laws provide a setting for labor problems rather than a solution.

Chapter 1 THE DYNAMICS OF LABOR LAW

Americans pride themselves on having maintained free collective bargaining and a free labor market in a world which is becoming increasingly regimented and collectivized. Our pride in this accomplishment is justifiable, for the freedom of the individual which has been preserved in these crucial areas strengthens the democratic processes upon which our basic liberties depend.

But the degree of freedom of our collective bargaining is relative. It is relatively unrestricted when compared with labor relations in the Soviet Union and other countries in the Communist bloc. On the other hand, any unbiased factual appraisal of labor relations in this country would reveal a patchwork of laws and regulations which have continually eroded and narrowed the field of individual action. So all-pervasive is the influence of government in the labor arena that a text on the subject of "labor and government" would be little different from a textbook on the general subject of labor. For whether we discuss the history and development of organized labor, collective bargaining, strikes, picketing, injunctions, wages and hours, social security and unemployment compensation, or any of the other subjects customarily covered in such treatises, the influence of government—federal, state, or local—has become of paramount importance.

This book has a limited objective. It does not seek to explore all of the possible ramifications of government and labor. It is concerned only with government control of union-management relations. In order to treat this subject in depth, we shall be compelled to omit consideration of minimum wage and hour legislation, social security and unemployment compensation, child labor, and aid to the indigent and aged, even though it can be argued that government intervention in these various areas affects the scope of bargaining between labor and management, and therefore is relevant to a discussion of government control of union-management relations.

GOVERNMENT AT THE BARGAINING TABLE

The government is always present at the bargaining table whenever labor and union representatives meet. The importance of this proposition cannot be understood by a mere cataloguing of various statutes relating to collective bargaining. Labor legislation does not affect collective bargaining piecemeal. The student must attempt to gain an insight into the impact on day-to-day union-management relations of the totality of legislation in this field.

In subsequent chapters, we shall have occasion to consider in detail the major statutes affecting collective bargaining. As each of these statutes is presented and reviewed in turn, the general provisions seem to be clear, and the reader is apt to get the impression that labor legislation in this country constitutes a coherent set of guideposts for unions and management to follow in the process of collective bargaining. Unfortunately, the guideposts are not clear; the statutes reflect conflicting philosophies enacted during widely separated periods of time; and there are conflicts and inconsistencies between various sections of individual statutes and among the various statutes themselves.

Much of the language of the Taft-Hartley Act, for example, was left deliberately vague, since Congress recognized the impossibility of spelling out in detail all the various possible circumstances which might arise in the complexity of actual events. The application of the general statutory purpose was left to an administrative board, the National Labor Relations Board. This principle is sound, but what Congress did not foresee is that the Board, whose members are appointed by the President, would change its interpretation of the law with each change in political administration! For example, the Board in power during the Eisenhower administration overturned more than thirty important precedents of the predecessor Truman and Roosevelt boards.[1] In October, 1961, the newly reconstituted Kennedy administration Board, with a new chairman and a newly appointed liberal member, overturned two decisions handed down only the previous February by the Eisenhower Board. These two cases—the General Motors decision involving the legality of an agency shop in a state having a "right-to-work" law, and the Calumet Contractors case involving the legality of informational picketing—both involved important policy matters in the field of labor relations. The statutes were not clear on either of the points involved; and, as can be seen from the reversal of opinions, the issues cannot

[1] 48 LRRR 95 Anal, October 9, 1961.

have been very clear to the National Labor Relations Board, either. Unfortunately, this sort of cloudy issue frequently occurs in collective bargaining. Each case as it arises is always different enough so that there is some question as to whether or not the statutory language covers it.

The reader should therefore approach labor legislation with a critical eye and with an appreciation of its basic inadequacy to cope with the complex factual situations of our economic environment. It may, perhaps, assist the reader to gain an insight into the complexity of these problems by imagining himself in the position of a director of industrial relations for a large steel plant which is negotiating a contract with the United Steelworkers. What are some of the practical problems which might arise during such negotiations which would relate to the influence of government on the collective bargaining process?

1. If the company is a major supplier of steel—and particularly if negotiations are proceeding on an industry-wide basis—a basic question for management is whether the dislocations to industry in general which might be caused by a strike would be sufficient to authorize the government to invoke the national emergency provisions of the Taft-Hartley Act. After how many weeks of a strike would the government seek to invoke the Taft-Hartley Act, and what pressures would be brought to bear by government officials short of invoking that Act? Even if no emergency were created by a strike, would the government appoint an *ad hoc* board and attempt to dictate a settlement? What action would the President take to prevent a long strike which, through an adverse effect on corporate profits, could sharply curtail government tax revenues? How much advantage would the union gain from the presence in key governmental positions of leaders whom the union had openly supported in the recent election campaign? As can be seen from the foregoing enumeration, these questions are primarily political in nature, but they indicate an important aspect of governmental influence on union-management relations.

2. The company is insisting in its negotiation with the union that in order to minimize the possibility of future strikes, a secret ballot should be taken, submitting the employer's last offer to the employees for acceptance or rejection before a strike vote can be taken. Can the company legally insist on inclusion of such a clause in the contract? It may strike the reader as odd that this should even be a question. He may assume that negotiators for labor or management can press demands for any type of clause as long as it does not contravene public policy and is relevant to collective bargaining. However, this is not the case. On the contrary, this is one area where government affects not

only the procedure of collective bargaining, but also the substance of what may be bargained for. We shall explore this problem in greater detail in Chapter 5.

3. The union has demanded an agency contract since the law of the state in which the plant is located forbids the union shop. Under the agency contract, employees are not required to join the union as a condition of employment, but they must pay a "fee" to the union for representing them in negotiations with the employer. The "fee" is equal to the amount of union dues, and failure to pay can result in dismissal from employment. Is this demand lawful, or is it contrary to the purpose and intent of the state "right-to-work" law? This question involves an understanding of the conflict in purpose between the federal labor law, which has encouraged union organization, and state legislation, which has in many cases sought to impede and discourage it.

4. A union member claims that the president and a majority of the officers of the local union who are represented on the union bargaining committee were elected in a "rigged" election in violation of law. He says that they do not reflect the true wishes of the membership and should be ousted. Can the company refuse to deal with the elected officials until an investigation is made of these charges? This question grows out of the enactment of the Landrum-Griffin Act of 1959, which purports to regulate the internal activities of unions and whose full implications for union-management relations are still little understood.

5. While negotiations are still in progress, the union is attempting to bring pressure on management for settlement by deliberate slowdowns and "quickie" strikes. Is there anything that the company can do to stop such action? The complexity of our current labor law is well illustrated by the fact that an answer to this relatively simple question was forthcoming only after extensive litigation culminated in a decision of the United States Supreme Court which clarified the application of the Taft-Hartley Act good-faith bargaining provisions to such union tactics.

6. The company has laid off men in its maintenance department and subcontracted to an outside company the work formerly done by the laid-off employees. The union claims that this is a violation of contract and demands that the issue be submitted to arbitration. The existing contract contains an arbitration clause calling for the arbitration of disputes as to the meaning and application of the provisions of the agreement. Another clause provides that matters which are strictly a function of management shall not be subject to arbitration. Does the company have to go to arbitration on a matter which it considers a man-

agerial prerogative? Who is to decide whether the question raised is an arbitrable issue? What law governs—state or federal? How can an arbitration award be enforced? Can the union strike to upset an unfavorable decision of an arbitrator? These questions involve an understanding of Section 301 of the Taft-Hartley Act and the Pandora's box of problems it has opened up in the entire field of labor arbitration.

7. Let us assume that the union has already called a strike, and that the strikers have placed tacks on company driveways and overturned company vehicles. Can the company get an injunction in state or federal court to compel the union to halt such tactics? In order to obtain a better understanding of the problems raised by this question, we shall delve into labor history and explore the labor injunction and labor's efforts to curb this effective employer weapon.

8. The city, state, and federal mediation agencies have all proffered their services in an effort to settle the dispute. Which, if any, of these agencies should be brought in, and how can satisfactory public relations be maintained with such diverse agencies? This is a problem to which relatively little attention has been given in the literature, but which poses real difficulties to both management and union leaders involved in a labor dispute. We shall discuss the mediation process in detail in Chapters 10 and 11.

9. The union has advised management that unless the strike is immediately settled to the union's satisfaction, it will set up picket lines around the plants of automobile manufacturers which use steel produced by this steel company in order to bring pressure to bear on the company to meet the union demands. Can the union get away with this action? To find the answer to this question, we shall examine the prohibitions against secondary boycotts in both the Taft-Hartley Act and the Landrum-Griffin Act.

10. The company has notified the union that it intends to install a new automated process which will displace 50 per cent of the men in the plant. The union has countered by stating that the new process can be introduced only if all the men whose jobs are eliminated are retained as "machine watchers" whose function would be to notify management if a breakdown occurs which might endanger the safety of the men working in the plant. The company says that there is no need for such positions and that this is a pure case of "featherbedding." The union threatens to strike to compel management to comply with its demands. What are management's rights? This question will involve us in a review of the application of the antitrust laws to organized labor and a consideration of the merits of proposed legislation which would bring

featherbedding activities under the purview of the antitrust laws.

Here are ten questions which run the gamut of the type of problem presented in the course of labor negotiations. These questions have, for the sake of illustration, been phrased as if they were management problems. Actually, all of them are of equal concern to labor officials. As the reader will learn as the discussion in this book progresses, these questions involve knowledge of and application of a variety of federal statutes. But more than that, they indicate how sensitive management and union representatives must be to the possible action of government officials whose influence and impact on union-management relations extend far beyond mere statutory language.

The discussions in this text will attempt to cast light upon the twin problems of where we have been and where we stand today in the crucial area of government regulation of union-management relations. In following the text, the reader should have one more question in mind: Where are we going in collective bargaining in this country? Vociferous voices are heard today crying that collective bargaining has failed and that government compulsion is required in order to curb the power of unions to shut down entire industries or vital projects or areas through the weapon of the strike. Other spokesmen take a contrary position and maintain that there is too much government intervention already in collective bargaining, that government should withdraw to the side lines without aiding or restricting either of the protagonists and should let the forces of the market place function again without government regulation. Interestingly enough, some of the same persons who favor increased government regulation in order to restrict various powers and activities of organized labor also argue equally convincingly for government withdrawal from the collective bargaining process when they seek to eliminate the advantages conferred on labor through the Norris–La Guardia Act and the Wagner Act. They do not seem to be aware of the basic philosophic inconsistency in these two positions—and yet this is understandable, for the same inconsistency underlies our present patchwork of labor laws.

Labor law is a fascinating field for study, for it involves the fundamental conflict between groups of people seeking to earn their livelihood. It is a continually evolving subject, for our views on what is "right" and "wrong" in terms of action by management, labor, and government in this area have undergone gradual modification over the years. Labor law is also a highly technical field—there is an element of truth in the contention that the Taft-Hartley Act might more aptly have been called the "Lawyers' Full-Employment Act"!

This book does not purport to be a substitute for a legal text on labor law; the mere brevity of this work alone precludes such a purpose. The emphasis throughout the discussion will be upon the economic implications of various statutes and their application to the collective bargaining process. Nevertheless, the authors have recognized that one cannot understand "what the fuss is all about" in connection with the free speech amendment or mandatory bargaining subjects, for example, without being familiar with the specific statutory language which is basic to these problems. Likewise, such cases as the Lincoln Mills decision have such momentous significance for the future of labor relations in this country that a labor economist would be working with blinders on if he were not fully aware of the nature of this decision and its aftermath in federal case law. Therefore, in the following pages the writers have attempted to mix labor law and labor economics judiciously so as to give the student a broad yet penetrating understanding of the latest developments in the field of government regulation of collective bargaining.

The discussion in the text is divided into five parts. The purpose of this introductory Part I has been to demonstrate that labor law is a dynamic subject, that the problems raised by the relationship of government to labor and management are everyday problems which vitally concern the policies and decisions of American industry, and that labor law is not a set of clear and distinct precepts which control the conduct of management and union officials but rather a patchwork of guidelines, sometimes clear but often obscure.

In Part II, we shall explore the changing nature of the role of government in union-management relations. In the course of this historical exegesis, we shall review the major federal statutes which affect the conduct of labor relations today: the Norris–La Guardia Act, the antitrust laws, the Wagner Act, the Taft-Hartley Act, and the Landrum-Griffin Act. In addition, we shall consider state labor relations legislation and the controls which states have imposed on various aspects of the collective bargaining process.

In Part III, we shall be concerned with direct intervention by government in labor disputes. In this context, we shall discuss mediation, arbitration, seizure, and emergency strike control legislation. Railway and air-line labor legislation will be analyzed in detail because of the lesson it affords as to the efficacy of comprehensive governmental regulation of labor relations.

Part IV is devoted to the discussion of a highly controversial problem which is of growing importance because of the increasing number of men and women who work for government—municipal, state, or federal. This is the question of what rights employees should have to bargain collectively and to strike when their employer is the government.

Finally, in Part V, we shall take a critical look at labor relations as a whole in our current economy and discuss the role which government should play in the future in order to make collective bargaining function effectively in a democratic society.

PART II
Government Control of Union-Management Relations

In Part II, we shall consider how government has attempted to regulate union and management tactics, weapons, and behavior, and has thus significantly affected the pattern of collective bargaining in our economy.

We shall observe how the role of government has evolved over the years: The Norris–La Guardia Act, discussed in Chapter 2, was primarily laissez-faire in outlook; the purpose of the statute was to prevent law from interfering with union-management relations. Then came the Wagner Act, discussed in Chapter 3, in which government intervened to assist organized labor to establish collective bargaining in the face of stiff resistance from hostile employers. With the enactment of the Taft-Hartley law, government placed itself in the position of policing actions of both labor and management. Chapters 4, 5, 7, and 8 consider some of the problems which arise out of this new role for government. Finally, in the Landrum-Griffin Act, discussed in Chapter 6, we find government prescribing detailed regulations for the internal conduct of labor unions.

Since much useful experimentation by government in labor relations occurs at the state level, Part II concludes with an analysis in Chapter 9 of state controls on labor-management relations.

Chapter 2 NORRIS–LA GUARDIA JUDICIAL REVOLUTION AND THE ANTITRUST LAWS

In order to achieve their economic objectives, workingmen have found it necessary to join together and to take action together against employers. Labor's weapons of self-help, therefore, involve combinations and concerted action which run counter to the basic principles of our system of free competition. The American public has always had a deep distrust of powerful combinations which, through the potent force of collective action, can interfere with the normal working of competitive markets. This outlook is reflected in the Sherman Antitrust Act, which, though directed primarily at big business, purported to outlaw all combinations in restraint of trade. It is not surprising, then, that during the early years of union organization, trade unions found that the techniques which they adopted to obtain members and to improve working conditions met with a hostile reception in the courts and were often equated with conspiracy.

It is against this kind of historical background that we now turn to examine labor's struggle to free its organizing activities from the restraining hand of the judiciary. In this connection, we shall discuss in detail the provisions of the Norris–La Guardia Act and the various Supreme Court cases construing it which have, through liberal interpretation of that legislation, given organized labor a measure of freedom in the economic arena which critics declare detrimental to the public interest. Finally, we shall consider how the Norris–La Guardia Act, by freeing labor from regulation under the antitrust laws, has given rise to a demand for new legislation which would apply the antitrust laws to certain aspects of organized labor's activities.

Labor and the Courts in Early America

The basic economic and social environment in the United States has, on the whole, been hostile to the development of union organization. In a land of opportunity, rich in natural resources and capable of providing a high standard of living to its wage earners, trade unions have been unable to draw their membership from a proletariat with strong class allegiance, as in most European nations. On the contrary, class lines have been fluid; and even among wage earners, there has been continuing respect and support for the institution of private property. Union leaders have come to recognize this difference in outlook among our workers and have had to adopt a new kind of unionism—antisocialistic and business-oriented—in order to attract and retain membership.

This same strength of private property rights which is a product of the free enterprise of the American environment is reflected in the attitude of both employers and courts toward union organization. In their struggle for recognition of the right to organize, unions have had to combat not only antagonistic employers, vehemently committed to defend their right to run their own businesses without interference from their employees, but also an unfriendly judiciary and an inimical common law. Members of the judiciary tended to be selected from the propertied classes of the community and therefore reflected a conservative attitude in their opinion in labor disputes. But even had their personal predilections been liberal, the fact remains that the controlling precedents of common law were generally restrictive of organized labor's actions.

Our common law, which is based upon the customs of the land as reflected in the accumulated decisions of the judiciary, dates back to medieval England when employer-employee relationships were truly that of master and servant. In that era the serf was bound to the land, and the rules of guilds governed the artisans. When a shortage of labor occurred, as, for example, after the Black Death plague in the fourteenth century, laws were passed so that one employer who enticed another's workers away by offers of higher wages would be heavily punished. The legal enforcement machinery was in the hands of the employing class, and both law and the judiciary were decidedly unfriendly to any efforts of workers to raise their standards above what was deemed to be their "correct station in life."

The rise of modern factory production found that the law was still concerned with preserving an archaic "master-servant" relationship, while workers were turning to organization to correct the ills suffered under emerging capitalism. Following their notions of ethics and economics, English courts (and later Parliament) outlawed labor combinations which exerted pressure to increase wages or to secure the closed shop as a means toward that end. British courts and statesmen considered such combinations among workmen to be inimicable to the public interest because they interfered with the free working of market forces. In the famous Philadelphia Cordwainers case of 1806, and in numerous others during the next thirty years, American state courts adopted this same viewpoint and held that concerted action by combinations of workmen to better their wages and working conditions represented an illegal conspiracy against the public and against employers.

Rulings of this and similar nature caused considerable unrest among working groups in early America. Judges were sometimes hung in effigy on street corners by mobs of workmen who showed their resentment at being classed as criminals because of union activity. Nevertheless, until 1842 the courts continued to move in the direction of completely outlawing all union activity. Then, in the case of *Commonwealth* v. *Hunt,*[1] the Supreme Judicial Court of Massachusetts decided that a strike in support of a closed shop was not, per se, illegal, and that unless it could also be shown that the workers' objectives were bad, the conspiracy doctrine did not apply. Although the conspiracy doctrine continued to be utilized occasionally for some years to break up strikes, the decision in *Commonwealth* v. *Hunt* dealt it a blow from which it never recovered.

The "Motive" Test

After the decision in *Commonwealth* v. *Hunt,* the courts tended to judge the legality of union activity on the basis of "motive" and "intent." Because the motives or intentions of workingmen engaging in union activity are mixed and difficult to ascertain, determinations of the legality of union activity in terms of its possible objectives are subject to as many interpretations as there are judges. One judge, for example, might find that all strikes are malicious because the object is to bring economic pressure upon the employer in violation of his property rights; on the other hand, an equally learned judge might decide that the purpose of the strike was merely to improve the economic standards of the working people and that any harm which might accrue to the employer was incidental and unintentional. The difficulties and impasses which resulted from such efforts to probe into motive and intent led many courts to abandon the attempt to determine cases on that basis and, instead, to place their emphasis on the means used.

The "Means" Test

Even the means test, however, did not take the uncertainty out of judicial determination of the legality of concerted union activity.

[1] *Commonwealth* v. *Hunt,* 4 Metcalf 111 (1842).

While the difference between lawful means and unlawful means may seem clear in principle—combination and persuasion are lawful, while violence, coercion, force, and intimidation are unlawful—the difficulty comes in applying these principles to actual practice. Who is to say where persuasion ends and intimidation begins? Is the employee who is faced by a picket line persuaded or coerced into not going to work? Faced by the difficult task of making such decisions, courts have frequently—consciously or unconsciously—looked to the objective of union activity in order to decide whether the means were lawful. Justice Holmes is said to have observed: "The lawfulness of threats depends on what you threaten." In the same way, courts have sometimes been influenced by the purpose of union action in determining whether to declare the means adopted unlawful.

Restraint of Trade

A further theory utilized by courts in labor cases in these early years was the doctrine of restraint of trade. This doctrine assumed much greater importance in judicial decisions with the subsequent enactment of the Sherman Antitrust Act, which will be discussed below. The doctrine of restraint of trade, however, also existed in common law. In general, the common-law doctrine was based on the premise that everyone should have equal access to the market and that when two or more persons combined to block access to the market and thereby inflicted injury upon the public, a conspiracy in restraint of trade existed. All restraints, whether inspired by labor or industry, were not considered illegal per se. The legality of such restraints was held to depend upon their "reasonableness," which was determined by the courts by weighing the extent of coercion exercised, if any, and the effect of the restraint on the volume of business and access to the market.

The Injunction

By the late part of the nineteenth century the courts had generally recognized the right of employees to organize in unions without civil or criminal liability. However, the use of concerted economic weapons —the strike, boycott, and picketing—was generally held unlawful on the basis of one of the theories referred to above in the text. The most effective weapon which management was able to utilize to restrain such action by unions was the injunction. When this tool was implemented by the so-called "yellow-dog" contracts—which we shall discuss more fully below—the right to organize was virtually made meaningless.

The major objective of organized labor in the latter part of the nineteenth and the early part of the twentieth century was to free itself from the shackles of the injunction. The injunction is a legal technique developed in equity courts to provide relief against continuing injury where recovery in the form of monetary damages does not suffice. Upon a showing that "irreparable damage" might occur to the party requesting the relief unless certain acts of the defendant are stopped, the judge may issue an order forbidding the defendant from doing such acts. If the defendant disobeys the court order, he may be fined or imprisoned for contempt of court.

The effectiveness of the injunction was based upon the speed with which it could be secured and the manner in which it could be applied. An employer could go into court and secure what is known as an ex parte injunction by alleging that grave and irreparable damage would occur to his business or property if the injunction were not granted. Such an ex parte injunction could be obtained by the employer or his attorney appearing before a single judge, without notice to the union and giving the judge only his side of the story. If the judge granted the request for an injunction—as he usually did—he would issue an order of the court forbidding the union officers and members from doing a long list of prohibited acts. Such an order would completely tie up union organizational activities, and at the same time leave the employer free to discharge union members and otherwise act to destroy union organization in his plant before the union could be heard in court. By the time the case was brought to a hearing to determine whether the injunction should be dissolved or made permanent, the employer could often whip the union. Moreover, if union officials violated any part of the injunction, they could be held in contempt of court and fined or jailed by the court, without trial by jury. This was true whether or not the injunction was made permanent.

English courts granted such injunctions only if there was evidence of actual or threatened damage to physical property—buildings, machinery, and so forth. American courts, however, went much further and issued injunctions where there was evidence only of damage, threatened or actual, to the employer's business. Judges tended to fall into the habit of assuming that practically any form of union activity directed against the employer was enjoinable since it threatened "irreparable damage" to valuable interests of the employer. As there was no statutory law to speak of, stating what union activity was lawful and what was unlawful, concerted action by unions was taken under an ever-present threat of possible injunction.

The language of the court order containing the injunction was frequently drawn by attorneys for employers and signed by the court. Sometimes the injunction was directed against named individuals, sometimes against the world in general!

Some idea of the manner in which an injunction could tie up union activities may be gained by studying the following paragraphs from the injunction granted against the unions in the 1922 nationwide strike by the railway shopmen. The order restrained workers from

> inducing or attempting to induce by the use of threats, violent or abusive language, opprobrious epithets, physical violence or threats thereof, intimidations, display of numbers or force, jeers, entreaties, argument, persuasion, rewards, or otherwise, any person or persons to abandon the employment of said railway companies or any of them, or to refrain from entering such employment. . . .
>
> . . . in any manner by letters, printed or other circulars, telegrams, telephones, word of mouth, oral persuasion, or suggestion, or through interviews to be published in newspapers or otherwise in any manner whatsoever, encourage, direct or command any person whether a member of any or either of said labor organizations or associations defendants herein, or otherwise, to abandon the employment of said railway companies, or any of them, or to refrain from entering the service of said railway companies or either of them; . . .[2]

The sweeping scope of this injunction is further indicated by the fact that a barber who put a sign in his shop stating that "scabs" would not be served was held in contempt of court!

The application of injunctions to labor disputes developed rapidly after the Debs case of 1895.[3] In that case, Eugene Debs, leader of the Pullman strike,[4] was enjoined by an order obtained by the United States government from continuing a boycott of Pullman cars which, the government alleged, interfered with interstate commerce and the transportation of the mail. Although injunctions had been used in labor disputes prior to this time, the case focused nationwide attention on the injunction technique as a weapon against union organizational activities.

A further development which contributed to the popularity of the injunction as a management tool in labor disputes was the so-called "yellow-dog contract." This is a contract which an employer requires a worker to sign stating that, as a condition of employment, he agrees not to join a union. The phrase "yellow dog" was applied by unionists

[2] *United States* v. *Railway Employees' Dept.*, 238 Fed. 479 (1922).

[3] *In re Debs*, 158 U.S. 654, 15 S. Ct. 900 (1895).

[4] The strike involved an abortive attempt to establish industrial unionism on the railroads.

at an early date to workers who signed such contracts, and the contracts have been known by that appellation ever since.

In practice, employers made no real attempt to enforce such contracts against the individual workers who signed them. The importance of the contracts was that if they were legal, then attempts by union organizers to compel workers who had signed such contracts to join a union was a deliberate attempt to cause a breach of such contracts, and such action could be enjoined by the courts. Unionists maintained that because workers had no choice but to sign such agreements, they were without force or effect. The majority of state courts rejected this view, holding instead that mere inequality of bargaining power did not preclude enforcement of contracts. The New York courts, however, accepted labor's point of view.

Because of the general antagonistic attitude of the courts, labor unions attempted at an early date to secure passage of legislation which would outlaw yellow-dog contracts and thus curb the use of this effective antiunion organization weapon. Between 1890 and 1914, no less than fourteen states enacted legislation making it a misdemeanor or otherwise unlawful for employers (1) to exact yellow-dog contracts from their employees and (2) to interfere with the right of the employees to join or otherwise belong to a legitimate union. In addition, in 1898, Congress passed the Erdman Act, which contained similar provisions for the benefit of operating employees of the railroads.

The courts, however, declined to view with favor this legislation, which contained the principles of the Wagner Act forty years before that law was conceived. The Supreme Court found that both the state laws and the pertinent section of the Erdman Act were unconstitutional because the Fifth and Fourteenth amendments to the Constitution guarantee freedom of contract as a property right.[5] According to the courts, an employer had a constitutional right to request his employees to sign yellow-dog contracts and to enforce such contracts, and also to discharge his employees because of union activities. In short, the courts held that furthering union activities or even preventing interference therewith was not a sufficient promotion of the general welfare to permit interference with the sanctity of contracts, not even if they were yellow-dog contracts. Furthermore, in 1917, in the Hitchman Coal and Coke case,[6] the United States Supreme Court completely supported the

[5] *Coppage* v. *Kansas,* 236 U.S. 1, 35 S. Ct. 240 (1915), which nullified the state laws; and *Adair* v. *United States,* 208 U.S. 161, 28 S. Ct. 277 (1908), which nullified Section 10 of the Erdman Act.

[6] *Hitchman Coal and Coke Co.* v. *Mitchell,* 245 U.S. 229, 38 S. Ct. 65 (1917).

enforceability of yellow-dog contracts. It ruled that a court of equity could issue an injunction restraining attempts to organize employees bound by contracts with their employer not to join a labor union. Needless to say, these decisions caused unionists to take an extremely jaundiced view of the judiciary and to redouble their efforts to curb judicial interference in labor-management relations.

The Application of the Antitrust Laws to Organized Labor

When people speak of the "antitrust laws," they have reference to three major statutes. These are the Sherman Act of 1890; the Clayton Act, adopted in 1914; and the Federal Trade Commission Act, passed in 1914. Section I of the Sherman Act states: "Every contract, combination in the form of trust, or otherwise, or conspiracy in restraint of trade or commerce among the several States, or with foreign nations, is hereby declared to be illegal."

The Clayton Act attempted to define specifically certain unreasonable restraints on trade, such as price cutting to eliminate competition, the granting of rebates, and a long list of other abuses. The Federal Trade Commission Act created the Federal Trade Commission to co-operate with the Department of Justice in the enforcement of the antitrust laws. The Act gave the Commission authority to prevent unfair competitive practices.

For some years after the Sherman Act was passed, there was speculation as to whether or not it applied to labor. Finally, in 1908, in the case of *Loewe* v. *Lawlor,*[7] commonly known as the Danbury Hatters case, the United States Supreme Court ruled that a nationwide boycott organized by the union to persuade wholesalers and retailers to refrain from buying the company's products was an illegal restraint on commerce. The Court interpreted the statutory phrase, "restraint of trade or commerce," to apply to interference by a union with the interstate shipment of goods. The Court ordered the union to pay treble damages amounting to over half a million dollars, and individual members of the union were held responsible for their share of such damages.

Labor leaders were justifiably concerned about this result and immediately commenced pressure for exemption of labor from the antitrust laws. This drive culminated in the passage of the Clayton Act. Section 6 of that Act declared:

> . . . nothing contained in the antitrust laws shall be construed to forbid the existence and operation of labor . . . organizations, instituted for the purposes of

[7] 208 U.S. 274, 28 S. Ct. 301 (1908).

mutual help, and not having capital stock or conducted for profits, or to forbid or restrain individual members of such organizations from lawfully carrying out the legitimate objects thereof; nor shall such organizations, or the members thereof, be held or construed to be illegal combinations or conspiracies in restraint of trade under the antitrust laws.

Section 20 of the Clayton Act barred issuance of federal injunctions prohibiting activities such as strikes, boycotts, or picketing "in any case between an employer and employees, or between employers and employees, or between employees, or between persons employed and persons seeking employment, involving or growing out of, a dispute concerning terms or conditions of employment."

Section 20 concludes with a broad statement that none of the acts specified in this paragraph shall be considered violations "of any law of the United States."

Despite this broad language, the United States Supreme Court in 1921, in the case of *Duplex Printing Company* v. *Deering,*[8] held that the Clayton Act did not give labor unions a complete exemption from the antitrust laws. In that case the union sought to organize the Duplex plant and succeeded in getting members of other unions to refuse to handle the products of that company. In holding that such action was an illegal restraint of trade and a violation of the antitrust laws, the Court ruled that Section 20 of the Clayton Act applied only in cases where the relationship of employment existed between the company and the union members involved. Furthermore, the Court stated that the Clayton Act did not exempt unions "from accountability where it or they depart from . . . normal and legitimate objects and engage in an actual combination or conspiracy in restraint of trade."[9]

By this decision the Supreme Court nullified what appears to have been the clear purpose of Congress and set up the judiciary as the judge of what actions by unions were "normal" and "legitimate." It is hard to believe that Congress, by use of the phrase "in any case between an employer and employees," meant to limit the protection of the statute to concerted action by labor only when it was carried out by employees of the employer involved in the dispute, for this would obviously make organization of a nonunion plant almost impossible. Nevertheless, the Supreme Court adopted a narrow construction of the statutory language which boiled down to saying that the only activities of organized labor that were protected by the Clayton Act were those that had been lawful before its enactment! As a result of this decision,

[8] 254 U.S. 443, 41 S. Ct. 172 (1921).

[9] 254 U.S. 443, 469; 41 S. Ct. 172, 177.

employers stepped up their use of the injunction as a weapon to curb labor's organizing efforts.

THE NORRIS–LA GUARDIA ACT

In 1932, when the membership of the American Federation of Labor was the lowest in twenty years, the AFL achieved its greatest legislative triumph to date. After almost fifty years of sustained effort the AFL succeeded in making the federal judiciary "neutral" in labor disputes. The law which accomplished this result was the Norris–La Guardia Anti-injunction Act passed by a Democratic-controlled House of Representatives and a Republican Senate, and signed by the then Republican President, Herbert Hoover.

We have seen how labor had been frustrated in its aim to secure passage of legislation which would effectively make lawful the use of union tactics deemed necessary by labor for its survival and successful growth. The Norris–La Guardia Act represented a new approach to this problem. It did not legalize union action; it simply deprived the federal courts of jurisdiction in most situations involving labor disputes. It reflected essentially a laissez-faire philosophy: The law should intervene only to prevent damage to tangible property and to preserve public order; otherwise, the disputants should be left to their own resources to work out their problems. Both labor and business would now be free to promote their own interests in the field of labor policy through self-help without interference of the courts. The Act thus represented a reaction to judicial policy making which had produced the anomalous result of the same action being enjoinable in one state and not in another. Henceforth, all federal courts were barred from passing judgment as to the lawfulness or unlawfulness of the objectives of labor's actions. This same principle was soon extended to many state courts, for the federal act was immediately copied by a dozen or more state legislatures.

The Norris–La Guardia Act commences with a statement of public policy which affirms the right of workers to engage in collective bargaining through unions of their own choosing. Yellow-dog contracts are declared to be against this public policy, and the federal courts are instructed not to enforce such contracts. Then Section 4 of the Act establishes the following rules for the courts:

> No court of the United States shall have jurisdiction to issue any restraining order or temporary or permanent injunction in any case involving or growing out of any labor dispute to prohibit any person or persons participating or in-

terested in such dispute (as these terms are herein defined) from doing, whether singly or in concert, any of the following acts:

a) Ceasing or refusing to perform any work or to remain in any relation of employment; . . .

. . . .

e) Giving publicity to the existence of, or the facts involved in, any labor dispute, whether by advertising, speaking, patrolling, or by any other method not involving fraud or violence.

f) Assembling peaceably to act or to organize to act in promotion of their interests in a labor dispute;

g) Advising or notifying any person of an intention to do any of the acts heretofore specified;

h) Agreeing with other persons to do or not to do any of the acts heretofore specified; and

i) Advising, urging, or otherwise causing or inducing without fraud or violence the acts heretofore specified. . . .

The Norris–La Guardia Act has been aptly called "the last monument to the spirit of complete free enterprise for unions."[10] It left unions pretty much free to use their tactical weapons without judicial interference. As we shall see, a "liberalized" Supreme Court interpreted the statute broadly so as to confer almost complete immunity on labor leaders in labor disputes. As long as violence was not used, unions could resort to threats, coercion, boycotts, picketing, strikes, and so on without fear of federal court action. Some labor critics say that the Act went too far in this direction and that the problems we face today in terms of abuse of union tactics would not have resulted had the Norris–La Guardia Act attempted to make a distinction between lawful and unlawful union objectives, as did the Clayton Act. This is a debatable issue which we shall better understand after discussing the Norris–La Guardia Act and its aftermath.

The Act defines "labor dispute" in the broadest possible way so as to preclude judicial constructions, such as occurred in the Clayton Act, which whittled away the effect of the latter law: "The term 'labor dispute' includes any controversy concerning terms or conditions of employment, or concerning the association or representation of persons in negotiating, fixing, maintaining, changing or seeking to arrange terms or conditions of employment, regardless of whether or not the disputants stand in the proximate relation of employer and employee." It will be observed that Congress specifically took account of the fact that organized labor had a valid interest in conditions of employment even where it did not represent a single employee and that although

[10] Charles O. Gregory, *Labor and the Law* (2d rev. ed.; New York: W. W. Norton & Co., Inc., 1961), p. 197.

such a situation did not involve a dispute technically between "an employer" and its "employees," nevertheless the protection afforded by the Norris–La Guardia Act was applicable.

The Act, in effect, outlawed injunctions in labor disputes except where violence is involved. Even in such cases the granting of injunctions is severely restricted. The Act provides that except for a five-day restraining order, no injunction may be granted restraining unlawful activities of a union in labor disputes cases except on a full hearing in open court. Furthermore, before the court can issue an injunction, it must find that unlawful acts have been and will be committed unless restrained; that the plaintiff will suffer substantial and irreparable injury; that as to each item of relief sought, greater injury will be inflicted upon the plaintiff by the denial of relief than will be inflicted upon the defendants by granting it; that the plaintiff has no adequate remedy at law; and that the police officers of the community are unwilling or unable to furnish adequate protection. Moreover, even if the above findings are made, the Act provides that no relief shall be granted a plaintiff who has failed to comply with any obligation imposed by law involved in the labor dispute, or who has failed to make every reasonable effort to settle the dispute by negotiation or any available governmental machinery of mediation or voluntary arbitration. It is understandable after reading this long catalogue of conditions that union attorneys are generally able to frustrate the attempt of management attorneys to secure injunctions even in cases where the union may have engaged in violence, intimidation, and other unlawful acts which were not intended to be protected by the Act.

The Norris–La Guardia Act and the Courts

With a single piece of legislation, Congress thus repealed a century of judicial interpretation and created *laissez faire,* or economic free enterprise, for organized labor as well as for business. Henceforth the courts were not to interfere with strikes, boycotts, and picketing which were conducted peacefully and otherwise within the law. Moreover, by defining "labor dispute" in a broad fashion, Congress insured labor's right to engage in sympathy strikes, secondary boycotts, stranger picketing, and other activities where nonemployees of a concern come to the aid of the concern's employees in labor disputes directly or by applying pressure upon third parties.

Despite the clarity of its language, the Norris–La Guardia Act might either have been misconstrued or declared unconstitutional by the courts if the attitude of the courts had not altered fundamentally on labor matters by the time litigation arising out of the Act reached the Supreme Court. Between the dates when the Act was passed by Congress and reviewed by the highest Court, the New Deal of Franklin D. Roosevelt had intervened, and the thinking of the highest Court had been altered. As a result, the Norris–La Guardia Act and similar state laws were interpreted to preclude injunctive relief in peacefully conducted labor disputes.[11]

Reversal of Sherman Act Decisions

The combined effect of the Norris–La Guardia Act and the liberalized view of labor disputes which the Supreme Court took after 1937 resulted in a revision of precedents on the application of the Sherman Act to labor. In 1940 the Supreme Court, in the case of *Apex Hosiery Co.* v. *Leader,*[12] handed down the first of a group of landmark decisions which delineate the present legal status of unions under the antitrust laws. In that case the union, in the course of an organizational strike against a hosiery company, seized the company's plant, engaged in a sit-down strike on company property, and refused to let the company make a shipment of hosiery, most of which was destined to out-of-state customers. Despite the fact that there was clear evidence of a restraint on interstate shipment of goods similar to that involved in the Danbury Hatters case, the Court held that such action did not violate the antitrust laws. The Court reasoned that the Sherman Act was aimed at restraints upon commercial competition in the marketing of goods or services, whereas the union's purpose was not restraint upon commerce, but only to compel the employer to accede to its demands.

According to the majority opinion, "in order to render a labor combination effective it must eliminate competition from nonunion made goods, . . . an elimination of price competition based upon difference in labor standards is the objective of any national labor organization. But this effect on competition has not been considered to be of the kind of curtailment of price competition prohibited by the Sherman Act." This decision is generally interpreted to mean that trade unions do not violate the Sherman Act if their activities do not actually result

[11] The Supreme Court has held, however, that the Norris–La Guardia Act does not bar the United States government from obtaining an injunction in a labor dispute in which it technically is the employer. In 1947, in the case of *United States* v. *United Mine Workers,* 330 U.S. 258, 67 S. Ct. 677, the Supreme Court held that an injunction could validly be issued by a federal court at the request of the United States government to prevent the Mine Workers from continuing to strike after the government had seized the coal mines.

[12] 310 U.S. 469. 60 S. Ct. 982 (1940).

in price fixing or restraint on competition unless this was the primary intention of their activities. While the Court attempted to reconcile earlier decisions, in effect it overruled them by making it clear that mere interference with interstate commerce was not sufficient to make such union action unlawful.

The effect of the next decision by the Supreme Court was to grant an even more sweeping immunity to labor organizations. In the case of *United States* v. *Hutcheson,*[13] decided in 1941, the court had before it a national boycott of the products of the Anheuser-Busch Brewing Company instituted by the carpenters' union because the company had contracted with machinists to dismantle certain equipment. Here was a boycott similar to those organized and held unlawful in the Danbury and Duplex cases. How could this new "liberal" Court hold such action lawful without overruling those early cases?

The Court accomplished this objective through a feat of circuitous reasoning. The conduct in question was held lawful because it fell within the general language of Section 20 of the Clayton Act, which, after describing various union activities, concludes with the statement that none of such acts shall be considered violations of "any law of the United States." Recognizing that the Supreme Court in the Duplex case had refused to apply this same language to legalize similar union action, the Court now ruled that Congress, by enacting the Norris–La Guardia Act, had breathed new life into this exemption! Since the action in question could not have been enjoined in federal court under the terms of that Act, the Court argued that it should not therefore be held unlawful under the Sherman Act. Labor union conduct of the type described in Section 4 of the Norris–La Guardia Act was henceforth not only nonenjoinable, but lawful for all purposes under federal law.

Justice Frankfurter, in speaking for the majority of the Court, did suggest one exception to this sweeping exemption: "So long as a union acts in its self-interest, and does not combine with non-labor groups, the licit and the illicit under Section 20 [of the Clayton Act] are not to be distinguished by any judgment regarding the wisdom or unwisdom, the rightness or wrongness, the selfishness or unselfishness of the end of which the particular union activities are the means." In this dictum, he suggested that if unions conspired with employers to control the supply and price of commodities for their mutual benefit and thus departed from legitimate union objectives, they might still be liable under the Sherman Act.

[13] 312 U.S. 219, 61 S. Ct. 463 (1941).

The third major case in this series, *Allen-Bradley Co.* v. *Local 3, International Brotherhood of Electrical Workers,*[14] was decided by the Supreme Court in 1945. In this case a union of electrical workers in the New York area agreed with contractors to purchase equipment only from local manufacturers who had closed shop agreements with Local 3. It also obtained agreement from manufacturers to confine their New York sales to contractors employing Local 3 members. The Supreme Court found that the contracts were "but one element in which contractors and manufacturers united . . . to monopolize all the business in New York City." The Court therefore held that the union and the employers were both guilty of violating the antitrust laws.

The extended immunity granted to labor from the antitrust laws and the injunction was followed to its logical conclusion in other decisions further elaborating the laissez-faire attitude. The American Federation of Musicians was permitted to maintain a nationwide boycott of recordings by refusing to have its members make such recordings;[15] a hod carriers' union was permitted to prevent usage within its jurisdiction of a low-cost cement-mixing machine except under conditions which made the use of such machines financially impossible;[16] building trade unions were permitted to boycott materials because they were produced by companies where rival unions were bargaining agents or because they were prefabricated instead of being put together on the job;[17] unions were allowed to picket or boycott a company solely on the grounds that it dealt with a rival union and despite the fact that if the employer recognized the picketing or boycotting union, he would violate the National Labor Relations (Wagner) Act;[18] and finally, a union could with immunity have its members refuse to work for an employer ready and willing to deal with the union, because of a grudge against the employer, even though the effect was to force the employer out of business.[19]

While there are still many gray areas in application of the antitrust laws to labor, these cases—and in particular the Apex, Hutcheson, and Allen-Bradley decisions—broadly define the permis-

[14] 325 U.S. 797, 65 S. Ct. 1533 (1945).

[15] *United States* v. *American Federation of Musicians,* 318 U.S. 741, 63 S. Ct. 665 (1943).

[16] *United States* v. *International Hod Carriers' Union,* 313 U.S. 539, 61 S. Ct. 839 (1941).

[17] *United States* v. *Building & Construction Trades Council,* 313 U.S. 539, 61 S. Ct. 839 (1941).

[18] *National Labor Relations Board* v. *Star Publishing Co.,* 97 F. (2d) 465 (1938).

[19] *Hunt* v. *Crumback,* 325 U.S. 821, 65 S. Ct. 1545 (1945).

sible limits of concerted union activity, and suggest that unions are subject to the antitrust laws under existing legislation only:[20]

1. Where the union intends to achieve some commercial restraint primarily and not as a by-product of its essential intent to advance its own cause (Apex case).
2. Where union activity is not in the course of a labor dispute as broadly defined by the Norris–La Guardia Act (Hutcheson case).
3. Where a union combines with some nonlabor group to achieve some direct commercial restraint (Allen-Bradley case).[21]

The Apex case, at first glance, appears to establish a workable criterion for distinguishing lawful and unlawful union action, but closer inspection reveals that the distinction is illusory. Just what is a "commercial restraint"? Can unions picket retail establishments without producing a "commercial restraint"? Is a secondary boycott of retail outlets in order to secure organization of a manufacturing business violative of this standard?

The Hutcheson decision, in practical effect, made the antitrust laws inapplicable to unions regardless of their objective as long as they did not conspire with nonlabor elements. There was no need to make such a sweeping pronouncement on the subject, and there are undoubtedly members of the Court today who regret the Court's largesse in granting such a broad exemption to labor. It should be remembered, however, that the Court in 1941 was dealing with a labor movement which during the thirties had never numbered more than 8.5 million members. Perhaps a different decision would have resulted had the Court first been presented with the Hutcheson case today, when union members number 19 million. In any case, it is difficult to see why labor should have a right to fix prices or allocate markets even without direct employer conspiracy. These are objectives which the antitrust laws and public policy generally condemn and should be unlawful when carried out by any group in the community.

The Allen-Bradley case amplifies the loophole in existing antitrust law. Unions cannot fix prices in combination with employers, but presumably they can do it alone. Courts and commentators have interpretated this case to mean that negotiation of parallel collective

[20] See "Should Labor Unions Be Subject to Antitrust Laws?" *Congressional Digest*, Vol. 61 (October, 1961), p. 231.

[21] In *Los Angeles Meat and Provision Drivers Union, Local 626* v. *U.S.*, 9 L. ed. 2d 150 (November, 1962), the United States Supreme Court held that the Norris–La Guardia Act did not bar a federal court from ordering a union to terminate the union membership of self-employed grease peddlers who, the court found, conspired with the union to fix the purchase and sale price of grease, allocate territories, and otherwise violate the antitrust laws.

bargaining agreements effecting market control, when sponsored by the union, do not violate the Sherman Act.[22] For example, in one large city the contract between the painters' union and painting contractors required all contractors to adhere to a minimum price scale. Should such union-induced price fixing be lawful?

Unions and Monopoly Power

We have seen how the Norris–La Guardia Act, passed at a time when organized labor was relatively weak and impotent, has today clothed organized labor with power that is denied to other groups in the market place. The contention is frequently urged that a union monopoly is no better than a business monopoly and that both should be subject to the restrictions contained in our antitrust laws, which were enacted to deal with monopolies and restraints on trade. Are unions monopolies? Do unions restrain trade? Consideration of the conflicting arguments relative to proposals to extend the antitrust laws to unions can best be analyzed by enumerating the various kinds of alleged union monopoly power.

1. ***Exclusive Jurisdiction.*** Every union can be said to be a monopolist, for the purpose of a union is to eliminate competition in the labor market. This would be true even if union organization did not have statutory support. In addition, a union is like a monopoly because, once certified by the National Labor Relations Board (and unless decertified), a union has, by law, an area of operation in representing workers in the bargaining unit in which competition from other unions is prohibited. Under the Taft-Hartley Act, employees bargain through unions of their own choosing which the employer must recognize as the exclusive bargaining agent. A majority of persons voting in the election determine the bargaining agent for all of the workers in the bargaining unit. As long as a union remains the certified bargaining agent, it has the exclusive right to represent workers in their relations with the employer. When this power is combined with a union shop, which requires new workers to join the union after 30 days as a prerequisite to holding their jobs, the union has in effect obtained a monopoly over job opportunities with the particular employer. Nonunion workers or members of other unions cannot work for the employer after expiration of the 30-day period.

Many of the staunchest friends of labor—including the late President Franklin D. Roosevelt—have publicly expressed doubts con-

[22] Archibald Cox, "Labor and the Antitrust Laws—A Preliminary Analysis," *University of Pennsylvania Law Review,* Vol. CIV (1955), pp. 252, 271.

cerning the merits of such "compulsory unionism." There is no doubt that the compulsory aspect of the union shop strengthens the power of union leaders and creates circumstances which may be used by labor bosses to enrich themselves at the expense of the rank-and-file employees. Justice Brandeis, certainly a friend of labor, felt that the ideal condition for strong unionism was to have an appreciable number of men outside the union. As he put it: "Such a nucleus of unorganized labor will check oppression by the unions as the unions check oppression by the employer."[23]

Many supporters of the extension of antitrust laws to unions earnestly believe that such legislation is meaningless unless the "source of union monopoly power" is eliminated, namely, the principle of exclusive representation and the union shop. They concur with the language of the Taft-Hartley Act, which states that "employees shall have the right to self-organization . . . for the purpose of collective bargaining or other mutual aid or protection, *and shall also have the right to refrain from any or all of such activities,*" but they would add as a basic tenet of public policy that employees shall have the right to join—*or not to join*—unions. Advocates of this position have actively promoted the adoption of so-called "right-to-work laws" banning the union shop. Because of a provision in the Taft-Hartley Act giving state law precedence in such matters, the union shop can be outlawed within state boundaries even though it is lawful under federal law. As of March 1, 1963, right-to-work laws of general application had been adopted in twenty states.

Some proponents of "voluntary unionism" believe that in the long run, unions will be more representative of their membership and more responsible to society if they have to hold employees on the basis of actual merit and performance than if they can rely on legal compulsion, which gives them a guaranteed flow of dues. Others, of course, are primarily interested in weakening unions. There are many pros and cons with respect to the union shop, which will be discussed in greater detail in Chapter 8. As for the principle of exclusive representation, it seems too firmly imbedded in our labor relations practice today to permit it to be removed without serious damage to the collective bargaining process.

2. ***Industry-wide Bargaining.*** The practice of so-called "industry-wide bargaining" has seemed to many people to be a major source of union monopoly power. Actually, the term is a misnomer,

[23] Quoted in Donald R. Richberg, *Labor Union Monopoly* (Chicago: Henry Regnery Co., 1957), p. 118.

for cases of actual industry-wide bargaining are rare. The coal industry is often pointed to as an example of industry-wide bargaining, but it is not. For example, in the bituminous coal industry, bargaining is conducted partly with the Bituminous Coal Operators' Association, partly with the Southern Coal Producers' Association, partly with some smaller groups, and partly with individual operators who do not bargain through the associations. Even in steel, bargaining is normally carried on with individual employers, although the pattern bargaining which has resulted in recent years gives the appearance of industry-wide bargaining. Closer examination of legislative proposals aimed at this type of bargaining indicates they are really concerned with multiunit bargaining—that is, collective bargaining arrangements covering more than one plant—particularly where the effect of a breakdown in bargaining can substantially curtail production and employment in an industry.

A typical example often cited to support the need for such legislation is the 1959 breakdown in negotiations between the United Steelworkers and the major steel companies, which resulted in idleness for 500,000 steelworkers and enforced layoffs for 100,000 other persons in related industries such as mining and railway transportation.[24] To many people, the struggle between the United Steelworkers and the major steel companies—and similar conflicts in other key industries—seems like a battle between Goliaths from which the public is bound to emerge the loser.[25]

It is wrong to assume, however, that multiunit bargaining is a device foisted on industry by strong unions. On the contrary, the development of different types of multiunit bargaining varies from industry to industry, depending upon the basic characteristics of the particular industry. While industry-wide bargaining frequently develops in oligopolistic industries where there are a few relatively large producers, it has also become established in highly competitive industries with many producers, such as the garment industries and bituminous coal.

Frequently, multiunit bargaining evolves because of employer preference for this kind of bargaining. One of the most important reasons why employers have defended or initiated multiunit bargaining is the protection it gives them against loss from strikes. In industries

[24] *Economic Report of the President, January, 1960* (Washington, D.C.: U.S. Government Printing Office, 1960), p. 14.

[25] The issues of public policy raised by so-called "national emergency" strikes will be discussed in Chapter 13.

such as transportation, building construction, amusements, services, or occasionally retail trade, a strike can result in a loss of business which is never regained because the company deals in a perishable good or service. If a union can pick off employers one by one, employers are, more often than not, helpless to prevent the union from achieving even the most outrageous demands. On the other hand, when the companies form a common front, the union power is blunted because a strike means a strike of the entire industry.

Unions frequently prefer multiunit bargaining because it enables them to equalize wage costs in industries where wages are an important cost factor. This is the case, for example, in the men's clothing industry. If wage rates were not equalized on a national basis, employers who compete with one another in the national market would have cost advantages attributable to a diversity of settlements in wage rates.

In industries in which an employee typically works for more than one employer, multiunit collective bargaining is virtually essential for both employer and union. These trades include the maritime trades, the building trades, and the needle trades. In such industries, failure to equalize wages and working conditions would have the effect of permitting some employers to pay lower wages to employees who also work for other employers paying higher wages. From the union and employer points of view, this is a chaotic situation. For example, in the building industry the low-wage employer would be able to outbid high-wage competitors solely because the union allowed him a favorable rate. Employers prefer that wage competition be neutralized and that competition rest upon efficiency, service, and similar considerations.

It is impossible to explore the rationale and full complexities of multiunit bargaining in this limited review. Nevertheless, it should be apparent that such bargaining practices cannot be eliminated by legislative fiat without seriously affecting industry competitive structure and practices. The national bargaining in certain industries was created by the national character of the market for the industry. The real question is not "Shall we have national bargaining?" but rather "Shall it be national bargaining with a strong union or without a strong union?" It is difficult to imagine effective collective bargaining between General Motors and a union if, on the union side, all negotiations had to be conducted on a plant basis between the local union and the company. Furthermore, proposals to atomize labor unions are completely unrealistic.

Nevertheless, this type of remedy is embodied in several of the bills now pending in Congress. Labor contracts, with certain exceptions, would be required by law to be negotiated only between individual employers and local unions. International union officials could no longer negotiate contracts for their locals; the international union would be put in the position of a trade association giving advice to its locals but taking no active role in labor-management negotiations. Obviously, such legislation, if enacted, would disrupt long-standing relationships in many industries and would also prohibit bargaining through employer associations which many employers feel has done much to stabilize labor-management relations.

Industry-wide bargaining has produced two problems which require solution. The first is the industry-wide strike which may imperil the national health or safety. We shall discuss this problem in detail in Chapters 13 and 15. The second is the wage-price spiral resulting from industry-wide settlements negotiated by a few men representing industry and labor which produce an industry-wide adjustment of both wages and prices. While the requirement of local bargaining would disrupt pattern wage and price adjustments, it might in the end produce even more inflationary results. As inflationary as steel settlements have been over the years, it is possible that the results would have been worse if there had been a series of local settlements with union vying with union to win the largest wage adjustment for its membership.

Proponents of legislation aimed at prohibiting industry-wide bargaining maintain that they are trying to protect our free collective bargaining institutions and that unless action is taken to bring back competition in the labor market, the government will be forced to intervene in nationwide strikes, with the result that compulsory arbitration or government dictation of the terms of settlement will result. This is a possibility that must be reckoned with. Nevertheless, there is a strong suspicion that supporters of this type of legislation are more interested in weakening labor than in restoring competition. None of these proposals have contained provisions which would require the breaking-up of industrial giants such as the United States Steel Corporation, for example. The requirement that all collective bargaining be carried out through local unions would generate widespread disorganization in industrial relations and raise problems of enforcement that stagger the imagination. It is unlikely that we can by legislative fiat establish a competitive labor market in our economy, and there is considerable doubt whether such objective, if it could be accomplished, would be desirable.

A case whose outcome may significantly affect the future of

industry-wide bargaining is now pending before the Sixth Circuit Court of Appeals. This suit—the so-called Phillips case—is one of a number of actions brought by small mine operators against the United Mine Workers Union alleging a violation of the Sherman Antitrust Act on the ground that the 1950 coal agreement between the UMW and the Bituminous Coal Operators' Association was an unlawful conspiracy to force high contract rates on all mines in the industry, large and small alike, and thus freeze out many small operators. A United States district court jury in Tennessee found the union guilty, and the lower court fined the union $325,000. The case is now pending on appeal and will undoubtedly be further appealed to the United States Supreme Court because of its importance not only to the coal industry but also to all industries in which multiunit bargaining exists. The United Steelworkers of America and the AFL–CIO Industrial Union Department have joined the UMW in defending the coal agreement. Union lawyers state that if UMW practices are held to constitute an antitrust violation, then other unions may be subject to possible antitrust liability when they engage in activities which heretofore have been considered legitimate union conduct.[26]

3. ***Market Control.*** While the viewpoints of organized labor and management frequently clash, nevertheless there are many situations in which their objectives may coincide. In an industry where a strong union continually seeks and obtains large wage increases, the normal pattern of adjustment is in price increases sufficient to offset the increases in cost resulting from the wage increases. Employers look with disfavor on those firms in the industry which do not go along with this trend, and union leaders are likely to be concerned at price-cutting efforts or aggressive attempts to move into territory of other firms on the ground that this will "upset" the industry and endanger the union's wage program. It is easy to visualize, therefore, a situation in which a union will become, in effect, a policeman in an industry and will be able to achieve, through the various pressures on management that only unions can use, maintenance of price policy, market sharing, and other policies affecting the market for the product which the employers themselves could not accomplish without being in violation of the antitrust laws. As the Supreme Court intimated in the Allen-Bradley case, a union can lawfully accomplish such results so long as it does not actually conspire with management to achieve such objectives.

[26] *Business Week*, November 3, 1962, p. 49.

As a consequence, there are many situations in which unions have been able to exert pressure on marketing policies which, in effect, restrain competition. In some industries—the building trades especially—it has been alleged that the very right to do business is openly controlled by unions; the unions decide who can operate, what wages are to be paid and hours worked, and who may be hired.[27] Numerous examples have been reported of unions in the laundry and dry-cleaning industry preventing "unfair competition" by eliminating price-cutting independents. In the clothing industry the unions have established so-called "industry stabilization programs," which impose controls on manufacturers' prices and also place limits on the companies with which the manufacturer may do business. In other industries, unions have refused to work for companies which are not members of a trade association and do not abide by the commercial practices decreed by the union.

A similar type of market control is exerted by unions through geographical restrictions on the permissible area of an employer's business. For example, in Chicago, Illinois, a roofing contractor was told by a union business agent that he was not to solicit or accept any jobs north of 47th Street. When he disobeyed this instruction and sought to extend his area of operations, he found that he could not get supplies or labor to operate his business.[28] The union had established a market-sharing arrangement to prevent price cutting and to make it possible for it to maintain high wages. No single employer had the power to upset this union-maintained monopolistic arrangement.

Unions have also been involved in direct price-fixing activities. For example, the labor agreement between painters and painting contractors in Peoria, Illinois, provided that all contractors must adhere to minimum prices approved by a local board and granted to such board the right to prevent the execution of any work obtained at prices below this minimum.[29]

Union interest in the product market and in the prices received by an employer for his product is, of course, understandable. Price cutting, declining profits, a disorganized market, too many competitors —all of these threaten the union's objective of maintaining high wage

[27] Statement of National Association of Manufacturers in *Congressional Digest*, Vol. 61 (October, 1961), p. 244.

[28] *Hearings before the Committee on Education and Labor*, House of Representatives, 83d Congress, 1st session, Vol. VIII (Washington, D.C.: U.S. Government Printing Office, 1953), p. 2809.

[29] Cox, *op. cit.*, p. 266.

rates. It is difficult to see, however, how union efforts to control prices, market share, or other aspects of the product market can be sanctioned when such action is forbidden to businessmen.

Most knowledgeable students of this problem who seek a limited application of the antitrust laws to unions have centered their attention upon market control or commercial restraint as the critical factor requiring governmental action. For example, after a long study of the problem, the Attorney General's National Committee to Study the Antitrust Laws concluded:

> . . . we believe that where the concession demanded from an employer as prerequisite to ceasing coercive action against him is participation in or submission to such a scheme for market control or commercial restraints, this union conduct should be prohibited by statute.
>
> Regarding such legislation this Committee recommends:
>
> *a*) It should cover only specific union activities which have as their direct object direct control of the market, such as fixing the kind or amount of products which may be used, produced or sold, their market price, the geographical area in which they may be sold, or the number of firms which may engage in their production or distribution. . . .[30]

4. ***Union Featherbedding Practices.*** Union featherbedding practices involving make-work rules and restrictions on output have increasingly become a matter of public concern in recent years. At a time when we are in a production battle with the Soviet Union and our overseas markets are threatened by new, efficient plants in West Germany, Japan, and other nations, the question is being raised whether we can any longer afford the luxury of featherbedding, which has as its objective inefficiency rather than efficiency in production. This issue has been injected in the antitrust debate on the ground that featherbedding rules constitute an unreasonable restraint of trade beyond the legitimate scope of union activity.

Examples of featherbedding practices are legion. The railroad brotherhoods have carried make-work rules to the extreme, as a result of their position that every item of work *belongs* to a particular employee. If that employee is deprived of the opportunity to work, he is entitled to be paid, and so of course is the man performing the job. The result in many cases is that two days' pay must be given as compensation for a trivial amount of work. Because of retention of archaic rules going back to a time when trains were not as speedy as today, five different crews may have to be used on a train between New York

[30] *Report of the Attorney General's National Committee to Study the Antitrust Laws* (Washington, D.C.: U.S. Government Printing Office, 1955), p. 304.

and Chicago. The building trades are also strong proponents of featherbedding rules. Local 3 of the International Brotherhood of Electrical Workers in New York has insisted that its members rewire apparatus that has come already wired from the manufacturer, even though the employees of the manufacturer are members of the same international union.[31] It is standard practice for the plumbers' union to require that pipes be threaded on the job, even though it is far more economical to do threading in the shop. Similar policies are frequently followed by the plasterers, electricians, and carpenters in the building trades and the stagehands in the amusement industry. In the printing industry, certain advertisers prefer to supply their copy in the form of a mat or cut, with the type already set. The International Typographical Union requires that an exact duplicate of these forms be set up by its members in the plant, proofread, and corrected. This so-called "bogus" type is then junked and melted down.

Union make-work rules have been particularly burdensome where they have excluded improved products, services, or inventions from the market. For example, in the Joliet, Illinois, area, the Glaziers' Local Union No. 27 undertook a comprehensive campaign to eliminate the use of preglazed window sash and doors on building work. Since it completely controlled the labor supply in this area for glazier work, it was able to cut off the supply of this skilled labor until use of preglazed sash was discontinued. Similarly, the plumbers' union in many areas has been able to prevent use of plastic pipe. This new product is superior to metal piping for some uses, is cheaper, and involves considerably less labor and skill in installation, but the union control of installation has kept it off the market. The painters' union in Chicago has applied restrictions on the use of roller coaters as well as spray guns. These rules not only prevent the use of certain improved paint products but have been estimated to add as much as $100 per house unit in federal housing projects.[32]

The employment of unneeded personnel is most closely associated with the activities of James Caesar Petrillo, former president of the American Federation of Musicians. The contracts of this organization have required the employment of musicians in radio stations, theaters, and elsewhere when no artistic commercial need existed. These practices led to the passage of the Lea Act in 1946, making it unlawful to compel a licensee under the Federation Communications Act (1) to

[31] Sumner H. Slichter, J. Healy, and E. Robert Livernash, *The Impact of Collective Bargaining on Management* (Washington, D.C.: Brookings Institution, 1960), p. 320.

[32] *Hearings before the Committee on Education and Labor,* Vol. VI, p. 2225.

employ or pay for more employees than are needed, (2) to refrain from carrying educational programs with unpaid performers on a noncommercial basis, and (3) to interfere with the production or use of records. According to one recent study, this legislation has been effective, so that "the employment of unwanted staff musicians is no longer a problem in broadcasting."[33]

On the other hand, the attempt to deal with this problem in industry at large in the Taft-Hartley Act has not been particularly successful. Section 8 *b* (6) of that Act makes it an unfair labor practice for a union "to cause or attempt to cause an employer to pay or deliver or agree to pay or deliver any money or other thing of value in the nature of an exaction, for services which are not performed or not to be performed." While this provision was aimed at "featherbedding practices" generally, the Supreme Court has greatly narrowed its scope and has, in effect, ruled that employers can be forced to pay for services that are not wanted or needed.

Make-work practices represent an extremely complicated problem in industrial relations. They are essentially an expression of employees' insecurity relative to their jobs. For this reason, they are most frequently found in industries faced by shrinking employment, either because of contracting markets or because of technological change, and in industries such as construction, entertainment, and stevedoring where employment is intermittent. Although featherbedding practices are wasteful and costly to the public, there is a real question whether they can be dealt with effectively by legislation. What agency, for example, is to pass judgment on how fast a man should work or how many men should be required to operate a given machine? Moreover, if a union is barred from actually prohibiting use of an improved device, it can still achieve the same objective by charging a prohibitory rate for employees who use it. To be sure, extreme cases are easy to detect, and it is possible that some form of legislation may be enacted to prohibit such practices. But where is the line to be drawn between practices which clearly make work and those which retard the speed of work in order to prolong the employees' working life, or as a health measure, etc.? Should a union be liable for treble damages under an antitrust statute because it forbids members to use spray guns, which it contends are injurious to health? It is extremely doubtful whether the courts could cope with this kind of a problem. Yet the complicated and diverse patterns of work practices in industry at large would be

[33] Slichter, Healy, and Livernash, *op. cit.*, p. 329.

dumped in their laps if such practices were brought under the antitrust laws. If, on the other hand, the job of policing a new antifeatherbedding law is given to an administrative agency, it will have to pass judgment on a variety of labor relations matters that are intimately related to management production policies. The great danger, therefore, is that such legislation will result in further injection of government into industrial relations to a degree which neither labor, business, nor the public would find desirable.

There is, furthermore, a basic question of public policy which must be considered. Restriction of output is a characteristic of our economy which is not limited to labor organizations. Many businessmen restrict output in order to keep prices high. Numerous professional societies have obtained enactment of legislation which would permit only licensed personnel to pursue certain professions, with the objective of limiting the supply of workers. In New Jersey, the State Bar Association attempted unsuccessfully to have the negotiation of labor-management contracts declared the practice of law. Farmers continually restrict production, plow under crops, and ask to be paid for crops not marketed. How different is all this from union make-work policies? Is it fair to single out labor alone for remedial legislation?

PROPOSALS FOR APPLICATION OF ANTITRUST LAWS TO LABOR

At this writing, four separate bills are pending before Congress aimed at restricting alleged union monopolistic activities.[34] Management spokesmen, having achieved some success through the Landrum-Griffin Act in eliminating abuses in the internal administration of unions, are now determined to make an all-out fight to curb union abuses which they contend amount to the uncontrolled use of monopoly power. Supporters of this viewpoint include union haters who see in such legislation a means of weakening organized labor. They also include many thoughtful public-minded individuals who are friends of organized labor, but who are also seriously concerned about any uncontrolled aggregation of power, whether it be labor or capital, which can be used to the detriment of the public interest. As a matter of fact, there is evidence of considerable public support for some legislation to curb excesses of unrestricted union power. The Opinion Research Corporation of Princeton, New Jersey, recently conducted a

[34] See Table 1, page 40.

TABLE 1

COMPARISON OF ANTIMONOPOLY BILLS

	Martin (H.R. 9271)	McClellan (S. 2573)	Thurmond-Alger (S. 2292–H.R. 8407)	Hiestand-Alger (H.R. 228–H.R. 4573)
General purpose	To ban union restrictive practices, multiemployer monopolistic bargaining, and national strikes.	To outlaw strikes in the transportation industry.	To prevent restraints of trade or actions tending to create a monopoly.	To prevent industry-wide bargaining and national strikes.
Scope of bargaining	Union agents can only bargain for employees of a single company, except in metropolitan areas where city-wide negotiations are allowed.	A union may not combine with another in a strike or plan to substantially restrain transportation.	A union may not combine with another where it would constitute a restraint of trade or tend to create a monopoly.	A union may not combine with another, whether an international or a local, to plot concessions to be won from employers.
Effect on union practices	It would be unlawful for a union to (1) interfere with production, (2) restrict the number of persons entering a trade, or (3) control prices or impose featherbedding practices. Featherbedding practices are specifically defined.	It would be unlawful to strike, picket, black-list, or commit any act against an employer which substantially restrains transportation of people or property. "Hot cargo" secondary boycott clauses, whereby a union reserves the right to refuse to handle products, would be illegal.	It would be unlawful for a union to strike or seek contract provisions which constitute a combination in restraint of trade.	It would be unlawful for a union to strike or seek contract provisions that will substantially or materially affect the production, use, cost, handling, or sales of a product or service.
Effect on employer practices	It would be illegal for any employer to join with another in bargaining, except in metropolitan areas where city-wide negotiations are permitted.	An employer would be prohibited from making an agreement which would require him to cease doing business with another employer.	It would be unlawful for an employer to make a labor agreement in restraint of trade.	It would be unlawful for an employer, in concert with a union, to engage in any conduct to restrain trade or tend to create a monopoly.
Coverage	All unions and employers except those subject to the National Railway Labor Act.	Applies only to employers and unions involved in transporting persons or goods in interstate commerce.	Applies to all employers and unions.	Applies to all employers and unions.

SOURCE: Chamber of Commerce of the United States, *Labor Relations Letter*, Extra Issue (Washington, D.C., January, 1962), p. 4.

poll which found that 62 per cent of the public favored bringing unions under the antitrust laws. Nine per cent were opposed, and 29 per cent were undecided. According to the same survey, 57 per cent of union members support such legislation, 20 per cent oppose it, and 23 per cent have no opinion.[35]

The idea of the free competitive economy is still very much a part of the American ideal and strongly affects our national economic policy. While this principle has been compromised many times—in subsidies to industries, support prices in agriculture, tariffs for favored industries, and regulated monopolies in the case of utilities—nevertheless a politician is assured of a favorable audience if he enunciates today the same doctrine embodied in the Sherman Act over seventy years ago, namely, that "*Every* contract, combination in the form of trust, or otherwise, or conspiracy in restraint of trade or commerce" (emphasis supplied) is unlawful. Our national labor policy, therefore, is inconsistent with our general views on economic policy, for in the area of labor relations, we have adopted as our public objective the encouragement and strengthening of monopoly.

The Wagner Act (and its successor, the Taft-Hartley Act), in purpose and application, runs counter to the objectives expressed in the antitrust laws. The Wagner Act fostered the growth of industry-wide unionism and encouraged the organization of 100 per cent of an industry without concern for the impact which such extensive organization would have upon prices and the product market. As a consequence, a dual standard in antitrust policy has developed: A union can probably negotiate separate but parallel labor agreements with all employers in an industry and thus effectively police the product market, yet the employers cannot take this action among themselves, nor can the union make such an agreement with all employers as part of one master contract.

Legitimate union action designed to stabilize wage rates in organized companies often necessarily involves an impact on the product market. A union cannot permit low-wage, low-price firms to enlarge their share of the market, for this will endanger the competitive position of the unionized firms and ultimately weaken union control in the industry. Furthermore, union efforts to organize, raise wages, and improve working conditions, when supported by strikes, picketing, boycotts, and similar tactics, all have the tendency to restrain trade. How can we permit legitimate union activity and still bar restraints

[35] Chamber of Commerce of the United States, *Labor Relations Letter,* Extra Issue (Washington, D.C., January, 1962), p. 1.

which are so monopolistic in nature as to run counter to our basic ideas of what is allowable economic strife in a free economy?

This is the problem, and it seems clear that there is no easy solution. Probably the worst thing that could be done would be enactment of a general amendment to the antitrust laws making some distinction between "legitimate" and "illegitimate" labor activities, and then leaving to the courts the amplification of policy through case-by-case decisions. Our existing antitrust laws have not been particularly successful in preventing monopoly in industry, and court decisions have in fact been notably unsuccessful in clarifying in businessmen's minds what is lawful and unlawful in this complicated field of law. To inject the courts into the labor monopoly issue would simply add confusion rather than solve the problem.

What is needed is specific labor legislation aimed at eliminating particular abuses upon which there is general agreement that governmental action must be taken. The Taft-Hartley and Landrum-Griffin provisions prohibiting secondary boycotts are examples of this type of legislation. Caution must be exercised to avoid extreme legislation—such as abolition of industry-wide bargaining—which would raise havoc with long-standing collective bargaining practices and create more problems than it would solve.

Furthermore, any workable approach to the problems raised by union monopoly and other restrictive practices of organized labor must include a thorough revision of the Norris–La Guardia Act. Some labor experts question whether the reason for its being any longer exists. In the words of Charles O. Gregory, distinguished professor of labor law: "Its original purpose—enabling unions to organize by recourse to economic pressures—has long since been fulfilled; and in many ways the statute has become obsolete."[36] When the Norris–La Guardia Act was passed, there was no Wagner Act or Taft-Hartley Act, no procedure for peacefully determining representation disputes, no government agency whose job it was to enable employees freely and without coercion to choose their bargaining representatives. All this has now been changed. Furthermore, as we shall note in later chapters,[37] the Norris–La Guardia Act actually conflicts with certain provisions of statutes enacted in later years, notably Section 301 of the Taft-Hartley Act. In view of the momentous change which has occurred since adoption of the Norris–La Guardia Act, both in the economic power of organized labor and in the statutory regulation of labor relations, it is

[36] Gregory, *op. cit.*, p. 551.

[37] See Chapters 5 and 7.

apparent that the Norris–La Guardia Act requires a careful and comprehensive review to adapt it to the current labor scene.

QUESTIONS FOR DISCUSSION

1. Why was the injunction so effective as a weapon against union organizing activities? How did the Norris–La Guardia Act restrict its use in labor disputes?
2. Suppose the Norris–La Guardia Act were repealed and the Clayton Act were in force in its original form. What kinds of union concerted activities could be enjoined? What kinds would be protected from injunction by the terms of that Act?
3. Discuss the pros and cons of each of the antimonopoly bills summarized in Table 1 (p. 40). How would each of these proposed measures affect legitimate union collective bargaining activities?

SUGGESTIONS FOR FURTHER READING

AARON, BENJAMIN. "The Labor Injunction Reappraised," *Labor Law Journal,* Vol. XIV (January, 1963), pp. 41–81.

A scholarly review of the injunction from the pre-Norris–La Guardia period to the complexities raised by Section 301 of the Taft-Hartley Act, in which the writer concludes that the Norris–La Guardia Act is "urgently in need of amendment."

DAVENPORT, JOHN. "Labor Unions in the Free Society," *Fortune,* April, 1959, pp. 132 ff.; "Labor and the Law," *Fortune,* May, 1959, pp. 142 ff.

Two thoughtful articles analyzing the present status of unions in our economy and advocating specific measures to control union power.

"Labor Monopoly Myth," *Labor's Economic Review* (AFL–CIO publication), February, 1956.

Labor's official answer to the union monopoly charge.

"Should Labor Unions Be Subject to Antitrust Laws?" *Congressional Digest,* Vol. 61, October, 1961.

An entire issue devoted to a discussion of the pros and cons of application of the antitrust laws to organized labor.

TELLER, LUDWIG. "The Labor Injunction," *Proceedings of New York University First Annual Conference on Labor,* pp. 327–57. New York: Matthew Bender & Co., 1948.

An historical review of the role of the injunction from the Debs case to Taft-Hartley.

Chapter 3 THE WAGNER ACT

The National Labor Relations Act of 1935, more commonly known as the Wagner Act, ranks without a doubt as the most significant labor law ever enacted in the United States. For the first time, the full power of the federal government, exercised through an administrative agency of that government, was arrayed on the side of labor to promote the organization of employees into unions of their own choosing. The Norris–La Guardia Act of 1932 was prolabor in outlook, but it did not make government a partisan in the struggle between labor and management. It simply denied to employers the right to use the federal courts to obtain injunctions which could tip the scales in their favor in opposing union organization. It did not affirmatively promote union organization of employees. The Wagner Act, however, marked a complete departure from pre-existing labor policies. Not only did it state that the policy of government was to encourage unionism, but it also virtually ordered employers to stop resisting the spread of unionism and to let their employees do what they wished as far as representation by a union was concerned. Employers' hands were tied, in effect, but union tactics were left virtually unrestricted.

Economic and Legislative Background

The Wagner Act was enacted largely because of the failure on the part of American employers to modernize their concepts of industrial relations. By 1935, the year in which the Wagner Act was passed, significant changes had occurred in the rate of expansion of employment and in the character of the work force. As the rate of growth in the labor force slackened, opportunities for advancement diminished, and employees became more concerned with improving hours, wages, and working conditions of their existing jobs. The onset of the depression sharply cut the resignation rate of employees in industry. Since jobs were scarce, employees could not hope to better their condition by shifting to other companies. Furthermore, the widespread unemployment of the depression developed a feeling among workingmen that layoffs were handled unfairly. All of these factors contributed to a growing interest on the part of labor in collective bargaining as a means of bettering conditions of work and protecting their rights.

As changes in employment opportunities were occurring, the character of the labor force was also changing. The annual number of high school graduates increased twenty-fivefold between 1890 and 1935. By the latter date, 40 per cent of American children were completing a high school education, and most of the others were obtaining one or two years of it. Educated and thoughtful workmen brought up on the history of American democracy expect as a matter of right to have a voice in the determination of the conditions of employment under which they labor. American employers, however, were heedless of the changes which had taken place. Desirous of holding on to their prerogatives, and bred in the fierce individualism of the nineteenth century, they were unwilling to share determination of the terms and conditions of employment with organizations of their employees. The result was the passage of the Wagner Act.[1]

The failure of industry to alter its industrial relations policies and voluntarily to recognize unions of its employees was all the more remarkable in view of the ample warnings that if industry did not act, government would be compelled to do so. Commencing in 1885, a long list of government commissions and agencies reported favorably in behalf of collective bargaining. In 1898, Congress passed the Erdman Act, which contained provisions making discriminations against union activity on the railroads a misdemeanor. Although this provision was declared unconstitutional, later railway legislation, including the Railway Labor Act of 1926, endorsed unionism and collective bargaining. And between 1890 and 1914, no less than fourteen states enacted legislation similar to the Erdman Act, only to have the courts declare such laws unconstitutional.

Nor was official governmental approval of collective bargaining confined to opinions of commissions or to railway labor legislation. During World War I a committee composed of representatives of labor and management established a War Labor Board which not only recognized the right of collective bargaining but forbade discrimination because of union activity and conducted secret elections to

[1] Sumner H. Slichter, "The Development of National Labor Policy," *Studies in Economics and Industrial Relations,* University of Pennsylvania Bicentennial Conference (Philadelphia: University of Pennsylvania Press, 1941), p. 143.

determine bargaining agents. The Norris–La Guardia Act of 1932 was primarily concerned with judicial procedure involving labor injunctions, but it contained a statement of policy which endorsed the right of the individual unorganized worker "to full freedom of association, self organization, and designation of representatives of his own choosing, to negotiate the terms and conditions of . . . employment . . . free from the interference, restraint or coercion of employers. . . ."

With the advent to power of the Roosevelt administration, legislative endorsement of the right to unionism and collective bargaining went forward rapidly. The National Industrial Recovery Act, approved on June 6, 1933, was fundamentally an attempt on the part of the Roosevelt administration to promote economic recovery by permitting business to establish its own regulations, including control of prices. In order to secure labor support, however, the NIRA included the famous Section 7 (*a*).

> . . . (1) That employees shall have the right to bargain collectively through representatives of their own choosing, and shall be free from the interference, restraint, or coercion of employers of labor, or their agents, in the designation of such representatives or in self-organization or in other concerted activities for the purpose of collective bargaining or other mutual aid and protection; (2) that no employee and no one seeking employment shall be required as a condition of employment to join any company union or to refrain from joining, organizing, or assisting a labor organization of his own choosing. . . .

Although this provision involved the most complete governmental endorsement of the collective bargaining outside of the railway industry up to that time, it carried with it no effective penalties in case of employer disinclination to comply. A large number of employers did alter their policies in accordance with the spirit of Section 7 (*a*), but the great bulk did not. Many employers, for example, took Section 7 (*a*) as an invitation to establish company unions or employee representative plans in order to prevent the unionization of their employees. On the other hand, the American Federation of Labor regarded Section 7 (*a*) as public encouragement of collective bargaining. This clash of viewpoint led to strikes and industrial unrest as immature unions clashed with antiunion employers.

In an attempt to cope with this situation, President Roosevelt appointed a tripartite National Labor Board under the chairmanship of the late Senator Robert Wagner of New York. The National Labor Board became an agency which took on the functions of settling labor disputes by mediation and voluntary arbitration, of determining whether unions represented employees in a given instance, and of determining whether employers unfairly interfered with the organizational rights of their employees. In carrying out these functions, the National Labor Board developed many of the policies later followed by the National Labor Relations Board under the Wagner Act in regard to the appropriate bargaining unit and the meaning of unfair labor practices. The National Labor Board, however, had no authority to penalize employers for unfair labor practices except by referral to the Attorney General's office, where the maximum penalty was revocation of the right to place the NRA blue eagle on the product of the alleged unfair employer.

In June, 1934, Congress passed Joint Resolution No. 44, which created a National Labor Relations Board as a substitute for the National Labor Board. This agency, not to be confused with the NLRB created under the Wagner Act, continued the work of the National Labor Board and attempted without too much success to overcome the opposition of business within the framework and the limited sanctions of the National Industrial Recovery Act. Its work ceased when the NIRA was declared unconstitutional in 1935.

Besides these two labor boards of the NIRA period, others were in existence for special purposes. They included agencies established in the textile, automobile, petroleum, and newspaper fields. In addition, both the National Labor Board and its successor agency established regional boards throughout the country, thus foreshadowing the administrative structure of the National Labor Relations Board under the Wagner Act.

THE WAGNER ACT

Purpose and Philosophy

The Wagner Act was based upon the philosophy that the failure of employers to accept collective bargaining results in strikes and interferes with the flow of commerce, that the inequality of bargaining power between individual employees and employers who are organized as corporations aggravates depressions by depressing wage rates and reducing purchasing power, and that the protection of the right of employees to organize into unions of their own choosing removes most of these difficulties.

Congress, in effect, now stated that government could not remain neutral because of the great disparity of power between the individual employee and his employer. It should be noted that at the time of enactment of the Wagner Act, unions themselves were relatively weak and incapable of launching large-scale organizing efforts in the face of strong antiunion employers. In 1935, less than four million employees were members of unions, out of a total labor force of over fifty million workers.

The enumeration of "Findings and Policies" contained in the introductory section of the Wagner Act concludes with this statement of governmental policy:

> It is hereby declared to be the policy of the United States to eliminate the causes of certain substantial obstructions to the free flow of commerce and to mitigate and eliminate these obstructions when they have occurred by encouraging the practice and procedure of collective bargaining and by protecting the exercise by workers of full freedom of association, self-organization, and designation of representatives of their own choosing, for the purpose of negotiating the terms and conditions of their employment or other mutual aid or protection.

The heart of the substantive provisions of the Wagner Act is contained in Section 7, which embodies the preceding statement of policy in these words: "Employees shall have the right to self-organization, to form, join, or assist labor organizations, to bargain collectively through representatives of their own choosing, and to engage in concerted activities, for the purpose of collective bargaining or other mutual aid or protection."

The reader will observe that the above-quoted language bears a close resemblance to the language contained in Section 7 (*a*) of the NIRA. However, unlike its predecessor NIRA, the Wagner Act provided effective machinery for implementing the policy stated in the Act.

Administration and Coverage

The administration of the Wagner Act was given to a three-man National Labor Relations Board. The NLRB developed a large staff to enable it to carry on its work, including attorneys, investigators, hearing officers, review officers, and the many clerical personnel that are required to perform the detailed work in a nationwide administrative agency. The NLRB had jurisdiction only over employers engaged in interstate commerce. The Supreme Court has given the phrase "interstate commerce" an elastic definition, so that the jurisdiction of the Board has been held to apply not only to companies actively engaged in shipping products across states lines, but also to intrastate businesses which use a substantial quantity of raw materials shipped across state lines or sell products a substantial portion of which are destined for shipment across state lines.

The broadening of the jurisdiction of the NLRB reflects a growing recognition by the courts, by Congress, and indeed the public at large of the increasing interdependence of our complex industrial economy. It was not so many years ago that manufacturing and mining were held by the Supreme Court to be intrastate in character. However, in 1937, in the famous case of *National Labor Relations Board* v. *Jones and Laughlin Steel Corporation,*[2] the Supreme Court, by a 5–4 decision, turned its back on the past and held that the Wagner Act was constitutional and applicable to the steel industry.

Section 9 (*c*) of the Wagner Act provided that whenever a petition was filed with the NLRB, the Board was to investigate the petition, and "if it has reasonable cause to believe that a question of representation affecting commerce exists," a hearing on the merits was to be held. It is obvious from the foregoing language that the first issue which the Board must itself resolve when a petition is filed is whether or not the case has a sufficient relation to interstate commerce to give the Board jurisdiction under the Act. Furthermore, even if the Board can legally take jurisdiction, it has as a matter of internal policy laid down definite standards for the assertion or refusal of jurisdiction based upon the dollar amount of goods purchased or sold out of state and similar criteria relating to the flow of interstate commerce.

UNFAIR LABOR PRACTICES

Enactment of the Wagner Act occurred at a time when the labor market was vastly different from that which exists in industry today. Organized labor numbered only four million union members, primarily concentrated in the construction trades, transportation, mining and needle trades. The great basic industries of the country were either unorganized or were characterized by bargaining with company unions dominated by management. In 1935, for example, industries such as basic steel, agricultural implements, petroleum refining, rubber products, electrical machinery, and meat packing had from 50 to 80 per cent of their employees covered by company unions.[3]

Employers were openly hostile to unions and used every weapon at their command to prevent union organization. Lockouts, intimidation, black lists, yellow-dog contracts, spying, and discrimination were commonplace. The La Follette Committee investigation of industrial

[2] 301 U.S. 1, 57 S. Ct. 615 (1937).

[3] H. A. Millis and E. C. Brown, *From the Wagner Act to Taft-Hartley* (Chicago: University of Chicago Press, 1950), p. 110.

espionage reported that 1,475 companies were clients of detective agencies during the years 1933–36 for "espionage, strike-breaking, guards in connection with labor disputes, or similar services."[4] Expenditures on espionage, arms, and strike breaking by about three hundred companies in the years 1933–37 amounted to nearly $9.5 million.[5]

In drafting the Wagner Act, Congress recognized that business hostility to unions was a fact to be reckoned with and that pious pronouncements of policy in favor of union organization, unbuttressed by sanctions against violators of Congressional policy, would achieve nothing. The Act therefore enumerated so-called "employer unfair practices" and made such conduct unlawful. Furthermore, it empowered the NLRB to issue cease and desist orders against such illegal conduct and to enforce such orders in the courts. During the twelve years of the Wagner Act administration until its amendment in 1947, employees and their representatives filed more than 45,000 charges of unfair labor practices against employers with the NLRB. It is therefore apparent that protection of employees against management unfair labor practices constituted a major function of the Board.

The unfair labor practices prohibited by the Wagner Act (in each case directed against employers) are the following:

1. *To interfere with, restrain, or coerce employees in the exercise of rights guaranteed in Section 7.*

This is an all-inclusive provision which actually covers all of the more specific unfair labor practices enumerated below. However, it was specifically aimed at such employer practices as spying on unions, questioning employees about their union affiliation, using black lists or yellow-dog contracts, or favoring one union over another.

A number of problems arose as a result of administration of this section of the law which subsequently gave rise to amendments in the Taft-Hartley Act. One of the major problems stemmed from the broad definition of "employer" contained in the Wagner Act, namely, "any person acting in the *interest* of an employer, directly or indirectly." Because of this broad definition, companies were held liable for the action of supervisors and foremen in intimidating employees, even though these actions would not normally have been attributable to the employer under the usual rules of agency. This construction, in effect,

[4] *La Follette Committee Reports, Industrial Espionage,* Report No. 46, Part 3, 75th Congress, 2d session (Washington, D.C.: U.S. Government Printing Office, November 16, 1937), pp. 26, 89.

[5] Millis and Brown, *op. cit.,* p. 101.

required employers affirmatively to act to prevent foremen from engaging in antiunion activities.

A second problem which arose under this section involved the question of freedom of speech. Since unions were weak during the early years of the Wagner Act, the NLRB considered the effect of antiunion speeches by employers as an important part of a totality of conduct which might interfere with the rights of employees under the Act. In one leading case,[6] for example, it was held a violation of this section of the act for an employer to deliver an antiunion speech, to which every employee was required to listen, in a plant during working time. Employers complained that such action by the NLRB deprived them of rights of free speech guaranteed by the Constitution.

2. *To dominate or interfere with the formation or administration of any labor organization or contribute financial or other support to it.*

This section was designed to prevent the formation or use of company unions which were supported by and subservient to the employer. As has already been mentioned, company unions were commonly used by employers in the early thirties as a device to deter legitimate independent unionism. One Department of Labor study indicated that in 1935, company unions or organizations confined to workers of a particular plant or company covered 20 per cent of manufacturing workers.[7] Numerous charges of domination of unions were brought under this section in the first few years of administration of the Act, but as a result of the effective enforcement of this provision, employer-controlled company unions gradually disappeared from the labor scene. Charges of domination or interference with the formation or administration of unions were involved in about 20 per cent of complaint cases brought before the Board in the first three years of the Wagner Act, but rapidly decreased in numerical importance so that they were less than 10 per cent of the charges filed in the last five years of the Wagner Act period.[8]

It should be noted that at the time the Wagner Act was passed, the CIO had not yet come into existence. The AFL was therefore thought of as the independent-type union, whereas company unions bore the taint of domination by employers. Subsequently, however,

[6] *Clark Brothers Co., Inc.,* 70 NLRB 802 (1946), 163 F. (2d) 373 (CCA [2d] 1947).

[7] U.S. Department of Labor, Bureau of Labor Statistics, *Characteristics of Company Unions* (Washington, D.C.: U.S. Government Printing Office, 1935), p. 3.

[8] Millis and Brown, *op. cit.*, pp. 78–79.

as a result of the rivalry between the AFL and the CIO, cases arose in which an employer preferred one of these unions to the other and assisted it in organizing his employees in order to keep the other union out.

Orders issued by the Board in cases of violation of this section required the employer to cease and desist from interfering with the administration of the dominated union and also required the employer to withdraw recognition from that union. The Board also had the power to order disestablishment of the dominated union, an action which, in effect, nullified its effectiveness as a bargaining agent. The Board in general applied the remedy of disestablishment only to unions not affiliated with a national organization—in other words, primarily to so-called "company unions." Where the union that had been assisted by the employer was affiliated with the AFL or the CIO, the Board would usually order the company to withhold recognition from the union as exclusive bargaining agent pending certification. After a sufficient waiting period deemed necessary to restore freedom of choice to the employees in the bargaining unit, the union was again permitted to participate in representation proceedings.

3. *By discrimination in regard to hire or tenure of employment or any term or condition of employment to encourage or discourage membership in any labor organization.*

This section was designed to make it unlawful for employers to use black lists, yellow-dog contracts, or other devices to discourage membership in unions. Employers were forbidden to inquire of job applicants whether they were union members or favored unions, and employers could not fire employees because of union membership or lawful concerted activities protected under the Act. However, it was held not an unfair labor practice for an employer to discharge employees who engaged in unlawful concerted activity such as a sit-down strike, or who struck in violation of a no-strike agreement in a contract.

A proviso was contained in this section permitting an employer who had entered into an agreement with a union duly representing his employees to require membership in the union as a condition of employment. This was the so-called "closed shop" proviso which was amended by the Taft-Hartley Act and will be more fully discussed in Chapter 8.

This section relating to discriminatory employer practices has frequently been called the "heart of the Act." About 30,000 or two thirds of all unfair labor practice charges filed during the twelve-year administration of the Wagner Act included charges of discrimination.[9] In the early years of the Act, acts of discrimination were frequently open and blatant; but as the years progressed, antiunion employers became more astute in their tactics, and discrimination against unions became more refined.

Frequently, cases arose in which an antiunion employer discharged an employee because of union activity and the employees went out on strike in protest. Could the employer replace the striking employees with strikebreakers and thus deter union organization? This obviously would undermine the basic purpose of the Act. The NLRB over the years developed rules of reinstatement applicable to two classes of strikes:

> *a) Unfair Labor Practice Strike.* Those who strike because of or following the employer's unfair labor practices, or who participate in a strike which is prolonged or aggravated by the employer's unfair labor practices, have an absolute right to reinstatement if the strike is for a lawful purpose and lawfully conducted. The employer must reinstate the strikers when they apply for jobs, even if their jobs are filled by replacements. In the case of an unfair labor practice which prolongs what began as a simple economic strike, the strike becomes an unfair practice strike, and the strikers must be reinstated when they request to return to work. Replacements hired after the date the strike was converted into an unfair labor practice strike must be discharged, if necessary, to make room for the strikers.[10]
>
> *b) Economic Strike.* Those who strike for higher wages and other improvements in working conditions have a limited right to reinstatement. They can reclaim their jobs if permanent replacements have not been hired.[11]

Both economic and unfair labor practice strikers who engage in serious misconduct during a strike are not entitled to reinstatement.[12]

A typical reinstatement order issued by the Board would require the employer to offer to the improperly discharged employees immediate and full reinstatement to their former or substantially equivalent positions without prejudice to seniority or other rights. A typical back-pay order would require the employer to compensate the employee for any loss of pay he might have suffered by reason of the employer's unlawful discharge. In determining the amount of back pay due, the Board normally took into consideration the amount of

[9] *Ibid.*, p. 78.

[10] *Kohler Co.*, 46 LRRM 1389.

[11] *National Labor Relations Board* v. *Mackay Radio & Telegraph Co.*, 304 U.S. 333, 58 S. Ct. 904 (1938).

[12] *National Labor Relations Board* v. *Fansteel Metallurgical Corp.*, 306 U.S. 270, 59 S. Ct. 490 (1939).

money the employee might have earned elsewhere subsequent to the discharge.

The rule on replacement of strikers followed by the Board has considerable merit and may well be essential to carry out the basic Congressional intent. It is instructive, however, to examine its operation in practice so that the student can understand the problems it poses to an employer attempting to carry on his business in the face of labor troubles.

In the business world, unfortunately, there is no clear line between an "economic" strike and an "unfair labor practice" strike. This is a distinction the members of the Board draw long after the events have taken place. Let us suppose that there has been an impasse in negotiations between a union and an employer over the terms of a new contract, and the employees strike for higher wages. So the strike begins as an economic strike. Violence erupts around the plant as a result of the picket line interfering with supervisory personnel going into the plant. The employer has the police arrest a number of the strikers on charges of various acts of violence and notifies these men that they are discharged. Among these men are the chief officers of the union. The union immediately brings a charge before the NLRB that the employer discharged these men because of his desire to weaken the union and because of their positions of union leadership. The employer claims that they were the men guilty of the major acts of violence. Meanwhile the strike drags on, and the employer decides to reopen the plant and hires new employees to take the jobs of the striking workers. After a few more months the striking employees realize they are fighting a losing battle and ask to be reinstated to their jobs. What should the employer do?

A wrong answer to this question can cost the employer millions of dollars! If he fires the men who worked in the plant during the strike and takes back his former employees, he minimizes his damages; but he is being unfair to men who were willing to risk the wrath of the union by taking jobs during the strike and who, in all probability, were promised that their jobs would be permanent. If he refuses to reinstate the former employees, and if the NLRB upholds the union claim that the discharges were discriminatory, then the strike will be viewed as an unfair labor practice strike, and the former employees are entitled to reinstatement from the time they terminated the strike. The employer can, of course, appeal such a decision to the courts, but at a tremendous risk, for court appeals take time, and if a year or so later the Court upholds the Board, the employees who were entitled to reinstatement would normally be eligible for back pay for the whole period between their application for reinstatement and the actual date when they are given jobs. Since presumably during this period the "strikebreakers" were employed at these same jobs, the employer is in the position of having to pay double time for work during this entire period. In large companies where perhaps a thousand or more strikers may be involved in a strike, such back-pay liability can amount to millions of dollars.

Employers argue that the threat of onerous back-pay awards plus the tendency of the NLRB to find discriminatory motives in employer discharge policy during strikes have curtailed the ability of employers to operate their plants during strikes. NLRB back-pay award policy has not only acted as a deterrent to discriminatory discharges by employers —which was the statutory intent—but also has strengthened union bargaining power by making the strike more effective as a weapon to close down an employer's operations.

4. *To discharge or otherwise discriminate against an employee because he has filed charges or given testimony under this Act.*

This section was deemed necessary by Congress in order to assure immunity to employees who invoked the provisions of the Act against employers. The problems involving this section that arose in practice were much like those discussed under the preceding section. An employer would demote an employee or shift him to a less desirable job, and then the question would arise whether such action had been taken in retaliation for the employee's bringing a charge under the Act or assisting fellow employees to utilize the procedures of the Act, or, alternatively, whether the action of the employer was motivated by purposes quite unrelated to union organization. Orders issued by the Board under this section were similar to those involved in cases of discrimination under the preceding section.

5. *To refuse to bargain collectively with the representatives of his employees duly chosen pursuant to other provisions of the Act.*

Interpretation of this section must be viewed against the backdrop of antiunion hostility which existed at the time the Wagner Act was adopted. It would serve no useful purpose to promote the organization of unions in response to employee wishes if employers would not meet with union representatives and discuss wages, hours, and other working conditions. And many employers in those early years would not talk to a union representative unless compelled to do so by a court of law. This attitude reflected the strong emphasis on private property rights and individual initiative which characterized our industrial development prior to the thirties. You can visualize the purple rage of a self-made tycoon who has worked himself up by his own bootstraps to a position of authority over thousands of employees and is suddenly told that a union business agent who is not even one of his own employees wants to sit down with him to tell him how to run his business!

This section of the law was inserted to require employers to meet and negotiate with representatives of their employees. It is clear from the legislative history of the Act that Congress did not intend to compel employers to agree to anything; it did want to assure that they would at least sit down and bargain. The language of this section has been the subject of violent criticism, both by management and by union spokesmen. Employers objected to the fact that the obligation to bargain was imposed only on them and not on unions. Furthermore, they criticized the manner in which the NLRB established criteria as to what was "good-faith" bargaining, claiming that such rules, in effect, required employers to come to an agreement contrary to the original statutory purpose.[13] Unions criticized the lack of any effective enforcement procedure under this section. When confronted by a violation of this section of the law, all the Board could do was to issue an order requiring the employer to bargain collectively with the representative of his employees. If an employer was determined to resist union organization, he could draw out the administrative proceedings by demanding a full hearing before the Board, disregarding the Board's order, and appealing the NLRB decision to the courts. Two or three years might elapse before a final order would be handed down which the employer would obey. During this entire period the employer was in a position to weaken the union by refusing to meet with it and ignoring the demands of its representatives. Obviously, many local unions would disintegrate during such a long period when subjected to strong employer pressure.

Nevertheless, despite its ambiguous language, and despite its weak enforcement provisions, the good-faith bargaining requirement was an essential part of the original Wagner Act. While many employers sought means to avoid its strictures and were brought before the Board on unfair labor practice charges,[14] many more employers abided by its provisions and therefore enabled the statutory purpose to become a reality. Without this section as an integral part, the Wagner Act

[13] The problems involved in the good-faith bargaining requirements of the Act will be discussed in detail in Chapter 5.

[14] About 15,000 "refusal to bargain" cases were filed with the NLRB prior to 1947. See Millis and Brown, *op. cit.*, p. 79.

would have been less effective in promoting collective bargaining between labor and management through unions representing employees. Whether or not this statutory language serves a useful purpose today is a question which will be explored in a subsequent chapter.

The prohibition of specific unfair labor practices in the Wagner Act ushered in a new era in labor relations. Whereas, in earlier years, labor leaders found the power of the courts interfering with their organizing activities, with the advent of the Wagner Act the courts, in effect, became an ally of labor, standing ready to enforce valid orders of the NLRB in cases where the Board had found an employer guilty of unfair labor practices and the employer ignored the Board's cease and desist order. Despite its shortcomings, and despite the delays attendant upon its enforcement, the unfair labor practice procedure contained in the Act represented such an improvement from organized labor's point of view over pre-Wagner Act conditions that organizing activity was greatly enhanced.

Unfair labor practice charges were brought by labor before the NLRB to curb unlawful practices of antiunion employers. Labor also soon found that filing such charges was an excellent propaganda device in an organizing campaign. In the heat of an organizing campaign, when tempers were frayed on both sides, it was not difficult for union business agents to find some evidence of employer unfair practices sufficient to warrant an NLRB investigation. Thus the statutory unfair labor practice procedure became a sword as well as a shield for labor in its struggle with management over the right to organize employees. It is perhaps significant that in the twelve-year period of administration covered by the original Wagner Act, in the more than 43,000 complaint cases closed by the NLRB, employers were actually found guilty of violation of the law in only 45 per cent of the cases.[15] Labor spokesmen cite this record as evidence of the ineffectiveness of the Board because of its inadequate staff and lack of funds; management spokesmen argue that these statistics show how unwarranted most union-filed charges were in reality; defenders of the Board claim that this record shows how the Board leaned over backwards to be fair to employers!

REPRESENTATION PROCEDURES

Equally as important as unfair labor practice cases in the work of the NLRB and every bit as controversial as a result of the split in

[15] *Ibid.*, p. 83.

the American labor movement which existed until 1955 have been representation cases. Section 9 (*a*) of the Wagner Act provided: "Representatives . . . selected for the purposes of collective bargaining by the majority of the employees in a unit appropriate for such purposes shall be the exclusive representatives of all the employees in such unit for the purposes of collective bargaining. . . ."

Election Procedures

The language quoted above from Section 9 (*a*) of the Act contains the entire Congressional dictate concerning the matter of selection of bargaining representatives. Obviously, the Board was called upon to improvise many rules to govern the complicated situations which actually presented themselves.

In the first place, the Board soon learned that it could not process every request received from a union for an election. Union business agents are notoriously optimistic when it comes to representation cases, and sometimes a union which claims a majority of employees in a plant may actually have relatively few adherents. Therefore the Board adopted a rule requiring a "showing of interest" as a prerequisite to an election. Specifically, it would not entertain an election petition of a union unless the union could show that it represented at least 30 per cent of the employees involved. The usual method of determination was by comparing cards authorizing the union to represent particular employees with a count of the total number of employees in the unit as revealed by the employer's payroll records.

The Act said nothing about employer petitions for elections, and therefore the NLRB adopted the policy of permitting employer applications for elections only if two or more unions were claiming to represent the employees. The Board's reluctance to permit employer applications founded on claims for representation by only one union was probably based on the notion that in this early period, when many unions were relatively weak and in the formative stages of organization, employers would take advantage of the right to petition for elections by calling for such elections prematurely, before unions had completed their organization campaigns.

Early in its life the NLRB was forced to determine whether a majority meant a majority of those eligible to vote or a majority of those who actually voted. At first, it adopted the former interpretation, but it soon found that this inspired coercion by employers to keep employees from voting. The NLRB then altered its policies and certified unions as bargaining agents if they received a majority of votes cast.

This meant that a union which received approval of only a minority of the total number of employees in a bargaining unit could become the exclusive bargaining agent for *all* employees in the unit, whether members of the union or not. This proved a wise move, for it compelled all interested groups to vie in getting out the vote. As a result, votes cast in NLRB elections averaged 80–90 per cent of those eligible, as compared with the average 50–65 per cent of those eligible who vote in national political elections.

Representation elections were held by secert ballot in enclosed voting booths under the close supervision of NLRB officials. The names of the union or unions seeking certification were placed on the ballot along with "No Union." If a union won a majority of these votes, it was certified as the bargaining agent with which the employer had to bargain as the exclusive agent of the employees involved. If "No Union" received a majority, no certification was made.

The conflict between AFL and CIO unions greatly complicated election procedures for the Board. When Congress passed the Wagner Act, it did not, of course, foresee the split in the labor movement. Therefore, it anticipated that in those situations where employees wanted to be represented by a union, a petition for an election would be filed with the Board by the union (normally an AFL affiliate), and a prompt, peaceful determination of the question of the representation would be made through the administrative procedures of the Board.

This procedure broke down when AFL and CIO unions engaged in a bitter struggle with each other over the right to represent employees in given bargaining units. Instead, the plant became a battleground, with both employer and employees as casualties. If one union felt confident enough to move for an early election, the other union would use all sorts of pressures to defer it. If it appeared that one union was successfully signing up members in a plant, the other might institute a boycott of the products of the company, picket the premises, threaten workers, or use similar pressures to weaken the hold of the rival union. The employer could do nothing to protect his business or employees against such tactics, for the Norris–La Guardia Act had deprived employers of their most effective weapon—the injunction. Since the Wagner Act imposed no prohibition on the activities of unions similar to the unfair labor practices proscribed for employers, employees had no way to protect themselves against such union pressures.

Even after one union was certified as the exclusive bargaining agent, there was nothing in the Wagner Act which prohibited a rival union from continuing its organizing and harrassing activities, including picketing and boycotting. Employers were bound by the results of an NLRB election; but a rival union which lost an election was not bound by such results as a practical matter, since it could still attempt to achieve through economic pressure what it could not accomplish through peaceful procedures under the Act.

In holding an election where rival unions were involved, the Board had to formulate its own procedures for deciding the victor, since the Act did not spell out such details. The Board decided that in such cases the ballot should give the employees an opportunity to vote for either of the two unions and also for "No Union." Suppose AFL union A and CIO union B both claimed the right to represent the employees in a given unit. The ballot would contain A, B, and "No Union" (or "Neither"). If either A, B, or "No Union" obtained a majority of the votes cast, that determined the final outcome of the election. But suppose that out of 500 votes cast, A received 150, B 160, and "No Union" 190. Then the Board would hold a runoff election with only the two highest choices on the ballot, namely B and "No Union." On the other hand, if A and B each polled more than "No Union," but neither had a majority, the runoff would be between the two unions. The Act itself laid down no rules for this type of circumstance, and the Board was continually under attack by both union and management representatives for decisions it found necessary to make in hotly contested elections involving more than one union.

Another controversial issue involved the question of who is entitled to vote in an election. Usually, the payroll period immediately preceding the date on which the direction of election issued governs. There is almost always a debate about the eligibility of seasonal employees, part-time employees, and those ill or temporarily laid off. On each of these issues the Board may be called upon to make an individual determination.

We have already discussed the problem of reinstatement orders, which depend upon whether or not the Board puts the label of "economic" or "unfair labor practice" on a particular strike. A similar controversial issue is raised when an election is called after an employer has replaced striking employees with so-called "strikebreakers." Who should be entitled to vote in such a case—the new employees, the replaced employees, or both?

Suppose that employer A has been negotiating with union B. The union demands a large wage increase and other benefits which the employer refuses to grant. An impasse develops, and the employees strike. The employer decides to attempt to continue to run the plant and succeeds in hiring new employees. He is able to get these employees only by promising them that they will be permanent employees and will not be fired if the strikers decide to return to their jobs. Now, the union, seeing that the jobs of its members are threatened, requests an election. The union claims its members have a continuing status as employees—they are not at work but are still employees of the company. The new employees say they are working and have every right to determine whether or not they are to be represented at the place of their work by a union.

The NLRB wrestled with this problem and decided that where an economic strike was involved—that is, one not involving unfair labor practices by the employer—both the strikers and the men who replaced them were eligible to vote.[16] On the other hand, if the strike was the result of unfair labor practices by the employer—such as a refusal to bargain, interference with the union, discrimination against union employees, etc.—then only the strikers were entitled to vote. As we shall see in a subsequent chapter, the right of strikers to vote in representation elections was substantially altered by the Taft-Hartley amendments to the NLRA.

Bargaining Unit Problems

If the majority rule question posed difficult problems for the NLRB, they were relatively easy to solve compared with the problems involved in deciding which group of employees should be designated as a unit for the purpose of determining their wishes with respect to a bargaining representative. Congress delegated this problem, known as the question of the "appropriate bargaining unit," to the NLRB, giving it almost unlimited authority[17] in Section 9 (*b*) of the Wagner Act, which stated that "the Board shall decide in each case whether, in order to insure to employees the full benefit of their right to self-organization and to collective bargaining, and otherwise to effectuate the policies of this Act, the unit appropriate for the purposes of collective bargaining shall be the employer unit, craft unit, plant unit, or subdivision thereof." This wide authority was given to the NLRB in the belief, based on experience of the NRA labor boards, that the various problems which arise in practice are not foreseeable and can

[16] *Rudolph Wurlitzer Co.*, 32 NLRB 163 (1941).

[17] This authority has been restricted to some extent in the Taft-Hartley Act with respect to craft units, guards, and professional employees.

best be determined by the NLRB. The AFL supported this viewpoint —not, of course, being able to predict that a full-fledged rival would arise to have equal status and different views on bargaining unit problems.

In most cases, however, the NLRB was able to secure agreement from the parties on the bargaining unit. Although the Board decided each case on its merits, it grouped the facts determining its bargaining unit decisions around two basic criteria—the history of collective bargaining, if any, and the mutuality of interest of the employeees.

In the first group were such factors as the past relationships between unions and employees, the unit covered by such relationships, the jurisdictional rules of the unions, and past unsuccessful efforts of self-organization. Strike histories were also important, for strikes show relationships and test the homogeneity of groups.

Around mutuality of interest, the Board placed a variety of factors, such as geographical location, manner of wage payment, degree of skill, comparability of wages, working conditions, etc. This meant that the typical bargaining unit was composed of production and maintenance employees in a single plant. Foremen and supervisors were excluded from the production workers' unit because of their peculiar relationship to management. Likewise, office, clerical, and white-collar workers were separated from production and maintenance employees, as were professional employees. In addition, guards and watchmen were placed in separate units because of their unique position, and temporary employees were often deemed outside the bargaining unit because they had no permanent status in the plant. All these decisions were based on the fact that production and maintenance employees have a basic common denominator which was lacking among other plant groups, especially since many of the latter have a special and different relation to the employer.

Determination of the bargaining unit, which at best was a most difficult problem, was further complicated by the rivalry between the AFL and the CIO. The struggle between these two groups was reflected in two major types of contested cases.

Craft-Industrial Problems. It will be recalled that at the time of enactment of the Wagner Act, the great basic industries of the country—steel, automobile, electrical, chemical, oil, etc.—were largely unorganized. It was in these industries that the CIO concentrated its organizing drives as it sought to organize on an industrial basis. Here it came into conflict with the AFL, which frequently represented strategically placed individual crafts in such industries. For example, in the metal industries a CIO union might ask that all production and maintenance workers be placed in one unit, but the CIO's petition might be contested by the AFL, which already represented the patternmakers and did not want them to be submerged in the larger unit.

In shaping policy in such cases, the Board had only vague guidance from Congress—"in order to insure to employees the full benefit of their right to self-organization and to collective bargaining, and otherwise to effectuate the policies of this Act." The right to self-organization might be best served by permitting the patternmakers to be represented by a separate union, but the policy of the Act was to strengthen unions, and fragmentation of bargaining units would seem to be contrary to this purpose.

In resolving this issue, the Board would consider the claims of both parties, and if it found, upon the basis of all the factors, that the craft could logically lay claim to consideration as a separate bargaining unit, and if there was reasonable doubt as to whether the majority of this craft preferred representation by the craft union, or by the union claiming wider jurisdiction, the NLRB permitted the workers in the craft to determine the issue for themselves. The Board accomplished this by providing that the workers in the craft would have a choice in an election of the craft union, the industrial union, or no union, whereas the other production and maintenance workers would vote only for the industrial union or no union. If the craft union won the election among the patternmakers and the industrial union among the other workers, the Board would then divide the plant into two units and certify the craft union as bargaining agent for the craft and the industrial union as bargaining agent for the remaining production and maintenance workers. If, however, the industrial union won bargaining rights for both the craft and the other production and maintenance workers, the NLRB would place the craft in the same unit as the other production and maintenance workers, and would certify the industrial union as the bargaining agent for the single large unit. Finally, if either group voted for no union, no certification would be issued where the workers did not wish to be represented by a union.

Multiunit Problems. A bargaining unit could be a department of a particular plant, or an entire plant, or an entire company encompassing many plants. It could be limited to one location, or to a region, or to many cities. In cases where a multiunit company was being organized, the NLRB had to consider whether the policy of the Act was best effectuated by a company-wide or by a more restricted bargaining unit. This frequently created a bitter clash between CIO and AFL unions, since one union may have had strength in one plant and not in others. A good example of how the bargaining unit determination affected the bargaining strength of a union in a particular industry is provided by the West Coast longshoremen's case. The CIO union headed by Harry Bridges had the most members on the whole West Coast, but there were four ports which were organized by the AFL. When the issue of the appropriate bargaining unit first came before the NLRB in 1938, it decided that the entire West Coast was the appropriate bargaining unit,[18] thus destroying AFL control in the four ports. In making this decision, the Board undoubtedly was motivated by a desire to create a strong union which could deal effectively with the employers, who were organized on a multiunit, multicity basis. However, the decision was bitterly attacked by the AFL as evidence of bias on the part of the Board and of its intention to shape the labor movement according to its own wishes. Subsequently, in 1941, after a change in membership of the Board, this case was reconsidered, and the ports with AFL locals were allowed to bargain separately.[19]

APPRAISAL OF THE WAGNER ACT

This chapter began with the observation that the Wagner Act was the most significant labor law ever enacted in the United States. We might now add that it was also the most controversial. From the date of its enactment the Wagner Act and its administrative agency, the National Labor Relations Board, were subject to constant attack and criticism by both labor and management. In retrospect, this is not really surprising. The Board was charged with a monumental task—to promote collective bargaining by enabling workers to select representatives of their own choosing in an industrial and business milieu charged with employer hostility to organized labor. To carry out this purpose, the Board had a minimum of personnel, no landmarks in the law to add flesh to the bare bones of the statute, and a continuing inadequate appropriation reflecting Congressional distrust of its actions. In no year of its administration of the Wagner Act did the Board ever have more than $4.5 million to spend, nor did its staff ever reach as high as one thousand members, though its responsibility extended from coast to coast and from Maine to Florida. Little wonder that delay in accomplishing its work was a constant problem throughout its administration.

[18] *Shipowners' Association of the Pacific Coast*, 7 NLRB 1002 (1938).

[19] 32 NLRB 668 (1941); 33 NLRB 845 (1941).

To make matters worse, the Board never really had a chance to function in what might be called a "normal" period. Its early years were beset by problems arising from the contest of the law's constitutionality; then came the division in the labor movement, with both the AFL and the CIO charging the NLRB with bias; finally, there were the myriads of unforeseen problems associated with defense, war, and a postwar economy.

Despite these problems the Wagner Act achieved its basic purpose—to promote collective bargaining. In 1935, when the Act became law, union membership stood at 3.9 million. In 1947, when the Wagner Act was amended, union membership exceeded 15 million. In 1935, about 19 per cent of workers in manufacturing were covered by collective bargaining agreements; in 1946, coverage had risen to 69 per cent.[20] Although this tremendous union growth must be attributed to many factors, it was without doubt substantially hastened by the Wagner Act. If the Wagner Act is judged in terms of fulfillment of its stated policy of "encouraging the practice and procedure of collective bargaining," it was eminently successful.

On the other hand, the Wagner Act cannot be said to have minimized the causes of industrial disputes except in one important respect. The representation procedure of the Act provided a peaceful and democratic means of determining whether a union had the right to represent a group of employees. The substitution of NLRB procedure for the use of force in determining this question was one of the great contributions of the Act.

In so far as strikes generally are concerned, however, the Wagner Act had little contribution to make. Congress gave the NLRB no authority to interfere in disputes over terms and conditions of employment. Once the union was certified as bargaining agent and the employer's conduct was purged of unfair labor practices, the Wagner Act left matters to the parties themselves. But since the protection of the Act spurred union activity, the period 1935–41 saw a great surge of union growth. A combination of immature unions and management inexperienced in industrial relations resulted in numerous strikes which more mature and experienced parties might have avoided. Critics of the Wagner Act blamed either the Act or its administration by the NLRB as the cause of the strife. Proponents of the Act blamed management opposition both to the Act and to unions as the cause. Perhaps a more accurate analysis would place the blame mainly on growing pains of unions and learning pains of employers.

[20] Millis and Brown, *op. cit.*, pp. 76–77.

A major criticism directed against the NLRB under the Wagner Act was its alleged bias—a charge, interestingly enough, joined in by both labor and management spokesmen. For example, the Hartley Report issued in connection with consideration of the Taft-Hartley amendments to the Act in 1947 stated: "The committee's investigations, as well as those of preceding Congresses, have shown bias and prejudice to be rampant in the Board's staff, and among some members of the Board itself."[21]

When employers complained that the NLRB was biased, what they really meant was that the Board tended to favor unions rather than employers in findings of fact and procedural issues before it. This was probably so. Indeed, it can be argued that the Board could not have carried out the statutory policy had this not been so. It should be remembered that the Wagner Act itself was a biased Act in basic concept—it was prounion, and therefore necessarily antiemployer in purpose and outlook, bearing in mind the attitude of most employers at the time. Unions were the underdog, the victims of discrimination by large, strong employers. Against this backdrop of circumstance and statutory purpose, it is not surprising that many employers came to feel that they did not get a fair hearing before the Board.

The union charges of bias came primarily from the AFL, which alleged that the Board favored the CIO in elections and was opposed to carving out craft splinter units from large industrial groups, despite the wishes of the craft workers. Actually, the statistics indicate that AFL affiliates won about the same number of elections over the years as did CIO affiliates—12,353 for the AFL compared to 13,837 for the CIO. Moreover, on the issue of severance of craft units, the statistics indicate that the AFL had little to complain about:

> In contested cases where the Board had to decide the unit, requests for craft units were granted in the great majority, outright in nearly 30 per cent of the cases, and provisionally with Globe elections in another 42 per cent. Moreover, the AFL fared far better before the Board in contested cases. It received the unit it wanted, outright or provisionally in 64.5 per cent of the cases compared to only 50 per cent for the CIO in their cases. In 260 cases where craft Globe elections took place, craft won in 80 per cent.[22]

[21] U.S. House of Representatives, Committee on Education and Labor, *Labor-Management Relations Act, 1947*, Report No. 245, 80th Congress, 1st session (Washington, D.C.: U.S. Government Printing Office, April 11, 1947), p. 26.

[22] Millis and Brown, *op. cit.*, p. 144. These results are based on an analysis of statistics for 1943–44. Globe elections are those in which craft groups are permitted to vote separately to determine whether they shall be represented by a craft union in a separate craft unit or by an industrial union in a larger plant-wide unit. The name derives from the case of *Globe Machine and Stamping Co.*, 3 NLRB 294 (1937).

The Prelude to Amendment

In appraising the Wagner Act, it should be observed that laws are merely imperfect instruments through which men attempt to impose rules of conduct on other men. If the mores, the basic beliefs of a large segment of the community, are hostile to such laws, the laws will usually not work (one has only to think back to Prohibition days to find a vivid illustration of this maxim). The Wagner Act was imposed upon a hostile employer community; yet despite this circumstance, it achieved its major objectives. It fostered the organization of unions; it reduced the number of strikes arising out of the issue of union recognition; it contributed to a rise in the level of wages and prices.

Indeed, it accomplished its objectives so well that it created new problems requiring new legislation. Unions grew so large and strong under its favorable shelter that the pendulum in industrial relations shifted radically. From a position of underdog, unions were able to dictate terms to small employers in many industries. Union leaders could call strikes which could paralyze whole industries, deprive large cities of necessary services, and possibly endanger the national health or safety. Union-induced wage increases, which had been viewed with favor during the deflationary era of the thirties, now became a major source of concern in the inflationary postwar period.

At the same time, too, a gradual change occurred in the public attitude toward the role of law in industrial relations. The Wagner Act, like its predecessor Norris–La Guardia Act, was essentially laissez-faire in attitude toward labor relations. Norris–La Guardia simply eliminated the courts as a convenient ally for employers in union-management conflicts; the Wagner Act went a step further in providing an administrative agency to assist the organization of unions. But neither act purported to govern the substantive terms of labor agreements or to impose the power of government upon the parties in disputes arising over wages, hours, and other working conditions.

But by 1946, public opinion had come to the recognition that the power of government would have to be exerted to curb some of the abuses which had been created as a result of inadequacies of the Wagner Act. For example, even the most outspoken proponent of *laissez faire* in labor relations would find it difficult to defend the situation which arose under the Wagner Act wherein an employer was compelled to bargain with a union certified as bargaining agent for his employees, yet a rival union was free to strike his plant and thereby destroy his business with impunity. Furthermore, the great strikes of the year 1946 convinced the majority of the public that the Wagner Act was responsible for much industrial unrest. Therefore, when the Republican Party captured control of Congress in 1946, its leaders believed that they had a mandate to enact legislation which would lessen the number of strikes and eliminate the inequities of the Wagner Act. This, then, was the background for the Taft-Hartley amendments, which we shall now examine in detail.

QUESTIONS FOR DISCUSSION

1. How did the conflict between the CIO and the AFL complicate the task of the NLRB in its determination of appropriate bargaining units?
2. What is the difference between an unfair labor practice strike and an economic strike? Is the distinction a meaningful one? How are the rights of employer and employee affected by NLRB determination as to the nature of a strike?
3. Enumerate the employer unfair labor practices prohibited by the Wagner Act. Discuss the reasons why each of these prohibitions was necessary in order to encourage free collective bargaining.

SUGGESTIONS FOR FURTHER READING

Cox, Archibald, and Dunlop, J. T. "Regulation of Collective Bargaining by the National Labor Relations Board," *Harvard Law Review,* Vol. LXIII (January, 1950), pp. 389–432.

An analysis of the extent to which the NLRB, under the original Wagner Act, regulated the terms and processes of collective bargaining.

Gregory, Charles O. *Labor and the Law,* chap. xii, pp. 341–85. 2d rev. ed. New York: W. W. Norton & Co., Inc., 1961.

A review of the most significant court decisions which interpreted and clarified various provisions of the Wagner Act.

Millis, H. A., and Brown, E. C. *From the Wagner Act to Taft-Hartley,* Part I, pp. 1–268. Chicago: University of Chicago Press, 1950.

A basic treatise on the Wagner Act, including a detailed discussion of controversial issues in administration of the Act.

Chapter 4 THE TAFT-HARTLEY ACT: ITS CONTENT AND MEANING

The Taft-Hartley Act was for many years a subject of controversy between representatives of labor and management. Union leaders called it a "slave labor law" and the "Lawyers Full-Employment Act." Industry spokesmen hailed it as a Magna Charta of employees' rights and complained that it did not go far enough in outlawing various undesirable union practices. In this chapter, we shall consider in detail the various provisions of the Act and its effect upon employers, unions, individual employees, and the general public. In the following chapter, we shall appraise the Act and the record of the National Labor Relations Board in administering it, and consider its implications for the future of effective collective bargaining in this country.

Economic and Legislative Background

We have seen that by the year 1946 the tide of public opinion was running against organized labor's unrestricted use of the bargaining power conferred upon it by the Wagner Act. The average American was appalled by the power of a union which, twice within the space of one year, could tie up a vital industry such as coal. Public utility strikes, like the lengthy strike of electric light and power workers in Pittsburgh, were particularly damaging to the union cause. Results of the Congressional election in November, 1946, reflected strong public dissatisfaction with current labor policies. Congress was in the mood for restrictive labor legislation; and on June 23, 1947, it passed the Labor Management Relations Act—more popularly called the Taft-Hartley Act—over President Truman's veto.

Thus ended an important stage in the development of national labor policy in this country. The attitude of government toward collective bargaining by employees had passed through a succession of stages from active hostility in the early 1800's, when labor organizations were prosecuted as conspiracies, to active encouragement of union organization under the Wagner Act. Enactment of the Taft-Hartley Act represented a new stage in government treatment of both management and labor. The metamorphosis which had occurred in public thinking on the subject of collective bargaining is well exemplified by a comparison of the original phraseology of Section 7 of the Wagner Act with its revised wording in the Taft-Hartley Act: "Employees shall have the right to self-organization . . . for the purpose of collective bargaining or other mutual aid or protection, and shall also have the right to refrain from any or all of such activities. . . ." Whereas formerly the weight of government influence had been placed behind union organization activities, the Taft-Hartley Act appeared to place the government in the position of a neutral, recognizing the right of employees to organize or not to organize. In theory, the government was to be not a partisan but a policeman, protecting both management and labor from unfair labor practices. However, as we shall observe in the later discussion, critics have alleged that the actual administration of the Act has deviated from this apparent statutory policy.

The Taft-Hartley Act also qualified the principle that organized labor should be free to use its economic weapons without restriction. Secondary boycotts, strikes, and picketing for certain purposes were all subjected to regulation by the Act. In this and other respects which will be discussed in the text, the Taft-Hartley Act established the principle that law, protecting the interest of management, labor, and the public, plays a necessary role in labor relations.

Scope and Administration of the Act

The Labor Management Relations Act of 1947 was, in form, an amendment of the Wagner Act. Title I incorporated the text of the Wagner Act—with, however, a number of major modifications and additions. Title II, which dealt with conciliation of labor disputes and national emergency strikes, is discussed in Chapter 13. Title III authorized suits by and against unions, and Title IV created a joint committee to study and report on basic problems affecting friendly labor relations and productivity.

Administration

Administration of the Act remained under the National Labor Relations Board, but a number of important changes were made in the composition and power of the NLRB. Section 3 of the Act enlarged the Board from three to five members. To remedy the oft-repeated charge made against the Board under the Wagner Act that it was both judge and prosecutor, the prosecuting function was removed from the Board and vested in a General Counsel who in this respect was made completely independent of the Board. In the handling of cases the General Counsel has final authority, subject neither to appeal to the Board nor to the courts, both as to institution of formal unfair labor practice proceedings and dismissal of charges. The General Counsel is also responsible for the administration of the Board's field offices and field personnel, but not the staff of trial examiners who hear unfair practice cases. For a time, it appeared that the effective operation of this agency would be impaired by disagreements between the General Counsel and the Board as to what employers and employees were subject to the Act. In early 1950 the Board revoked its prior issuance of administrative functions to the General Counsel and issued a modified substitute which subjected the General Counsel to the Board's direction in matters of basic policy.

The personnel of the NLRB has mushroomed since its early days. Whereas, in 1935, this agency had only 62 field employees, by 1963 the number had swelled to about 1,100. In addition to field personnel, there are about 700 NLRB employees in the Washington office today, compared with the 53 who originally made up the headquarters staff. Despite this increase in administrative staff, the NLRB has continually been plagued with time-consuming delays in the handling of cases. For example, in fifty-seven unfair labor practice cases decided by the Board in March, 1961, it was found that the median time from filing the unfair practice charge to the issuance of the decision by the NLRB was 402 days.[1] In addition, it takes a typical case 396 days more to reach the state of effective judicial decree compelling compliance with the Act.[2] Justice delayed so long is frequently justice denied. By the time a final decision is rendered by a court enforcing a Board order, the employer involved may have gone out of business, or the union may have disintegrated.

A good example of the time-consuming red tape which has slowed down the Board's processes is evidenced by the celebrated Kohler case which was finally decided by the NLRB in 1961. This was one of the longest and most extensively litigated cases in the history of the Board. Charges of unfair labor practices were first filed by the UAW against the company in April, 1954. The written record in this case formed a stack of documents 16 feet high. The transcript consisted of more than 20,000 pages, and there were 1,900 exhibits.[3]

[1] LRR, 48 Anal 52.

[2] 45 LRR 336.

[3] National Labor Relations Board, *Twenty-sixth Annual Report* (Washington, D.C.: U.S. Government Printing Office, 1962), p. 3.

The NLRB has sought to speed up its handling of cases by delegating decision-making authority to the Board's twenty-eight regional directors. Acting pursuant to authority given the Board by Congress in the 1959 amendments to the Taft-Hartley Act, the NLRB in 1961 delegated decision-making authority in election cases to its regional directors. This delegation includes decisions as to whether a question concerning representation exists, determination of appropriate bargaining unit, direction of elections to determine whether employees wish union representation for collective bargaining purposes, and rulings on other matters such as challenged ballots and objections to elections. Under the new procedure the regional directors decide all election cases, and the Board in Washington considers appeals[4] only

1. Where a substantial question of law or policy is raised because of the absence of or departure from officially reported precedent.
2. Where the regional director's decision on a substantial factual issue is clearly erroneous, and such error prejudicially affects the rights of a party.
3. Where the conduct of the hearing in an election case or any ruling made in connection with the proceeding has resulted in prejudicial error.
4. Where there are compelling reasons for reconsideration of an important Board rule or policy.

The significance of this new procedure is demonstrated by the fact that the regional directors disposed of the first fifty-two cases under the new arrangement in an average of 34 days from filing to direction of election; whereas during the preceding six months under the old procedure it had taken the NLRB an average of 113 days to dispose of such cases.[5]

When a petition for an election is filed, it is first assigned to a regional office employee, usually a field examiner, for investigation. He checks on the relationship of the business to interstate commerce, the necessary showing of employee interest, and related issues. Such investigation may lead the regional director to dismiss the petition, in which case the matter is closed unless there is an appeal. If, on the other hand, the investigation discloses that there is merit to the petition, then the examiner tries to get the parties to utilize the Board's informal machinery. This is of two types. Under one procedure, the agreement for a consent election, the parties agree to waive all rights

[4] Up to January 1, 1962, one thousand contested election decisions were handed down by regional directors; and of these, only 3 per cent were granted appeal by the NLRB. See the speech of Frank W. McCulloch, Chairman of the NLRB, before the American Management Association, Chicago, Illinois, February 15, 1962.

[5] *Twenty-sixth Annual Report,* p. 2.

to a hearing at any stage, and the regional director makes binding rulings on all questions related to the election. Under the second procedure, the stipulation for certification upon a consent election, the parties waive only the right to pre-election hearings and agree that the Board itself shall rule on election issues. By encouraging consent elections, the Board has been able to dispose of three out of every four election cases in its field offices.[6]

If the parties decide not to utilize the informal procedures outlined above, the regional director schedules a hearing before an NLRB regional employee as hearing officer. The latter produces a full record of factual issues. On the basis of this record the regional director then decides whether or not an election shall be held.

It might be thought that after the holding of representation elections for more than twenty-five years, there would be a slackening of cases of this type. On the contrary, in recent years there seems to have been an actual increase in petitions for election. In the fiscal year 1961, for example, 10,559 representation cases were filed with the Board—the largest number in its history.[7]

In 1961 the NLRB sought approval from Congress to delegate decision-making authority in unfair labor practice cases as well as election cases, but the legislature would not grant such approval for the former category of cases. The time-consuming pattern of handling unfair labor practice cases therefore continues as in the past. This poses a real problem to the Board because the case load of unfair labor practice charges has sharply increased. Unfair labor practice case filings more than doubled in the last five years—from 5,606 in fiscal 1957 to 12,132 in fiscal 1961.[8]

Extent of Coverage of the Act

Under both the original Wagner Act and the Taft-Hartley Act, the NLRB was granted jurisdiction extending to any business "affecting commerce." Because of its limited budget, however, the Board has never exercised fully the powers granted to it by Congress. In 1950, 1954, and 1958,[9] the Board laid down general standards intended to

[6] LRR, 48 Anal 3.

[7] *Twenty-sixth Annual Report,* p. 8.

[8] *Ibid.,* p. 5.

[9] Under Section 701 of the Landrum-Griffin Act, which limits the discretion of the Board in declining jurisdiction, reference is made to "standards prevailing upon August 1, 1959." These standards incorporate the general standards announced on October 2, 1958, referred to in part above in the text, and standards affecting the hotel and motel industry set forth in the case of the Florida Hotel of Tampa, Inc. (44 LRRM 1345) on July 30, 1959.

exclude "local businesses" from the Board's jurisdiction. These standards, based upon sales volume and similar criteria, were intended to keep the Board from being inundated with a flood of cases involving small companies with relatively few employees. For example, under the new standards the Board will not take jurisdiction of cases involving retail concerns unless they do a gross volume of business of $500,000 or more. Nonretail concerns must show at least $50,000 "outflow or inflow, direct or indirect."[10] Office buildings must have gross revenue of $100,000, of which $25,000 or more is derived from organizations which meet any of the new standards. Public utilities must have $250,000 gross volume or $50,000 outflow or inflow, direct or indirect. Wholesale utilities are subject to the general nonretail standard; transit systems require $250,000 gross volume; radio, television, telegraph, and telephone must have $100,000 gross volume; and newspapers, $200,000 gross volume. The Board will take jurisdiction of cases involving instrumentalities, links, and channels of interstate commerce only if $50,000 is derived from the interstate (or linkage) part of the enterprise, or from services performed for employers in interstate commerce.

The action of the Board in thus limiting its jurisdiction nullified in practice certain aspects of the protection which the Act attempted to afford to small employers. For example, the Taft-Hartley Act makes it an unfair labor practice to coerce an employer or self-employed person to join a union. Obviously, this provision is most meaningful in the case of small employers or self-employed persons working without hired help; yet the Board would not ordinarily take jurisdiction of such cases because the business involved did not normally meet the Board's jurisdictional requirements. To make matters worse, the United States Supreme Court held in a series of decisions that state labor relations boards had no power to act in cases involving interstate commerce where the National Labor Relations Board had refused to assert jurisdiction. The High Court reasoned that Congress, by vesting in the NLRB jurisdiction over labor relations matters affecting interstate commerce, had completely displaced state power to act. The net result

[10] Direct outflow refers to goods or services furnished to customers outside the state. Indirect outflow refers to goods or services furnished to customers within the state who themselves meet a jurisdictional standard other than indirect outflow. Direct inflow refers to goods or services furnished directly to the employer from outside the state in which the employer is located. Indirect inflow refers to the purchase of goods or services which originated outside the employer's state but which he purchased from a seller within the state. Direct and indirect outflow may be combined, and direct and indirect inflow may also be combined to meet the $50,000 requirement. However, outflow and inflow may not be combined.

of NLRB policy and the Supreme Court's interpretation of the law was the creation of a no man's land in the field of labor relations where the small employer was without a forum to hear his case. This serious defect in the administration of the Taft-Hartley Act was not remedied until enactment of the Landrum-Griffin Act in 1959.[11]

The Taft-Hartley Act made important changes in the definition of "employer" and "employee" as these terms were used in the Wagner Act. Formerly, the term "employer" included "any person acting in the interest of the employer." Now it was redefined to include any person acting as "agent of an employer directly or indirectly." The reason for this change was that the NLRB had held employers liable for unfair practices when these practices had actually been engaged in by minor supervisory employees who sometimes acted without authority and even contrary to express instructions from their employers. Union leaders, however, charged that this change in terminology had gone too far, since it would make it difficult for the NLRB to take action against employers' associations which engage in "open-shop drives" or other unfair practices unless it could be proved that the employer had actually constituted the association his agent for this purpose. In actual practice the change in language has made little difference, because the NLRB has utilized the statutory phrase "directly or indirectly" to give the term "agent" a broad interpretation.

Most important, perhaps, was the removal of supervisors from the protective coverage of the Act. Under the Wagner Act the NLRB vacillated as to whether or not that Act protected the right of supervisors to form unions and engage in collective bargaining, but it consistently held that the Act protected supervisors as employees from discriminatory practices by employers. Under the Taft-Hartley Act, however, supervisors were deprived of both of these protections and were therefore compelled to rely solely on economic weapons to achieve their objectives. Supervisors could still join unions, but employers were free to use any means to intimidate and forestall such organization. In practice, the Taft-Hartley Act dealt unions of supervisors a hard blow. After its enactment, contracts of the Foreman's Association of America with Ford Motor Company and other important firms were not renewed. However, the Act has had little effect in printing and other industries in which it was customary to include foremen in unions of employees. The Act distinguished between straw bosses, lead men, setup men, and other minor supervisory employees, on the one hand,

[11] See Chapter 6 for a discussion of the manner in which the 1959 Act dealt with this problem.

and supervisors vested with such genuine management prerogatives as the right to hire, fire, or discipline, on the other. Only the latter were excluded from the Act.

The treatment of supervisors under the Taft-Hartley Act has been criticized on the ground that it disregards past history and practice, and attempts to assimilate to management a group whose fears and hopes and needs are in many cases more akin to those of employees than employers. Foremen and other classes of supervisors are in an anomalous position in American industry. They are supposed to be the representatives of management in the shop, but they also have problems concerning their own wages and hours which tend to put them in the position of employees versus management. Under the Wagner Act the NLRB certified unions of foremen. In doing so, the Board did not distinguish between independent and affiliated unions of foremen. It did, however, place foremen in separate bargaining units from those of rank-and-file employees. This separation was more apparent than real in instances in which the same union was certified as the representative of the foremen and of the rank and file. The problem that concerned Congress was this: If employees belong to an AFL union and strike, and the foremen also belong to an AFL union, will the foremen be loyal to management or to the AFL? The Taft-Hartley Act seeks to discourage organization of supervisors and thus solve this problem of divided loyalties. The fact is, however, that foremen will not be loyal representatives of management unless management pays them adequately, hears their grievances, and through training and indoctrination makes them feel a part of the management group.

HOW THE EMPLOYER WAS AFFECTED

In form, the Taft-Hartley Act retained the five unfair labor practices specified in the Wagner Act; and therefore, to a casual reader, it might appear that the employer is still subject to the same restrictions as under the Wagner Act. Actually, however, a number of newly added provisions were intended to afford the employer new privileges and freedoms. As the subsequent discussion will indicate, restrictive interpretations by the NLRB and the courts have robbed these provisions of some of the benefit which it appears Congress intended to confer upon employers.

Free Speech

The Taft-Hartley Act accepted in principle employers' complaints on the "free speech" issue. Under the original Wagner Act the employer was prohibited from interfering with employee concerted activities. This was so construed that practically any opinion expressed by an employer against union organization was held to be an unfair labor practice. In the years immediately prior to enactment of the Taft-Hartley Act, however, the Board modified its views so as to permit some employer opinions to be stated in the interest of preserving the right of free speech. During the time of the Wagner Act, NLRB policy toward employer free speech went through three distinct phases:

> The first was characterized by the requirement that the employer maintain strict neutrality by remaining silent; the second, by the concession that the employer could express his anti-union views, so long as they were not accompanied by threats or promises, and so long as employees were not required to listen; and the third, by the refinement that the employer could make non-coercive anti-union speeches to compulsory audiences of his employees, provided that similar opportunities were afforded union representatives to express their views.[12]

The Taft-Hartley Act attempted to clarify employer rights of free speech by specifically providing in Section 8 (*c*) that the expression of any views, arguments, or opinions could not be considered evidence of an unfair labor practice unless there was an actual threat of reprisal or force or promise of benefit.

The protection afforded by this provision is capable of acting as a serious deterrent to union organizing activity in those areas, such as parts of the South, where unions are not yet entrenched. The employer no longer has to remain neutral in a bargaining representative election, and can actively campaign for "no union." Thus, for example, it is not an unfair labor practice under the Act for an employer to compel employees to meet on company time to hear an attack on unions, as long as the address is phrased in terms of "opinion" rather than "threats." However, under the Democratic Truman administration the NLRB sought to limit such freedom of speech by requiring employers who addressed employees on company time and property to make equal time and facilities available for union organizers. This requirement, which became known as the Bonwit Teller doctrine, was in keeping with the concept of the Board that "laboratory conditions" should prevail in an election, with the employees not being subject to undue persuasion. It is interesting to note that the proportion of "no union" votes in representation elections, though greater today than in the early days of the Wagner Act, was not greater in the first four years

[12] J. Shister, B. Aaron, and C. W. Summers (eds.), *Public Policy and Collective Bargaining*, Industrial Relations Research Association Publication No. 27 (New York: Harper and Row, 1962), p. 35.

of the Taft-Hartley Act than in the last four years of the Wagner Act.[13]

In late 1953 the NLRB, reflecting the views of a Republican-appointed chairman and member, reversed[14] the Bonwit Teller doctrine and held that up to 24 hours before a representation election, the employer may address his employees on the subject of union organization without giving the union the same privileges, provided he makes no threats or promises of benefit. If he speaks within the 24-hour period, a new election may be held, but he will not be charged with an unfair labor practice. In reversing its previous decisions, the NLRB took the position that it was not the intent of Congress that "one party must be so strangely open-hearted as to underwrite the campaign of the other." The Board questioned whether the union would permit the employer to take over a meeting in the union hall to present his views.

We shall have occasion in the next chapter to discuss how Board decisions gradually effect a change in national labor policy over the years even though there may have been no change in statutory law during the same period. This transition is particularly evident in the development of labor policy relating to employer free speech. In the early years of the Wagner Act, the Board viewed as intimidatory even such employer statements as "We don't want no outside union to come in and run our business for us"; yet by the time the Taft-Hartley Act was enacted, the NLRB had taken a much more liberal attitude toward employer rights to talk to employees. The change in policy of the NLRB was itself a reflection of the change in public attitude toward the need for union organization and, in particular, the need for restricting employer rights in order to encourage such organization. The view that employers and unions should be treated equally by government without special concessions to either side would, as a practical matter, give the employer an advantage in the area of influencing employee opinion, for the employer can, while the union cannot, compel attendance of employees to hear his views on organization.

The new Board, reflecting the views of two members appointed by President Kennedy, has moved in the direction of restricting employer statements, even though they technically are permissible under the free speech provision of the Taft-Hartley Act, if, as part of an entire

[13] See Sumner H. Slichter, "Revision of the Taft-Hartley Act," *Quarterly Journal of Economics*, Vol. LXVII (May, 1953), pp. 154–55.

[14] The present Board holds that this reversal applied only to manufacturing establishments and that the Bonwit Teller rule is still applicable to department stores which enforce broad "no solicitation" rules on company property. See *May Department Stores Co.*, 49 LRRM 1862.

environmental situation, they can be viewed as restraining employee freedom of choice.[15] In the words of Board member Gerald A. Brown:

> . . . employer statements that union victories may result in plant shutdowns and/or transfer of operations to other geographical locations are no longer automatically equated to "predictions" nor are they automatically considered protected campaign oratory. . . . For, as the present Board well recognizes, the question upon which each case should turn is whether when viewed in proper context the employer's words, even if couched in terms of a "prediction," or statement of legal position, render employee free choice impossible.[16]

Furthermore, the present Board has made clear its position that the so-called "free speech amendment," Section 8 (*c*) of the Taft-Hartley Act, has relevance only to unfair labor practice cases, and has no application in representation cases.[17] In an unfair labor practice proceeding the question at issue is whether an employer statement has interfered with employee rights to make a free choice to join or not to join a union. If the NLRB finds that there has been employer interference, a formal cease and desist order is issued against the employer which is enforceable in federal court. On the other hand, in election cases the question is whether employees have had an opportunity to cast uncoerced ballots which represent their true wishes on whether or not to join a union. If the Board makes a finding that employer statements have prevented such free choice, it can set aside the election and direct a new one.

The NLRB has indicated that it will require a much higher standard of conduct from employers in election cases than in unfair labor practice cases, where employers can invoke the protection of Section 8 (*c*). Thus the Board has set aside elections where an employer made the following statements in pre-election talks, none of which would appear to involve a "threat of reprisal or force or promise

[15] The Board's policy on employer statements has been attacked by employer spokesmen, who allege that it is contrary to Congressional intent as evidenced by inclusion of the so-called "free speech amendment" in the Taft-Hartley Act. As one persistent critic puts it: "Although Section 8 (*c*) of the Taft-Hartley Act was designed to put it to rest, the 'totality of conduct' doctrine is now identifiably back in action, doing yeoman work to hold employers guilty of unfair practices whether or not they have actually violated the law" (Sylvester Petro, "Labor Relations Law," *Labor Law Journal*, Vol. XII [May, 1961], p. 460).

[16] Address by Gerald A. Brown at Institute on Labor Law, Duke University Law School, Durham, North Carolina, February 9, 1962.

[17] This distinction was made by the NLRB as early as 1948 in the General Shoe case (21 LRRM 1337), where it observed that "conduct that creates an atmosphere which renders improbable a free choice will sometimes warrant invalidating an election even though the conduct may not constitute an unfair labor practice." While some subsequent cases suggested that Section 8 (*c*) might have some application to election cases, the present Board has re-emphasized the clear distinction between the two. See *Dal-Tex Optical Co.*, 50 LRRM 1489 (1962).

of benefit": "There is no doubt in my mind, because of terrific demands, there will be a strike." "Whether we go out of business or not, I am not saying now." "Demands of the union cannot and will not be met."[18] On the other hand, no violation of the unfair labor practice prohibition (Section 8 [*a*] [1]) was found where an employer characterized a union as a Communistic, strike-causing, trouble-making organization.[19]

It can truthfully be said that neither employers nor unions are happy about the so-called "free speech amendment." Employers complain that freedom of speech is freedom of speech whether it is involved procedurally in an unfair labor practice case or in an election case. They argue that the present Board has adopted a restrictive attitude relative to employer statements reminiscent of the Wagner Act era. Union spokesmen, on the other hand, complain that the freedom from prosecution afforded employers by the free speech amendment has resulted in many more pre-election speeches which are responsible for union losses when the ballots are counted. It should also be mentioned that the language of Section 8 (*c*) is applicable by its terms to union statements as well as employer statements. Unions had hoped that this section would protect all forms of peaceful picketing in which union men carry placards expressing their opinions in a labor dispute. However, both the Board and the Supreme Court have adopted the view that picketing is more than mere expression of opinion, and that Section 8 (*c*) does not limit other sections of the Taft-Hartley Act which restrict picketing.

A picket line does involve an aspect of freedom of speech, since it seeks to disseminate information about a labor dispute. It is also coercive. The same can be said about employer statements. Words as well as acts can have a coercive effect upon employee actions. As the United States Supreme Court has observed: ". . . employers' attempts to persuade to action with respect to joining or not joining unions are within the First Amendment's guaranty. . . . When to this persuasion other things are added which bring about coercion, or give it that character, the limit of the right has been passed. . . ."[20] The courts have indicated that the NLRB is vested with the power to balance these conflicting rights—freedom of speech and freedom of choice to join a union—and to determine when freedom of speech may have to be curtailed, within the statutory limits, in order to protect employees'

[18] *Somoso, Inc.,* 49 LRRM 1030.

[19] *Grand Central Aircraft Co.,* 31 LRRM 1616; enforced, 35 LRRM 2052.

[20] *Thomas* v. *Collins,* 323 U.S. 516, 537–38; 65 S. Ct. 315, 326 (1945).

rights. The task is a difficult one and is certain to involve the Board in controversy for years to come.

Reinstatement

Section 10 (*c*) of the Act prohibited the Board from ordering reinstatement or back pay in any case where the discharge was made "for cause." This provision was included, according to the majority report of the House Labor Committee, in order to "put an end to the belief, now widely held and certainly justified by the Board's decisions, that engaging in union activities carries with it a license to loaf, wander about the plant, refuse to work, waste time, break rules and engage in incivilities and other disorders and misconduct." The basis for this charge does not appear to have been factual. President Truman, in his message vetoing the Taft-Hartley Act, expressed the fear that this clause would permit an employer to dismiss a man on pretext of a slight infraction of shop rules, even though his real motive was to discriminate against the man for his union activity. However, the NLRB has indicated that it will not allow this clause to be used as a subterfuge. For example, in one case a company reduced its force by 150 men because of economic conditions, and it included in this number a disproportionately large number of union members and participants in a recent strike. The Board held that these discharges could not be camouflaged as "for cause."[21] The NLRB has continued to order reinstatement where circumstances warrant this remedy for workers illegally discharged. During the fiscal year of the NLRB ended June 30, 1961, in cases filed against employers, a total of 2,507 workers were ordered reinstated in their jobs, and a total of $1,508,900 in back pay was recovered for employees.[22] In September, 1962, for the first time in twenty-seven years, the NLRB commenced adding 6 per cent interest to back-pay awards granted to employees who were illegally discharged. While there is no specific authorization in the Taft-Hartley Act for such action, the Board relied on "accepted legal and equitable principles" as justification for adding interest to back-pay awards.[23]

Disestablishment

The Taft-Hartley Act required modification in NLRB practice with regard to disestablishment of unions as bargaining agents. After

[21] *National Labor Relations Board* v. *Sandy Hill Iron & Brass Works,* 21 LRRM 2021.

[22] *Twenty-sixth Annual Report,* p. 8.

[23] NLRB Press Release, September 21, 1962.

passage of the Wagner Act, employers sought to satisfy the collective bargaining provisions by inducing employees to bargain through so-called "company unions," unaffiliated with national unions. Frequently, such company unions were dominated by employers, who paid their expenses and appointed their officers. Where this condition was found to exist, it was the practice of the Board to order disestablishment. An organization affected by such an order, no matter if its members and officers subsequently purged themselves of the taint of employer domination, would not thereafter be permitted recognition. By contrast, when an employer assisted an AFL union to get a majority in order to keep out a CIO union, the Board merely directed the offending employer to cease giving such assistance. The Taft-Hartley Act sought to compel uniform treatment of both unaffiliated and affiliated unions.

The NLRB policy under the Taft-Hartley Act has been to disestablish a union, whether it is affiliated or unaffiliated, if the employer dominated it; or to cut off its bargaining rights temporarily, if the employer gave it illegal assistance. While this policy is applied uniformly to both unaffiliated and affiliated unions, there has been, in practice, little change from the earlier procedure under the Wagner Act, since affiliated unions are seldom found to be "dominated," and therefore the most that will be done to them is a temporary withdrawal of bargaining rights, subject to certification in a new election. However, in one case the NLRB ordered disestablishment of a local of the Teamsters' Union on the ground that it had been unlawfully dominated and assisted by an employer in order to prevent a CIO union from organizing the company's employees.

Procedural Privileges

Employers were also granted important procedural rights. Whereas, previously, employers could petition for an election only when confronted with demands for bargaining rights by two or more competing unions, they could now seek an election whenever a union made a demand for recognition. The grant of this privilege to the employer restrained premature claims of representation by unions attempting to organize a plant; for if the union failed to secure a majority vote in an election called by the employer, the Act prohibited the holding of another election for twelve months. The right to request an election has been frequently utilized by employers. During the fiscal year ended June 30, 1961, employers petitioned for elections in 739 cases.[24]

[24] *Twenty-sixth Annual Report,* p. 217.

Another important right provided in the Taft-Hartley Act is the privilege to sue unions in federal court for breach of contract. Section 301 (*a*) of the Act provides: "Suits for violation of contracts between an employer and a labor organization representing employees in an industry affecting commerce as defined in this Act, or between any such labor organizations, may be brought in any district court of the United States having jurisdiction of the parties without respect to the amount in controversy or without regard to the citizenship of the parties."[25]

Furthermore, Section 303 of the Act provides that whoever is injured in his business or property by reason of certain enumerated unfair labor practices[26] of a labor organization may sue in federal district court "and shall recover the damages by him sustained and the cost of the suit." While, contrary to the grim prognostications of union leaders, there has been no rush by employers to sue unions[27] in federal court, nevertheless this section of the Act carries with it implications of great significance for the development of labor relations in this country. We shall have occasion to consider this section in more detail in the next chapter.

One direct result of the inclusion of Section 301 (*a*) in the Taft-Hartley Act has been an increase in frequency of clauses in labor contracts protecting the union against financial liability in the event of unauthorized strikes. Contrary to expectations, however, there appears to have been no reduction in the frequency of no-strike clauses in labor agreements negotiated since enactment of the Taft-Hartley amendments.

Suppose a collective bargaining contract contains a no-strike clause and an agreement to arbitrate disputes. The union strikes in violation of its contractual agreement. Can an employer require the union to desist from such action by bringing suit in federal court under

[25] While Section 301 (*a*) is considered above in connection with employer procedural rights, it should be noted that equal rights are accorded to unions to bring suits against employers.

[26] The Landrum-Griffin Act amendments to the Taft-Hartley Act broadened this provision so that today an employer can sue a union for damages sustained as the result of any activity or conduct defined as an unfair labor practice in Section 8 (*b*) (4) of the Taft-Hartley Act, as amended.

[27] One purpose of the legislation was to enable unions to be sued as entities so as to protect individual members and officers from damage suits. In *Atkinson* v. *Sinclair Refining Co.* (50 LRRM 2433), the United States Supreme Court dismissed a claim for damages against individual union members included in a suit against the union brought by an employer under Section 301 of the Taft-Hartley Act. The Court said, at 50 LRRM 2438: "The national labor policy requires, and we hold, that when a union is liable for damages for violation of the no-strike clause, its officers and members are not liable for these damages."

Section 301 (*a*) for specific performance of the agreement not to strike?

Enforcement would, of course, require a court order equivalent to an injunction, which would seem to be prohibited by the Norris–La Guardia Act. However, it can be argued that an exception should be made in order to carry out the statutory purpose of the Taft-Hartley Act. Since a major statutory purpose of the Taft-Hartley Act was to reduce the number of strikes, and since the United States Supreme Court has already ruled that Section 301 of the Taft-Hartley Act enables a union to bring a suit in federal court against an employer for specific performance of an agreement to arbitrate,[28] should not the employer be held to have the same right against the union?

Whatever the logic or justice in this argument, the United States Supreme Court has seen fit to disagree with it. In *Sinclair Refining Co.* v. *Atkinson,*[29] decided in June, 1962, the Court held that the Norris–La Guardia Act barred a suit by an employer under Section 301 of the Taft-Hartley Act for an injunction against a union's breach of a no-strike pledge contained in an agreement requiring arbitration of disputes. The Court held that the case involved a labor dispute within the meaning of the Norris–La Guardia Act and therefore the federal courts were deprived of jurisdiction. The Court intimated that it was up to Congress to resolve the discriminatory pattern of law which has resulted from the conflict between the Taft-Hartley and Norris–La Guardia acts.

Justice Brennan, speaking for the dissenting three justices, argued that the Taft-Hartley Act should be accommodated to the Norris–La Guardia Act by permitting injunctions against unions for breach of contract. In his words, the decision of the majority

> deals a crippling blow to the cause of grievance arbitration itself. Arbitration is so highly regarded as a proved technique for industrial peace that even the Norris LaGuardia Act fosters its use. But since unions cannot be enjoined by a federal court from striking in open defiance of their undertakings to arbitrate, employers will pause long before committing themselves to obligations enforceable against them but not against their unions.[30]

The Sinclair decision leaves unanswered a number of pertinent questions. In the Sinclair case, although the collective bargaining agreement contained a provision for arbitration of disputes, this was not directly at issue. The central problem facing the Court was whether to

[28] *Textile Workers' Union* v. *Lincoln Mills,* 353 U.S. 448, 77 S. Ct. 912 (1957).

[29] 82 S. Ct. 1328 (1962).

[30] 82 S. Ct. 1328, 1345 (1962).

permit the power of the Court to be used to prevent a union from striking in violation of a no-strike covenant in its contract. Suppose the union goes to arbitration, loses the decision, and then strikes to upset the award. Could an employer obtain a court order confirming the award so that if the union continues to strike, it would be in contempt of court? Or suppose an employer gets a court order directing a union to arbitrate in accordance with its contractual obligation, and the union refuses and strikes. Would a court order the strikers back to work? It would seem that both of these cases are still farther removed from the evils sought to be remedied by the Norris–La Guardia Act, and that a court could use its power to end the strike on these facts, despite a contrary holding in the circumstances of the Sinclair case. An arbitration award—and indeed the arbitration procedure itself—is a result of the agreement of the parties, so there would seem to be no public policy reasons for denying resort to court enforcement in such cases.

An even more fundamental question posed by the Sinclair decision is whether the Norris–La Guardia Act is out of date and requires modification to conform to governmental policy embodied in labor laws enacted since its passage. The Norris–La Guardia Act is inconsistent with the Taft-Hartley Act in a number of important respects:

1. The Norris–La Guardia Act rejected the injunction as a remedy in labor disputes. The Taft-Hartley Act incorporates it as part of its basic pattern of regulation. Thus, injunctions against unions are permitted to be obtained by the NLRB under sections 10 (*j*) and 10 (*l*) against suspected unfair labor practices and under sections 206 to 210 in so-called "national emergency" strikes. It is true that these sections do not permit injunctions by private parties and therefore seek to avoid some of the evils which grew out of the hasty use of the injunction as a private weapon and which ultimately led to enactment of the Norris–La Guardia Act. But nevertheless the injunction is embodied in the law as a government-sanctioned means of dealing with labor disputes. Furthermore, Section 302, dealing with employer payments to union representatives and management of pension and welfare funds, expressly allows private parties to seek injunctions although, admittedly, these areas may be considered peripheral to what the Norris–La Guardia Act considered involved in labor disputes.

2. The Norris–La Guardia Act established the policy of government neutrality in labor disputes. Government was to stay on the side lines and let the parties fight it out with their own tactical weapons. This view has now been replaced with the attitude that the government, while being relatively neutral, should police the activities of

both management and labor in order to protect the public interest.

3. The Norris–La Guardia Act reflects the view that the federal courts are not proper agencies to formulate substantive labor policy. That Act, in effect, repudiated the federal common law of labor relations which had been devised by the courts and was hostile to the interests of organized labor.[31] By contrast, as we shall note further in the next chapter, the Taft-Hartley Act, through Section 301, has given the federal courts the task of formulating a new federal law of contract administration—or at least this is what the United States Supreme Court interprets Section 301 to mean!

Professor Charles O. Gregory, in an article written prior to the Sinclair decision,[32] stated his opinion that the Norris–La Guardia Act had nothing to do with the enforcement of contract provisions, that there was a strong public policy in favor of such enforcement, and that the United States Supreme Court should make it clear that no-strike agreements by unions are enforceable in federal court. Now that the Supreme Court has held to the contrary, the question remains whether Congress intended that Section 301 operate as an exception to the Norris–La Guardia Act and, if so, whether further legislation will now be passed to accomplish this result. While the legislative history of the Act is full of conflicting indications,[33] on balance it appears that Congress did not intend to render the Norris–La Guardia Act inoperative by its enactment of Section 301 of the Taft-Hartley law. Furthermore, there is considerable doubt whether a specific amendment, standing alone and intended to emasculate the Norris–La Guardia Act, could now pass Congress. That Act is a keystone in the emotionally charged tradition of organized labor; an attack on it would be considered a frontal attack on labor, and few politicians are prepared to take such a step at this time.

Some commentators have pointed out that while there is an unfairness in permitting injunctions to one side and not to the other, this

[31] See Note on "Labor Injunctions and Judge-Made Labor Law: The Contemporary Role of Norris–La Guardia," *Yale Law Journal,* Vol. LXX (November, 1960), p. 73.

[32] Charles O. Gregory, "The Law of the Collective Agreement," *Michigan Law Review,* Vol. LVII (March, 1959), p. 645.

[33] For example, the Senate Report (Committee on Labor and Public Welfare, "Federal Labor Relations Act of 1947," Senate Report No. 105, 80th Congress, 1st session [Washington, D.C.: U.S. Government Printing Office, 1947], p. 15) made collective bargaining agreements "equally binding and enforceable on both parties." This would seem to require an exception from the Norris–La Guardia law. On the other hand, no less an authority than Senator Taft, Chairman of the Conference Committee on the law which bears his name, stated that the conferees rejected the repeal of the Norris–La Guardia Act. A detailed legislative history of the Act as it applies to Section 301 is contained in the Appendix to the Lincoln Mills decision (1 L. ed. [2d] 997–1027).

to some extent compensates for the imbalance in damages.[34] If an employer refuses to arbitrate a grievance, a union's only real remedy is specific performance of the agreement to arbitrate, for it has been held that damages for breach of promise to submit a dispute to arbitration are only nominal. On the other hand, when a union strikes and refuses to arbitrate a dispute in accordance with its contractual agreement, the factor of strike losses makes the damage award a substantial deterrent.

One possibility of strengthening the employer's position in collective bargaining contracts requiring arbitration of disputes would be to make a failure to abide by such an agreement an unfair labor practice and give to the NLRB the power to obtain injunctive relief as it does in other unfair labor practice cases. The Taft-Hartley bills as they originally passed the House and Senate[35] contained such a provision, but they were dropped in conference.

In any case, as matters now stand, the procedural advantages which Section 301 afforded to employers appear to have boomeranged. While employers can now sue unions in federal court, they cannot obtain injunctive relief. On the other hand, unions can obtain specific enforcement by federal courts of decisions rendered by arbitrators under the grievance machinery.

HOW UNIONS WERE AFFECTED

Unfair Labor Practices

The Wagner Act sought to overcome the disparity of bargaining power between employers and employees which existed at the time of its enactment. Therefore, its restrictive provisions were all directed at employers, while unions were left free to engage in strikes, picketing, and various forms of coercion short of violence, in order to achieve organization of the workers. For this reason the Wagner Act was criticized as being a one-sided law. The Taft-Hartley Act was designed to remedy this one-sidedness. It proceeded on the assumption that substantial equality of bargaining power had been achieved and that therefore both union and management should be subject to similar prohibitions regarding unfair practices.[36] The bulk of unfair labor practice cases handled by the Board continue to be brought against em-

[34] Note on "Labor Injunctions . . . ," *op. cit.*, p. 99.

[35] Committee on Labor and Public Welfare, "Federal Labor Relations Act of 1947," pp. 20, 21, 23; U.S. House of Representatives, Committee on Education and Labor, *Labor Management Relations Act, 1947,* Report No. 245, 80th Congress, 1st session (Washington, D.C.: U.S. Government Printing Office, April 11, 1947), p. 21.

[36] Despite this change in emphasis, more than 80 per cent of the Board's time under the Taft-Hartley Act has been spent in handling cases submitted by unions, not employers.

ployers, but a substantial number now involve complaints against unions. In the fiscal year ended June 30, 1961, the Board disposed of 1,772 unfair labor practice charges against unions filed by employers.[37] Of these, 223 were contested, and violations were found in 174, or 78 per cent, of these cases.[38] The unfair labor practices to which unions are subject are six in number, enumerated in Section 8 (*b*) of the Act:

1. ***Restraint or Coercion.*** It was made an unfair labor practice for a union to restrain or coerce employees in the exercise of the rights guaranteed them in Section 7. The latter guarantees the right to bargain collectively through representatives of the employees' own choosing and also the right to refrain from such activity (except where a union shop has been authorized by law). This section was intended to protect individual employees from the strong-arm tactics of union "goon squads" which, allegedly by threat and intimidation, sometimes secured a majority vote which did not reflect the preference of the workers. Union officials, however, argued that if this section was directed at physical assaults and threats of violence, state and local laws were already adequate to deal with this problem, whereas if it applied to conduct short of physical coercion, it could be used by antiunion employers to obstruct the organizing activities of unions. Most of the unfair labor practice charges filed against unions involve alleged violations of this section of the law. In fiscal 1961, over 2,000 cases were filed with the NLRB against unions for alleged violation of this section. Union activities which have been found violative of the provisions of this section include mass picketing, blocking ingress to and egress from struck plants, and threatened physical violence toward employees. Recently the statutory language has been construed to impose an obligation upon a labor organization, when acting as exclusive bargaining agent, to refrain from taking any "unfair" action against employees in matters affecting their employment. The NLRB has held that a union was guilty of an unfair labor practice where it unfairly reduced an employee's seniority classification.[39]

The broad scope which has been imputed to the phrase "to restrain or coerce" is well illustrated by the following set of facts: Suppose that a union conducts an organizing campaign and obtains signature cards from what it believes is a majority of the employees in the bargaining unit. There is no other union attempting to organize the employees. The union contacts the employer, tells him that it has a

[37] *Twenty-sixth Annual Report,* p. 217.

[38] *Ibid.,* p. 17.

[39] *Miranda Fuel Company, Inc.,* 51 LRRM 1585.

majority of the employees signed up, and requests that he recognize the union as exclusive bargaining agent. The employer signs an agreement with the union recognizing it as bargaining agent for his employees. It turns out that the union was wrong in its estimate of support among the employees and that actually at the time the agreement was signed, it had the consent of only a minority of the employees.

This set of circumstances has undoubtedly occurred many times in many sections of our economy. A case involving similar facts recently came before the United States Supreme Court,[40] which held that both the employer and the union were guilty of unfair labor practices in recognizing a minority union. Such recognition restrained employees in the exercise of their rights granted under Section 7 of the Taft-Hartley Act. The Court agreed with the Board that the contract was unlawful, that the parties must cease giving effect to it, and that the union was barred from representing any of the employer's employees—even its members only—until after a Board election was held. In the case actually litigated, the contract did not contain any union security provisions. Suppose, however, that the contract had provided for a checkoff of union dues. Since the employer and the union had no right to enter into the collective bargaining agreement, all attributes of that contract presumably would be subject to challenge, and both union and employer might be liable for reimbursement of such amounts. It can be seen that the penalty for guessing wrong in the matter of recognition may be high. Consequently, both unions and employers are likely to rely almost entirely on Board-sponsored elections, rather than self-help, which will result in a substantial increase in the case load facing the NLRB.

2. ***Illegal Demands for Union Security.*** It was made an unfair labor practice for a union to cause an employer to discriminate against an employee for nonmembership in a union unless there was a union security contract with the employer which was recognized under the Act.

The closed shop was prohibited even though both employer and employees were satisfied with its operation. A union shop provision in a collective agreement was recognized under the Act if it allowed at least thirty days after hiring before new employees were required to become members of the union. However, before a union could negotiate such a security provision, it was required to fulfill a number of conditions: (*a*) file all required reports and affadavits, (*b*) receive

[40] *International Ladies' Garment Workers' Union, AFL-CIO* v. *National Labor Relations Board,* 366 U.S. 731, 81 S. Ct. 1603 (1961).

designation as bargaining representative by a majority of the employees, (*c*) show that at least 30 per cent of the employees in the bargaining unit wish to authorize the union to make a union security agreement, and (*d*) secure a majority vote of all employees in the unit in favor of such a clause in a specially conducted NLRB election. The requirement of a special election proved to be a time-consuming and costly formality. In October, 1951, after a period of four years in which the NLRB held 46,146 union shop elections, of which 97 per cent authorized the union shop, the Act was amended by the so-called "Taft-Humphrey amendments" so as to permit voluntary union shop contracts without elections.

Even if a union satisfied all the requirements enumerated above, and even if an employer engaged in interstate commerce was willing to grant the union shop, its inclusion in a collective bargaining agreement was prohibited under the Act if the particular state in which the business was located imposed more drastic conditions on union security clauses or forbade them entirely.[41] Despite dire predictions by labor leaders, there is no strong evidence that this latter provision seriously weakened the labor movement, although it did accelerate enactment of "right-to-work" laws by a number of states. As of March 1, 1963, the union shop was prohibited in twenty states that have passed right-to-work laws.

If a labor organization succeeds in winning a union shop, the power of the union officials to dismiss a member from the union and hence from his job is circumscribed by a provision of the Act which makes it illegal for a union (or an employer) to enforce a union security clause against anyone for any reason other than nonpayment of dues or initiation fees. The inclusion of this clause in the Act is evidence of the concern of Congress that the union shop, by giving the union a monopoly of job opportunities in the particular establishment, might be used as a club to intimidate workers who disagreed with the policies of union officials.

Although the union shop has been a part of the labor scene for many years, it still remains a highly controversial issue. Because of its importance as a friction point in union-management relations, the union shop and various adaptations of the union security principle will be discussed in depth in Chapter 8.

[41] This provision ran counter to the usual principle that state laws are superseded by federal legislation on the same subject matter. The Taft-Hartley Act not only applied the state law but declared further that the state law should apply to employers engaged in interstate commerce as well as those whose business was purely local.

3. ***Refusal to Bargain.*** It was made an unfair practice for a union to refuse to bargain collectively with an employer. This provision was apparently directed at those unions which had become so powerful that their "bargaining" activities consisted of presenting demands with a "take it or leave it" attitude. It is doubtful, however, that this provision has brought about any change of attitude by unions in negotiations, since the Act makes it clear that the obligation to bargain in good faith does not compel a union (or an employer) to "agree to a proposal or require the making of a concession." Furthermore, bargaining by ultimatum has been sanctioned by the NLRB under certain circumstances.

For example, in one recent case[42] the Board held that the unions involved did not refuse to bargain in good faith by giving the employer an ultimatum backed by a strike threat to sign certain contract proposals immediately, without any further opportunity to consult with its bargaining agent. The ultimatum was the culmination of protracted bargaining which had extended over a period of five months and resulted in an impasse.

The statutory mandate to management and unions to bargain in good faith raises serious questions of public policy which are worthy of further scrutiny. In the next chapter, we shall consider in depth how these simple statutory precepts have resulted in detailed regulation by the NLRB of the substance and conduct of collective bargaining negotiations.

4. ***Illegal Strikes and Boycotts.*** Section 8 (*b*) (4) of the Act made it an unfair labor practice for a union to engage in or to encourage any strike[43] or refusal by employees to use, manufacture, transport, work, or handle goods if an object of such action was one of the following:

a) *To require an employer or self-employed person to join a union or an employer organization.* The purpose of this clause was to prevent unions from forcing independent businessmen, such as plumbers, bakery deliverymen, and others, to join a union. Congress believed that the economic independence of these groups should be protected, even though their hours of work and earnings might affect the standard of employees who work for hire in the same occupation.

b) *To force the employer or any other person to cease dealing in the products of another employer or to cease doing business with any other person.* This clause was directed at the so-called "secondary boy-

[42] *Lumber and Sawmill Workers' Union,* 47 LRRM 1287.

[43] The Act defined "strike" to include a concerted stoppage or slowdown.

cott." If employees in plant A strike to compel employer A to grant higher wages or to grant a union shop, this involves direct action against the employer primarily involved in the dispute; but if the employees, having a grievance against employer A, picket, or induce a strike in company B which uses the products of plant A, then a secondary boycott or secondary action is involved. Congress not only made the secondary boycott an unfair labor practice, but it also directed the NLRB to seek federal court injunctions against its continuance under certain circumstances and, furthermore, authorized damage suits to be brought in federal court by employers against unions which engage in secondary boycotts. However, the antiboycott provisions of the Act were poorly drawn and left a number of loopholes which Congress attempted to close by the Landrum-Griffin Act of 1959.

c) *To force or require an employer* (*including the employer of the strikers*) *to recognize or bargain with one union if another union is the certified bargaining agent, or to force another employer* (*not the employer of the strikers*) *to recognize an uncertified union.* This clause was intended to protect employers from strikes by an uncertified union aimed at compelling the employer to deal with it rather than with another union already certified. Under the Wagner Act, many companies found themselves in a disastrous dilemma as a result of rivalry between CIO and AFL unions. If the employer yielded to the pressure of the uncertified union, he violated the Wagner Act and was subject to sanctions for so doing. If he did not yield, his business could be destroyed. He could get no injunction or court relief against the picketing because of the anti-injunction provisions of the Norris–La Guardia Act.

The dilemma to the employees was as real. Because they had exercised their right of free choice, they stood to lose their jobs through the efforts of the union they had rejected.

The Teamsters' Union, which employed picketing as its method, and the International Brotherhood of Electrical Workers of America, AFL, which instituted boycotts through its control of building construction workers, were the principal offenders in attempting to compel disregard of NLRB certifications. The latter, in the last days of the Wagner Act, invoked a nationwide boycott of the products of the Westinghouse Electric Company because most of the production workers of the company had chosen to be represented by a rival CIO union. In many cities, this boycott was quite effective because members of the International Brotherhood of Electrical Workers of America controlled all electrical installation and construction work. The attempts on the part of unions to nullify the right of workers to join unions of their own choosing were indefensible and completely at variance with the basic principles of the Wagner Act. Such activities were also, of course, part of the basic conflict between the principle of exclusive jurisdiction upon which American unionism had been built and the principle of self-determined organization which the Wagner Act made law.

The Taft-Hartley Act made such strikes illegal and made it mandatory for the NLRB to seek injunctive relief in the courts if, after a preliminary investigation, there was reason to believe that the union was engaging in a strike prohibited by this section.

d) To force or require an employer to assign particular work to employees in one union or craft rather than to employees in another union or craft. This clause was intended to outlaw the so-called "jurisdictional strike." Such strikes, growing out of controversies as to which craft has the right to perform a particular job, were particularly common in the construction industry and evoked widespread public criticism. As a direct result of the enactment of the Taft-Hartley law, the building trade unions set up machinery to adjust jurisdictional disputes among the various crafts.

A union which engaged in any of the activities banned in the above four situations committed an unfair labor practice and rendered itself liable in damages to anyone whose business or property was injured as a result of the strike. Moreover, when a charge was filed alleging that a union was engaging in activities under (*a*), (*b*), or (*c*), above, it was made mandatory that the Board seek an injunction against the union if the Board had reasonable cause to believe the charge was true. In the case of jurisdictional disputes, however, the Board had to hear and "determine" such cases itself unless, within ten days after the charge had been filed, the parties agreed to voluntary adjustment of the dispute. The mandatory injunction provision mentioned above did not apply to jurisdictional disputes, but the NLRB could seek an injunction in situations where such relief was appropriate.

In the fiscal year ended June 30, 1961, injunctions were granted in 18 cases involving jurisdictional disputes; 11 of these related to conflicting claims to assignment of work in the building and construction industry.[44] It is obvious from this record that the machinery set up by the building trades to handle its disputes is not fully effective.

Although the Board has often been attacked for injecting itself

[44] *Twenty-sixth Annual Report,* p. 197.

into the substance of collective bargaining, it religiously refrained from making determinations of work assignments in jurisdictional dispute cases coming before it. In 1961, however, in the Columbia Broadcasting case,[45] which involved a dispute between a union of television technicians and a union of stage employees over which union would control the work of providing electric lighting for television shows, the United States Supreme Court held that the NLRB could not "duck" this responsibility imposed upon it by Congress and that it must make an affirmative award of disputed work in such cases. In March, 1962, the Board handed down three unanimous work assignment decisions to end jurisdictional disputes that were accompanied by strikes or threats of strikes. One involved the government's atomic energy plant at Hanford, Washington. These were the first decisions of this type handed down in the twenty-six years of the Board's existence. It is expected that the assumption by the Board of the role of arbiter in such disputes will add pressure on unions to settle such controversies through their own dispute machinery.

5. ***Excessive Initiation Fees.*** It was made an unfair labor practice for a union which had a union shop agreement to charge membership fees in an amount which the Board found excessive or discriminatory under all the circumstances. In a number of cases the Board has ordered a union to reduce its admission fees, but the total effect of this provision has been minor.

6. ***Featherbedding.*** It was made an unfair labor practice for a union to "cause or attempt to cause an employer to pay or deliver or agree to pay or deliver any money or other thing of value, in the nature of an exaction, for services which are not performed or not to be performed." This clause is sometimes referred to as the "antifeatherbedding" provision; but actually, its scope is much more limited than the practice of make-work rules which is ordinarily encompassed within the term "featherbedding." If some work is performed in return for the compensation—even though it is mere standing around during a recorded broadcast—then the statutory requirement of "services which are not performed" is not satisfied, and the provision is not applicable. Thus the Supreme Court ruled that the practice of the International Typographical Union in requiring pay for setting so-called "bogus" type which is not used and the practice of the American Federation of Musicians of requiring pay for "stand-by orchestras" when outside bands play in local theatres were both lawful under this provision.

[45] *National Labor Relations Board* v. *Radio and Television Broadcast Engineers' Union,* 364 U.S. 573, 81 S. Ct. 330 (1961).

Loyalty Affidavit

One of the most controversial provisions of the Act was directed at Communist officers who had been in power in a few American unions. Section 9 (*b*) of the Act disqualified a labor organization both as a bargaining agency and as a complainant under the Act unless there was on file with the Board an affidavit executed "by each officer of such labor organization and the officers of any national or international labor organization of which it is an affiliate or constituent unit that he is not a member of the Communist Party or affiliated with such party, and that he does not believe in, and is not a member of or supports any organization that believes in or teaches the overthrow of the United States Government by force or by any illegal or unconstitutional methods."[46]

This provision evoked considerable criticism from both unions and other sources, on the ground that it was unconstitutional to discriminate on the basis of membership in the Communist Party when the Party was a legal organization entitled to a place on our electoral ballots. However, the Supreme Court settled this issue in 1950 by ruling that Congress had a right to require the oaths to protect the public against the "evils of conduct." Union spokesmen also argued against the one-sided nature of the affidavit provision which required the loyalty oath from union officers but not from employers.

Some critics questioned whether the most effective method of driving Communists from unions was to deny locals all over the country the protection of the Act simply because one officer in the parent international refused to sign the affidavit. Consequently, a number of the largest and strongest unions—among them the United Steelworkers, International Typographical Union, and the United Mine Workers—initially declined, as a matter of principle, to comply with this provision. Such noncompliance meant that these unions could not seek the aid of the Board in requiring an employer to bargain with them, nor could they be certified in an NLRB election. However, these unions were sufficiently well entrenched in their respective industries so that, by and large, employers did not refuse to bargain with them on the ground of their noncompliance with this affidavit provision.

Noncompliance by many Communist-dominated unions did, however, prove very detrimental to these organizations. The noncomplying

[46] Settling an issue which was once much debated, the United States Supreme Court in 1951 held that under Section 9 (*b*), the AFL and CIO are "national or international organizations" whose officers must file non-Communist affidavits if their subsidiary organizations are to be permitted to use the processes of the NLRB.

United Electrical, Radio and Machine Workers of America, and other left-wing unions, lost thousands of workers to AFL–CIO unions, such as the International Union of Electrical, Radio and Machine Workers. Severe membership losses were also suffered by the International Union of Mine, Mill and Smelter Workers, the United Farm Equipment and Metal Workers of America, and the United Office and Professional Workers of America, all former left-wing CIO unions. After several defections, the latter two organizations complied technically with the Act by removing officers with direct Communist connections, electing alleged "stooges" in their places, and placing the former officers in appointive jobs which held the real power but which did not come within the purview of the affidavit. This gave these unions access to the NLRB once more. These two unions have ceased to function, but some of the left-wing organizations such as the International Union of Mine, Mill and Smelter Workers and the West Coast Longshoremen's and Warehousemen's Union have continued to maintain sizable memberships because of their entrenched positions in their industries.

The loyalty affidavit provision of the Taft-Hartley Act clearly strengthened the hand of non-Communist elements in unions. However, the provision was frequently evaded by use of "front" men and "fellow travelers," as we have already observed.

Reports and Financial Accounts

The Act also required unions to file with the Secretary of Labor copies of their constitutions, bylaws, reports showing salaries of officers above $5,000, initiation fees, and annual financial statements. The only sanction applied for failure to file reports was denial of use of the machinery of the NLRB. Unfortunately, the unions which did not voluntarily file financial reports were concentrated in the building and amusement trades, and were so well entrenched that they had little need to use the NLRB and therefore did not have to comply with such provisions. However, these provisions are significant because they mark the entry of the federal government into regulation of internal union affairs and therefore foreshadow the more detailed regulations incorporated in the Landrum-Griffin Act twelve years later.

Restrictions on Political Contributions

The Act made it unlawful for any labor union to make a contribution or expenditure in connection with any election to any federal political office. The prohibition as to contributions corresponded to a similar prohibition applicable to corporations under the Corrupt Practices Act. Addition of the broad term "expenditures," however, in the restriction applicable to unions raised doubts as to the constitutionality of the provision. The Supreme Court has held that the ban of this section does not apply to expenditure of union funds in publishing the *CIO News,* which advised members to vote for certain candidates in a Congressional election.[47]

Contributions to Union Welfare Funds

In recent years, health and welfare funds supported in whole or in part by employer contributions have become increasingly popular as a subject of union-management negotiation. Such funds require the collection of very large sums of money. Consequently, Congress felt the need for legislation which would hold union leaders to strict accountability in the administration of such sums. Section 302 of the Act attempted to accomplish this purpose by permitting welfare funds maintained by employer contributions only when the payments are held in trust and the fund is administered jointly by employer and employee representatives, with neutral persons available to settle possible disputes. However, funds in existence prior to January, 1946, were exempted. Employer payments to such welfare funds were permitted only for the purpose of "medical or hospital care, pensions, compensation for injuries or illness resulting from occupational activity or insurance to provide any of the foregoing, or unemployment benefits or life insurance, disability and sickness insurance, or accident insurance." In 1959, as a result of the Landrum-Griffin Act amendments, these purposes were broadened to include "pooled vacation, holiday, severance or similar benefits, or defraying costs of apprenticeship or other training programs." Experience has demonstrated that employers evidence little interest in the administration of such joint funds, with the result that in some industries, corrupt union officials were able to utilize the tremendous sums which build up over a period of time in such funds to their own personal gain. Congressional investigation of the handling of certain of these welfare funds led to such shocking disclosures that it became clear that further legislation would be required in order to conserve and protect such funds against possible abuses. The Teller Act of 1958 (amended in 1962) and the Landrum-Griffin Act were direct results of such investigations.

[47] *United States* v. *Congress of Industrial Organizations,* 335 U.S. 106, 68 S. Ct. 1349 (1948).

HOW THE INDIVIDUAL WORKER WAS AFFECTED

A major objective claimed by the framers of the Taft-Hartley Act was to protect individual employees from the arbitrary power wielded by some labor leaders. Consequently, a number of important new privileges were granted to employees, with corresponding limitations on unions, on the theory that the actions of the latter have not always been truly representative of the will of the workers in the collective bargaining unit. In addition, the Act contained language concerning bargaining unit determination which had significant repercussions upon the rights of particular groups of employees.

Elections

The Taft-Hartley Act made a number of important changes in election procedure. Under the original Wagner Act procedure, if two or more unions were on the ballot in an election to choose a bargaining representative, the employees voting in a "runoff" election did not have an opportunity to cast a negative vote (i.e., no union) in the runoff, unless the no-union choice had received a plurality of votes cast in the first election. In other words, the employees were limited in the runoff election to a choice between two unions, even though one of these unions might have run in third place. Later, the NLRB changed this procedure by requiring the two highest choices to be placed on the runoff ballot so that the "no union" choice could appear on the runoff ballot even if it had not received a plurality of votes in the first election. The Taft-Hartley Act made this procedure a matter of law.

The Act also gave employees the right to seek elections to decertify a bargaining representative which no longer represented the majority of workers. In decertification elections held under the Act, the bargaining representative has been decertified in about two out of every three elections, indicating that in many cases, unions, in the course of time, cease to represent the will of the majority of workers.[48]

Representation elections still require a major portion of the Board's time. In the fiscal year ended June 30, 1962, the Board conducted 7,355 representation elections, over twice as many as in fiscal 1948.[49] More than 50 per cent of all elections involved less than thirty employees—indicating the difficulty that organized labor now faces in organizing the thousands of small employers. Labor lost a

[48] See Table 2.

[49] See Table 3.

TABLE 2

RESULTS OF DECERTIFICATION ELECTIONS UNDER THE TAFT-HARTLEY ACT

Fiscal Year	Total Elections	Per Cent Won by Union	Per Cent Lost by Union	Number of Eligible Voters	Per Cent of Eligible Voters Voting
1948	97	36	64	8,836	89
1949	132	38	62	18,773	91
1950	112	33	67	9,474	90
1951	93	29	71	6,111	88
1952	101	27	73	7,378	89
1953	141	31	69	9,945	90
1954	150	32	68	10,244	89
1955	157	35	65	13,002	91
1956	129	31	69	11,289	91
1957	145	32	68	11,018	92
1958	153	39	61	10,124	90
1959	216	34	66	16,231	90
1960	237	31	69	17,421	88
1961	241	33	67	18,364	90
1962	285	35	65	19,253	87

SOURCE: NLRB statistics.

greater percentage of elections than in the past years. In 1962, unions won majority designation in 58 per cent of elections, as compared with 62 per cent in 1957 and 73 per cent in 1952.[50] It is interesting to note that in fiscal 1958, for the first time since 1941, charges of unfair labor practices constituted a majority of all cases filed with the Board—that is, the number of charges of unfair labor practices exceeded the number of petitions for collective bargaining elections. This proportion continues to exist as of 1963.

The Taft-Hartley Act also made an important change in the rule governing the right of employees on strike to vote in representation elections. Under the Wagner Act the Board had ruled that in a strike caused by employer unfair labor practices, only strikers were eligible to vote, since they were entitled to reinstatement, whereas in a strike over economic issues, both replacements and strikers were eligible to vote. The Taft-Hartley Act, however, contained a specific provision that "employees on strike who are not entitled to reinstatement shall not be eligible to vote." In an economic strike the employer has the legal right to fill jobs of strikers with permanent replacements. Therefore, in an economic strike, strikers who are replaced could lose the right to vote in a representation election. This provision was attacked by

[50] See Table 3.

TABLE 3

RESULTS OF NLRB REPRESENTATION ELECTIONS, 1936–62

FISCAL YEAR	ELECTIONS		EMPLOYEES INVOLVED		
	Total	Per Cent Won by Unions	Total Eligible	Total Valid Votes Cast	Per Cent for Union
1936	31	81	9,512	7,572	81
1937	265	94	181,424	164,135	87
1938	1,152	82	394,558	343,687	82
1939	746	77	207,597	177,215	78
1940	1,192	77	595,075	532,955	82
1941	2,568	83	788,111	729,933	81
1942	4,212	86	1,296,567	1,067,037	84
1943	4,153	86	1,400,000	1,126,501	82
1944	4,712	84	1,322,225	1,072,594	77
1945	4,919	83	1,087,177	893,758	79
1946	5,589	80	846,431	698,812	76
1947	6,920	75	934,553	805,474	77
1948	3,222	72	384,565	333,900	77
1949	5,514	70	588,761	516,248	73
1950	5,619	74	890,374	786,382	83
1951	6,432	74	666,556	587,595	75
1952	6,765	73	771,346	667,878	75
1953	6,050	72	737,998	639,739	78
1954	4,663	66	511,430	449,673	70
1955	4,215	68	515,995	453,442	74
1956	4,946	65	462,712	414,568	65
1957	4,729	62	458,904	410,619	64
1958	4,337	61	351,217	315,428	60
1959	5,428	63	430,023	385,794	64
1960	6,380	59	483,964	436,723	64
1961	6,354	56	450,930	403,310	59
1962	7,355	58	536,047	482,558	62

SOURCE: NLRB statistics.

union spokesmen, who claimed that it would enable antiunion employers to provoke a strike, recruit nonunion replacements, and then call for an election. The strikebreakers could elect "representatives," and this would bar an independent, effective union from calling an election for a year, or they might vote for decertification of the existing union. This provision, which became known as a "union-busting" provision, was amended by the Landrum-Griffin Act, as explained in Chapter 6.

While the Taft-Hartley provision admittedly created problems for unions on the losing end of an economic strike, it seems unfair to dub this clause "union busting." While one may not agree with the basic philosophy which underlies this provision, certainly a valid argument can be made that where an employer has lawfully hired permanent replacements for economic strikers, these new employees should be the ones to vote in the election, since they—and not the men who have been replaced—will continue in the employ in the company.

Ban on Compulsory Checkoff

The Act prohibited the compulsory checkoff, the method by which union dues are deducted by the employer from the worker's wages and paid directly to the union treasury. The checkoff of membership dues was made lawful only where individual employees execute a written assignment of wages for not longer than one year, or for the duration of the applicable union contract, whichever is shorter.

Bargaining Unit Problems

Under the Taft-Hartley Act, as under the Wagner Act, the NLRB continued to be vested with the authority to determine the appropriate bargaining unit. This authority, however, was limited in the case of professional employees, craft workers, and guards.

Craft-Industrial Problems. As we have noted in our discussion of the Wagner Act, one of the most difficult problems faced by the NLRB was the contest between AFL and CIO unions as to whether the appropriate bargaining unit should be a craft or an industrial unit. Congress, of course, had been concerned primarily with the question whether employees wanted *any* union to represent them, rather than *which* union. This highly explosive issue was dumped into the lap of the NLRB with little statutory guidance to assist it in its determination. Section 9 (*b*) of the Wagner Act simply directed the Board to "decide in each case whether, in order to insure to employees the full benefit of their right to self-organization, and otherwise to effectuate the policies of the Act, the unit appropriate for the purposes of collective bargaining shall be the employer unit, craft unit, plant unit, or subdivision thereof."

Out of this simple declaration the NLRB, in hundreds of decisions involving thousands of pages of complex and technical rules, established policies which significantly affected the size, strength, and structure of organized labor in American industry. The action of the Board in this field affords a graphic example of how an administrative agency becomes involved in policy formulation because of the lack of detail in statutory language. The NLRB found that it had to weigh and balance two often conflicting objectives of labor policy: self-determination and stability in industrial relations.[51] Self-determination, which favored craft severance, could, if carried to an extreme, result in the fragmentation of collective bargaining into a myriad of small, ineffective units. Moreover, it raised the problem of multiplicity of negotiations, more jurisdictional disputes, and possible weakening of industrial unions. On the other hand, the policy of stability, which was frequently synonymous with favored treatment for industrial unions, could mean that individual crafts would be submerged in a large union without regard to their peculiar problems. Moreover, preference for larger industrial unions could lead to dissatisfaction among substantial groups of employees within the union.

The Board wrestled with this problem throughout the Wagner Act period. In the early years, it tended to favor large industrial unions as most conducive to effective collective bargaining. Then, in 1937, this trend was reversed, and the "Globe"[52] doctrine evolved, which in most instances allowed craftworkers in initial representation elections to determine whether they wanted to be in a plantwide union or have a separate craft. The Board was for a time more reluctant to allow craft severance where craftsmen had already been included in a large industrial union; but by 1942 the Board's policy shifted, and severance was permitted where a "true" craft was involved.

However, the Board's policies on bargaining units did not satisfy either the CIO or the AFL. The Taft-Hartley Act sought to settle this issue by writing into law the restriction that the Board may not decide that a craft unit is inappropriate on the ground that an industrial unit had already been established by a prior Board determination, unless a majority of employees in the proposed craft unit voted against the craft unit. This clause was criticized by CIO officials, who argued that it could be used to permit various splinter craft groups to break off from

[51] The gradual formation of the Board's rules regarding contracts as a bar to an election is a further example of policy formulation by the Board to insure stability in collective bargaining relations. Under the Board's present practice, as promulgated in November, 1962, a contract is held to bar a determination of representatives for the term of the contract where the contract is for a definite duration of three years or less. Contracts having longer fixed terms will be treated for bar purposes as three-year agreements and will bar an election for their initial three-year period, except that longer contracts will bar, for their entire term, elections requested by the contracting employer or the contracting certified union. See *General Cable Corp.*, 51 LRRM 1444.

[52] The "Globe" doctrine, which involves the principle of self-determination by a particular group of employees as to their bargaining unit, is so called because it was first enunciated in the case of the *Globe Machine and Stamping Co.*, 3 NLRB 294 (1937).

established industrial unions. These fears proved groundless, however; and in actual practice, this provision produced little change in NLRB procedure with regard to representation of skilled crafts. The NLRB wisely interpreted this provision as prohibiting it from using a prior unit determination as the sole ground for decision as to the appropriateness of a craft union, but as still giving it discretion to include skilled workers in a larger industrial union where the work of the skilled group is so integrated with that of production workers that a separate unit would be inappropriate. Thus the Board has allowed severance of traditional crafts not closely integrated with production employees, but it has denied severance of craft units in highly integrated industries such as basic steel, basic aluminum, lumbering, and wet-milling industries.

In 1954 the Board adopted a policy of allowing craft units whenever employees within such a group constitute a true craft and the union seeking to represent them traditionally represents employees of that type on a craft basis. In adopting this policy, the NLRB abandoned such guides as bargaining history and plant integration. In 1959, however, in the Pittsburgh Plate Glass case,[53] the Circuit Court of Appeals for the Fourth District held that this policy was arbitrary and discriminatory, and directed the Board to decide each case on its merits by considering all the relevant factors rather than relying on a general formula.

Under its present practice, therefore, in passing on petitions for the establishment of craft units or the severance of craft or craftlike groups from existing larger units, the Board does not follow any automatic rules, but instead utilizes "the case-by-case analysis based upon such factors as the desires of the parties, bargaining history, similarity of skills, job functions and working conditions, common supervision and/or interchange of employees, type of industry, organization of the plant, and whether any union seeks to represent the technical employees separately."[54]

The same case-by-case approach typifies the attitude of the present Board toward most problems involving the appropriate bargaining unit. While there is merit in such attention to the particular details of each case, it is also important to both management and labor that rules and precedents evolve in this important field, so that there can

[53] *National Labor Relations Board* v. *Pittsburgh Plate Glass Co.*, 270 F. (2d) 167 (CCA 4).

[54] From speech by NLRB member Gerald A. Brown at Institute on Labor Law, Duke University Law School, Durham, North Carolina, February 9, 1962.

be advance planning and stability in employee relations. The Board has been making bargaining unit determinations for almost thirty years, so one would expect that by now there would be some established pattern in Board decisions on this subject. On the contrary, so sweeping is the present Board's re-examination of its basic policies that bargaining unit decisions are in a complete state of flux, and important precedents topple day after day.

Typical of the significant modifications in Board policy on the subject of appropriate bargaining units is the recent Sav-On Drugs case.[55] In that case the Retail Clerks' International Union sought to represent employees of the Edison, New Jersey, chain store of Sav-On Drugs, a subsidiary of the Kroger Company. The union's petition for election was dismissed by the NLRB regional director, who relied on prior Board decisions which would make the single store an inappropriate bargaining unit.[56] He supported the company's contention that the appropriate unit should take in all employees in the nine stores in New Jersey and New York which comprised an administrative subdivision of the Kroger Company. The Board, however, upheld the union and ordered a secret ballot of employees in the one store to determine whether they should be represented by the Retail Clerks' International Union. In commenting on this decision, the Board stated that henceforth "whether a proposed unit which is confined to one of 2 or more retail establishments making up an employer's retail chain is appropriate will be determined in the light of all the circumstances of the case."

A continuation of this policy by the Board will provide a significant stimulus to union organization,[57] for it is obviously much easier for a union to organize retail chains one store at a time than to have to achieve sufficient strength to win an election for an entire group of stores. Concern has been expressed, however, that this policy may eventually give rise to jurisdictional disputes within a chain operation among rival unions where none now exist. The case serves to illustrate how the power of the Board to determine the appropriate bargaining

[55] *Sav-On Drugs, Inc.*, 51 LRRM 1152.

[56] Prior to the Sav-On Drugs case, the Board had generally ruled in chain store cases that the appropriate unit for collective bargaining should embrace employees of all stores located within an employer's administrative division or geographic area. See *Daw Drug Co., Inc.*, 46 LRRM 1218.

[57] A similar rule has been applied in the insurance industry with similar significance for union organization. Unions seeking to organize insurance agents no longer will be required to do the job all at once by a state-wide or company-wide campaign. The old rule that only state-wide or employer-wide units are appropriate has been discarded. See *Quaker City Life Insurance Co.*, 49 LRRM 1281.

unit can affect the rate of union growth as well as the nature and structure of union-management relations in a company and in an industry.

The power of the Board in this area is particularly impressive because it is normally not subject to court review. Although Section 10 of the Act provides for court review in the case of any person "aggrieved by a final order of the Board," the Supreme Court has decided that certifications of a bargaining agent are not "final orders" in this sense and therefore cannot be appealed to the courts.[58] Normally, the only way an employer can obtain judicial review of an NLRB order in an election case is to refuse to bargain with the union certified by the Board. When the union brings an unfair labor practice charge, the NLRB's order to bargain can be appealed, and at such time the certification of the bargaining agent and the record of the election are subject to review by the court. However, this process is not open to a union that wishes to challenge an election ruling.

Professional Employees. Under the Wagner Act the NLRB customarily excluded professional employees from all bargaining units of production and maintenance workers. The Board based its policy on the fact that professional employees and production workers had no common history of collective bargaining, and that, from the standpoint of education, experience, economic interest, relation to their employer, and method and amount of compensation, there was little, if any, mutuality of interest between the two groups.

When the bargaining unit problems involved professional employees and subprofessional technicians and/or white-collar workers rather than production workers, the policy was somewhat different. In such instances the Board ruled that its so-called "Globe" doctrine applied. In a key case the Board stated: "Upon the entire record we find that the professional employees might properly be considered either as a separate unit or as part of a larger unit composed of professional and nonprofessional employees. Under such circumstances, we apply the principle that the determining factor is the desires of the professional employees. We shall, therefore, direct separate elections in order that we may ascertain the wishes of the professional employees."[59]

Despite the apparent fairness of this policy, a number of profes-

[58] If, however, a Board certification violates an express provision of the statute such as improperly grouping together professional and nonprofessional employees in the same bargaining unit, the courts will set aside the action of the Board (*Leedom* v. *Kyne,* 358 U.S. 184, 79 S. Ct. 180 [1958]).

[59] *Shell Development Company, Inc.,* 38 NLRB 192, 196–97 (1942).

sional associations felt that the NLRB was not giving due consideration to the problems of professional employees. This view, even though based upon a misunderstanding of the NLRB's policies, resulted in a growing demand on the part of various professional agencies for amendment of the Wagner Act.

Such amendment was secured in the Taft-Hartley Act, which provided that the NLRB shall not decide that any unit including professional and nonprofessional workers is appropriate for collective bargaining unless a majority of such professional employees vote for inclusion in such unit. In effect, this wrote into law the NLRB's "Globe" doctrine as far as professional employees are concerned.

Guards. The Act also provided that no union could be certified as a bargaining representative if it included both guards or watchmen and other employees or was affiliated with an organization which included both groups. This section accepted *in toto* the arguments of employers that the same union should not be permitted to represent both guards and the rank and file. As a result, unions which included both guards and others had to disaffiliate locals of guards, which under the Taft-Hartley Act could be represented only by independent unions, unaffiliated with the AFL or the CIO. This weakened somewhat the union movement among guards.

Discrimination against Minority Groups

The Act provided (Section 8 [*a*] [3]) that an employer was not justified in discriminating against an employee for nonmembership in a labor organization if he had reasonable grounds for believing that such membership was not available to the employee on the same terms and conditions generally applicable to other members. At first glance, this appears to mean that a union shop contract could not be applied to Negro employees unless Negroes were fully and equally admitted with whites to union membership. However, another section (8 [*b*] [1]) provided that a union shall have the right to prescribe its own rules with respect to the acquisition or retention of membership. Moreover, the Conference Report expressly declared that the Act did not disturb arrangements in which Negroes were relegated to an auxiliary local.[60] Thus, it appears that the Act merely requires a union to apply its admission rules—whatever they might be—uniformly to

[60] The Conference Report refers specifically to the case of *Larus and Brother Co.*, 62 NLRB 1075 (1945), as an example of an arrangement not disturbed by the Act. Any other interpretation would have alienated southern Democrats, who were among the Taft-Hartley Act's most ardent supporters.

all applicants.[61] This provision had little or no effect on existing discriminatory membership policies of unions.

Other Procedural Safeguards

Among other important rights given to individual employees to strengthen their positions relative to the union was the power to sue the union for damages resulting from an illegal strike. Also, the employee was given the right to present grievances directly to his employer and to have such grievances adjusted without the intervention of the union representative. The adjustment could not be inconsistent with the terms of the collective bargaining agreement, and the union was given the right to have its representative present at the adjustment.

HOW THE PUBLIC WAS AFFECTED BY THE LAW

One of the major reasons for enactment of the Taft-Hartley Act was the general recognition on the part of the public and lawmakers that some means had to be devised to protect the community from stoppages of the flow of essential commodities and services such as characterized the wave of strikes in 1946. The Wagner Act itself had contained no prohibition against strikes of any kind; instead, it provided a peaceful alternative[62] to the costly strikes which had been fought over the denial of basic rights of union recognition. In 1937, 60 per cent of the workers on strike were involved in organizational disputes. In 1945, only 22 per cent of the strikers were out on organizational strikes.[63] Thus the Wagner Act was successful in reducing this particular form of work stoppage. At the same time, however, strikes over economic issues—wages, hours, and working conditions—increased in importance. Moreover, industry-wide bargaining led to walkouts involving an entire industry instead of merely one plant. Thus the same number of strikes in 1946 as in 1937 produced four times as many man-days lost in the later year. The Taft-Hartley Act attempted by a number of pro-

[61] In November, 1962, at a special White House Conference called by President Kennedy, leaders of more than one hundred AFL–CIO unions signed pledges to eliminate race discrimination in the labor movement. As part of the pledge the unions agreed to accept all applicants without regard to race, creed, or color; not to charter any new segregated local unions; and to integrate those now existing.

[62] From 1936 to 1945, 10,058,872 employees resorted to the orderly procedures of the Act in 32,615 separate representation cases in order to establish their rights to recognition (*Matter of Packard Motor Car Co.*, 61 NLRB 14 [1945]).

[63] National Labor Relations Board, *Eleventh Annual Report* (Washington, D.C.: U.S. Government Printing Office, 1946), p. 2, n. 1.

cedures and prohibitions to narrow and restrict the use of the strike weapon by organized labor.

Prohibited Strikes

Certain types of strikes deemed unduly oppressive to employers and the public were outlawed. These have been considered earlier in this chapter and included secondary strikes and boycotts, jurisdictional disputes, and strikes to upset the certification of a rival union. Any person injured in his business or property as a result of such unlawful strikes could bring suit for damages against the offending union.

Strikes against the federal government were likewise forbidden, and any individual employed by the United States who went on strike was subject to immediate discharge and loss of civil service status. We shall discuss this section in Chapter 16.

Strikes called in violation of no-strike clauses in collective bargaining agreements were not prohibited, but the Act provided a procedure whereby the union could be sued by the employer in federal court for damages due to breach of contract. It was hoped that the Act, by facilitating the bringing of suits against unions, would make for stricter observance of such clauses and thus lessen the number of work stoppages.

National Emergency Strikes

Finally, the Taft-Hartley Act established procedures to govern so-called "national emergency" strikes. This procedure, which is discussed in Chapter 13, did not, however, forbid such strikes but merely provided for their postponement.

Cooling-Off Periods

The Act also required that at least 60 days' notice had to be given by unions and employers desiring to terminate or modify an existing contract. Within 30 days following such notice, if no agreement had been reached, a second notice was to be given to the Federal Mediation and Conciliation Service and to whatever mediation agency there was within the state.

The difficulties involved in this procedure will be discussed in Chapter 10. Criticism has been directed, in addition, at the sanctions imposed by this section. Employees who walk out in violation of the cooling-off period—the 60 day prior to contract termination—lose their status as employees under the Act and therefore are deprived of any protection against unfair practices by an employer. As a practical matter, however, the notice provisions have been of little importance. Notices are perfunctorily given, and the sanctions are so drastic that they are rarely invoked.

QUESTIONS FOR DISCUSSION

1. In what ways is the Norris–La Guardia Act inconsistent with the Taft-Hartley Act? How does this conflict affect the utilization of arbitration provisions in collective bargaining agreements?
2. Enumerate briefly each of the union unfair labor practices contained in the Taft-Hartley Act. Discuss the reasons why each of these prohibitions was deemed necessary by Congress.
3. Discuss the issue of employer free speech and the changing attitude of the NLRB on this problem. Should the restrictions on employer speech be relaxed or made more stringent?

SUGGESTIONS FOR FURTHER READING

AARON, BENJAMIN. "Employer Free Speech: The Search for a Policy," in J. SHISTER, B. AARON, AND C. W. SUMMERS (eds.), *Public Policy and Collective Bargaining,* pp. 28–59. Industrial Relations Research Association Publication No. 27. New York: Harper and Row, 1962.

A concise summary and analysis of the major NLRB and court decisions relating to the issue of employer free speech.

COX, ARCHIBALD. *Law and the National Labor Policy,* chap. i, pp. 1–19. Institute of Industrial Relations Monograph Series, No. 5. Los Angeles: University of California, 1960.

A brief, clear exposition of the evolution of national labor policy which led to enactment of the Taft-Hartley Act.

JONES, D. L. "Self-Determination v. Stability of Labor Relations," *Michigan Law Review,* Vol. LVIII (January, 1960), pp. 313–46.

A review of the changing policy of the NLRB on the subject of craft severance and determination of bargaining units.

Chapter 5 THE TAFT-HARTLEY ACT: IMPLICATIONS AND APPRAISAL

The Taft-Hartley Act is the single most important labor law in this country. Its provisions vitally affect the conduct and status of union-management relations in all industry affecting interstate commerce. Its impact upon industrial relations depends not only on what the Act provides in its statutory language, but also upon the manner in which this language is applied by the National Labor Relations Board and construed by the courts. In this chapter, we shall consider in detail two technical provisions of the Taft-Hartley Act: the one dealing with the good-faith bargaining requirement provided in Section 8 (*a*) (5), the other with the jurisdiction to bring suits involving collective bargaining agreements in federal court as provided in Section 301 of the Act. An analysis in depth of these two provisions is instructive, for it pointedly illustrates how seemingly innocuous language in a statute can be amplified and enlarged by an administrative board or court until it bears little relation to the original legislative intent. Furthermore, this discussion will indicate how far the Taft-Hartley Act has involved government in the control and regulation of the substantive aspects of collective bargaining.

At the conclusion of this discussion, we shall attempt to step back from the detail of the Act and look at the law as a whole. How has the Act been administered by the NLRB? Is it a "good" Act or a "bad" Act in terms of its impact on collective bargaining? These are the questions to which we shall address ourselves in an appraisal of the Taft-Hartley Act.

Government Involvement in the Collective Bargaining Process

In years to come, historians may look back upon the Taft-Hartley Act as the first major step down the road to compulsory arbitration of labor disputes. This is a rather surprising statement because the Act itself is notoriously weak in handling even national emergency disputes. Nevertheless, it is true that the Act has injected government into every vital aspect of union-management relations, and history demonstrates that once government commences to control a field of human endeavor, its scope of influence always grows. The Act has involved government in the negotiation of collective bargaining agreements, the content of collective bargaining agreements, the administration of union-management relations under such agreements, and strike settlement. In the following discussion, we shall consider the impact of the Taft-Hartley law on the first three of the above-mentioned phases of the collective bargaining process. In Chapter 13, we shall discuss the Taft-Hartley Act and strike settlement procedures.

As we have already noted in the preceding chapter, the Taft-Hartley Act itself spelled out what employers and unions could and could not include in labor contracts with respect to welfare plans, union security clauses, and checkoff of union dues. There is no need to repeat the analysis of these provisions in this discussion. But beyond the clear words of the statute, the NLRB has utilized the "good-faith bargaining" provisions contained in the Act to lay down rules respecting the content and conduct of collective bargaining negotiations. The development of the law on the subject of what constitutes bargaining in good faith provides a revealing example of how a simple statutory precept has been used as a wedge for government intervention in collective bargaining. The question is no longer: "Should the government intervene at the bargaining table?" We have gone too far down the road of regulation to retrace our footsteps to completely free collective bargaining. The government, in the person of the National Labor Relations Board, is already at the bargaining table. The question now is simply: "How great should its influence be?"

THE CONTROL OF BARGAINING TACTICS

The original Section 8 (*a*) (5) of the Wagner Act provided merely that it was an unfair labor practice for an employer to refuse to bargain collectively with representatives of his employees. Congress was primarily concerned that employers bargain with collective bargaining representatives. How they bargained once they sat down together was not then considered a problem requiring government interference. As Senator David I. Walsh, then Chairman of the Senate Committee on Education and Labor, stated: "When the employees have chosen their organization, when they have selected their representatives, all the bill proposes to do is to escort them to the door of the employer and say, 'Here they are, the legal representatives of your employees.' What happens behind those doors is not inquired into, and the bill does not seek to inquire into it."[1]

However, antiunion employers sought to weaken this provision by listening to union demands and rejecting all of them. As a consequence, the National Labor Relations Board, with the sanction of the courts, found it necessary to establish a series of rules as to what constituted bargaining in good faith. For example, it held that there had to be a "common willingness among the parties to discuss freely and fully their respective claims and demands and, when these are opposed, to justify them on reason."[2] Furthermore, the Board held that an employer could not simply listen and reject all union demands, but had to make counterproposals.[3]

While some affirmative action by the NLRB was undoubtedly necessary to make the bargaining provision of the Wagner Act effective, many employers claimed that the NLRB frequently went too far and used the threat of an unfair labor practice charge to compel employers to accede to union demands. Thus, in the course of the Congressional hearings preceding enactment of the 1947 Taft-Hartley amendments of the Wagner Act, it was stated that the National Labor Relations Board had "gone very far, in the guise of determining whether or not employers had bargained in good faith in setting itself up as the judge of what concessions an employer must make and of the proposals and counterproposals that he may or may not make."[4]

The Taft-Hartley amendments enacted by Congress in 1947 sought to counteract the prolabor provisions contained in the Wagner Act. With respect to good-faith bargaining, two important changes were made. In the first place, Congress added a new Section 8 (*b*) (3), which made it an unfair labor practice for a labor organization or its agents to refuse to bargain collectively with an employer. This provision was intended to impose an obligation to bargain in good faith upon unions, which had in many cases adopted the same kind of "take it or leave it" attitude which the NLRB had condemned in management in the early years of administration of the Wagner Act.

In the second place, a new provision, Section 8 (*d*), was added, applicable to both unions and employers alike, which sought to define

[1] 79 *Congressional Record* 7660, 74th Congress, 1st session, May 16, 1935.

[2] *National Labor Relations Board* v. *George Pilling & Son Co.,* 119 F. (2d) 32, 37 (3d Cir. 1941).

[3] *Rex Manufacturing Co., Inc.,* 24 LRRM 1653.

[4] U.S. House of Representatives, Committee on Education and Labor, *Labor Management Relations Act, 1947,* Report No. 245, 80th Congress, 1st session (Washington, D.C.: U.S. Government Printing Office, April 11, 1947), p. 19.

the obligation to bargain collectively. As the United States Supreme Court has pointed out: ". . . it remains clear that Section 8 (*d*) was an attempt by Congress to prevent the Board from controlling the settling of the terms of collective bargaining agreements."[5]

Section 8 (*d*) states:

> . . . to bargain collectively is the performance of the mutual obligation of the employer and the representative of the employees to meet at reasonable times and confer in good faith with respect to wages, hours, and other terms and conditions of employment, or the negotiation of an agreement, or any question arising thereunder, and the execution of a written contract incorporating any agreement reached if requested by either party, but such obligation does not compel either party to agree to a proposal or require the making of a concession. . . .

A number of labor authorities contend that this statutory language is inherently self-contradictory. Professor Archibald Cox, for example, suggests that the statutory duty to bargain must either simply require union recognition and the formalities of negotiation, or else it must require that plus the making of objectively reasonable proposals.[6] The NLRB has generally held that bad faith in bargaining depends upon a totality of conduct and, despite the statutory language which states that concessions are not required, has tended to view a refusal to make a counterproposal as evidence of bad faith. Thus, it appears that the NLRB has tended to lean in the direction of the second of Professor Cox's viewpoints. Moreover, the Board has continued to amplify the good-faith bargaining requirement by regulating various aspects of the collective bargaining process.

Thus, for example, the NLRB has over the years marked out certain actions as constituting per se violations of the good-faith requirement of the law. A refusal to sign a written agreement,[7] or unilateral changes in wages during negotiations,[8] or the withholding of information on wages and hours necessary for collective bargaining[9] have all been held to be per se indications of bad faith. In this manner the NLRB has attempted to set up standards of conduct which negotiators must follow behind closed doors.

[5] *National Labor Relations Board* v. *Insurance Agents International Union, AFL–CIO,* 361 U.S. 477, 487; 80 S. Ct. 419 (1959).

[6] Archibald Cox, "The Duty to Bargain in Good Faith," *Harvard Law Review,* Vol. LXXI (June, 1958), p. 1416.

[7] *National Labor Relations Board* v. *Highland Park Manufacturing Co.,* 110 F. (2d) 632 (4th Cir. 1940).

[8] *General Motors Corp.,* 81 NLRB 779, enforcement granted 179 F. (2d) 221 (2d Cir. 1950).

[9] *National Labor Relations Board* v. *F. W. Woolworth Co.,* 352 U.S. 938, 77 S. Ct. 261 (1956).

Furthermore, the Board has seemingly adopted the notion that it is its function to attempt to maintain "laboratory" conditions for the bargaining process. It has therefore condemned attempts by unions or employers to use economic pressure during negotiations on the ground that this would disrupt the negotiations process. For example, in one recent case,[10] during the course of negotiations between a large insurance company and a union representing insurance agents, the agents refused to write new contracts, slowed down in their work, and adopted various tactics to harrass and embarrass the company. The NLRB ruled that such tactics constituted an unfair labor practice on the part of the union, but on appeal the United States Supreme Court disagreed.

The Court, in its decision, criticized the NLRB for its attempts to regulate the bargaining process. It stated that it was the intent of Congress that the parties approach bargaining with the proper attitude, but "apart from this essential standard of conduct, Congress intended that the parties should have wide latitude in their negotiations, unrestricted by any governmental power to regulate the substantive solution of their differences."[11] The Court held that the use of economic pressure was not inconsistent with bargaining in good faith. "We see no indication that Congress has put it to the Board to define through its processes what economic sanctions might be permitted negotiating parties in an 'ideal' or 'balanced' state of collective bargaining."[12] Expressing a fear reminiscent of employer charges in the pre-Taft-Hartley era, the Court noted that if the Board could regulate the use of bargaining tactics under the guise of policing the good-faith requirement, it would be in a position to exercise considerable influence on the substantive terms of bargaining.

The difficulty of applying the "good-faith" doctrine to complicated patterns of bargaining tactics is well illustrated by the issue of "Boulwarism" which is presently before the Board. Boulwarism is the name given to the hard bargaining policy of the General Electric Company first carried out by Lemuel R. Boulware, now retired as a vice president of that company, and consistently used with considerable success in negotiations with the International Union of Electrical Workers. Its foundation is a fair offer by the employer and a refusal to go beyond that offer—whatever the consequences—unless new economic

[10] *National Labor Relations Board* v. *Insurance Agents' International Union, AFL–CIO,* 361 U.S. 477, 80 S. Ct. 419 (1959).

[11] 361 U.S. 477, 488.

[12] 361 U.S. 477, 499.

facts are developed to demonstrate that changes are necessary. The union argues that this is a form of bargaining by ultimatum—a denial of the very essence of bargaining, which implies the process of give-and-take, conciliation, and compromise of opposing viewpoints. The Company argues with equal vigor that it does change its position where justified, but that if the basic offer is fair, there is no statutory requirement that it continually improve it in response to union demands. Furthermore, the Company raises the fundamental question of how it can be accused of failure to bargain when it did actually sign a contract with the union making the complaint and with over a hundred other unions on substantially the same terms! The NLRB's decision on the union's charge that the bargaining tactics used by General Electric constitute an unfair labor practice may have important ramifications on bargaining practices in the future, not only in this particular company, but also in other industries where employers have been watching and appraising the success of Boulwarism.[13]

THE CONTROL OF BARGAINING CONTENT

We have seen that both labor and management are subject to regulation as to *how* they bargain with each other. In addition, Congress, the NLRB, and the courts have regulated *what* the parties can bargain about. The content of bargaining can now be divided into three categories: (1) mandatory subjects of bargaining, (2) prohibited subjects of bargaining, and (3) nonmandatory but lawful subjects of bargaining.

1. *Mandatory Subjects of Bargaining*

Under the Wagner Act the subjects over which there was a duty to bargain were defined by the NLRB and the courts through interpretation of the statutory language which refers to "bargaining in respect to rates of pay, wages, hours . . . or other conditions of employment." In the famous Inland Steel case[14] the Court held that even such matters as pensions and compulsory retirement were encompassed by this statutory language. Since that time, such varied issues as merit

[13] In *Philip Carey Mfg. Co.*, 52 LRRM 1184, the NLRB held that an employer was not guilty of a failure to bargain in good faith where the company during eleven meetings with the union made counterproposals, then made a so-called final offer, and refused to modify it in seven succeeding meetings.

[14] *Inland Steel Co.* v. *National Labor Relations Board*, 170 F. (2d) 247 (7th Cir. 1948).

increases, group insurance, Christmas bonuses, rentals for company housing, and stock purchase plans have been held to be within the scope of collective bargaining.[15]

Employers ask with some concern where are the limits to the matters over which there is a statutory obligation for them to bargain. They fear that the continually broadening view of what is encompassed by "wages, hours, or other conditions of employment," plus the Board's tendency to require counterproposals as part of the totality of conduct constituting good-faith bargaining, is gradually whittling away managerial prerogatives.

This problem is graphically illustrated by the recent decisions of the NLRB on the subject of subcontracting. In March, 1961, the NLRB held, in the Fibreboard Paper Products case,[16] that an employer had no obligation under the Taft-Hartley Act to bargain with a union representing its maintenance employees concerning the company's decision to contract out maintenance work. Subsequently, in April, 1962, after a change in membership of the Board, this decision was overruled, and the Board held that an employer must bargain with the union representing his employees regarding a decision to subcontract bargaining unit work, even if the decision to subcontract was motivated solely by economic considerations. Such a decision, the NLRB said, falls within the statutory phrase "other terms and conditions of employment" and is a mandatory subject of collective bargaining.[17] The Board emphasized, however, that the obligation to bargain did not prevent the employer from going ahead with a decision to subcontract made for valid business reasons.

The full significance of this decision is not yet clear. Does the Board mean that the employer can make up his mind, and then simply go through the motions of talking it over with the union, or must he actually "bargain"? Employers generally take a dim view of the Board's action. They contend that if the law requires them to talk about an issue with union representatives, it is almost impossible to avoid some compromise on it. The result will be new provisions on subcontracting in collective bargaining agreements, and managerial freedom to adjust to changing economic circumstances will be further restricted. As Professor Charles O. Gregory states: "The difference be-

[15] See Leon M. Despres and Samuel D. Golden, "The Duty to Bargain," *University of Illinois Law Forum* (Spring, 1955), p. 15.

[16] 47 LRRM 1547.

[17] *Town & Country Manufacturing Co.*, 49 LRRM 1918.

tween this and a direct statutory command from Congress that certain matters be included in contracts is only one of degree."[18]

On the other hand, Board members justify the decision on the ground that the twin problems of chronic unemployment and automation have reached such proportions today that subcontracting and the curtailment of operations and employment which it may entail must be subjected to the deliberation of the collective bargaining process.[19]

The process of erosion of managerial prerogatives may have been slowed by the United States Supreme Court by its decision in the American National Insurance Company case,[20] in which it held that management insistence upon a managerial prerogatives clause was not bad-faith refusal to bargain. The content of collective bargaining must, of course, be kept flexible and fluid. But it is likewise important to avoid the use of governmental power to take away prerogatives which industry requires for sound management of its business.

2. *Prohibited Subjects of Bargaining*

Under the Wagner Act the substantive terms of collective bargaining contracts were almost entirely free of statutory regulation. The Taft-Hartley amendments, however, prohibited bargaining concerning certain matters even if both labor and management were agreeable to the inclusion of such provisions in a contract. Thus the amended Act made it an unfair labor practice for an employer or a union to enter into or to effectuate closed shop or preferential hiring agreements. Congress, in effect, stated that public policy considerations superseded the wishes of the parties concerned when they bargained over such issues.

3. *Nonmandatory Subjects of Bargaining*

Congress has thus stated that the parties must bargain over certain issues and cannot bargain over others. What about all the issues which do not fall in these two categories—are they free of regulation?

Assume the following set of facts: An employer bargaining with a union insists, as a condition to entering into any contractual agree-

[18] Charles O. Gregory, *Labor and the Law* (2d rev. ed.; New York: W. W. Norton & Co., Inc., 1961), p. 413.

[19] See address of John H. Fanning, NLRB member, "The Duty to Bargain in 1962," reported in *Daily Labor Report* (Washington, D.C.), October 19, 1962.

[20] *National Labor Relations Board* v. *American National Insurance Co.,* 343 U.S. 395, 72 S. Ct. 824 (1952).

ment, that such agreement contain (*a*) a "ballot" clause calling for a prestrike secret vote of employees, both union and nonunion, as to the employer's last offer; and (*b*) a "recognition" clause which excludes as a party to the contract the international union which had been certified by the NLRB as the employees' exclusive bargaining agent and substitutes for it an uncertified local union.

Now, it can be argued that the second demand involves an illegal objective, since the Wagner Act, as amended, requires the employer to bargain with the certified representative of the employees, and the employer circumvents this purpose by substitution of an uncertified local. But what about the first demand—is there anything wrong with that? The employer's argument, of course, is that he is interested in avoiding strikes resulting from hasty action by the employees and therefore wants to make sure that employees have time to consider his last offer and to vote for or against it by secret ballot.

This set of facts came before the NLRB in the Wooster Division of Borg-Warner Corporation case and subsequently was appealed all the way to the Supreme Court.[21] The Supreme Court upheld an NLRB order that the employer's insistence upon either clause was violative of the good-faith requirement of Section 8 (*a*) (5) of the amended NLRA. Justice Burton, speaking for the majority, stated that neither clause related to a matter which under the amended Act was a subject of mandatory collective bargaining. He enunciated the view that the parties could talk about other things, but if they *insisted* on inclusion of such matters in a contract, it violated the good-faith requirement of the law!

Justice Harlan, speaking for the minority, raised some penetrating questions concerning the practicality of the majority position. He agreed with the majority as to the employer's insistence upon the recognition clause, but disagreed on the matter of the secret ballot clause. He stated:

> . . . I am unable to grasp a concept of "bargaining" which enables one to "propose" a particular point, but not to "insist" on it as a condition of agreement. The right to bargain becomes illusory if one is not free to press a proposal in good faith to the point of insistence. Surely adoption of so inherently vague and fluid a standard is apt to inhibit the entire bargaining process because of a participant's fear that strenuous argument might shade into forbidden insistence and thereby produce a charge of an unfair labor practice. . . .[22]

[21] *National Labor Relations Board* v. *Wooster Division of Borg-Warner Corp.*, 356 U.S. 342, 78 S. Ct. 718 (1958).

[22] 356 U.S. 342, 352; 78 S. Ct. 718, 724.

The Supreme Court had open to it in this case three possible avenues of decision:[23]

a) The Court could decide that the ballot clause was a mandatory subject of bargaining falling within the meaning of the statutory language "wages, hours, and other terms and conditions of employment." This position would give the parties the maximum latitude over subjects which could be included in collective bargaining. Specifically, it would mean that the employer could bargain to an impasse on the issue of the ballot clause. By the same token, it would mean that a union could bargain to an impasse on issues which employers in future cases might feel should not be included in normal collective bargaining negotiations. Furthermore, once an issue is determined to fall in the mandatory bargaining category, the power of government can be brought to bear to force a recalcitrant party to negotiate on this subject. As a practical matter, once an issue falls in the mandatory class, it is only a question of time before it becomes embodied in written contracts, for it is almost impossible to bargain in good faith on an issue in accordance with Board standards and not be led into compromises and settlements with respect to it. From this point of view the Court, in the Borg-Warner case, by refusing to hold that the ballot issue fell within the mandatory class, may have set a precedent which will tend to slow the invasion by unions of the critical area of managerial prerogatives. For while, in this case, it was the employer who was pressing an unusual demand, in general it can be anticipated that unions in the future will be more aggressive and more imaginative in devising new demands[24] than management. The Borg-Warner decision sets up a protective bar against such novel demands unless by some elasticity of language they can be made to fall within the statutory class of mandatory subjects of bargaining.

b) The Court could decide that the issue was nonmandatory, but that bargaining to an impasse on it was not per se an unfair labor practice. Determination that an unfair labor practice existed would

[23] See, for an excellent analysis of this problem, R. W. Fleming, "The Obligation to Bargain in Good Faith," in J. Shister, B. Aaron, and C. W. Summers (eds.), *Public Policy and Collective Bargaining*, Industrial Relations Research Association Publication No. 27 (New York: Harper and Row, 1962), pp. 60–87.

[24] A new demand which a number of unions are currently pressing involves employer contributions to "industry development funds," the proceeds of which are to be utilized for education of employees, retraining, advertising, research, and promotion of the products of the industry. In *Carpenters' Union* (McCloskey & Co.), 50 LRRM 1431, the Carpenters' Union demanded that an employer sign a contract which provided for contributions to the Industry Advancement Fund for education, research, and industry relations. The NLRB held that contribution to such a fund was a nonmandatory subject of bargaining and that the union's insistence on inclusion of this provision constituted a refusal to bargain.

then depend upon an examination of the total circumstances of the case, in which bargaining to an impasse on one issue would simply be an element to be considered. This approach would mean that superior bargaining power would ultimately dictate what terms were included in collective bargaining contracts. Suppose the United Steelworkers were to seek to obtain agreement from a steel producer that it would not follow a wage increase with a price increase for a period of at least six months on the ground that the wage-price spiral hurt the public image of the union. Such an argument might be pressed in good faith, and the union might be strong enough to compel the company to accede to it, in which case unions would become involved in a key aspect of managerial prerogative—price policy. Perhaps Congress, by defining collective bargaining in terms of "wages, hours, and other terms and conditions of employment," intended that bargaining power by management or labor be limited to these areas. In any case, application of the Borg-Warner viewpoint would permit the union to raise the price issue but would prohibit it from bargaining to an impasse over it.

c) The Court could decide—as it did—that bargaining to an impasse on the ballot clause was per se an unfair labor practice, even though the trial examiner had made a finding that the company had bargained in good faith. This approach effectively narrows the area of permissible collective bargaining. It places the government in the position of more or less preserving the *status quo* as to what is a bargainable issue. The Court, in effect, says to the parties: "This issue does not seem to fall within the statutory language referring to 'wages, hours, and other terms and conditions of employment,' and therefore you cannot press this demand too far." This approach does not take the government out of collective bargaining, for there is little significant difference between having the government tell parties what they *must* bargain about and what they *cannot* bargain about. In either case the government exercises a major control over the substantive content of collective bargaining.

The Borg-Warner decision tends to put collective bargaining in a strait jacket and seems inconsistent in outlook with the Insurance Agents' case referred to on page 114. In the latter case the Supreme Court flatly said that "Congress intended that the parties should have wide latitude in their negotiations, unrestricted by any governmental power to regulate the substantive solution of their differences." Yet in the Borg-Warner case the power of the government has been used to deprive the parties of the right to bargain to an impasse over issues which the Court feels are outside of the "norm." But collective bargaining is an evolving institution; many issues which are now considered normal were unheard of when the Wagner Act was first passed. Certainly, Congress would have been surprised to know that pensions, for example, would fall within the statutory reference to "wages," but so the courts have held. In years to come, there will be many new issues raised, particularly in the field of job security as a result of the rapid application of automation in industry. There will be many cases involving the closing-down of plants, subcontracting work,[25] transfer of employees, and the multitude of problems that result from the impact of major technological change. These all involve delicate decisions of investment and fall in the jealously guarded realm of managerial policy. They also concern job rights, seniority, and other valid union claims. If it should be held that these issues do not fall in the mandatory area, and if the Borg-Warner criterion is followed so that bargaining to an impasse on them is per se unlawful, how are differences over these matters to be resolved, if they cannot be part of normal collective bargaining?

SHOULD THE DOCTRINE OF GOOD-FAITH BARGAINING BE SCRAPPED?

The present status of the law of good-faith bargaining is wholly unrealistic. The distinctions between mandatory and nonmandatory bargaining are satisfactory for the courtroom but not for the smoke-filled conference room. Charges of unfair labor practices serve merely to delay effective collective bargaining and further to burden the NLRB and the courts with time-consuming litigation. With these problems in mind the Independent Labor Study Group of the Committee for Economic Development, in its recent report entitled *The Public Interest in National Labor Policy,* concludes:

> The subjects to be covered by bargaining, the procedures to be followed, the nuances of strategy involving the timing of a "best offer," the question of whether to reopen a contract during its term—such matters as these are best left to the parties themselves. Indeed, the work load of the National Labor Relations Board and of the parties could be substantially reduced by returning these issues to the door of the employer or union, where Senator Walsh wisely left them.[26]

The simple fact seems to be that the government can compel parties to talk over their problems, but it cannot legislate good faith.

[25] The position of the NLRB on plant shutdowns and subcontracting work is discussed in Chapter 7.

[26] Committee for Economic Development, *The Public Interest in National Labor Policy* (New York, 1961), p. 82.

This can come only from a growing maturity on the part of labor and management—a maturity which is already evident in some industries but sadly lacking in others. Where there is a disparity of bargaining power between the parties, the present doctrine of good-faith bargaining, in theory, tends to afford some protection to the underdog, whether it be labor or management. In practice, however, it has simply brought increasing governmental regulation and litigation into the collective bargaining sphere.

THE CONTROL OF CONTRACT ADMINISTRATION

In the previous chapter, we observed that the Taft-Hartley Act made it possible for employers and unions to bring suits involving collective bargaining agreements in federal court. Section 301 (*a*) of the Act provides: "Suits for violation of contracts between an employer and a labor organization representing employees in an industry affecting commerce as defined in this Act, or between any such labor organizations, may be brought in any district court of the United States having jurisdiction of the parties, without respect to the amount in controversy or without regard to the citizenship of the parties."

This innocuous-appearing provision, which on its face seems only to provide a new forum for trying cases involving disputes over labor contracts, promises to have far-reaching effects upon a vital area of union-management relations—contract administration. As a matter of fact, some labor experts believe that this provision may well be one of the most important in the entire Act. As Professor Archibald Cox states: "Until the Taft-Hartley Act was enacted, collective agreements were negotiated without much regard to whether they were enforceable contracts or merely treaties resting upon mutual interdependence backed by moral force and fear of economic reprisals. . . . History will mark the Taft-Hartley Act as the turning point at which law began to play a large role in contract administration."[27]

Prior to 1947, unions and management generally took the position that the courts should be kept out of contract administration. Grievances were generally resolved informally between company representatives and union business agents or shop stewards. At the same time, most contracts contained a formal procedure for resolving differences over contract interpretation during the term of the bargaining agreement. The grievance machinery usually included a series of steps,

[27] Archibald Cox, *Law and the National Labor Policy,* Institute of Industrial Relations Monograph Series, No. 5 (Los Angeles: University of California, 1960), p. 17.

with a higher level of union and management authority participating at each step.[28] To induce settlement without a work stoppage, contracts customarily provided for a terminal step of arbitration, to which disputes were referred which the parties could not settle in any of the earlier stages. Bureau of Labor Statistics studies indicate that more than 90 per cent of the contracts which it examined provide for such arbitration. In consideration of the employer's agreement to refer such disputes to arbitration, the union customarily agrees not to strike over such issues during the life of the contract. The arbitrator may be an individual or a state or federal board named in the agreement, or an individual or a board selected *ad hoc* by union and management representatives for each dispute reaching the terminal point in the grievance machinery.

Arbitration of disputes over contract administration has become so common on the American labor scene that literally thousands of decisions are handed down by arbitrators every year interpreting various clauses in collective bargaining agreements under a variety of factual circumstances. These decisions are for the most part rendered by men who are economists or labor lawyers, or who have some special familiarity with the customs and practices in the particular industry. The hearings before the arbitrators are less formal than in a court of law, and the rules of evidence which are controlling in court cases do not apply. Arbitration decisions are compiled and printed,[29] and are consulted by arbitrators who wish to see how other arbitrators have dealt with similar factual situations. Thus, there has developed outside the courtroom a "law of contract administration" which has no legal force as such but which serves as a body of technical precedents in the field of arbitration.

Since Section 301 (*a*) of the Taft-Hartley Act purports to apply to suits for violation of collective bargaining agreements, it obviously applies to disputes involving the applicability of the grievance machinery terminating in arbitration. For example, the union may claim that a dispute on a certain issue should go to arbitration, because the business agent does not want to "stick his neck out" to make an unpopular decision. The employer, on the other hand, may not want to go to arbitration on a matter because of a conviction that it is solely a

[28] For a discussion of typical grievance machinery, see Gordon F. Bloom and Herbert R. Northrup, *Economics of Labor Relations* (4th ed.; Homewood, Ill.: Richard D. Irwin, Inc., 1961), pp. 181–87.

[29] See, for example, *Labor Arbitration Reports,* published by the Bureau of National Affairs, Inc., Washington, D.C.

matter of managerial prerogative and was not intended to be covered by the grievance machinery.

Suppose an employer refuses to refer such a dispute to arbitration and the union brings suit in federal court to require the employer to do so. Section 301 (*a*) might have been construed simply as a procedural provision permitting such suits for enforcement of an agreement to arbitrate to be brought in federal court. But the United States Supreme Court has read into the statutory language much more than that. In the famous Lincoln Mills case and its companion cases,[30] the United States Supreme Court established that an arbitration agreement in a collective bargaining contract in an industry affecting interstate commerce was enforceable in federal court, and *that the law to be applied in determining the intent of the parties and in interpreting the contract provisions was federal law.* The Court stated unequivocally that a *whole new body of substantive federal law* now has to be devised applicable to the arbitration process in collective bargaining.

This decision has aroused grave misgivings on the part of some labor experts and labor arbitrators. The fear has been expressed that litigation over contract administration will increase and that judges, who are generally unfamiliar with labor practices in industry, will tend to construe collective bargaining agreements literally without sufficient attention to practice and custom. It has been pointed out that collective bargaining agreements are unlike most contracts—they are the basis of a continuing relationship and typically are not complete instruments. As a consequence, arbitrators, after investigating practices and customs in an industry, frequently read things into contracts which are not there. What does "discharge for just cause" mean? This is the kind of cryptic phrase that arbitrators must wrestle with. Are courts equipped to deal with the shorthand phraseology of collective bargaining agreements? Justice Frankfurter, who dissented in the Lincoln Mills case, voiced the opinion that "judicial intervention is ill-suited to the special characteristics of the arbitration process in labor disputes."[31]

ARBITRABILITY AND MANAGEMENT RIGHTS

The dangers of judicial intervention in collective bargaining contract administration are well illustrated by two important decisions

[30] *Textile Workers' Union* v. *Lincoln Mills of Alabama,* 353 U.S. 448, 77 S. Ct. 912 (1957); *General Electric Co.* v. *Local 205, United Electrical Workers,* 353 U.S. 547, 77 S. Ct. 921 (1957); *Goodall-Sanford, Inc.* v. *United Textile Workers,* 353 U.S. 550, 77 S. Ct. 923 (1957).

[31] 353 U.S. 448, 463.

rendered by the Supreme Court in June, 1960, involving arbitration under collective bargaining agreements.[32] These decisions concern the basic authority of the arbitrator to arbitrate—a technical issue which on its surface appears to affect only the phraseology of the arbitration clause. The implications of these decisions, however, are much more profound and may well affect the entire area of managerial control in industrial relations.

Let us suppose that management in a particular company makes a decision that it is more profitable to contract out certain maintenance work than to perform the work with its own employees. It therefore lays off nineteen men and subcontracts to an outside company the work previously done by the laid-off employees. The union claims that this action violates the collective bargaining agreement and demands that management submit the matter to arbitration. The contract contains a no-strike agreement by the union and an arbitration clause calling for the arbitration of disputes "as to the meaning and application of the provisions of this agreement." Another clause provides that "matters which are strictly a function of management shall not be subject to arbitration." While the matter of subcontracting work is not specifically mentioned in the contract, the company takes the position that this is strictly a management decision. The company emphasizes that for nineteen years the union has attempted to make changes in the contract which would have limited this right, and the company has always defeated such attempts as an invasion of managerial prerogative. Should the company now have to go to arbitration on this issue?

It should be noted that the issue is initially only a procedural one: Is this an arbitrable issue? Even if the issue is found to be arbitrable, the company might still be sustained by the arbitrator in its action in laying off the men. But a corollary result would be that management could no longer act freely in this sphere and would have to be prepared to justify its action to an arbitrator whenever it made similar decisions. Thus, procedural decisions tend to affect the substance of employer-union relations.

The facts set forth above were involved in the case of *United*

[32] *United Steelworkers of America* v. *American Manufacturing Co.*, 363 U.S. 564, 80 S. Ct. 1343 (1960); *United Steelworkers of America* v. *Warrior and Gulf Navigation Co.*, 363 U.S. 574, 80 S. Ct. 1347 (1960). A third case, decided the same day, *United Steelworkers of America* v. *Enterprise Wheel and Car Corp.*, 363 U.S. 593, 80 S. Ct. 1358 (1960), involved the question of whether an arbitrator had exceeded his authority in making an arbitration award after a voluntary submission to arbitration by both parties to the contract.

Steelworkers of America v. *Warrior and Gulf Navigation Company.*[33] The union brought suit under Section 301 of the Taft-Hartley Act to compel the Company to go to arbitration on the issue of subcontracting out work. The lower courts sustained the management's position that the issue was not arbitrable, but on appeal the United States Supreme Court reversed and sided with the union. The High Court set forth at length its theory of the nature of a collective bargaining agreement: "It is a generalized code to govern a myriad of cases which the draftsmen cannot wholly anticipate,"[34] and the parties utilize arbitration as a means of filling in the gaps and taking care of unforeseen circumstances. The Court reasoned that in selecting the system of arbitration for the resolution of differences over contract interpretation and administration, management and labor intend that *every* dispute or grievance be arbitrated unless they have *specifically* excluded it from the arbitration provisions. The Court emphasized that federal policy is to promote industrial stability through collective bargaining agreements and that giving arbitration clauses the broadest possible coverage furthers this policy.

In dissenting, Justice Whittaker stated:

> I understand the Court thus to hold that the arbitrators are not confined to the express provisions of the contract, that arbitration is to be ordered unless it may be said with positive assurance that arbitration of a particular dispute is excluded by the contract, that doubts of arbitrability are to be resolved in favor of arbitration, and that when, as here, the contract contains a no-strike clause, everything that management does is subject to arbitration.
>
> This is an entirely new and strange doctrine to me. I suggest with deference, that it departs from both the contract of the parties and the controlling decisions of this Court.[35]

In a companion case, decided the same day, *United Steelworkers of America* v. *American Manufacturing Company,*[36] the Supreme Court further amplified its doctrine favoring broad coverage of arbitration in contract administration. In this case the union sought to compel the company to arbitrate the question of whether an employee who had been injured should be reinstated to his job by virtue of the seniority provisions of the collective bargaining agreement. The employee had already obtained a permanent workmen's compensation award based upon 25 per cent permanent partial disability which clearly established

[33] 363 U.S. 574, 80 S. Ct. 1347.

[34] 363 U.S. 574, 578; 80 S. Ct. 1347, 1351.

[35] 363 U.S. 574, 589; 80 S. Ct. 1347, 1356.

[36] 363 U.S. 564, 80 S. Ct. 1343.

that he was unable to perform his previous work. The arbitration clause stated that all disputes "as to the meaning, interpretation and application of this agreement" should go to arbitration. The Company's refusal to arbitrate was upheld by the lower courts, which found the union's claim to be a "frivolous, patently baseless one, not subject to arbitration under the collective bargaining agreement."

The Supreme Court reversed and held that the issue was arbitrable. In so holding, it again emphasized that it was attempting to implement the federal policy in favor of settlement of grievances, as expressed in Section 203 (*d*) of the Taft-Hartley Act. That section states: "Final adjustment by a method agreed upon by the parties is hereby declared to be the desirable method of settlement of grievance disputes arising over the application or interpretation of any existing collective bargaining agreement. . . ." The Court felt that this policy could best be effectuated by giving the arbitration clause "full play." In the words of Justice Douglas: "There is no exception in the 'no-strike' clause and none therefore should be read into the grievance clause, since one is the quid pro quo for the other."[37] Furthermore, the Court indicated that the processing of even frivolous claims may have a therapeutic value in labor relations. One writer has commented that as a result of these two decisions, an employee who wants to compel management to let him hang a collection of butterflies in the main lobby to promote employee morale has probably raised an arbitrable issue![38]

Where do these decisions leave the delicate issue of managerial prerogative? The Supreme Court apparently takes a very narrow view of this area and would require a specific exclusion in a written agreement, or "the most forceful evidence" indicating that the parties intended the arbitration clause not to be applicable. Practical labor practitioners will recognize the difficulty in a collective bargaining agreement of enumerating specific subjects which are to be solely the prerogative of management. As a matter of fact, most companies have preferred to rely on a general management clause and would prefer not even to discuss what it encompasses for fear that this will give the union an opportunity to whittle away at managerial authority. Some companies do not even have management rights provisions in their labor contracts and prefer to rely on the so-called "residual rights" theory. Under this theory, management is presumed to have retained

[37] 363 U.S. 564, 567; 80 S. Ct. 1343, 1346.

[38] Franklin B. Snyder, "What Has the Supreme Court Done to Arbitration?" *Labor Law Journal,* Vol. XII (February, 1961), p. 97.

all rights governing the conduct of its business that are not limited by the labor agreement. It is doubtful that the Supreme Court would subscribe to this view, for it has defined management rights as only those over which the contract gives management "complete control and unfettered discretion."

What began in the Lincoln Mills case as a simple test of the application of Section 301 of the Taft-Hartley Act has now opened a vista for unions of a major assault on managerial prerogatives. Union claims which were previously held not arbitrable will now be pressed again, and courts following the guidelines set down by the Supreme Court will now tend to consider many of them arbitrable. The result will be a gradual extension of union control over areas previously reserved for exclusive managerial determination. Coming at a time when employers are faced by difficult decisions arising out of automation, the Common Market, and general intensified competition, the result may well be a shifting of the major area of industrial discord from wages to a broad range of issues intertwined with managerial decisions and ranging from layoffs to investment policy.

Some critics contend that the Taft-Hartley Act should be amended in order to prevent more and more judicial intrusion into the substance of collective bargaining.[39] On the other hand, it can be asked: What is the alternative? Certainly, great damage could be done to the entire system of private arbitration in labor disputes if the parties believed they could, with legal impunity, ignore an agreement to arbitrate. Court enforcement of such agreements is not, therefore, the real problem. As one labor spokesman comments: "The question presented by the Lincoln Mills case is not really whether there should or should not be judicial intervention but whether the judicial intervention should be state or federal."[40] The Lincoln Mills case and other decisions have established that state courts have concurrent jurisdiction in such matters, but must apply federal law. The real problem is that the Supreme Court has enunciated a theory of contract administration which is at variance with what many company and union negotiators have believed was meant by a labor agreement. As a practical matter, it would be extremely difficult for Congress to deal with this problem—even if it were so disposed, which is unlikely. We can, therefore, in

[39] See, for example, W. J. Isaacson, "Lincoln Mills Revisited: Caution, Judges Inventing," *Twelfth Annual Conference on Labor* (New York: New York University, 1959), p. 210.

[40] D. Feller in *Arbitration and the Law*, Proceedings of the Twelfth Annual Meeting of the National Academy of Arbitrators (Washington, D.C.: Bureau of National Affairs, Inc., 1959), pp. 14–15.

summation conclude that the Taft-Hartley Act, through court interpretation of Section 301 (*a*), will have a major influence on the nature of contract administration in the years to come.

APPRAISAL OF THE ROLE OF THE NLRB UNDER THE TAFT-HARTLEY ACT

From its very first days of administration under the Wagner Act, the NLRB has been under attack by various groups in our economy. These criticisms continue to this day. Current complaints against the Board fall into three major categories:

1. The Board has become a policy-making body and has in effect usurped the authority of Congress in legislating in the field of labor relations.
2. The function of the Board is quasi-judicial, but it acts more like a political agency than a court.
3. The Board is biased in favor of organized labor and has not properly reflected the spirit of the Taft-Hartley Act, which intended that government be a neutral.

Let us consider each of these criticisms in turn.

Is the NLRB a Policy-Making Body?

There is no doubt that the answer to this question is yes. The Board has taken a statute which sets forth certain general rules, and has sought to implement and amplify this Act by applying it to the multitude of diverse circumstances which arise in case-by-case progression before the Board. Take the so-called "free speech amendment" as an example. We have already observed that Section 8 (*c*) of the Taft-Hartley Act states that "The expressing of any views, argument, or opinion, or the dissemination thereof, whether in written, printed, graphic, or visual form, shall not constitute or be evidence of an unfair labor practice under any of the provisions of this Act, if such expression contains no threat of reprisal or force or promise of benefit."

The legislature has spoken, but what does it mean?

Free speech problems arise, of course, in unfair labor practice cases, but principally in representation proceedings when the losing party to an election protests the results on the theory that prejudicial conduct rendered it impossible for the employees to register a true and meaningful sentiment on their choice of union representation. This type of case raises the question whether employer or union speech "goes too far." Suppose the employer wrongfully libels the union leadership as Communistic, or truthfully states that he cannot meet union wage demands and that the advent of a union would probably result in a strike during which he would be forced to hire replacements. Are these statements merely permissible views and opinions, and hence protected free speech; or are they threats of reprisal, and therefore illegal interference with the rights of employees to self-organization?

Obviously, no statute could spell out all the nuances which develop in the complicated industrial world we live in. It is in this area that the Board is a policy maker and, subject to court review, wields great power over the destinies of the many employers and unions whose names become entries in the voluminous dockets of the NLRB. There are many vociferous critics who contend that the NLRB should not have such policy-making power, but closer examination of their arguments will usually reveal that their animus is directed not so much at the Board for making policy as for making what they believe is the *wrong* policy. Such difference of opinion is, of course, inevitable. While it is conceivable that the policy-making power could be taken away from the Board and given to the courts, critics of the Board would probably not be any happier with the eventual result if the courts rendered decisions which reflected a philosophy or a statutory interpretation contrary to the critics' own.

Although the Board has inevitably been drawn into policy making, it has not always done so willingly and on many occasions has taken a more limited construction of its powers in this regard than have the courts. A case in point is the recent Supreme Court decision involving interpretation of the Board's function under Section 10 (*k*) of the Taft-Hartley Act. That section states that when a union is charged with an unfair labor practice growing out of a jurisdictional dispute, "the Board is empowered and directed to hear and determine the dispute out of which such unfair labor practice shall have arisen. . . ." In this case the Board refused to make a determination as to whether a union of television technicians or a union of stagehands was entitled to work involving electric lighting for television shows. In support of its contention that it could not make such a decision, the Board argued that Section 10 (*k*) sets forth no standards to guide it in determining jurisdictional disputes on their merits. The United States Supreme Court, however, held that the Board was bound to inquire into the merits of the dispute and make a binding award of the work. The Court stated:

> It is true that this forces the Board to exercise under sec. 10 (*k*) powers which are broad and lacking in rigid standards to govern their application. But administrative agencies are frequently given rather loosely defined powers to cope with problems as difficult as those posed by jurisdictional disputes and strikes.

It might have been better, as some persuasively argued in Congress, to intrust this matter to arbitrators. But Congress . . . decided to intrust this decision to the Board. It has had long experience in hearing and disposing of similar labor problems. With this experience and a knowledge of the standards generally used by arbitrators, unions, employers, joint boards and others in wrestling with this problem, we are confident that the Board need not disclaim the power given it for lack of standards.[41]

The government has taken a major role in the regulation of collective bargaining relationships in this country. Despite mistakes and weaknesses in administration of our labor laws, probably neither labor nor management would wish to return to an era of pure *laissez faire.* This being the case, the complicated task of applying general statutory provisions to day-to-day labor negotiations almost necessarily requires the intervention of an administrative agency which must "fill in the blanks" left by the legislators in enacting a general statute. The problem with the NLRB is that in the view of many of its critics it has gone beyond "filling in the blanks" and has written new law, sometimes in a manner which appears contrary to Congressional intent.

Our national government is tripartite in form. The determination of general policy is a function of Congress. The executive branch, which includes such administrative agencies as the NLRB, is charged with the responsibility of implementing such policy and rendering it workable in the complex factual situations of everyday life. An important function of the courts is to review decisions and actions of administrative agencies to make sure they do not stray from the declared statutory purpose. In this connection, it is noteworthy that the United States Supreme Court has frequently disagreed with the NLRB. During 1959–60 the NLRB lost five out of six cases in which it appeared before the High Court. In 1960–61 the Board made nine appearances in the Supreme Court and won three and a half cases. Furthermore, as Frank W. McCulloch, Chairman of the Board, recently admitted: "Our losses involved much more significant issues than did our victories."[42]

Is the NLRB a Quasi-Judicial Body or a Political Agency?

Management spokesmen have consistently maintained that the functions of the Board are very much like that of a court; yet the Board is not constituted like a court, nor does it function like one. For example, in hearing unfair labor practice cases, the NLRB, in effect, de-

[41] *National Labor Relations Board* v. *Radio Engineers' Union*, 47 LRRM 2332, 2334.

[42] Speech before the American Management Association, Chicago, Illinois, February 15, 1962.

termines the guilt or innocence of the parties charged with violating the law. The orders it enters can require payment of large sums of money and can have drastic effects upon the operation of business and union organizations, large and small. While, technically, a Board order has no binding force until it is enforced in a court of law, as a practical matter it has great coercive power, since defendants frequently cannot run the risk of violating it because of the delays incidental to court review of such orders. Furthermore, even where an appeal is taken to the courts, findings of fact made by the Board are, within broad limits, accepted as final by the courts. Therefore, there is substantial basis for the contention that in such cases the Board is performig a quasi-judicial function.

Criticism of Board action in this capacity stems primarily from the fact that the members of the NLRB, like the members of most administrative agencies, are short-term political appointees. As one critic puts it: "They are an essential part of the political equipment of the administration which gives them their office."[43] Whereas judges in a court of law usually have life tenure and are thus removed from the direct pressures of the political scene, the members of the NLRB must answer to the administration which appointed them and can have little hope of reappointment if they displease the administration in power. This leads to the type of situation wherein the Eisenhower-appointed Board overturned over thirty important precedents of the preceding Truman and Roosevelt boards, and the newly reconstituted Kennedy-appointed Board reversed an equal number of key decisions handed down by prior Boards.

Because Board members are political appointees, management spokesmen in particular have questioned whether they should have a right to make quasi-judicial decisions which may reflect the bias of a particular political point of view. Furthermore, the value of appeal to the courts—which is, of course, always open to an employer who believes a decision of the Board was unfair—is weakened by the fact that the Board does not have to follow the rules of evidence like a court of law. Therefore, it is argued, a Board with a bias in favor of one of the parties can permit evidence to become part of the record which would have been excluded in a court of law and can thus substantiate an unfair decision.[44]

[43] Sylvester Petro, *The Kohler Strike* (Chicago: Henry Regnery Co., 1961), p. 104.

[44] Recently, a number of circuit courts have been critical of findings of fact made by the Board. In *National Labor Relations Board* v. *Cosco Products Co.*, 272 F. (2d) 23 (CA–5, 1959), the Court accused the NLRB trial examiner of a "misunderstanding of his independent function as an impartial trier," of "active and partisan participation in the hearing," and of "misunderstanding . . . what was relevant and what was not."

In defense of the Board, it should be noted that only a small portion of its work consists of this controversial quasi-judicial nature. Most of its staff time is devoted to investigation, negotiation, and settlement of problems through informal procedures. For example, in the fiscal year ended June 30, 1961, there were 22,691 new cases filed with the NLRB. In this same year, only 3,746 cases of all types went to decision by the full Board.[45] The twenty-eight regional offices of the Board usually dispose of about 90 per cent of all complaint cases by dismissals, withdrawals, and settlements.[46]

Some critics believe that the Board should continue to handle investigation, negotiation, and settlement of matters coming within the purview of the Act, but that quasi-judicial functions, such as those involved in unfair labor practice cases, should be taken away from the Board and given to the courts. For example, in a recent press release the United States Chamber of Commerce recommended that most of the functions of the NLRB be abolished, that unfair labor practice cases should be transferred to the courts, and that the NLRB should confine its activities to holding union elections among employees.[47]

These spokesmen argue that one of the reasons these functions were given to the Board in the first place was because the judicial process was alleged to be too slow and the administrative process was thought capable of providing more speedy relief to an aggrieved party. Actually, the delays which have bogged down the processes of the Board have belied this supposed advantage. Board members are cognizant of the long delays which have developed in administrative procedure, and point with pride to the recent decentralization of decisions in election cases and the resultant reduction in elapsed time for final disposition of such cases. However, the problem still remains and will be further aggravated by the mounting case load facing the Board.

On the subject of political outlook, some Board members would deny that their political affiliation affects their attitude toward cases coming before them. On the other hand, other Board members openly acknowledge that the Board is a political arm of the executive branch of the federal government, and therefore should reflect in some measure the views of the party in power. In the words of Frank W. McCulloch, Chairman of the National Labor Relations Board: "Congress has refused to give Board Members long-term tenure. It constituted

[45] National Labor Relations Board, *Twenty-sixth Annual Report* (Washington, D.C.: U.S. Government Printing Office, 1962), p. 6.

[46] Speech by McCulloch, *op. cit.*

[47] *Boston Globe,* March 1, 1962, p. 39.

the Board with five-year terms, which are staggered so as to permit each President to make appointments. The obvious conclusion is that while it laid down the basic charter and policy to be applied, Congress recognized and intended that the President should have some influence through the appointive process on the broad direction taken by the agencies which 'execute' the law."[48]

The responsiveness of an administrative agency such as the NLRB to the wishes of the chief executive can present serious problems to a litigant appearing before the agency who is seeking an unbiased determination of the merits of a particular case. On the other hand, in terms of the gradual evolution of labor policy, there are some advantages which follow from an agency which "bends with the prevailing wind." Changes in the National Labor Relations Act have been made at infrequent intervals. As a matter of fact, major changes have been made at intervals of twelve years. If the Board did not gradually change its outlook in the intervening years, the amendments would have a tremendous impact upon collective bargaining because Congressional action, since it is infrequent, tends to go to extremes. The Taft-Hartley Act, while quite far removed from the original Wagner Act in spirit and purpose, was nevertheless foreshadowed by many of the decisions of the Board. For example, the so-called "free speech amendment" in effect wrote into law the decisions of the Board which had gradually evolved from the strict regulation of employer speech in the early days of the Act when labor was relatively weak to a more liberal attitude in the postwar years.

Is the NLRB Biased in Favor of Organized Labor?

Management spokesmen frequently complain that despite the fact that the Taft-Hartley Act was passed by Congress to restrict certain detrimental practices of unions and to eliminate the one-sided nature of the Wagner Act, the NLRB has continued to administer the Act in the Wagner Act tradition—that is, *for* labor and *against* management. Many examples of this alleged bias can be cited. The following discussion includes a few of the instances most frequently raised by critics of the NLRB.

The NLRB has frequently appeared to be prolabor in its interpretation of the good-faith bargaining provision which we have already discussed earlier in this chapter. Part of the problem here arises from the fact that bargaining in labor negotiations since World War II has been pretty much a one-sided affair. Unions always ask for somthing

[48] Speech by McCulloch, *op. cit.*

more. Employers either give in or hold the line. It has been rare for an employer to ask the union for anything, although in the last few years we have seen the beginning of an effort by management, particularly in the railroad industry, to wring concessions on work rules from unions. But generally, it is the union which makes requests, for requests cost nothing. It is the employer who pays; and even small requests, if granted, can, over a year's time, amount to hundreds of thousands of dollars. Even though the Taft-Hartley Act specifically states that neither party is required to make a concession in negotiations, the NLRB has seemed to employers to take the view that if a company continually says no, it is either out to break the union or is antiunion.

The present Board has been subject to particularly sharp attacks for alleged bias because of its action in reversing many of the key decisions of the prior Board. Mention was made in Chapter 1 of two of these decisions. In the General Motors case the Eisenhower Board had held that an agency contract was not a permissible form of union security under the Taft-Hartley law. The Kennedy Board reversed this decision. Now the United States Court of Appeals for the Sixth Circuit has reversed the Board[49] and ruled that the earlier decision by the Board was proper. In the Calumet Contractors case[50] the former Board had ruled that it was unlawful for a union to picket to force an employer to adopt that union's contract rates where the employees of the employer were already represented by another union certified by the Board. The present Board reversed this decision[51] and held that picketing to establish union standards was not picketing for recognition, and was therefore not banned by the Landrum-Griffin amendments to the Taft-Hartley Act. The Board admitted that this decision might result in "unwarranted harrassment" of the employer, but suggested that this problem be addressed to Congress. In the Barker Bros. case,[52] in which the majority of the Board held that mere isolated interferences with pickups and deliveries were not sufficient to make picketing unlawful, the dissenting members bitterly attacked the majority and argued that by this and other decisions they were virtually nullifying Congressional purpose in enacting the picketing restrictions contained in the 1959 amendments.

In the field of employer free speech, the Board has seemed to many employers to have eviscerated the free speech amendment in-

[49] 50 LRRM 2396.
[50] 47 LRRM 1253.
[51] 48 LRRM 1667.
[52] 51 LRRM 1053.

cluded in the Taft-Hartley Act and to have adopted a restrictive attitude reminiscent of the early days of the Wagner Act. This viewpoint is reflected in the following statement made by Gerald A. Brown, NLRB Board member, in a recent address: "Our role in election cases is, as the Board cogently stated in General Shoe many years ago 'to provide a laboratory in which an experiment may be conducted, under conditions as nearly ideal as possible, to determine the uninhibited desires of the employees.' It is our duty to establish these conditions. . . ."[53] In implementing this view, the Board has ruled, contrary to prior practice, that the employer can no longer discuss union matters with workers on his own time and property unless he gives equal time and equal facilities for the union to reply. Furthermore, the Board has relied on the doctrine of totality of conduct to render unlawful what to many observers appear to be employer utterances permitted by the express language of Section 8 (*c*) of the Taft-Hartley Act.[54]

In bargaining unit determination the Board has broken with precedent and, as discussed in the previous chapter, has held that a single store in a retail chain may be an appropriate bargaining unit.[55] Critics of this decision contend that it was motivated by a desire on the part of the Board to assist the lagging union drive for organization. Whatever the motivation, there is no question that this decision, if followed in future cases, will make it much easier for unions to pick off stores in presently unorganized chain establishments. Moreover, this is no isolated decision. The record shows that the present Board has reversed or modified some 30 prior Board decisions in representation matters.[56]

It is apparent that the outlook of the present NLRB differs from that of its predecessor and that many of its decisions tend to favor organized labor. These favorable decisions have fallen in three major areas:

1. Blunting restrictions on union tactical weapons, such as the picket line.
2. Restricting employer counterweapons, such as employer speech.
3. Defining the bargaining unit to facilitate organizing.

[53] Speech delivered to the State Bar of Texas, July 5, 1962, reported in 50 LRR 251.

[54] For example, in the Cole Manufacturing Company case (49 LRRM 1033) an election lost by a union was set aside because the employer stated factually that prior organizing efforts had resulted in business being lost and that business would improve if the union lost the election.

[55] *Sav-On Drugs, Inc.,* 51 LRRM 1278.

[56] Harry L. Browne, "The National Labor Relations Board: Labor Law Rewritten," *American Bar Association Journal,* Vol. 49 (January, 1963), p. 68.

The attitude of the NLRB in administering the Taft-Hartley Act is influenced, as we have already noted, by the fact that it is a Board some of whose members are appointed by the current chief executive; and therefore, to some extent, it must necessarily reflect the policies of the party in power. Beyond that, however, is the fact that the Board has historically considered its primary purpose to be the encouragement of collective bargaining as the democratic method of solving labor problems. This is consistent with the statutory language contained in Section 1 of the Taft-Hartley Act, which states:

> It is hereby declared to be the policy of the United States to eliminate the cause of certain substantial obstructions to the free flow of commerce and to mitigate and eliminate these obstructions when they have occurred *by encouraging the practice and procedure of collective bargaining* and by protecting the exercise by workers of full freedom of association, self-organization, and designation of representatives of their own choosing, for the purpose of negotiating the terms and conditions of their employment or other mutual aid or protection [italics supplied].

Within this context of policy, some of the so-called "bias" of the NLRB becomes more understandable. For the Board—rightly or wrongly—apparently feels that collective bargaining can best be preserved and strengthened by actively assisting labor. Many friends of organized labor feel that this is not a sound basis upon which to build a labor movement and that the sooner organized labor learns to solve its difficulties itself without having to run to the government for solutions, the better off it will be. Professor William Gomberg, for example, in commenting on the Board's interpretation of the good-faith bargaining requirements of the Act, states: "It is my conviction that the so-called good faith bargaining clause has made the NLRB an extension of the tactics of the parties. It provides a whipping boy for the frustration of a party to the bargain who refuses to face the consequences of overplaying his hand and then goes running to papa government."[57] Similarly, Gomberg questions whether it is sound to permit a union to bring an unfair labor practice action to the NLRB in a case such as that involving the General Electric Company, where company strategy was simply to make an offer and then stick to it. As Gomberg puts it: "Is it the function of the government or the National Labor Relations Board to provide a miasma of busy work so that the weaker party is spared the pain of looking squarely at his own problem, the consoli-

[57] William Gomberg, "Government Participation in Union Regulation and Collective Bargaining," *Labor Law Journal,* Vol. XIII (November, 1962), p. 944.

dation of this organization and the formulation of a rational strategy?"[58]

Any fair appraisal of the supposed bias on the part of the Board must recognize that despite the tremendous strength of organized labor in many industries today, there are still many areas and situations where unions are weak and employers are hostile, and where, therefore, maintenance of a strictly neutral attitude on the part of the NLRB would probably be promanagement in effect. Take, for example, the very sensitive area of free speech. The same words spoken by an employer and by a union agent do not have the same import to an employee. The employer is the source of the employee's livelihood, his promotion, his success in business life. Unions, despite efforts to control entrance to a trade, and despite their formidable power, cannot match the employer's influence in these respects. Moreover, the employer has the power, derived from the employment relationship, to compel his employees to listen to his opinions on union organization, whereas a union has no such control over its membership. For these reasons the NLRB has tended to be much more restrictive of employer utterances on the subject of union organization and has, as a consequence, been accused of a prolabor bias.

This attitude on the part of the NLRB may be commendable if one favors the particular economic and social philosophy which it supports. But the question still remains whether under our labor laws, as they exist today, the NLRB has any legal right to use the power of its position to compensate for the deficiencies in bargaining power which labor may suffer in particular situations. If the literal application and enforcement of the free speech amendment included in the Taft-Hartley Act after long and careful deliberation by Congress would have the effect of weakening labor's bargaining position, does the NLRB have the right to interpret this language so as to soften its impact on unions which are in a weak or formative stage? In this connection the language of the United States Supreme Court in the recent Insurance Agents decision may be pertinent. The Court criticized the NLRB for attempting to regulate the economic weapons which labor and management could utilize and then stated that the Taft-Hartley Act does not contain "a charter for the National Labor Relations Board to act at large in equalizing disparities of bargaining power between employer and union."[59]

No satisfactory balance sheet of cases can be drawn up which

[58] *Ibid.*, p. 945.

[59] *National Labor Relations Board* v. *Insurance Agents' International Union, AFL–CIO*, 361 U.S. 477, 490; 80 S. Ct. 419 (1959).

will concretely establish the bias or lack of bias of the Board. Many decisions of the Board have been vehemently attacked by union representatives as antilabor, so the record is certainly not entirely one-sided. The Board has had an extremely difficult task in administering the Taft-Hartley Act, for the law itself is extremely broad and provides a minimum of statutory guidelines. Any final conclusion as to favoritism on the part of the Board will reflect the individual's own bias and particularly his preference for collective bargaining or individual determination as a goal of national policy.

While the bias or lack of bias of the Board is arguable, the fact that it has—rightly or wrongly—reversed many key precedents of long standing in labor relations law is undeniable. The lack of regard for *stare decisis* by the present Board has made it difficult for management and labor leaders to make policy decisions with any assurance that they will comply with what the Board considers lawful practice. The Board might well heed the advice of one of its own members who in a dissent stated:

> . . . an agency such as the National Labor Relations Board has the responsibility of establishing guideposts, which are as clear and understandable as the circumstances in the Board's organic act permit. Once such guides have been established they should not be obliterated without good, sufficient and carefully weighed reasons. Employers and labor organizations alike should be able to follow the Board's guideposts with some degree of assurance that they are on the right road. It should not be a game of chance.[60]

APPRAISAL OF THE TAFT-HARTLEY ACT

Whether the Taft-Hartley Act is considered a "good" law or a "bad" law depends in large measure upon the standard by which it is judged. If it is deemed desirable to afford greater freedom and privileges of self-determination to the individual worker, then it would seem that the Act constituted a rather hesitant advance in labor legislation. On the other hand, if one believes that progressive social policy requires strengthening labor organizations on the theory that all but a few unions are still at a disadvantage in bargaining with employers, then the various restrictions imposed upon the activities of unions appear less desirable.

Standards, therefore, affect one's view of the Act, and such standards frequently reflect the social bias of the individual. However, one

[60] Fanning, dissenting in *American Cyanamid Co.*, 48 LRRM 1152.

standard is at hand which lends itself to a fairly objective appraisal. That is the extent to which the Act facilitated the process of effective collective bargaining.

Ways in Which the Act Encouraged Effective Collective Bargaining

Effective collective bargaining may be defined as bargaining which in general represents the will of the majority of workers. The decertification procedure provided by the Taft-Hartley Act enabled employees to rid themselves of a union which, because of corrupt leadership or other causes, no longer represented the majority of workers. Likewise, the Communist affidavit requirements may have served to lessen industrial disputes which reflected not the bona fide grievances of workers but rather the planned intrigues of Communist officials. The prohibition against the closed shop and restrictions on the union shop were intended to eliminate practices such as the selling of jobs through issuance of work permits, which benefited the union bosses rather than the union membership, but these provisions were largely ineffective.

Effective collective bargaining assumes also a balance of power between labor and management. Under the Wagner Act, however, the balance of power in some industries had been so turned in labor's favor that individual employers had no choice but to accept the union's demands. The Taft-Hartley Act sought to remedy this situation by imposing an obligation to bargain upon both the union and the employer. Moreover, on the premise that effective collective bargaining requires responsible parties to the agreement, the Act made unions subject to court actions for breach of contract. But this premise ignored the fact that sound industrial relations are not built by running to the courts.

Effective collective bargaining assumes that the democratic privilege of self-determination of wages, hours, and working conditions will be reasonably exercised so as not to inconvenience the public by widespread work stoppages. Such union devices as the secondary boycott, jurisdictional strikes, and industry-wide strikes in essential industries unnecessarily burden the public. Therefore the Taft-Hartley Act narrowed the use of the strike weapon within limits deemed consistent with the public interest.

Ways in Which the Act Impeded Effective Collective Bargaining

The Act enabled employers to delay peaceful determination of a bargaining representative through the NLRB machinery and therefore encouraged unions to strike to obtain recognition. An employer bent on delaying an election for certification of a bargaining representative could delay proceedings by charging the union with unfair labor practices, and since most organizing campaigns usually involve some "high-pressure" salesmanship by union advocates, a prima-facie case of coercion frequently could be made out. Time-consuming delays are still one of the great unsolved problems of the NLRB. As we have noted in the previous chapter, a typical contested unfair labor practice case will take more than two years from date of filing with the NLRB to entry of a court decree requiring compliance.

The Act used as a sanction in a number of provisions the deprivation of rights under the Act. Thus, for example, employees who struck in violation of the cooling-off period provisions, and unions which failed to sign non-Communist affidavits, were forbidden to use the machinery of the Board. Obviously, however, these men and these unions would continue to take part in industrial relations, and their unprotected status only invited attacks by antiunion employers. If the objective of the Act was equality between management and unions in collective bargaining, sanctions for enforcement should not have been put in the hands of employers. Such a policy invites industrial unrest rather than compliance with the Act.

The Act was intended to restore the balance of power in collective bargaining relations. But Congress had in mind the circumstances which exist in highly organized industries, without fully recognizing that in some areas, organization is still in an incipient state and that in such areas the Act gave an antiunion employer power to prevent the emergence of effective collective bargaining. Particularly potent in this respect were the provisions which guaranteed the employer "free speech" and enabled him to sue a union in federal court (and thus weaken it financially) and to charge it with unfair labor practices in organizing. Under other provisions of the Act an employer could invite a walkout over economic issues and then be free to replace the strikers with nonunion men. The Act stated that the strikers could not vote in an election, but the strikebreakers were given this privilege. Antiunion employers could thus use a strike over wages to change the bargaining representative in their plants.

Effect of Taft-Hartley Act on Growth of Union Organization

There is no question that the rate of growth of unions has slowed down in recent years and that from 1947 to the present, contrary to experience in prior years, unions have grown at a slower rate than the labor force.[61] It is not clear, however, whether the full blame for labor's organizing woes can be put on the Taft-Hartley Act, although labor leaders find this piece of legislation a convenient excuse for lack of progress.

For example, Solomon Barkin, director of research for the Textile Workers Union of America, lists the "unfriendly Taft-Hartley Act and Eisenhower Board" as a major cause of the decline in union membership.[62] In the same vein, Lester Spielman, an official of the International Ladies Garment Workers' Union, concludes in a recently published article that "the major barrier to the growth of union membership in the United States has been the Taft-Hartley Law with its 'progenies,' the 'right-to-work' laws."[63] Spielman relies heavily on a comparison of Canadian and American statistics to reach his conclusion. He finds that from 1947 to 1957, Canadian unions increased membership at a faster rate than the increase in the labor force, while a contrary pattern was observable in the United States. However, he neglects to point out that since 1958, union membership has been declining in Canada, both in absolute numbers and relative to the labor force.[64] This trend has developed in Canada despite the absence of restrictive legislation comparable to the Taft-Hartley Act and suggests that more fundamental factors may be responsible for the decline in union membership in both the United States and Canada.

Of primary importance in this regard are the following factors:

1. There has been a shift of employment from manufacturing to service industries. Whereas during the early Wagner Act period the majority of wage earners were employed in production of goods, by 1959 a striking change had occurred in our employment structure, with the result that the majority of workers were employed in the service sector of the economy. Unions have been unable to gain acceptance readily among the white-collar, management-oriented workers in the service industries. At the same time, unions in highly organized basic industries such as mining, transportation, textiles, metals, coal, and petroleum have suffered sharp reductions in membership because of the decline in production jobs in these industries.
2. There has been a tremendous growth in white-collar employment. The increase in white-collar employment from 1947 to 1959 was more than

[61] Union membership rose about three million from 1947 to 1960.

[62] Solomon Barkin, *The Decline of the Labor Movement* (Santa Barbara, Calif.: Center for the Study of Democratic Institutions, 1961), p. 20.

[63] Lester Spielman, "The Taft-Hartley Law: Its Effect on the Growth of the Labor Movement," *Labor Law Journal,* Vol. XIII (April, 1962), p. 300.

[64] Allan A. Porter, *The Fourth Canadian Labour Congress Convention* (Montreal, Can.: National Industrial Conference Board, 1962), p. 2.

twice as great as the increase for manual workers. By 1959, white-collar employment constituted 42 per cent of total civilian employment. The growth in white-collar employment is *not* primarily due to the shift from manufacturing to service. On the contrary, the increase in white-collar employment has been even sharper within manufacturing industries than in business as a whole. In many of the manufacturing industries in which production jobs and union membership have decreased in recent years, nonproduction white-collar jobs have actually increased as a result of the greater utilization of research and automation. Unions have been unable to make organization attractive to such white-collar workers.

3. Most large companies are now organized. New organizational efforts must be directed against smaller units where employee loyalty to the employer may be greater and organization is more difficult and time-consuming.
4. The geographical shift of industry to the South and Midwest, where public opinion as reflected in newspapers, city and police administration, and other strategic areas is hostile to unions, has retarded union organization efforts.
5. There has been a stiffening of resistance by employers to union efforts which would have made organization more difficult even if the Taft-Hartley Act had not been passed.
6. Leadership of many unions has become more mature, older, and less willing to deplete treasury funds in organizing drives.

The foregoing circumstances are the major barriers to the growth of union organization in this country. It is to these factors, rather than the Taft-Hartley Act, that organized labor must direct its attention if it is to regain its drive and influence in industry.

QUESTIONS FOR DISCUSSION

1. What is meant by "mandatory" and "nonmandatory" subjects of collective bargaining? Give examples of each. Does this distinction make sense in practical collective bargaining? Comment.
2. Discuss the significance of the Lincoln Mills decision on the administration of collective bargaining agreements.
3. In what ways have recent decisions by the NLRB tended to facilitate union organization? Is this action consistent with the statutory purposes set forth in the Taft-Hartley Act?

SUGGESTIONS FOR FURTHER READING

Committee for Economic Development. *The Public Interest in National Labor Policy.* New York, 1961.

An analysis by an independent study group under the chairmanship of

Professor Clark Kerr of the extent to which our present national labor policy serves the public interest.

FLEMING, R. W. "The Obligation to Bargain in Good Faith," in J. SHISTER, B. AARON, and C. W. SUMMERS (eds.), *Public Policy and Collective Bargaining,* pp. 60–87. Industrial Relations Research Association Publication No. 27. New York: Harper and Row, 1962.

An excellent discussion of the "good-faith bargaining" problem which questions how various current union demands can be handled under existing interpretation of the law.

MCMANEMIN, J. P. "Subject Matter of Collective Bargaining," *Labor Law Journal,* Vol. XIII (December, 1962), pp. 985–1008.

The most up-to-date and thorough exposition of the various topics which fall into the categories of mandatory, permissive, and nonbargainable subjects of collective bargaining.

"National Labor Relations Board: A Symposium," *George Washington Law Review,* Vol. XXIX (December, 1960), pp. 1–489.

A collection of short articles by experts in labor relations law covering many controversial aspects of the National Labor Relations Act.

Chapter 6 THE LANDRUM-GRIFFIN ACT

In the preceding chapters, we have seen how the role of law and government has evolved in the field of union-management relations. The Norris–La Guardia Act was essentially laissez-faire in attitude. The purpose of the statute was to prevent law—in the form of the court injunction—from interfering with union-management relations. Then came the Wagner Act, in which the force of law was used to assist organized labor. Government power was committed to protect the right to organize and to restrict employer interference with such rights. Union tactics were left virtually unregulated. As a result of its favored position, organized labor grew so strong that abuses developed, and the need was recognized for restrictions on the power of unions. The Taft-Hartley Act was enacted, with government now placed in the role of policing certain actions of both labor and management. However, abuses continued to come to light in the internal administration of unions. Since much of the power wielded by unions over individual workers stems from union monopoly over job opportunities provided under both the Wagner and the Taft-Hartley acts, government has felt a responsibility to safeguard the rights of individual union members. As a result, the conduct of internal union affairs has come to be viewed as a federal problem. And so, while the Norris–La Guardia Act still remains on the books as an anachronistic landmark of a philosophy of labor-management relations now outmoded, the role of law in labor relations has evolved so far that the regulation of both local and international union internal procedures has now become a proper subject of government concern. Such regulation is the purpose of the Labor-Management Reporting and Disclosure Act of 1959, more popularly known as the Landrum-Griffin Act.

If ever the name of a Congressional enactment was a misnomer, it is the Labor-Management Reporting and Disclosure Act of 1959. While it is true that the Act broadens reporting requirements for both unions and employers, the reporting provisions of the new law are, by and large, the least controversial and probably among the least significant features of the new reform law. The new law is sweeping in its coverage; imposes new obligations on unions and their officers which are prescribed in minute detail; curtails picketing, "hot cargo" agreements, and secondary boycotts; and restricts many other activities in the field of labor-management relations.

It is interesting to observe that a 12-year cycle seems to characterize federal enactments on the subject of labor. The Taft-Hartley Act was passed 12 years after the Wagner Act; and the new labor law was enacted on September 14, 1959, approximately 12 years after passage of the Taft-Hartley law. The intervening 12 years since Taft-Hartley was enacted were marked by a series of attempts to amend that law and by increasing Congressional concern with labor racketeering. In 1956, Senator John L. McClellan (Democrat, Arkansas) began an investigation of malpractices in the Teamsters' Union. From 1957 to 1959, he continued his investigation of improper activities in the labor and management field as Chairman of a special Senate Committee. The well-publicized hearings of this Senate Select Committee on Improper Activities in the Labor or Management Field indicated that many union officials were guilty of coercion, violence, and denial to union members of basic rights; that small employers were being victimized through use of secondary boycotts, extortion, picketing, and similar techniques; and that employers were guilty of interfering with employee rights through use of "sweetheart contracts" and bribery of union officials by hired consultants.

It was the disclosures of the McClellan Committee and the dramatic appeal to the nation made on television by President Eisenhower for a strong labor bill that set the stage for enactment of a law that was more stringent than the bills reported out by the House and Senate labor committees. For the first time, the federal government undertook the task of policing the internal affairs of labor unions, from the international down to the smallest local union. While the new labor law affects all unions, many of its provisions have reference to abuses that were particularly prevalent in the Teamsters' Union.

In analyzing the provisions of this new law (which we shall refer to as the Landrum-Griffin Act), it will be convenient to follow a procedure similar to that utilized in the text in connection with the Taft-Hartley Act. The analysis which follows does not purport to be all-inclusive, but it does summarize the major provisions of the new law.

SCOPE AND ADMINISTRATION OF THE ACT

The Landrum-Griffin Act comprises seven different sections, called "titles," each of which deals with a different phase of the Act's coverage. Title I contains a Bill of Rights for members of labor organizations. This section guarantees every union member equal rights to nominate candidates and vote in union elections, guarantees certain rights of free speech and assembly subject to reasonable union rules concerning the conduct of meetings, and regulates the manner in which dues and initiation fees can be increased. Title II requires unions to file with the Secretary of Labor reports on union finances and copies of their constitutions, together with statements spelling out in detail various provisions required by the new law. This title also requires employees of unions to file reports on any remuneration they receive from employers with whom the union is bargaining or whom the union is seeking to represent, and requires employers to file reports concerning payments made to unions or union officials and certain classes of payments to labor relations consultants.

Title III requires filing of semiannual reports by unions which assume a trusteeship over any subordinate labor organization and regulates the administration of such trusteeships. Title IV contains detailed provisions with respect to the term of office of union officials, election procedures, and procedures for removal of union officers. Title V contains provisions relating to the fiduciary responsibility of union officials, requires the bonding of such officials, prohibits loans by unions to employees of such organizations resulting in a total indebtedness in excess of $2,000, and prohibits certain classes of persons with records of crime or Communist affiliation from holding union office. Title VI contains a number of miscellaneous provisions, among them a prohibition against extortionate picketing and a grant of power to the Secretary of Labor to investigate violations of the Act.

Title VII contains a number of amendments to the Taft-Hartley Act relating to federal-state jurisdiction, voting rights of economic strikers, and secondary boycotts and recognition picketing. Many congressmen believed that the Landrum-Griffin Act should stand on its own feet and deal only with new areas of regulation, leaving to later enactments the complex task of amending the Taft-Hartley Act. However, so much pressure was brought to bear upon Congress, particularly with respect to the inadequacies of the Taft-Hartley Act prohibitions against secondary boycotts and picketing, that Title VII, embodying such amendments, was finally incorporated in the law as passed.

Administration and Enforcement

Each title of the new law contains provisions to insure enforcement of the regulations contained therein. The Act provides both civil remedies and criminal penalties for violations of various sections of the law.

Of major significance for the future is the power given to the Secretary of Labor in Title VI of the Landrum-Griffin Act to make investigations whenever he believes it necessary in order to determine whether any person has violated or is about to violate any provisions of the Act, except in the case of Title I or amendments made by the Act to other statutes (Title VII). The exception for the Bill of Rights means that Congress felt it should be up to the individual union members to utilize private suits to enforce the rights guaranteed them in Title I. The exception for Title VII was inserted in order to avoid conflicts with the National Labor Relations Board, which is charged with enforcement of the Taft-Hartley Act.

The investigatory powers given to the Secretary are unusually broad and permit him to enter places, inspect records, and question such persons as he may consider necessary to determine the facts. The Secretary is given the power to call upon other agencies and departments of the United States government for co-operation in providing information which he may require in performing his functions under the Act. It is worthy of note that the Teamsters' Union named these powers of investigation as one of the principal grounds for their opposition to passage of the Act. The Union claimed that these powers were far broader than those usually granted administrative agencies and would permit the Secretary of Labor "to keep under constant surveillance and harrassment any labor organizations he chooses to descend upon."

EXTENT OF COVERAGE OF THE LAW

Like its predecessor, the Taft-Hartley Act, the Landrum-Griffin Act relates to employers and labor organizations in industries "affecting commerce." However, the coverage of the new law is broadened by the fact that many of its provisions are applicable to employees and employers covered by the Railway Labor Act, who were expressly excluded from the Taft-Hartley provisions. The definition of "employer" includes anyone considered an employer under any federal law. The definition is thus the most comprehensive to be found in federal law.

HOW THE EMPLOYER WAS AFFECTED

The new labor law imposes new obligations as well as new benefits upon employers.

Restrictions on Employers

Although the McClellan Committee devoted most of its attention to abuses of labor organizations, it uncovered a number of examples of malpractice by employers in their dealings with employees and unions. Thus, some companies paid union officials in order to obtain so-called "sweetheart contracts" which permitted continuation of substandard working conditions, or conspired with officials of a "friendly" union to permit organizing of the company's workers to the exclusion of other more belligerent unions. The Committee also found evidence that some companies were interfering with the rights of employees to organize by using so-called "labor consultants." The Committee noted that the Taft-Hartley Act could not deal effectively with such activity because the NLRB had no power to act against independent contractors serving as labor consultants.

Title II of the Landrum-Griffin Act requires employers to file annual reports with the Secretary of Labor disclosing payments and loans to unions, union officers, shop stewards, and employees of unions. The reporting requirement applies to payments and loans, whether direct or indirect, whether in cash or other things of value. However, in order to eliminate reporting of valid employer payments, the Act states that reports need not be filed with respect to payments or loans by a credit institution, compensation paid to a union officer or employee by reason of his services as an employee of the employer, payments to satisfy or settle a legal judgment or arbitration award, the deduction of union dues pursuant to a checkoff agreement, the purchase of an article at the then prevailing market value, and payments into a valid employee benefit fund.

Other subsections of this title require reports by employers of payments to employees or employee committees if the purpose was to cause the employee or employee committee to persuade other employees to exercise or not to exercise their right to organize and bargain collectively *and* if the payments were not disclosed to such other employees when they were made. It was the intent of this second condition to exempt payments by employers to foster good will such as payments to bowling leagues, picnics, clinics, etc. Employers must also file reports concerning expenditures made to restrain employees in the exercise of their bargaining rights or to secure information concerning the activities of employees or a union in connection with a labor dispute with such employer. Reports are also required by the employer of arrangements with labor consultants. It is apparent from these various provisions that Congress wanted to keep a close check on employer expenditures and activities which interfered with employees' free choice in exercising their rights to organize and bargain collectively.

Labor consultants who, pursuant to an arrangement with an employer, undertake to persuade employees in the exercise of their organizing or bargaining rights, or to supply information to the employer concerning employee or union activity in connection with a labor dispute, except information solely for use in legal or arbitration proceedings, must also file detailed reports. These reports have to be filed within thirty days after the making of the arrangement. Such prompt filing was required by Congress in order to give employees and unions an opportunity to use such information before it was too late. Consultants must also file annual statements listing receipts from employers and disbursements.

Title V of the new law expands Section 302 of the Taft-Hartley Act by broadening the types of payments which are criminal offenses. Payments are now unlawful, for example, if they are made by an employer or his agent to:

1. Any representative of his employees.
2. A union, or its officers or employees, which is seeking to represent or represents or would admit to membership employees of the employer.
3. Employees or committees of employees of the employer in excess of their normal compensation for the purpose of causing them to influence other employees in the exercise of their organizing or bargaining rights.
4. Any officer or employee of a union with intent to influence him with respect to his actions or duties as a union representative or official.

Lawyers have expressed concern that these criminal provisions are very broad—in fact, broader than the corresponding reporting provisions contained in Title II, so that, technically, certain payments which need not be reported may actually be criminal offenses! Furthermore, since certain acts which must be reported are subject to criminal penalties, there is some question as to the constitutionality of these reporting requirements in view of the protection against self-incrimination guaranteed under the Fifth Amendment.[1]

Relationship to Teller Act

It is apparent from the foregoing discussion that the Landrum-Griffin Act imposes detailed reporting requirements upon both employers and unions. None of these reports, however, relate directly to the operation of employee welfare and pension plans. Reporting on the operation of such funds is covered by a different statute—the Welfare and Pension Plans Disclosure Act of 1958, more commonly known as the Teller Act.

The mushrooming of employee welfare and pension plans during the decade of the forties led to a series of Congressional investigations into the administration and operation of such funds. These investigations revealed substantial evidence of corruption and mismanagement of welfare funds. As a result of these findings and the obvious need for regulation on a uniform basis by one agency, Congress passed the Teller Act in 1958. Although the Act contained detailed reporting requirements for welfare and pension plans, it was sharply criticized for its ineffective enforcement provisions. The Secretary of Labor was given no authority to issue rules and regulations, make investigations, or institute enforcement proceedings. He was empowered only to put the reports on file, while enforcement was left to the beneficiaries of the funds.

In March, 1962, the Act was amended and materially strengthened. The Secretary of Labor, who had been little more than a custodian of reports under the original law, was now given interpretive, investigative, and enforcement powers. In addition, administrators of such plans were required to be bonded, and criminal penalties were provided in cases of embezzlement of funds, knowingly making false statements on reports, and giving or receiving "kickbacks" in connection with administration of the funds.

The Teller Act covers all employee welfare and pension plans in industries affecting interstate commerce, whether the plan is collectively bargained or unilaterally established by the employer, whether jointly administered by employer and union or employer alone, and whether financed in part by employee contributions or entirely by the employer. The Act requires that a description of every plan be filed

[1] In Senate hearings, Senator Wayne Morse (Democrat, Oregon) stated that in his opinion these reporting requirements were "plainly unconstitutional" (*Congressional Record*, September 3, 1959, p. 17871).

with the Secretary of Labor; and thereafter, annual reports must be filed, giving details of operation of the fund.

A number of states have followed the lead of the federal government and now require filing of information regarding such plans. As of January 1, 1963, such laws were in effect in Connecticut, Massachusetts, New York, Washington, and Wisconsin.

Benefits of Landrum-Griffin Act to Employers

Although the reporting requirements of the Landrum-Griffin Act are onerous to employers already burdened by reporting requirements of many other federal agencies, nevertheless the benefits to employers conferred by the new law far outweigh its disadvantages.

Thus, for example, employers sought a "tough" law with respect to secondary boycotts—and they got it. The Taft-Hartley Act purported to outlaw secondary boycotts; but as we have seen, many loopholes developed in practice. Thus, if a Teamster business agent attempted to persuade Mr. X's employees not to handle the goods manufactured by Mr. Y, this was unlawful; yet the Taft-Hartley Act did not prohibit the business agent from warning Mr. X directly that he had better not handle Mr. Y's product! Likewise, the former law permitted boycott action applied through inducement of employees individually, instead of in concert, and inducement of employees of railroads, municipalities, and governmental agencies. The Landrum-Griffin Act closed all of these loopholes.

Under the Taft-Hartley Act, it was common practice for unions to induce employers to sign collective bargaining agreements which contained a so-called "hot cargo" clause. In accepting this provision, the employer agreed that his employees would not handle the goods of anyone with whom the union was having a labor dispute. The new Act makes it an unfair labor practice for any labor organization and any employer to enter into such agreements. Two exceptions are made, however: agreements in the construction industry relating to contracting or subcontracting of work done at the construction site[2] and agreements relating to jobbers, subcontractors, and the like in the apparel and clothing industry.

Of great benefit to employers are the Landrum-Griffin restric-

[2] While voluntary agreements are permissible in the construction industry, whereby the contractor can bind himself not to use nonunion subcontractors, the NLRB has ruled that a union may not strike to compel a contractor to enter into such an agreement. See *Construction, Production and Maintenance Laborers' Union, Local 383,* 50 LRRM 1444.

tions on picketing. The Act makes extortionate picketing—picketing intended to "shake down" an employer for the personal profit of a union agent rather than for the benefit of employees—a federal offense. Furthermore, in perhaps the most controversial section of the new law, major restrictions are imposed upon recognition and organizational picketing and secondary boycotts. These provisions will be examined in detail in Chapter 7.

While these provisions of the new law materially strengthen management's position, it remains to be seen whether such bare words will really be effective against unions with such tremendous economic strength as the Teamsters. Some observers believe that the average small employer is so fearful of the truck union's economic muscle that they are more likely to "knuckle under to" the exactions of Hoffa's lieutenants than they are to avail themselves of the new law's remedies.

Another important employer benefit conferred by the labor reform act is the elimination of the so-called "no man's land" created by the refusal of the National Labor Relations Board to assert jurisdiction over certain labor disputes which did not meets its jurisdictional standards. Under the Taft-Hartley Act the NLRB found it had neither the time nor the money required to handle the great number of labor disputes involving small employers; therefore, it imposed certain jurisdictional limitations on itself, stating in effect that it would not become involved in a dispute if the employer's sales volume was less than a certain prescribed figure. But when the small employer then went to the state court for relief, the United States Supreme Court ruled that the state court had no right to hear the case if the NLRB *could* have taken jurisdiction, even if it *did* not! As a consequence, small employers were denied a forum to give them relief from union coercive tactics, even though their larger competitors were protected by the NLRB.

The Landrum-Griffin Act seeks to solve this problem by amending the Taft-Hartley Act so as to permit the states to assert jurisdiction over labor disputes in interstate commerce over which the NLRB declines to take jurisdiction. The new law authorizes the NLRB to decline to assert jurisdiction over any labor disputes which it determines would have only a slight impact upon interstate commerce, but it cannot reduce its jurisdiction below the standards prevailing on August 1, 1959. The Board is free, of course, to expand its jurisdiction at any time. The states have always had jurisdiction of labor disputes in intrastate commerce and cases involving violence, mass picketing, or other coercive conduct. This jurisdiction has now been broadened to include cases in interstate commerce which formerly fell in the "no man's land" area.

While the Landrum-Griffin Act appears to have eliminated the question of conflicting jurisdiction over cases of labor disputes, it does not necessarily follow that either management or labor will find that turning these problems back to the states is wholly satisfactory. At this writing, only 13 states and Puerto Rico have comprehensive codes regulating labor relations. In 37 states, parties excluded from protection of the Taft-Hartley Act by reason of the Board's jurisdictional standards do not have recourse to comprehensive labor laws governing labor-management relations. In such states, these excluded parties will have to rely upon common-law doctrines or their own economic power.[3] The small businessman and the weak union are thus still penalized by lack of size. This problem can be met only by enactment of labor relations laws in all of the states or by a major expansion of the personnel of the NLRB so as to enable that agency to enlarge its jurisdiction. Neither of these possibilities appears to be very likely at this time.

HOW UNIONS ARE AFFECTED

The Landrum-Griffin Act is based upon the premise that unions, and officials of unions, have in many instances disregarded the rights of individual employees and that individual union members have been powerless to protect themselves against such tactics. The Act therefore contains numerous restrictions on unions and union officials while conferring new rights and privileges upon individual union members.

Restrictions on Internal Union Affairs

The Landrum-Griffin Act repeals those provisions of the Taft-Hartley Act that required the filing of information as to the union's constitution, bylaws, and financial reports and also the filing of non-Communist affidavits. It substitutes new provisions requiring more detailed reports concerning the internal operation and financial condition of the union. Most important is the change in approach relative to enforcement. Whereas the Taft-Hartley Act punished failure to file required reports with a denial of the right to use the procedures of the

[3] G. W. Hardbeck, "Federal-State Jurisdictional Issues and Policies under the New Labor Law," *Labor Law Journal*, Vol. XII (February, 1961), p. 106.

National Labor Relations Board, the Landrum-Griffin Act imposes direct and severe criminal penalties.

Every labor organization is required to adopt a constitution and bylaws and file a copy with the Secretary of Labor. Furthermore, to the extent that the constitution and bylaws do not cover these points, the union must file a detailed statement as to qualifications for or restrictions on membership, procedures with respect to such matters as levying of assessments, audit of the financial transactions of the organization, discipline or removal of officers and agents for breaches of trust, imposition of fines, suspensions and expulsions of members, and numerous other details as to the internal administration of the union. Unions must also file annually financial reports which, in addition to the usual balance sheet, must disclose loans aggregating more than $250 made to any officer, employee, or member; direct and indirect loans to any business enterprise; payments, including reimbursed expenses, to officers and employees who during the fiscal year received more than $10,000 union compensation; and "other disbursements including the purposes thereof."[4]

Both types of reports which were referred to above must be made available on request to all members of the union. Some union spokesmen have expressed the fear that this provision will enable employers to gain access to such reports and learn the details of their financial condition, which may weaken union bargaining power in negotiations. If a union member desires "for just cause" to examine books, records, and accounts of the union and is denied this right by a union official, the member can go to court, and the statute provides that in such action the court may, in its discretion, "in addition to any judgment awarded to the plaintiff or plaintiffs, allow a reasonable attorney's fee to be paid by the defendant and costs of the action." Unions are fearful that this clause may be an invitation to disgruntled union members and their attorneys to have a field day in court at union expense.

Restrictions on Union Officials

Under the provisions of many state laws, officers and directors of business corporations are held accountable to strict standards of fiduciary responsibility. The Landrum-Griffin Act applies this principle to officials of unions and states that officers, agents, stewards, and other representatives of labor unions must conduct themselves in accordance

[4] The latter catch-all phrase probably requires reporting on expenditures for political purposes and may therefore provide information on a little-known subject.

with the rules of law generally applicable to the dealings of a trustee with other people's money. The Act establishes a new federal crime—embezzlement or other unlawful conversion of a union's assets by an officer or employee of the union—punishable by a fine up to $10,000, imprisonment up to five years, or both. Drawing on the principle of minority stockholder suits in corporation law, the Act provides that if an officer or other representative is accused of violating his fiduciary responsibilities and the union fails to take action against such officer or representative in a reasonable time after being requested to do so by a union member, the latter may, with the court's permission, bring his own suit in state or federal court for an accounting, and attorney's fees may be awarded out of any recovery.

The Act establishes detailed bonding requirements for officers, agents, shop stewards, or other representatives of employees of unions (other than a union whose property and annual financial receipts do not exceed $5,000 in value) who handle funds or other property of the union. The bond must be for an amount not less than 10 per cent of the funds handled by the individual during the prior fiscal year, but no more than $500,000. No bond can be placed through an agent or broker or with a surety company in which any labor organization or any officer, agent, shop steward, or other representative of a labor organization has any direct or indirect interest. Willful violation of this section of the Act is punishable by a fine of not more than $10,000 or imprisonment for not more than one year, or both. Union officials have complained bitterly that this section of the Act is poorly drawn and will saddle unions with excessively high bonding costs. For example, because the statutory language refers to the furnishing of a "corporate surety," such sound institutions as Lloyds of London cannot be used because it functions as a partnership. Furthermore, the requirement that the surety be one in which the union has no interest has destroyed low-cost self-insurance surety programs such as that utilized by the United Automobile Workers' Union. However, this prohibition was badly needed, for the record of testimony before the McClellan Committee is replete with examples of "kickbacks" and special concessions gained by union officials in handling insurance for their unions.

A major objective of the 1959 legislation was to stamp out racketeering, crime, and corruption in labor unions. To this end the Act contains provisions designed to bring to light possibile conflicts of interest and similar shadowy transactions through which unscrupulous union officials and employers sacrifice the welfare of employees to personal advantage. Thus the Landrum-Griffin Act requires officers and employees of labor unions (other than employees performing exclusively clerical or custodial duties) who have engaged in certain transactions enumerated in the Act to file annual reports with the Secretary of Labor, covering not only themselves but their wives and minor children, and disclosing payments, stock, or other interests acquired in or from companies which the union represents or seeks to represent. Payments and other benefits received as a bona fide employee of an employer and bona fide investments in securities traded on a registered exchange need not be reported. The filing of false reports is made punishable by a fine of up to $10,000, a year in jail, or both. These reports, as well as the reports which employers and labor consultants must file, as discussed previously, are required to be available for public inspection.

Unions are also prohibited from making, "directly or indirectly," any loan or loans to officers or employees which result in a total indebtedness of such individual to the labor organization of more than $2,000. The phrase "directly or indirectly" is included in the Act to bar deals such as those used by James Hoffa to camouflage his financial manipulations. Hoffa's own Local 299 in Detroit, according to McClellan Committee testimony, once loaned $25,000 to a man who immediately reloaned it to Hoffa!

Persons convicted of serious crimes are barred for a period of five years after conviction from holding any union position other than a clerical or custodial job. Members of the Communist Party and ex-Communists for a period of five years after they have quit the Party are likewise barred from all but clerical and custodial jobs.[5] Violation of these provisions is punishable by a fine of not more than $10,000 or imprisonment for not more than one year, or both. Whether these severe penalties will prove more effective than the affidavit requirements formerly included in the Taft-Hartley Act in ridding unions of Communist officials remains to be seen.

The Landrum-Griffin Act prohibits union representatives from requesting or receiving various types of payments from employers or their consultants. The use of force or threats of force against union members to interfere with the exercise of any of their rights under the Act is made a federal offense. The Act also requires every labor organization

[5] The prohibitions stated in this paragraph also apply to labor relations consultants and officials and employees (other than employees performing exclusively clerical or custodial duties) of employer associations dealing with labor organizations.

"to inform its members concerning the provisions of this Act"—a provision which has led many unions to reproduce the Act verbatim in union newspapers.

Trusteeships

The constitutions of many international unions authorize the international officers to suspend the normal processes of government of local unions and other subordinate bodies to supervise their internal activity and to assume control of their property and funds. These so-called "trusteeships" have been widely used by responsible officials to prevent corruption, mismanagement of funds, and infiltration of Communists, and to preserve order and integrity within the union. However, the hearings before the McClellan Committee revealed that trusteeships have been used in some cases as a means of consolidating the power of corrupt union officials, of plundering and dissipating the resources of local unions, and preventing the growth of competing political elements within the organization. For example, the McClellan Committee found that of the Teamsters' 892 locals, 113 were under "trusteeship"!

Title III of the Landrum-Griffin Act requires national or international unions to file reports with the Secretary of Labor concerning all trusteeships.[6] These reports must be filed every six months while a trusteeship is in existence. The reports must state the name and address of the trusteed local, the date the trusteeship was established, the reason for the trusteeship, and the nature and extent of participation by members of the local in the selection of delegates to conventions and in the election of national and international union officers. The initial report must also contain a full account of the local's financial condition at the time the trusteeship was established. The Act expressly limits trusteeships so that they can be established only in accordance with the constitution and bylaws of the national or international union and can be imposed only for the purpose of "correcting corruption or financial malpractice, assuring the performance of collective bargaining agree-

[6] A total of 777 trusteeships were reported to the Department of Labor during two and a half years following enactment of the Landrum-Griffin Act. As of March 13, 1962, 590 of these had been terminated, leaving 187 subordinate bodies still in trusteeship. These 187 contrast with 487 unions under trusteeship on September 14, 1959, the effective date of the Act. During the past two and a half years, new trusteeships have continued to be imposed at a rate averaging about 10 per month, and indications are that the Act has not substantially hindered national unions in the establishment of trusteeships for legitimate purposes. See U.S. Department of Labor, Bureau of Labor-Management Reports, *Union Trusteeships,* Report of the Secretary of Labor to Congress upon the Operation of Title III of the Labor-Management Reporting and Disclosure Act (Washington, D.C.: U.S. Government Printing Office, September, 1962).

ments or other duties of a bargaining representative, restoring democratic procedures, or otherwise carrying out the legitimate objects of such labor organizations."

The Act recognizes the element of coercion and force which has characterized the existence of many trusteeships in the past and therefore provides that the Secretary of Labor, upon the written complaint of any member of a union alleging that a trusteeship has been wrongfully imposed or that the statutory provisions have not been followed, shall investigate, and if he finds probable cause to believe that a violation has occurred and has not been remedied, he is to bring a civil suit in federal court for such relief as may be appropriate. The Act specifically provides that the identity of the complainant is not to be disclosed.

In order to limit the duration of trusteeships without imposing a fixed term which would interfere with the legitimate activities of the union, the Act merely provides that after a period of eighteen months a trusteeship shall be "presumed invalid," and the court is directed to decree its discontinuance unless it is shown by clear and convincing proof that continuation is necessary for an allowable purpose.

Restrictions on Union Organizing and Bargaining Tactics

As has already been pointed out, the Landrum-Griffin Act imposes prohibitions and limitations on the use of picketing and boycott tactics by unions. Union spokesmen believe that if the amendments to the Taft-Hartley Act had been brought in as a separate enactment in a different session of Congress, less restrictive provisions would have resulted. However, since the picketing and boycott sections were considered as part of an over-all labor reform program aimed primarily at a few corrupt unions, the entire union movement is now saddled with provisions which will certainly render new organizing activities considerably more difficult.

Special Privileges for Unions in Construction Industry

The casual and occasional nature of the employment relationship between employer and employees in the construction industry caused many problems to develop in that industry because of the restrictive provisions of the Taft-Hartley Act. The Landrum-Griffin Act—in one of its few provisions intended to loosen restrictions on unions—recognizes these problems and amends the Taft-Hartley Act so as to make lawful so-called "prehire" agreements in the construction industry. Such agreements may now make union membership compulsory seven days after employment (rather than thirty days as is the case in other industries) in states where union shops are permitted. Union contracts also can require an employer to notify the union of job opportunities and give the union an opportunity to refer qualified applicants for such employment, and can specify minimum training or experience qualifications for employment.

HOW THE INDIVIDUAL WORKER WAS AFFECTED

A major objective of the Landrum-Griffin Act was to rid unions of gangster control and corrupt practices generally. The legislators believed that if they could provide the union member with information about what was happening to union funds and other vital aspects of union activities, and if they could protect individual rights through a Bill of Rights and procedures insuring secret elections, union members would rid themselves of untrustworthy or corrupt officers.

The Bill of Rights

Title I of the new law purports to legislate into the internal laws and procedures of unions certain of the essential guarantees contained in the Bill of Rights of the Constitution of the United States. The Act provides that every member of a union shall have equal rights to nominate candidates, to vote in elections or referendums of the union, to attend membership meetings, and to participate in the deliberations and voting upon the business of such meetings, subject to reasonable rules and regulations in the union's constitution and bylaws. Furthermore, every member is guaranteed the right to meet and assemble freely with other members, and to express views, arguments, or opinions, and to express at meetings of the labor organization his views upon candidates in a union election or upon any other business before the meeting, subject to the organization's established and reasonable rules pertaining to the conduct of meetings.

Congress wanted to strengthen the hand of the individual member who sought to "buck the machine." Yet at the same time, it recognized that it could not restrict the legitimate right of unions to carry on business at meetings in an orderly fashion. Therefore the Landrum-Griffin Act subjected the exercise of individual union members' rights to "reasonable rules" and furthermore provided that nothing in this section of the Act should be construed to "impair the right of a labor organization to adopt and enforce reasonable rules as to the responsibility of every member toward the organization as an institution and to his refraining from conduct that would interfere with its performance of its legal or contractual obligations." Union officers may have the right by virtue of the foregoing proviso to silence a member at a meeting who advocates dual unionism or a wildcat strike.

The language of the Act is so general and ambiguous that the impact of the statute will depend in large measure upon what courts decide to read into the statutory language. What, for example, did Congress intend by the statement contained in Section 101 (*a*) (1) of the Act that "Every member of a labor organization shall have equal rights and privileges within such organization . . . to attend membership meetings, and to participate in the deliberations and voting upon the business of such meetings, subject to reasonable rules and regulations in such organization's constitution and bylaws." Does this section give to union members a statutory right to vote on the acceptance or rejection of a collective bargaining agreement, or can a union bylaw reserve such determination to an executive committee or other select group? Since a major purpose of union membership is to achieve the benefits which flow from a collective bargaining agreement, it can be argued that union members should have the right to pass on the terms of such agreements. However, in one recent case a federal court has ruled that the Landrum-Griffin Act does not confer this right. In the words of the court: "The statute does not require that members of a labor organization have the right to vote on the business of negotiating and executing contracts of employment unless such negotiation and execution might become the business of a membership meeting."[7] This decision may be justified by the facts of the particular case, since it appeared that the practice in the musicians' union was for members to vote on minimum wage scales, but not on specific collective agreements, which typically remained in effect for a relatively short time. The fear has been expressed by one observer, however, that the narrow judicial construction evidenced by this decision may sap most of the vitality from the Bill of Rights.[8]

The new Act seeks to limit the extent to which union dues and assessments can be raised without the will of the membership. The Act also states that no member of any union may be fined, suspended, expelled, or otherwise disciplined except for nonpayment of dues by such organization or by any officer thereof unless such member has been served with written specific charges, given a reasonable time

[7] *Cleveland Orchestra Committee* v. *Cleveland Federation of Musicians,* 193 F. Supp. 647 (N.D. Ohio 1961).

[8] Benjamin Aaron, "The Union Member's 'Bill of Rights': First Two Years," *Industrial Relations,* Vol. I (February, 1962), p. 57.

to prepare his defense, and afforded a full and fair hearing.[9] Furthermore, unions are prohibited from limiting the right of any union member to sue in court, except that such member may be required to exhaust reasonable hearing procedures (not to exceed a four-month lapse of time) within the union before instituting legal or administrative proceedings against the union or its officers.

Many persons who favored adoption of other sections of the Landrum-Griffin Act opposed inclusion of the Bill of Rights in this enactment. They questioned whether or not unions should—or could—operate as model democratic institutions. Unions, they argued, are fighting organizations; in many disputes with employers the very existence of the union may be in danger. In such cases, organizations typically require strong direction from the top. Furthermore, as unions mature, the role of professionals will become more and more important in determining policy, in much the same way that professional management of corporations has reduced the role of stockholders in decision making. Whether or not democracy is desirable or feasible in unions, it seems likely that the Landrum-Griffin Act, by encouraging dissent within the local union, will promote some unrest and factionalism which may spill over into more grievances at the plant level. Moreover, some employers have expressed concern that union representatives, who may now have to contend more strongly to maintain their jobs as union officials, will be more inclined to make extreme demands and less likely to strike a bargain which might subject them to criticism by their rivals.

In this connection the director of a large employer's council recently observed that the Bill of Rights has already impinged upon collective bargaining. According to William H. Smith, Executive Vice President of the Federated Employers of San Francisco, local union leaders are showing more care in making their proposals, and union bargaining demands have become more lengthy and detailed. There is a conscious effort by union leaders to include "something for everyone." Furthermore, there has been more referring of counterproposals to the general membership. As Smith puts it: "There is a greater use of union committees to spread the risk of unfavorable reaction by rank and file to counterproposals and to a final settlement which is short of the original demands."[10]

[9] Senator Kennedy pointed out in the Conference Report that these procedural safeguards apply to union members *as members.* They do not relate to suspension or removal from a union office. See *Congressional Record,* September 3, 1959, p. 17899.

[10] Address of William H. Smith at Institute of Industrial Relations, May 11, 1960, reprinted in *Current Trends in Collective Bargaining* (Berkeley: Institute of Industrial Relations, University of California, 1960), p. 18.

Certain provisions of the Act will undoubtedly hamper union government. For example, suppose the president of a union local believes that one member is an informer for the employer. Technically, he cannot suspend such member nor even keep him from attending meetings until the full statutory requirements have been complied with—written charges, time for defense, and full hearing. As a practical matter, however, in this and similar circumstances where the Bill of Rights impedes union action, the officers will probably go ahead and do what they think best, and then "see what happens." The Act significantly omits any criminal penalties for violation of the Bill of Rights section, except where there is use of force or threat of violence. Civil remedies, such as an injunction, may not be very effective relief for a member, since there is no way a court can afford a member the right to attend or to speak at a meeting that has already been held. Therefore, although in theory the Bill of Rights section of the new law might be burdensome to unions, in practice this is not likely to be so.

Fair Elections

Under both the Taft-Hartley Act and the Railway Labor Act, the union which is the bargaining agent has the power, in conjunction with the employer, to fix a man's wages, hours, and working conditions. The individual employee has no right to negotiate directly with the employer if he is dissatisfied with the contract made by his union representatives. The federal government, which conferred these exclusive rights upon unions, has an obligation to insure that the officials of unions who wield this power are responsive to the desires of the membership they represent. The best assurance of this is free and periodic elections—a fact recognized by the AFL–CIO Ethical Practices Committee which wrote into its Code a requirement for frequent elections.

With these principles in mind, the legislators incorporated in the Landrum-Griffin Act detailed provisions relating to union elections. Every national or international union, except a federation of national or international unions, is required to elect its officers not less than once every five years either by secret ballot among the members in good standing or at a convention of delegates chosen by secret ballot. Local unions are required to elect officers not less often than once every three years by secret ballot among the members in good standing. Officers of intermediate bodies between the internationals and the locals must be elected not less often than once every four years by secret ballot among the members in good standing or by labor organization officers representative of such members who have been elected by secret ballot.

The Act provides that in any election required to be held by secret ballot, a reasonable opportunity shall be given for the nomination of candidates, and every member in good standing shall be eligible to be a candidate, subject to reasonable qualifications uniformly imposed (except for Communists and persons convicted of certain crimes, who are barred from holding office). Union members are guaranteed the right to vote for or otherwise to support the candidate of their own choice without being subject to penalty, discipline, improper interference, or reprisal. All candidates have to be treated equally, and every bona fide candidate is given the right, once within thirty days prior to the union election in which he is a candidate, to inspect the list of names and addresses of "all members of the labor organization who are subject to a collective bargaining agreement requiring membership therein as a condition of employment."[11] Unions are forbidden to spend dues money in support of any candidate, and employers likewise are forbidden to spend money in support of candidates for union office. Detailed requirements are spelled out in the Act as to the manner of sending election notices, counting votes, and other safeguards to insure a fair election. The Act also establishes a procedure insuring that union officers guilty of serious misconduct may be removed by secret ballot elections.

The Secretary of Labor has ruled that unions may prescribe reasonable rules and regulations with respect to voting eligibility. They may "in appropriate circumstances defer eligibility to vote by requiring a reasonable period of prior membership, such as 6 months or a year, or by requiring apprentice members to complete their apprenticeship training, as a condition of voting." The Secretary of Labor has expressly stated that such union rules may not be used to create special classes of nonvoting members.

Suppose a union member claims that the president of a local was elected in a "rigged" election in violation of the law. Meanwhile, the union continues to carry on its business, and the new president must sign collective bargaining agreements and similar contracts by reason of his office. Can he do so? Congress considered this question and concluded that a union election should be presumed valid until the contrary can be established. A union member who attacks an election must first go through the union channels provided by the union constitution. If, at

[11] In twenty states which have so-called "right-to-work" laws, union shop contracts are unlawful. In these states, it would appear that the lists above referred to would not have to be maintained by the union or made available to candidates. While the language of this particular section raises questions as to both its applicability and its usefulness, another section of the Act requires unions to "refrain from discrimination in favor of or against any candidate with respect to the use of lists of members." Therefore, if *any* list of members is available, even in the "right-to-work" states, it presumably must be made available on equal terms to all candidates.

the end of three months, he has either received an adverse decision or no decision at all, he has one month in which to file a complaint with the Secretary of Labor. The Secretary is then required to investigate such charges, and if he finds probable cause to believe that a violation of the Act has occurred, he takes the matter to court. Meanwhile, however, "the affairs of the organization shall be conducted by the officers elected," even though they have been challenged.

The perpetuation of what are in effect union dictatorships depends upon stifling democratic elections at the local level. The late Senator Taft once said that "the employee has a good deal more of an opportunity to select his employer than he has to select his labor-union leader." Certain unions—particularly the Teamsters—have been able to keep the ruling clique in power by various devices which have disqualified opposition candidates or put them at a substantial disadvantage in obtaining votes. The Landrum-Griffin Act strikes at these unfair methods and attempts to insure free and honest elections in unions. The safeguards contained in the new law will permit rank-and-file union members to express their wishes more freely than was possible in the past. Whether they will exercise this privilege remains to be seen. In most unions, there is a general apathy among the membership with respect to union elections. On the other hand, there is among union leaders a strong desire for power and a repugnance to resuming status as an ordinary worker member. The result is what one writer has called "the iron law of oligarchy,"[12] with union leadership becoming more and more entrenched. It seems clear that legislation, without active interest on the part of union members, will not suffice to make unions democratic.

As we have noted at the beginning of this section, Congress apparently believed that if it could provide union members with information about the operation of their unions and could protect individual rights through requirement of democratic procedures, union members themselves would rid their unions of corruption. Congress thus assumed that a democratic union would be less inclined to corruption. However, experience suggests that this relationship does not always hold. The United Steelworkers, for example, would hardly be classed as a democratic union, yet it handles tremendous trust funds without a hint of corruption. On the other hand, some unions with substantial local autonomy have been infected with corruption. It has been suggested that corruption in a union is more related to economic factors

[12] C. Peter MacGrath, "Democracy in Overalls: The Futile Quest for Union Democracy," *Industrial and Labor Relations Review*, Vol. XII (July, 1959), p. 508.

in the industry—such as severe competition and a highly mobile labor force—than to election procedures contained in the union constitution.[13]

Voting by Strikers

Through an amendment of the Taft-Hartley Act the new law eliminates the so-called "union-busting" provision contained in the Taft-Hartley Act. Section 9 (*c*) (3) of that Act provided that employees on strike who are not entitled to reinstatement shall not be eligible to vote. This provision had the effect of preventing any "economic striker" (an employee striking for higher wages, better conditions, or any reason other than his employer's unfair labor practices), who had been replaced by a new employee hired during the strike, from voting in an NLRB election conducted during the strike. For example, in a case in the rubber industry the United Rubber Workers were certified as bargaining representative in an NLRB election. Following months of fruitless negotiations for a contract, the union struck, and the company replaced the strikers with new employees. Thereafter the employer filed for a new election and succeeded in throwing out the union, because the strikers were not permitted to vote. Under the amendment added by the Landrum-Griffin Act, such economic strikers retain their right to vote in any NLRB election conducted within twelve months of the start of the strike, subject to regulations established by the NLRB. In applying this new statutory provision, the NLRB has ruled that it will presume that economic strikers have retained their interest in struck jobs, and that replacements were employed on a permanent basis, and that both therefore are eligible to vote. This means that the mere fact that a striking worker has taken a job elsewhere does not mean that he cannot vote in an election held in the company at which he and other union men are on strike. The NLRB places the burden of proof on the party challenging his vote to show that he is disqualified from voting.

HOW THE PUBLIC WAS AFFECTED

Because the Landrum-Griffin Act deals primarily with the internal administration of unions, its impact upon the general public will be somewhat limited. It is to be hoped, however, that the procedures it requires, by eliminating corrupt influences in unions, together with the

[13] David Previant, "Have Titles I–VI of Landrum-Griffin Served the Stated Legislative Purpose?" *Labor Law Journal,* Vol. XIV (January, 1963), p. 31.

provisions designed to tighten restrictions on picketing and boycotts, will reduce the area of industrial strife. Beyond this is the strengthening of our democratic processes in the nation as a whole which comes from the practice of unionism under conditions where each union member is free to speak his mind and help to determine the over-all policies of union government. Democracy is not something which can be trotted out on rare occasions—like a treasured antique—and then put back in mothballs. It must be lived daily to survive. We cannot expect democracy in government to survive when employees in their daily lives see democratic forces subverted through intimidation and corruption.

APPRAISAL OF THE ACT

The Landrum-Griffin Act is a law with a very limited purpose. Its primary object is the reform of labor unions. It does not purport to be a law covering the broad aspects of collective bargaining, as did the Taft-Hartley Act. Nor is it intended to effect a broad revision of that Act. The provisions which it includes amending the Taft-Hartley Act were added as an accident of its legislative history and for the most part bear some relation to the abuses which were the main object of the legislators' concern.

Interestingly enough, it is the amendments of the Taft-Hartley Act—particularly those which deal with restrictions on picketing and secondary boycotts—that have given rise to the most litigation and controversy. The main body of the Landrum-Griffin law has been incorporated in our industrial life with a minimum of court action. This does not mean that this Act of Congress has reformed unionism or that many abuses still do not exist. The fact is, however, that the Labor Department has been called upon to handle fewer complaints of violation of the Act than many labor experts had anticipated.

In the first thirty months of enforcement of the Landrum-Griffin Act, the United States Department of Labor handled about 10,000 cases of alleged violation. Over half of these involved failure to file reports required by the new law. In view of the extensive reporting requirements contained in the Act and the fact that many small unions were not equipped to provide the requested information promptly, this high proportion of delinquents is not surprising. As of June 30, 1962, the Bureau of Labor-Management Reports had on file about one quarter of a million reports, mostly from the over 50,000 unions subject to the Act.

During the fiscal year 1961–62 the Bureau conducted 5,408 investigations either as a result of complaints or as part of a routine sampling of repors filed. Of 3,174 investigations closed during the year, about 60 per cent disclosed some deficiency in reports or some other violation of the Act. Voluntary compliance has been obtained in 96 per cent of these cases. In 76 cases the Bureau found willful violations and instituted legal action. Of these cases, 48 involved embezzlement, 15 violation of reporting requirements, nine election cases, three instances of ineligible persons holding union office, and one deprivation of member rights through use of violence.[14]

Analysis of the legislative history of the Landrum-Griffin Act indicates that three basic principles motivated the legislators in drafting it:

1. There should be a minimum of interference by government in the internal affairs of any private organization; only essential standards of conduct should be established by legislation.
2. Given the maintenance of minimum democratic safeguards and availability of detailed essential information about the union, individual members are fully competent to regulate union affairs.
3. Remedies for abuses should be direct. Where the law prescribes standards, sanctions for the violation should also be direct.

There can be little argument with the first principle, although there will be considerable dispute as to whether the labor reform act goes too far or far enough in establishing minimum standards. Union spokesmen contend that the Act will permit labor spies to obtain confidential information about union finances and to hamstring the internal operation of the union. They contend that the Bill of Rights provisions go so far that they convert the union into a debating society and weaken it as a fighting organization. On the other hand, eight members of the House Labor Committee filed a minority report bitterly attacking the proposed labor reform bill for its omission of a guarantee of civil rights. In their words, "if there is to be a bill of rights in this legislation it must most assuredly include a guarantee of equal rights—the right of every workingman to join a union and not to be segregated within that union because of race, creed, color or national origin." Some union officials oppose the free admission requirement on the ground that a voluntary association such as a union should have a right to choose its members. Others fear that adoption of a Bill of Rights as recommended by the minority report would be equivalent to forced integration and would inhibit unionization of southern members.

With respect to the second principle, some skeptics wonder

[14] 51 LRR 213–14.

whether the rank-and-file union member is really concerned about graft and corruption in his union any more than the average citizen really concerns himself about graft and corruption in government. Surveys have indicated, for example, that many Teamster members, despite the disclosure of corruption among their officers, still approve their leadership because they have "produced" for them in terms of high wages and excellent working conditions. Perhaps the conditions affecting the relationship of the average worker and his union are such that we should not expect democratic action to flourish in such an environment. As one writer puts it: ". . . the conditions that currently characterize unions—the complexity of their organization, the increasing tendency to assume functions complementary to those of management, the status and salary gap existing between leaders and members, not to mention the psychological compulsion of the leaders to retain power, and the members' expectation that their union is primarily a service institution rather than a way of life—do not provide the soil in which the democratic process can operate."[15] Nevertheless, maintenance of minimum democratic safeguards seems necessary to protect the rights of individuals and to insure that union action reflects the desire of the membership.

On the subject of the third principle, the new law takes a different approach than that of the Taft-Hartley Act. The latter penalized violation by unions of various provisions of the law by denying the union access to the procedures of the NLRB. This has the effect of punishing all the union members for violations of their officials. The Landrum-Griffin Act, by contrast, imposes direct sanctions in the form of fines, imprisonment, and/or civil remedies through court action to insure compliance with the Act. This is certainly a more mature and realistic approach.

The type of legislation embodied in the Landrum-Griffin Act was probably inevitable. Abuses in other aspects of business life—such as the securities market, banking, drugs—have likewise brought forth detailed federal regulation. Unions thus far have been remarkably free from such internal regulation, despite the fact that they enjoy benefits and privileges under the income tax laws and the antitrust laws which are unique. No association or organization can long expect to enjoy such privileges without assuming major obligations.

Unions in our society are no longer mere private clubs or fraternal organizations whose internal affairs, admission, and fiscal policies are matters of concern to their membership only. On the contrary,

[15] MacGrath, *op. cit.*, p. 524.

they bear more resemblance to public utilities or governmental entities, subject to legal control of their internal affairs.[16] When a union is certified as a collective bargaining agent, it has conferred upon it a government-sanctioned monopoly and the unusual powers that flow from this privilege. It is incumbent upon government, which granted this power to unions, to insure that it is not abused. Even without special statutory regulation of their internal affairs, there is precedent for holding unions to rules of conduct requiring fair and equal treatment of employees represented by the union. For example, in *Steele* v. *Louisville & Nashville Railroad,*[17] the United States Supreme Court decided that a union certified under the Railway Labor Act could not lawfully make an agreement with an employer which would arbitrarily deprive nonmember Negro employees of their seniority rights. In so holding, the Court stated: "We think that the Railway Labor Act imposes upon the statutory representative of a craft at least as exacting a duty to protect equally the interests of the members of the craft as the Constitution imposes upon a legislature to give equal protection to the interests of those for whom it legislates."[18] Similarly, some state courts have enunciated the view that where a union is acting as a bargaining representative, it is acting as an agency created and functioning under provisions of federal law; therefore, exclusion of persons on grounds of race, for example, deprives such persons of rights guaranteed under the federal Constitution.[19]

Unions have an obligation to maintain democratic processes. They control the conditions under which their members spend most of their productive lives. More and more, they have a captive audience. A truck driver may move from one city to another, but he cannot long escape the far-flung power of the Teamsters' Union. The Landrum-Griffin Act takes a long step in the direction of attempting to insure democratic conditions in unions. Its success in achieving this objective will depend upon the support afforded this legislation by union leaders who profess to be interested in "clean" union government and, most important, upon the rank-and-file union membership who must want dem-

[16] See Joseph R. Grodin, "Legal Regulation of Internal Union Affairs," in J. Shister, B. Aaron, and C. W. Summers (eds.), *Public Policy and Collective Bargaining,* Industrial Relations Research Association Publication No. 27 (New York: Harper and Row, 1962), p. 183.

[17] 323 U.S. 192, 65 S. Ct. 226 (1944). See also *Miranda Fuel Co.,* 51 LRRM 1585.

[18] 323 U.S. 192, 202; 65 S. Ct. 226, 232.

[19] *Betts* v. *Easley,* 161 Kans. 459 (1946); *Thorman* v. *International Alliance of Theatrical & Stage Employees,* 49 Cal. (2d) 629 (1957).

ocratic government enough to use the tools which Congress has given them.

QUESTIONS FOR DISCUSSION

1. Discuss the "no man's land" problem of jurisdiction which existed prior to enactment of the Landrum-Griffin Act. How did the latter attempt to solve this problem? Is this solution likely to be satisfactory? Discuss.
2. Discuss the so-called "Bill of Rights" incorporated in the Landrum-Griffin Act. In what way could these provisions handicap union action? Should the Bill of Rights have been broadened to include other rights, such as the right of free admission to a union? Discuss.
3. Assuming that there were abuses in the internal administration of unions, do you think that the power of the federal government should be invoked to cure such abuses? What other measures might have been taken to accomplish the same objective?

SUGGESTIONS FOR FURTHER READING

AARON, BENJAMIN. "The Union Member's 'Bill of Rights': First Two Years," *Industrial Relations,* Vol. I (February, 1962), pp. 47–71.

A review of the first two years' experience under the Bill of Rights, including a thorough analysis of various court decisions interpreting provisions of the new law.

PREVIANT, DAVID. "Have Titles I–VI of Landrum-Griffin Served the Stated Legislative Purpose?" *Labor Law Journal,* Vol. XIV (January, 1963), pp. 28–41.

A critical appraisal of the Landrum-Griffin Act in which the writer concludes such legislation was unnecessary.

U.S. DEPARTMENT OF LABOR, BUREAU OF LABOR-MANAGEMENT REPORTS. *Report for the Fiscal Year 1961.* Washington, D.C.: U.S. Government Printing Office, 1962.

A comprehensive, detailed, and readable summary of the activities of the Bureau of Labor-Management Reports.

WYLE, BENJAMIN. "Landrum-Griffin: A Wrong Step in a Dangerous Direction," *Proceedings of New York University Thirteenth Annual Conference on Labor,* pp. 395–406. New York: Matthew Bender & Co., 1960.

A critic of the new law reviews its provisions and indicates how they may harass effective union operation.

Chapter 7

GOVERNMENT CONTROL OF THE WEAPONS OF CONFLICT

A line of men slowly parade back and forth in front of the main gate of a factory, bearing placards which state: "Ace Factory Unfair to Organized Labor," "Ace Factory Refuses to Recognize Union." Another group of workers attempts to enter the plant through the gate. There are taunts of "Scab," fists fly, and violence erupts. The police enter the fray, and a battle royal ensues.

Such incidents have occurred time and time again in American labor history. They exemplify what is in many respects a phenomenon unique to the American labor scene. Other democratic countries have labor unions; they have strikes; they have picket lines. But only in America has the picket line become of such paramount importance as an organizing device for unions.

The reasons are twofold. In the first place, the basic economic environment in this country has been hostile to organized labor. As we have already noted in Chapter 2, this antagonism is a reflection of the strength of private property rights, the identification of the middle class with the capitalistic system, the fluidity of class lines, and the general orientation of our economic life in terms of free competition and *laissez faire.* American employers have been more reluctant than employers in other countries to accept collective bargaining as a permanent institution and over the years have fought labor organization with an arsenal of weapons—injunctions, yellow-dog contracts, spies, black lists, open-shop drives, paternalism, lockouts, and a variety of other stratagems, including violence. In the second place, American labor has had to rely primarily on self-help to achieve its gains. Whereas other countries have had widespread social legislation, nationalization of industry, political parties representing labor's interest, and other aspects of government intervention on behalf of labor, our government has been much less partial to labor. Unions in this country have had to struggle long and hard to obtain legislative recognition of labor's right to organize and to use its economic weapons freely.

In this chapter, we shall examine in detail some of the major weapons of conflict in the struggle for power between unions and management. On the labor side, we shall trace the law of picketing from the pre-Norris–La Guardia era to the present and shall also consider how other union tactical weapons, such as the strike and secondary boycott, have been affected by legislation. On the management side, we have already discussed in detail in the preceding chapters the steps which government has taken to curb many of the techniques formerly used by employers to prevent union organization. Thus, the yellow-dog contract, discriminatory hiring and discharge practices, subsidization of company unions—all of these and other similar activities have been declared unlawful by the federal and many state governments. Likewise, the Norris–La Guardia Act and state acts modeled after it have effectively curtailed the use of the injunction as an anti-union weapon in labor disputes. In this chapter, we shall discuss an employer weapon which is not subject to any specific legislative regulation, but which is nevertheless very effective in labor disputes. This is the lockout—the employer's counterpart of the strike.

The inquiry undertaken in this chapter cuts across the years and involves analysis of the impact of many of the statutes we have already discussed in preceding chapters. The purpose of this broad review is to give a sense of historic perspective to the struggle between labor and management in the labor market and to focus attention on the clearly defined trend toward increasing governmental regulation in the arena of economic conflict.

STRIKES, BOYCOTTS, AND PICKETING BEFORE 1932

In Chapter 2, we observed that the courts in the years prior to 1932 tended to interpret both the common law and the statutory law in a manner unfavorable to the development of organized labor. Whether courts applied the doctrine of "conspiracy" or "restraint of trade," or purported to examine the motive of the strikers or the means employed, the simple fact was that the legality of union tactics was determined by the members of the judiciary, who, by and large, represented a conservative element in the community and were prone to value private property rights more than the social gains which might derive from union organization. As a consequence, union tactics were severely hampered.

Strikes

As has already been mentioned in Chapter 2, in the early part of the nineteenth century, strikes by workers were considered unlawful on the ground that they were an illegal conspiracy against the public and employers. Then, in the case of *Commonwealth* v. *Hunt,* decided in 1842, the Supreme Judicial Court of Massachusetts decided that a strike in support of a closed shop was not illegal per se, and that unless it could also be shown that the workers' objectives were bad, the conspiracy doctrine did not apply. After the decision in *Commonwealth* v. *Hunt,* the courts tended to judge the legality of union activity on the basis of "motive" and "intent." Because the motives or intentions of workingmen engaged in union activity are mixed and difficult to ascertain, determinations of the legality of union activity in terms of possible objectives are subject to as many interpretations as there are judges. One judge, for example, might find that all strikes are malicious because the objective is to bring economic pressure upon the employer in violation of his property rights; on the other hand, an equally learned judge might decide that the purpose of the strike was merely to improve the economic standards of working people and that any harm which might accrue to the employer was incidental and unintentional. Moreover, courts differed in their judgments as to whether or not a particular objective was in the public interest and therefore lawful. As a consequence of this diversity in viewpoint, a union could lawfully strike for a closed shop in California but not in Massachusetts.[1]

On certain types of strikes, however, there was general agreement among the courts. Thus, most courts prior to 1932 held that sympathetic strikes were unlawful. These are strikes by one group of workers in support of another, such as a strike of plumbers out of sympathy for striking gravediggers. Judges found no possible justification for inflicting loss on the employers of plumbers merely because of a dispute between gravediggers and their employers.

On the other hand, in the case of strikes against technological change and jurisdictional strikes, courts have usually adopted a "hands off" attitude. Although most courts have indicated that they regard strikes aimed at preventing technological advance as harmful to society, they have recognized the problem that such progress often creates for workers and have usually not interfered, in the absence of legislative

[1] Compare *J. F. Parkinson Co.* v. *Building Trades Council,* 154 Cal. 581 (1908), with *Plant* v. *Woods,* 176 Mass. 492 (1900).

enactment, with the attempts of unions to retard technological change. Likewise, in the case of jurisdictional strikes—which are contests between unions over which group of workers shall perform a specified piece of work—most courts have declined to enjoin such strikes per se. They have regarded jurisdictional strikes as a matter for regulation by the legislative branch of the government.

Boycotts

A former Chairman of the National Labor Relations Board recently wrote: "The most effective union weapon in organizing and collective bargaining has been the secondary boycott, implemented by the hot cargo agreement."[2] A boycott is an organized refusal to deal with someone in order to induce him to change some practice which he follows. Such a boycott may be in the form of a "we do not patronize" list or in other forms of pressure designed to prevent sales of particular products; or it may be a refusal to handle certain goods. A "hot cargo" agreement involves an agreement by an employer with a union that he will not handle or compel his employees to handle the goods or merchandise of another employer with whom the union has a labor dispute. A secondary boycott usually involves an effort by employees to induce their employer not to deal with another party against whom they have a grievance.

The boycott has been most utilized as a tactical weapon by the teamster unions. For example, about 34 per cent of all secondary boycott cases brought before the National Labor Relations Board under the Taft-Hartley Act in the years 1947–59 involved the International Brotherhood of Teamsters, which represents only about 10 per cent of all organized workers.[3] However, other unions have also found the boycott a useful weapon against employers. Recently, the United Automobile Workers resorted to a nationwide boycott of Kohler products in its bitter battle against this manufacturer of plumbing wares. In another case, this same union asked its members not to use fishing tackle manufactured by a firm which allegedly had locked out members of the United Steelworkers. Union building tradesmen have usually refused to handle materials manufactured under nonunion conditions.

Before 1932 a majority of American courts held secondary boycotts unlawful per se—"as if it were a separate category of tort liabil-

[2] Guy Farmer, *Strikes, Picketing and Secondary Boycotts under the Landrum-Griffin Amendments,* Industrial Relations Counselors Research Monograph No. 19 (New York, 1960), p. 9.

[3] Farmer, *op. cit.,* p. 3.

ity."[4] This attitude, founded in the common law, was strengthened by enactment of the Sherman Antitrust Act in 1890. In the famous Danbury Hatters case[5] the United States Supreme Court in 1908 held that a secondary boycott organized by a union of hatworkers against hat manufacturers violated the Sherman Act. The manufacturer who brought the suit against the union, claiming triple damages, was awarded a judgment of over half a million dollars. Thereafter, until passage of the Norris–La Guardia Act, the federal courts generally held that boycotts by organized labor were unlawful under the Sherman Act. In the face of this judicial attitude, it is understandable why from 1908 until the mid-thirities, boycott action by unions greatly diminshed.

Picketing before the Norris–La Guardia Act

One of the most controversial questions of public policy in the field of labor relations today concerns the extent to which picketing by labor unions should be regulated. A companion question upon which conflicting views are found in the field of labor law involves the extent to which such limitations on the right to picket are constitutionally permissible.

Picketing is a familiar form of pressure utilized by unions which has become an indispensable adjunct of the strike. Picketing usually involves the patrolling of a struck establishment by one or more persons bearing signs or placards stating that the workers are on strike or that the employer is unfair to organized labor, or words to similar effect. The average worker will not pass a picket line. This is based partly on the fear of social ostracism; partly on the feeling that unless he supports this group on strike, they may not support him some day when his union is out on the street; partly on fear of physical violence; sometimes because of fear of sanctions contained in the constitution of his own union. Whatever the motivations, it is clear that the picket line is a most effective weapon. In our highly unionized economy a picket line, manned even by a small group in a large company, can completely paralyze a plant or establishment because other union men who work in the plant, or deliver it supplies, will not cross the picket line.

Picketing may be thought of in two ways. It is a form of expression, letting the public and labor supporters know that a controversy exists and giving labor's side of that controversy. It is also a form of pressure intended to dissuade persons from patronizing or entering a

[4] Charles O. Gregory, *Labor and the Law* (2d rev. ed.; New York: W. W. Norton & Co., Inc., 1961), p. 122.

[5] *Loewe* v. *Lawlor*, 208 U.S. 274, 28 S. Ct. 301 (1908).

place of business. The fact that picketing is at one and the same time a method of communication and a method of persuasion bordering on the coercive contributed to judicial confusion as to the lawfulness of this important labor technique.

Right up to the passage of the Norris–La Guardia Act, many state and federal courts took the position that all picketing was coercive in intent and unlawful, and that there could be no such thing as truly peaceful picketing. As one federal court put it: "There is and can be no such thing as peaceful picketing, any more than there can be chaste vulgarity, or peaceful mobbing, or lawful lynching."[6] Other courts grudgingly conceded that picketing was legal as long as it was peacefully conducted and did not bar entrance to and exit from a place of business, and as long as it did not obstruct traffic on a public thoroughfare. But while some courts conceded the legality of picketing, they also stringently regulated it, often limiting the number of pickets permitted and generally outlawing "stranger picketing," that is, picketing by persons who were not employed in the plant or business involved in the labor dispute. The attitude of the courts on stranger picketing was conditioned by their belief that workers had no interest in a labor controversy unless they were employees of the business involved in the dispute—a theory which ignores the relation of labor conditions in one plant with those in another.

Supporters of organized labor who believed in labor's right to picket freely argued that picketing was a form of expression and hence, if peacefully conducted, was protected by the First Amendment, as are other forms of communication. That viewpoint, however, was almost unanimously rejected by the courts prior to 1932. Indeed, the tendency right up to passage of the Norris–La Guardia Act was to limit rather than to expand the right of labor to picket in support of its interests.

PICKETING AFTER THE NORRIS–LA GUARDIA ACT

As was pointed out in Chapter 2, the Norris–La Guardia Act did not purport to legalize picketing or any other labor technique. All that it did was to remove the jurisdiction of the federal courts to issue injunctions against picketing except under limited and closely regulated circumstances. Nevertheless, the same shift of public opinion which made possible enactment of such prolabor legislation as to the Norris–La Guardia and Wagner acts gradually filtered through to the courts.

[6] *Atchison, Topeka & Santa Fe Railway* v. *Gee,* 139 Fed. 582, 584 (C.C.S.D. Iowa 1905).

During the depression years the nation as a whole was concerned with the economic status of labor; much of the prolabor legislation of this period was motivated by the desire to increase labor income and purchasing power and thus achieve a recovery from the depression. Furthermore, the ultimate arbiter of the lawfulness of picketing—the Supreme Court of the United States—was liberalized by President Roosevelt's appointment of a number of prolabor justices. As a consequence of these developments, court decisions tended to give labor more leeway in using the picket line; and, as we shall note in the following discussion, the Supreme Court soon put its blessing on picketing as a form of communication protected by the First Amendment.

The Legality of Recognition Picketing

In passing judgment on the legality of strikes, courts sometimes made a distinction between organizational picketing and recognition picketing. The former is said to involve picketing by a minority union directed to the employees of an employer in order to persuade them to become union members or to win their adherence to the union cause. The latter is directed to the employer in order to compel him to recognize the minority union; in effect, it brings pressure on the employer to force the employees to join the picketing union. In practice, it is difficult to make a valid distinction between the two forms of picketing, for either type of picketing, if effective, will bring economic pressure to bear upon both employer and employees with the objective of compelling recognition of the minority union as the bargaining representative for the employees.

Before considering the attitude of the courts toward picketing since enactment of the Norris–La Guardia Act, it may be helpful to explore the conflicting arguments pro and con advanced by union and management spokesmen on the subject of picketing. Should recognition picketing be permitted, prohibited, or restricted, and under what circumstances? For the purpose of this discussion, we shall consider organizational and recognition picketing as being substantially the same, since the same arguments are in general applicable to the two types of picketing.

Arguments Favoring Unrestricted Recognition Picketing

Union spokesmen argue that the picket line is labor's most effective organizing device. They contend that many employers are still extremely hostile to labor and that such employers, armed with the protection afforded by the Taft-Hartley Act's provisions relating to free speech, can prevent employees from really expressing their desires unless the union can apply economic pressure. They argue further that unions must have the right to picket even after dismissal of a representation case or loss of an election because employers sometimes maneuver unions into an election proceeding before the union is really ready and therefore the union must be able to continue to try to get its message across to employees. Finally, union spokesmen contend that they have a basic right to try to cure conditions which threaten the maintenance of wages and other working conditions in organized companies. If most of an industry is organized, for example, but a few employers are nonunion, pay low rates, and cut prices, they can demoralize the entire industry. Unions maintain that under such circumstances, they must have the right to continue to picket and bring pressure on the nonunion employer until he has been organized. If attaining his objective requires some employees to join the union against their will, union spokesmen feel that this is still in accord with democratic procedures because the union must look to the wishes of the majority of workers in the industry, not in an individual plant.[7]

Of course, these arguments are also sprinkled with comments that the picket line is merely informational, and that the picket line never forces the employer to do anything—he just finds it is to his economic benefit to sign up. These latter arguments will not stand up under analysis, but the need to protect union wages and hours through pressure on nonunion employers is a very basic one and difficult to counter. Moreover, it cannot be denied that the picket line is more effective than other media in communicating the union message to employees, for the picket line demonstrates in concrete fashion to nonunion employees that by joining the union, they need not fear the employer's economic power.

Arguments Favoring Restriction of Recognition Picketing

Management spokesmen who contend that recognition picketing should be prohibited usually begin with the Taft-Hartley Act itself (or similar state labor relations acts) as the basis for their argument. That Act and its predecessor (the Wagner Act) were intended to reduce the many industrial disputes arising out of the problem of selection of a collective bargaining representative. Furthermore, it was made clear in the Taft-Hartley Act that employees were to be free *not* to join a union if they did not want to. In view of these acts, the argument runs,

[7] Benjamin Wyle, "The New Law of Picketing," *Labor Law Journal,* Vol. X (December, 1959), p. 893.

recognition picketing should be prohibited. Union organizers can still distribute literature at plant gates and hold meetings to explain their position to employees. Beyond that, the peaceful machinery of the NLRB and state labor relations boards should be substituted for the economic pressure and violence generated by the picket line. This argument is particularly forceful when the peaceful machinery has been used and the union has lost. The management viewpoint is put cogently by NLRB member Jenkins, who, in his concurring opinion in the Curtis case, said: "I do not believe that Congress intended to or did write a statute providing for elections conducted at public expense which are to be considered binding if the union wins, but not binding if the union loses."[8]

If recognition picketing can continue indefinitely even after a union has been decisively rejected by employees in an NLRB election, a small employer cannot possibly withstand the pressures which can be applied by a powerful union. Opponents of unrestricted picketing emphasize the coercive aspects in picketing and the tremendous power this weapon confers on union leaders, who can break many businesses at their whim. They question whether the picket line, as an organizing device, is entitled to the same protection today, when organized labor numbers eighteen million strong, as when its membership was a weak three million.

Picketing and Free Speech

As we have seen, the enactment of the Norris–La Guardia Act in 1932 substantially limited the power of the federal courts to issue injunctions in labor disputes. State courts, however, continued to enjoin picketing under a variety of circumstances and for a variety of reasons, except where the power of state courts had been circumscribed by the enactment of state "little Norris–La Guardia acts," modeled after the federal statute.

Commencing in 1937, a series of cases was brought before the United States Supreme Court involving the question whether picketing could be restricted by state legislatures and courts or whether it was protected from such regulation as a form of free speech guaranteed by the First Amendment of the federal Constitution. These cases are of major interest to students of labor problems not only because they concern a major union weapon—picketing—but also because they indicate how the changing views of the Supreme Court may influence the pattern of state legislative and judicial control of labor relations and thus

[8] *Curtis Brothers, Inc.*, 41 LRRM 1025, 1033.

profoundly affect the evolution of collective bargaining in our society. As will appear more fully in the following discussion, it seems in retrospect that the Supreme Court first became intrigued with the idea of treating picketing as a form of free speech entitled to constitutional protection and then retreated from this position when it recognized the coercive elements present in picketing and the legitimate right of the states to limit picketing in certain instances to protect the public interest.

In 1937, in a case which affirmed the right of a state to enact a "little Norris–La Guardia Act," Justice Brandeis remarked: "Members of a union might without special statutory authorization by a State make known the facts of a labor dispute, for freedom of speech is guaranteed by the Federal Constitution."[9] This statement was misconstrued by many lawyers and judges to mean that picketing was a form of free speech guaranteed by the Constitution. Actually, Justice Brandeis merely said that union members might make known the facts of a dispute, without stating what means they might use for this purpose. He did not say that union members had a constitutional right to make known facts by means of a picket line. Nevertheless, three years later, in the case of *Thornhill* v. *Alabama,*[10] the Supreme Court completely accepted the doctrine that picketing was a form of free speech. An Alabama law, which termed picketing a form of loitering and made it a misdemeanor, was held unconstitutional on the ground that picketing is a form of speech protected by the First Amendment and that a penal statute which makes picketing a misdemeanor without regard to the manner in which it is conducted is unconstitutional on its face. In the companion case of *Carlson* v. *California*[11] the Supreme Court elaborated the doctrine of picketing as a form of speech in the following words: "Publicizing the facts of a labor dispute in a peaceful way through appropriate means, whether by pamphlet, by word of mouth or by banner, must now be regarded as within that liberty of communication which is secured to every person by the Fourteenth Amendment against abridgement by a State." And in 1941, in *American Federation of Labor* v. *Swing,*[12] the Supreme Court held unconstitutional the decision of the Illinois Supreme Court enjoining peaceful stranger picketing of a beauty parlor when none of the employees of the beauty parlor were members of the union conducting the picketing.

However, the notion that picketing is merely a form of free speech

[9] *Senn* v. *Tile Layers' Protective Union,* 301 U.S. 468, 57 S. Ct. 857 (1937).

[10] 310 U.S. 88, 60 S. Ct. 736 (1940).

[11] 310 U.S. 106, 113; 60 S. Ct. 746, 749 (1940).

[12] 312 U.S. 321, 61 S. Ct. 568 (1941).

did not prove very satisfactory in view of the coercive elements usually present in picketing. As a result, the United States Supreme Court slowly began to modify its views. In 1941 the Supreme Court refused to set aside an Illinois injunction which forbade all picketing by a milk drivers' union where there had been a background of previous violence.[13] In three important cases handed down in 1950, the Supreme Court held that the state courts could constitutionally restrict picketing which had as its objective action which violated a state statute or was deemed contrary to public policy.[14]

Finally, in *Vogt* v. *Teamsters,*[15] the Supreme Court upheld the action of a Wisconsin court in enjoining simple stranger picketing, thus fully acknowledging the retreat from the Thornhill doctrine and amounting, as the dissenters observed, to "formal surrender." Speaking for a majority of the Supreme Court, Justice Frankfurter stated that picketing is fully subject to the right of the states to balance the social interests between employers and unions, provided only that the states' policies are rational. Although Justice Frankfurter noted that the states could not, under the Thornhill doctrine, proscribe all picketing per se, he made it clear that state courts and legislatures are free to decide whether to permit or suppress any particular picket line for any reason other than a blanket policy against picketing.[16] One commentator concludes that this decision "sounded the death knell for organizational picketing in intrastate commerce, as far as the federal constitution is concerned."[17]

Picketing under the Taft-Hartley Act

The cases referred to above all arose as the result of efforts of state courts and legislatures to prohibit or restrict picketing. The federal

[13] *Milk Wagon Drivers* v. *Meadowmoor Dairies, Inc.,* 312 U.S. 287, 61 S. Ct. 552 (1941).

[14] *Building Service International Union* v. *Gazzam,* 339 U.S. 532, 70 S. Ct. 784 (1950); *Hughes* v. *Superior Court of State of California,* 339 U.S. 460, 70 S. Ct. 718 (1950); *International Brotherhood of Teamsters* v. *Hanke,* 339 U.S. 470, 70 S. Ct. 773 (1950).

[15] 354 U.S. 284, 77 S. Ct. 31 (1956).

[16] However, states cannot enact laws restricting peaceful picketing in a manner which deprives workers of rights guaranteed under the Taft-Hartley Act. Thus, for example, the United States Supreme Court has held unlawful a Virginia statute which imposed a fine on any person participating in picketing who was not a "bona fide" employee of the business or industry being picketed. Such a law against stranger picketing would be inconsistent with the Taft-Hartley Act, which makes no distinction as to whether a person picketing is an employee or not. See *Waxman* v. *Commonwealth of Virginia,* 51 LRRM 2221, October 8, 1962.

[17] T. L. Bornstein, "Organizational Picketing in American Law," *Kentucky Law Review,* Vol. XLVI (1957), pp. 25, 56.

government has also passed legislation restricting labor's right to picket. These restrictions are embodied in the Taft-Hartley Act and in the Landum-Griffin Act. At this point, in order to complete the picture of the attitude of the United States Supreme Court toward picketing, reference should be made to two recent cases involving picketing under the Taft-Hartley Act which were decided by the Supreme Court.

In 1951 the Supreme Court, in a decision consistent with its changed point of view toward picketing, held that the provisions of the Taft-Hartley Act banning certain types of picketing in connection with secondary boycotts did not violate constitutional guarantees of free speech.[18] This decision made it clear that Congress *could* restrict picketing. The next question was just how far had Congress intended to restrict picketing of an organizational nature when it enacted the Taft-Hartley law.

This question was answered in *National Labor Relations Board* v. *Drivers, Chauffeurs, Helpers, Local Union No. 639.*[19] In that case (which came before the NLRB prior to enactment of the Landrum-Griffin Act), a teamsters' union, after losing an election proceeding 28 to 1, continued to picket an employer's establishment. Only two pickets were involved, and they carried signs saying: "Curtis Bros. employs nonunion drivers, helpers, warehousemen, etc. Unfair to Teamsters' Union No. 639 AFL." On the other side, the picket signs stated: "Teamsters' Union 639 AFL wants employees of Curtis Bros. to join them to gain union wages, hours and working conditions." The employer filed a complaint with the NLRB, charging the union with a violation of Section 8 (*b*) (1) (*A*) of the Taft-Hartley Act, which makes it an unfair labor practice for a union to "restrain or coerce . . . employees in the exercise of rights guaranteed under section 7. . . ." Section 7 guarantees employees the right freely to choose to join or not to join a union. The NLRB, in a reversal of its previous policy, held that the peaceful organizational picketing violated Section 8 (*b*) (1) (*A*) because it was designed to cause the employer to coerce the employees into joining the union against their will. Upon appeal, however, the Supreme Court disagreed with the Board and held that peaceful picketing by a minority union under the circumstances of this case does not amount to conduct intended to restrain or coerce employees in the exercise of their right to organize and bargain collectively or to refrain from such activities, as provided in Section 7

[18] *International Brotherhood of Electrical Workers* v. *National Labor Relations Board,* 341 U.S. 694, 71 S. Ct. 954 (1951).

[19] 362 U.S. 274, 80 S. Ct. 706 (1960).

of the Taft-Hartley Act. The Court concluded that Congress had intended that the Board regulate peaceful picketing only when it is employed to accomplish specific objectives prohibited in Section 8 (*b*) (4) of the Act, and that Section 8 (*b*) (1) (*A*) became applicable only in cases of violence, intimidation, reprisals, and threats thereof. The Court referred to the Landrum-Griffin Act[20] and stated: "While proscribing peaceful organizational strikes in many situations, it also establishes safeguards against the Board's interference with legitimate picketing activity. See 8 (*b*) (7) (*C*). Were 8 (*b*) (1) (*A*) to have the sweep contended for by the Board, the Board might proceed against peaceful picketing in disregard of these safeguards."[21]

The language of the Court therefore indicates that under federal law, peaceful organizational picketing is permissible except as prohibited in specific situations by the provisions of the Taft-Hartley and Landrum-Griffin acts.

Present Status of Picketing

As far as federal law is concerned, it seems clear from reading the legislative history of the Act that Congress, in passing the Landrum-Griffin Act in 1959, intended to restrict both organizational and recognition picketing.[22] The new law makes it an unfair labor practice to picket or cause to be picketed, or threaten to picket or cause to be picketed, any employer where an object thereof is forcing or requiring an employer to recognize or bargain with a labor organization as the representative of his employees, or forcing or requiring the employees of an employer to accept or select such labor organization as their collective bargaining representative, unless such labor organization is currently certified as the representative of such employees.

The statute then sets out in Section 8 (*b*) (7) three circumstances in which picketing for the above purposes constitutes an unfair labor practice. These are:

(*A*) Where an employer has lawfully recognized another union and the question of representation may not be legally raised at this time;

[20] It should be mentioned that three justices were of the opinion that the new Section 8 (*b*) (7) added by the Landrum-Griffin Act "seems squarely to cover the type of conduct involved here." They would have remanded the case for consideration by the NLRB in the light of the new Act.

[21] 362 U.S. 274, 291, 80 S. Ct. 706, 716.

[22] The original Kennedy-Ervin bill contained no new restrictions on organizational or recognition picketing, but the measure was amended during Congressional debate to limit both types of picketing.

(*B*) Where a Taft-Hartley Act election has been held within the past 12 months;

(*C*) Where the picketing has been conducted without a petition for a representation election being filed within a reasonable period of time not to exceed 30 days from the commencement of the picketing.

Then follow two important provisos. The first states that when such a petition has been filed, the NLRB shall forthwith, without regard to the provisions of Section 9 (*c*) (1) of the Act or the absence of a showing of a substantial interest on the part of a union, direct an election in such unit as the Board finds to be appropriate and shall certify the results thereof. The second proviso deals with so-called "consumer picketing" and has been the source of much controversy. It states:

> *Provided further,* That nothing in this subparagraph (*C*) shall be construed to prohibit any picketing or other publicity for the purpose of truthfully advising the public (including consumers) that an employer does not employ members of, or have a contract with, a labor organization, unless an effect of such picketing is to induce any individual employed by any other person in the course of his employment, not to pick up, deliver or transport any goods or not to perform any services.

Paragraph (*A*), above, by its reference to legally raising a question of representation, incorporates the current practice of the NLRB, which states that where one union has a contract in effect with an employer, a petition for an election by a rival union can only be filed within a period of not more than 90 days and not less than 60 days prior to the termination date of the then current agreement. Thus, picketing can only occur during this limited 30-day period, and if it occurs outside this period, it can be immediately enjoined.

Paragraph (*B*) is intended to bar picketing where within the past 12 months the employees voted "no union" in a valid representation election. Picketing for recognition in the face of a Board certification of another union as bargaining representative is barred by another section of the Act (8 [*b*] [4] [C]).

Paragraph (*C*) is applicable to situations in which neither (*A*) or (*B*) control. The first proviso means that when recognition or organizational picketing is followed within 30 days by the filing of a representation petition by the union, the NLRB may dispense with its normal requirement of a pre-election hearing and the requirement that the union show, by signed cards or otherwise, that it has the support of at least 30 per cent of the bargaining unit. Union leaders have for years been seeking a way to obtain quick representation elections. Does this provision require that an election be held immediately if a union merely pickets and then files a petition without any showing of interest by the employees in the bargaining unit? The NLRB has attempted to solve this problem by providing that such a "quickie" election will be held only if the employer files an unfair labor practice charge under Section 8 (*b*) (7). This rule, at least, gives the employer the chance to make the decision, but he is apt to find himself on the horns of dilemma. It is the Board's policy to permit picketing to continue where a petition for election has been filed until the results have been certified. If the employer wants to avoid the "quickie" election and have the Board follow the more time-consuming regular election procedure, he must endure the picketing that much longer. If he cannot withstand the picketing and files the unfair labor practice charge, he must accept the speedy election.

While there may be sympathy for the employer's dilemma, it seems obviously unfair to curtail a union's right to picket unless an alternative means is provided of determining whether or not the employees wish to be represented by this union. From this point of view, the inclusion of the "quickie" election provision is not a "booby trap," as it has been referred to by some writers,[23] but a logical outcome of the legislative intent underlying our labor legislation.

It is apparent that Congress weighed the conflicting arguments concerning the desirability or shortcomings of unrestricted recognition picketing and concluded that further governmental regulation was necessary in order to safeguard the rights of employees and to give meaning to the action of the NLRB authorized by law. Congress has, in fact, stated that it will recognize the right of a union to apply coercion and pressure to organize a nonunion plant only for a reasonable time, and once a valid election has been held, a union can no longer utilize coercive measures to achieve its objective, even though a result may be the disruption of union wage standards[24] in an entire industry.

The Landrum-Griffin Act, however, leaves many questions about picketing unanswered, and its full impact on labor relations will not be clearly understood for some time to come. Much of the confusion is created by the so-called "consumer picketing" proviso referred to above. At first glance, this second proviso seems to ban all consumer picketing which is effective, in the sense that it interrupts the flow of goods in or out of an establishment. However, it must be remembered

[23] See, for example, Farmer, *op. cit.*, p. 26.

[24] Whether "wage standards picketing" is restricted by the Act is presently a subject of controversy. See subsequent discussion in this chapter.

that this is merely a proviso and that the effective prohibition would have to be found in other language of the Act. Actually, these prohibitions are aimed at recognition and organizational picketing, and it is therefore possible that even if informational picketing does interfere with deliveries, it will not be held unlawful under this clause if it does not have recognition or organization as an objective. This is the interpretation given this language by the NLRB, as we shall see from the discussion which follows, but there is foundation for a contrary construction in the legislative history of the Act. For example, in commenting on the language of the proviso, Representative Griffin (Republican, Michigan), whose name the Act bears, stated flatly that any type of publicity aimed at consumers, including picketing, which interfered with deliveries and pickups was not protected by the statutory language.[25]

While this statement may reflect Congressional intent, there is some question whether peaceful picketing intended solely to inform the public about a labor dispute can be constitutionally prohibited by a statute whose criterion of lawfulness is not the conduct of the strikers themselves, but the manner in which other persons react to the picket line. For example, in a number of cases which have recently come before the NLRB, the unions involved have gone to great lengths to insure that the picket line does not affect deliveries or pickups of merchandise;[26] nevertheless, some deliverymen have elected not to cross the picket line. In such circumstances, one possible view is that all picketing, even when conducted with the best of intentions to inform the consumer, is necessarily coercive; therefore, if it in fact results in coercion of deliverymen and others, this is a natural consequence of the conduct itself, which should be enjoined. The contrary view would hold that labor should have the right to inform the public that certain employers are nonunion or pay low wages, and that this right, which involves the right of free speech, is so important that it should not be circumscribed unless there is a substantial interference with the employer's right to carry on his business freely. Therefore, if the union takes reasonable precautions to prevent any interference with deliveries, the mere fact that a few deliveries are not made would not render the picketing unlawful.

The final word as to interpretation and constitutionality of the picketing restrictions contained in the Landrum-Griffin Act must await decision by the United States Supreme Court. Meanwhile, the NLRB, in

[25] *Congressional Record*, September 4, 1959, p. 18153.

[26] See, for example, *Barker Bros. Corp. and Golds, Inc.*, 51 LRRM 1053.

a series of influential decisions, has laid out these guidelines based upon its construction of the statutory language:

1. ***Informational Picketing.*** If the sole object of the picketing is to inform the public, and recognition of the union is not an objective of the picketing, the picketing is lawful and is not barred by any of the subsections enumerated above. Furthermore, even if such picketing interferes with deliveries or pickups, it is lawful nonetheless.[27]

2. ***Dual-Purpose Picketing.*** A picket line frequently has as its purpose both informing the public and securing recognition by an employer. Such picketing is presumably unlawful where the circumstances set out in subsections (*A*) and (*B*) above prevail. If (*A*) or (*B*) is not applicable, such picketing is entitled to the protection of the second proviso to subsection (*C*) unless it interferes with deliveries, etc.[28] The NLRB has further held that mere isolated interferences with deliveries are not enough to make the picketing illegal. Despite the fact that the second proviso expressly refers to "*an* effect" and "*any* individual" (italics added), the NLRB has read the language as if Congress were concerned only with a "substantial" effect and has held that there is a violation of the law only if picketing has "disrupted, interfered with or curtailed the employer's business."[29]

3. ***Recognition Picketing.*** Picketing intended to compel the employer to recognize the union as bargaining representative for his employees is subject to the prohibitions of subsection (*C*), and the picketing will be enjoined if it continues more than thirty days without a petition for an election being filed.[30] The Board has held, however, that so-called "union standards" picketing is not recognition picketing. Therefore, even if an employer has signed a contract with another certified labor organization, it is not unlawful, according to the NLRB, for another union to picket where the signs carried by the pickets merely state that the employer pays wages lower than the standards set by the picketing union, and there is no attempt by the union to obtain recognition from the employer.[31]

It is apparent from the foregoing brief outline that the NLRB has greatly narrowed the scope of the restrictive provisions contained in

[27] *Crown Cafeteria,* 49 LRRM 1648, reversing 47 LRRM 1321.

[28] *Ibid.*

[29] *Barker Bros. Corp. and Golds, Inc.,* 51 LRRM 1053.

[30] The statutory criterion is a "reasonable period of time not to exceed thirty days." The NLRB has held 17 days is a reasonable time in which to file in one case (*International Brotherhood of Teamsters,* 127 NLRB 958, enforced 289 F. [2d] 41) and 18 days in another (*Sapulpa Typographical Union,* 45 LRRM 2400).

[31] *Claude Everett Construction Co.,* 49 LRRM 1757.

the Landrum-Griffin Act as they apply to picketing. Many of the key decisions have been handed down by a divided Board, with the two dissenting members sharply in disagreement with the majority. In the Barker Bros. case,[32] in which the majority introduced the notion of "curtailment of business" as a criterion of the lawfulness of the impact of the picket line—despite the fact that this concept is nowhere to be found in the statutory language—the dissenters, Rodgers and Leedom, declared that the majority had completed "the virtual nullification of the Congressional purpose in enacting 8 (*b*) (7) (*C*)." The application of the statute is obviously not clear to the members of the Board, and it is even more uncertain for the average union member. Gone are the simple days when the Norris–La Guardia Act granted automatic immunity to such action. By contrast, a union leader who today determines to place a picket line around a plant needs a lawyer at his side to guide him. The legality of the picketing may depend upon the wording of placards which the pickets carry and how people react to them. It may depend upon the relationship between the employer and the union, between the employer and a rival union, or between the employer and other employers with whom the union has a dispute. Most of all, the lawfulness of the picket line may hinge upon what the NLRB interprets the objective and purpose of the picket line to be.[33] To the average laboring man, such examination of motives and objectives seems like a return to the old doctrine of lawful and unlawful objectives, motives, and other mystical criteria which courts found so convenient in the past to justify injunctions against union activity.

Boycotts after the Norris–La Guardia Act

We have seen that the Norris–La Guardia Act deprived the federal courts of jurisdiction in most cases involving labor disputes. However, its effect upon such union tactics as boycotts was even broader, for the United States Supreme Court interpreted the Norris–La Guardia Act as

[32] Barker Bros. case, *op. cit.*

[33] The Crown Cafeteria case is a good illustration of how subjective judgments—which reflect the particular bias of the Board member or judge—now determine the lawfulness or unlawfulness of a picket line. In that case a union picketed a new cafeteria which had refused to hire through a union hiring hall or to sign a contract. The picket signs were addressed to "members of organized labor and their friends," stated that the cafeteria was "nonunion," and asked them not to patronize it. No stoppage of deliveries or services took place. In its first hearing of this case a majority of the NLRB concluded that despite what was said on the signs, the picketing was really conducted for recognition purposes and was therefore not protected by the consumer picketing proviso (47 LRRM 1321). Subsequently, two new members were appointed to the Board, and upon reconsideration of the case the Kennedy Board held that the picketing was lawful because it was conducted merely to advise the public and caused no stoppages (49 LRRM 1648).

not only depriving the federal courts of jurisdiction to enjoin labor tactics enumerated in Section 4 of that Act, but also making such acts lawful for all purposes under federal law. This momentous decision was enunciated by the Court in the Hutcheson case,[34] which involved a secondary boycott organized by a carpenters' union against the Anheuser-Busch Brewing Company. The Court held that because of the intervention of the Norris–La Guardia Act, which had "infused new spirit" into the Clayton Act, such union conduct did not violate the Sherman Act, even though in 1908 it had reached a contrary conclusion on similar facts in the Danbury Hatters case.

As a result of a more liberal judicial attitude reflecting the spirit of the Norris–La Guardia and Wagner acts, by the late thirties and early forties union boycotts were no longer repressed by federal courts.[35] The result was a major expansion in the use of the secondary boycott by organized labor. Strategically placed unions, particularly in the field of distribution, were able to expand their sphere of organization by bringing pressure on persons whose only relation to the dispute was that they did business with the particular employer involved. The Teamsters exerted additional pressure on nonunion employers by obtaining "hot cargo" agreements, in which employers agreed not to deal with nonunion employers.

Taft-Hartley Restrictions on Secondary Boycotts

The abuses which arose from the widespread use of such tactics by organized labor, together with the rash of strikes in 1947, led to a demand for restrictive labor legislation. The Taft-Hartley Act, passed in that year, had as one of its prime objectives the outlawing of all secondary boycotts. Section 8 (*b*) (4) of that Act made it an unfair labor practice for a union to engage in or to encourage any strike or refusal by employees to use, manufacture, transport, work, or handle goods if an object of such action was to force an employer or any other person to cease dealing in the products of another employer or to cease doing business with any other person. Congress not only made the secondary boycott an unfair labor practice, but also it directed the NLRB to seek federal court injunctions against its continuance under certain circumstances; furthermore, it authorized damage suits to be brought in federal court by employers against unions which engage in secondary boycott action. Congress thus condemned secondary boycotts

[34] *United States* v. *Hutcheson*, 312 U.S. 219, 61 S. Ct. 463 (1941).

[35] J. James Miller, "Legal and Economic History of the Secondary Boycott," *Labor Law Journal*, Vol. XII (August, 1961), p. 755.

on the ground that they unduly widen the area of industrial disputes by interrupting the operations of employers only remotely connected with the chief cause of the controversy.

Congress may also have been concerned about the secondary boycott because it had become a potent weapon in the hands of strong labor unions to force union membership on unwilling employees. Since the national labor policy now stated that employees should have the right to join or to refrain from joining a union (unless there was a compulsory union shop provision in effect), it is not surprising that Congress found it necessary to restrict boycotts in order to make employee rights of self-determination effective.

Union leaders objected vehemently to these provisions of the Act. They pointed out that the Act even outlawed such traditional union action as a concerted refusal to handle "scab" products made in a nonunion shop or in a shop in which a strike was in progress. Even where one nonunion employer threatened the working standards of an otherwise fully organized industry, a refusal on the part of employees in the organized plants to handle or process goods intended for or coming from the nonunion plant would violate the Act.

Common Situs Problems

Some of the most difficult cases which the NLRB and the courts have been called upon to decide under the Taft-Hartley Act ban on secondary boycotts have been those in which the picketing has occurred at premises where employees of both the struck employer and a neutral employer are engaged in work. Situations involving work by two or more employers at the same premises have become known as common situs cases.

The essence of the problem is the determination as to where primary action ends and secondary action begins. Generally, primary picketing against a struck employer is lawful, while secondary picketing against a so-called "neutral" is unlawful. Section 8 (*b*) (4) of the Taft-Hartley Act is intended (among other things) to prohibit strikes or picketing where an object is to force what we may call "neutral" employers to stop doing business with the struck employer. Both the NLRB and the courts have recognized that the broad statutory prohibitions cannot be applied literally, for almost every picket line has as an object to deter employees of neutral employers from crossing the picket line. Suppose a picket line around plant A, in which a labor dispute exists, prevents drivers of employer B's trucking company from entering and picking up merchandise. Is the picket line unlawful because of its effect on employees of employer B? The NLRB has answered no, since the strike against A is privileged activity and the repercussions on B are only incidental. But suppose the primary dispute is with the trucking company, employer B. Can the employees of that company picket the trucks which are being loaded and unloaded on the premises of employer A? This raises the question of the so-called "ambulatory situs"—the trucks are in a sense an extension of the employer's business site. The Board has ruled that such picketing is permissible where it is confined to one employer and conducted at the only place where the union could picket effectively.[36]

In the Moore Drydock Company case,[37] the Board established four criteria which unions must observe when picketing against a primary employer is conducted on the premises of another employer:

1. The picketing must be limited to times when the primary (struck) company's employees are actually present at the common situs.
2. At the time of the picketing the primary employer must be engaged in its normal business at the situs.
3. The picketing must be limited to places reasonably close to the operations being conducted by the primary employer's workers.
4. The picketing must clearly disclose that the dispute is only with the primary employer.

Subsequently, in the Washington Coca-Cola case,[38] the NLRB added a fifth criterion. It held that picketing at premises at which employees of neutral employers are working is unlawful, even though the four tests above enumerated are satisfied, if the primary employer has a permanent place of business in the area at which the union could adequately publicize the dispute.[39] This last requirement, however, has been rejected by several courts of appeals as being too rigid, and the present Board has recently repudiated the doctrine as an automatic rule of application.[40] The present Board's view appears to be that the existence of a common situs and of another place which can be picketed is a factor to be considered in determining whether or not there has been a violation of law; but this factor is not conclusive, and other factors may be held to be controlling.

[36] *Schultz Refrigerated Service, Inc.*, 87 NLRB 502 (1949).

[37] *Sailors' Union of the Pacific* (Moore Drydock Co.), 27 LRRM 1108.

[38] *Brewery & Beverage Drivers* (Washington Coca-Cola Bottling Works), 33 LRRM 1122.

[39] In the words of one commentator, this requirement would practically destroy the ambulatory situs doctrine. See M. J. Segal, "Secondary Boycott Loopholes," *Labor Law Journal*, Vol. X (March, 1959), p. 178.

[40] *Electrical Workers, IBEW* (Plausche Electric, Inc.), 49 LRRM 1446.

The extent of application of the secondary boycott ban has been a controversial issue in the so-called "reserved gate" cases. Suppose that an industrial establishment is organized on an industrial unit basis, so that all employees are represented by one union. However, the employer from time to time uses independent contractors for a variety of tasks on the premises, such as construction, retooling, and maintenance work. The employees of the independent contractor are, for the most part, skilled craftsmen organized on a craft union basis. In order to avoid conflict between the two groups of workers, the industrial concern reserves one of the gates leading into the plant site for the exclusive use of employees of independent contractors who work on the premises and posts a notice to this effect. Subsequently, the industrial union gets into a dispute with the company and goes on strike. It pickets all of the gates, including the one reserved for use of independent contractors; and as a result, employees of the independent contractor refuse to enter the premises. Is the picketing of the reserved gate unlawful because it has the objective and effect of forcing the neutral independent contractor to cease doing business with the struck employer?

In the recent General Electric Company case,[41] on facts similar to these, the Supreme Court had to decide whether or not the NLRB had properly ruled that the picketing of the reserved gate involved an illegal secondary boycott. In reaching a decision, the High Court considered whether or not the independent contractor was truly a neutral or whether the work that was being done on the premises of the struck employer was so intimately related to the work performed by the striking employees that the effect of the picketing on the independent contractor should simply be treated as incidental to lawful primary action. The Court laid down the following rules as guides for determining whether the independent contractor should be treated as a neutral and the picketing of the reserved gate prohibited:

1. There must be a separate gate, marked and set apart from other gates.
2. The work done by the men who use the gate must be unrelated to the normal operations of the employer.
3. The work must be of a kind that would not, if done when the plant was engaged in its regular operations, necessitate curtailing those operations.
4. If the gate is used by contractors who perform some conventional maintenance work, such use must be relatively insignificant.

Since the record in the General Electric case showed that independent contractors performed some maintenance work that was related to

[41] *Local 761, IUE* v. *National Labor Relations Board* (General Electric Co.), 48 LRRM 2210.

normal operations of the employer, but did not indicate whether this was substantial, the Supreme Court remanded the case to the Board for a determination of this point. The NLRB on remand subsequently held that the picketing was lawful because the work performed by the independent contractor did involve work which was not unrelated to the employer's normal operations, and such work was not *de minimus.*[42]

The problems raised by the common situs cases reflect more than a difference of opinion among lawyers as to the meaning of the statutory prohibitions on secondary boycotts. Actually, in many cases the controversy is basically a contest of unions for members—frequently a clash between industrial and craft unions for the same work. The nature of this power struggle is brought out in the briefs filed with the appeals court by two union groups in a recent case. The Building Trades Department, representing the viewpoint of the craft union employees working for independent contractors, summarized the issue as follows: "The question, as it affects both the [building trades] workers and their contractor employers, is whether they will be permitted to work in or around the plant premises of an employer . . . without interference at the hands of the incumbent plant union which seeks, by its illegal activity, to restrict the rights of the employees of these independent construction contractors to perform work contracted out by a plant employer to construction contractors."[43] On the other hand, the Steelworkers, in their reply brief, stated: "This is not 'the question' at all. Rather, the question is whether a union may use traditional, peaceful concerted activities in connection with a legitimate dispute concerning the contracting out of work of the kind which could be, and in the past has been, performed in the bargaining unit."[44] Behind the conflicting viewpoints revealed by these statements lies a basic economic fact: The industrial unions have been losing membership due to automation and technological unemployment, and are now seeking to retain for members of their bargaining unit jobs which many companies would prefer to contract out to independent contractors. The reserved gate issue is typical of the complex problems which arise in the field of labor relations where the influence of government legislation, management business needs, economic and technological trends, and internal union conflicts must all be resolved if a satisfactory pattern of collective bargaining is to emerge and endure.

The common situs problem has also been a major source of

[42] 51 LRRM 1028.
[43] LRR, 48 Anal 11.
[44] LRR, 48 Anal 11–12.

friction in the construction industry, where it is customary for a general contractor and various subcontractors to work on the same premises. Suppose employees of the general contractor or union subcontractors picket the premises in protest over another subcontractor using non-union labor. Under the Board and court interpretations of Section 8 (*b*) (4) (*A*), such action has been held to be a secondary boycott. It is not surprising that the building trades unions are the most frequent users of the secondary boycott technique. For the calendar year 1960, NLRB records show that 707 secondary boycott charges were filed with the Board. Unions in the building and construction field were charged with 52 per cent of such charges, while the Teamsters were involved in 16 per cent of the cases. The building trades unions contend there is no secondary boycott action involved because there is really only one employer—the general contractor—and all of the subcontractors are so related to him by the nature of the work that they cannot be considered to be "neutrals" as far as picketing is concerned. The United States Supreme Court, however, has held that the subcontractors are to be treated as independent employers in considering the applicability of Section 8 (*b*) (4) (*A*).

The so-called "ally doctrine" is another principle which has been established by the NLRB in handling secondary boycott cases. The late Senator Taft had foreshadowed this doctrine by his remark that the secondary boycott ban was not intended to apply to a case "where the third party is, in effect, in cahoots with or acting as a part of the primary employer." The Board has taken the position that the secondary boycott prohibitions are not applicable where there is a common ownership and management of two companies, or where a company transfers struck work to another company which is aware of the primary dispute.

The Landrum-Griffin Amendments

While it is clear from the foregoing discussion that the Taft-Hartley Act effectively curtailed many forms of union secondary boycott activity, nevertheless it also left major loopholes. Thus, if a Teamster business agent attempted to persuade Mr. X's employees not to handle the goods manufactured by Mr. Y, this was unlawful, yet the Act did not prohibit the business agent from warning Mr. X directly that he had better not handle Mr. Y's product! Likewise, the Act permitted boycott action applied through inducement of employees individually, instead of in concert, and inducement of employees of railroads, municipalities, and governmental agencies. Inducement of supervisors was also not barred by the original Taft-Hartley language, because the statute referred to inducements to the "employees of any employer" and the definition of "employee" in the Act excluded supervisory personnel. One other loophole resulted from NLRB rulings on "hot cargo" agreements. After some vacillation the Board held that "hot cargo" agreements could validly be included in collective bargaining agreements and presumably could be enforced by appropriate court action, but not by strike action or appeals to employees. However, the fact that they were sanctioned as a subject of collective bargaining and were included in contracts enforceable in law strengthened the hands of unions in making secondary boycott action effective.

The Landrum-Griffin Act was aimed at the Teamsters' Union more than any other labor organization. It is not surprising, therefore, that specific provisions were included intended to close each of the loopholes in the secondary boycott prohibitions mentioned above. The problem of threats to employers directly was dealt with by adding a new section which makes it an unfair labor practice for a union to "threaten, coerce, or restrain *any person*" (italics added) where the purpose is prohibited secondary boycott action. Just where the Courts will draw the line between unlawful threatening action and lawful persuasion of an employer remains to be seen. The problem of inducement to individual employees, employees of railroads, municipalities, and governmental agencies, and supervisors was handled by deleting the language in this section of the Act which referred to "employees of any employer" and substituting "any individual employed by any person engaged in commerce or in an industry affecting commerce." Despite this change in language, the NLRB has continued to maintain that "any individual" does not include corporate officers, high-ranking supervisors, and others who are high up in the management ladder.[45] In the recent Servette case, the NLRB held that inducements made by a union to retail store managers not to carry certain products distributed by a struck wholesaler were not a prohibited secondary action against "any individual employed by any person," but the United States Supreme Court, while agreeing on the facts with the final decision of the Board, plainly stated that the Board had erred in making any such distinction between lower ranking and supervisory employees.[46] The controversy indicates the difficulty that exists in spelling out legislative purpose clearly in statutory language even in a case where the amendment was intended to close this very loophole

In the case of "hot cargo" agreements, a new Section 8 (*e*) was

[45] The Second Circuit had adopted a similar construction. See *National Labor Relations Board* v. *Local 294, Teamsters,* 49 LRRM 2315.

[46] *National Labor Relations Board* v. *Servette, Inc.,* 55 LRRM 2957, 2958.

added to the National Labor Relations Act, making it an unfair labor practice for both unions and employers to enter into such agreements. Two exceptions are made, however—agreements in the construction industry relating to contracting or subcontracting of work done at the construction site; and agreements relating to jobbers, subcontractors, and the like in the apparel and clothing industry.

Despite problems of interpretation, the statutory restrictions against secondary boycotts have been greatly strengthened by the Landrum-Griffin Act. Still untouched are the various ramifications of the ally and roving situs doctrine, which depend to some extent upon administrative determination of the degree of neutrality involved in a secondary employer's status. A further complication is introduced by the so-called "publicity proviso" contained in the Landrum-Griffin Act.

This proviso appears in the amended Section 8 (*b*) (4) of the National Labor Relations Act after enumeration of prohibitions on various forms of strikes and boycotts. The proviso states:

> Provided further, that for the purposes of this paragraph (4) only, nothing contained in such paragraph shall be construed to prohibit publicity, other than picketing, for the purpose of truthfully advising the public, including consumers and members of a labor organization, that a product or products are produced by an employer with whom the labor organization has a primary dispute and are distributed by another employer, as long as such publicity does not have the effect of inducing any individual employed by any person other than the primary employer in the course of his employment to refuse to pick up, deliver, or transport any goods, or not to perform any services, at the establishment of the employer engaged in such distribution.

It will be observed that this proviso expressly refers to "publicity, other than picketing." It has generally been thought, therefore, that its protection does not extend to picketing, in contrast to the proviso earlier considered in connection with consumer informational picketing. However, in a recent decision handed down by a divided court, the United States Supreme Court has stated that the statutory words do not mean what they say. In that case a teamsters' union which had a primary dispute with an organization of fruit packers set up picket lines in front of retail stores which sold fruit purchased from the packers. The picket signs advised consumers not to buy the fruit because it was nonunion. Pickets were instructed not to patrol delivery entrances or exits, and other precautions were taken not to interfere with the flow of merchandise in and out of the stores. No employees stopped work, and deliveries were not affected. Nevertheless, the NLRB found the union action was unlawful secondary boycott action intended to force the stores to cease doing business with the packers. The Board took the position that the Landrum-Griffin provisions completely ban picketing on the premises of the secondary employer, and no protection is afforded picketing in this regard.[47] However, when the case reached the United States Supreme Court, the High Court reversed the Board and held that so-called consumer picketing at neutral stores for the purpose of persuading customers to cease buying the products of a struck primary employer does not violate the Act even though it may cause economic loss to the stores of the neutral third party.[48] The Court concluded that Congress had not intended to ban all consumer picketing and that it was necessary to distinguish between a union appeal to the public not to trade with the secondary employer (presumably unlawful) and what the Court found existed in the present case—a union appeal to the public not to buy merchandise of the primary employer.

While the full significance of the Court's decision on the application of this proviso is not fully apparent, it may still be important to define picketing in future cases. This is not as easy as it may appear at first glance. The NLRB has held that the distribution of "do not buy" handbills to customers on public property adjoining retail stores that purchased merchandise from a distributor with whom a union had a dispute comes within the protection of the "publicity proviso."[49] Apparently, giving out handbills is not picketing. Suppose that instead of giving out the handbills, union members simply stand in front of a store and hold them up so customers can read them. Is this a picket line? Do they have to move around to become a picket line?[50] This is the kind of abstruse problem which is raised by the complicated verbiage of the statute. Little wonder that union officials yearn for the good old days when you did not have to call a lawyer to see if pickets could move their feet in a picket line!

Another problem raised by the publicity proviso involves the interpretation to be given to the words "product or products are produced by an employer . . . and are distributed by another employer." By its terms, it would appear that the protection afforded by the language of the proviso is applicable only when a product is actually produced or manufactured by one company and distributed by another. The

[47] *True Fruits Labor Relations Committee*, 48 LRRM 1496.

[48] *NLRB* v. *Fruit Packers Local 760*, 55 LRRM 2961 (1964).

[49] *Teamster Union* (Schepps Grocery Co.), 49 LRRM 1011.

[50] In *NLRB* v. *Local 182, Teamsters Union* (*Woodward Motors, Inc.*), EB *LRRM* 2354 (CA[2d]1963), pickets had planted two signs in snowbanks, stationed themselves in autos parked near the highway, and emerged whenever a truck approached the premises. In upholding a cease and desist order issued by the NLRB against the Teamsters for illegal picketing, the court stated: "Movement is thus not requisite, although here there was some." 52 LRRM 2356.

NLRB, however, has taken a much broader view and has held, for purposes of applying the protection of the proviso, that a radio broadcasting station "produced" automobiles advertised on its programs and that a wholesale distributor of grocery products "produced" those items which it distributed to retailers. The Ninth Circuit Court of Appeals has disagreed with the Board and reversed the Board in both cases.[51] In the opinion of the Circuit Court, if Congress had wanted to give the publicity proviso broad coverage, it would have been simple enough to refer to the production *or distribution* of goods by an employer engaged in a labor dispute, rather than using the narrow phraseology. However, the United States Supreme Court appears to have resolved this controversy in favor of the Board by holding in its review of the Servette case[52] that "products produced by an employer" includes products distributed as well. After reviewing the statutory history of this terminology, the Court concluded that there was no evidence that Congress intended to narrow the application of this language to producers only and it pointed out that similar language in other federal statutes has also been given the broader construction.

It is apparent from the foregoing discussion that while the Landrum-Griffin amendments further tightened restrictions on secondary boycott activity, the new language contains its own "loopholes." There will be many years of litigation and possible further Congressional legislative revision before the limitations on secondary boycotts are clarified.

Limitations on the Right to Strike

Writers are often prone to equate the right to strike with democracy and a free labor market. It has been said that preservation of the right to strike is what distinguishes our economy from those of Communist nations and that if this right is compromised, then other individual rights will also suffer. Actually, however, the right to strike has been limited in a number of important respects by the Taft-Hartley and Landrum-Griffin acts, and yet economic democracy still flourishes in our country. The change from the era of uninhibited union action under the Norris-La Guardia Act is a rather remarkable one and is deserving of closer scrutiny.

Strike action can be divided into two general categories—primary and secondary. A primary strike is a strike which occurs in connection with a labor dispute and directly involves the employer of the striking

[51] *Great Western Broadcasting Corp.* v. *National Labor Relations Board,* 51 LRRM 2480; *Servette, Inc.* v. *National Labor Relations Board,* 51 LRRM 2621.

[52] *NLRB* v. *Servette, Inc.,* 55 LRRM 2957.

workers. A secondary strike is a strike which is aimed at an employer other than the employer of the striking workers. Suppose the carpenters on a construction job strike for higher wages. This is a primary strike directed against their employer who, let us say, is the general contractor on the job. Now, a nonunion flooring subcontractor brings in nonunion men to put down asphalt tile flooring in the building. The carpenters go on strike in protest against the use of nonunion workers on the job. This is a secondary strike.

While it is difficult to generalize in such a complicated field, it can be said that the law generally permits primary strike activity and prohibits secondary strike activity. A similar rule applies to picketing. There are, however, important exceptions. All secondary strike activity is not unlawful; and on the other hand, there are many kinds of primary strike activity which are either prohibited or subject to limitations under our statutes. Let us examine some of the major types of primary strike activity which are restricted by federal law.

1. ***Strikes against Public Policy as Set Forth in Federal Statutes.*** In this category would fall strikes which directly violate, or compel an employer to violate, restrictive provisions contained in labor laws such as the Taft-Hartley law. Thus, for example, it is unlawful for a union to strike to compel an employer to recognize one union when another union has already been certified as collective bargaining agency by the NLRB. The NLRB recently held that it was unlawful for a union to strike to compel an employer to sign a "hot cargo" contract in the construction industry, even though the statute expressly permits such contracts if voluntarily made. A strike for a closed shop is unlawful under the Taft-Hartley Act, and it is also unlawful in many states under common law.

2. ***Strikes Arising Out of Jurisdictional Disputes.*** The Taft-Hartley Act makes it an unfair labor practice for a union to engage in a strike to force or require any employer to assign particular work to employees in a particular labor organization or in a particular trade, craft, or class rather than to employees in another labor organization or in another trade, craft, or class, unless such employer is failing to conform to an order or certification of the Board determining the bargaining representative for employees performing such work. The law further provides that whenever it is charged that there has been a violation of this section, "the Board is empowered and directed to hear and determine the dispute out of which such unfair labor practice shall have arisen." The United States Supreme Court has held that this provision means that the Board must inquire into the merits of the dispute

and then make a binding award of the work.[53] The Board has discretionary authority to seek an injunction against jurisdictional strikes in violation of the statute. As a result of these statutory provisions, the NLRB is now required to determine jurisdictional disputes by what amounts to compulsory arbitration.

3. ***Strikes during the Term of a Valid Collective Bargaining Agreement.*** A strike to compel a change in the terms of a contract prior to the expiration date of the contract has been held to be unlawful under the Taft-Hartley Act. This is true whether or not the contract contains a no-strike agreement. A strike in violation of a collective bargaining agreement is not protected concerted activity under the Taft-Hartley Act, and may constitute an unfair labor practice.[54] A strike during the term of a contract over grievances or in protest over employer unfair labor practices is not, however, unlawful.

Section 301 of the Taft-Hartley Act provides that suits for violation of contracts between an employer and a union may be brought in any district court of the United States. The remedy of the employer would normally be damages for breach of contract, for the United States Supreme Court has held that the Norris–La Guardia Act bars issuance of an injunction in such cases.

The Taft-Hartley Act specifically prohibits strikes called before the end of a sixty-day notice period prior to the expiration of collective bargaining agreements. This provision was included in the law in order to give conciliation agencies sufficient time to meet with the parties and attempt to resolve disputes before a walkout occurs.

4. ***Strikes against the Government as Employer.*** Most governmental bodies—federal, state, and municipal—forbid strikes by employees on the ground that this is a strike against the sovereign and therefore against the public interest. Section 305 of the Taft-Hartley Act makes it unlawful for any individual employed by the United States or any agency thereof, including wholly-owned government corporations, to participate in any strike. The problem of government employees and the right to strike will be more fully explored in Chapter 16.

5. ***National Emergency Strikes.*** The Taft-Hartley Act contains provisions enabling the government to obtain a temporary injunction in cases involving strikes which imperil or threaten to endanger the national health or safety. After such an injunction is obtained, the strike

[53] *National Labor Relations Board* v. *Radio Engineers Union,* 47 LRRM 2332.

[54] *United Mine Workers of America* (Boone County Coal Corp.), 117 NLRB 1095 (1957); enforcement denied, 257 F. (2d) 211 (D.C. Cir. 1958). Cf. *Boeing Airplane Co.* v. *National Labor Relations Board,* 174 F. (2d) 988 (D.C. Cir. 1949).

action becomes unlawful. These provisions will be discussed in Chapter 13.

The foregoing brief outline describes the status of strikes in interstate commerce where federal labor laws are applicable. Where state law is applicable to a local dispute, the results will depend upon the provisions of the state statute, or upon common law in the absence of an applicable statute. Basically, courts, in the absence of statutes to guide them, still apply the old rule of ends and means. If the ends are illegal, the court is likely to enjoin the strike, no matter how peaceful the means used may be. This result reflects the historical judicial attitude that a strike is fundamentally an intentional tortious interference with an advantageous business relationship and therefore should only be permitted if it is carried on for a proper purpose. Strikes to improve working conditions are generally held to be a valid purpose, but a strike for a closed shop may still be held lawful in one state and illegal in another.

LIMITATIONS ON THE RIGHT TO LOCK OUT

Labor legislation in this country has gradually deprived employers of most of the effective tactical weapons which employers used in the past to combat efforts of unions to organize their employees. We have seen how the Norris–La Guardia Act outlawed the yellow-dog contract and barred injunctions against unions in federal court—thus eliminating two devices which had been widely used to discourage union organizing efforts. Likewise, the unfair labor practice provisions of the Wagner and Taft-Hartley laws restricted other tactics frequently utilized by antiunion employers, such as discriminatory hiring and firing practices, spying on employees, antiunion speeches, and so forth. While this restrictive legislation was primarily intended to prevent employers from obstructing the efforts of employees to organize and bargain through representatives of their own choosing, it also had the effect of weakening the tactical position of employers who reach an impasse in bargaining with unions over economic issues. For example, the Norris–La Guardia Act and the state statutes patterned after it have made it extremely difficult—and sometimes impossible—to halt mass picketing, vandalism, and other violence which sometimes results from efforts of management to bring employees through a picket line into a struck plant. As a consequence, most employers are reluctant to run a plant with strikebreakers, even though they have a legal right to do so. The Norris–La Guardia Act, therefore, tends to make the picket line a more effective weapon for imposing economic losses upon the employer and consequently gives the union a strategic advantage in collective bargaining.

There is another effective employer tactical weapon which is relatively little used and about which little has been written. That is the right to lock out. In some respects the employer's right to lock out his employees may be thought of as paralleling the employees' right to withhold their services through strike action. Just as the right to strike has been subjected to restrictions where it contravenes certain purposes, so the employer's right to shut down operations has been held to be a limited managerial prerogative. Although, with minor exceptions,[55] there are no statutory prohibitions against use of the lockout, nevertheless, as a result of decisions of the NLRB and the courts, the lockout has been so circumscribed by restrictions that an employer involved in a labor dispute would be ill advised to shut down or move his plant without first obtaining competent legal advice.

The Lockout as a Device to Avoid Union Organization. The Taft-Hartley Act prohibits discharges of employees where the purpose is to discourage membership in a labor organization. Since an employer cannot discharge individual employees in order to deter unionization, it is not surprising that both the NLRB and the courts have held that he cannot shut down an entire plant and lay off all employees in order to accomplish the same result. Of course, employers will generally point to some economic reason for the shutdown, while union spokesmen will claim the action was taken to break the union. Cases which come before the NLRB on this issue usually involve factual situations susceptible of either interpretation, which tends to complicate the problem presented to the Board for determination.

Today, it is not uncommon for companies to shut down an entire operation and move to the South and other less industrialized areas, where they are being wooed by tax concessions and other advantages promoted by local industrial development commissions. Suppose an employer has been in business in a northern city for many years, and has been continually receiving attractive offers to move to the South, where a local municipality will build a new plant for him and lease it at a very low rental. When a union organizer comes into the picture and the employer realizes his labor costs are likely to rise still further, can he now make the decision to shut down his existing operation and move to the South?

While the result will depend upon the particular factual situation

[55] The Taft-Hartley Act prohibits lockouts (and strikes) for a period of sixty days after notice is given of a proposed modification or expiration of a collective bargaining agreement (Section 8 [*d*] [4]). In addition, lockouts (and strikes) which imperil the national health and safety are subject to injunction for a limited period of time during the fact-finding procedure prescribed by Section 206 of the Taft-Hartley Act.

involved, it can safely be said that the NLRB will look at such employer action with a jaundiced eye. As the NLRB has recently pointed out: "The mere coincidence of union organization of a plant with the shutting down thereof is not conclusive evidence of a discriminatory motive in shutting down that plant, although the coincidence itself is evidence bearing upon discriminatory intent."[56] The same rule applies where a company seeks to avoid its commitment under an existing union contract or to wrest bargaining concessions from a union by moving a plant to another area. In these cases the NLRB usually requires the employer to offer employment to the former employees at the new location, to pay their moving expenses to such location, and, in addition, to make the employees whole for the loss they may have suffered by reason of the unlawful discharge. Even if the employer's motives are wholly legitimate, the Board has imposed the minimum requirement that an employer with an existing contract talk things over with the union before pulling up stakes. While this requirement may be exasperating to an employer who has made a decision based upon cold facts and figures, it may make sense from the point of view of maintaining stability in a community and minimizing loss of skills to labor. Sometimes, employees faced by an imminent move of a plant to another area have been able to persuade an employer to remain in his existing facilities by agreeing to a wage cut, accepting new production standards, or even arranging a loan for the company.

Does an employer have an absolute right to go out of business regardless of the motives responsible for this decision? The NLRB has answered "No" if a reason for the termination of business is employees' union activities. In the Darlington Manufacturing case[57] a parent corporation liquidated a subsidiary company by selling the assets at auction and terminating the employment of about five hundred workers. The Board held that the Darlington Company did not have the right to go out of business since its decision to close down was in part attributable to the fact that the Textile Workers' Union had just won a hotly contested election in the mill. The Board assessed back-pay damages not only against Darlington, but also against the parent company. How the Board would enforce a remedy against a corporation which was not affiliated with any other and which ceased business operations is not clear. Would the stockholders or officers have any liability? Can a company

[56] National Labor Relations Board, *Twenty-sixth Annual Report* (Washington, D.C.: U.S. Government Printing Office, 1962), p. 98.

[57] *Darlington Manufacturing Co.,* 51 LRRM 1278. The United States Court of Appeals at Richmond has refused to enforce the Board order in the Darlington case (54 LRRM 2499) and the Board is now seeking certiorari to the Supreme Court.

be forced to reopen its plant? It is apparent that the Darlington case decision raises a host of intricate problems.[58] Yet the result in this case was foreshadowed by the related decisions reviewed above.

A variation of the lockout which has become increasingly common involves contracting out certain operations which had previously been performed by the employer's own employees. In one recent case the employer abolished its automotive service department, farmed out the work to others, and terminated all employees in this department. The NLRB directed that the department be reopened and that the terminated employees be reinstated to their former positions and be made whole of any losses suffered because of the employer's action.[59] In another important decision the Board has ruled that an employer has a mandatory obligation to consult with a union on the company's decision to subcontract some of its work that employees have been doing, even though the subcontracting is motivated by economic considerations.[60]

The Lockout as a Device in Collective Bargaining Negotiations. Suppose that an employer has dealt with a union for many years and has no desire to discourage union organization among his employees, but honestly believes he cannot afford to meet union wage demands presented in collective bargaining negotiations. When the union threatens him with a strike unless he meets union terms, can he lock out his employees in reprisal? The answer to this question is not clear. Despite the importance of the lockout as a weapon in such circumstances, the rights of an employer to use it remain shrouded in doubt.

Three different types of lockout situations may be distinguished:[61]

1. *Single Employer Bargaining Lockout.* This is the simple case of a single employer, bargaining individually with a union, who is faced by a bargaining impasse and shuts down his plant in order to bring the

58 Suppose an employer goes out of business rather than deal with a union. One member of the current NLRB believes that this is a privileged action and that it does not and should not involve any violation of law. (See dissenting opinion of Rodgers in *Star Baby Co.,* 52 LRRM 1094, 1097.) The majority of the Board apparently believes that such action does constitute an unfair labor practice. The question then arises: what remedy should be applied for the benefit of the discriminatorily discharged workers? In the Star Baby Co. case referred to above, the partners in a children's wear business, who had dissolved their business and sold all their assets, were ordered to pay back pay to discharged workers from the date of sale of such assets to such time as the employees secure "substantially equivalent employment elsewhere." Theoretically this liability could continue forever, although the Board emphasized it required such employees to seek work with due diligence.

59 *Jays' Foods, Inc.,* 47 LRRM 1042.

60 *Town & Country Manufacturing Co.,* 49 LRRM 1918; see also *Fibreboard Paper Products Corp.,* 51 LRRM 1101, reconsidering 47 LRRM 1547.

61 See, for a more complete discussion of this problem, Bernard D. Meltzer, "Lockouts under the LMRA: New Shadows on an Old Terrain," *University of Chicago Law Review,* Vol. XXVIII (Summer, 1961), pp. 614–28.

union to terms. While no specific statutory provision is violated by such employer action, nevertheless the NLRB has generally condemned such conduct. The rationale of the Board is that collective bargaining and the strike are "protected concerted activities," and since the lockout is a reprisal against employee resort to such activities, the lockout is inconsistent with statutory purposes. Yet it is well-accepted law that an employer in an economic strike can lay off and replace strikers with permanent replacements. Is not such action equally a reprisal for protected concerted activity? Moreover, replacement of strikers and the attempt to operate a plant with strikebreakers is likely to lead to violence, whereas a lockout avoids these problems. The Board's position on individual employer lockouts is also difficult to understand in the light of its more permissive attitude where multiemployer bargaining is involved, as discussed below. To date, the United States Supreme Court has not passed on this question, and therefore the legality of the lockout as a tactical weapon in individual employer-union negotiations remains unresolved.

2. *Defensive Multiemployer Lockout.* Suppose that a number of employers in an industry bargain jointly with a union and sign a master contract covering all the companies. In negotiations for a new contract an impasse is reached, and the union strikes one of the companies. Can the other companies lock out their employees in retaliation for the union's selective strike? In 1954 the NLRB abandoned its earlier position condemning such employer action and ruled that such defensive action was lawful. In the Buffalo Linen case[62] the United States Supreme Court upheld the Board's position and stated: "We hold that in the circumstances of this case the Board correctly balanced the conflicting interests in deciding that a temporary lockout to preserve the multi-employer bargaining basis from the disintegration threatened by the Union's strike action was lawful."[63]

In view of the Court's language, should not lockouts by individual employers also be held to be a lawful use of economic power?

Despite the Court's language, lockouts even by multiemployer groups have continued to be restricted by the Board and the courts. In the Utah Plumbing and Heating Contractors' Association case,[64] a lockout, after expiration of a contract but during the course of collective

[62] *National Labor Relations Board* v. *Truck Drivers' Union*, 353 U.S. 87, 77 S. Ct. 643 (1957).

[63] 353 U.S. 97.

[64] *Utah Plumbing and Heating Contractors' Association* v. *National Labor Relations Board*, USCA (10th) 1961, 294 F. (2d) 165.

bargaining by members of a multiemployer bargaining association in an attempt to compel a group of unions to accept the employers' last offer on a wage issue, was held to be unlawful. The union had authorized its officers to call a strike, but no strike had been called at the time of the lockout. The United States Court of Appeals, sitting in Denver, refused to equate the employers' right to lock out with the union's right to strike and said: "Under these circumstances, the threat at the bargaining table to resort to a lockout unless the representatives of the unions would give assurance of their endeavor to bring about acceptance of the last offer and the prompt effectuating of the lockout constituted wrongful interference with the right of collective bargaining under Section 7 of the Act and therefore an unfair labor practice under Section 8."[65]

Furthermore, the NLRB has ruled that where circumstances are such that a defensive lockout by an association is lawful, the employers must actually shut down their businesses during the lockout. If they lock out their employees and attempt to carry on business temporarily by use of supervisory personnel as replacements, the lockout becomes illegal.[66]

3. *Lockout to Prevent Extraordinary Losses.* The Board has recognized that in certain industries an employer, in order to avoid extraordinary economic or operational losses threatened by an imminent strike, may shut down his plant in the face of a strike threat. As stated by the Board:

> An employer is not prohibited from taking reasonable measures, including closing down his plant, where such measures are under the circumstances necessary for the avoidance of economic loss or business disruption attendant upon a strike. This right may, under some circumstances, embrace the curtailment of operations before the precise moment the strike has occurred. . . . The nature of the measures taken, the objective, the timing, the reality of the strike threat, the nature and extent of the anticipated disruption, and the degree of resultant restriction on the effectiveness of the concerted activity, are all matters to be weighed in determining the reasonableness under the circumstances and the ultimate legality of the employer's action.[67]

Recently, this rule was invoked[68] to sanction the action of a manufacturer of television and radio receivers who subcontracted his service work and laid off or terminated his service employees upon learning

[65] 294 F. (2d) 165, 168.

[66] *Brown Food Store et al.*, 50 LRRM 1046.

[67] *Betts Cadillac-Olds, Inc.*, 28 LRRM 1509; National Labor Relations Board, *Seventeenth Annual Report* (Washington, D.C.: U.S. Government Printing Office, 1952), p. 155, n. 20.

[68] *Packard Bell Electronics Corporation*, 47 LRRM 1455.

that his employees had voted for a strike that was supposed to take place within forty-eight hours. The justification found was that the manufacturer had a legitimate interest in taking the steps it did to make sure that its customers' television sets would not be tied up during the strike; that if it had waited until the authorized strike was actually in progress, the movement of its customers' partially dismantled sets to other shops would have presented an extreme hardship; and that it had no assurance other companies would take the sets after the strike was in progress.[69]

Is the distinction which the Board attempted to draw between a permissible and an unlawful lockout a valid one? Certainly, there is nothing in any statute which says that a strike which will cause an employer great loss permits him to take action which would be unlawful if the strike presented only minor inconveniences. Every strike presents an employer with hardships, and it appears doubtful that the degree of hardship should be the criterion for judging the employer's right to retaliate against the union.

The Board's hostile view toward the lockout is a throwback to the earlier days of union organization when unrestricted use of the lockout would have seriously weakened unions which were then in their infancy. Today, most unions have fat treasuries and strike insurance for members out on strike. It would seem that a fresh appraisal is required as to the validity of restricting an employer's right to close down his plant where no issue of deterring union organization is involved.[70]

Subcontracting as a Device in Economic Strikes

We have seen that an employer's ability to take action to combat a strike is stringently circumscribed. This is because strike activity is a protected form of employee concerted action under our federal labor laws. However, the law is clear that in an economic strike—that is, where the employees are striking over economic issues such as wages, hours, and conditions of work—an employer may protect his business

[69] Similarly, the Board, in a split decision, recently ruled that a lockout by an association of building contractors in the face of an imminent strike was not unlawful because "a work stoppage which occurs on a construction project once in progress submits the contractor to serious economic loss and threatens lives, safety, and welfare of the public." See *Building Contractors' Association of Rockford,* 51 LRRM 1211. The dissent questioned whether any unusual operational problems or hazards would have resulted from a strike.

[70] Some courts appear to be in the process of making such a reappraisal. Recently the Fifth Circuit set aside a Board finding that a lockout by an employer constituted an unfair labor practice and stated that a "lockout may not be made a violation simply on the ground that this gives advantage to the employer, or takes advantage away from the employees, or tips the scales one way or the other." *NLRB* v. *Dalton Brick and Tile Corp.,* 301 F.(2d) 886 (CA[5th]1962).

by hiring replacements for the strikers. If permanent replacements are hired before the strikers apply for reinstatement, the employer can lawfully refuse to discharge the replacements and rehire the strikers. This is the rule laid down by the United States Supreme Court in the Mackay Radio case.[71]

Suppose that an employer in an economic strike wants to reopen his plant and resume operations, but cannot get sufficient replacements. Can he subcontract out some of the work previously done by the men on strike? At first glance, one would think that if an employer can lawfully hire a permanent replacement for a striking worker, he ought to be able to assign that work to an independent outside contractor to perform. The NLRB, however, has taken a contrary view. In the recent Hawaii Meat Company case[72] a union of meatcutters, which represented delivery department employees in a meat company, went on strike over economic issues. The employer, who was concerned about maintaining deliveries of a perishable product, entered into an agreement with an outside trucker to deliver the employer's products in the employer's trucks using the contractor's employees. The employer then notified his striking employees that he intended to reopen his plant but that the jobs as drivers would not be available. The NLRB, in a split decision, held that the employer was guilty of an unfair labor practice in subcontracting work without negotiating this issue with the union, even though the employees were on strike. We have already observed earlier in this chapter that the NLRB considers subcontracting a mandatory subject of bargaining. According to the NLRB, the employer has a right to replace *men,* but he cannot eliminate *jobs*—and thus threaten the status of the bargaining representative—without bargaining with the union.

The result in this particular case was that the Board held that the employer's unlawful action converted an economic strike into an unfair labor practice strike, so that the strikers were entitled to reinstatement upon their unconditional application to return to work. The employer was ordered to re-establish the subcontracted work and reinstate the strikers with back pay, with 6 per cent interest! This decision, if supported by the courts, considerably narrows the limits of permissible employer activity in an economic strike as laid down in the Mackay Radio case. Like the Board's decisions in lockout cases, it enhances the power of the strike as an economic tactic while depriving the employer of effective countermeasures.

[71] *National Labor Relations Board* v. *Mackay Radio & Telegraph Co.,* 304 U.S. 333, 58 S. Ct. 904 (1938).

[72] *Hawaii Meat Co.,* 51 LRRM 1430.

In the recent Insurance Agents' case[73] the United States Supreme Court held that harassing tactics, including a slowdown, used by insurance agents during collective bargaining negotiations with their employer did not constitute a violation of the duty to bargain in good faith. The Court went on to state: "The use of economic pressure by the parties to a labor dispute is not a grudging exception to some policy of completely academic discussion by the Act; it is part and parcel of the process of collective bargaining."[74] If a union can use a slowdown and similar tactics to bring economic pressure to bear upon an employer during negotiations, should not an employer be able to counter with effective pressure in the form of a lockout or subcontracting, where an economic strike is involved? Are we not being unrealistic about the facts of economic warfare in requiring that an employer, in the midst of a strike, bargain with the union over the abolition of jobs formerly held by men on strike?

During the latter part of 1962 and early 1963, the ports on the East Coast of the United States were shut down as a result of a crippling strike of longshoremen, and the newspaper strike in New York City caused losses to the retail trade running into millions of dollars. Strikes such as these produce a clamor for government restrictions on the right to strike. Such a solution would certainly be injurious to the cause of free labor unions in the long run. Perhaps another avenue should be investigated—the possibility of eliminating some of the restrictions on employer activity which hinder management's ability to combat such economic strikes. While legislative action which would seek to achieve this result would be construed as "antiunion," it might, in the long run, by making unions more concerned about the ability of employers to "win" strikes, diminish the number of strikes and thus make unnecessary a more stringent program of strike regulation by the federal government.

QUESTIONS FOR DISCUSSION

1. What is the distinction between organizational picketing, recognition picketing, and union standards picketing? Should the law recognize any differences between these various types of picketing? Discuss from the point of view of the union, the employer, and the public.
2. What is meant by common situs picketing? Why does this raise a problem of secondary boycotts? Should the law be amended so that subcontractors

[73] *National Labor Relations Board* v. *Insurance Agents' International Union, AFL–CIO,* 361 U.S. 477, 80 S. Ct. 419 (1959).

[74] 361 U.S. 477.

on construction jobs are not treated as independent contractors in considering whether the Taft-Hartley Act prohibitions against secondary boycotts are applicable?

3. Is an employer's right to lock out his employees comparable to the right of employees to strike? What are the important differences? Discuss the legality of lockouts by employers, both individually and as part of a bargaining group.

SUGGESTIONS FOR FURTHER READING

ANKER, J. "Organizational Picketing and Our National Labor Policy," *George Washington Law Review*, Vol. XXIX (December, 1960), pp. 466–78.

A criticism of the imposition of legal restrictions on labor's right to use the picket line for organizational purposes.

BURSTEIN, H. "Picketing—A Management Point of View," in *Proceedings of New York University Fourteenth Annual Conference on Labor*, pp. 11–24. New York: Matthew Bender & Co., 1961).

A defense of the Landrum-Griffin Act restrictions on picketing on the ground that picketing is a coercive weapon.

FARMER, GUY. "The Status and Application of the Secondary Boycott and Hot Cargo Provisions," *Georgetown Law Review*, Vol. XLVIII (Winter, 1959), pp. 327–45.

Analysis of the scope and meaning of the Landrum-Griffin restrictions on secondary boycotts by a former Chairman of the NLRB.

MELTZER, BERNARD D. "Lockouts under the LMRA: New Shadows on an Old Terrain," *University of Chicago Law Review*, Vol. XXVIII (Summer, 1961), pp. 614–28.

A concise summary of the law on employer lockouts.

Chapter 8 THE VEXING UNION SECURITY ISSUE

A unique, persistent, and vexing question affecting union-management relations and public policy on the American scene is the issue of "union security"—an agreement between employer and union requiring union membership as a condition for employment (see Table 4 for definitions). This issue is as sharp and emotion-packed in many areas of our country today as it was a century ago. This chapter explains public policy pertaining to this issue.

BACKGROUND OF THE UNION SECURITY ISSUE

Union development was hindered in the United States by a variety of factors which emphasized individual rather than collective activity as the best method of achieving economic progress. Class fluidity bred individual opportunity. The "rags to riches" stories still occur; but in the nineteenth century, when there existed an abundance of free land, open doors to ambitious immigrants, and the development of a continent-wide market, union partisans found neither sympathy nor economic strength for their philosophy. Hindered also by the heterogeneity of races and nationalities, the fierce individualism of employers, and the antagonism of public policy, especially as expressed in the courts, unions also found that they could not depend on class solidarity, so often in evidence in other countries, to maintain union membership, dues, and strength. Instead, they turned to contractual provisions requiring the employer to maintain union membership for them. Today, as in 1875, a primary aim of most unions is "union security," and this has been achieved in the overwhelming majority of union contracts (Figure 1). But although the union objective has been highly successful, the issue of whether compulsory union membership should be permitted remains very much alive.

Whether a union will demand a "closed shop" (under which employees must join a union as a prerequisite to employment) or a "union

TABLE 4

Types of Union Security and Checkoff

Union-Security Terms

Closed Shop—Employer agrees that all workers must belong to the union to keep their jobs. He further agrees that when hiring new workers he will hire only members of the union.

Union Shop—Employer agrees that all workers must belong to the union to keep their jobs. He can hire whom he wants; but the workers he hires must join the union within a specified time (usually 30 days) or lose their jobs.

Modified Union Shop—Employer agrees that all present and future members of the union must remain in the union for the duration of the contract in order to keep their jobs. (Present workers who are not in the union and who do not join the union in the future can keep their jobs without union membership.) The employer further agrees that all new employees must join the union within a specified time (usually 30 days) or lose their jobs.

Agency Shop—The employer and the union agree that a worker shall not be forced to join or stay in the union to keep his job. The worker has the choice of joining or not joining. But if he elects not to join he must pay to the union a sum equal to union dues. This sum represents a fee charged him by the union for acting as his agent in collective bargaining and in policing the union contract.

Maintenance of Membership—Employer agrees that all present and future members of the union must remain in the union for the duration of the contract in order to keep their jobs. (Workers who are not in the union and who do not join the union in the future can keep their jobs without union membership.)

Revocable Maintenance of Membership—Employer agrees that all present and future members of the union must remain in the union to keep their jobs. But he specifies that workers can leave the union during specified periods (usually 10 days at the end of each year) without losing their jobs.

Preferential Hiring—Employer agrees that in hiring new workers he shall give preference to union members.

Checkoff Terms

Voluntary Irrevocable—Employer agrees to deduct union dues and other monies from the worker's wages only if the worker signs a form authorizing him to do so. This generally requires that the worker's authorization shall not be irrevocable for more than 1 year or beyond the termination date of the contract, whichever is sooner.

Year-to-Year Renewal—Employer agrees to deduct dues and other monies from the worker's wages if the worker signs a checkoff authorization. If the worker does not revoke his authorization at the end of a year or at the contract termination date, it goes into effect for another year.

Voluntary Revocable—Employer agrees to deduct union dues and other monies from the worker's wages if the worker signs a form authorizing him to do so. The worker can revoke this authorization any time he sees fit.

Automatic—Employer agrees automatically to deduct dues and other monies from the worker's wages and turn the money over to the union.

Involuntary Irrevocable—Employer agrees that to secure and keep his job a worker must sign a form authorizing the employer to deduct union dues and other monies from his wages.

Source: J. J. Bambrick, Jr., *Union Security and Checkoff Provisions*, Studies in Personnel Policy, No. 127 (New York: National Industrial Conference Board, 1952).

shop" (under which the employer may hire anyone he chooses, but after a probationary period of 30–90 days, all employees must join the union as a condition of employment) will vary with the type of employment and labor market. In general, the closed shop is found among skilled and strategically located trades and in industries in which employment is

FIGURE 1

UNION SECURITY PROVISIONS IN MAJOR COLLECTIVE BARGAINING AGREEMENTS*

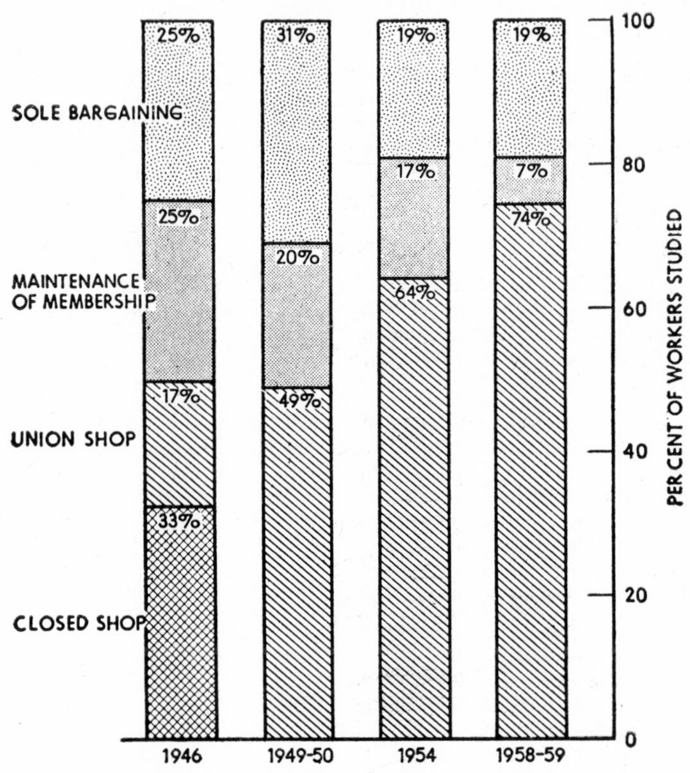

* The 1946 estimates relate to the proportion of all workers under agreement covered by each type of union status. Closed and union shop clauses are not shown separately for subsequent years. Buraeu reports issued since passage of the Taft-Hartley Act have classified the closed shop as a type of union shop.

SOURCE: U.S. Department of Labor, Bureau of Labor Statistics.

casual or intermittent. The closed shop differs from the union shop primarily in that it is not only a means of "union security" but also a method of controlling entrance to the trade or industry. The closed shop is utilized primarily by unions which cannot control layoffs because a layoff occurs when the job ends. For example, a building contractor lays off bricklayers when the brickwork is completed. Hence, if the union is to enforce its agreements, it must control the hiring end.[1] In such industries, unions, in effect, act as employment agencies supplying labor to employers.

Whether closed shop or union shop, however, early unions came to believe passionately that the closed or union shop was necessary to their survival. Only if union security was achieved could the union count on effective protection from employer discrimination against union members. Indeed, unions argued, often with considerable evidence, that union security provisions were necessary to induce workers to join a union, not so much because of their reluctance to join but because of their fear of consequences in the form of employer retaliation if they joined voluntarily.

In England, unions found little need of union security. The English unions grew at a more rapid rate than those in the United States and encountered much less employer opposition. Complete union membership was achieved not by union security provisions in contracts but by direct action among employees. Men unwilling to join unions in England are usually compelled to do so either because union men will not work with them or because they find that failure to join unions means social ostracism or other types of effective pressure. Such methods proved ineffective in America in the face of employer opposition to unions and the lack of class consciousness on the part of employees.

In Sweden the union security issue was taken out of collective agreements by industrial relations statesmanship. The central employer and union federations agreed in 1906 that employers would recognize unions as bargaining agents for workers, and unions in turn would not demand the closed or union shop. At the same time, in the United States, the National Association of Manufacturers was waging a "holy" war on unions under the slogan that the "open" shop was the "American way." Small wonder that in the United States the refusal of employers to grant the closed or union shop has often been taken by unions as proof that the employer would like to destroy the union!

Theoretically, the passage of the National Labor Relations (Wagner) Act in 1935 eliminated much of the need for union security. This Act outlawed employer discrimination against workers because of union membership and required employers to bargain with duly certified unions. Nevertheless, union security demands lost none of their intensity. This was true partly because union leaders and members

[1] For a more complete discussion, see Gordon F. Bloom and Herbert R. Northrup, *Economics of Labor Relations* (4th ed.; Homewood, Ill.: Richard D. Irwin, Inc., 1961), pp. 227–40.

believed, often with considerable justification, that employers were opposed to unions and could circumvent the law; partly because, emotionally, they could not imagine successful unionism without the closed or union shop; and partly because of a new development—the rise of rival unionism on a scale previously unknown. The existence of a union security provision deters raiding by rival unions, and thus gives unions "security" from another angle.

Arguments pro and con the closed or union shop are actually matters for individual determination. If one believes that under no condition should a person be compelled to join a union in order to have the right to work, one is opposed to union security. If one believes that persons should be compelled to support an organization which has won certain benefits in which they share, one favors union security provisions. These are irreconcilable value judgments.

The most fundamental charge against union security provisions is that they encourage dictatorial union administration. In recent years, federal regulation of union security has been aimed primarily at such abuses. But federal policy has also encouraged complete state curbs of all union security provisions. The development of this policy and its present status and effect are analyzed in the remainder of this chapter.

DEVELOPMENT OF PUBLIC POLICY

Like much of the early public policy toward union activity, the first issues involving union security were determined by the courts under the common law. The closed shop was considered by the courts as a part of the "illegal conspiracy" of unionism until the famous 1842 Massachusetts case of *Commonwealth* v. *Hunt,* which introduced the questions of "motive," "intent," and "means" to judge union tactics.[2] This improved the union potential for achieving union security but at the same time caused a split in judicial opinion. The courts of some states, for example, ruled that a strike for a closed shop was a legitimate objective for a union; the courts of other states disagreed.[3]

On the other hand, most state and federal courts did not find that the "closed nonunion shop" was illegal. As was noted in Chapter 2, this was achieved by the "yellow-dog" contract. Such contracts were not

[2] See Chapter 2, pages 14–17.

[3] For a good discussion of this background, see Paul E. Sultan, *Right to Work Laws: A Study in Conflict,* Industrial Relations Monograph No. 2 (Los Angeles: University of California, 1958), pp. 12–43.

only deemed enforceable by the courts, but state and federal legislation aimed at preventing their enforcement was declared unconstitutional.[4]

A significant influence on public opinion and public policy at the turn of the century was the campaign waged by American business against unionism, utilizing the union security issue as the focal point. Led by the National Association of Manufacturers and the National Metal Trades Association, employer groups fought union recognition in the name of the "open shop"—which to them meant no union recognition. Unionism and the closed shop were equated as one and the same and found anti-American, if not unholy. Antiunion sentiment of farmers and small businessmen was reinforced and solidified, and union growth was brought to a standstill by this business drive against unionism.

World War I and Aftermath

World War I saw a temporary truce in the fight over union recognition. As war approached, tripartite industry, union, and public boards were established to handle labor problems and to avoid strikes. Union recognition and growth resulted. A National War Labor Board to settle unresolved disputes was established, also on a tripartite basis. The thorny union security issue was shelved by an agreement guaranteeing the right to organize and providing for a freeze on the compulsory union issue which stated that open shops were to remain open and closed shops closed for the duration of the emergency. Aided by this agreement, government recognition, and the shortage of labor, union membership reached a pre-New Deal high of 5.5 million, more than double that which prevailed before the war.

A labor-management conference called by President Wilson after hostilities ended to continue labor-management co-operation failed primarily on the combined issues of union recognition and union security, which by now both unions and industry considered as almost one and the same. Employers once more took the offensive, combining their "open-shop" program with the first ingredients of scientific personnel administration, and often company unions or employee representation plans. The open shop was once more widely advertised as the "American way," and unions and the closed shop as alien in concept and form. By 1930, union membership had fallen to pre-World War I levels.

[4] *Coppage* v. *Kansas,* 236 U.S. 1, 28 S. Ct. 277 (1915), which nullified the state laws; and *Adair* v. *United States,* 208 U.S. 161, 35 S. Ct. 240 (1908), which nullified a federal statute.

The New Deal and Union Security

On June 16, 1933, President Franklin D. Roosevelt signed the National Industrial Recovery Act. It contained the famous Section 7 (*a*), which provided that labor should have the right to join unions without employer discrimination. It also contained a proscription against employer requirement for membership in company-dominated unions, but otherwise did not impinge on the closed shop or other forms of union security. Although this law did not provide effective protection for labor's right to organize or to gain its union security objective, it set the policy stage for the National Labor Relations (Wagner) Act of two years later.

Before the Wagner Act was passed, Congress pursued a different approach for railway labor relations. The Railway Labor Act was amended in 1934 to outlaw not only employer unfair labor practices, but all union security provisions as well. Here the aim was clearly to eliminate company-dominated unions supported by compulsory checkoff of dues.[5]

The Wagner Act furthered union security considerably, but it also limited it to some extent. It furthered it by assisting and encouraging unionization, and therefore opening up the opportunity for the attainment of closed and union shops. By 1940, union membership had risen to 8.5 million, and about 40 per cent of all union agreements contained union security provisions.[6]

But the Wagner Act also placed some limits on the legality of union security provisions. Section 8 (3) made it an unfair labor practice for an employer to discriminate against an employee because of union membership, or to encourage or discourage membership in a labor organization. If this provision had not been modified, it would have completely outlawed all forms of the closed and union shop. However, Section 8 (3) contained a proviso which stated that nothing therein would "preclude an employer from making an agreement with a labor organization (not established, maintained, or assisted by any action defined in this Act as an unfair labor practice) to require as a condition of employment membership therein, if such labor organization is the representative of the employees as provided in Section 9 (*a*), in the appropriate collective bargaining unit covered by such agreement when made."

This proviso had the effect of permitting closed or union shops

[5] See Chapter 12.

[6] Sultan, *op. cit.*, p. 44.

except where the union had been dominated or assisted by the employer, and except where the union did not represent the majority in the appropriate bargaining unit. The effect of the Act, therefore, was to place two important limitations upon the right of unions to sign compulsory membership agreements. These limitations caused dissatisfaction on the part of the AFL with the administration of the Wagner Act. In a number of instances, for example, AFL leaders signed compulsory union agreements with employers who preferred the AFL to the CIO. Upon charges filed either by individual workers or by a CIO union, the National Labor Relations Board abrogated some of these agreements on the ground that they violated Section 8 (3) on two counts—that the AFL union had won its contract through company assistance, and that the AFL did not represent a majority of the workers involved. In a few cases, in addition, CIO unions and, quite often, independent unions also signed contracts in violation of Section 8 (3) which the Board abrogated.

The statutory limitations of the closed and union shop which were imposed by the Wagner Act were extended by interpretation of the NLRB. In a number of interesting cases the Board ruled that a union which either refused admission to members of a rival union or, just prior to the expiration of a contract, used its compulsory union agreement to cause the discharge of those who were seeking to change the bargaining agent was in fact violating the Wagner Act. Because, however, there was no provision in the Wagner Act for enforcement of unfair labor practices against unions, the NLRB issued orders against the employer, who was ordered to cease and desist from discharging persons in contravention of this Board policy. The employer was also liable for back pay to such persons whom he had discharged. Many persons saw considerable justice in the claims of employers that they should not be penalized for carrying out the terms of an agreement with the union, but rather that such penalties should be assessed against the union itself.

World War II Policies

As the international situation became more ominous, strikes in defense industries gave rise to more concern; and once again, union security loomed large in defense and war labor policy. A tripartite National Defense Mediation Board, set up in 1941 to deal with the defense labor situation, developed the "maintenance of membership" doctrine (see Table 4, page 213) as a compromise between the union or closed shop and no compulsory membership. But when John L. Lewis demanded the full union shop for coal miners working in mines owned by steel companies (a demand which had already been secured in most other bituminous mines), the National Defense Mediation Board declined to go further than maintenance of membership. The CIO members of this Board then resigned, the miners struck the mines of the steel companies, and the Board ceased to function effectively.

President Roosevelt backed up the National Defense Mediation Board by declaring: "I tell you quite frankly that the Government of the United States will not order, nor will Congress pass legislation ordering, a so-called closed shop. . . . The Government will never compel this 5 per cent to join the union by a Government decree. That would be too much like the Hitler methods toward labor."[7]

Nevertheless, the union won its demand. The strike was settled by an agreement to arbitrate, with John R. Steelman, then Director of the United States Conciliation Service, as the arbitrator. Steelman ruled in favor of the union shop on the ground that only one of every two hundred miners was not already a union member.

The Steelman award was handed down on December 7, 1941—Pearl Harbor Day—and soon the same problem was in the lap of the National War Labor Board. With employer members dissenting, the NWLB adopted maintenance of membership as its compromise policy. At first the NWLB tended to award this type of union security upon a showing that it was necessary to protect the union, deprived of its strike weapon by the emergency, against loss of membership because of employer opposition or rival union raiding. In return for this protection, the NWLB demanded adherence to the no-strike pledge, democratically conducted union elections, audited financial reports to members, and a fifteen-day escape period between the time when the NWLB order was handed down and the time when the maintenance-of-membership provision became effective, so that anyone wishing to resign could do so without penalty. As time wore on and a flood of cases passed through the NWLB's national and regional offices, the granting of maintenance of membership became largely pro forma, with the only real restriction kept being the escape period. By the end of World War II, union membership, buoyed up by the increased employment of war production, had risen to 15 million. One fourth of these were working under maintenance-of-membership contracts and another 40 per cent under closed or union shops. Compulsory union agreements thus covered a majority of unionized employees by 1946.[8]

[7] Quoted by Sultan, *op. cit.*, p. 46.

[8] Data from U.S. Bureau of Labor Statistics reports (see Figure 1, page 214).

UNION SECURITY—TAFT-HARTLEY AND THEREAFTER

Despite union gains in achieving compulsory union membership, the issue remained unsettled, especially in the political arena. The result was a series of provisions in the Taft-Hartley Act which permitted union gains on this issue to continue (and may even have furthered them), but at the same time opened the door to effective restrictions against any type of union security. This paradoxical result was achieved because the Taft-Hartley Act was a compromise both between the advocates of federal and state regulation, and between those who wished to outlaw union security and those who desired to control it.

Taft-Hartley Background

Beginning in the late 1930's, a number of state legislatures reacted to public concern over union tactics and excesses by enacting laws which controlled union activity, often severely. Of particular interest here was the passage of legislation in a number of states which restricted or outlawed union security provisions. In some states, such as Wisconsin and Pennsylvania, this legislation took the form of amendments to state laws which were originally modeled on the Wagner Act; in others, such as Colorado, it was largely new legislation; in Florida, the first "right-to-work" law became operative in 1944—that is, a law completely outlawing all forms of union security.

Meanwhile, as union security provisions became more common, widespread disquiet developed over the fact that a union could fine, discipline, or cause the discharge of an employee, who then usually had no recourse or court of appeal.[9] That such acts were being committed by union officials who insisted on the impartial arbitration and review of employer disciplines and discharges served to emphasize the need for a review of public policy relating to union security provisions. The general consensus in Congress was either to prohibit union security provisions altogether or to regulate the admission and disciplinary policies of unions.[10] The Taft-Hartley Act did some of both. The Act imposed restrictions on types of union security clauses which could be negotiated, established conditions for the negotiation of union security clauses, and permitted states to legislate union security clauses out of

[9] A discussion of this issue will be found below, pages 229 ff.

[10] Sultan, *op. cit.*, pp. 48–50.

existence regardless of federal law. Once a union security provision was legally negotiated, the union was not restricted in its admission or disciplinary actions, but the teeth were withdrawn from the latter by the requirement that a union could require the discharge of an employee pursuant to a legal union security provision only on the ground that the employee had failed to tender the regularly required initiation fee or dues.

Discharges and Checkoff

The last provision has undoubtedly been significant. Expelling a man from a union for nonfiscal reasons, or for declining to pay a special fine or assessment, cannot thus expel him from his job unless an employer conspires with a union to violate the Act. Undoubtedly, this happens when the parties mutually agree to rid themselves of a "troublemaker" to both. Nevertheless, the existence of this provision has been a powerful restraint against arbitrary union discipline of members, and especially arbitrary union-inspired discharge of members.[11]

The Taft-Hartley Act in this respect did not attempt to protect a person's right to belong to a union. It protected the person's right to remain on the job under a union shop provision as long as he tendered his regular union dues. The sections of the Landrum-Griffin Act dealing with individual union rights, which are discussed in Chapter 6, added protection to the individual against arbitrary expulsion from the union. Such protection is vital if the worker is to have a voice in determining his wages and working conditions where a union has bargaining rights with or without union security provisions, but the factor of compulsory membership certainly adds emphasis to the need for democratic union procedures.

Closely allied to this union security restriction in the Taft-Hartley Act was the Act's ban on the compulsory checkoff. The checkoff of membership dues was made lawful only where individual employees execute a written assignment of wages for not longer than one year, or for the duration of the applicable union contract, whichever is shorter. In general practice, such assignments are in effect until revoked, which is rarely. But it is now unlawful for an employer and union to agree to turn over a portion of an employee's wages to a union without that employee's express written permission—certainly a highly defensible public policy.

[11] For a discussion of cases and NLRB and court rulings enforcing this protection, see Sultan, *op. cit.*, pp. 85–95.

Ban on Closed Shop

The restriction placed by the Taft-Hartley Act on the types of union membership clauses which were henceforth to be permitted was the outlawing of the closed shop (see Table 4, page 213, for definitions) and other forms of pre-employment preferential treatment of union members. The writers of the Act were impressed with the fact that unreasonable denial of work had occurred as a result of union control of hiring, and this they were determined to eliminate.

There is general agreement, however, that this provision tended largely to drive the closed shop underground instead of out of existence. Without control of hiring, it is almost impossible for unions in the construction, maritime, and other casual trades to exert effective control over working conditions. Employees in such industries typically work for several employers, and leave the job when it is finished. Seniority or other controls over layoffs are therefore ineffective.

When it enacted the Landrum-Griffin Act, Congress recognized the problem of the closed shop in the building construction industry. This Act loosened Taft-Hartley restrictions applied to the construction industry by legalizing so-called "prehire" agreements (that is, arrangements to employ union personnel before a job starts). Such agreements may now make union membership compulsory seven days after employment (rather than thirty days, as is the Taft-Hartley requirement in other industries), provided that the state law permits union security provisions. Construction union contracts also can require an employer to notify the union of job opportunities and to give the union an opportunity to refer qualified applicants for employment, and can specify minimum training or experience qualifications for employment. The net effect of these provisions is probably to restore a considerable amount of legality to practice in the construction industry.

In the maritime industry the Taft-Hartley restrictions on the closed shop caused considerable litigation in so far as the hiring hall was affected. The hiring hall is an employment office, usually financed by employers and a union, but frequently controlled by the union, to which men off work from ships or docks report and are assigned to jobs as work opens up in these industries. The purpose of the hiring hall system is to "decasualize" the work. It is frankly aimed to give first choice of work to regular employees (who are nearly always union members) and to give only extra employment to stragglers or newcomers. In the absence of such a system, or one devised on similar principles, the docks and ships give a little work to a lot of people, and job selling and racketeering flourish as workers are taken advantage of in their anxiety to work.

Of course, the hiring hall can result in favoritism and unfair dealing, too, although it is generally conceded that it is a preferable system to an unregulated, casual maritime labor market. The question which the parties, the NLRB, and the courts had to decide was whether the closed shop ban of the Taft-Hartley Act in effect also banned hiring halls.

The NLRB ruled that hiring halls could not confine applicants and referrals to union members, that employers must retain the right to reject applicants referred by union-run hiring halls, and that notices had to be conspicuously posted in hiring halls containing these and similar provisions designed to assure nondiscrimination against those not union members.[12] Where these safeguards were not included, the NLRB held that a hiring hall violated the closed shop proscription in the Act.

The Supreme Court, however, interpreted the law more liberally for the hiring hall protagonists. It ruled, in effect, that hiring halls will be found discriminatory, and therefore illegal, "only upon proof of actual discrimination in its application, and not upon the basis of any per se doctrine."[13] This is the same rule applied to other closed shop situations. It requires a complaint by an individual, a union, or a company, followed by proof that the discrimination (i.e., closed shop condition) did take place. As in the case of the closed shop the overt rules of the hiring hall have changed, but the practice today does not materially differ from the practice of the pre-Taft-Hartley period. So long as a union or an employer does not obviously discriminate against a job applicant in some provable manner, the closed shop and the hiring hall are difficult to attack under the Act, and will remain so.

Union Shop Polls and Deauthorizations

Union shop and maintenance-of-membership provisions were permitted by the Taft-Hartley Act, but initially only after a special vote of the membership, a provision first adopted by Wisconsin and Colorado, and copied by the framers of the Taft-Hartley Act. Expressions by witnesses before Congressional Committees and by members of Con-

[12] The pertinent NLRB and court cases are discussed by Stuart Rothman, then General Counsel of the NLRB, in "The Development and Current Status of the Law Pertaining to Hiring Hall Arrangements," *Virginia Law Review,* Vol. XLVIII (June, 1962), pp. 871–82.

[13] *Ibid.,* pp. 875–76, commenting upon *Local 337, Teamsters' Union* v. *National Labor Relations Board,* 365 U.S. 667 (1961).

gress in debate indicated that there was a belief that employees would reject compulsory unionism. The opposite proved to be the case, however, with over 75 per cent of the 6,545,001 eligible employees voting for the union shop and authorizing negotiations for it in 97 per cent of the cases.[14] The net effect was twofold—a bipartisan movement to repeal this voting requirement, which was accomplished by the Taft-Humphrey amendments of 1951; and a general spread of union shop agreements throughout industry. Companies such as General Motors and United States Steel, which had accepted maintenance-of-membership provisions only under National War Labor Board compulsion, now agreed to the union shop after their employees had voted in favor of it.

The Taft-Humphrey amendments, which permit negotiations for union shop and maintenance of membership without prior special vote, retained the ban on the closed shop and preferential hiring (later modified by the Landrum-Griffin construction amendments), and also retained the little-known and little-utilized union shop deauthorization poll. This is conducted by the NLRB if 30 per cent of the employees in a bargaining unit petition to rescind the union's authority to make union security agreements. If a majority of these employees vote to rescind the authority in a deauthorization election, it becomes illegal for the parties to negotiate a union security contract for one year.

Deauthorization elections have been relatively uncommon. One study of the period from 1947 to 1958 indicates that there were only 89 deauthorization elections conducted, involving 9,067 eligible voters.[15] Except in one year the majority of deauthorization polls conducted resulted in rescission of the union shop.[16] In the fiscal year 1961 a total of 51 requests for union shop deauthorization polls were filed with the Board, up 28 per cent from the previous year,[17] but whether this is significant is doubtful. Employees who are unhappy with unions are more likely to decertify them altogether than to deauthorize their right to negotiate for compulsory union membership.

Nevertheless, the right of employees to rescind the union shop requirement is probably a worth-while escape clause, the presence of which tends to keep union business agents alert to the needs of their members. Since the AFL–CIO merger and the resultant no-raiding

[14] An analysis of these votes is presented later in this chapter. Data from *Monthly Labor Review,* Vol. LXXVI (August, 1953), p. 837.

[15] C. A. Morgan, "The Union Shop Deauthorization Poll," *Industrial and Labor Relations Review,* Vol. XII (October, 1958), p. 84.

[16] *Ibid.,* p. 80.

[17] National Labor Relations Board, *Twenty-sixth Annual Report* (Washington, D.C.: U.S. Government Printing Office, 1962), p. 6.

agreement have largely eliminated active rivalry between unions for employee loyalty, it is important that an employee have this alternative to continued membership in a union without jeopardizing his job status, if the union leadership fails to represent its membership satisfactorily.

Railway Labor Act Union Shop Amendments

In the same year that Congress rescinded the union shop election poll, it further advanced the cause of the union shop by amending the Railway Labor Act to permit its negotiation in the railway and air-line industries, where it quickly spread following these 1951 amendments to this law. The Railway Labor Act's union security provisions have no provision for deauthorization. Moreover, they follow the traditional policy of railway labor legislation by overtly favoring the so-called "standard" railway labor organizations.[18] To accommodate the situation where an employee may join the locomotive firemen's or the trainmen's unions, and remain a member thereof after being promoted to engineer or conductor, the Railway Labor Act now provides that membership in any union "national in scope" in these crafts must be deemed to meet the requirements of a compulsory membership provision. Since "national in scope" has been defined to include the standard railway unions, this has meant that membership in some unions who are not bargaining agents for a craft may be maintained as a condition of employment in place of membership in the union which is the bargaining agent; but membership in other unions which are not bargaining agents for the craft cannot be so substituted for membership in the bargaining agent union.[19]

In two other respects, the Railway Labor Act provisions parallel those of the Taft-Hartley Act. In both, the closed shop is forbidden; and in both, nonpayment of regular fees and dues is the only ground for discharge as a result of expulsion from the union.

Finally, it is noteworthy that Congress voted to permit the railway unions to bargain for compulsory unionism despite the record before it showing that several of these unions deny Negroes equal membership rights.

Union Security and the National Wage Stabilization Board

The Taft-Hartley union shop elections occurred just prior to and during the Korean War Period. Having received authorization to

[18] For a discussion of the Railway Labor Act, and of this point, see Chapter 12.

[19] For an analysis of these Railway Labor Act provisions in practice, see D. M. Levinson, "Union Shop under the Railway Labor Act," *Labor Law Journal,* Vol. VI (July, 1955), pp. 462–82, 494.

negotiate such provisions from the membership, unions were in a strong position to demand them in collective bargaining and in cases brought before the National Wage Stabilization Board, a tripartite agency established initially to control wages, and later given authority over labor disputes by Presidential executive order. With industry members dissenting, the NWSB usually agreed with the union case, basing its rationale strongly on the Taft-Hartley votes.[20]

THE STATES AND RIGHT-TO-WORK LAWS

In the long run, the most significant provision of Taft-Hartley relating to union security is probably Section 14 (*b*), which provides that "Nothing in this Act shall be construed as authorizing the execution or application of agreements requiring membership in a labor organization as a condition of employment in any State or Territory in which such execution or application is prohibited by State or Territorial Law." This provision ran counter to the usual principle that state laws are superseded by federal legislation on the same subject matter. The Taft-Hartley Act not only applied the state law but declared further that the state law should apply to employers engaged in interstate commerce, as well as those whose business was purely local.

Thus the clear purpose of Section 14 (*b*) was to give states the right to legislate in this field, and many did, outlawing union security provisions altogether. Twenty states now prohibit such agreements;[21] and a twenty-first, Louisiana, which once had such legislation, repealed it, except in so far as it applies to agriculture. Three other states have repealed statutes of this nature which were in effect for a short period,[22] while others[23] have defeated attempts to enact "right-to-work" laws. In short, the big political battle over union security is now at the state level, with opponents largely successful in the more rural states, the proponents having a clear edge in all big industrial states except Indiana, and the issue is still very much alive in a number of states.[24] The significance of the right-to-work issue will be discussed in the general analysis of the issue below.[25]

[20] Sultan, *op. cit.*, pp. 54–55.

[21] Alabama, Arizona, Arkansas, Florida, Georgia, Indiana, Iowa, Kansas, Mississippi, Nebraska, Nevada, North Carolina, North Dakota, South Carolina, South Dakota, Tennessee, Texas, Utah, Virginia, and Wyoming.

[22] Delaware, Maine, and New Hampshire.

[23] California, Colorado, Massachusetts, Ohio, Oklahoma, and Washington.

[24] For example, in Oklahoma, the issue was a factor in the 1962 gubernatorial race.

[25] See pages 229 ff.

The Agency Shop

Some unions have sought to circumvent this prohibition by securing so-called "agency shop" agreements with employers. Under the agency shop (see Table 4, page 213), an employee does not have to join the union as a condition of employment, but he must pay it a fee—usually equivalent to the amount of union dues—for acting as his bargaining agent. Failure to pay the fee is a dismissal offense under the contract.

Should agency contracts of this nature be lawful? Of the twenty right-to-work laws, all but one outlaw the agency shop, either by the language of the law or by court or state attorney general opinions. In Indiana a state court has held that the state right-to-work law does not prohibit the agency shop.[26] In a recent case involving a plant in Indiana, General Motors Corporation refused to execute an agency shop agreement on the ground that it was an unlawful form of union security under the Taft-Hartley Act. The National Labor Relations Board agreed with General Motors in a decision handed down in February, 1961, and then reversed itself in September of the same year after two new appointments were made to the Board by President Kennedy. Subsequently, on appeal to the United States Court of Appeals for the Sixth Circuit, the Court held that the agency shop is not a form of union security lawfully permitted under the National Labor Relations Act and therefore was not a mandatory subject of collective bargaining.[27] Then, in June, 1963, the Supreme Court reversed the Court of Appeals. Agency shop contracts are therefore mandatory bargaining subjects.

The agency shop is, of course, a rather questionable device, since it is taxation without representation. Unions counter this argument by saying that those who receive services should pay for them. To force people who refuse to join to support an organization does not, however, seem like a sound way to obtain their moral support, so necessary in a crisis.

Union Label Approach

Another approach to surmount state right-to-work laws is the provision in the contract between the Byer-Rolnick Hat Corporation of Texas and the United Hatters, Cap, and Millinery Workers. It grants

[26] *Meade Electric Co.* v. *Hagberg,* Indiana Superior Court, Lake County, May 19, 1958; affirmed, Indiana Court of Appeals, June 19, 1959.

[27] *General Motors Corp.* v. *National Labor Relations Board,* 303 F. (2d) 428 (1962); reversed, U.S. Supreme Court, June 3, 1963.

the union label to the company only if 97 per cent of those eligible become union members. This union has advertised "union-made" hats, and the company admits that "naturally we will be interested in workers joining the union, but it will not be mandatory."[28] Not many unions are in a position to offer this inducement to counteract compulsory membership prohibitions.

Other State Union Security Restrictions

Besides the states which prohibit union security altogether, a number prescribe conditions which must be met before such a provision can be negotiated. Wisconsin initially required a three-fourths majority of those voting in a special election before a union security clause could be negotiated, and now requires only a two-thirds majority. Hawaii had a similar provision, but now requires only a simple majority. Colorado has maintained its three-fourths majority requirement. Massachusetts prohibits the application of compulsory membership provisions to employees who are not eligible for full union membership and full voting rights in the union; Colorado and Wisconsin provide that a union which is a party to a union security provision must not "unreasonably" refuse to accept as a member any employee covered by the contract; Pennsylvania makes it an unfair labor practice for an employer to enter into a union security contract with a union which excludes workers from membership because of race, color, creed, or political affiliation; and the states which have enacted fair employment practice laws,[29] of course, ban such discrimination. Oregon has a deauthorization procedure similar to the Taft-Hartley provision.

Recently, the General Counsel of the National Labor Relations Board has initiated a test case to determine whether these state restrictions short of an outright ban on union security are valid.[30] If the courts rule that the federal government has pre-empted the regulation of union security agreements when such agreements are *not* banned by state law, then, to regulate them, a state must ban them entirely—a seemingly anomalous situation.

THE REAL RIGHT-TO-WORK ISSUES

In a very real sense, no one has a constitutional or even moral right to work at a particular job or business. What is at stake is the extent to

[28] *Business Week,* June 3, 1961, p. 103.

[29] See Chapter 9, pages 247–49, for a discussion of these laws.

[30] *Matter of Hribar Trucking Co.,* NLRB Press Release R–889, September 30, 1962.

which an organization endowed with authority by Congress or state legislatures should also be permitted to exert coercive power to require contributions to its maintenance and well-being, and the extent to which such an organization should be permitted to determine whether workers, otherwise employable, should be denied or be forced out of work.

From these, several corollary questions flow, relating (1) to the extent that such coercive power should be limited either directly through limits on that power itself, or indirectly through restraints on the conduct of the organization wielding the power; and (2) to the extent to which the union security issue represents a real or an emotional power issue in the field of union-management relations.

Power over Members

That the union security issue is concerned with union coercive power over its members seems undeniable. Power over the membership involves, of course, the right of a union to fine, to discipline, or to effectuate the discharge of a member for violation of union rules or conduct, or for the completely indefensible reasons of opposing, antagonizing, or otherwise offending union leadership. Students of labor relations have always recognized that a union must have some authority over its members, particularly when a majority has taken a legitimate position in favor of a legitimate objective. Otherwise, anarchy in industrial relations could result. For example, few disagree with the right of a majority to accept a settlement offered by an employer, or to reject the settlement and to choose a strike. But should a union have the power to fine or to discipline a member who crosses a picket line, returns to work during a strike, and thus makes the achievement of the strike goal more difficult for the majority? Questions like this involve complex moral and economic issues which each citizen may answer differently, and which the legislatures and the courts likewise find difficult to determine.

Historically, the courts have regarded unions as voluntary organizations, into the affairs of which they have preferred not to tread.[31] A worker expelled from a union, and in consequence deprived of the opportunity to work where he might otherwise be employed, could expect little relief from the courts. Even in the few cases in which the courts might be disposed to question the action of the union, they were inclined to insist that the complaining member (or ex-member) first

[31] For a good discussion of the course of judicial action in this regard, upon which this section is based, see Joseph R. Grodin, "Legal Regulation of Internal Union Affairs," in J. Shister, B. Aaron, and C. W. Summers (eds.), *Public Policy and Collective Bargaining*, Industrial Relations Research Association Publication No. 27 (New York: Harper and Row, 1962), pp. 182–211.

exhaust his internal or administrative remedies. This could mean following union constitutional requirements for appeal from the action of the local union to an intermediate body, thence to the national executive board, and finally to the union convention, which might not meet for two to four years. A long-drawn-out procedure such as this, with the complainant out of work, was, and often still is, an effective bar against seeking judicial remedy.

After unions were clothed by law with the right to act as exclusive bargaining agent for employees if certified as the representative of the majority by a governmental agency, and, as a result of such governmental assistance, grew in numbers, influence, and power, the courts began to question and to qualify their noninterference principles. The United States Supreme Court ruled that a union which has been duly certified as a bargaining representative by a government agency must represent all workers in the bargaining unit without discrimination, or be subject "to the usual judicial remedies of injunction and award of damages when appropriate for breach of that duty."[32]

The Supreme Court of California has ruled that a closed union and a closed shop are incompatible—the union may have one, but not both, and thus may not effectively bar a man from work with the combination.[33] The Supreme Court of Kansas has held that discriminatory union practices combined with exclusive bargaining rights under the Railway Labor Act violate the Fifth Amendment.[34]

A most significant recent case has been the ruling of the United States Supreme Court which restricted the use of union funds obtained from dues pursuant to a union shop contract under the Railway Labor Act.[35] The Court ruled such dues money could not be used to support political candidates if the individual objected. Although it is difficult to set up standards to determine whether union funds are used for union or political purposes, this decision does mark a further step in the judicial protection of the union member and his rights in relation to the union under compulsory union conditions.

Of special importance to the right-to-work issue is the ruling of a California appeals court ordering the International Association of Machinists to reinstate two former members who had been expelled for "conduct unbecoming a member." The "conduct" involved was, as the

[32] *Steele* v. *Louisville & Nashville Railroad Co.,* 323 U.S. 192, 65 S. Ct. 226, (1944).

[33] *James* v. *Marinship,* 155 P. (2d) 329 (1945).

[34] *Betts* v. *Easley,* 169 P. (2d) 831 (1946).

[35] *International Association of Machinists* v. *Street,* 108 S.E. (2d) 796 (Ga. 1959); affirmed, U.S. Supreme Court, 48 LRRM 2345 (1961).

court described it, their "peaceful, open, public, active and vigorous campaign and support" in behalf of a measure for a right-to-work law in California.[36]

Other courts have restrained union disciplinary and expulsion policies. But judicial restraint of either union administration or union expulsion policies without statutory regulation has been neither certain nor common in most jurisdictions.[37] Hence the Congress and the state legislatures have tended to move into this field of regulation—either by a "Bill of Rights" guarantee, such as is contained in the Landrum-Griffin Act, or by limiting or controlling union security provisions. The latter approach stems from the obvious reason that union security provisions give the union leadership greatly added power over their members.

Power in Union-Management Relations

From a strictly union-management relations viewpoint, how much substance is there to the union security issue? Despite the heat of controversy surrounding this vexing issue, it seems more of a symbol or a sham to many observers. The proponents of individual freedom—of "right to work"—are business managers who want no interference with their right to hire and fire. The opponents of "right to work" are union officials who base their reason to exist on the democracy which their organizations bring to the work force, but who also want the right to coerce people into forced membership and forced dues payment. Proponents of right-to-work laws are usually opposed to laws outlawing discrimination because of race, color, or creed. Opponents of right-to-work laws usually favor such fair employment practice restrictions. The irony of this situation is further compounded by the fact that in only one industrial state—Indiana—is compulsory unionism forbidden. The other nineteen states outlawing union security are all heavily weighted by the rural vote. Where unions are the weakest, right-to-work laws have been most easily enacted. In industrial states, such as California, Ohio, and Massachusetts, the voters have rejected such legislation by overwhelming margins.

Studies of right-to-work laws in various states have shown that their direct effects on union strength have not been discernibly sharp. Professor Frederic Meyers found that union growth in Texas was not significantly slowed by the passage of a right-to-work law. On the

[36] *Mitchell* v. *International Association of Machinists,* 49 LRRM 2116 (1962).

[37] For an examination of cases in which the courts declined to interfere decisively in union governmental questions of this character, see Grodin, *loc. cit.;* and Sultan, *op. cit.,* pp. 102–9.

contrary, union membership grew faster in Texas after the law was passed than it did in the country as a whole because the rate of industrialization was more rapid in Texas than in the country as a whole.[38] In Virginia a study found that the right-to-work law forced union security provisions "underground." This author emphasized that although union security requirements disappeared from union contracts, "the practices formerly set forth openly in such documents continue."[39]

Professor Fred Witney adds to the evidence in favor of this viewpoint by noting that the Indiana right-to-work law did not result in mass union membership resignations or any observable changes in the union-management relationship.[40] Moreover, he reported that when faced with a deal to repeal the right-to-work law on condition that it support a state law of the Landrum-Griffin type, the Indiana AFL–CIO declined with the comment that such reform legislation "could probably be much more effective in destroying the Indiana labor movement than the present compulsory Open Shop Law."[41]

On evidence such as these studies present, Professor Meyers concludes a major study of right-to-work controversies with the statement that " 'right to work' proposals are of much less importance than either side to the controversy has been willing to admit. The issue is a symbolic one. What is at stake is the political power and public support of management and unionism."[42]

If this view is correct, many managers of businesses and labor union officials are spending a great deal of time, money, and energy battling windmills. When right-to-work proposals were before the voters of five states in 1958, the Chamber of Commerce of the United States estimated that unions spent $70 million to attempt to defeat them, and proponents spent $2 million in their support. The Teamsters alone spent $800,000.[43] Were these foolish expenditures on the part of hardheaded businessmen and tough-minded labor officials?

There is, first of all, no doubt that unions are correct in noting that

[38] See Frederic Meyers, "The Growth of Collective Bargaining in Texas," *Proceedings of Seventh Annual Meeting,* Industrial Relations Research Association (1954), pp. 286–97; and *ibid., "Right to Work" in Practice* (New York: Fund for the Republic, Inc., 1959).

[39] J. M. Kuhlman, "Right to Work Laws: The Virginia Experience," *Labor Law Journal,* Vol. VI (July, 1955), pp. 453–61, 494.

[40] Fred Witney, *Indiana Labor Relations Law,* Bureau of Business Research Report No. 30 (Bloomington: Indiana University, 1960), pp. 81–98.

[41] *Ibid.,* p. 92.

[42] Meyers, *"Right to Work" in Practice,* p. 45.

[43] Quoted by James W. Kuhn, "Right to Work Laws—Symbols or Substance?" *Industrial and Labor Relations Review,* Vol. XIV (July, 1961), p. 588. Professor Kuhn's excellent analysis has contributed much to this discussion.

the passage of a right-to-work law creates an "atmosphere" hostile in some way to unionism. This is true when any union control law is enacted. It marks a public defeat for the prounion forces, and is both a result in itself and a creator of a political atmosphere unfavorable to unionism to some extent, even though such legislation has the support of those who would "reform," not curtail, legitimate unionism. Because of the emotion engendered by right-to-work legislation, the passage of such laws usually both reflects and results initially in strong feelings on questions relating to unions and union-management relations.

But union security restraints limit union power in more direct ways —by reducing control of the leadership over the membership and by reducing the income of the union. The first type of restraint may have an unexpected or perverse effect on union-management relations. Its justification is, as noted in the previous section, based upon the need to improve the chances of fair treatment or civil rights for the union member in the latter's relationship to the organization and its leaders. Such improved democracy may not redound to management's advantage. The more democratic an organization is, the more factional conflict there is likely to be within it. Such conflict has the advantage of keeping the leadership sensitive to membership opinion. But a democratic union is also more easily infiltrated by Communists and other groups who are experienced factionalists. Factionalism may weaken a union in its dealings with employers. But factionalism can also increase industrial strife because of the fear of union leaders to agree to a bargain that is subject to criticism by rivals.

Probably the average employer does not want too much democracy in a union. Most employers want agreements with union leaders to stick, and not be overturned by the rank and file. To the extent that right-to-work laws reduce leadership control over the rank and file, they can boomerang against management in this respect.

On the other hand, if management attempts to influence the rank and file directly by communication, then a democratic union is essential for the success of such efforts. Otherwise, the rank and file, if persuaded by management's communications, cannot exert influence on union leadership. General Electric Company, the leading exponent of direct communication to its employees, is an avowed exponent of both union reform (Landrum-Griffin type) and right-to-work laws.

Effect on Union Membership

Perhaps the basic question in determining whether the union security issue is a real or a symbolic one in union-management relations is whether the absence of compulsory unionism reduces union membership and income sufficiently to make a difference in the relationship of unions and companies. Both proponents and opponents of right-to-work laws believe that this is the case. There is certainly no proof that this is true. The preponderant evidence, however, indicates that their reasoning is based upon fact, not fancy.

In the first place, unions need income to conduct their operations, and the main source of union income is dues. Automation, industry dispersion, and other factors in recent years have had an adverse effect on union membership in steel, automobiles, rubber, and electrical products. Unions in these industries have been forced to curtail programs, lay off representatives, and reduce organizing efforts because of the reduced income from a declining membership. Lack of funds in union treasuries to pursue goals designed to organize new shops or to educate members to the union point of view or to pay strike benefits can certainly be a factor in relative union-management power. Moreover, requests to the membership to increase dues in order to offset loss of income from a declining membership put union officials in an unpopular position, and this too can reduce union bargaining power.

What, then, is the effect of compulsory membership provisions on union membership and hence on union power? Although the proved data are sparse, the following facts appear accurate:

1. In the absence of compulsory membership provisions, a substantial percentage of American workers will not join unions.
2. Union security provisions thus add significantly to union membership and dues.
3. Once workers join unions, they tend to remain members even absent union security provisions.
4. Unions which control hiring through a closed shop appear able to maintain such arrangements despite legal proscriptions.
5. The absence of a compulsory membership provision in 1963 may well be more significant to unions than it was in 1950.

American workers, as befits their individualistic heritage, have less class solidarity and are less likely to join unions than their counterparts in most other democratic countries. This is, of course, a prime reason for the existence of the union shop controversy. If workers would join willingly, the Wagner Act, outlawing employer opposition to union membership, would have ended the controversy. For example, when Chrysler and General Motors gave a modified union shop in 1950, it added 50,000 workers—5 per cent of the union's total membership—to the rolls of the United Automobile Workers.[44] Yet, by then the

[44] Kuhn, *op. cit.*, p. 589.

union had been bargaining agent for employees in these companies for a dozen years.

The union shop elections conducted under Taft-Hartley provisions between 1947 and 1951 are generally cited as proof that worker support for compulsory unionism is overwhelming. The union shop was authorized in 97 per cent of the 46,146 elections, and about 92 per cent of those voting favored the union shop. In addition, state elections on the same issue have also resulted in impressive support for the union shop.[45]

Certainly, these elections were decisively won by union shop proponents. But the issue is by no means so clear as it seems—for again, if it were, the need for unions to press compulsory unionism would not exist. In the first place, as many careful observers have noted,[46] the unions made the issue support of unions; and in the absence of any employer communications to the contrary, many workers thought they were voting for unions, rather than just for the union shop. More important perhaps, as Professor James W. Kuhn has emphasized, the majorities were not as impressive as the 90 per cent figure seems. The rules provided that a union had to win a majority of those in the unit in order to win, not a majority of those voting. The unions publicized this fact and made strenuous efforts to get out the vote, but 15 per cent of the 6,545,000 did not vote, in addition to the 8 per cent who voted "No." A minority of about 23 per cent is a substantial number of members (and dues)—enough to affect a power balance, to pay the costs of a lot of strike benefits, or to employ a squad of union organizers.

Table 5 shows the results of the Taft-Hartley union shop vote in

[45] In New Hampshire, between 1947 and 1949, pursuant to that state's short-lived Willey Act, only two elections opposed the union shop in all of the state's most important industries. About 90 per cent of the workers eligible voted, and 95 per cent of these favored the union shop (J. A. Hogan, "The Meaning of Union Shop Elections," *Industrial and Labor Relations Review,* Vol. II [April, 1949], pp. 322–23).

In Colorado, between 1945 and 1960, unions won 314 elections for the union shop and lost 33, a majority of 90.5 per cent in a state where a three-fourths majority is required to authorize the union shop. (See H. Seligson and George E. Bardwell, *Labor-Management Relations in Colorado* [Denver: Sage Books, Alan Swallow, Publisher, 1961], p. 147).

In Wisconsin, where until recently a three-fourths majority was also required (now it is two thirds), unions won approval of the union shop in 2,498 cases out of a total of 2,956 between 1939 and 1960, an 85 per cent record (data from reports of the Wisconsin Employment Relations Board).

In Kansas, between the enactment of the law in 1955 and its replacement by a right-to-work provision in 1958, the union shop won in 34 out of 37 cases, or a 92 per cent record (Kansas Department of Labor, *Biennial Report* [Topeka, 1960], p. 21).

[46] Hogan, *op. cit.,* pp. 324 ff.; and S. Cohen, "Union Shop Polls: A Solution to the Right to Work Issues," *Industrial and Labor Relations Review,* Vol. XI (January, 1959), p. 254.

TABLE 5

PER CENT OF ELIGIBLE WORKERS VOTING "NO" OR NOT VOTING IN NLRB-CONDUCTED UNION SHOP ELECTIONS 1947–51

	Voted "No"	Did Not Vote	Sum of "No" and No Vote
Total NLRB elections	7.6	15.2	22.8
Small plants, 1948–49*	5.1	12.0	17.1
Large plants, 1950–51*	12.1	18.6	30.7
General Motors	7.0	13.3	20.3
Ford	1.2	7.5	8.7
Boeing Aircraft	11.6	24.2	35.8
Curtis-Wright	8.7	5.6	14.3
Local 131, UAW	7.1	7.8	14.9
Local 644, UAW	9.5	4.1	13.6
162 steel plants	14.2	19.6	33.8

* The break between "large" and "small" is defined as one thousand workers.

SOURCE: Calculated from various sources by James W. Kuhn, "Right to Work Laws—Symbols or Substance?" *Industrial and Labor Relations Review*, Vol. XIV (July, 1961), p. 592.

specific areas. The relatively high "No" and "No Vote" percentages in steel plants, at Boeing, and in "large plants" emphasize the point that although unions did indeed win the votes, they find union security provisions a valuable asset in enrolling a substantial number of members who are otherwise not easily enrolled. The size of this figure is not known, but in some cases, it may range as high as 40 per cent[47]—Professor Kuhn believes it would average between 6 and 25 per cent.[48]

Table 5 also illustrates the fact that workers "get used" to compulsory unionism. The highest vote for union security set forth there is at Ford, where the union shop was in effect nearly a decade before the vote was taken. When maintenance of membership is in effect with an escape period, the number of escapees has always been small.[49] This is also undoubtedly why Professor Witney found that the Indiana law had so little immediate effect on union membership. There was no rush to resign from unions.[50]

The fact that workers get used to belonging to unions under compulsory unionism is, from the union point of view, a sound reason for desiring union security. When it is removed, as it was in Indiana, the threat to union membership rolls is not immediate, but rather in the future. If right-to-work advocates are correct, new employees will be the problem for union recruiters. A follow-up study on Indiana in 1968—

[47] See the discussion of the Aerospace cases, below, pages 238–41.

[48] *Op. cit.*, p. 5.

[49] *Ibid.*, p. 591. This conclusion is in line with the writers' experiences.

[50] Witney, *op. cit.*, pp. 88–89.

ten years after that state's right-to-work law was enacted—may well show that it has cost the unions there a substantial loss of membership and dues from the new entrants to the labor market.[51]

The study of the Virginia law[52] which reached the conclusion that the right-to-work law's principal effect was to drive union security underground does not change this analysis because its examples primarily involved the building trades and the closed shop. The Taft-Hartley Act's attempt to outlaw the closed shop has, as already been noted, had this effect, and Congress recognized the problem at least in so far as the building trades are concerned. A spot check of manufacturing enterprises in Virginia by one of the authors between 1960 and 1962 revealed no union plant with a membership estimated in excess of 85 per cent, and many between 50 and 65 per cent. The outlawing of union security in Virginia appeared to have a substantial effect in industrial plants. But it is most likely that in Virginia, and in other states with right-to-work laws, the under-the-table closed shop remains a significant factor because of the union's ability to control hiring by control of the skilled personnel. Since the number of workers involved in closed-shop conditions is small as compared with those in all manufacturing where the closed shop is largely inapplicable, the right-to-work laws seem very real issues in the union-management relationship, however symbolic they may also be.

THE AEROSPACE DISPUTE OF 1962

Fresh evidence of the pervasiveness of the union security dispute, as well as some unexpected developments pertaining to it, occurred in 1962 in the cases affecting the aerospace industry and the International Association of Machinists and the United Automobile Workers. The West Coast sector of this industry is one of the few large industrial groups which have declined to grant union security beyond the maintenance-of-membership provisions originally ordered by the National War Labor Board during World War II. With a friendly administration in Washington, the unions decided that 1962 was the year to push for the union shop. Moreover, their desire to attain the complete union shop was furthered by the rapid expansion and high turnover which have featured the industry.

The Kennedy administration succeeded in getting the parties to

[51] To the extent that the agency shop spreads in Indiana, the net effect of the law will be lessened.

[52] Kuhlman, *op. cit.*

agree on the appointment of a special fact-finding board, headed by Dr. George W. Taylor, to make recommendations in the dispute.[53] Before the Taylor board had reported, the Douglas Aircraft Company agreed on an agency shop contract, but the other companies declined to move beyond maintenance of membership.

To settle the case, the Taylor board proposed a vote conducted by the National Labor Relations Board, with a proviso that the union shop would become effective if the employees voted by a two-thirds majority in favor of it. North American Aviation, Convair Division of General Dynamics Corporation, and Ryan Aeronautical agreed to the vote only after intense pressure by President Kennedy.[54] Lockheed Aircraft refused to accept the recommendation to put the issue to a vote.[55]

The votes proved to be quite shocking to the unions, for in none of the three companies did two thirds of the employees vote for a union shop, and in Convair a majority of those in the unit did not even favor it. At Ryan Aeronautical the union did not win the union shop vote, even though it had an 85 per cent membership of the unit. (See Table 6.)

Does this mean that employees are less likely to vote for the union shop today than they were in the early 1950's? The answer seems to be a qualified yes. There were several special conditions in the aerospace case. First of all, communication by the employers and others in the communities clearly showed that the companies would yield to the union shop only under the intense governmental pressure which was being exerted by President Kennedy and members of his administration. In the second place, the unions had been praised by Kennedy and others for "accepting a smaller increase." This left the feeling on the part of some of the employees that their wages had been traded for an opportunity to expand union treasuries. Third, the high turnover in the industry, resulting from dynamic changes in technology, cancellation and awarding of government contracts, and rapid expansion to meet the accelerated missile program, have made it difficult for the unions to enroll new employees.

Of general significance, however, is the fact that the employees in

[53] An analysis of the use of such *ad hoc* boards will be found in Chapters 14 and 15, below.

[54] In his press conference of September 11, 1962, President Kennedy publicly stated that if the companies failed to agree to the Taylor board recommendations, they would bear responsibility for any stoppage which occurred.

[55] The President later invoked the emergency provisions of the Taft-Hartley Act in the Lockheed case. Before the last offer vote occurred, the International Association of Machinists agreed to a contract without the union shop, believing apparently that the employees would back the company's position. See Chapter 14, pp. 362–65.

TABLE 6

AEROSPACE UNION SHOP VOTES, 1962

Company	Eligible Employees	Per Cent of Union Members	Number Voting	Number for Union Shop	Number against Union Shop	Per Cent Voting for Union Shop	Per Cent Voting against Union Shop	**Per Cent of Total Employed Voting for Union Shop**
North American Aviation	35,029	62	32,131	19,232	12,899	59.8	40.2	**54.8**
Convair Division, General Dynamics	19,392	55	17,080	9,268	7,822	54.2	45.8	**47.8**
Ryan Aeronautical	1,459	85	1,377	833	544	60.5	39.5	**57.5**

SOURCE: *Business Week*, November 10, 1962, p. 144.

the aerospace industry are a young group without a heritage of union experience or interest. To the extent that these employees are typical of employees of the future in new industries, it seems likely that prounion sentiment will be less among new entrants to the labor force, and that therefore the absence of a union shop will be a more serious problem for unions in the future than it was a dozen years ago.

This analysis is not altered by the events which took place at Boeing Aircraft after these aerospace votes. There, a second extralegal panel, headed by Saul Wallen, a well-known arbitrator, "changed the rules" of the vote procedure. The vote was held *prior* to the settlement of other issues; and the union, the International Association of Machinists, campaigned for a vote in favor of the union shop on the ground that an affirmative vote was necessary to obtain a good contract. The IAM went so far as to declare that it would cost each employee $500 if a substantial union shop majority was not obtained. The employees voted in favor of the union shop by a 73.8 per cent majority. The Boeing company refused to accept the results as an indication of the real sentiments of the employees on the union shop issue alone, the panel issued a report castigating the company for its position (which it has maintained for many years), and the dispute was later settled without the union shop.

The union security dispute is thus still very much alive and is capable of unexpected developments. The belief on the part of unions that they have had the battle won from their point of view is, at best, premature. One may expect right-to-work laws to be adopted in a few other states from time to time, and one may also expect that unions will have great difficulty in repealing any such laws now in existence. If anything, it is likely that the American people will become less tolerant of compulsory unionism in the future than they are today.

QUESTIONS FOR DISCUSSION

1. What are the arguments, pro or con, which might be used in a political campaign waged in your state to enact or to prevent repeal of a right-to-work law?
2. Do right-to-work laws guarantee anyone a right to work; and if so, under what conditions? Do such laws really weaken unions? If so, how? If not, why not?
3. President Kennedy has appointed boards which have conducted votes on the union shop issue in a number of aerospace plants. Do you think it would be wise to have this issue determined in this manner? In explaining your answer, analyze the aerospace votes referred to in this chapter and those conducted by the National Labor Relations Board before 1951, and explain their significance.

SUGGESTIONS FOR FURTHER READING

KUHN, JAMES W. "Right to Work Laws—Symbols or Substance?" *Industrial and Labor Relations Review,* Vol. XIV (July, 1961), pp. 587–94.

A realistic and incisive analysis of the basic issues in the right-to-work controversy.

MEYERS, FREDERIC. *"Right to Work" in Practice.* New York: Fund for the Republic, Inc., 1959.

An analysis of the right-to-work issues developed in the state controversies, with emphasis on the emotional impacts and arguments.

SULTAN, PAUL E. "The Union Security Issue," in J. SHISTER, B. AARON, and C. W. SUMMERS (eds.), *Public Policy and Collective Bargaining.* pp. 182–211. Industrial Relations Research Association Publication No. 27. New York: Harper and Row, 1962.

An excellent summary and review of the facts and issues involved in union security and right-to-work debates.

Chapter 9 STATE LABOR RELATIONS ACTS AND CONTROLS

Modern state labor relations legislation dates from the 1930's after federal legislation in the field was held to be consistent with the Constitution. In 1937, the year in which the Supreme Court sanctioned the Wagner Act, Massachusetts, New York, Pennsylvania, Utah, and Wisconsin adopted legislation patterned on the Wagner Act.

In 1939, however, the Pennsylvania and Wisconsin laws were amended to incorporate restrictions on employers and unions, as well as on employees, thus foreshadowing the Taft-Hartley Act. "Little Taft-Hartley" acts were also adopted by Minnesota and Michigan in 1939, Colorado and Kansas in 1943, Hawaii in 1945, and North Dakota in 1961. In 1947, Utah also converted its law to a Taft-Hartley type, but laws modeled on the Wagner Act were passed by Rhode Island in 1941 and by Connecticut and Puerto Rico in 1945. Oregon passed a labor relations act in 1953, repealed it in 1959, and then in 1961 passed a new labor-management relations act which provides for the selection of bargaining agents and mild restraints against both employers and unions.[1] The Massachusetts Act remains basically a Wagner Act type, although it limits union entrance requirements and union security provisions, as noted in the previous chapter.[2]

Figure 2 shows the states having laws of the Wagner or Taft-Hartley type. In addition to these comprehensive labor relations laws, a number of states have enacted special or limited-purpose laws, some of the Landrum-Griffin type, as well as legislation designed to prevent dis-

[1] There is considerable literature on state labor relations acts upon which we have drawn for this chapter, supplemented by our own research. This includes Charles C. Killingsworth, *State Labor Relations Acts* (Chicago: University of Chicago Press, 1948); Harold A. Katz, "Two Decades of State Labor Legislation: 1937–1957," *Labor Law Journal*, Vol. VIII (November, 1957), pp. 747–67, 818; Illinois Legislative Council, *State Labor Relations Laws*, Publication No. 131 (Springfield, 1958); and U.S. Department of Labor, Bureau of Labor Standards, *State Labor Relations Acts*, Bulletin No. 224 (Washington, D.C.: U.S. Government Printing Office, 1961).

[2] See above, page 229.

crimination because of race, sex, or age. State legislation of both the general and the limited type will be reviewed in this chapter.

FIGURE 2

STATE LABOR RELATIONS ACTS

January, 1963

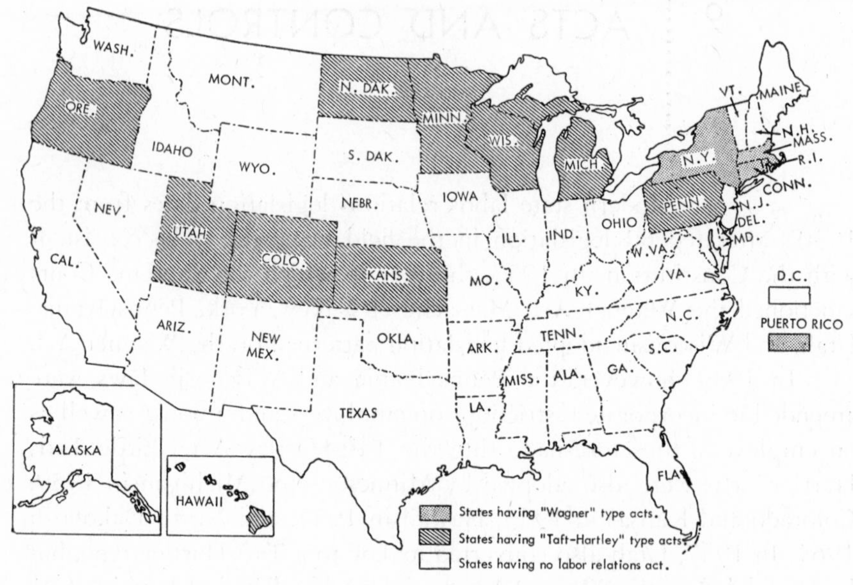

COMPREHENSIVE STATE LABOR RELATIONS LAWS

The comprehensive state laws usually commence with policy statements similar either to that contained in the original Wagner Act or to that of the present Taft-Hartley law. Laws modeled on the latter usually include the right to "refrain from" as well as to join unions.

Jurisdiction

Coverage of the state labor relations acts is limited by (1) the extent of federal pre-emption and (2) restrictions imposed in the state laws. Between the passage of the Taft-Hartley Act in 1947 and the enactment of the Landrum-Griffin Act of 1959, the jurisdiction of state laws was severely limited to intrastate commerce business not within the purview of the Taft-Hartley law. Amendments contained in the Landrum-Griffin Act specifically gave the states jurisdiction over cases which might fall within the Taft-Hartley Act's jurisdiction, but which the National Labor Relations Board declined to accept under its jurisdictional standards of August 1, 1959, as set forth in Table 7. Since only fourteen states and Puerto Rico have labor relations laws, this area left to the states is still under common law in most state jurisdictions.

TABLE 7

REVISED NLRB STANDARDS FOR ASSERTING JURISDICTION, EFFECTIVE AUGUST 1, 1959

Following are the standards which show the volume of business the Board requires before it will exercise its jurisdiction. Eleven categories have been established:

1. *Nonretail.* $50,000 outflow or inflow, direct or indirect.*
2. *Office Buildings.* Gross revenue of $100,000, of which $25,000 or more is derived from organizations which meet any of the standards, exclusive of the indirect inflow standard.
3. *Retail Concerns.* $500,000 gross volume of business.
4. *Instrumentalities, Links, and Channels of Interstate Commerce.* $50,000 from interstate (or linkage) part of enterprise, or from services performed for employers in commerce.
5. *Public Utilities.* $250,000 gross volume, or meet Standard 1 (nonretail).
6. *Transit Systems.* $250,000 gross volume (except taxicabs, to which the retail test [$500,000 gross volume of business] shall apply).
7. *Newspapers and Communication Systems.* Radio, telegraph, television, and telephone, $100,000 gross volume; newspapers, $200,000 gross volume.
8. *National Defense.* Substantial impact on national defense.
9. *Business in the Territories and the District of Columbia.* Plenary in the District of Columbia; standards applicable in the territories.
10. *Associations.* Regarded as single employer.
11. *Hotels and Motels.* $500,000 gross revenue (excluding permanent or residential hotels or motels, i.e., one as to which 75 per cent of its guests remain one month or more).

* Direct outflow refers to goods shipped or services furnished by the employer outside the state. Indirect outflow includes sales within the state to users meeting any standard except solely an indirect inflow or indirect outflow standard. Direct inflow refers to goods or services furnished directly to the employer from outside the state in which the employer is located. Indirect inflow refers to the purchase of goods or srvices which originated outside the employer's state but which he purchased from a seller within a state. Direct and indirect outflow may be combined, and direct and indirect inflow may also be combined to meet the $50,000 requirement. However, outflow and inflow may *not* be combined.

SOURCE: National Labor Relations Board.

Interstate industries covered by state labor relations laws include the fast-growing service trades, many retail and wholesale establishments, and, as will be discussed in Chapter 16, in some states, nonfederal governmental employment. Exemptions from coverage under these laws, as set forth in Table 8, include domestic employees, persons employed by parent or spouse, and various other specific categories.

TABLE 8

EXEMPTIONS EXPRESSLY MENTIONED IN STATE ACTS

Exemption	Colorado	Connecticut	Hawaii	Kansas	Massachusetts	Michigan	Minnesota	New York	North Dakota	Oregon	Pennsylvania	Puerto Rico	Rhode Island	Utah	Wisconsin
State and political subdivisions	X	X	X	...	X	X[1]	X[1]	X	X[1]	X	X	X[2]	X	X	X[1]
Specified charitable, religious, educational, or other non-profit organizations	X[3]	X	...	...	...	...	...	X	X[5]	X	X[4]	...	X	X[5]	...
Federal agencies	...	...	...	...	...	X	...	...	X	X	X	...	...	X	...
Employers of seven or fewer	X	...	X	...	...	...	...	...	...	...	...	...	...	...	...
Employers subject to Railway Labor Act	X	X	...	...	...	X	X	...	X	X	X	...	...	X	...
Employees subject to Railway Labor Act	X	...	X	X	X	X	...	X	X	X	...	...	X	...	X
Employers subject to Labor Management Relations Act	...	X[6]	...	...	...	...	...	...	...	...	...	...	...	...	...
Employees subject to Labor Management Relations Act	...	...	X[6]	...	X[6]	...	...	X	...	...	...	...	X	...	...
Executives and supervisors	X	...	X	...	...	X	...	...	X[8]	X	...	X	...	...	X
Domestic employees	X	X	X	...	X	X	X	X	X	X	X	X	X	X	X
Person employed by parent or spouse	X	X	X	...	X	X	X	X	X	X	X	X	X	X	X
Agricultural employees	X	X	X[7]	...	X	X	X	X	X	X	X	...	X	X	...
Persons employed to replace strikers for duration of dispute	...	X	...	...	...	...	...	X	...	...	...	...	X	...	...
Independent contractors	X	...	X	...	...	...	...	...	X	X	...	...	...	...	X
Labor unions, except when acting as employers	...	X	...	...	X	X	...	...	...	X	X	...	...	X	X

[1] These states provide for a representation and/or bargaining procedure for state and local government employees which is administered in part by the agency administering the state labor relations act.

[2] Corporate instrumentalities of the government of Puerto Rico, as defined, are covered, however.

[3] Charitable private hospitals (*St. Luke's Hospital* v. *Industrial Commission*, 349 P. [2d] 995 [1960]).

[4] Public nonprofit hospitals (*Western Pennsylvania Hospital* v. *Lichliter*, 340 Pa. 382, 17 A. [2d] 206 [1941]) and nonprofit colleges (*Washington and Jefferson College* v. *Clifford*, 55 Dauph. 182 [1944]).

[5] Hospitals only.

[6] Law includes, however, cases where the NLRB has declined to assert jurisdiction.

[7] Only those engaged in the milking and feeding of milk cows.

[8] Also excludes guards.

The number of cases coming before these agencies is not large, nor are the number of employees involved, when compared with the case load of the NLRB and the number of employees affected by NLRB decisions and orders. In any given year the case load of the NLRB, for both representation and unfair labor practice cases, is almost ten times that of all the state agencies combined. In 1959, total NLRB cases were approximately 22,000; state agency cases totaled about 2,600, half of which were New York cases. Moreover, whereas many NLRB cases involve large numbers of employees, the typical state case is a small shop with less than one hundred employees.[3]

EMPLOYER UNFAIR LABOR PRACTICES

As the summary in Table 9 shows, both the "little Wagner" and the "little Taft-Hartley" acts follow the unfair labor practice provisions of the Wagner Act in so far as employer unfair labor practice provisions are concerned. Some include in their proscriptions specific prohibitions against the black list, employer espionage, and other matters which were included within the Wagner Act's general restrictions on restraint of employees for union activity.

On the other hand, the state laws of Minnesota, Michigan, and Oregon do not specifically prohibit the employer from restricting or coercing employees in the exercise of their rights. The Wisconsin, Minnesota, and Colorado statutes limit the protection of workers against unions which could conceivably be found to be company-dominated under the Taft-Hartley regulations, while the Oregon law provides only the slightest protection in this regard—i.e., the Oregon board may order another election if one has not been conducive to free choice.

Most of the state laws permit union security provisions unless—as in Kansas, North Dakota, or Utah—the state has a right-to-work law. As noted in the previous chapter, the acts of Colorado, Hawaii, Massachusetts, Pennsylvania, and Wisconsin require conditions before union security provisions can be negotiated, and Oregon has a deauthorization provision. Except in Massachusetts and Oregon, these conditions are in fact directed against the employer, since he commits an unfair labor practice by signing an illegal compulsory membership agreement or by discharging an employee pursuant thereto. Perhaps this accounts for the fact that only in Wisconsin have there been a significant number of cases brought to hearings under these provisions, but the Wisconsin Supreme Court has ruled that the Wisconsin Employ-

[3] Data from annual reports of state agencies and National Labor Relations Board.

TABLE 9

Principal Unfair Labor Practices Forbidden by State Labor Relations Acts

Prohibited Practice	Colorado	Connecticut	Hawaii	Kansas	Massachusetts	Michigan	Minnesota	New York	North Dakota	Oregon	Pennsylvania	Puerto Rico	Rhode Island	Utah	Wisconsin
For employers:															
Interference	X	X	X	X	X	X	...	X	X	X	X	X	X	X	X
Domination of union	X	X	X	X	X	X	...	X	X	...	X	X	X	X	X
Discrimination for union activity	X	X	X	...	X	X	X	X	X	...	X	X	X	X	X
Discrimination for testifying	X	X	X	X	X	X	X	X	X	...	X	X	X	X	X
Refusal to bargain	X	X	X	...	X	...	...	X	X	...	X	X	X	X	X
Espionage	X	X	X	X	...	...	X	X	...	...	...	...	X	...	X
Black-listing employees	X	X	X	...	...	...	X	X	...	...	...	...	X	...	X
Deducting dues not authorized individually	X	...	X	X	...	...	...	...	...	...	X	...	...	...	X
Breach of contract	X	...	X	...	...	...	X	...	...	...	...	X	...	...	X
Bargaining with minority	...	...	X	...	...	...	...	...	...	...	...	X	...	X	X
Lockout contrary to agreement	...	...	...	...	...	...	X	...	...	...	...	...	...	...	...
Ignoring final determination of tribunal	X	...	X	...	...	...	...	...	...	...	...	...	...	...	X
For employees or unions:															
Secondary boycott	X	...	X	X	...	...	X	...	X	...	X	...	...	X	X
Picketing in minority strike	X	...	X	X	...	...	...	...	...	...	...	...	...	X	X
Coercing employees	X	...	X	X	X	X	X	...	X	X	X	X	...	X	X
Coercing employers to engage in interference	X	...	X	...	...	...	...	...	X	X	...	...	...	X	X
Ignoring final determination of tribunal	X	...	X	...	...	...	...	...	...	...	...	...	...	...	X
Breach of contract	X	...	X	X	...	...	X	...	...	...	...	X	...	...	X
Sit-down strike	X	...	X	X	X	X	X	...	...	...	X	...	...	X	X
Mass or violent picketing	X	...	X	X	...	X	X	...	X	...	...	...	...	X	X
Intimidating employee's or employer's family	X	...	...	X	...	...	X	...	X	...	X	...	...	X	X
Picketing beyond industry	...	...	...	X	...	...	...	...	X	...	...	...	...	...	...
Insistence on hiring stand-by employees	X	...	...	...	...	...	...	...	X	...	...	...	...	...	...
Acting as union agent without license	...	...	...	X	...	...	...	...	...	...	...	...	...	...	...
Forcing union membership	X	...	X	X	X	X	...	X	...	...	X	...	...	...	X
Jurisdictional strike	...	...	...	X	...	...	...	...	...	...	X	...	...	...	X

Source: Compilation by Bureau of National Affairs, Inc., with addenda by authors.

ment Relations Board has no authority to force unions to share in any back-pay award made to an employee discharged under an illegal union security provision. The union may, however, be ordered to cease inducing the employer to enter into an illegal union security agreement.

The Kansas, Michigan, Minnesota, and Oregon statutes make no provision for reinstatement or back pay for any reason, but the courts could conceivably require both as a remedy. These four states also do not require the employer to bargain with the representative of the employees; but here again, courts could presumably order an employer to do so in order to effectuate the purposes of the laws.

UNFAIR LABOR PRACTICES OF EMPLOYEES AND UNIONS

The unfair labor practices in the "little Taft-Hartley" laws which are directed against employees and unions are summarized in Table 9. They may be divided into four categories:

1. Prohibitions of violence and similar activities which were almost universally unlawful before the passage of the labor relations acts—for example, sit-down strikes, sabotage, and mass picketing.
2. Restrictions on peaceful tactics such as picketing and organizing campaigns, especially where coercion is alleged.
3. Limitations on union objectives which make illegal all efforts to achieve a forbidden objective, such as a make-work rule.
4. Regulation of the internal affairs of unions, such as financial matters, election procedure, and eligibility for union office.[4]

Prohibition of Violence

In making violence and other already unlawful acts unfair labor practices, the "little Taft-Hartley" laws provide new procedures and penalties to control such conduct. The laws which are enforced by administrative agencies can be utilized to restrain violence or illegal picketing, or the protection of the law may be withdrawn from unions. This latter is a severe penalty, for it leaves the employer free to commit any and all unfair labor practices against the union, and this amounts to a doctrine that two wrongs make a right. Moreover, in case the same penalty is invoked against the employer, he has little to lose, since he can apply for police protection against activities which were always unlawful. As a matter of fact, however, the withdrawal of the protection of the law is a penalty rarely, if ever, utilized. Restraint by injunction is far more effective. Moreover, these laws have been enacted largely

[4] Killingsworth, *op. cit.*, pp. 42–43.

because of the failure or inability of local law enforcement agencies to cope with law violations during strikes.

Picketing and Boycotts

The second group of state employee unfair labor practices restricts activities such as peaceful picketing, boycotting, and jurisdictional strikes which would otherwise be lawful. As we noted in Chapter 6, the extent to which the states may regulate peaceful picketing in interstate commerce is not clear, although it is certain that some regulation is permissible, provided there is no conflict with the Taft-Hartley Act.

Wisconsin has apparently had at least as much experience with these sections as any other state, and appears to have had fairly good success in enforcing provisions of laws which, as was noted in the discussion of federal statutes,[5] are difficult to construe. The records of the Wisconsin Employment Relations Board contain many decisions dealing with mass picketing, secondary boycotts, violence, etc. The author of a very thorough study of the Wisconsin Act reported that one union official told him that the Wisconsin law's regulation of strike and picketing conduct "allow[s] us to keep a firm hand on our people with the result that violence has been kept down."[6] The same author reported that management representatives were also reasonably satisfied with experience under the Wisconsin legislation, but they felt that action on boycott cases was too slow to be helpful.[7] The experience under the Wisconsin statute was probably in the minds of the drafters of the Taft-Hartley Act when they provided that the NLRB must give prior treatment to and seek an injunction in boycott cases.

Kansas makes it unlawful to strike, picket, boycott, or otherwise engage in concerted activity for the purpose of a jurisdictional strike. Minnesota provides that if, upon due notice, the unions do not cease a jurisdictional strike and determine the issue peacefully, the governor may appoint a referee and force the matter into compulsory arbitration. This provision has never been invoked.[8] A somewhat similar Michigan law has been invoked only rarely.[9] And a section in the Wisconsin law makes it an unfair labor practice for employees "to engage in, pro-

[5] See Chapter 7, above.

[6] Quoted by Justin C. Smith, "Unfair Labor Practices in Wisconsin," *Marquette Law Review*, Vol. XLV (Fall, 1961), p. 250.

[7] *Ibid.*

[8] Based on a study of the reports of the Minnesota Division of Conciliation through 1960.

[9] Benjamin Aaron, "The Mediation of Jurisdictional Disputes," *Labor Law Journal*, Vol. VII (August, 1956), p. 472.

mote, or induce a jurisdictional strike," but no case has reached the decision stage under these provisions.[10] If state prohibitions of jurisdictional disputes have been of any importance, it has been to induce unions to settle such disputes more quickly. It is likely that the Taft-Hartley provision on the same subject has had overriding importance here, but fortunately to the same ends.

Defying Awards and Certifications

Wisconsin and Colorado make it an unfair labor practice for a union to refuse to accept a final and binding award of the state labor relations agency, an arbitration tribunal, or a court. This has had the effect of outlawing picketing or boycotting to upset labor board certifications. North Dakota's new law contains broad restrictions against boycotts, blocking or hindering entrance and egress to plants, or picketing a worker's home.

Oregon specifically outlaws picketing or threats aimed at overturning certifications of bargaining agents, or otherwise forcing an employer to bargain with a union not certified as a bargaining agent. North Dakota makes such coercion an unfair practice.

In 1947, Massachusetts specifically amended its law to prevent union defiance of labor board certifications. In New York the state courts have ruled that the state anti-injunction law, which is modeled on the Norris–La Guardia Act, does not limit the right of the courts to enjoin picketing which is aimed at nullifying a state labor board certification. Hence, New York has felt no need to legislate on this subject.

In a related problem the New York area has been plagued with a rash of "paper" unions—local unions set up by racketeers which enter into agreements with employers as a means of enriching the racketeering promoters of such unions and defrauding the employees, sometimes with the connivance of employers. New York has adopted a number of rules designed to prevent such unions from getting certified as bargaining agents,[11] but as a Wagner-type law, it has no direct sanctions against unions.

Minnesota, Wisconsin, and Colorado provide that strikes in violation of collective agreements are unfair labor practices. In addition, most of the states which have legislation similar to the Taft-Hartley Act require strike notices prior to the calling of a strike.

Kansas, Wisconsin, Utah, Minnesota, North Dakota, and Colo-

[10] Smith, *op. cit.*, p. 255.

[11] Jay Kramer, "Law and Policy in State Labor Relations Acts: The New York Board as Innovator," *The Annals*, Vol. CCCXXXIII (January, 1961), pp. 59–75.

rado have outlawed nearly all types of primary or secondary boycotts. Utah, Wisconsin, and Minnesota exempt sympathy strikes in support of employees in similar occupations working for other employers in the same type of work, but the other states even omit these provisions. Picketing in support of boycotts which are illegal in these states is also outlawed for industries which come under the states' jurisdictions.

Finally, Wisconsin, Colorado, Utah, Michigan, Kansas, North Dakota, Pennsylvania, and Oregon prohibit employee interference or coercion in the right of employees to join or not to join unions.

Restrictions on Union Objectives

The most important regulation classified in the third group is that of compulsory union agreements. Since this applies as an unfair labor practice to employers as well as to unions, it has already been discussed above. In addition, however, the laws of three states—Wisconsin, Colorado, and Pennsylvania—have, like the Taft-Hartley Act, outlawed the automatic or general checkoff of union dues and permit only the voluntary checkoff after the individual has authorized it in writing.

Two other restrictions are contained in this type of legislation. The first is the provision in the Colorado Act which makes it an unfair labor practice for a union to require the hiring of unnecessary employees. A similar provision was later placed in the Taft-Hartley Act which, as in the Utah law, has not proved enforceable. The other is the restriction in the Utah law which makes it an unfair labor practice for an employer to bargain with a minority union. This is applicable not only where there is a majority union but also where there is a union to which a minority of the employees belong, but no majority union has been certified.

Regulation of Union Internal Affairs

The final group includes some provisions such as those which were included in the Landrum-Griffin Act, as well as provisions similar to the Taft-Hartley type. In either case, they seem to have had very little effect, since little or no action has been recorded pursuant to them.

Wisconsin's statute requires unions to provide financial reports in writing to all members, but makes no penalty for violations. Kansas prohibits the collection of dues, assessments, etc., in excess of those authorized in the constitution of the union. Colorado's financial requirements are severe, in that they require the state Industrial Commission to pass upon initiation fees and dues, and to change or to alter any fees if the Commission thinks such changes are proper. Conceivably, the Industrial Commission could cut off all revenues of the union, but the provisions cannot now be enforced, since they were included in a compulsory incorporation section which was held unconstitutional.[12] North Dakota makes it an unfair labor practice for a union to require "excessive or discriminatory fees."

Kansas, Wisconsin, and Colorado regulate union elections. Kansas merely makes it an unfair labor practice to prevent or prohibit an election of union officers. Minnesota's unique union democracy law is discussed later in the chapter, as is the New York law. Colorado's regulations, which were the most drastic, have been rendered unenforceable by the court decision in the compulsory incorporation case.

Pennsylvania, Wisconsin, Colorado, and Massachusetts regulate union membership policies in cases where the union holds a closed shop or other form of compulsory membership contract, as has already been discussed. The Massachusetts law of 1947 provides that no compulsory membership agreement can be applied to an employee who is not eligible for full membership and voting rights in the union. In addition, the employer cannot discharge such an employee except under restricted conditions; and the employee can appeal to the Massachusetts Labor Relations Commission to have a discharge overturned if (1) the discharge violated the union's rules, (2) the employee was denied a fair trial, (3) the penalty imposed was not justified by the offense, or (4) the penalty was inconsistent with the established public policy of the state. It is also an unfair labor practice in Massachusetts to strike against or boycott an employer to force him to discharge an employee in violation of the state law.

Kansas makes it a misdemeanor for a union to deny an employee the right to petition courts concerning any agreement, to publicize facts concerning such agreement or violation of law, and to assemble peaceably or to speak freely. Colorado permits an employee to take any complaint regarding any union matter to the state Industrial Commission and thus suspend any disciplinary action of any kind that a union might impose upon a member until the Commission could interfere. Here again, however, the law is inoperative because of its tie-in with the unconstitutional compulsory incorporation feature.

Representation Disputes

All the state labor relations laws except that of Michigan provide that in case of a dispute over representation the appropriate agency shall have authority to determine which union, if any, is the representative of

[12] *American Federation of Labor* v. *Reilly*, 155 P. (2d) 145 (1944).

a given group of employees. In Michigan the state mediation board can conduct elections but only if all parties agree.

In general, the state boards handle representation matters in a manner similar to the National Labor Relations Board (see Figure 3).

FIGURE 3

GENERAL PROCEDURE FOLLOWED IN REPRESENTATION CASES UNDER STATE LABOR RELATIONS ACTS

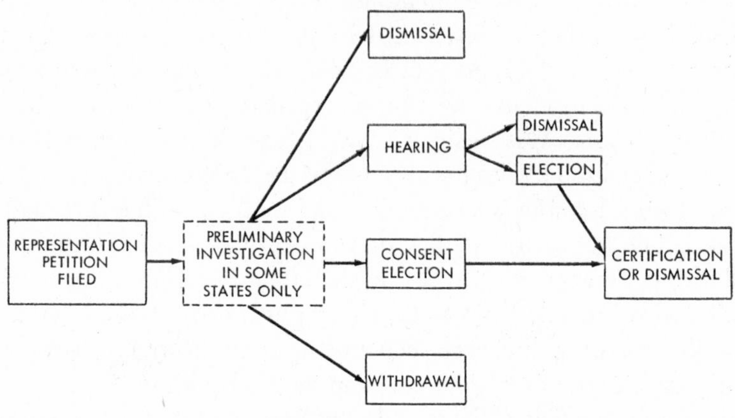

SOURCE: U.S. Department of Labor, Bureau of Labor Standards, *State Labor Relations Acts,* Bulletin No. 224 (Washington, D.C.: U.S. Government Printing Office, 1961).

There are, however, some statutory and administrative variations. The first of these is the so-called "craft proviso," which was written into many of the state laws at the request of the American Federation of Labor. Thus the New York law, Section 705 (2), provides that "in any case where the majority of employees of a particular craft shall so decide, the [New York State] board shall designate such craft as a unit appropriate for the purpose of collective bargaining." This is similar to, but goes beyond, the craft unit policies of the NLRB. In effect, it extends to all crafts the right of separate representation such as the Taft-Hartley Act gave to professional employees. State agencies may, however, deny a separate election to an employee group if the agency decides that the group is composed of various employees rather than being a "true craft."

The appropriate unit is generally one plant, but multiplant units are not unknown, particularly in industries—for example, retail trade—where multiunit bargaining on a local basis is common.

All the laws follow the Taft-Hartley rather than the Wagner Act in permitting employers to petition for representation elections, although the latitude permitted employers to petition varies considerably. In addition, Pennsylvania and Wisconsin permit employees to file petitions to prove that they do not want representation by a union. This is an approach somewhat similar to the decertification procedure of the Taft-Hartley Act.

ADMINISTRATION OF STATE LABOR RELATIONS LEGISLATION

Administration of the state labor relations acts is vested in several different types of administrative establishments. In some, typified by the state labor relations boards of New York and Pennsylvania, a single-purpose agency modeled on the National Labor Relations Board was created to handle only unfair labor practice and representation matters arising under the state labor relations acts of the states. A second type of administrative agency, such as that in Colorado, Wisconsin, or North Dakota, is multipurpose. It administers the labor relations act in addition to several other functions—such as mediation of labor disputes, or even functions like workmen's compensation, safety, minimum wages, and other protective legislation. Minnesota, Michigan, and Kansas vest the representative function of their acts in the state mediation agency, but leave unfair labor practice enforcement to the courts. Oregon provides for division of the responsibility among a part-time agency, the state attorney general, and the state labor conciliator.

The relative merits of a specialized versus a multipurpose agency appear to center on the question of the need for specialized agency and personnel. The argument has been made that the prosecuting and judicial function required by an agency administering a state labor relations statute is at odds with the mediation function in labor disputes, and that such an agency, by the very requirements of decision making, must alienate labor or management at times, thus making it less effective in mediation. That there is some truth in these points is illustrated by conflicts between decision making and mediation which have occurred under the Railway Labor Act and under the Colorado statute.[13]

On the other hand, the number of state labor relations board cases does not seem large enough to support separate agencies from a taxpayer point of view. The work of multipurpose agencies like the Wisconsin Employment Relations Board would seem to indicate that conflicts are easily avoided by good administration, and an agency which is charged with various responsibilities can do all quite well.[14]

[13] See below, Chapter 12.

[14] For the pros and cons of this subject, see the discussion by Morris Slaveny of the Wisconsin Board and Frank Zorilla of the Puerto Rico Department of Labor, in U.S. Department of Labor, Bureau of Labor Standards, *Labor Laws and Their Administration*, Bulletin No. 238 (Washington, D.C.: U.S. Government Printing Office, 1961), pp. 49–61.

No matter what type of administrative agency, the agency itself, as in the case of the National Labor Relations Board, cannot enforce an order. Enforcement must come from the courts. This affords an opportunity for court review, which also may be sought by the losing party.

In enforcing unfair labor practice provisions, the New York courts have permitted the State Labor Relations Board wide latitude to draw inferences from hearsay and to make other variations from accepted courtroom procedure along the lines of the procedure utilized by the NLRB under the Wagner Act. In most of the other states, however, either the laws or the state courts have been more restrictive, and have forced the state agencies to adhere more rigorously to court procedure.

In the three states—Minnesota, Michigan, and Kansas—in which no special agency is delegated authority to handle unfair labor practice procedure, an aggrieved party must secure his remedy by direct application to the courts for relief. This is the same procedure which is set forth under the Railway Labor Act, and discussed in Chapter 12.[15] It means that unfair labor practice matters are rarely litigated. Thus the protection afforded by the law to the parties is minimized. On the other hand, so is government interference minimized. Unfair labor practice proceedings in these three states, as under the Railway Labor Act, have afforded only the barest protection to the parties; but the administration of the law has not become embroiled in bargaining tactics, either.

The unfair labor practice laws which are administered by agencies are of two general types—the preliminary investigation and the compulsory hearing. In the former type, which includes the "little Wagner" acts plus the Utah and North Dakota laws, an agent of the state investigates the dispute and usually tries to settle it informally, but if not, prepares the case for hearing before the agency. This is similar to the old Wagner Act procedure, where the same agency acts, in effect, as prosecutor and judge.

To divide the responsibility for prosecution and judgment, Congress split the National Labor Relations Board into a bifurcated agency, with the General Counsel independent of the Board itself. Oregon accomplishes this by having the state attorney general investigate cases and a board hear them.

Colorado, Hawaii, Pennsylvania, and Wisconsin attempt to achieve this result by still another route. Their laws provide that when a complaint is filed, a hearing must be held unless the complaint is withdrawn. Upon the filing of a charge, a copy of it is sent to the party alleged to

[15] See below, pages 338–40.

have committed the unfair labor practice, and a hearing is held before the agency, at which the two parties argue the merits of their case. The state agency's role is confined to deciding the case.

These two procedures are compared graphically in Figure 4. The

FIGURE 4

GENERAL PROCEDURE FOLLOWED BY STATES IN UNFAIR LABOR PRACTICE CASES

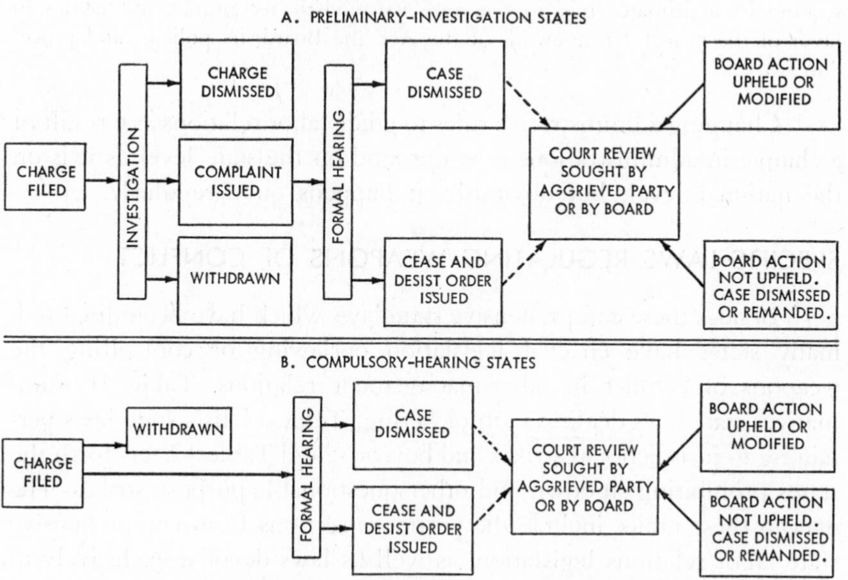

SOURCE: U.S. Department of Labor, Bureau of Labor Standards, *State Labor Relations Acts,* Bulletin No. 224 (Washington, D.C.: U.S. Government Printing Office, 1961).

disadvantage in the compulsory hearing technique is that it places the burden on individuals and organizations to handle their own cases. This means that the weakest and the poorest are the least likely to succeed against more powerful adversaries. On the other hand, the compulsory hearing discourages the trivial complaint or the use of the procedure as a bargaining "gimmick," because it places the burden and costs of prosecution on the complainants themselves.

As was noted in the discussion of the Taft-Hartley Act, there also is a tendency for political alignment to guide the administration of unfair labor practice provisions of state laws. Thus the *Nineteenth Annual Report* of the Pennsylvania State Labor Relations Board noted:

> Striking is the fact that 1955 has seen the second largest case load since the creation of the Board, eighteen years ago. The causes for a case load of such magnitude exist, probably, in the multitudinous variables which make up the

labor-management complex. Nevertheless, we may speculate that substantial impetus is being supplied by certain outstanding developments in government, politics and in the labor movement itself.

Properly attributable to the case load is what we may speculate to be the renewed confidence enjoyed by the labor movement in the legal processes of a Board staffed by an Administration which has received substantial endorsement by that movement for its announced commitment to foster, to the fullest extent, the collective bargaining policies of the Pennsylvania Labor Relations Act. Seen in that light, it would seem there is a greater willingness on the part of Labor, in seeking its legitimate ends, to renounce its atavistic techniques and tactics in favor of the peaceful framework of the Act, the Board, its policies and procedures.[16]

Changing administrative rules to guide labor relations as a result of a change in administrations is as unsound on the state level as it is on the national level; but obviously, it happens quite regularly.

SPECIFIC LAWS REGULATING WEAPONS OF CONFLICT

Besides these comprehensive state laws which have been discussed, many states have enacted legislation outlawing or controlling the weapons of conflict in labor-management relations. Table 10 summarizes state laws dealing with picketing; Table 11 lists state laws pertaining to jurisdictional strikes and boycotts; and Table 12 sets forth the states prohibiting sit-down and other questionable-purpose strikes. The data in these tables include the pertinent sections from comprehensive state labor relations legislation, as well as laws devoted exclusively to the specific regulation or prohibition.

Of related interest to the laws summarized in Tables 10, 11, and 12 is one enacted in Montana guaranteeing sole proprietors and partnerships of two persons in the retail and amusement business the right to work without union interference. Such small businesses are unusually subject to coercive picketing and boycotts.

On the other side have been the several new laws which prohibit any person not directly involved in a labor dispute from recruiting persons to replace workers on strike or locked out. These laws were enacted in Delaware, Maryland, Massachusetts, New Jersey, and Washington in 1961, and Louisiana and Michigan in 1962. Pennsylvania has had such a law since 1937. In Massachusetts the law was tightened in 1962 to proscribe such importation by anyone but the employer, who in turn must register and file detailed data with the state. Such laws have also been enacted by several cities, including Manchester, New

[16] Pennsylvania State Labor Relations Board, *Nineteenth Annual Report* (Harrisburg, 1956), pp. 1–2. This Board was composed of a majority of members selected by a Democratic administration, the first in Pennsylvania in sixteen years.

TABLE 10

State Regulation of Picketing

State and Date of Law	Mass Picketing	Picketing by Nonemployees	Picketing Where No Labor Dispute	Picketing of Homes	Other Picketing
Alabama: 1943	....	....	....	....	Unlawful to prevent pursuit of lawful vocation by force or violence or threat thereof.
Arizona: 1952	....	....	X	....	....
Arkansas: 1943	X	....	....	....	....
Colorado: 1943	X	....	....	....	Picketing illegal, except after strike vote.
Connecticut: 1947	....	....	....	X	....
Florida: 1943	....	....	....	X	Unlawful to restrict entrance and exit. Must confine picketing to area where dispute arises.
Georgia: 1947	X	....	....	....	....
Hawaii: 1949	....	....	....	X	Unlawful to restrict ingress or egress.
Kansas: 1955	....	....	....	X	Unlawful to restrict entrance, exit. Must confine picketing to area where dispute arises.
Louisiana: 1950	....	....	....	....	Picketing of courts.
Maine: 1961	....	....	....	....	No mass picketing, coercion, or force to hinder work in connection with perishable food products.
Massachusetts: 1950	....	....	....	....	Picketing of courts.
Michigan: 1949	X	....	....	X	Unlawful to restrict entrance, exit; to interfere with roads, means of travel.
Minnesota: 1939	....	X	X	....	Restriction on picketing where no strike is in progress.
1945	....	....	....	....	No picketing to deny right of certified union to act.
Mississippi: 1942	X	....	....	....	....
Nebraska: 1949	X	....	....	....	....
New Mexico: 1959	....	....	....	....	No picketing by minority union.
North Dakota: 1949	....	X	....	....	....
1961	X	....	X	X	Unlawful to obstruct entrance, exit; or to use roads and public conveyances, or to hinder lawful employment
Oregon: 1961	....	....	....	....	No picketing to upset choice of representatives; no picketing by other than regular employees where perishable farm products are being harvested.
Pennsylvania: 1947	....	X	....	....	....
South Carolina: 1954	X	....	....	....	Unlawful to obstruct or threaten to obstruct plant entrances, exits, or use of roads and public conveyances.
South Dakota: 1943	....	....	....	X*	....
1947	....	X	X	X	Unlawful to obstruct entrance, exit, or act with violence.
Texas: 1947	X	....	X	....	Picketing illegal if there is misrepresentation or breach of contract; no picketing of public utilities.†
1955	....	....	....	....	Unlawful for union to picket unless it represents majority of employees.
Utah: 1947	X	....	....	X	Picketing permitted only if majority have voted in favor of a strike.
Virginia: 1952	....	X	....	....	Unlawful to obstruct entrance and exit.
Wisconsin: 1939	X	....	X	X	....

* No picketing of homes on agricultural premises.

† No picketing of public utility when intent is to disrupt service; no sabotage of public utility; no picketing to secure a violation of a valid labor agreement.

Source: Compilation by Bureau of National Affairs, Inc., with addenda by authors.

TABLE 11

Jurisdictional Strikes and Boycotts

State and Date of Law	Provision against: Jurisdictional Strike	Secondary Boycott	Other Boycotts
Alabama: 1943	....	....	Unlawful to prevent employer from obtaining or using materials.
Arizona: 1952	....	X	....
California: 1947	X	....	....
Colorado: 1943	....	X	....
Florida: 1943	X	....	....
Georgia: 1947	....	....	Unlawful to prevent any employer from lawfully conducting his business or acquiring materials.
Idaho: 1947	....	X	....
Iowa: 1947	X	X	....
Kansas: 1955	X	X	....
Massachusetts: 1947	X	....	Illegal to boycott to bring about an unfair labor practice, to coerce employees in choice or rejection of bargaining representative after commission has determined that they do not desire to be represented by such union.
Michigan: 1949	X†	....	....
Minnesota: 1943	X‡	....	....
1945	....	....	Restriction on boycotting to deny right of certified union to bargain.
Nebraska: 1947	....	X§	....
1959	....	X	....
North Dakota: 1953	....	X	....
1961	....	....	All boycotts unfair labor practices.
Oregon: 1947	....	X	....
1961	....	....	Similar to Massachusetts.
Pennsylvania: 1947	X	X	....
South Dakota: 1953	....	....	Illegal to interfere with movement of farm products because not union-made.
Texas: 1947	....	X	Certain boycotts are in restraint of trade.
Utah: 1947	....	X°	....
Wisconsin: 1939	....	X	....
1947	X*	....	....

† No strike pending attempt to mediate. If this fails, election must be held to determine the issue.
‡ No strike pending determination by labor referee appointed by the governor.
§ No boycott to coerce an employer to encourage or discourage union membership.
° Does not prevent sympathetic strikes of workers in the same craft.
* Does not outlaw jurisdictional strikes but provides injunctive relief when one party fails to comply with an arbitration award.
Source: Compilation by Bureau of National Affairs, Inc., with addenda by authors.

TABLE 12

State Regulation of Strikes

State and Date of Law	Prohibition against: Sit-Down Strike or Seizure of Property	Prohibition against: Other Strikes
Colorado:		
1943	X	
Florida:		
1943	X	
Kansas:		
1943	X	
Maryland:		
1941	X	
Massachusetts:		
1947	X	No strike or slowdown to bring about an unfair labor practice.
Michigan:		
1939	X	
Minnesota:		
1943	X	
1945		No strike to deny right of certified union to bargain.
1947		No strike to coerce other employer to encourage or discourage union membership.
North Dakota:		
1953		Sympathy strike.
1961		No strike to deny right of certified union to bargain; no strike to coerce, encourage, or discourage recognition of bargaining agent.
Oregon:		
1961		No strike to deny right of certified union to bargain.
Pennsylvania:		
1947	X	
Utah:		
1947	X	
Vermont:		
1937	X	
Washington:		
1937	X	
Wisconsin:		
1939	X	

Source: Compilation by Bureau of National Affairs, Inc., with addenda by authors.

Hampshire; Newark, Dunellen, Morristown, and Perth Amboy, New Jersey; Rochester and New York City, New York; Wilmington, Delaware; and Akron, Ohio—all aimed at strengthening union bargaining power by making it difficult for the employer to obtain replacements. They have been especially sponsored by the International Typographical Union, with AFL–CIO support. The ITU has had a number of strikes against newspapers and printing firms defeated by strikebreakers from out of state, who are willing to work after having been displaced themselves by the closing-down of newspapers and printing firms unable to compete profitably under the twin impact of high union-imposed costs and cheaper substitute methods of composing.

"Little Norris–La Guardia" Acts

Following the passage of the Norris–La Guardia Act, similar laws were enacted by twenty-four states[17] and Puerto Rico. As on the national scene, these laws have caused the number of injunctions issued in labor disputes to decline sharply. There is, however, tremendous variation in these state anti-injunction laws, partially because many have been amended over the years to permit curbs on boycotts, picketing, and other weapons of conflict, and also because some state courts have tended to interpret these laws very narrowly, while others have interpreted them very broadly.

Although there are some exceptions—notably in Massachusetts—the trend seems to be a tendency on the part of state legislatures to reduce the immunities in state anti-injunction acts and a tendency on the part of state courts to interpret laws so as to grant relief when they feel it is warranted. In view of the size and strength of labor unions today as compared with the 1930's and 1940's, when most of these anti-injunction laws were adopted, it is not surprising that both legislatures and courts perceive a greater need to restrain strikes, boycotts, and picketing than was the case twenty-five years ago.[18]

[17] Arizona, Colorado, Connecticut, Idaho, Illinois, Indiana, Kansas, Louisiana, Maine, Maryland, Massachusetts, Minnesota, Montana, New Jersey, New Mexico, New York, North Dakota, Oregon, Pennsylvania, Rhode Island, Utah, Washington, Wisconsin, and Wyoming.

[18] For accounts of the role of the injunction in labor disputes in three states having "little Norris–La Guardia" acts, see Jacob Seidenberg, *The Labor Injunction in New York City, 1935–1960* (Ithaca: Cornell University, New York State School of Industrial and Labor Relations, 1953); Fred Witney, *Indiana Labor Relations Law,* Bureau of Business Research Report No. 30 (Bloomington: Indiana University, 1960), pp. 19–38; and H. Seligson and George E. Bardwell, *Labor-Management Relations in Colorado* (Denver: Sage Books, Alan Swallow, Publisher, 1961), pp. 156–69. A summary of the provisions of state "little Norris–La Guardia" acts is found in the *Monthly Labor Review,* Vol. LXXXV (September, 1962), pp. 1019–21.

"Little Landrum-Griffin" Laws—Reporting, Disclosure, and Democracy

A number of states[19] require unions to file organizational data, or financial statements, or both, with a state official, or to make available to members certain financial information. Most of these laws appear to require only perfunctory reporting. The laws of Alabama, Connecticut, Hawaii, Minnesota, New York, and Wisconsin provide that unions must make information on their financial activities available to the membership, as well as to a state official. Only Kansas, Massachusetts, and New York require that such records be kept open to the public.

In addition, six states—California, Connecticut, Massachusetts, New York, Washington, and Wisconsin—have enacted legislation requiring disclosure about the activities of health and welfare funds set up by labor-management agreements. These laws require full disclosure of the income, disbursements, and operations of the covered funds, but they all lack effective enforcement mechanisms. In 1962, Congress amended a similar federal law to facilitate more effective enforcement of racketeering, malfeasance, or maladministration involving the millions of dollars collected by such funds. It is likely that the task of policing these funds will become largely a federal one as a result of the failure of the states to move more effectively into this field.

An unusual law is that enacted in 1952 by both New Jersey and New York to regulate waterfront conditions in the port of New York. It established a bistate Authority to control crime on the waterfront by barring those convicted of felonies from serving as waterfront union officials, and by regulating waterfront hiring practices. Although considerable success has been achieved by this Authority, particularly in bringing stability and fairness in the hiring of longshoremen, the Authority's own reports emphasize that crime on the waterfront, in New York as in many other ports, still flourishes. Pilfering, loan-sharking, and "kickbacks" remain problems difficult to eliminate in a labor market where more men want jobs than there are jobs available, and where the opportunity for preying on the job seeker, the customer, and the public is great.

The two most comprehensive state laws aimed at furthering union democracy are the Minnesota Labor Union Democracy Act of 1943, and the New York Labor and Management Improper Practices Act of 1959.

[19] Alabama, Connecticut, Florida, Hawaii, Kansas, Massachusetts, Minnesota, New York, Oregon, South Dakota, Texas, Utah, and Wisconsin. As noted above, the reporting requirements of the laws of Hawaii, Kansas, Massachusetts, Utah, and Wisconsin are not separate laws, but are included in the "little Taft-Hartley" laws of these states.

The Minnesota law regulates the details of union elections, providing that they must be held at least once every four years by secret ballot. The state can disqualify the union as a bargaining agent in case of violation. The law also gives the state the right to appoint a temporary labor referee to take charge of a union and conduct a fair election.

When Minnesota enacted its law, it was hailed as a major advance toward insuring union members their full rights as members. Actually, it has been completely dormant except in so far as its existence on the statute books may have encouraged unions to amend their constitutions or actions to conform to its requirements. In 1958 the Minnesota Division of Conciliation reported: "In general, the requirements of law are less rigid than the requirements prescribed by the constitutions and by laws of the labor organizations operating in Minnesota. There have been no instances in which it was necessary to appoint a Labor Referee under this portion of the law."[20]

The New York law is very similar to the financial reporting sections of the Landrum-Griffin Act. It requires financial reporting by both employers and unions, imposes a fiduciary obligation on union officers and agents, and forbids conflict-of-interest transactions. The law also applies to employers and to labor relations consultants in a similar manner as the Landrum-Griffin Act by requiring annual reports on expenditures related to interference, restraint, or other attempts to sway employees away from their rights to choose unions as bargaining agents.[21]

The passage of the Landrum-Griffin Act, immediately after New York enacted its legislation, has tended to overshadow the New York law. Because of the broad coverage of its provisions, few unions are outside the purview of the Landrum-Griffin Act. Congress decided, however, not to bar concurrent state legislation, for it provided in Section 603 (*a*) of the Landrum-Griffin Act that "except as explicitly provided to the contrary, nothing in this statute shall reduce or limit the responsibilities of any labor organization . . . or take away any right or bar any remedy to which members of a labor organization are entitled under any other federal law or law of any state." What role a concurrent law like New York's Labor and Management Improper Practices Act can and will play in view of the far-reaching character of

[20] State of Minnesota, Division of Conciliation, *Biennial Report, 1956–1958,* (St. Paul, 1958), p. 8.

[21] For a pro and con analysis of this law, see C. R. Katz, "New York's Improper Practices Act," *Labor Law Journal,* Vol. X (August, 1959), pp. 557–61; and B. Rubenstein, "A Critique of the New York Improper Practices Act," *ibid.,* pp. 563–65.

the Landrum-Griffin Act still remains to be determined. It is likely, however, that since Congress decided to exercise the full scope of federal jurisdiction in regulating internal union affairs, few states will find it desirable to legislate further in this field.

Limits on Union Political Expenditures

A final group of laws aimed at controlling union finances are those which limit a union's right to utilize regular union income from membership dues, fees, etc., for political purposes. Four states—Pennsylvania, Texas, Indiana, and Wisconsin—limit union political contributions. The first two are rather narrowly construed, the latter two rather broad in their restrictions.[22] Like the proscription in the Taft-Hartley Act, however, their aim is to force unions to raise money for political purposes voluntarily and directly, instead of utilizing dues money which may be contributed by employees who oppose the aims or people for which the contribution is given.

FAIR EMPLOYMENT PRACTICE LEGISLATION

The efforts of Negroes and other minorities to obtain a fair chance at employment opportunities, coupled with the manpower requirements of the armament program, led in early 1941 to the issuance of a Presidential executive order establishing a Fair Employment Practices Committee. During the war the committee attempted to integrate minority workers into war industries and otherwise effectuate the policy of nondiscrimination on grounds of race, color, creed, or national origin.

The work of the FEPC dramatized the possibilities of such legislation and led a number of states and municipalities to pass laws, either modeled on the federal FEPC or less broad in coverage. Some of these laws have enforcement powers, and others do not (Table 13).

Under state fair employment laws with enforcement powers, agencies are required to investigate and to hear charges of discrimination in much the same manner as the NLRB handles unfair labor practice cases. These laws also provide, however, that conciliatory methods to secure compliance must be attempted before enforcement is invoked.

The state laws have already had effects upon policies of employers and unions. A number of unions, such as the Brotherhood of Railway and Steamship Clerks, Freight Handlers, Express and Station Em-

[22] W. R. Brown, "State Regulation of Union Political Action," *Labor Law Journal*, Vol. VI (November, 1955), pp. 769–76.

ployees and the Brotherhood of Maintenance of Way Employees, have removed discriminatory provisions from their rules and have adopted nondiscriminatory policies. Others, however, such as the Brotherhood of Railroad Trainmen and the Brotherhood of Locomotive Firemen and Enginemen, have modified their rules but not their policies.

TABLE 13

State and Municipal Fair Employment Practice Legislation, January, 1963

State Laws with Enforcement Powers		State Law with Only "Educational" Powers
Alaska	Missouri	Indiana
California	New Jersey	
Colorado	New Mexico	
Connecticut	New York	
Delaware	Ohio	
Idaho	Oregon	
Illinois	Pennsylvania	
Kansas	Rhode Island	
Massachusetts	Washington	
Michigan	Wisconsin	
Minnesota		

Municipal Ordinances with Enforcement Powers			Municipal Ordinances with Only "Educational" Powers
Illinois:	Minnesota:	Warren	Ohio:
Chicago	Duluth	Youngstown	Akron*
	Minneapolis	Cincinnati†	
Indiana:	St. Paul		Arizona:
East Chicago			Phoenix†
Gary	Missouri:	Pennsylvania:	
	St. Louis	Braddock	Virginia:
Iowa:		Clairton	Richmond†
Des Moines	Ohio:	Duquesne	
Sioux City	Campbell	Erie	
	Cleveland	Farrell	
Maryland:	Girard	Johnstown	
Baltimore	Hubbard	Monessen	
	Lorain	Philadelphia	
Michigan:	Lowellville	Pittsburgh	
Ecorse	Niles	Sharon	
Hamtramck	Steubenville		
Pontiac	Struthers	Wisconsin:	
River Rouge	Toledo	Milwaukee	

* Applicable only to municipal agencies and firms doing business with municipality.
† Applicable only to municipal agencies.
Source: New York State Commission against Discrimination.

State fair employment practice laws have also resulted in considerably increased employment, especially for Negroes but also for other minorities. The most far-reaching effects have occurred in New York State and in the cities of Baltimore and Philadelphia. The progress in New York may be a result of various complex social, political, and economic factors all favorable to Negro employment. After a careful study of the effects of all fair employment practice laws, however, Dr. Paul H. Norgren concluded that the main reason was the work of the New York State Commission against Discrimination.[23] Not only was SCAD the first agency of its kind in the field, but its policies have produced the most effective results. Noteworthy among these have been its broad program of investigating industry employment patterns and its generous budget for conducting its operations. Since workers look for jobs, not insults, lawsuits, or rejections, minority groups tend to stay away from industries which have a reputation for not hiring them. The New York SCAD program has opened up such industries to a remarkable degree with an absolute minimum of litigation or controversy.

In other jurisdictions, considerable, but much less, progress is the rule under fair employment practice legislation. Where the agency does not take the lead in altering employment patterns, there is no social organization to play the role which unions have in unfair labor practice cases. A worker who believes that he has been discriminated against because of race or color may secure some assistance from a race relations organization or a legal aid group, but no such organization exists which is primarily engaged in handling such matters before fair employment practice agencies. As a result, many complainants do not follow through even if they make complaints. Nevertheless, there have been substantially improved employment opportunities for minorities as a result of these laws.

Use of Weapons of Conflict to Achieve Minority Employment

In recent years, Negro groups in a number of areas have adopted union-devised weapons of conflict to achieve their goal of equal rights. "Sit-ins" in restaurants to achieve service and boycotts of urban transit facilities to end segregated seating have been widely publicized and quite successful in achieving equalitarian goals.

Now a movement has developed to utilize the boycott and the

[23] Paul H. Norgren, "Governmental Fair Employment Agencies: An Appraisal of Federal, State, and Municipal Efforts to End Job Discrimination," in Industrial Relations Research Association, *Proceedings of the Fourteenth Annual Meeting* (1961), pp. 120–38.

picket line to gain more jobs. In areas around New York City and Philadelphia, this has achieved widely publicized success. A picket line on a store in a Negro community can destroy that store's business; an appeal to boycott a company's product in a city like Philadelphia, which has a 25 per cent Negro population, can significantly hurt that company.

But the very success of these boycotts raises questions of public policy on two accounts: What is fair employment? And can abuses be avoided? In answer to the first point, the demand is usually for a proportion of Negro employees similar to that in the population. Yet often, skill mixes, existing seniority rules, and lack of qualified Negroes make this impossible to fulfill. Fair employment requires no set proportion, but equal treatment of all applicants on the basis of competence, regardless of race, color, or creed. And second, too often one hears of a racketeering group boycotting a small business and settling for a payoff —not for Negro employment. Just as union use of the strike and boycott raises questions of policy and demands for regulation, and just as free speech and coercion are intertwined in union tactics, so can the use of these weapons by minority groups become a focus of public policy, debate, and perhaps legislation.

Other Nondiscrimination Legislation

Fair employment legislation of another kind exists in nine states[24] which outlaw discrimination because of age. As far as can be determined, these laws represent a statement of public concern, and not much more. Enforcement is extremely difficult, since age and requirements for a job are often closely intertwined with specifications for performance, making age a problem.

In addition to these laws, fourteen states[25] forbid discrimination in rates of pay between the sexes for equal work. Such legislation is sponsored both by female "equal rights" groups and by unions, which fear that women will be employed at lower rates than men.

CONCLUDING REMARKS

State labor relations legislation thus includes a wide variety of laws. In most states, however, no state labor relations act exists. Companies in intrastate commerce in a majority of the states operate their

[24] Colorado, Connecticut, Louisiana, Massachusetts, New York, Oregon, Pennsylvania, Rhode Island, and Wisconsin.

[25] Alaska, California, Connecticut, Illinois, Maine, Massachusetts, Michigan, Montana, New Hampshire, New Jersey, New York, Pennsylvania, Rhode Island, and Washington.

labor relations under the old rules of common law. The failure of the states to act encourages federal jurisdiction over primarily local situations.

Where state labor relations legislation has been enacted, some state laws seem at odds with federal enactments, some seem to complement federal enactments, and others are experiments in new and untried areas. The tendency on the part of the federal government to pre-empt the field reduces state experimentation, from which valuable lessons can be drawn. In the next part of this book the roles of the federal and state governments in other significant areas of labor relations will likewise bear out this point.

QUESTIONS FOR DISCUSSION

1. If you were managing a business, would you prefer to locate the business in a state which has a Wagner-type labor relations act, a state which has a Taft-Hartley-type labor relations act, or a state which has no labor relations act? Would your answer differ if you were a union business agent instead of a business manager? Explain.
2. In view of the passage of the Landrum-Griffin Act by the federal government, do you think there is a role to be played by the states in legislating to protect democracy in unions? If so, how? If not, why not?
3. Fair employment practice laws have been compared to state labor relations acts. How do they differ, and how are they similar? Do you think that boycotts by minority groups to obtain more work should come under the same laws as union boycotts? Explain.

SUGGESTIONS FOR FURTHER READING

KRAMER, JAY. "Law and Policy in State Labor Relations Acts: The New York Board as Innovator," *The Annals,* Vol. CCCXXXIII (January, 1961), pp. 59–75.

An analysis of the role of the New York State Labor Relations Board by its Chairman.

SMITH, JUSTIN C. "Unfair Labor Practices in Wisconsin," *Marquette Law Review,* Vol. XLV (Fall, 1961), pp. 223–56.

———. "Selected Aspects of the Wisconsin Employment Peace Act," *Marquette Law Review,* Vol. XLV (Winter, 1961–62), pp. 338–65.

Two very informative articles dealing with the administration and practices of the Wisconsin Employment Relations Board.

U.S. DEPARTMENT OF LABOR, BUREAU OF LABOR STANDARDS. *State Labor Relations Acts.* Bulletin No. 224. Washington, D.C.: U.S. Government Printing Office, 1961.

A description of all state labor relations acts (except the new Oregon and North Dakota laws), with clear explanations of how they work.

PART III

Intervention in Labor Disputes

In Part II the activities of the government in controlling union and management tactics and behavior and the weapons of conflict were analyzed. The discussion indicated that although this type of regulation was initially designed to bring the parties to the bargaining table, but not to regulate bargaining itself, it has in fact exerted considerable control over the conduct of the participants at the bargaining table.

In Part III the subject of governmental intervention frankly aimed at the collective bargaining process itself is the subject of discussion. The nature of mediation, fact finding, arbitration, and seizure (see Figure 5, page 274, for definitions) is examined, and the implications of the use of these tools are analyzed. Included in Part III is an analysis of the Railway Labor Act, which combines provisions similar to the Wagner Act with a detailed procedure for governmental control of dispute settlement.

Chapter 10 MEDIATION: THE FUNCTION, THE AGENCIES, AND THEIR JURISDICTION

A recent dispute involving supermarkets in Camden, New Jersey, and Philadelphia, Pennsylvania, brought out headlines in the papers to the effect that mediators from the federal government and from the state governments of New Jersey and Pennsylvania were endeavoring to help settle the dispute. In other cases throughout the country at the same time the newspapers called attention to the fact that strikes existed or were threatened and that federal, state, or even municipal mediators were on the job.

Mediation or conciliation (see Figure 5 for definition) is the most frequent and, to the majority of persons, the most accepted form of government intervention in labor disputes. This chapter explains the mediation function, describes the agencies which are engaged in this area, and examines the jurisdiction of the various agencies. A subsequent chapter deals with the problems of the mediators and of the mediated.

Mediation as an Intervention Process

Collective bargaining is a method of setting the terms and conditions of the employment process by negotiation between representatives of an employer or employer group, on the one hand, and of a unionized employee group or groups on the other. Before agreement is reached, strife or strikes may occur. As noted in Figure 5, mediation and conciliation are used interchangeably to denote intervention by a third party who, without power to compel agreement, attempts by persuasion, compromise, etc., to assist the parties to come to an agreement.

A famous mediator and arbitrator has written that "mediation is inseparable from collective bargaining; it is an integral part of dispute settlement, and it can exert an important influence on government's role in labor relations. It potentially bears on how union or industry

FIGURE 5

DEFINITIONS

MEDIATION AND CONCILIATION are used interchangeably to mean an attempt by a third party, typically a government official, to bring disputants together by persuasion and compromise. The mediator or conciliator is not vested with power to force a settlement.

STRIKE-NOTICE laws require the union and company to notify each other and certain public officials a specified number of days prior to striking or locking out.

STRIKE-VOTE laws require an affirmative vote of either the union members or the employees in the bargaining unit before a strike may be called.

FACT FINDING involves investigation of a dispute by a panel, which issues a report setting forth the causes of a dispute. Usually, but not always, recommendations for settling the dispute are included in the report. Laws requiring fact finding usually provide that the parties maintain the status quo and refrain from strikes or lockouts until a stipulated period after the fact finders' report has been made. Once the procedure has been complied with, however, the parties are free to strike and to lock out.

COMPULSORY ARBITRATION requires the submission of an unsettled labor dispute to a third party or board for determination. Strikes or lockouts are completely forbidden, and the arbitrator's decision is binding on the parties for a stated length of time.

SEIZURE involves temporary state control of a business which is, or threatens to be, shut down by a work stoppage. Strikes or lockouts are forbidden during the period of seizure, which lasts until the threat of work stoppage is abated.

power is exercised and, thus, becomes an important factor in deciding whether additional regulating legislation is needed."[1]

This quotation not only points up the importance of mediation as an intervention process, but it also illustrates the views of many authorities who think of mediation and collective bargaining as almost one and the same; others regard mediation as an "adjunct to collective bargaining."[2] We believe that it is more accurate to look upon mediation as a form of intervention because mediation involves the introduction of a third party into the bargaining process. Once the mediator enters, bargaining is never the same as it was before he came.

[1] David L. Cole, "Government in the Bargaining Process: The Role of Mediation," *The Annals*, Vol. CCCXXXIII (January, 1961), p. 43.

[2] See, for example, Howard S. Kaltenborn, *Governmental Adjustment of Labor Disputes* (Chicago: Foundation Press, 1943).

To be sure, the government—or at least its shadow—is never absent from the bargaining table. There are always restrictions, or potential ones, on the parties. There is always the threat of intervention by one level of government or another. But once that intervention takes place, the situation changes. The constraints are there and visible, and must be considered by the parties. If this remains collective bargaining, it is a different kind of bargaining than it was before the mediator entered. To call it simply by the name of the pure process is likely to be confusing rather than descriptive.

Nor can mediation be considered as merely an "adjunct to collective bargaining," that is, a supplemental assistant. Again, to be sure, it is often that; and in its most constructive form, mediation is utilized to carry the parties to agreement when they are almost there by themselves. This, however, requires that mediation be utilized at precisely the right time and in the right way. But if mediation is introduced too early, the mediator can become an obstacle to overcome. Likewise, mediation too often or too regularly introduced can induce the parties to save a little to give to the mediator. In such instances, mediation is no adjunct but a hindrance. In any case, mediation is intervention and can only be correctly understood as such. For however clever the mediator, he is helping to do what the parties should have the courage to do themselves—settle their differences. The better he does it, the less the parties will need him; the more the parties rely on mediation, the greater will be the propensity for more complete intervention to come in, particularly as mediation, like an old hat, loses its novelty and charm.

FEDERAL MEDIATION AND CONCILIATION SERVICE

The act of 1913 which created the United States Department of Labor contained a paragraph authorizing the Secretary of Labor to mediate disputes and to appoint commissioners of conciliation for that purpose. This phase of the Department's work quickly expanded until a special division known as the United States Conciliation Service was established in 1917. At its World War II peak, the Service employed 250 persons. Its headquarters were in Washington, D.C., but it established regional offices in the chief industrial centers of the nation. In 1947, it was abolished by the Taft-Hartley Act; and an independent agency, whose functions and structure remained basically the same, was substituted for it.

The Federal Mediation and Conciliation Service is by far the largest, most important, and most active agency engaged in mediation. It was set up as a separate agency largely at the behest of employer groups, who felt that if the Conciliation Service were to remain a division of the Department of Labor, conciliators themselves would inevitably reflect what many employers feel is a prolabor bias of the Department of Labor.

In establishing a separate Mediation and Conciliation Service, the Taft-Hartley Act gave the Service the statutory base which it previously lacked. In addition, Section 201 of the Taft-Hartley Act set forth the policy of the federal government as the peaceful settlement of labor disputes by collective bargaining; Section 203 directed the Service to minimize work stoppages by mediation and encouragement of voluntary arbitration; Section 204 admonished labor and industry to co-operate fully with the efforts of the Service to settle strikes; and Section 205 established a labor-management advisory panel for the Service (which has never been very active). Finally, Section 8 (*d*) of the Taft-Hartley Act required labor and management to notify each other of intent to modify a collective agreement at least 60 days prior to the termination date of the agreement, and to notify the Service and any appropriate state agency 30 days later if no agreement has been reached.

The fact that the Mediation and Conciliation Service now has a statutory base has been cited by some observers as a reason for its greater acceptability in labor disputes in recent years. Other observers, however, point to an improvement in the caliber of mediators through experience and better pay, and greater sophistication on the part of labor and management in utilizing the services of mediation agencies than was the case when the former Conciliation Service was young and collective bargaining relatively infrequent.

The Mediation and Conciliation Service may be called into a dispute by either labor or management, or it may proffer its services. It has, however, no authority to force itself upon a recalcitrant employer or union. Of course, as a federal agency, it carries with it the prestige of the government, so that refusal to participate in a conference called by the Service is not usual.

The Taft-Hartley Act also declared it to be national policy for the parties to settle disputes arising out of the interpretation of contracts by voluntary arbitration and to provide for such arbitration in their agreements. The FMCS, like most state mediation agencies, maintains a panel of arbitrators and assists the parties in selecting arbitrators if necessary.

In the fiscal year 1961–62, the FMCS received approximately three thousand requests for the appointment of arbitrators under this provision. This is in addition to appointments made by state mediation agencies or by the private nonprofit organization which does this work, the American Arbitration Association.

FIGURE 6

FEDERAL MEDIATION AND CONCILIATION SERVICE ORGANIZATION

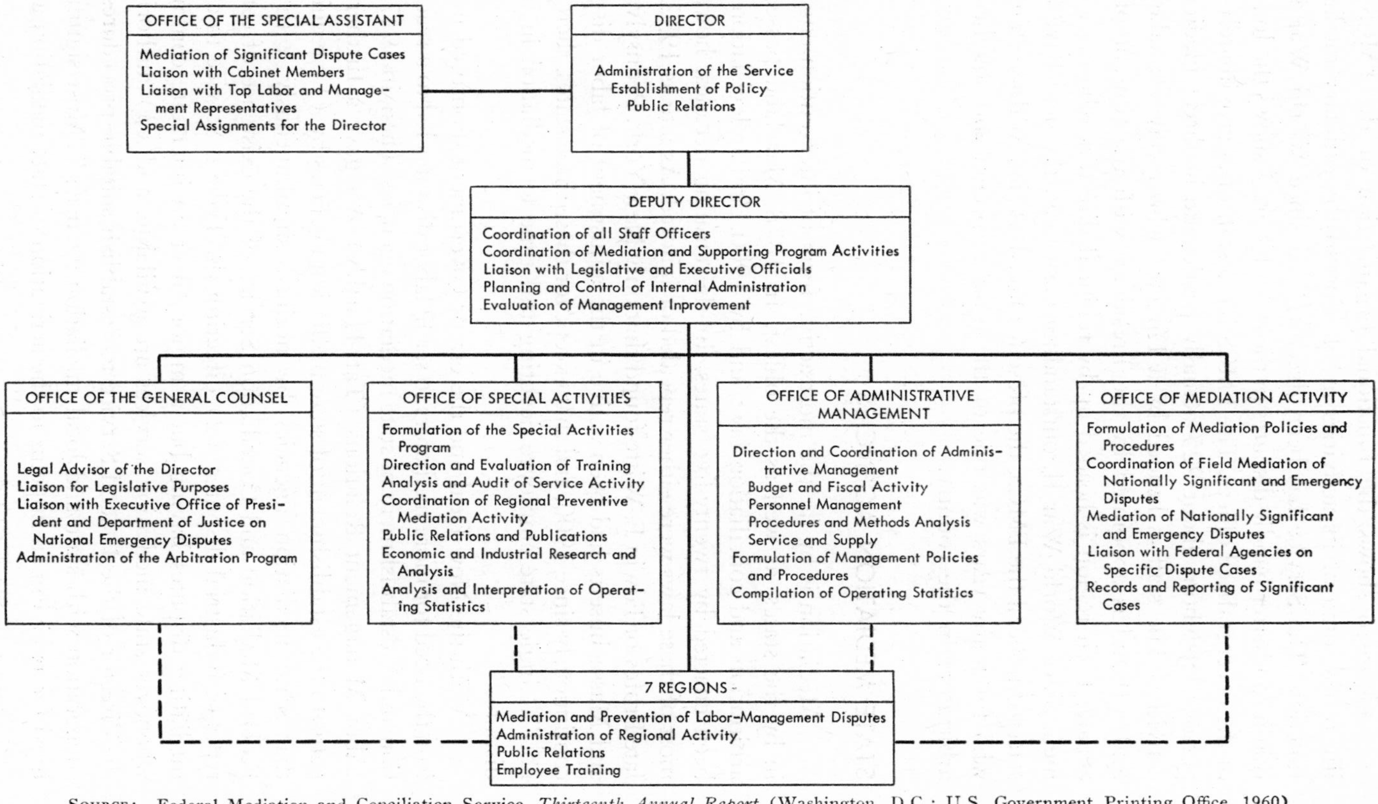

SOURCE: Federal Mediation and Conciliation Service, *Thirteenth Annual Report* (Washington, D.C.: U.S. Government Printing Office, 1960).

Figure 6 shows the functional organization of the FMCS and illustrates some of its activities in addition to the ordinary mediation function. The Service has been decentralized since World War II so that it can better handle disputes in the field. Figure 7 shows the location of the decentralized offices. The FMCS has a staff of approximately 350 persons, of whom about 225 actually participate in direct meditation activities. The staff is headed by a Director who receives a salary of $20,500 and is appointed by the President, with the consent of the Senate. Each region is headed up by regional directors who are career men. Since World War II, outstanding persons in the field have been selected to head the FMCS, the present Director being William Simkin, who for many years was one of the most respected and sought-after arbitrators in the country.

STATE MEDIATION AGENCIES

Mediation is by far the most active form of intervention engaged in by the states, as well as the oldest. In 1878, Maryland passed an arbitration and conciliation law; and by 1900, similar legislation had been enacted by twenty-five states. In the ensuing decades, however, most of these laws were either repealed or ignored. As late as 1932, the late Professor Edwin E. Witte found that only New York, Pennsylvania, and Massachusetts had been active in the adjustment of labor disputes continuously since 1900, and that except for these three states, there was not "a single state employee devoting full time to mediation in labor disputes."[3]

With the New Deal and the era of government-sponsored unionism, the need for more mediators to settle labor disputes led to a reactivation and re-establishment of state mediation agencies. Then, in 1947, the Labor Management Relations (Taft-Hartley) Act gave a further impetus to the establishment of state mediation agencies by (1) requiring that state mediation agencies be notified simultaneously with the Federal Mediation and Conciliation Service of the existence of certain types of industrial disputes, (2) directing the Federal Service to avoid mediating disputes having but a minor effect on interstate commerce whenever state mediation services are available, and (3) authorizing the director of the Federal Service to "establish suitable procedures for cooperation with state and local mediation agencies."[4] Most significant in so far as giving an impetus to the activation of state mediation agen-

[3] Edwin E. Witte, *The Government in Labor Disputes* (New York: McGraw-Hill Book Co., Inc., 1932), p. 252.

[4] Sections 8 (*d*), 202 (*c*), 203 (*b*).

cies was the advance notification requirement to the pertinent state mediation agency.[5]

At present, forty-six states and Puerto Rico have some kind of facilities, established by law or practice, for mediating labor disputes in industry generally; and two states, Missouri and Nebraska, have set up facilities for mediating disputes in "critical" or public utility industries only. In all but seven of these states, mediation is done pursuant to a specific statute; but in seven, it is done by state labor departments by interpretation of their broad general powers. Only Mississippi

FIGURE 7

REGIONALIZATION PLAN, FEDERAL MEDIATION AND CONCILIATION SERVICE
July 1, 1960

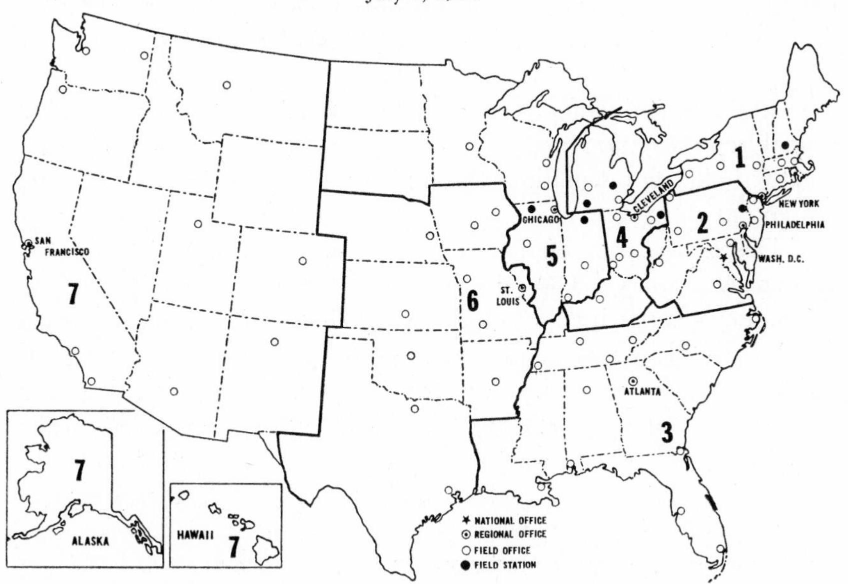

SOURCE: Federal Mediation and Conciliation Service, *Thirteenth Annual Report* (Washington, D.C.: U.S. Government Printing Office, 1960).

and Texas have no agency to mediate labor disputes, and in Texas the governor is authorized to refer labor disputes of public concern to a specially appointed industrial commission for investigation, hearing, and report.

In addition to the notice requirements of the Taft-Hartley Act, a number of states, as will be pointed out below, have special notice provisions. This notice may or may not require the state mediation agency

[5] U.S. Department of Labor, Bureau of Labor Standards, *A Guide to State Mediation Laws and Agencies,* Bulletin No. 176 (Washington, D.C.: U.S. Government Printing Office, 1958).

to intervene. In some states, however, it is mandatory that the agency intervene when it has knowledge of a strike or when it has been notified that a strike impends. This is the case in Connecticut, Illinois, Massachusetts, Ohio, Pennsylvania, and Puerto Rico for all types of disputes, in New Hampshire for disputes involving 10 or more employees, and in Oklahoma for those involving 25 or more employees. In Michigan, New Jersey, New York, and North Carolina the agency must proffer its services when so directed by the governor; and in New Jersey, California, Maine, and Oregon the agency must mediate whenever requested to do so by one or both of the parties. In other states and/or situations the agency can usually proffer its services on its own motion or at the request of either of the parties, or at the behest of a state official. A few state agencies, however, do not proffer their services, but act only at the request of one or both of the parties; and in Utah and West Virginia the agencies may intervene only if both parties so request.[6]

In the majority of states, where no state labor relations act and no formal representation machinery exist, state mediation agencies will usually hold representation elections if all parties so request and consent to the procedure.

Despite the proliferation of state agencies, the work load of most of them is not large. Those in the less industrialized states do not, of course, have as much opportunity for activity as others. Where mediation is handled by the state labor commissioner or by a similar official who has many other duties, intervention in labor disputes is less common than in states where there is a separate agency devoted to mediation. In Maryland, for example, where state mediation of labor disputes was born, the state agency has a very small budget, publishes no reports, and mediates only when called in on some special occasion.

In Rhode Island the director of the Department of Labor is apparently always selected from the top ranks of organized labor in the state; and the state mediators, who are under his jurisdiction, are former associates. Some employers in Rhode Island appear to regard the Rhode Island state mediation service as a virtual adjunct of organized labor and therefore do not welcome its services.[7]

On the other side of the coin is the Georgia situation. According to the official write-up in the United States Department of Labor's *Guide to State Mediation Laws and Agencies,* the Georgia Commission of Labor is "authorized to do all in its power to promote mediation, conciliation, and voluntary arbitration . . . may designate a mediator

[6] *Ibid.*

[7] Interviews, October, 1960, and May, 1962.

. . . [and] also appoint temporary board of arbitration. . . . Upon receipt of a notice of a labor dispute, the Commission immediately offers conciliation services. . . ."

In actual fact, the Commission made it clear that no mediation was performed because "that gave recognition to unions."[8] No mention of mediation is made in the annual reports of the Georgia Department of Labor. Several states in the Midwest and South reflect a similar attitude. Mediation services in such states are pure window dressing, not to be used, and usually not staffed by persons capable of mediating any serious dispute.

In Florida, no mediation was performed for years by the director of the Florida Mediation and Conciliation Service. Then, in 1961, he died; and the office was taken over by a new director, who, although totally inexperienced, has attempted to "learn the trade" and to perform a service. In 1961 the Florida Mediation and Conciliation Service was active in sixty cases—probably more cases than it had handled in the previous decade.

The experience of Indiana "demonstrates that employers and unions will use the mediation function of a state when full-time and qualified conciliators are avilable."[9] Indiana established a mediation agency in 1897, which was quite active for a state, but fell into disuse and was abolished in 1911. For four years, mediation became one of the functions of a Bureau of Inspection; and then, for twenty-two years, mediation was provided for only by special commissions appointed by the governor—but none were appointed. Finally, in 1937, Indiana established a permanent mediation agency which since then has been quite active in the field.[10] Mediation in Indiana has, however, been limited in the past by inadequate salaries and the lack of an effective training program.[11]

Antagonism to a law by one party can greatly reduce the activity of state mediation bodies. In Colorado, for example, mediation has operated first under the Compulsory Investigation Act of 1915, and then under the Labor Peace Act of 1945. Organized labor's antagonism to both laws has resulted in a reluctance by unions to utilize the Industrial Commission's mediation functions.[12]

[8] Interview in Atlanta, Georgia, March 13, 1962.

[9] Fred Witney, *Indiana Labor Relations Law,* Bureau of Business Research Report No. 30 (Bloomington: Indiana University, 1960), pp. 49–50.

[10] *Ibid.,* pp. 41–52.

[11] *Ibid.,* pp. 56–57.

[12] H. Seligson and George E. Bardwell, *Labor-Management Relations in Colorado* (Denver: Sage Books, Alan Swallow, Publisher, 1961), pp. 151, 189.

On the other hand, some states have become very active in mediation when "activist" mediators, or governors propelling mediators, were in office. Other states have developed very active agencies by doing an effective job. The most active state agencies are Connecticut, Massachusetts, New York, New Jersey, and Pennsylvania in the East; Michigan, Minnesota, and Wisconsin in the Midwest; and California in the West. North Carolina has the most active mediation service in the South. Illinois and, as noted above, Indiana are also quite active in the Midwest.

MUNICIPAL MEDIATION AGENCIES

In addition to the states, a number of municipalities have at one time or another established machinery for the adjustment of labor disputes. Most have depended upon the volunteer services of public-spirited citizens and have ceased to exist after these citizens retired. Their success has been varied. Experienced mediators have not been available to municipalities, and inexperienced ones have frequently done more harm than good. Strikes which occur on the outskirts of a city, or in its suburbs, may vitally affect a city, yet be outside the jurisdiction of its adjustment agency. And if state and federal agencies are already in operation, the intrusion of a municipal board may only complicate matters.[13]

Among the cities which have been most active in this field are Toledo, Ohio; Newark, New Jersey; and New York City. The boards of Toledo and Newark both resulted from the failure of states to establish effective machinery to service highly industrial cities. In both cities, these boards had considerable success in maintaining peace. Both agencies, however, ceased to function during the war. The Newark agency's work was taken over by the New Jersey State Mediation Board, and the work of the Toledo agency was largely taken over by the Conciliation Service and the War Labor Board.[14] After World War II, however, Toledo reorganized its board, and it is now again active.

Other cities which have been quite active at one time or another in the mediation field include Louisville, Kentucky; Pittsburgh, Pennsylvania; Tacoma, Washington; and South Bend, Indiana.[15] In all of these cities, however, the state mediation service is more active. Only in New

[13] W. L. Nunn, "Local Progress in Labor Peace," *National Municipal Review,* Vol. XXIX (December, 1940), pp. 784–91.

[14] W. L. Nunn, "Municipal Labor Boards of Toledo and Newark," *Monthly Labor Review,* Vol. XLIX (November, 1936), pp. 1045–49; Kaltenborn, *op. cit.,* pp. 208–17.

[15] Victor H. Rosenbloom, "How Cities Keep Industrial Peace," *Labor Law Journal,* Vol. III (October, 1952), pp. 663–76.

York City is there a mediation service maintained which actively competes with state and federal agencies.

The New York City Labor Relations Division dates back to 1937 when Mayor La Guardia created a city industrial relations board and appointed a full-time labor secretary. This board lasted for only a few months before it went out of existence when the New York State Board of Mediation began operations; but at the same time, Mayor La Guardia appointed the secretary of the city board as his personal labor secretary. At first, the Mayor made an agreement with the State Board of Mediation to the effect that his labor secretary would not intervene in the case until the Board certified that it could not settle the dispute by mediation. Nevertheless, the labor secretary was very active in city disputes until 1942, when the Mayor allowed the position to disappear.

After William O'Dwyer succeeded La Guardia as Mayor, he resurrected the position of labor secretary and then in 1946 reorganized a New York City Division of Labor Relations which still exists today.[16] This Division is presided over by a director who now receives $25,000 per year and is permitted to engage in private activities on the outside. In addition, considerable use is made of *ad hoc* tripartite mediation boards composed of prominent persons from the ranks of labor and industry, and so-called "neutrals," if direct mediation by the labor secretary or his staff is unsuccessful.

The relations of the New York City Division of Labor Relations with state and federal agencies are intricate, and depend upon the fact that within New York City the mayor is in many ways a more powerful figure than the governor of the state. Many of the disputes which occur in New York City are directly involved in city activities. For example, construction, hauling, fuel, sand, and gravel, etc., all involve city licenses to do business or other direct or indirect relations with the city government. Moreover, whereas the state and federal mediators are usually merely mediators, the city labor relations head is apparently empowered to and, in fact, does speak in the name of the mayor. Consequently, many disputes in New York are not settled until the mayor's voice is heard through his labor division.

Thus the New York City Division of Labor Relations has added a complicating dimension to dispute settlement by taking jurisdiction in areas where state and federal mediators are already available. This has a direct bearing on the jurisdictional problem discussed in the next section.

[16] See Victor H. Rosenbloom, "The New York City Division of Labor Relations," *Labor Law Journal,* Vol. III (August, 1952), pp. 528–41, 571.

THE QUESTION OF JURISDICTION

What is the jurisdiction of the state mediation agencies over matters affecting interstate commerce? How much should the Federal Mediation and Conciliation Service involve itself in essentially intrastate or local disputes? Where do local mediation leaders fit in the picture? The answer to these questions seems to be that there are neither definitive legal guidelines nor co-operative resolution of mutual problems. Instead, there is a hodgepodge of overlapping jurisdictions and jurisdictional claims dating back to World War II.

Background of Jurisdictional Problem

Before a case could go to the War Labor Board during World War II, the Secretary of Labor had to certify that the United States Conciliation Service had been unable to settle the dispute by mediation. Because several states had by then built up mediation organizations, these agencies were permitted to act for the Federal Service in certifying cases to the War Labor Board. In Pennsylvania, co-operation in peacetime was pioneered by an agreement whereby all notices of strikes or threatened strikes received by either the federal or the state agency were transmitted to the other, and the agency which could reach the scene first, or which could act most effectively, was to assume sole jurisdiction.

Despite the success of some of these co-operative ventures, there was enough competition between federal and state agencies—and occasionally local agencies as well—to cause concern in Congress. In 1947, Congress attempted to solve the problem by placing in the Taft-Hartley Act provisions for notification of contract negotiations to state agencies as well as to the Federal Service, by directing the Federal Service to avoid disputes having a minor effect on interstate commerce if state agencies were available, and by authorizing the Federal Service to work out co-operating procedures with state agencies. In 1948 the Federal Service reported that it had agreements with nearly all active state agencies, outlining jurisdictions and formulating a policy of co-operation.[17] In December, 1955, the Federal Service reached an understanding with officials of the Association of State Mediation Agencies, an organization to which most state mediation officials belong, and with the individual officials of state mediation agencies, and issued general regulations to replace the individual agreements previously reached with various state agencies. (See Figure 8.)

In some states, co-operation between the FMCS and the state

[17] *Business Week,* January 29, 1949, p. 74.

FIGURE 8

Policies of the Federal Mediation and Conciliation Service

(Sec. 1403.2). It is the policy of the Federal Mediation and Conciliation Service:

(*a*) To facilitate and promote the settlement of labor-management disputes through collective bargaining by encouraging labor and management to resolve differences through their own resources.

(*b*) To encourage the states to provide facilities for fostering better labor-management relations and for resolving disputes.

(*c*) To proffer its services in labor-management disputes in any industry affecting commerce, except as to any matter which is subject to the provisions of the Railway Labor Act, as amended, either upon its own motion or upon the request of one or more of the parties to the dispute, whenever in its judgment such dispute threatens to cause a substantial interruption to commerce.

(*d*) To refrain from proffering its services: (1) in labor-management disputes affecting intrastate commerce exclusively; (2) in labor-management disputes having a minor effect on interstate commerce, if state or other conciliation services are available to the parties; or (3) in a labor-management dispute when a substantial question of representation has been raised, or to continue to make its facilities available when a substantial question of representation is raised during the negotiations.

(*e*) To proffer its services in any labor-management dispute directly involving government procurement contracts necessary to the national defense, or in disputes which imperil or threaten to imperil the national health or safety.

(*f*) To proffer its services to the parties in grievance disputes arising over the application or interpretation of an existing collective bargaining agreement only as a last resort and in exceptional cases.

Obtaining Data on Labor-Management Disputes (Sec. 1403.3). When the existence of a labor-management dispute comes to the attention of the Federal Service upon a request for mediation service from one or more parties to the dispute, through notification under the provisions of Section 8 (*d*) (3), Title 1 of the Labor Management Relations Act, 1947, or otherwise, the Federal Service will examine the information to determine if the Service should proffer its services under its policies. If sufficient data on which to base a determination [are] not at hand, the Federal Service will inquire into the circumstances surrounding the case. Such inquiry will be conducted for fact-finding purposes only and is not to be interpreted as the Federal Service proffering its services.

Assignment of Mediators (Sec. 1403.4). The Federal Service will assign one or more mediators to each labor-management dispute in which it has been determined that its services should be proffered.

Relations with State and Local Mediation Agencies (Sec. 1403.5). (1) If under state or local law a state or local mediation agency must offer its facilities in a labor-management dispute in which the Federal Service is proffering its services, the interests of such agencies will be recognized, and their co-operation will be encouraged in order that all efforts may be made to prevent or to effectively minimize industrial strife.

(2) If, in a labor-management dispute, there is reasonable doubt that the dispute threatens to cause a substantial interruption to commerce or that there is more than a minor effect upon interstate commerce, and state or other conciliation services are available to the parties, the regional director of the Federal Service will endeavor to work out suitable arrangements with the state or other conciliation or mediation agency for mediation of the dispute. Decisions in such cases will take into consideration the desires of the parties, the effectiveness and availability of the respective facilities, and the public welfare, health, and safety.

(3) If requested by a state or local mediation agency or the chief executive of a state or local government, the Federal Service may make its services available in a labor-management dispute which would have only a minor effect upon interstate commerce when, in the judgment of the Federal Service, the effect of the dispute upon commerce or the public welfare, health, or safety justifies making available its mediation facilities.

agency appears quite good. In Illinois, except for a six-month period in 1954, when it referred no cases, the FMCS referred an average of about six hundred cases per year to that state's Conciliation and Mediation Service between 1949 and 1961.[18] In California, state and federal agencies appear to work together reasonably well. And in states having relatively inactive mediation agencies, the FMCS handles nearly all mediation by clear consent of the state.

The problem, however, is far from resolved. In New Jersey, antagonism between the state and federal agencies is not disguised. In many other states, competition, not co-operation, is the rule. Some state agencies have maintained to the authors that the FMCS has recently assumed an even more vigorous jurisdictional position involving less significant disputes than is indicated by its 1955 general regulations.[19] On the other hand, at the 1959 annual meeting of the Association of State Mediation Agencies, the state mediation agencies voted unanimous and complete lack of support for the position of the Federal Service. (See Figure 9.) There are several reasons why this problem remains unsolved.

FIGURE 9

RESOLUTION ADOPTED AT THE EIGHTH ANNUAL CONFERENCE OF THE ASSOCIATION OF STATE MEDIATION AGENCIES ON JULY 31, 1959

WHEREAS collective bargaining in a free enterprise system is predicated on the freedom to contract, and whereas any proposal to impose Federal mediation under the threat of being charged with an unfair labor practice does violence to established concepts of freedom and the voluntary mediation process; and

WHEREAS it is recognized that labor disputes dealing with the hours and conditions of work are basically local disputes: *Therefore be it*

RESOLVED, That the Association of State Mediation Agencies go on record as supporting an amendment to section 203 (*B*) of the Taft-Hartley Act which would limit Federal jurisdiction in such labor disputes to matters involving two or more employers located in two or more States and disputes involving the public health and welfare and national defense.

Bases for the Problem

In the first place, it does not appear that the Federal Mediation Service has carried out the intent of Congress "to avoid attempting to mediate disputes which would have only a minor effect on interstate

[18] Illinois Department of Labor, *Annual Report* (Springfield, 1960), p. 7.

[19] In interviews with the authors.

commerce if state or other conciliation services are available to the parties." A glance at any FMCS annual report will show that the vast majority of cases over which the Service asserts jurisdiction involve a small number of employees. Usually, about 80 per cent of the cases involve less than 1,000 employees; about 70 per cent involve less than 500 employees; about 25 per cent involve less than 100 employees; and about 10 per cent involve less than 50 employees. Size is, to be sure, no absolute criterion of importance or effect on interstate commerce. Yet it is difficult to quarrel with the statement that "The vast majority of FMCS cases just do not have a 'substantial' impact on interstate commerce."[20]

Moreover, there is some evidence that the FMCS varies its jurisdictional position, depending on the aggressiveness of its leadership and the number of cases on hand. For example, mediators of the Federal Service have recently been encouraged to make early contacts with labor and management, and to employ "more aggressive and affirmative mediation methods."[21] This seems to mean asserting federal jurisdiction early and often, regardless of the availability of other mediation services; and in practice, it does seem to have worked out in this manner.

According to one observer, who charges that the FMCS has interpreted "substantial impact" on interstate commerce to mean all but the most trivial of disputes, the FMCS interest in small disputes varies "with the caseload of the Federal mediators. During busy seasons the term has a definition that differs from slack seasons."[22] Such a charge is difficult to prove, but most state mediators certainly seem to believe it.

State mediation agencies also have the impression that the Federal Service has "understandings" with a number of unions—the International Association of Machinists is one frequently mentioned—to the effect that all mediation conducted in disputes involving these unions will be done by the FMCS, regardless of the number of persons involved or the impact of the dispute on interstate commerce.

On the other hand, the fault of the jurisdictional problem is by no means solely the tendency of the Federal Service to become involved in essentially intrastate disputes. Members of three very active state mediation services advised the authors on separate occasions that they re-

[20] W. Weinberg, "The Jurisdictional Problem between State and Federal Mediation Agencies," *Labor Law Journal,* Vol. XII (March, 1961), p. 203.

[21] *Business Week,* January 13, 1962, p. 93. See also the address by S. I. Schlossberg, Special Assistant to the Director of the FMCS, "Philosophy and Procedures of Labor Mediation," *Labor Law Journal,* Vol. XIII (October, 1962), pp. 828–32.

[22] Weinberg, *op. cit.,* pp. 202–3. Weinberg is a mediator on the staff of the New Jersey Board.

garded any dispute, regardless of its nature, which occurred within their state to be within the province of the state agency.[23] This view would include within state jurisdiction companies of the size of General Motors, General Electric, and United States Steel, which are obviously in and substantially affect interstate commerce.

Part of the problem has resulted from the increasing competence of state agencies. Before the Pennsylvania service was reorganized in 1958, the FMCS could, without protest, take jurisdiction over most any dispute in the commonwealth. Now, Pennsylvania has a much abler staff, who want to assert their jurisdiction, but FMCS personnel are loath to give up areas handled in the past. In other states, too, the problem has grown more acute as the effectiveness of the state personnel has improved.

In Indiana the governor has been sending out letters announcing the availability of the Indiana Mediation Service and, in effect, inviting industry and labor to use state instead of federal mediators. In other areas an informal "first come, first served" arrangement is in effect. One mediator termed this sort of thing "mediation ambulance chasing."[24]

Another reason why state mediators attempt to assert jurisdiction in clearly major interstate situations is likely to be their frustration over the fact that the most important disputes affecting the people and industries of their states are really beyond their power to act. Consider this comment by the Minnesota Division of Conciliation:

> . . . there are many instances in which neither the union nor the employer file a petition for conciliation with this office. Particularly where industry-wide bargaining covers employees in several states and where the negotiations are carried on in a location outside the State of Minnesota is this true. Nevertheless, such cases can, and sometimes do have a tremendous impact on the economy within the state. By way of illustration, the steel negotiations affecting over 14,000 employees in the Iron Range area can be cited as an outstanding example.[25]

An official who is charged with keeping the peace likes to be able to handle breaches; his rewards, his staff, and his general standing are usually more favorable the busier he is and the better the strike record looks. This, of course, is the kernel of the problem. Moreover, mediators are often prodded by public figures who want their administrations to receive credit for settlement. "Those intimate with the problem recognize an increasing awareness of the 'exploitability' of labor disputes. Strikes make headlines; the bigger the strike, the bolder the headlines. Strike

[23] Interviews, March and April, 1962.

[24] Interview, May, 1962.

[25] State of Minnesota, Division of Conciliation, *Biennial Report, July 1, 1958–June 30, 1960* (St. Paul, 1960), p. 25.

settlements bring public acclaim to the peacemaker. 'Agreement reached at the office of . . .' are pleasant words to read on the front page of today's paper."[26]

In some areas, difficulties are further complicated by having more than two jurisdictions represented. Where a dispute crosses state lines, two state agencies and the FMCS may all have a hand in the dispute. In New York City, there have been several occasions when the FMCS, the State Board, and the New York City Labor Division were all involved. In one case, three state agencies, the New York City agency, and the FMCS all participated. Yet few would claim that mediation is made more effective because of the number of mediators.

The reason why this jurisdictional hodgepodge has not resulted in open fighting among the agencies is that it has been disguised from the public by an uneasy accommodation known as "the duet" or, in New York City, "the trio." What this means in practice is that in virtually all significant cases, when a dispute arises in states—for example, Connecticut and Michigan, and in the Boston area of Massachusetts—two mediators appear on the scene, one state and one federal. Usually, the mediators are friendly toward each other and sometimes work well as a team. Sometimes, they are downright antagonistic and work at cross purposes. Either way, it gives both agencies an opportunity to service the entire jurisdiction, and avoids at least the outward manifestations of hostility among agencies whose prime job is the furtherance of labor peace.

A spokesman for the Connecticut State Board of Mediation has commended the formal mediation duet as practiced in his state as an ideal solution of the jurisdictional question which recognizes the jurisdictional interests of all concerned and which provides sound mediation.[27] Others have been highly critical of dual mediation as a bureaucratic solution which, in effect, amounts to mediation featherbedding and which wastes taxpayer dollars without increasing the effectiveness of mediation.[28]

A Proposed Solution

One possible solution would be that all disputes involving five hundred or less employees be considered within the province of state mediation services except (1) where the dispute also involves more

[26] Arthur Stark, "Are There Too Many Mediators?" *Labor Law Journal,* Vol. VI (January, 1955), p. 33.

[27] Robert L. Stutz, "Troikas, Duets and Prima Donnas in Labor Mediation," *Labor Law Journal,* Vol. XIII (October, 1962), pp. 845–52.

[28] Weinberg, *op. cit.;* and J. J. Manson, "The Sunset of Mediation: Prima Donnas, Duets and Troikas," *Labor Law Journal,* Vol. XIII (October, 1962), pp. 841–45.

than one plant in more than one state; (2) where the dispute pertains to a collective agreement or business covering more than one plant in more than one state; (3) where a specific federal law (for example, the Railway Labor Act) has assigned jurisdiction to a specific agency; (4) where a qualified state agency does not exist; or (5) where the parties jointly otherwise request.

A qualified state mediation agency could be defined as one which performs the mediation function as its sole obligation, and which employs an adequate full-time staff on a competitive, civil service basis. To improve competence, a committee of two—the president of the Association of State Mediation Agencies and the director of the Federal Mediation and Conciliation Service—could be designated to certify whether a state mediation service is qualified to perform its mediation function in any state. If they cannot agree, they should be required to designate a third party from a list of experts in the labor relations field.

The Notice Problem

In order to insure the success of this proposal, the Taft-Hartley Act would have to be amended to include the jurisdictional criteria. Such amendments could also forbid the agency which does not have jurisdiction from intervening after receipt of the required contract termination notices. The present notice provisions which now must be sent to both the federal and state services were designed to insure that some mediation body would know of a possible dispute before it became a work stoppage. Although the notice provisions do have this effect, they now invite jurisdictional disputes among mediation agencies.

A union will almost always advise the federal and state agency of contract termination and failure to settle in order to free itself for possible strike action. Upon receipt of these notices, some federal and state mediators have made a habit of acknowledging receipt in a manner which indicates to the parties that jurisdiction has been asserted. The FMCS often advises the parties that a commissioner of conciliation has been "assigned" to the disputes. Many state agencies follow up receipt of Taft-Hartley notices with telephone calls to the parties inquiring about the situation. "It is not uncommon for employers and unions, peacefully negotiating a contract, to receive calls from two or more mediation services, inquiring about the progress of negotiations and asking to be kept 'informed of developments.' "[29] This, too, often amounts to solicitation, interference, or premature mediation.

[29] Stark, *op. cit.*, pp. 38–39.

No notice might well be preferable to the present system—but it might also be sound if notice went to one agency. A clear determination of the jurisdictional question—by this proposal or by any other reasonable one—would either permit a single notice to be sent to a single agency or at least let only one agency follow it up without fear of the need to get there first.

Federal legislation dividing mediation jurisdiction on some reasonable basis would probably by pre-emption also determine the jurisdictions of state mediation agencies, although not disputes between state and city agencies. The laws of many states—Connecticut and Michigan are examples—now require the state mediation agencies to intervene if a strike is threatened or if one of the parties so requests, or require the parties to confer with the mediation board if it assumes jurisdiction.[30] It would be most helpful, of course, if the FMCS and the state agencies in harmony resolved the mediation jurisdiction question, and Congress and the state legislatures then enacted appropriate legislation. If only Congress acted, however, this would, by pre-empting the sphere of federal jurisdiction, resolve the problem except where state and city conflicts exist. These conflicts state legislatures must resolve, particularly in New York, the only state where a municipal agency actually competes with federal and state agencies.

As the situation now exists, the greater the degree of labor peace, the more mediation agencies are tempted to invade each others' jurisdictions. The proposal made here would permit a decrease in the number of federal mediators, and perhaps those in several states as well. Studies have shown that mediators in the federal service have a smaller average case load than their counterparts in several industrial states.[31] This may be because the FMCS cases involve larger numbers of employees and require more time, although the FMCS data do not support such a thesis. It may also be because mediators are not utilized as efficiently where the budget is larger. In any case, if jurisdiction were better defined, the race to mediate would be lessened, and the mediators could better concentrate on serving the parties and the public effectively.

[30] There is a constitutional question here which is discussed in Chapter 15 in connection with a recent decision affecting the Massachusetts agency. Briefly, as long as the intervention is solely concerned with voluntary mediation, there is no federal pre-emption. See J. Lazar, "Concurrent Jurisdiction of Federal and State Mediation Agencies," *Labor Law Journal,* Vol. XIII (March, 1962), pp. 254–61. But if mediation is accompanied by required investigation or fact finding, the jurisdiction of the states is doubtful. (See below, pages 446–48.)

[31] Weinberg, *op. cit.,* p. 205.

QUESTIONS FOR DISCUSSION

1. How do you conceive that mediation can help in a labor dispute with which you are acquainted? Explain how, if you were the mediator, you would handle yourself in such a situation.
2. How would you resolve the jurisdictional question involving federal and state mediators? Explain whether you think that the plan presented here is workable and, in any case, how it could be improved.
3. What role do you think is available for mediators attached to municipal governments? In explaining your answer, state whether such mediators should be full-time government employees or private citizens called upon in time of crisis to devote their energies and abilities to public service.

SUGGESTIONS FOR FURTHER READING

FEDERAL MEDIATION AND CONCILIATION SERVICE. *Annual Reports.* Washington, D.C.: U.S. Government Printing Office, 1957–62.

The 1957 annual report contains a summary of the FMCS activity and philosophy for the first ten years of its existence as an independent agency; the reports since then contain valuable information on the work and thinking of those who have been in charge of the Service.

"Proceedings of the Eleventh Annual Conference, Association of State Mediation Agencies," *Labor Law Journal,* Vol. XIII (October, 1962), pp. 801–73.

A number of practicing mediators and scholars analyze and describe various problems in mediation from different points of view. The jurisdictional question, duets in mediation, philosophies of mediation, and a comparison of mediation in Canada and the United States are among the topics explored.

U.S. DEPARTMENT OF LABOR, BUREAU OF LABOR STANDARDS. *A Guide to State Mediation Laws and Agencies.* Bulletin No. 176. Washington, D.C.: U.S. Government Printing Office, 1958.

A good summary of the official activities of the various state mediation agencies.

Chapter 11 MEDIATION: EVALUATIONS, TECHNIQUES, AND PROBLEMS

How and how well does the mediator accomplish his task? What are some of the problems he faces? With the previous chapter's background, describing the mediation agencies and their jurisdictional problem, this chapter turns to an analysis of the mediation process in action.

EVALUATING THE MEDIATOR

Expert mediation has been described by David L. Cole as acting as "a lubricant, perhaps a catalyst." The essential function of the mediator "is to keep the parties in intelligent discussion with each other." Cole continues:

> How the mediator accomplishes his purpose is another matter. Techniques which work in one case will not necessarily work in another. Things proposed by one mediator will be emphatically rejected if proposed by another. The effectiveness of the mediator depends mainly on the confidence he can inspire and on certain indefinable qualities he possesses. Among the latter is his intuitive ability to do what will arouse favorable response and to know when to make his moves. He must be able to anticipate unfavorable reactions and to help temper them so they do not divide the parties further in the search for agreement.
>
> Basically, the mediator proceeds on the theory that a strike is undesirable and that there exists a community, or public interest as well as a private interest in avoiding or shortening a strike. This fortifies him; he speaks to the embattled parties as the voice of the community. He has the delicate task of preserving for the parties their resort to economic force while not allowing the economic threat to destroy their ability to reason with each other.[1]

No one can deny that this is a difficult task indeed. How well do mediation agencies handle this function? The answer must, of course, be something of a personal evaluation based upon study and experience. The experience of the authors has been largely that of the

[1] David L. Cole, "Government and the Bargaining Process: The Role of Mediation," *The Annals*, Vol. CCCXXXIII (January, 1961), pp. 50–51.

"mediated" and the researcher. Perhaps Cole or other fine mediators would look at the problem quite differently.[2]

First of all, there is wide variation in competence and effectiveness among mediation agencies and personnel. There are, of course, many competent men from both the federal and the state agencies. In some very difficult situations, these mediators have proved most constructive and helpful in attempting to assist the parties to move toward agreement. They are serving the public interest and continue to do so.

On the other hand, there are indications that such competence may be in the minority among state agencies and among regional offices of the Federal Service. There are several reasons why this may be true.

In the first place, as has already been noted, most states assign mediation as an auxiliary duty to the state labor commissioner or director. He is more often than not selected on the basis of political expediency, usually a union functionary being rewarded for organized labor's share in the election spoils. If he has a staff, it is likely to be composed of his friends from union ranks, or of allies of his sponsor. Special qualification requirements or training programs for mediators in such agencies are largely absent. Competence and impartiality in the mediation field sometimes develop in such agencies, but not too often. Political upheaval usually means a new staff regardless of competence or experience developed.

In Pennsylvania, for example, the mediation service was allowed to lapse into mediocrity for a number of years, with appointments made without too much concern for individual qualifications. Then, in 1958, Charles Douds, formerly Regional Director of the National Labor Relations Board in New York City, was named head of the Pennsylvania service. He has upgraded it considerably by the character of his appointments, instituted qualifying examinations, and utilized training programs to increase the knowledge and effectiveness of the staff.

California is a state which has been very successful in developing high competence in mediation. Since its inception in 1947 the California Conciliation Service has been careful to build a qualified staff, to keep the staff trained, and to endeavor conscientiously to perform the services for which it was created.[3]

On the federal level, good mediators, particularly those who are

[2] For other views, see the bibliography at the end of the chapter, as well as the above-cited article by Cole.

[3] For an examination of the qualifications of mediators in several states, see J. J. Manson, "Mediators and Their Qualifications," *Labor Law Journal,* Vol. IX (October, 1958), pp. 755–64.

reasonably young, are often employed by industry for industrial relations positions. Others leave the Service because they prefer different work or less "firemen"-type hours—little to do one day, no rest another. Like other government agencies, the FMCS has difficulty holding good young men, although many of its senior members have become sophisticated, expert mediators.

Moreover, the status of mediation work is not sufficient in many instances to attract first-class personnel. Despite the public service rendered by mediation when a strike is prevented in a constructive manner, the tributes to the mediator do not seem to last long. He and his work are soon forgotten—at least until another headline makes the public once more aware of his existence. Since the effective mediator must not be a headline seeker lest he alienate the parties whom he is supposed to serve in the public interest, quiet appreciation is his best hope for nonpecuniary award. Few glory hunters have the requisites of the sound mediator, or are even attracted to the profession.

Salaries and Status

Perhaps the unrecognized glory of the mediator's status could be overcome if salaries were paid which could attract the best personnel; but for the most part, this is far from the case. Most states do not pay mediators in excess of $7,500, with some labor commissioners receiving as high as $12,000, but such state officials are responsible for a host of other functions besides mediation.

Table 14 shows the salaries paid mediators in the nine states where state mediation agencies are most active, and compares such salaries with those paid by the Federal Mediation and Conciliation Service. Despite continued low pay in Pennsylvania and Massachusetts, these salaries indicate that state legislatures in key industrial states and the federal government have commenced to appreciate the need for salaries sufficient to attract able personnel. Also, except possibly for Massachusetts, these states are the ones which have given the most attention to establishing qualifications for and maintaining a mediation agency not dependent on political machines or appointment.

Selection and Training

The greatest difficulty in the path of obtaining improved competence in state mediation is closely related to, but not wholly dependent upon, the status and salary situations, that is, the method of selection and training. A large number, if not a majority, of state mediators are selected on the basis of political patronage instead of competence; and

TABLE 14

SALARY RANGES, QUALIFICATIONS, AND DUTIES OF MEDIATORS, NINE STATES AND FEDERAL SERVICE, 1962

Jurisdiction	Salary Range	Qualifications	General Duties
California	$9,384–$11,400	College degree or four years' experience	Mediation, representation votes, and public employee disputes
Connecticut	7,480– 10,360	College degree plus four years' experience	Mediation
Massachusetts	7,553– 9,581	Four years' experience	Mediation
Michigan	7,871– 12,319	College degree and/or four to six years' experience	Mediation, public employee fact finding and mediation, representation votes
Minnesota	8,004– 9,744	College degree	Mediation, representation votes, public employee disputes, compliance hearings
New Jersey	7,369– 11,645	College degree plus four to six years' experience	Mediation
New York*	9,975– 12,768	College degree plus two years' experience	Mediation and arbitration
Pennsylvania	6,090– 9,923	College degree plus three to five years' experience	Mediation
Wisconsin	7,512– 9,732	College degree plus four years' experience	Mediation, representation and referendum hearings and vote, public employee disputes
Average, nine states	7,915– 10,830		
Federal Mediation and Conciliation Service†	7,560– 16,295	College degree and/or equivalent experience plus two to four years' experience	Mediation

* District supervisors also do mediation and are paid $12,296–$14,585 per year.

† Regional directors receive $15,255–$16,295, and assistant regional directors receive $13,730–$15,030. Both actively mediate important cases.

SOURCE: Association of State Mediation Agencies, and Federal Mediation and Conciliation Service.

once they are selected, the mediators are put on the job with insufficient training as to the delicate and important nature of their function. Yet most authorities would agree with David L. Cole that mediation, to succeed, "must be completely and utterly divorced from politics in its every aspect and feature. . . ."[4]

The fact that a person is a political appointee does not, of course, connote his competence or lack thereof. Nevertheless, management representatives certainly are not inspired by contact with mediator after mediator who was appointed because he was the ex-business agent of a union whose leaders supported the winning state administration—and this seems to be the most obvious qualification of a great number of state mediators. For example, in Minnesota, in 1939, the then Governor, Harold Stassen, appointed an American Federation of Labor official to head up the newly created Division of Conciliation as an apparent means of softening union opposition to the Minnesota Labor Relations Act. This patronate has since "belonged" to labor, a situation which parallels that in many states.[5]

Management officials are not alone in complaining about appointment to mediation positions via the patronage instead of the competence route. Union officers have noted to the writers that there have been appointments to state mediation bodies of political cronies whose background is either solely managerial or who are wholly ignorant of labor relations, at least in terms of experience.[6] A person with a background in labor or management may be one-sided; but often, he can learn that there is some sense to the point of view or interest of the other party. But a person with no labor relations experience must learn both his trade and a sense of impartiality—and usually does this at the expense of the parties whom he is supposed to help reach an accord. The lack of competence of many political appointees to state mediation agencies prompted a prominent attorney who represents labor unions to tell a meeting of the Association of State Mediation Agencies that "many times it explains the reluctance of labor leaders and some labor lawyers to disclose facts which might accelerate the possibility of a solution of a threatened strike or an actual strike."[7]

[4] Cole, *op. cit.*, p. 52.

[5] J. W. Stieber, *Ten Years of the Minnesota Labor Relations Act* (Minneapolis: University of Minnesota, Industrial Relations Center, 1949), p. 31. The incumbent is the first who was not a full-time paid union official. He is a former reporter, who headed the negotiating committee of the American Newspaper Guild (AFL–CIO).

[6] Interviews during 1961 and 1962.

[7] S. E. Angoff, "Impartial Opinion and Constructive Criticism of Mediators, Mediation Agencies and Conciliators," *Labor Law Journal*, Vol. XII (January, 1961), p. 71.

The Federal Mediation and Conciliation Service has recognized the need for better selection and training of mediators since its organization in 1947. Mediators are now under civil service regulations and appointed on the basis of competitive examinations, with qualifications of experience and/or education required prerequisites, as noted in Table 14. In addition, the FMCS conducts regular training programs and workshops.[8] The high caliber of its successive directors, plus the emphasis that it now places on selection and training, are undoubtedly reasons why we have detected a general feeling among representative unions and management that the caliber of mediation and the personnel of the FMCS is on the upgrade.

New York is an example of a state which has attempted to overcome the weaknesses of selection and training which have caused many state agencies to suffer serious loss of prestige and confidence, by careful selection and training procedures, and the placing of mediators under civil service protection. New York has also pioneered in training on the job.[9]

Once mediators are appointed, training is a problem which, by the very nature of the function, is difficult. "A mediator is a lone operator—he knows more about the many facets of a labor dispute than anyone else. It is his ingenuity, persuasiveness, and personality that will help settle the dispute—not his superiors'. Mediation is essentially a personal art."[10]

This means that training and supervision must be on the job. But a careful assignment of cases, work with an experienced person, and careful consultation during a case are all used by the New York Board as training techniques. Nevertheless, "the test of efficiency remains success. . . . Supervisory judgment is . . . based on a negative quality: lack of complaints by unions or employers. . . . complaints may be unfounded, but . . . a mediator cannot long function if he becomes generally unacceptable."[11]

The blackball of either party is potent and has cost the country many a good mediator. Unions are especially prone to declare a man *persona non grata.* Moreover, the ease with which a man may become a failure as a mediator by alienating a single union or management which

[8] Federal Mediation and Conciliation Service, *Tenth Annual Report* (Washington, D.C.: U.S. Government Printing Office, 1957), p. 47.

[9] Arthur Stark, "Operations of the New York State Board of Mediation," *Industrial and Labor Relations Review,* Vol. V (July, 1952), p. 576.

[10] *Ibid.*

[11] *Ibid.*

is in a position "to spread the word," combined with the modest salary structure and the lack of nonpecuniary benefits, contributes not only to the reluctance of qualified personnel to enter the profession; even more unfortunate, this tends to place the mediator at the mercy of the parties and susceptible to their pressures. Where state mediation is primarily a political patronage situation, this means that the job of the mediator is clearly on the line if he opposes, or even fails to carry out, the wishes of the party who possesses more potent political power—which in the industrial states is usually the union. And in states like New York, where civil service regulations somewhat protect the mediator, the above quotation from the New York Board's then Executive Secretary illustrates the pressures on the mediator "to understand the situation."

The five members of the Board of Mediation in New York, in contrast to the staff, are appointed by the governor with the consent of the state Senate for three-year terms. Originally, all five members served only on a per diem basis. Now the chairman is full time. Over the years, governors of both parties have appointed persons of prestige and standing in the labor relations field, a fact which has contributed to the stature of the Board in furthering its work. Moreover, New York lawmakers have given their mediation agency a respectable operating budget. This is in sharp contrast to the situation in many other jurisdictions, which do not have the funds either to employ sufficient competent personnel or to do routine clerical or statistical functions.

One other facet of the New York experience deserves mention: Mediators on the staff of the New York Board, as well as Board members themselves, are regularly used as arbitrators. Only a few other states—for example, Indiana[12]—permit their mediators to perform arbitration functions. The FMCS does not. The reason is that the decision-making process of arbitration can often result in an award which alienates a party sufficiently to make the arbitrator *persona non grata* as a mediator or an arbitrator. New York defends this practice on the ground that it permits small employers and unions to have free arbitration service. To avoid the danger of assigning lengthy or potentially highly controversial arbitration cases to its own employees, these are assigned, if at all possible, to the arbitration panel which the New

[12] Fred Witney, *Indiana Labor Relations Law,* Bureau of Business Research Report No. 30 (Bloomington: Indiana University, 1960), pp. 53, 55–56.

The Wisconsin Board acts as an arbitrator either collectively or in the person of one of its members, but delegates mediation work to its staff. Recently the Minnesota agency announced a change of policy to permit its mediators to arbitrate under certain circumstances.

York Board (like the Federal Mediation and Conciliation Service and the American Arbitration Association) maintains.[13] The problem of conflicts between the mediation and arbitration function does not seem seriously to have affected the New York agency, but it could well do so. Emulation of this aspect of New York's procedure has not commended itself to similar agencies.

Other states have problems which can be handled in different ways with good success. For example, in California and in Pennsylvania, as well as in the FMCS, the administration of mediation seems to be very satisfactory with a single head rather than with a board. Indeed, there is a serious question whether the board approach as used in New York and New Jersey really adds anything to effective mediation.

New York and New Jersey, with their all-public boards, whose members serve only on a part-time basis, are not the only state mediation agencies headed by boards instead of individual directors or commissioners. In Massachusetts and Connecticut the mediation agencies are also headed by boards; but here, appointment is on a tripartite basis. In most other states, however, the mediation services are headed by single directors or commissioners, as in the Federal Mediation and Conciliation Service. Does the organizational make-up determine the effectiveness of a service? The answer must be that there is no evidence that this is so.

The most active agencies include a mixture of the public per diem board, the tripartite board, and the single director. The character, knowledge, and ability of the personnel, the state's appreciation of the importance of mediation, and the salary, status, and training of personnel all far dwarf the organizational structure of the agency.

On the other hand, considerations of cost and efficiency all favor the single director. Mediation originally profited in states like New York and New Jersey by having prominent people serve on the agency on a part-time basis. This is no longer needed. It is certainly more costly and less efficient to have an executive secretary act as the administrative head and a board make policy than it is to place in one man the responsibility and authority for both. New York has added to its administrative superstructure by appointing Joseph F. Finnegan, Director of the FMCS during the Eisenhower administration, as its full-time, $23,000 per year Chairman. Whether, as a full-time Chairman, Finnegan will take over some of the work of the executive secretary, whose top pay is now set at almost $17,000, remains to be seen, but this

[13] Stark, *op. cit.*, pp. 580–81.

seems to be a lot of administration to operate a fairly small, although very important agency.

Tripartite boards are even more cumbersome and expensive than public ones. They bring together persons with set views and with avowed interests to maintain. This requires much committee and conference work—internal mediation—before getting on with the business of mediating labor disputes. It is noteworthy that the most successful tripartite mediation agency—Connecticut's—actually functions principally as a voluntary board of arbitration and leaves most mediation to individual staff mediators.[14]

COMPULSORY, PREVENTIVE, AND GRIEVANCE MEDIATION

In 1959, when the Landrum-Griffin bill was before Congress, Joseph F. Finnegan, then Director of the Federal Mediation and Conciliation Service, and now Chairman of the New York State Board of Mediation, asked Congress to consider making it an unfair labor practice for a union or company representative to refuse to attend a mediation meeting called by the FMCS. This proposal is not new, having been suggested at one time or another by state and federal officials and private citizens over the years. It has not been adopted, however, by any jurisdiction. The Minnesota law, which comes closest to this position, is not administered in practice with any compulsory mediation features.

The argument behind these proposals was recently suggested to one of the authors by a member of a state agency. "The parties," he said, "are often surprised with what we can do to bring them to settlement. Our files bulge with letters attesting to this fact. On the other hand, too often, they think that to ask for, or even to accept, mediation is a sign of weakness. Perhaps Mr. Finnegan's suggestion goes too far. But I would require the parties to accept mediation if the chairman of our Board or the director of the FMCS assigned a mediator to assist them."[15]

Unfortunately, there is another side of the problem. Assigning a mediator does not produce mediation. The old story of leading the horses to water, but not being able to make them drink, is applicable here. Combined with this fact is the pressure which would be put on officials to assign mediators. It is bad enough now. We know of at least

[14] See, for example, A. Q. D. Emerzian, "An Evaluation of a State Tripartite Arbitration Agency," *Labor Law Journal*, Vol. VI (April, 1955), pp. 234–354; and Robert L. Stutz, "Troikas, Duets and Prima Donnas in Labor Mediation." *Labor Law Journal*, Vol. XIII (October, 1962), pp. 845–52.

[15] Interview, March, 1962.

one international union which makes it a practice to demand mediation almost as soon as it starts negotiations with a major concern. This company is strong enough to handle its own situation and knows it. The minute the mediators walk in, the company's chief negotiator states to the union and management committees something like this: "Gentlemen, I want you to meet federal mediators Jones and Smith. They are certainly welcome to join us. They will be the first to tell you that they have no authority to force a settlement, or otherwise to substitute government fiat for our deliberations."

Mediation has never contributed much to these negotiations. If the presence of the mediator were made compulsory, the company would not change its policy. The mediators might come even earlier, but their effectiveness would be no greater.

Compulsory mediation is not likely to be effective mediation. As the Independent Study Group authorized by the Committee on Economic Development noted: "Extensive experience with mediation has disclosed two facts of primary importance about it. The first is that mediation works best when the parties themselves decide that it would be helpful. The second is that the individual mediator must command the respect and have the confidence of the parties. When an unqualified or unwanted man is thrust upon the parties, not only is he less likely to be successful, but confidence in mediation as a whole may be shaken."[16]

Preventive Mediation

In its annual report for 1957 the Federal Mediation and Conciliation Service stated that "the basic industrial relations policy of the United States (as expressed in Section 201 of the [Taft-Hartley] Act) can be effectuated only if, in addition to dispute mediation, the mediators of the Service make an active effort to identify and help solve disruptive labor relations when the parties are not engaged in crisis bargaining . . . and the advantage of industrial peace can be more readily seen by both parties."[17] The FMCS defines "preventive mediation" as the "providing of advice and counsel to parties as needed and wanted by them." This means that the mediator may enter the case even before bargaining starts, or remain concerned with a case long after a strike has ended, working with the parties to identify causes of friction or to at-

[16] Committee for Economic Development, *The Public Interest in National Labor Policy* (New York, 1961), pp. 92–93.

[17] Federal Mediation and Conciliation Service, *Tenth Annual Report,* p. 48.

tempt to improve attitudes, practices, or other factors which might contribute to industrial peace.[18]

An example of preventive mediation was the assignment of J. Andrew Burke, a skillful and experienced mediator, to meet with representatives of the International Longshoremen's Association and the New York Shipping Association more than six months prior to the expiration of their contract on September 30, 1962. The success of these talks was questioned by one faction in the union, but applauded by another faction and by the industry.[19] Actually, this continued intervention served to emphasize to the parties that the government would "take care of things." There was no bargaining—not only before the contract expired, but actually not even after the eighty-day Taft-Hartley injunction had also expired and a strike of about one month had occurred. A final settlement was imposed by an extralegal board appointed by the President.

In Philadelphia, mediators kept in touch with the parties to the long Yale and Towne strike of 1961–62 almost weekly for some time after the strike ended, endeavoring to determine if anything could be done to improve a most hostile relationship.

On the face of it, preventive mediation seems like a sound idea. Why wait till the parties get into trouble before mediating their disputes? Cannot early entrance into the situation enhance opportunities for settlement by locating, as former President Eisenhower suggested, the "fever spots" of discord before they erupt into economic warfare?[20] The answer seems to be that the advocates of this technique have forgotten the basic fact that mediation is a form of intervention, and that therefore it is not the same as collective bargaining.

Preventive mediation means early intervention. Sometimes this can be helpful, but only if collective bargaining has already broken down. To intervene prematurely otherwise is more likely to insure failure of both collective bargaining and mediation.

The early entrance of the mediator upsets the power balance. With the consequences of either intransigence or ignorance—i.e., the strike—still in the distance, the early entrance by the mediator often results in a hardening of positions, instead of a realistic appraisal of the situation. Moreover, in such a situation the mediator can become, as a labor re-

[18] *Ibid.*, pp. 6, 7, 48.

[19] *New York Times*, April 16 and 18, 1962.

[20] From Eisenhower's speech to the AFL convention in 1952, allegedly written by M. S. Pitzele, later Chairman of the New York State Board of Mediation.

porter of the *New York Times* has appraised it, "as commonplace as the furniture and as useful."[21]

For any type of intervention to be successful, it must be properly timed as well as adroitly executed. Preventive mediation is too often only premature mediation. The parties are notified of third-party interest and, in effect, encouraged to save a little for the mediator. By the time the crisis stage of the dispute is reached, the mediator has likely lost both his novelty and his usefulness. The result is likely to be to set the stage for more intervention rather than to strengthen collective bargaining. Moreover, if the purpose of public policy should be to strengthen collective bargaining, not to set the stage for more intervention, then it follows that mediation can best serve as a remedial function rather than as a preventive function, which in many instances serves to hinder rather than to help collective bargaining.

Grievance Mediation

Closely allied with preventive mediation is the proposal that mediation services give attention to grievance settlement and, by aiding in the settlement of such grievances, prevent problems presented by such grievances from bursting into economic warfare. Proposals of this type have been made by the advocates of preventive mediation, who often do not distinguish it from preventive mediation,[22] or by state mediation administrators—for example, the Florida mediation director[23]—who are looking for a greater means of service for their organizations.

Ideas for mediation of grievance disputes seem to stem largely from the success of impartial chairmen or arbitrators in many industries or firms. Here the terminal point of the grievance process is arbitration before a permanent arbitrator, agreed upon by the parties. To a great extent, such arbitrators settle many disputes by mediation also. Why not use government mediators for this purpose, too?

The answer seems to be quite clear. It is very well established that parties to an agreement should determine their own means of settlement for disputes which result from actions or interpretations under the agreement. To compare an impartial chairman selected by the parties

[21] Quoted by Allan Weisenfeld, "Labor Dispute Settlement—Local or Federal Function?" *Labor Law Journal,* Vol. X (October, 1959), p. 704.

Weisenfeld, Secretary of the New Jersey State Board of Mediation, opposes preventive mediation, among other reasons, because he believes that FMCS activity of such nature tends to reduce still further state mediation activity.

[22] Federal Mediation and Conciliation Service, *Thirteenth Annual Report* (Washington, D.C.: U.S. Government Printing Office, 1960), pp. 23–26.

[23] Florida has been circulating literature stating the availability of its Service for this function.

with power to settle to a government mediator, who was neither selected by the parties nor given power to force settlement if the mediation fails, does not seem valid.

Congress considered the question of grievance mediation when enacting the Taft-Hartley Act and wrote the following into national policy as Section 203 (*d*) of the Act: "Final adjustment by a method agreed upon by the parties is hereby declared to be the desirable method for settlement of grievance disputes arising over the application or interpretation of an existing collective-bargaining agreement. The [FMC] Service is directed to make its conciliation and mediation services available in the settlement of such grievance disputes only as a last resort and in exceptional cases."

A legislative history of this provision indicates that Congress very definitely—and, we believe, quite rightly—wanted to force the parties to settle such disputes themselves by self-devised arbitration arrangements and, in order to encourage this, purposely made mediation largely unavailable except in highly special situations.[24] The net effect has been to establish arbitration as the terminal point of grievance machinery in more than 90 per cent of the nation's collective agreements.

The language of Section 203 (*d*) also raises the question whether state mediation agencies are left any role at all in grievance mediation. This is the one area where the Taft-Hartley Act definitely restricts mediation. At the very least, this restriction applies as much to state agencies as it does to the FMCS—and by mention of the limited role which the FMCS is to play, it might even be construed to preclude a role for state agencies in any case affecting commerce as defined in the Taft-Hartley Act.

There is, moreover, no factual basis to believe that grievance arbitration needs mediation assistance from government mediators. This includes such situations as contracts involving General Motors, General Electric, and others, in which arbitration of wages, standards, and other subjects have not been granted by the companies, but instead the union retains the right to strike over such issues if they are not resolved in the grievance machinery. Strikes do occur over these issues during the life of such contracts. These strikes serve a purpose of settlement. The parties to such agreements understand why they occur and prefer to

[24] Rolf Valtin, "'Preventive Mediation,' Grievance Disputes and the Taft-Hartley Act," *Labor Law Journal*, Vol. VII (December, 1956), pp. 773–75. Valtin, a federal mediator, concludes—despite his excellent evidence to the contrary—that the FMCS has a larger role of service in grievance mediation, although he concedes it would still be very limited.

make an investment in a strike rather than to arbitrate. Mediation, once the strike begins, is certainly in order. But at any time the parties feel strikes are too costly over such issues, they can arbitrate. They do not need government mediators to explain these truths to them. A few costly strikes usually establish the ground rules and keep things in a generally peaceful vein. Moreover, such small strikes often teach parties the value of peaceful settlement, and avoid the more difficult strikes over working conditions which are so hard to settle. Mediation is a substitute for neither experience nor decision making on the part of the parties themselves.

FINAL COMMENTS—TECHNIQUES AND MEDIATORS

A great mediator told the authors that expert mediation actually breaks down into four aspects: (1) understanding the what and why of the dispute, including the power structure; (2) raising doubts among the parties as to the correctness of their course or their chances of victory; (3) developing alternative solutions or even a consent to lose if that is warranted; and (4) recommending solutions if the parties mutually request or consent to have this done.

Other mediators may phrase their procedure differently, e.g., in terms of helping the parties save face, getting them out of untenable positions, etc. Generally speaking, however, the four categories not only sum up the mediation job, but illustrate its inherent difficulties. To guess wrong at any of these stages is likely to destroy the potential for success, or even to worsen the chance for constructive settlement. This is no role for the incompetent or the inexperienced to play. It requires knowledge, sensitivity, and experience—requisites that are not often enough present but are invaluable when they are.

Much of what is popularly thought to be sound mediation tactics is actually quite the opposite. For example, there is a widespread fallacy about mediation techniques to the effect that the way to settle a dispute is to lock the participants into a room and keep them there all night until a settlement is achieved. To the contrary is the following analysis of such tactics:

> The place to hold a meeting or conference quite often is important. We are all now quite used to the conveniences of air conditioning and things of that nature. We are not a nocturnal race. . . . If you want an irate person, keep him up night after night in a hot, crowded room. . . . Who knows who will surrender at the last minute when one is exhausted at about 4:00 A.M. after around-the-clock negotiations.

> Furthermore, the number of coronary thrombosis cases is increasing in . . . [the labor relations] field. Maybe the only good labor leaders, labor lawyers or management representatives are the dead ones. I don't think so and I state flatly that meetings after 6:00 P.M. are dangerous and unnecessary. Remember, irritated people are not susceptible to solution. This does not mean that occasionally such night sessions are not necessary; they are, but only in an extreme emergency.[25]

Too many meetings are also often more of a hindrance than a help. The collective bargaining novice may be surprised to learn that there is much more work done in negotiations by the parties separately than meeting together. Union and management representatives need time to discuss and work out solutions within the management or union organizations before meeting together in conference. This is not only true prior to negotiations; it is equally true all during bargaining and no less true while a strike or lockout is occurring. It is impossible to assess one's position while in constant meetings; moreover, the absence of meetings can be a source of worry and pressure on the parties, with each wondering what the other is planning and how he is faring, in fact, under the strike pressures and stresses.

In such an instance, mediation can be a great help or hindrance, and this is largely up to the skill and perception of the mediator. If the mediator insists on too many conferences, or on not letting the powder dry before he is pushing the parties to get together again, he is likely to be a nuisance rather than a catalyst. If he realizes the importance of timing, and pushes for meetings when they can move the participants toward settlement but understands that no meetings are preferable to sterile, time-wasting sessions, he can be of much greater assistance in achieving settlement when bargaining does occur.

Another widespread fallacy is the belief that mediators must be jolly fellows, who backslap and tall-story their way into the hearts and minds of irascible management representatives and irresponsible unionists, and cajole these unpleasant types into happy agreement. Actually, most good mediators are highly individualistic personalities, some extroverted, some introverted, some good storytellers, some very quiet. One of the best can hardly get along with anyone—except when he is mediating. Each has his own style, and no format or type describes success for a mediator.

Keeping Amateurs Out

In times of labor disputes, mediation agencies can often be of great assistance in precluding intervention by either well-meaning or publicity-

[25] Angoff, *op. cit.*, p. 71.

seeking private citizens or politicians by giving such persons a valid reason for declining to yield to the pressures frequently generated by the press or interested parties that "action be taken." The presence of a mediator on the scene can be used to block out the publicity seeker; the governor who does not want to be drawn in can point to the fact that his expert representative is already there. And the parties are saved the necessity of either turning away the self-appointed intervenor themselves or educating him to the detriment of settlement.

On the other hand, the presence of a mediator is often insufficient to prevent the insistent officials from intervening—especially if the mediator is a state or federal employee and a governor or cabinet member insists on "getting into the act." In such cases, David L. Cole sees an important function for the governor, and warns mediators that they should not resent the intrusion, but should treat it as the valuable help he assumes it is.[26]

To be sure, there are times when help from above, constructively given, may end an impasse. The long Westinghouse strike of 1956 and the Yale and Towne strike of 1961–62 are cases in point. Too often, however, such intervention by political figures is contrived to strengthen the hand of one of the parties, or just simply muddies the waters with amateur intervention. An example of the former was the attempt of a New England state governor to set up a governors' mediation committee in the 1960 General Electric strike after prearranging the matter with the union leadership. This failed because no other governor would go along, most declining on the ground that the Federal Mediation and Conciliation Service was already involved.

In the 1960 strike of the Long Island Railroad, federal, state, and local intervention occurred in both mediation and fact-finding form, while the strike went on to the annoyance, but not the disaster, of the commuters. Meanwhile, settlement was slowed while the parties concentrated on finding the most favorable intervenor, instead of looking for a settlement. Perhaps mediators should not resent such goings-on. On the other hand, most experts are not pleased to see a job bungled which they can perform if only they are permitted to do so. And most important of all, it would seem that the parties have an overriding right to expect mediation to be handled by mediators, not amateurs, however high their rank in other endeavors.

The Independent Study Group sponsored by the Committee on Economic Development has proposed that the FMCS activate groups of distinguished and qualified citizens to assist in mediation. They would

[26] Cole, *op. cit.*, p. 54.

utilize such groups apparently where the regular mediation services could not do the job, using such citizens as individuals on all public panels and on tripartite panels.[27] Again, cognizance must be taken of the fact that there have indeed been cases when such private mediation has achieved salutary results. Even tripartite panels, which usually fail in mediation because the interests appointed to the panel act as partisan representatives, not mediators, have succeeded where this did not occur, and, for example, a union man was able to persuade the union of the need to temper its stand.

Generally speaking, however, the success of such *ad hoc* panels is likely to be limited. If they are appointed more often than rarely, parties tend to wait for their appointment, instead of settling by collective bargaining or with regular mediation services. More important, the number of persons available for such mediation services are, as the Independent Study Group noted, indeed "rare." In fact, most of the really able ones—Clark Kerr, George W. Taylor, David L. Cole, and John Dunlop—were in the Independent Study Group. It is natural for such able men to believe that they are not alone, but their counterparts are actually very limited. In reading this aspect of their report, one has the feeling that they generalized too much from their individual experience and competence.

The Real Professionals

On the other hand, the Independent Study Group was very right in noting that a tremendous talent for mediation exists in the practicing ranks of labor and management. This chapter has dealt with the services rendered by governmental mediators. The great bulk of mediation, however, is done by private representatives of the individual parties to a negotiation. The industrial relations manager, or company negotiator or lawyer who takes the union demands, explains and sells his management on the fact that there is a logic behind them, and then sells the union on a constructive alternative, is in fact doing a first-rate mediation job. The national union representative who goes before a local union or committee, understands their needs and desires, but still notes the practical problems involved, and is able to turn the committee's impractical desires into an understanding approach and a practical solution, is also doing a first-rate mediation job.

When the experienced members of management and union negotiating committees meet, they mediate among themselves in the best sense of the word. Sometimes, they may need assistance from experi-

[27] Committee on Economic Development, *op. cit.*, pp. 92–95.

enced governmental mediators. They should not be harassed by premature intervention or by the need to educate inexperienced or incompetent mediators. They have a right to expect assistance occasionally by persons as expert as they. Anything else is inappropriate. And above all, quantity is no substitute for quality anywhere, but in mediation above all.

QUESTIONS FOR DISCUSSION

1. In 1962, preventive mediation was tried in the East and Gulf Coast longshore situation without apparent success. Does this mean that as a technique, it should never be used? Explain your answer carefully, using such specific examples as you may uncover.
2. Recently, a mediator in a dispute which was attracting wide attention stated: "I am going to lock the parties in a room till this thing is settled." If you were the management representative, what would be your reaction? Suppose that you were the union representative; would your reaction be different? Explain.
3. Are government mediators the principal source of mediation in labor disputes? Before answering this question, obtain data on the number of contracts which are negotiated annually, and compare that total with the total cases in which federal or state mediation is present.

SUGGESTIONS FOR FURTHER READING

ANGOFF, S. E. "Impartial Opinion and Constructive Criticism of Mediators, Mediation Agencies and Conciliators," *Labor Law Journal,* Vol. XII (January, 1961), pp. 67–72.

An attorney serving unions analyzes the work of mediators and some facts and myths about mediation.

COLE, DAVID L. "Government in the Bargaining Process: The Role of Mediation," *The Annals,* Vol. CCCXXXIII (January, 1961), pp. 42–58.

A famous mediator gives his views on the role of mediation, which he conceives as basically part of the bargaining process.

STARK, ARTHUR. "An Administrative Appraisal of the New York State Mediation Board," *Industrial and Labor Relations Review,* Vol. V (April, 1952), pp. 383–92.

———. "Operations of the New York State Board of Mediation," *Industrial and Labor Relations Review,* Vol. V (July, 1952), pp. 569–83.

Two articles describing the work, philosophy, and problems of one of the most important state mediation agencies by its then Executive Secretary.

Chapter 12 RAILWAY AND AIR-LINE LABOR LEGISLATION

The railway industry has served as an experimental laboratory for public control of labor relations. The strategic position of the railway industry in the American economy and the consequent inconvenience to the public if railway service is interrupted, the rapid rise of the railway train and engine service brotherhoods to economic and political prominence, and the early recognition by the judiciary that Congress had the right to regulate railroads, all led to agitation for federal intervention in railway labor matters. Then, in the 1930's, Congress placed the air-line industry under existing railway labor legislation. This chapter reviews the Railway Labor Act and examines the effects of this legislation on the two industries over which it has jurisdiction.

Early Railway Labor Legislation

In 1888 a law was passed which provided for voluntary arbitration under government auspices of any railway labor dispute and for investigation of the causes of and means for adjusting specific controversies by a board composed of the Commissioner of Labor and two additional persons appointed by the President. The arbitration section of this law was never invoked, and only one investigation was made—in the Pullman strike of 1894—and then not till the strike had been defeated with the assistance of the injunction and the use of federal troops.[1]

The failure of the 1888 legislation led to the enactment of the Erdman Act of 1898, which, as slightly amended by the Newlands Act of 1913, governed railway labor relations till World War I. Both laws stressed mediation and recourse to voluntary arbitration if mediation

[1] For a discussion of early railway labor legislation, see C. O. Fisher, *Use of Federal Power in Settlement of Railway Labor Disputes*, Bulletin No. 303 (Washington, D.C.: U.S. Department of Labor, Bureau of Labor Statistics, 1922); Harry D. Wolf, *The Railroad Labor Board* (Chicago: University of Chicago Press, 1927); and Howard S. Kaltenborn, *Governmental Adjustment of Labor Disputes* (Chicago: Foundation Press, 1943), chap. iii.

proved unsuccessful, and both applied only to operating employees. In addition, the Erdman Act outlawed "yellow-dog" contracts and discrimination by an employer against employees because of union activity. Although the latter two provisions were invalidated by the Supreme Court in 1908, they contained the basic ideas which were later incorporated into the Norris–La Guardia and National Labor Relations acts, as well as in the amended Railway Labor Act of 1934.

In 1916 the railway brotherhoods demanded a change from the ten-hour to the eight-hour day, without loss of pay, and refused to arbitrate the matter, although the carriers were willing to do so. Failing to achieve settlement by personal mediation, President Wilson went before Congress to insure passage of the Adamson Act, which gave the brotherhoods their demand. Like previous legislation, it did not apply to nonoperating employees, whose organizations were then small and politically impotent.

Soon after America entered the war, President Wilson, by virtue of a previous act of Congress, took over the railroads and established the Railroad Administration headed by a director-general, who gave immediate attention to the demands of labor. Commissions were established to pass upon questions of wages and working conditions. The antidiscrimination provision of the Erdman Act, which had been declared unconstitutional, was restored by an order providing that "no discrimination will be made in the employment, retention or conditions of employment of employees because of membership or nonmembership in a labor organization." And bipartisan boards of adjustment were established, consisting of an equal number of labor and management representatives, empowered to decide grievances and other disputes arising out of the interpretation of collective agreements. If an adjustment board deadlocked, it could refer a dispute to the director-general.

The most disputed acts of the Railroad Administration involved those pertaining to rules governing working conditions. The eight-hour day was universalized on the roads, and penalty overtime was added. The rates of Negro operating crews, who had previously been paid discriminatorily low rates, were equalized with those of whites, and equal pay for equal work was provided for temporary women employees. The rigid seniority system governing both promotions and demotions, which the operating crews had succeeded in establishing, was extended to all other crafts. Piecework in the railway shops was abolished. And most important, a detailed and extraordinarily rigid classification of shop craft employees and their duties was set forth and later made a part of national agreements which the director-general executed with most of the standard unions. This classification resulted in substantially increased costs, as well as a waste of manpower.[2]

Considering the treatment accorded them under government operation, under which all the railway unions had expanded their membership greatly, it was quite natural that these unions wholeheartedly opposed the return of the roads to private ownership. They supported the Plumb Plan, by which the government would purchase the railway system and run it through a tripartite commission on which labor would have representation. It had little support elsewhere. In March, 1920, the railroads were returned to private ownership under the terms of the Transportation Act (Esch-Cummings law), Title III of which established machinery for the handling of labor disputes. It remained in effect for six troubled years. Unlike previous legislation, it applied to all railway employees. A nine-man tripartite Railroad Labor Board was established, with the labor and carrier representatives chosen from a panel recommended by their respective groups. Disputes were required to be discussed by the parties before being brought to the attention of the Board, and provisions were made for the voluntary establishment of adjustment boards, whose function it would be to handle minor disputes. The law, however, contained no enforcement machinery.

The Railroad Labor Board began its work in the midst of a period of unrest occasioned by rising prices. Decision No. 2 of the Board gave railroad employees substantial increases. Soon thereafter, however, the depression of 1921 commenced. The carriers secured wage decreases, a revision of the rigid working rules, including permission to return to piecework, and abrogation of the national agreements. And when the downturn continued, the Board ordered further decreases in the rates of some nonoperating groups in 1922, but this time left intact the wages of the higher paid operating groups (who had threatened a strike as a result of the 1921 cut). The shop crafts then began their long nationwide strike, in which they were joined by large numbers of workers in other nonoperating classes, but in which they suffered a thorough defeat.

The Railroad Labor Board ruled that the representative of the majority of any craft or class should be the representative for all workers and that employees should be free to choose their representatives without interference from the employer. The Pennsylvania Railroad declined to recognize the standard unions except the operating brother-

[2] Wolf, *op. cit.*, pp. 14–50.

hoods, however, and established employee representation plans. The inability of the Board to enforce its decisions caused workers to lose confidence in it.

When the Transportation Act of 1920 was written, it was assumed that adjustment boards would be established without difficulty. However, the nonoperating unions insisted on national adjustment boards such as had existed during the war, whereas the railroads refused to consider anything broader in scope than regional boards. The result was that no boards were set up for the nonoperating groups, and all the petty grievances fell to adjudication by the Railroad Labor Board. The operating brotherhoods and the railroads, however, established four regional boards which remained in existence till 1934.

The Railway Labor Act of 1926

The dissatisfaction of both unions and management with the Railroad Labor Board induced them to agree on a bill which became the Railway Labor Act of 1926. This Act made it the duty of the parties to exert every reasonable effort to "make and maintain agreements concerning rates of pay [and] working conditions," and to attempt to adjust all differences by peaceful methods. A five-man, nonpartisan Board of Mediation was created, which attempted mediation if the parties could not agree among themselves. The board was further instructed to urge voluntary arbitration if mediation proved unsuccessful. If arbitration was refused and the dispute was such as "substantially to interrupt interstate commerce," the Board of Mediation was instructed to notify the President, who could create special emergency boards to investigate and publish findings. During the pendency of these various proceedings and until thirty days after the report of the emergency board, neither party was to alter "the conditions out of which the dispute arose" except by mutual agreement. The parties, however, were under no legal obligation to accept the recommendations of the emergency board.

The Act of 1926 also provided that "boards of adjustment shall be created" by the parties for the purpose of handling disputes arising out of the interpretation of agreements. Under this provision the boards established by the operating brotherhoods under the Transportation Act of 1920 continued in operation. In the case of the nonoperating groups, however, negotiations between the carriers and the unions broke down as to whether the boards should be regional or local in scope. Some three hundred adjustment boards were established, but many not until several years after 1926; and for many classes of employees, no boards were set up. Moreover, the adjustment machinery provided no means to break deadlocks, and since the boards were all bipartisan in character, deadlocks occurred with increasing frequency, so that by 1934, when the adjustment boards were abolished, some 2,500 disputes remained to be adjudicated.[3]

The Railway Labor Act of 1926 also provided (Section 2, Third): "Representatives, for the purpose of this Act, shall be designated by the respective parties in such manner as may be provided in their corporate organization or unincorporated association, or by other means of collective action, without interference, influence or coercion exercised by either party over the self-organization, or designation of representatives by the other." No specific machinery for the determination of employee bargaining representatives was contained in this law, however; nor did it compel carriers to deal solely with the representative of the majority. The Act also contained no specific penalties for carriers which violated prohibitions against interference with the free choice of representatives by employees, as guaranteed by Section 2, Third. The Supreme Court, however, ruled that such interference was subject to the injunctive process.[4]

The period 1926–34, during which railway labor relations were conducted under the 1926 legislation, was featured by peace on the rails. Only two strikes occurred, and but ten emergency boards were appointed, half of the latter during the last year of the Act's operation. The increased threats to railway labor peace during the last year of the Act's unamended incumbency have been attributed to inherent defects in the legislation.[5] A more realistic analysis, however, would probably find the causes of unrest in the Great Depression and the general political upheaval which took place after 1933.

The 1934 Legislation

Whatever its merits, the 1926 Act was found defective by the railway unions on several counts. They desired national adjustment boards with effective machinery for breaking deadlocks and for enforcing awards; they desired specific penalties, in addition to the injunctive process, to prevent carriers' influence over the choice of employees' representatives; they desired formal machinery by which bargaining agents could be selected; and they desired drastic changes in the per-

[3] William H. Spencer, *The National Railroad Adjustment Board,* Vol. VIII, No. 3, of "Studies in Business Administration" (Chicago: University of Chicago Press, 1938), pp. 11–12.

[4] *Texas and New Orleans Railroad Co.* v. *Brotherhood,* 281 U.S. 548 (1930).

[5] Kaltenborn, *op. cit.,* pp. 49–51.

sonnel of the Board of Mediation, which had fallen from their favor. All these objectives they achieved by the 1934 amendments to the Railway Labor Act, which were backed by the railway unions, assisted materially by the late Joseph B. Eastman, then Federal Coordinator of Transportation, and which were bitterly opposed by the carriers.

The amended Railway Labor Act maintains the basic structure of the 1926 legislation in so far as mediation, arbitration, and the appointment of emergency boards are concerned. The main difference in this respect is that the five-man Board of Mediation was abolished and replaced by a three-man National Mediation Board.

The 1934 amendments established the National Railroad Adjustment Board, which has jurisdiction over grievances and disputes arising out of the interpretations of agreements. The Adjustment Board is a bipartisan agency composed of thirty-six members, half of whom are selected and compensated by the carriers, and half by unions "national in scope." (Thus, smaller organizations of workers have no representation on the Adjustment Board.) The work of the Adjustment Board is divided into four divisions, each of which has jurisdiction over certain crafts. If a division deadlocks, referees are appointed by the National Mediation Board, or by the division if it can agree on a selection.

The 1934 amendments also provided elaborate safeguards for the free choice of employee representatives by setting forth a list of unfair labor practices similar to those contained in the National Labor Relations (Wagner) Act. In addition, any form of union security, as well as the checkoff was made a violation of the Act. Enforcement is also different from the Wagner Act, in that violations are punishable by criminal penalties and prosecution is under the jurisdiction of the Department of Justice. These penalties, of course, supplement the employees' right to use the injunctive process.

Formal machinery for the selection of employee representatives was also included in the 1934 amendments, which provided that the National Mediation Board must ascertain, if a dispute arises, who are the representatives of a craft or class and, upon finding, certify them. The National Mediation Board is entrusted with wide discretion in defining "craft" or "class" and in determining who shall participate in any election if the election method is used.

The Air Carrier Amendments of 1936

Soon after its formation in 1931 the Air Line Pilots' Association secured the introduction of a bill in Congress to place air carrier employees under the coverage of the Railway Labor Act. This bill failed of passage, but the Association kept trying. Finally, by 1935, the ALPA had obtained the backing of the American Federation of Labor, the Railway Labor Executives' Association, and the Roosevelt administration for its goal. Bills extending the Railway Labor Act to air transportation were reintroduced in 1935 and passed with little opposition in April, 1936.

When the air carrier amendments became law, the ALPA was the only active union in the field, although a few others were then attempting organization. Organized labor, fearful that the National Labor Relations (Wagner) Act, which then covered air transportation, would be either unconstitutional or ineffective, supported the pilots' case. The air transport industry was divided and, except for a few minor officials, did not testify.

The 1936 amendments place the air transport industry under all the provisions of the Railway Labor Act except those pertaining to the National Railroad Adjustment Board. That agency's jurisdiction is confined to the railway industry. Provision is made, however, for a National Air Transport Board when the National Mediation Board deems it desirable; but thus far, there has been no demand for the establishment of such an agency.

The Union Security Amendments of 1951

As already noted, the 1934 Railway Labor Act amendments prohibited all types of union security and checkoff agreements. This prohibition was placed in the Act with the support of the so-called "standard" unions,[6] which feared that unions formed after the 1922 strike of shop crafts was defeated, often with carrier support, would be "frozen in" by union shop and checkoff arrangements. In addition, the frequent transfer of personnel between the firemen's and engineers' brotherhoods, or between the trainmen and the railway conductors, contributed to the lack of interest in compulsory unionism.

By 1951, however, the standard unions had wrested bargaining rights for most railroad employees from their rivals and had worked out

[6] These unions include the Brotherhood of Locomotive Engineers, the Brotherhood of Locomotive Enginemen and Firemen, the Order of Railway Conductors, the Brotherhood of Railroad Trainmen, and the Switchmen's Union in the operating end; and the Brotherhood of Maintenance of Way Employees, the Order of Railroad Telegraphers, the Brotherhood of Railway and Steamship Clerks, Freight Handlers, Express and Station Employees, the American Train Dispatchers' Association, the Brotherhood of Railroad Signalmen, the Brotherhood of Railway Carmen, the International Association of Machinists, the International Brotherhood of Electrical Workers, the Brotherhood of Boilermakers, Shipbuilders, Welders, and Helpers, and the Brotherhood of Firemen and Oilers in the non-operating part of the industry. The last four include unions which now have only a small portion of their membership in the railroad industry; the remainder draw most of their members from the railroad industry.

suitable arrangements to effectuate transfers of members from one union to another under union shop conditions. As noted in Chapter 8, these unions were then able to persuade Congress to legalize union security and checkoff provisions, despite the discriminatory membership policies of several of them. Unlike the Taft-Hartley Act, the Railway Labor Act provides no machinery for voting out union security provisions if the workers so desire.

ANALYSIS OF THE RAILWAY LABOR ACT—THE DISPUTES PROCEDURE

The Railway Labor Act is thus a comprehensive code of labor legislation which (1) establishes definite provisions for the conduct of negotiations and provides for the postponement of strikes or lockouts until a variety of government intervenor techniques have occurred; (2) provides for compulsory arbitration of grievance disputes before a national, publicly supported bipartisan board; (3) provides for a method of selecting bargaining representatives and proscribes employer unfair labor practices; and (4) applies the principles and practices of the Act (except for compulsory arbitration of grievances) which were developed in the railroad industry to a new industry—air transportation. What have been the results?

Required Collective Bargaining

Section 2, First, of the Railway Labor Act establishes "the duty of all carriers, their officers, agents and employees to exert every reasonable effort to make and maintain agreements concerning rates of pay, rules and working conditions and to settle all disputes" peacefully. Ensuing paragraphs of the same section set forth a procedure for collective bargaining which includes (1) written request for a conference relating to a dispute served by one party on the other; (2) written reply by the second party, setting a time and place mutually agreeable for a conference; (3) requirement that the conference be held within twenty days after the receipt of the original notice at a location "upon the line of the carrier," except that the time and place may be altered by mutual agreement; and (4) prohibition of unilateral changes in contracts except in the manner prescribed in the Act.

Thus the first basic element in the Railway Labor Act's disputes settlement is the obligation of the carriers to make and to maintain collective agreements which, by custom, are written agreements. Corollary to this obligation is a second one—the duty to dispose of disputes quickly and peacefully.

The National Mediation Board, the Railway Labor Act's mediation agency, has placed much stress on the policy pronouncement and the procedure for collective bargaining embodied in the Act. The Board as well as many other authorities have argued that the Act's stated policy and procedure encourage collective bargaining and collective agreements which, it believes, are "primarily" responsible for the alleged "peaceful nature" of collective bargaining in the railroad industry.[7]

Undoubtedly, the Railway Labor Act has encouraged the making of collective agreements, particularly in the earlier years of its existence, when collective bargaining was so much less universally accepted. Few will also deny, however, that the National Labor Relations (Wagner) Act also resulted in a substantial increase in collective agreements. Is the strike record under the Railway Labor Act superior to that in many other industries because the Railway Labor Act makes it the duty of unions and employees to settle disputes peacefully, whereas the Wagner Act did not deal with labor-management disputes? One may well doubt that policy pronouncements have so compelling an influence. Rather, it seems wiser to conclude that although this portion of the Railway Labor Act has probably been of some value in maintaining industrial peace, its influence has not been nearly so significant as the Mediation Board claims.

Mediation

If the parties are unable to settle a dispute by collective bargaining, they may seek mediation by the National Mediation Board, or the Mediation Board "may proffer its services in case any labor emergency is found by it to exist at any time."

On the basis of statistics which show that mediation has settled far more cases than other forms of intervention, both the Mediation Board and many of the observers who have studied the Railway Labor Act have concluded that mediation is the most important and most effective method of intervention under the Act. There is no doubt that the National Mediation Board and its staff have enjoyed the respect and confidence of the parties in the railway industry, and to a lesser degree (as will be discussed below) in air transport as well. The availability of a mediation service which enjoys good relations with the parties is surely an aid to peaceful settlement. To that extent the National Mediation Board and its employees have performed a real service in aiding industrial peace.

[7] See Kaltenborn, *op. cit.*, p. 52, for an elaboration and endorsement of this view.

On the other hand, statistics of cases settled, and arguments based thereon, do not distinguish qualitatively among cases. A dispute involving all the standard unions and railroads and one involving three train dispatchers on a single road receive the same weight. Actually, very few nationwide railroad wage cases have been settled by mediation since 1936. In an industry like the railroads where national collective bargaining settles basic wage issues, it would be surprising indeed if most of the cases requiring government intervention were not settled by mediation. Hence the fact that mediation is used more than any other form of government intervention does not mean that it is either the most satisfactory or the most successful, but rather that it is the method most useful for minor controversies when the major issues have been disposed of.

One should not infer from this discussion that mediation is unimportant in railway labor disputes. Quite the contrary is true. The existence of a mediation agency having the respect of the parties has aided immensely in bringing about peaceful settlement of numerous cases. Some of these cases conceivably might have erupted into stoppages if such competent or influential mediation were not present. Undoubtedly also, mediation under the Railway Labor Act has prevented minor disputes from becoming major ones. Again, however, this does not make mediation the most effective or most important method of settlement, especially in view of the fact that mediation is not utilized very much where big issues or national disputes are involved, except as a step toward the appointment of an emergency board.

One other aspect of the availability of a special mediation agency deserves mention. On several occasions in its annual reports the National Mediation Board has noted that it is too frequently requested to mediate without any genuine attempt at settlement having been made by the parties themselves.[8] This, as will be noted below, is partially, if not largely, the result of the parties getting ready for an emergency board instead of bargaining. It is also the result of the very availability of a special agency, the National Mediation Board, which the parties feel is there to serve them, to assist them, or otherwise to suit their purposes of strategy, rather than just to mediate.

Arbitration

If the National Mediation Board is unable to settle a dispute by mediation, it must request the parties to arbitrate. Either or both may

[8] National Mediation Board, *Twenty-sixth Annual Report* (Washington, D.C.: U.S. Government Printing Office, 1960), p. 27.

refuse to do so without penalty. If, however, both agree, Sections 7, 8, and 9 provide detailed procedure for the establishment of an arbitration board and for the conduct and enforcement of the arbitration. This procedure was first worked out under the Erdman Act of 1898 and was later modified and refined under the Railway Labor Act of 1926. An award issued under this procedure is final and binding on the parties, as it is filed in the nearest federal district court and becomes a court order. It is enforceable as such unless overturned on one or more of the following three grounds: that either the award or the proceedings were not in conformity with the requirements of the Act, that the award did not conform nor confine itself to the stipulations of the agreement to arbitrate, or that fraud or corruption affected the result of the arbitration.

Under the Railway Labor Act, arbitration boards may be composed of either three or six members, who are evenly divided between those chosen by unions, those chosen by carriers, and those representing the public. Public members are selected by the partisan members or by the National Mediation Board if the partisan members are unable to agree. Arbitration boards may be reconvened to interpret any section of an award on which the parties disagree.

Arbitration under the Railway Labor Act is not utilized with great frequency. During the period 1926–34, a total of 538 disputes were settled by arbitration, but most of these disputes were over contract interpretation or involved unsettled grievances. Since 1934, such disputes have been handled by the National Railroad Adjustment Board.[9]

Between 1934 and 1962, when arbitration of disputes involving contract interpretation and arbitration of disputes arising from proposed contract changes have been processed separately, only 270 cases of the latter type were submitted to arbitration boards, an average of less than 10 per year for the railroad and air transport industries combined, with their multitude of carriers and unions.

The reason for this lack of interest in arbitration appears to be the existence of other means of settlement. Minor disputes have been settled mainly either by the parties or by mediation. This is, of course, all to the good, since the responsibility for settlement is directly on the parties. On the other hand, major disputes (as well as many minor ones) have tended to go to emergency boards rather than to arbitration boards. The reason for this is rather obvious. As the late Professor Slichter has pointed out, "it is easier for the representatives on one side or the other to . . . refuse to arbitrate if an immediate result is not a strike or a

[9] See below, pages 330–34. The statistics used throughout this chapter are taken from the annual reports of the National Mediation Board.

lockout, but the appointment of an emergency board which has no authority to make a binding award."[10]

Emergency Boards—The Record

If the parties, or one of them, reject arbitration, and the dispute threatens, in the opinion of the Mediation Board, to deprive an area of essential transportation, the Board notifies the President, who may than appoint an *ad hoc* emergency board to hear the dispute and make recommendations for its settlement. The emergency board has 30 days in which to make its report (unless, as is frequent, its time is extended), during which, and for 30 days thereafter, the parties are required to maintain the *status quo.* After that, there are no legal restrictions on the parties.

Between 1926 and 1934, when the Act was amended, only two minor strikes occurred, and only ten emergency boards were appointed. In at least one case a board's recommendation was disregarded by a carrier, but no strike occurred, although the resulting grievances did cause a stoppage in 1936.

Five of the ten boards appointed during this period were created in the fiscal year 1933–34. The fact that as many boards were appointed during the last year of the unamended Act as in the previous seven years is attributable to the increased organizing activity begun in that period and the disputes resulting therefrom, and also to the greater willingness on the part of President Roosevelt, as compared to his predecessors, to appoint emergency boards.

Of the ten emergency boards appointed prior to July, 1934, nine involved relatively minor cases concerning small segments of the railroad system, and only one involved a regional case of major importance.

Between 1933 and 1935 the Federal Coordinator of Transportation, an office established in the early 1930's to re-examine all federal transportation policies, took over the handling of most important railway labor disputes. Nationwide negotiations between carriers and unions were mediated by the Federal Coordinator and frequently by the President himself. In a period of turmoil in industrial relations the major disputes were thus handled outside the framework of the Railway Labor Act.

In 1937 the railway unions negotiated a general wage increase with the carriers with the help of mediation by the National Mediation Board. The following year, as a result of the recession, the carriers made

[10] Sumner H. Slichter, "The Great Question in Industrial Relations," *New York Times Magazine,* April 27, 1947, p. 5.

a demand for a 15 per cent nationwide wage reduction. The case went to an emergency board, which recommended that the demand be denied. The carriers acquiesced in the settlement. This was the last major dispute prior to 1941.

It was in the period 1933–41 that the Railway Labor Act achieved its reputation as a "model law." This reputation was based on an alleged relationship between railway labor peace and the procedures of the Railway Labor Act compared with strife in industry generally where this Act did not apply. A more sophisticated analysis would point to the absence of great organizing drives and new unionism on the railroads at a time when industry generally was involved in the difficult task of adjusting to unionism for the first time.

The tone of wartime labor relations on the railroads was set by the 1941 dispute, in which all the standard railway unions demanded substantial increases and an emergency board was appointed to hear the case on a national basis. The recommendations of the board did not meet the unions' desires. They appealed to President Roosevelt; he reassembled the board and, in effect, put pressure on the carriers and the board to grant further increases, which was done.

During the war and immediate postwar period, similar developments were common. The 1943 diesel case, the nonoperating employee dispute of the same year, the 1943–44 case involving operating employees, the Illinois Central case of 1945, and the 1946 and the 1947 wage cases were the most important of those which featured union repudiation of emergency board decisions, threatened or actual strikes, and usually government seizure, culminating on several occasions with more favorable terms to the unions than were recommended by the boards. Further union repudiations of emergency board recommendations were involved in the Pacific Electric, and the Chicago-Milwaukee interurban cases. Some of the emergency boards were appointed from the National Railway Labor Panel, which was established during World War II so that emergency boards could be created without a union strike vote, but otherwise the procedure was consistent with the provisions of the Railway Labor Act.[11]

Later in 1945, all the railway unions demanded substantial wage increases and rules (working conditions) changes. The nonoperating unions, and the conductors, switchmen, and firemen, agreed with the carriers to drop their demands for rules changes and to submit their

[11] For a history of railway labor relations during this period, see Herbert R. Northrup, "The Railway Labor Act and Railway Labor Disputes during Wartime," *American Economic Review*, Vol. XXXVI (June, 1946), pp. 324–43.

disputes to separate arbitration boards created pursuant to the Railway Labor Act. The engineers and the trainmen refused to drop their demands for rules changes, and their dispute was heard by an emergency board.

Both arbitration boards awarded the employees increases of 16 cents per hour. The emergency board, on the basis of these awards, recommended a like increase and, except for a few very minor ones, remanded the proposed rules changes back to the parties for further negotiation.

The unions were unanimous in condemning the awards and the recommendation. The nonoperating groups, and the conductors, switchmen, and firemen, having agreed to accept binding arbitration, accepted the awards in a technical sense only, for they immediately made new demands on the carriers. The trainmen and the engineers rejected the emergency board's recommendation and called a nationwide strike to commence on May 18, 1946.

When the impasse continued, President Truman took over the railroads. The leaders of the engineers and trainmen, however, refused to call off the strike until thirty minutes before it was scheduled to commence. Then they announced a postponement for five days. By then, trains had been canceled, express embargoed, and some union members had walked out, so that the nation's transportation system was thrown into a state of confusion. The President then recommended settlement on the basis of an additional increase of 2.5 cents per hour, which would bring the total to the 18.5 "pattern" established in mass production industries. His proposal was accepted by all carriers and unions except the trainmen and engineers, to whom it was made contingent on their waiving the seven minor rules changes which the emergency board had recommended. When these two unions refused the compromise, a nationwide railway strike, the only one in American history involving operating unions, began on May 23, 1946. It ended two days later on President Truman's terms, as he was asking Congress for a drastic strike law to deal with the emergency.

In 1947 the nonoperating unions arbitrated their demands with the carriers, and the trainmen and the conductors accepted a settlement based upon this arbitration without third-party intervention. The other three operating unions attempted to gain more, and rejected an emergency board report which recommended the same settlement. As a result, President Truman utilized his war powers to take over the railroads in May, 1948. This time the President declined to put pressure on the carriers for additional concessions, and in July the three holdout unions settled on basically the same terms as the others. The roads were then returned to private management.

Despite the use of arbitration in these few significant postwar cases, it was not continued in most other important disputes. Labor relations on the railroads continued in somewhat of an upheaval for the next several years, with strikes by the locomotive firemen over the extent and number of firemen (actually helpers) to be carried by diesel engines, and by the switchmen, trainmen, and others over the forty-hour week. In addition, numerous difficulties arose because of unsettled grievances pending before the National Railroad Adjustment Board, as will be discussed below.[12] During the latter part of the 1950's, however, the bigger cases were settled without great difficulty, although strikes resulting after recommendations of emergency boards had been rejected continued to occur on some railroads. This was a period in which unions could not count on favorable intervention from the White House. Moreover, as traffic and employment declined on the railroads, the carriers became more insistent on the elimination of obsolete work rules and featherbedding practices, and the weaknesses of the unions' case on these issues discouraged them from invoking the emergency board procedure.[13]

In its report involving a dispute between the larger railroads and the conductors' and trainmen's unions in 1955, an emergency board recommended a detailed study and review of the railroad industry's wage structure for the operating classifications, noting that this had not been done since World War I. James P. Mitchell, Secretary of Labor in the Eisenhower administration, succeeded in obtaining agreement between the railroads and the five operating unions to set up a tripartite commission, which was done by Presidential executive order. As with an emergency board, recommendations of the commission were not to be binding on the parties.

The Presidential Railroad Commission made an exhaustive study and report after a year spent in hearing evidence, having special studies made, and observing the matters at issue. It recommended many changes in existing practices, many favorable to employees, but also the elimination of wasteful practices and unproductive jobs, including the

[12] See below, pages 330–34.

[13] For a history of disputes during this period, see David M. Levinson, "Railway Labor Act—The Record of a Decade," *Labor Law Journal,* Vol. III (June, 1952), pp. 13–29; and Jacob J. Kaufman, "Emergency Boards under the Railway Labor Act," *Labor Law Journal,* Vol. IX (December, 1958), pp. 910–20, 949.

use of "firemen" on yard and switch diesels.[14] The carriers accepted the recommendations, but the unions did not. President Kennedy declined to throw the full weight of his office behind the Railroad Commission's recommendations. Instead, he appointed an emergency board to hear the dispute. After this board had made the recommendations more favorable to the unions, they again rejected them. Finally Congress ordered arbitration of the fireman issue; the others were settled favorable to the unions under pressure from President Johnson.

The manner in which President Kennedy handled the dispute growing out of the Railroad Commission report is reminiscent of Presidential intervention in railway labor disputes during the 1940's. A few weeks before the appointment of the emergency board to rehear matters that were before the Commission, the Order of Railroad Telegraphers struck the Chicago and North Western Railway. The issue was the demand of the union for a veto over job abolishments. An emergency board had recommended liberalized unemployment, retraining, and severance payments instead, which the carrier was willing to accept. The President demanded "sufficient concessions" from both sides to get an agreement.[15] A few days later the parties agreed to arbitrate, giving the union another "bite at the apple," although the arbitrator, in effect, sustained the carriers' position.

Emergency Boards—Analysis

From the time the Railway Labor Act was amended in 1934 to October 1, 1962, emergency boards were appointed to hear 125 railway cases (plus 27 air-line cases), and 58 additional boards were selected from the National Railway Labor Panel. These boards considered some cases involving nearly all the nation's railroads, as well as some involving one issue on a small, localized carrier. The record indicates three conclusions: (1) The appointment of emergency boards has become commonplace; (2) recommendations of emergency boards at critical times have been handled with political expediency; and (3) the procedure has severely inhibited collective bargaining.

1. The thinking which went into the creation of the Railway Labor Act assumed that the emergency boards would be appointed only in

[14] *Report of the Presidential Railroad Commission* (Washington, D.C.: U.S. Government Printing Office, February, 1962).

[15] From President Kennedy's news conference of September 13, 1962, as transcribed in the *New York Times*, September 15, 1962, p. 12. Several papers noted editorially that in the same press conference the President threw the full weight of his office behind the recommendation of a panel which he created without legislative sanction to handle a dispute in the aerospace industry, and which recommended a voting procedure in regard to the union shop, to the dismay of the industry and joy of the unions. See the editorials in the *New York Times*, Sept. 15, 1962, and the *Washington Post*, Sept. 16, 1962.

rare instances of genuine emergency. In other cases where disputes were not settled by collective bargaining or mediation, it was felt that arbitration would be utilized.[16] The late Dr. William M. Leiserson, for many years Chairman of the National Mediation Board, emphasized this thinking when he declared that emergency boards were merely an extension of arbitration:

> Such emergency boards have become known as fact-finding boards, but this is a misnomer. They are really arbitration boards who hear the parties, decide the issues, and publish the facts to support their decisions, but these are treated as recommendations, not awards binding on the parties. Pressure of public opinion is relied on to secure compliance, a process which makes it essential to center public attention on the awards and not on the facts as these might lead people to draw different conclusions from those of the board. Also, unless the number of such boards is strictly limited, the many decisions scatter the attention of the public and the expected pressure does not materialize.[17]

Contrast this view with that of a spokesman for the nonoperating unions in the 1948 wage case who termed the emergency board's report a "basis for negotiation"! To term emergency boards "arbitration" boards is as much a misnomer as to term them "fact-finding" boards, because public opinion usually is not nearly as effective as proponents of this view believe. It is correct that one reason why public opinion has not turned the emergency board procedure into an effective, binding-award-making mechanism is that far too many boards have been appointed. This was especially true when Presidents Roosevelt and Truman, partially because of the necessities of war, commenced appointing "emergency" boards to hear the most trivial disputes. Yet the ease with which many unions disregarded the recommendations of these boards during the war years, when a railroad strike was unthinkable, indicates that public opinion cannot bind participants.

It is, moreover, not practical to assume that any strict limit can be kept on the number of emergency boards which are to be appointed. As long as the emergency board procedure is available, one side or the other will create the "emergencies" if the possibility of gaining a better settlement exists. When that occurs, the pressure on the President, or whoever must appoint such boards, from well-meaning citizens and newspaper headlines to prevent the "emergency," plus added pressure from labor or industry to aid the emergency creator, usually results in the

[16] See, for example, the comments of the union spokesman advocating the original 1926 law in Kaufman, *op. cit.,* pp. 911–12.

[17] William M. Leiserson, "Public Policy in Labor Relations," *American Economic Review,* Vol. XXXVI (May, 1946), p. 345 (*Papers and Proceedings of the Fifty-eighth Annual Meeting of the American Economic Association,* Cleveland, January 24–27, 1946).

appointment of a board, the establishment of a precedent, and an ever-increasing number of "emergencies" and boards. In addition to railway labor experience, ample evidence to support this analysis is found in our war labor history and in the state experience discussed in Chapter 14, as well as in the experience of other countries which have utilized similar machinery.[18]

2. Great opportunities to make the Railway Labor Act's emergency procedure work have been lightly jettisoned. When President Roosevelt, first in 1941, and then repeatedly throughout the war years, assisted the railroad unions to gain additional benefits over and above emergency board recommendations, he set the tone for over a decade of railway labor relations. The failure of President Kennedy to place the full weight of his office behind the impressive findings of the Presidential Railroad Commission, and his lack of endorsement of the recommendations of other emergency boards, promise an acceleration of the "platform" approach to emergency board procedure—that is, use of the board recommendations as a departure point for further benefits.

This is, of course, not surprising if viewed in the context of political power, instead of industrial relations. The Railway Labor Act, and especially the 1934 and 1951 amendments, stand as testimony to the ability of the railway unions to achieve goals via the political route when the procedures of the Act fail to accomplish desired ends.

3. Preparing for an emergency board proceeding and bargaining collectively are quite different approaches to the task of either winning gains or achieving agreement. If one is doing the former, it is often wiser to ask for more than expected, in both amounts and quantity of demands, in the hope that the emergency board will recommend the maximum possible. Why bargain away anything when it might be granted? This is what has happened in the industry. The parties usually go through the procedure of the Act with little or no intention of yielding on anything till the emergency board stage is involved—and then too often, not till after the emergency board recommendations are issued.

Consider, for example, the comment of the emergency board in a 1948 case:

> The board was not asked, on this conversion rule issue, to resolve a question of principle. It was made, instead, the target for a barrage of conflicting arguments about a lot of little details. We were asked to find the answers to all these quibbles in a mass of evidence and testimony which covered 230 pages of exhibits and 150 pages in the record. This was to be done, within a 2-week

[18] See B. M. Stewart and W. J. Couper, *Fact Finding in Industrial Disputes* (New York: Industrial Relations Counselors, Inc., 1946).

period, as 1 little piece of a job which included the disposition of 36 other issues on the basis of well over 12,000 pages of testimony and exhibits.[19]

Fourteen years later, another emergency board gave this succinct summary of what passes for collective bargaining in the railroad industry:

The [union] Organizations, by letter dated September 25, 1961, invited the Carriers to meet on the issues. The Carriers replied on October 5, 1961 that they would consider the matter later. Five days later, the Organizations invoked mediation.

The parties after a strike vote had been taken, met in Washington, D.C., January 10, 1962 in what was or should have been intended as an effort to negotiate or otherwise settle the issues confronting them.

It should be noted and noted well that the principals involved in this matter, which is a labor dispute of the greatest magnitude and importance to the Nation, conferred with each other but four times in as many days.

The Organizations declined the National Mediation Board's proffer of arbitration; the Carriers, after the case had been closed out, advised the National Mediation Board they were agreeable to arbitration, providing a proper arbitration agreement could be reached. The certification of this dispute to the President and the appointment of this board then followed.

The board convened in Chicago, Ill., on March 6, 1962 to hear the positions and arguments of the parties. Hearings were held there and in Washington, D.C. on a total of fifteen days. The transcript of these hearings consists of 2,649 pages and the board received 24 exhibits from the Organizations and 26 from the Carriers, as well as data supplied by the parties at the board's request.

In addition, the board met with representatives of the parties in many sessions in Chicago and Washington in an effort to mediate the issues which separated them. Our efforts in this regard were unavailing. The will to agree was not present. . . .

It bespeaks a traditional failure to meet problems and an unwillingness to grapple with them without invoking the aid of outsiders. . . .[20]

Little need be added to this summary except to point out that the absence of bargaining before an emergency board is appointed not only insures the appointment of a large number of such boards, and therefore aids in making public opinion an ineffectual enforcement measure, but creates the real emergency—if such can occur—*after* the emergency board has reported and one of the parties has declined to accept the recommendations. This usually brings the Mediation Board back into the situation; or the Secretary of Labor, or even the President, enters

[19] *Report of the Emergency Board in re* [*Certain Railroads*] . . . *and the Brotherhood of Locomotive Engineers, et al.* (Washington, D.C., 1948).

[20] *Report to the President by the Emergency Board . . . in re* [Certain Railroads] *and . . . Eleven Cooperating Railway Labor Organizations* (Washington, D.C., May 3, 1962).

the picture, with either pressure on the carrier to accept the emergency board recommendations or pressure on the carrier to grant more in order to induce the union to accept peaceful settlement. In such cases the emergency procedure may even create the emergency—for if it were not in existence, the parties would have to settle the disputes themselves, as they do in most other industries.

In this respect, emergency board procedure may be less in the public interest than compulsory arbitration. Both inhibit collective bargaining. But compulsory arbitration at least affords a substitute method of settlement, whereas the railroad emergency board procedure, or other so-called "fact-finding" arrangements, do not.

NATIONAL RAILROAD ADJUSTMENT BOARD

The National Railroad Adjustment Board is "the only administrative tribunal, federal or state, which has ever been set up in this country for the purpose of rendering judicially enforceable decisions in controversies arising out of the interpretation of contracts."[21] The NRAB was created by the 1934 amendments to the Railway Labor Act and marked the return of the settlement of grievances on a national basis which had prevailed during World War I and which the railroads refused to continue in the interim period. The NRAB consists of thirty-six members, one half chosen by the carriers, and one half by unions "national in scope" and free from carrier domination. It is divided into four divisions and is actually four separate boards rather than a single agency.

Although in some cases, other unions have more members or

[21] Lloyd H. Garrison, "The National Railroad Adjustment Board: A Unique Administrative Agency," *Yale Law Journal,* Vol. XLVI (1937), p. 567.

[22] Herbert R. Northrup and M. L. Kahn, "Railroad Grievance Machinery: A Critical Analysis," Part I, *Industrial and Labor Relations Review,* Vol. V (April, 1952), pp. 370–72. The Secretary of Labor has the duty to determine if a union is eligible. The Brotherhood of Sleeping Car Porters is one nonstandard union found eligible, but the other unions do not permit it representation on the Third Division.

[23] The Second Division has always been able to agree on referees, the Fourth generally, the Third occasionally, and the First, which decides 70–80 per cent of the cases, almost never. The First Division has jurisdiction over operating employees, the Second over shop employees, the Third over all nonoperating groups except shop, waterborne, and supervisory, and the Fourth over waterborne employees of railroads, supervisory and miscellaneous groups.

[24] Although the Railway Labor Act seems to authorize submission by individuals, the union representatives, with few exceptions, vote not to hear them. This creates a procedural deadlock which there is no way to break, so they do not get heard. The First and Second divisions do not accept cases of nonstandard unions, but the Third and Fourth do. However, most nonstandard unions will not submit cases to a Board whose union members are controlled by rivals.

more contracts, only the standard unions have been designated "national in scope" or otherwise permitted to participate in the selection of employee representatives. This has proved a decided advantage to these unions in competitive organizing situations.[22]

When a Division of the NRAB cannot agree on a case, a referee is appointed either by the Division or, if it cannot agree, by the National Mediation Board.[23] If they so desire, carriers and unions can set up system regional boards, or special boards to hear their cases, instead of referring them to the NRAB. This has been done in a number of instances, sometimes because of the long wait for a decision on the part of the NRAB, on other occasions because of the desire of a nonstandard union to select its own employee representatives.

Procedure of the NRAB

Cases may be submittted to the NRAB by one or both of the parties, but 80 per cent are submitted by the standard unions.[24] Neither notice nor a right of hearing is given to any individual or organization which might be affected, other than the carrier or union involved, although awards of the NRAB have been enjoined or otherwise collaterally attacked on many occasions because of this lack of elementary due process.[25] The fact that the divisions operate in secrecy without stenographic records, reporters, or other outsiders present, accentuates the problems of due process or lack thereof.

When a Division issues an award, judicial review is provided only by the losing party refusing to put it into effect and the winning party instituting enforcement proceedings by suit in federal court. For years the operating unions frustrated this process by an agreement among themselves not to take such cases to court, but to threaten a strike. In addition, strike threats aimed at by-passing the NRAB altogether became increasingly common. The net effect was to invoke the Railway Labor Act's disputes procedure, and often emergency board proceedings. In some years, such cases were the leading cause of emergency boards being created.[26]

[25] For a list of cases, see Northrup and Kahn, *op. cit.,* pp. 373–74. Individual authorization, usually obtained through union constitutions and membership applications, is also required for an award to be binding upon employees. Merely being the bargaining agent does not confer the right to represent employees before the NRAB. *Elgin Joliet & Eastern Railway Co.* v. *Burley,* 325 U.S. 711 (1945).

[26] In 1949–50, for example, six of eleven emergency boards were actually concerned with matters properly within the jurisdiction of the NRAB, and one forty-five-day strike occurred. The Mediation Board noted that a "great amount of time of the [Mediation] Board and its mediators was spent in preventing strikes in such situations." See National Mediation Board, *Sixteenth Annual Report* (Washington, D.C.: U.S. Government Printing Office, 1950), pp. 24–25.

Legal proceedings may finally have checked this extralegal activity and enforcement. If a case is before the NRAB, the courts will enjoin a strike and require the union to rely solely on NRAB procedures.[27] If the NRAB has issued a decision, the courts will enjoin a strike aimed at enforcing an award, making judicial review a real instead of an empty route.[28] Of course, it is conceivable that a union can threaten to strike over an alleged wage matter, when the real underlying issue is still under NRAB jurisdiction. Thus legal processes might still be frustrated.

Case Load and Issues

From its inception in 1934 to June 30, 1962, the NRAB had received a total of 58,383 cases. Of these, approximately 70 per cent were First Division cases.[29] The proportion of First Division cases has been declining in recent years—for example, in 1960–61, only 44 per cent of the cases were within this Division's jurisdiction, as against 81 per cent in the years prior to 1947. Unfortunately, this has not been a real decline, since about 15,000 cases between 1951 and 1961 were referred to special regional or system boards of adjustment set up because of the awesome case load and ten-year backlog of the First Division. Had these cases been docketed by the First Division, it would have received about 80 per cent of the NRAB's cases in this period, too.

Although the number of grievances received by the Second, Third, and Fourth divisions is not small, these divisions do keep reasonably current. Not so the First. Despite the creation of many special boards to alleviate its load, it continues to maintain a four- to six-year backlog of cases. The number of cases involved and the length of time required to decide them are unprecedented and unique in American industrial relations practice. There are several reasons for this.

In the early days, when precedents were established, the unions clearly won the advantage, both in terms of numbers of claims sustained[30] and in the nature of the decisions, which the late Professor Sumner H. Slichter termed "among the strongest in the annals of in-

[27] *Brotherhood of Railroad Trainmen* v. *Chicago River Industrial Railroad Co.*, 353 U.S. 30 (1951). The courts will not enjoin a strike if the case has not been submitted to the NRAB, even though the matter is within the NRAB's jurisdiction (*Manion* v. *Kansas City Terminal Railway Co.*, 353 U.S. 927 [1956]); but presumably, to obtain an injunction, the carrier may merely submit the matter to the NRAB.

[28] *Denver and Rio Grande Western Railroad Co.* v. *Brotherhood of Railroad Trainmen,* 185 F. Supp. 369 (1960).

[29] Data are from Garth L. Mangum, "Grievance Procedures for Railroad Operating Employees," *Industrial and Labor Relations Review,* Vol. XV (July, 1962), pp. 474–99; and National Mediation Board, *Twenty-eighth Annual Report* (Washington, D.C.: U.S. Government Printing Office, 1962).

[30] Mangum, *op. cit.*, p. 491.

dustrial relations."[31] The unions were able to install the principle that each and every bit of work is "owned" by a craft or class of employees and that any deviation therefrom was at the carriers' risk. No matter how long a carrier had the practice of doing something differently, that carrier was liable—often as far back as the 1920's—for deviating from a practice deemed correct by a referee and five union representatives who made up a majority of the First Division. Thus, through the Adjustment Board the unions were able to apply, nationally, restrictive rules which obtained on one railroad, despite the wide variety of different conditions and history of bargaining which prevails on many railroads.

The carriers, however, refused to concede precedent, while the unions attempted to expand precedent as widely as possible. Moreover, to the outsider, the awards are written with such "telegraphic brevity"[32] that what was meant and what was not meant by an award is often difficult to determine, let alone apply as precedent. Hence the decision in one case still does not cause others to be decided on the basis of an outstanding award.

In recent years the carriers have succeeded in reversing the First Division box score and now win most cases, partly because they have already lost on the basic issues, and the interpretations sought by the unions are simply beyond any possibility of credibility; and partly because the carriers are now better and more thoroughly represented. This has not, however, reduced the grievance flow or backlog. It appears that union representatives still process cases they are certain to lose, but find it easier to "send to Chicago" than to settle and thereby possibly alienate some constituents.

The changing box score of the First Division and the court rulings which have estopped extralegal enforcement of awards have lessened the railway brotherhoods' opposition to regional and system boards of adjustment to relieve the First Division's case load. Many have been appointed, but the only effect is to increase the number of cases, for as soon as these boards are formed, a flood of cases is generated which maintains the four- to six-year backlog of the First Division.

The real basis of the First Division's backlog seems to be twofold: (1) the arthritic condition of the settlement process on the railroads in the light of the grave decisions and problems, and the long history of

[31] Sumner H. Slichter, *Union Policies and Industrial Management* (Washington, D.C.: Brookings Institution, 1941), p. 195, n. 80. The courts have been equally caustic about NRAB awards. See Northrup and Kahn, *op. cit.*, Part II, *Industrial and Labor Relations Review*, Vol. V (July, 1952), pp. 549–55, for analysis of awards and court citations.

[32] Mangum, *op. cit.*, p. 496.

having governmental decision machinery available; and (2) the financing of the costs of grievance settlement by the taxpayers instead of by the parties.

No industry faces more severe problems than those with which railway employers and unions must grapple. The carriers, supported by a Presidential Railroad Commission, demand relief from oppressive work rules, often expanded and reinforced by NRAB awards, as a means of helping to achieve solvency and to meet competition of rival carriers. The unions, with a membership decimated by unemployment, and dominated by old men desirous of working out their lives as nearly as possible in a manner to which they have grown accustomed, stand firm against change, and hope for more favorable governmental intervention to maintain the *status quo.* Both are so inured to governmental solutions that the need to step up to their problems is not given serious mutual consideration. The failure to settle grievances where most of them should be settled—at the local level—is just one aspect of a total situation.

Moreover, the single significant factor which (when all else fails) forces unions and companies to settle their disputes over contract interpretations is absent from the railroads. Only in this industry does the taxpayer support grievance settlement. "An arbitration rate of one per year for every 220 employees would bankrupt most local unions and would be a serious financial burden to most international unions and employers at the usual cost of private arbitration."[33] The NRAB procedures cost local unions nothing, and national unions and carriers only the salaries of their representatives on the divisions. All other costs are met by the taxpayers. In the fiscal year ended June 30, 1962, the NRAB cost the taxpayers $788,646, or more than $420 per case. When system, regional, or special boards of adjustment operate, the taxpayer pays the referee. There is no more basic reason for the failure to reduce the backlog of cases on the First Division than this. In the other divisions the issues are not so sharp, so that the availability of public support has not created so drastic a result. Nevertheless, as the Presidential Railroad Commission stated: "There is no reason for the public to continue to support from public funds"[34] grievance settlement in this industry any more than in any other. The "unique" National Railroad Adjustment Board requires many reforms—but none would be so important as to withdraw taxpayer support and to compel the parties to support their own industrial relations system, as do labor and management in every other industry in the United States.

[33] *Ibid.*, p. 499.

[34] *Report of the Presidential Railroad Commission,* p. 185.

REPRESENTATION AND UNFAIR LABOR PRACTICES

One year before Congress enacted the Wagner Act to provide a peaceful mechanism for determining representation disputes and to prohibit employer unfair labor practices, it included procedures to accomplish both in the railway industry. In this regard the 1934 amendments were merely an extension of long-time legislative and administrative experimentation. Under federal control during World War I the government instituted the principle of exclusive representation of the majority of any craft of workers and forbade carrier interference therewith. Following the war, both the Transportation Act of 1920 and the Railway Labor Act of 1926 contained policy statements aimed at similar results, but they lacked the mechanism for carrying out this intent.

Representation Matters

Section 2, Ninth, of the Amended Railway Labor Act requires the National Mediation Board to investigate representation disputes and determine, by secret ballot or other means, which organization or individual, if any, represents a "craft" or "class." By requiring that the bargaining unit be a craft or class, Congress limited the discretion of the Mediation Board to define the bargaining unit (and the freedom of employees to organize on other bases). Outside of specifying that the principle of majority rule should hold, Congress left the procedure and methods for determining bargaining agents, as well as the definition of "craft" or "class," to the Mediation Board.

As of June 30, 1962; the Mediation Board had decided 3,543 representation disputes. In recent years, about 65 of these have occurred per year, with a substantial number involving the air-line industry.[35] The Mediation Board has been very careful to define "craft" or "class" to match the jurisdictional claims of the standard unions. The net effect has been to assist these unions to eliminate and/or to resist raiding attempts from nonstandard organizations.[36] This has been defended by the Board on the ground that it encourages stability and therefore labor peace. The Board's policy is understandable in view of its prime concern,

[35] National Mediation Board, *Twenty-seventh Annual Report,* p. 26.

[36] Herbert R. Northrup, "The Appropriate Bargaining Unit Question under the Railway Labor Act," *Quarterly Journal of Economics,* Vol. LX (February, 1946), pp. 250–69; and J. J. Kaufman, "Representation in the Railroad Industry," *Labor Law Journal,* Vol. VI (July, 1955), pp. 437–40, 508–12. The National Mediation Board has published three volumes containing its key representation cases and decisions (*Determinations of Craft or Class of the National Mediation Board* [Washington, D.C.: U.S. Government Printing Office, Vol. I, 1948; Vol. II, 1953; and Vol. III, 1961]).

as a mediation agency, with the maintenance of peaceful collective bargaining. This favoritism of one group of unions over another is, as already noted, a feature of the Railway Labor Act and much of its administration.

A more serious question, perhaps, is whether Congress should have confined the bargaining unit to craft or class. The declining employment in the industry and the changing character of jobs has not left either crafts or unions in the same status as was the case in 1934. The Presidential Railroad Commission pointed out that the existence of five standard craft unions among the operating groups made employee relations problems in all aspects more difficult of solution.[37] Thus the confinement of the bargaining unit to a craft or class, plus the adherence to union jurisdictional claims as a basis of determining craft or class, may also tend to retard solutions to problems which must be solved if peaceful collective bargaining is to exist.

As to procedure, the Mediation Board at first acted very informally, and actually published no rules of procedure until it was forced to do so by the Administrative Procedures Act of 1946. In this early period the Board tended to certify unions on the basis of card authorizations obtained by unions. Its members and staff were, on occasion, otherwise not too careful to observe reasonable rules of conduct or to preserve rights of Negro employees or of nonstandard unions.[38] More recently, the procedure, rules, and practices governing representation cases have been aligned with more accepted standards, with the secret ballot election almost entirely relied upon to determine representation rights, but the problem of Negroes being denied membership in railway unions continues to exist and to be largely ignored by the National Mediation Board.

There remain, moreover, significant differences between National Labor Relations Board and National Mediation Board representation proceedings which illustrate shortcomings in Mediation Board procedure. Unlike the NLRB, the Mediation Board does not put "No union" on the ballot, so that employees who want this preference must write it in. The Mediation Board will not certify a union if 51 per cent of those eligible do not vote. The NLRB certifies on the basis of a majority of those voting. The NLRB procedure encourages voting; the Mediation

[37] *Report of the Presidential Railroad Commission,* pp. 184–85.

[38] For cases in point, see Herbert R. Northrup, "The Appropriate Bargaining Unit . . ."; and *ibid., Organized Labor and the Negro* (New York: Harper & Bros., 1944), pp. 58–62. The fact that many railway unions have historically denied Negroes membership rights means that the careless policies of the Mediation Board in the early years of its existence contributed substantially to union racial discrimination.

Board procedure does not. Since the Railway Labor Act, unlike the Taft-Hartley Act, makes no provision for decertification elections, this in effect reduces the nonunion potential. The Mediation Board does not make the employer a party to representation proceedings, thus effectively denying him a voice either in handling cases, in determining the bargaining unit, or in petitioning for an election, all of which rights the employer enjoys under the Taft-Hartley Act.

The Mediation Board's policies thus further union organization even if only a minority of employees desire a union. For if 51 per cent of the employees vote, and 26 per cent favor one of two unions, it will be certified. United Airlines has recently instituted a court suit challenging this extraordinary prounion approach and demanding that "No union" be placed on the ballot as a choice for the employees to vote along with two contending unions.

Determinations of the Mediation Board in representation matters, like those of the National Labor Relations Board, are not "final administrative orders" and are therefore not ordinarily reviewable unless combined with an unfair labor practice matter, such as the refusal of an employer to deal with a union certified as a bargaining representative as a result of a representation determination.[39]

A final difference between the Taft-Hartley Act and the Railway Labor Act is that supervisors, including the yard and road superintendents, stationmasters, and other management personnel, are "employees" under the latter law but would be excluded by the former. The fact that the Railway Labor Act furthers the unionization of managerial personnel has been severely criticized, because it interferes both with managerial effectiveness and with freedom of association of the rank and file.[40]

Unfair Labor Practice Prevention[41]

The legal proscription of employer attempts to interfere with union activity on the railroads dates back to 1898, when the Erdman Act included a section providing for severe penalties for such activity. Although this law was declared unconstitutional in 1908,[42] it was, in

[39] *Switchmen's Union* v. *National Mediation Board,* 320 U.S. 297 (1943).

[40] E. Dale and R. L. Raimon, "Management Unionism and Public Policy on the Railroads and Airlines," *Industrial and Labor Relations Review,* Vol. XI (July, 1958), pp. 551–71; and Northrup, "The Appropriate Bargaining Unit. . . ."

[41] For a more detailed discussion of this subject, see Herbert R. Northrup, "Unfair Labor Practice Prevention under the Railway Labor Act," *Industrial and Labor Relations Review,* Vol. III (April, 1950), pp. 323–40.

[42] *Adair* v. *United States,* 208 U.S. 161, 28 S. Ct. 277 (1908).

effect, reinstated during the World War I period of federal control. The postwar Railroad Labor Board attempted without success to effectuate a similar policy, but the first real protection for the right of free association came under the Railway Labor Act of 1926. Section 2, Third, of this Act provided that both carriers and employees should select their bargaining representatives without coercion or influence of the other party. Although this Act did not provide a mechanism for enforcement, the courts ruled that it conferred a right which could be judicially enforced. Accordingly, a carrier which attempted to substitute a company union for one of the employees' choice could be compelled to accept the latter as bargaining agent.[43]

The 1934 amendments went considerably further. Section 2, Third, was tightened, and new paragraphs were added which set forth a list of unfair labor practices similar to those governing management conduct under the National Labor Relations Act, but providing for criminal penalties instead of administrative enforcement for the "willful failure or refusal of any carrier, its officers or agents to comply with" these regulations.

The elimination of carrier influence in union organization was made possible on the railroads by the unfair labor practice proscriptions, in so far as these acted as deterrents and forced the withdrawal of carrier financial support of such unions. It was completed, however, by the representation procedure, where the standard unions steadily defeated their rivals in elections until, today, few of the nonstandard organizations have survived on any major railroad.

Despite the fact that the standard railway unions regarded the insertion into the Railway Labor Act of specific penalties for carriers committing unfair labor practices as a major accomplishment, they have been of little importance except perhaps as restraints on potential violators. There has been only one case brought to trial under this section, and no convictions. Nor is this difficult to explain. In the first place, railroads have been much more willing to recognize unions than has been the case in industry generally. Hence the number of potential cases was not large. Then, too, company unions were ousted in representation cases, rather than in unfair labor proceedings. And finally, in such instances where unfair labor practice proceedings might have been appropriate, it was soon discovered that criminal penalties were not practical. There are several reasons why this is so.

[43] *Texas and New Orleans Railroad Co.* v. *Brotherhood,* 281 U.S. 548 (1930).

The union security prohibitions, since repealed, were also included in this Act, as was a prohibition against modifying contracts other than after compliance with the Act's disputes procedure.

The Act provides penalties for "willful" violations. Willful intent is most difficult to prove ordinarily, but perhaps even more difficult in unfair labor practice proceedings in which subtle actions play so significant a role. Criminal penalties also require trial by jury. The average layman is likely to be unable to comprehend easily what constitutes an unfair labor practice; and even if he does, as a juror, he is apt to be hesitant to agree that the matter is a serious enough offense to merit fine or imprisonment. If the intent is proved, there is the additional problem of placing the responsibility. It is not easy to demonstrate to a jury that a foreman acted on orders in discriminating against a union member. Moreover, the punishment does not fit the crime in other ways. If an officer of a carrier is convicted of committing an unfair labor practice and jailed or fined, that does not provide affirmative relief for employees who may, for example, have been discriminated against or discharged because of union activity. Effective remedial action requires reinstatement with back pay for the employee, not jail for the employer.

On the other hand, the lack of an administrative remedy for unfair labor practice procedure has saved this procedure from being converted into "a tactical weapon used in many situations as a means of harassment"[44]—the fate which in substantial part has befallen the National Labor Relations Act procedure.[45]

Although the criminal penalites have proved relatively unimportant in unfair labor practice proceedings, civil suits have been much more significant. Following the lead of the Texas and New Orleans case, unions have appealed to the courts for injunctions ordering carriers to bargain and to refrain from coercing or intimidating employees in their choice of a bargaining agent. The courts, in turn, have adapted their rulings to the 1934 amendments. In a number of instances, they have ordered carriers to bargain with duly certified unions as the *exclusive* bargaining agency of a craft or class.[46] Moreover, discharges because of union activity are subject to the grievance procedure and hence can be carried to the compulsory arbitration machinery of the National Railroad Adjustment Board. Further, if a carrier attempts to influence the conduct of a representation election, the Mediation Board may set the results aside.[47]

[44] Committee for Economic Development, *The Public Interest in National Labor Policy* (New York, 1961), p. 82.

[45] The reader will recall that this same question—administrative versus criminal procedure—is an issue in state labor relations legislation.

[46] See, for example, *Virginian Railway* v. *System Federation,* 300 U.S. 515 (1937).

[47] *Chicago and Southern Airlines* (Case No. R–1955) and *Allegheny Airlines* (Case No. R–3470).

There is thus considerable protection for unions under the Railway Labor Act against unfair employer influence or coercion. The reverse is not the case. Unlike what was accomplished by the Taft-Hartley amendments to the National Labor Relations Act, there never were proscribed unfair acts for unions added to the Railway Labor Act. It is possible, however, that union coercion or refusal to bargain could be enjoined by the courts just as employer acts of this nature have been. The Act gives both parties the right of complete "independence" of the other, and protects for each the right of self-organization and selection of representatives. It also places the duty to bargain on both parties. Perhaps if a carrier requested such an order, a federal court would order a union to cease interfering with its designation of bargaining representatives, or order the union to bargain, but no such case has occurred.

APPLICATION OF RAILWAY LABOR ACT TO AIR TRANSPORT

The air transport industry was placed under the Railway Labor Act in 1936 at the behest of the Air Line Pilots' Association, then the only unionized group in the industry, supported by the American Federation of Labor. The industry was neither in favor nor opposed. Since then, the industry has grown tremendously and has become quite thoroughly unionized. The record indicates that it is at least questionable to attempt to transfer both a system of collective bargaining and a method of government control developed in one industry to another.

The disputes procedure in the air-line industry has had the same effect on collective bargaining as it has had on the railroads. The ability to get an emergency board appointed has inhibited collective bargaining and has resulted in more crises after the emergency board procedure has been exhausted. The first air-line emergency board was appointed in 1946; but in recent years, they have been appointed with increasing frequency. A total of twenty-seven air-line emergency boards had been appointed as of October 1, 1962, with the number showing decidedly increasing trends in recent years.

Despite the increased number of air-line emergency boards, it is difficult to find one case where a real emergency, or even a serious inconvenience, existed. Air-lines do not generally bargain as a group, and never have bargained industry-wide. In most cases, at least two lines serve an area, so that a strike involving one does not mean no air transportation. And almost always, other forms of transport are available. Since the appointment of an emergency board does not and has not meant the end of strikes, the practice of appointing them in air-line cases seems dubious.

Arbitration under the Railway Labor Act has been utilized by the unions and the air-line industry to an increasing degree. This is all to the good, but arbitration would be equally available if the industry were not covered by the Act, and is also used by many other industries, some more, some less, without being covered by the Railway Labor Act.

Mediation as provided under the Railway Labor Act has certainly been of service to the parties in air transport, but this is limited by the fact that nearly all mediators have had their major experience in the railroad industry. As one executive of a large air line stated: "The mediators know their business, but usually they are so steeped in solutions worked out in the railroad industry that they feel all we have to do is what is done there. I doubt that this attitude is helpful."[48]

It is difficult to believe that the Federal Mediation and Conciliation Service could not supply mediation facilities equal to those now supplied. Because of the varied conditions to which FMCS mediators are exposed, it is not improbable that such mediators would be receptive to special problems of the industry without relating them to solutions developed in just one industrial environment.

In the representation area a firm case exists against the decision which brought the air-line industry under the Railway Labor Act. For in so doing, Congress decreed that employees must organize by craft or class. In other industries, organization proceeded on a basis determined by employees and, in turn, resulted from various factors inherent in labor market and industrial conditions. Even on the railroads the craft or class rule was not decided till after it was largely a fact.

By limiting employee organization to craft or class, federal policy created a number of problems and aggravated others. For example, one result has been to establish separate bargaining units of each and every class of flight crews—pilots, flight engineers, radio operators, and navigators, and stewards or stewardesses. All but the first and last have become, or are becoming, technologically obsolete. Their organization into separate unions aggravates the technological displacement problem because the demise of the craft means the demise of the union. Several strikes of flight engineers have resulted from the attempts of a union to save itself after the problems of its members were at least reasonably met.

The craft or class problem on the air lines has been aggravated by

[48] Interview, August, 1962.

the rigidity of the National Mediation Board's interpretations and rulings. Basically, the Board applies regulations and policies developed on the railroads, and these are often of questionable applicability on the air lines.[49] It is difficult to see how this phase of the Railway Labor Act has contributed constructively to air-line employee relations.

The fact that the industry is under the unfair labor practice procedure of the Railway Labor Act instead of the National Labor Relations Act does not appear to have affected the industry too much one way or another. Certainly, unions have had no difficulty in growing in the industry and with the industry. More recently, the Civil Aeronautics Board has entered the picture firmly on the union side. It ordered Southern Airways, in effect, to stop maintaining its position that it would give pilots recruited after a strike seniority over those who struck. Although the strike was purely economic and the air line was functioning without difficulty, the CAB found Southern's position, adopted after the strike began, to be a violation of the Railway Labor Act. Compliance with the Railway Labor Act is a condition for an air line to maintain its operating license—a powerful weapon as the CAB's 3 to 2 majority have interpreted it.[50]

The air-line industry and its unions may be directed by the National Mediation Board under Section 205 of the Railway Labor Act to set up an eight-man bipartisan National Air Transport Adjustment Board. No action has been taken, however, and none is advocated by either side. For all the unions and all carriers in this industry to agree upon two representatives is not likely. Moreover, each group has observed the operations of the National Railroad Adjustment Board, emulation of which is not likely to be considered desirable.

Grievance settlement in the air-line industry has instead followed the more common and satisfactory method. Each air line and union which bargain collectively have established procedures to settle grievances. When they cannot agree on an arbitrator, they usually ask the National Mediation Board to make the appointment. Arbitrators so appointed are compensated by the parties, not by the government.[51] By failing to emulate the railroad industry and unions in this regard, the

[49] See, for example, cases involving clerical and store and stock clerks, such as C–1693, C–2252, C–2389, and R–1706.

[50] *Business Week,* June 2, 1962, p. 130, and September 29, 1962, p. 60. In reaching its decision, the CAB ignored the damage done to the air line by leaflets and other publicity warning the public not to fly the air line "because it was not safe." Southern had no accident during the twenty-seven-month strike which ended when the air line, as dictated by the CAB, returned the strikers with seniority over their replacements.

[51] National Mediation Board, *Twenty-seventh Annual Report,* p. 60.

managements and unions in the air-line industry have demonstrated good judgment for themselves and for the public.

CONCLUDING REMARKS

The Railway Labor Act involves the most complete form of government control of collective bargaining which has been developed for an industry in peacetime. It is noteworthy that the industries involved are also regulated in a variety of other ways—including supervision of pricing, business routes and location, and rights to initiate or abandon service.

The experience of the Railway Labor Act raises the serious question of whether the government can control collective bargaining without being forced into a position of complete dictation. As the situation now exists, the emergency board procedure has caused the parties to cease bargaining in order to await the appointment of a board. Then a crisis is likely to arise *after* the board has been appointed. This unfortunate situation has been common since 1941, and the propensity of the Kennedy administration to appoint emergency boards for disputes regardless of the seriousness of the potential stoppage to the public, and then to demand "concessions" from *both* sides after only the union has rejected a report,[52] indicates that it will worsen, not improve. The present crisis over outmoded and costly work rules is the culmination of years of refusal on the part of the parties to deal constructively with some of the underlying problems of the industry, but rather to rely on government aid or control.

Obviously, reform is in order. The emergency board procedure could be abolished altogether. Or compulsory arbitration could be substituted. If the former were done, the parties would have an opportunity to salvage their right to settle their disputes without intervention. In such a case, there would be no more threat to public health and safety then now exists after an emergency board has reported and its recommendations have been rejected. If the parties do not avail themselves of the opportunities thus afforded, compulsory arbitration could still be instituted in place of the emergency board procedure. For if collective bargaining is to be rendered unworkable, a substitute form of settlement should be imposed.

[52] In contrast, when the carriers expressed disagreement with the size of the increase recommended by the emergency board in the 1962 nonoperating dispute, the administration made it clear it would go "all out" in support of these recommendations, which pleased the unions. The carriers then acquiesced.

The National Railroad Adjustment Board is, of course, a monument to what can happen if grievance disputes are first invited and then settled on national precedent without regard to local variations. To reform this agency requires the drastic surgery of making the parties pay all costs and of abolishing national grievance settlement in favor of systemwide boards of arbitration except when the parties agree otherwise.

The methods of determining representation disputes and unfair labor practice matters under the Railway Labor Act are perhaps not superior to those under the Taft-Hartley Act, but their importance in the railroad industry is now too slight to consider change.

On the other hand, the subjection of collective bargaining in the air-line industry to the rigidities and inhibitions built into the Railway Labor Act can only be termed a sad error of public policy. This would be true even if the Railway Labor Act had worked beyond criticism in the railroad industry, where it reflects to some extent a codification of practice. But the structure and problems of the air lines require a collective bargaining system tailored to its own needs, not those of a different industry. No harm, and probably substantial benefit, could come from repealing Title II, which places the air-line industry under the Act.

In ending this chapter, it might be well to note that the Railway Labor Act is, in effect, special-privilege legislation. It confers rights and duties dissimilar to those conferred on the parties in other industries. The railroad industry and unions are specially treated in most other social legislation, including social security, unemployment, and health and safety legislation. The rationale has always been the "special nature" of the business and employment conditions.

On the other hand, each industry has its special conditions. Does the railroad industry deserve this special privilege?

Some analysts believe so. One observer, for example, found nine conditions which differentiated railroad employment from that in other industries.[53] Professor William Gomberg, in commenting upon these points, noted that far from being unique characteristics, they exist, often in greater severity, in many other industries which overcame equally difficult problems.[54] Perhaps the very existence of special-privilege legislation has so conditioned the parties in the railroad industry to governmentally imposed solutions that they cannot be expected to

[53] Jacob J. Kaufman, "Logic and Meaning of Work Rules on the Railroads," *Proceedings of the Fourteenth Annual Meeting, Industrial Relations Research Association,* 1961, pp. 378–88. Dr. Kaufman serves as consultant to the Switchmen's Union and other railroad union groups.

[54] William Gomberg, "Discussion," *ibid.,* pp. 413–16.

face up to their problems. The air lines may well be headed in the same direction under the impetus of the Railway Labor Act.

QUESTIONS FOR DISCUSSION

1. Suppose the railway emergency board procedure were abolished. What do you think would happen—more crises, less crises, or things just about the same as now? Explain your answer.
2. What is the justification for including the air-line industry under the Railway Labor Act? Do you agree with such inclusion? If so, why? If not, why not?
3. It has been charged that the Railway Labor Act is special-privilege legislation at the taxpayers' expense. Do you agree with this point of view? What are your reasons and evidence?

SUGGESTIONS FOR FURTHER READING

KAUFMAN, JACOB J. "Logic and Meaning of Work Rules on the Railroads," *Proceedings of the Fourteenth Annual Meeting, Industrial Relations Research Association,* 1961, pp. 378–88.

An attempt to show that the archaic work rules in the railroad industry are a function of the uniqueness of working conditions in the industry.

See also William Gomberg's discussion of the Kaufman paper in the above *Proceedings,* pp. 413–16—a succinct challenge of Kaufman's view.

MANGUM, GARTH L. "Grievance Procedures for Railroad Operating Employees," *Industrial and Labor Relations Review,* Vol. XV (July, 1962), pp. 474–99.

An up-to-date analysis of the problems and administrative complexities of the National Railroad Adjustment Board.

MASON, CHARLES M. "Collective Bargaining Structure: The Airlines Experience," in ARNOLD R. WEBER (ed.), *Structure of Collective Bargaining: Problems and Perspectives,* pp. 217–55. New York: Free Press of Glencoe, Inc., 1961.

An excellent analysis of collective bargaining in air transport, with emphasis on the limiting effects of the Railways Labor Act, by the chief personnel executive of United Airlines, with discussion by other authorities.

Report of the Presidential Railroad Commission. Washington, D.C.: U.S. Government Printing Office, February, 1962.

An exhaustive analysis of labor relations problems of railway operating employees and management, and suggestions for their reform.

Chapter 13 NATIONAL EMERGENCY STRIKE CONTROLS: WAR AND PEACE

In Chapters 10 and 11 the discussion centered on the government's mediation activities, that is, the attempts to assist the parties to reach agreement through persuasion and other noncompulsory methods. In Chapter 12 the long history of governmental intervention in the railroad industry and its more recent adaptation to air transport demonstrates how one type of "emergency procedure"—fact finding —can work out in practice.

Most early experience with government intervention to postpone or to prevent strikes in peacetime involved the railroad industry because of the importance of railway transport in the life and industrial development of the country, and because it was sufficiently organized for unions to be able at least to threaten an effective strike. As industry grew in independence and unions grew in strength, however, stoppages in other industries began to disrupt or inconvenience larger segments of the population. Experiences during World War II, when labor disputes were adjudicated by the National War Labor Board, followed in 1946 by the greatest strike losses in our history, led to considerable experimenting by both the federal and the state governments with laws and procedures aimed at providing methods of dispute settlement which would be substitutes for strikes. Attempts of the federal government to devise strike control or emergency strike provisions during both war and peacetime are discussed in this chapter; Chapter 14 deals with state experiments in this field; and Chapter 15 analyzes some of the problems and consequences of, and proposals for, federal and state regulation of strikes.

WARTIME ADJUSTMENT MACHINERY

Except for the railroad industry and for occasional *ad hoc* Presidential intervention, such as President Theodore Roosevelt's activities in the anthracite coal dispute of 1902, federal intervention designed to postpone or to prevent strikes prior to 1946 was largely a wartime phenomenon.[1] The needs of war production, combined with the psychological necessities of uniting for the war effort, mean that no industrial strike can be tolerated in wartime. During both World War I and World War II, therefore, compulsion substituted for voluntarism in the settlement of labor disputes. To lessen the degree of compulsion, prominent roles in wartime adjustment machinery were given to representatives of labor and industry. Nonetheless, the factor of compulsion remained, and the difficulty of restoring voluntary collective bargaining after compulsory controls are lifted is well illustrated by the great strike waves of both 1919–20 and 1945–46. Moreover, the principles and precedents developed by war labor agencies have had permanent influence on peacetime policy.

The World War I Labor Board

The industrial strains created by World War I—higher prices, expanding industry, and labor shortages—caused considerable unrest and strife even before the United States entered the conflict. To devise remedies, President Wilson called a conference of labor and industrial leaders to formulate a national industrial relations policy. The conference, after ten week's deliberation, agreed on an eight-point program, including a pledge of no strikes or lockouts, the freedom of workers to organize and bargain collectively, and, as noted in Chapter 8, the maintenance of the *status quo* on the question of the closed and the open shop. To effectuate these policies, the National War Labor Board of World War I was created in April, 1918. The Board was composed of five industry, five labor, and two public members.[2]

The World War I Board was in existence for approximately one year. Although its guiding rule was the maintenance of the *status quo* in industrial relations generally, it had the effect of encouraging unionism and collective bargaining. Through it, the American Federation of Labor won official governmental recognition on a par with employers' associations; and through it, peaceful collective bargaining was encouraged.[3]

[1] President Roosevelt succeeding in getting the parties to submit to an arbitration board which he established by agreement with the parties after a long strike.

[2] For a discussion of the World War I experience, see Alexander Bing, *War-Time Labor Disputes and Their Adjustment* (New York: E. P. Dutton & Co., 1921); and U.S. Department of Labor, Bureau of Labor Statistics, *National War Labor Board,* Bulletin No. 287 (Washington, D.C.: U.S. Government Printing Office, 1922).

[3] The World War I Board also pioneered in such questions as representation elections, appropriate bargaining unit, majority rule, etc., and thus established precedents for various NRA boards and the National Labor Relations Board.

The World War I Board was able to settle all cases referred to it with the exception of three, which were referred to President Wilson, who, as a means of enforcing the Board's awards, either took over plants or threatened to draft workers and bar them from war jobs. In view of the national emergency, labor and management generally showed a patriotic willingness to abide by the Board's awards.

In addition to its National War Labor Board, World War I saw the creation of several industry boards in industries which the federal government either took over directly or which were considered extremely crucial for the prosecution of the war. They included the United States Railroad Administration, the Shipbuilding Labor Adjustment Board,[4] the Emergency (building) Construction Wage Commission, the National (longshore) Adjustment Commission, and the Arsenals and Navy Yard Wage Commission, among others. On each, the AFL was granted official recognition, and peaceful collective bargaining was encouraged. Most of these special adjustment agencies were created prior to the World War I Labor Board. After the latter was established, appeal was provided to it from decisions of the industry agencies. An exception was railway labor relations, which were under the exclusive supervision of the director-general of the railroads, since the government took over railroad operation during the war. (See Chapter 12.)

With the end of the war, strikes flared up throughout the country. At the height of the strike wave, President Wilson convened a National Industrial Conference, composed of labor, industry, and public groups, to formulate principles for a "genuine and lasting co-operation between capital and labor." The conference broke down on the issue of union recognition. Moreover, both industry and the AFL were extremely wary of government-supervised collective bargaining and, unlike the situation on the railways, did not want it continued. Hence the World War I Labor Board had no immediate peacetime successor.

The National Defense Mediation Board

As the defense program got under way in 1940, strikes in crucial industries gave rise to increasing concern. By early 1941, it became apparent that emergency measures were necessary to cope with the situation. On March 19, 1941, President Roosevelt created the National Defense Mediation Board to adjust labor disputes in defense industries.

[4] For a discussion of the work of this agency, a typical wartime board, see W. E. Hotchkiss and H. R. Seager, *History of the Shipbuilding Labor Adjustment Board,* Bulletin No. 283 (Washington, D.C.: U.S. Department of Labor, Bureau of Labor Statistics, 1921).

The Mediation Board was tripartite in character, composed of four industry, four labor, and three public members, with alternates from all three groups. The labor representatives were equally divided between the American Federation of Labor and the Congress of Industrial Organizations. Disputes could be heard by the board only after the Secretary of Labor had certified that the United States Conciliation Service had been unable to settle them. "Three steps were set forth in the executive order for the Board to follow in settling these controversies: (1) Mediation in promoting collective bargaining between the parties before the Board; (2) if this fails, suggestion of voluntary arbitration; and (3) if both of these fail, findings of fact and recommendations, which may be made public."[5]

Thus the Defense Mediation Board was instructed, in effect, to follow a procedure similar to that of the Railway Labor Act, except that all steps were to be undertaken by one agency, which was tripartite in character.

Early in its career the Defense Mediation Board settled several very difficult strikes by mediation, but soon its procedure partook of compulsion. If it failed to mediate a case, it issued public recommendations. These recommendations carried with them threats of government seizure if either party refused to accept them, and a stoppage resulted. Four such seizures occurred during the Board's nine-month existence.

The most troublesome question which faced the Defense Mediation Board—and the one which led to its downfall—was that of union security. As discussed in Chapter 8, the Board attempted to solve this question by "maintenance of membership," thus setting the stage for the policy of its successor agency, the National War Labor Board. Industry generally opposed union maintenance, however, and when the Defense Mediation Board declined to go further and grant the all-union shop in the "captive mines" case, the CIO members resigned, and the Board collapsed.

The National War Labor Board of World War II

The collapse of the Defense Mediation Board was followed shortly by the Japanese attack on Pearl Harbor. To provide for the peaceful settlement of wartime labor disputes, President Roosevelt followed Wilson's example and convened a management-labor conference. The

[5] L. J. Jaffe and W. G. Rice, Jr., *Report on the Work of the National Defense Mediation Board,* Bulletin No. 714 (Washington, D.C.: U.S. Department of Labor, Bureau of Labor Statistics, 1942), p. 1.

conference agreed to settle disputes without resort to strikes and recommended the establishment of machinery for that purpose. Management delegates wished to have union security provisions frozen for the duration, but in effect the President accepted labor's view by committing all disputed questions to the wartime settlement machinery.

On January 12, 1942, the National War Labor Board of World War II was established by executive order. In June, 1943, it was given statutory backing by the War Labor Disputes Act, passed by Congress over the President's veto. During the previous October, the Board had been assigned wage control under the Stabilization Act. To aid in administering its functions, the WLB also established thirteen regional boards and several industry commissions. Its jurisdiction included virtually all American industry, except rail and air carriers subject to the Railway Labor Act.

Peaceful Settlement. The War Labor Board initially attempted to decide each industrial dispute case on its merits. Gradually, however, it developed official policies on virtually every issue under dispute between the parties. It attempted to maintain peace in settling disputes by using three basic approaches: (1) appeal to the legal framework governing industrial relations in wartime; (2) appeal to historical precedent, whenever possible; and (3) compromise.

The WLB used the "legal framework" method most frequently in wage cases. The Stabilization Act and the executive orders issued thereunder set forth the law. Hence, when a proposed increase exceeded the Little Steel Formula, the War Labor Board had merely to cite a higher authority as the basis of its decision.

The appeal to historical precedent as a basis for maintaining industrial peace is well explained by the following quotation:

> Where an arbitrator's decision is based on historical precedent, especially if this historical pattern has been created and/or perpetuated by collective bargaining, neither party to the dispute can logically accuse the arbitrator of attempting to innovate in the field of industrial relations. Where the parties are convinced of the negative fact that the arbitrator is not trying to impose any "revolutionary" change on either of them, the first step in avoiding conflict has already been taken. And when, in addition, the positive part of the arbitrator's action is molded along historical lines, the parties are very likely to go along with the decision.[6]

Thus the War Labor Board refused to disturb North-South wage differentials, or historical differentials between two plants of the same

[6] J. Shister, "The National War Labor Board: Its Significance," *Journal of Political Economy*, Vol. LIII (March, 1945), pp. 39–40.

company located in different parts of the country, or even local differentials between two neighboring plants. Likewise, the WLB refused to alter union or closed shop contracts voluntarily agreed to by management.

When the WLB had neither law nor historical precedent to guide it, compromise always remained. The best example is, of course, found in the issue of union security. The principle of maintenance of membership is an obvious compromise between the closed and the open shop. Likewise, compromise guided the War Labor Board when it acceded to unions' demands for such "fringe" issues as paid vacations, paid holidays, and night-shift bonuses, but denied demands for paid sick leave and compulsory health and welfare funds.

The Stabilization of Wages. Since changes in wages invariably affect industrial relations, the stabilization duties of the War Labor Board were closely interrelated with its job of maintaining industrial peace. The War Labor Board realized this quite clearly. For example, its attempt to eliminate interplant wage inequities was based not so much on stabilization principles (although the extent of the adjustments permissible under this concept was regulated by stabilization) as by a belief, as expressed by Chairman George W. Taylor, that "the absence of a proper internal rate alignment may often be more destructive of employee morale than interplant differences."[7]

But wage stabilization was not only related to peaceful labor relations; it often worked at cross purposes with it. The denial of a voluntary application for wage increases, jointly submitted by an employer and a union, usually caused unrest in a plant, and sometimes a work stoppage. Such stoppages were directed not against employers but against the War Labor Board.

Because of this conflict between wage stabilization and labor peace at a time when the latter was considered paramount, compromise was often permitted to weaken stabilization. For example, when a substantial general increase demand of the CIO Steelworkers was denied, a variety of fringe issues such as improved vacations, night-shift bonuses, and the elimination of interplant inequities was used to mollify the union. In sum, stabilization was made flexible to suit the immediate needs of labor peace.

The Heritage of the War Labor Board. The National War Labor Board of World War II rendered decisions for all industry on every conceivable aspect of industrial relations. For many years, its

[7] George W. Taylor, "Wage Regulation in Post-War America," *American Economic Review*, Vol. XXXIV (March, 1944, Supplement), p. 188.

decisions have served as a guide for rulings in labor disputes. The WLB established the historical precedents and the legal framework for arbitrators to follow, and both labor and management still turn to the WLB's rulings for precedents in solving disputed questions. And this will continue to be true whether the War Labor Board's decisions have been "sound" or not, primarily because the scope of such decisions includes all industry and all phases of industrial relations.

Likewise, War Labor Board decisions have furthered certain labor goals which became increasingly prominent in postwar years. They include the following: (1) that a "responsible" union deserves union security; (2) that paid vacations, paid holidays, paid sick leave, group health insurance, night-shift bonuses, and other benefit issues are proper union objectives; (3) that unions should have a voice in the establishment of benefit plans, and that such plans are a proper sphere of collective bargaining; (4) that wage rate structures should be simplified so as to eliminate intraplant differences; and (5) that similar occupations in neighboring areas should be similarly compensated.[8]

The effect of the War Labor Board on postwar labor relations was felt in still another important manner. After four years of setting terms and conditions of employment, the federal government was reluctant to retire from the field because large sections of management and labor found it difficult to return to collective bargaining. Moreover, many unions and many employers were anxious to "teach the other a lesson." This, combined with the pent-up resentment of wartime, did much to make 1946 the greatest strike year of American history in terms of man-days lost from work.

Both labor and management were surprised at the duration of some of the 1946 strikes. During the war, such strikes as occurred were usually "quickies." The emphasis was on uninterrupted production to the exclusion of all else. Union leaders found in the postwar period that management resistance was much greater, particularly when loss of business was compensated for by rebates of wartime excess profits taxes. On the other hand, those employers who felt that unions could not survive postwar strife miscalculated badly. One result of the postwar strike wave was a more realistic appraisal of the effectiveness, costs, and results of strikes on the part of both labor and management.

Another wartime heritage to which the 1946 strikes gave sharp emphasis was the increasing public concern with stoppages of work which interfered with "essential" services or even inconvenienced a portion of the population. Wartime hysteria over strikers was carried over

[8] The natural result of establishing "sound and tested" area rates.

into the postwar period. Moreover, a number of unions exhibited unparalleled irresponsibility and lack of understanding of public sentiment in striking essential services. One result was the election of a Congress with a Republican majority in 1946, which enacted the Taft-Hartley law; and another result was an increasing concern of state legislatures with "emergency" labor settlement machinery.[9]

ENFORCEMENT OF SETTLEMENT—WAR AND POSTWAR

The War Labor boards of both World War I and World War II were set up by Presidential executive orders, and therefore had, legally, only "advisory" power. In fact, however, defiance of the orders (legally, advice!) of these agencies could not be tolerated if general respect for the procedures was to be maintained. Hence, utilizing wartime emergency powers, Presidents Wilson, Roosevelt, and Truman were forced to handle compliance by decree and use, or potential use, of the armed forces.

The problem in World War I was minor. Only three cases of defiance of the War Labor Board of that period occurred. "Two were cases of company defiance and resulted in government seizures. The third was a defiant strike which led to President Wilson's famous 'work-or-fight' order. The workers returned to their jobs."[10]

Seizure in World War II became the recognized method of enforcing orders of the National Defense Mediation Board, the War Labor Board, and railway labor agencies, although in three cases other sanctions were also employed (for example, loss of material priorities for companies, loss of draft deferments for strikers). A total of forty seizure cases occurred during World War II, in addition to the four in the prewar Defense Mediation Board period.[11]

Government seizure, as noted in Figure 5, page 274, involves temporary government control of a business. Nationalization is not contemplated. In the absence of specific legislation the legal basis for seizure rests in the wartime and emergency powers of the executive to prevent a breakdown of essential services to the community.

In 1943, Congress passed the War Labor Disputes Act over Presi-

[9] State emergency strike control legislation is discussed in Chapter 14.

[10] Ludwig Teller, "Government Seizure in Labor Disputes," *Harvard Law Review*, Vol. LX (March, 1947), p. 1020.

[11] Nineteen of these seizure cases arose from employer noncompliance, twenty-one from union noncompliance. See W. E. Chalmers, "Voluntarism and Compulsion in Dispute Settlement," in *Problems and Policies of Dispute Settlement and Wage Stabilization during World War II*, Bulletin No. 1009 (Washington, D.C.: U.S. Department of Labor, Bureau of Labor Statistics, 1950), p. 59.

dent Roosevelt's veto. This law provided a statutory basis for seizure,[12] but many wartime and postwar seizures were made under executive emergency power without reference to the wartime law, which expired by its own terms on June 30, 1947.

Post-World War II Fact Finding and Seizure

Several efforts were made by both President Truman and the Congress to cope with major strikes in the period between the end of World War II and the passage of the Taft-Hartley Act in 1947. Both the President and the Congress leaned heavily on the procedures of the Railway Labor Act as a model for their proposals and activities, but both also advocated and strove to utilize more stringent measures when the more modest ones seemed to fail.

The President, obviously dismayed by the postwar strike wave, sought to abate it by the appointment of fact-finding boards, some set up by himself, others by his Secretary of Labor. These operated similarly to those under the Railway Labor Act, but without statutory basis. Their recommendations were not always acceptable, but with some "sweetening," usually after a White House conference in the manner of the Railway Act workings in this period (see Chapter 12, pages 318–25), they usually provided a basis of settlement. A Committee appointed by the governor of New Jersey to review emergency dispute laws was favorably impressed with these extralegal boards, maintaining that they helped to avoid strikes in some cases or helped to curtail them in others.[13] On the other hand, representatives of the industries involved, and probably most management personnel, felt that these boards were created as a result of "labor's easy access to the White House," and that the "boards' recommendations . . . were unduly generous to labor."[14]

Congress, too, favored the fact-finding approach. Two bills, Ball-Burton-Hatch, and Case, which received serious attention, were modeled in part on the Railway Labor Act. Congress passed the Case bill in May, 1946 (on the very day on which the railroad unions went out on a nationwide strike), but President Truman successfully vetoed it. The Ball-Burton-Hatch proposal, which did not get out of committee, added

[12] This law also provided rarely used penalties against union violation of War Labor Board orders, and a strike vote procedure, which is discussed in Chapter 14, pages 378–81.

[13] New Jersey Governor's Committee on Legislation Relating to Public Utility Labor Disputes, *Report to Governor Robert B. Meyner* (Trenton, 1954), p. 13. David L. Cole, who served on some of these fact-finding boards, was Chairman of this Committee.

[14] Industrial Relations Counselors, Inc., *Emergency Disputes: A National Labor Policy Problem,* Industrial Relations Monograph No. 138 (New York, 1961), p. 23.

a compulsory arbitration feature to the Railway Labor Act procedure.[15]

When fact finding did not succeed and White House conferences also failed, President Truman used his seizure powers which he retained under wartime emergency powers in effect through mid-1947. On nine occasions after the Japanese surrender, he seized properties, with the coal mines and the railroads the most frequent industries involved. In both the second 1946 coal strike and the 1947 railroad dispute, seizures were accompanied by injunctions, ordering the termination of the strike in the former and barring a strike in the latter. When John L. Lewis and the United Mine Workers defied the injunction secured by the federal government, both were heavily fined. On appeal, the United States Supreme Court upheld the fine, ruling that the coal miners were "government employees" during the period of the seizure and that therefore the Norris–La Guardia Anti-injunction Act[16] did not apply to such "government employees."[17] The Court ruled thus although seizure had resulted in only the most nominal government operation, with the coal mine owners designated as "government managers" of the mines, and with profits accruing to the private owners, although losses were assumed by the federal government.

War and postwar seizure was not always objectionable to unions, however. For example, in one of the dramatic confrontations between the government and John L. Lewis's United Mine Workers which occurred in this period, the mines were seized, and then the famous agreement between Lewis and Secretary of the Interior Julius Krug set up the welfare payments on the basis of a royalty per ton of coal mined. "When this kind of settlement is made, employees as a group are not required to work under unsatisfactory terms, but the position of the employers is most unenviable. Only by embracing a settlement to which they were not a party can they secure control of their plants."[18]

EMERGENCY DISPUTES AND THE TAFT-HARTLEY ACT

The emergency disputes provisions of the Taft-Hartley Act were shaped by wartime and postwar events. The Republican Party won con-

[15] For an examination of the proposed legislation of this period, see Donald R. Richberg, "The Proposed Federal Industrial Relations Act," *Political Science Quarterly,* Vol. LXI (June, 1946), pp. 189–204; and Herbert R. Northrup, "A Critique of Pending Labor Legislation," *ibid.,* pp. 205–21.

[16] See Chapter 2 for a discussion of the Norris–La Guardia Act.

[17] *United States* v. *United Mine Workers,* 67 S. Ct. 677 (1947).

[18] George W. Taylor, "Is Compulsory Arbitration Inevitable?" *Proceedings of the First Annual Meeting, Industrial Relations Research Association,* 1948, p. 76.

trol of Congress in 1946 on a platform which stressed labor reform. Although the chief attention of Congress was directed toward amending the Wagner Act, there was considerable interest in strike control in view of the big strike wave of 1946 and the general public disquiet with labor strife.

The postwar experience had, however, given some pause to those who advocated stringent strike control. The late Senator Robert Taft, Republican leader in the Senate, led the fight which prevented the adoption of President Truman's "draft labor" bill, aimed at ending the 1946 railroad strike.[19] The costly Krug-Lewis agreement pointed up the dangers of government seizure to management proponents. And the experiences under fact-finding boards appointed by President Truman, as well as the war and postwar record of the Railway Labor Act, discouraged too faithful emulation of the Railway Labor Act's procedures. The product was a series of compromises which left labor free to strike after a delaying procedure, provided for fact-finding boards but denied such boards the right to make recommendations, tried to make certain that employees really wanted to strike, and then required the President to request Congressional action if he believed more authority to deal with a situation was required. The result, like most compromises, has pleased very few, been administered quite differently under different administrations, and remained in effect because of lack of agreement on proposed changes, not because of lack of proposals for change.

Emergency Strike Provisions of Taft-Hartley

As already explained in Chapter 10, Title I of the Taft-Hartley Act provides that a sixty-day notice be required for changes in labor-management contracts. As noted earlier, this law resulted in automatic and perfunctory notices—and since these notices are sent to federal and state mediation services, they have probably contributed to the trend toward too early and too much mediation, as well as to jurisdictional disputes among mediation agencies.

Title II of the Taft-Hartley Act also provides that the President appoint a "board of inquiry" to investigate and to report on the issues of a dispute where he believes that such threatened or actual dispute "will, if permitted to occur or to continue, imperil the national health or

[19] See Chapter 12, pages 323–24, for an account of this strike. President Truman's proposal to draft strikers and subject them to severe penalties was quickly enacted by the House of Representatives, but was referred to committee in the Senate on the motion of Senator Taft, where it was allowed to die quietly. The strike was called off as the President was addressing the Congress and requesting his bill.

safety. . . ." The board of inquiry is required, after public hearings if it so desires, to report to the President, setting forth the pertinent issues in dispute and the positions of both parties, but the report "shall not contain any recommendations."

Upon receiving the report, the President may then direct the Attorney General to petition a federal district court for an injunction to prevent or to terminate a strike or lockout. If the injunction is granted, the conditions of work and pay are frozen for the time being, and the parties are obliged to make every effort to settle their differences with the assistance of the Federal Mediation and Conciliation Service. If these efforts fail, at the end of 60 days the board of inquiry, which the President reconvenes when the injunction is granted, is required to make another public report to the President, also without recommendations for settlement, which includes the current status of the dispute, the positions of the parties, and "the employer's last offer of settlement." The National Labor Relations Board is then required within 15 days to poll employees as to whether they would accept the last offer of the employer and to certify the result to the Attorney General within five days. The injunction must then be dissolved. By this time, 80 days have elapsed since the first application for an injunction. If the majority of workers refuse the employer's last offer, then the President may submit a complete report to Congress with or without recommendations for action, but the employees are free to strike or the employer to lock out once the injunction is dissolved. Table 15 shows that, as of April 1, 1963, boards of inquiry had been appointed, under this section, on 23 different occasions. In 11 cases a strike vote on the employer's last offer was taken; and in four cases, strikes occurred after the machinery of the Act had been completely utilized.

Presidents and Industries

An examination of the data in Table 15 shows that President Truman was a major invoker of the Act, utilizing it ten times in five years, seven of which came in the first year of its existence. President Kennedy could surpass this record, for he had already invoked Taft-Hartley emergency procedure six times in a little more than two years, whereas President Eisenhower utilized this procedure only seven times in eight years. It could be argued that times were more difficult for labor peace in the Truman and Kennedy administrations than in Eisenhower's. Given, however, the propensity of Presidents Truman and Kennedy to utilize extralegal emergency provisions in addition, and often in preference, to

TABLE 15

EMERGENCY DISPUTES UNDER THE TAFT-HARTLEY ACT, 1947–APRIL 1, 1963

Administration	Year	Industry, Company, and Union	Results
Truman	1948	1. Atomic energy, Oak Ridge, Tennessee (Union Carbide Company versus Atomic Trades and Labor Council, a local federation of AFL unions)	Agreement reached after Act had run its course and "last" offer rejected, on basis of an offer superior to "last" offer. No strike before or after Act was invoked.
	1948	2. Meatpacking (Swift, Armour, Cudahy, Morrell, and Wilson companies and United Packinghouse Workers)	Strike ended by agreement after board of inquiry made its report, but before injunction was issued.
	1948	3. Bituminous coal industry (most of industry and United Mine Workers)	Strike settlement by appointment of Senator Bridges of New Hampshire as neutral member of pension board. Meanwhile, John L. Lewis and United Mine Workers disobeyed court injunction and were heavily fined by district judge for contempt of court.
	1948	4. Telephone (American Telephone and Telegraph Company versus American Union of Telephone Workers [now Communication Workers of America])	Dispute settled without a strike after board of inquiry was appointed, but before hearings were held.
	1948	5. Maritime and longshore industry (all unionized shipping companies, plus Pacific stevedoring industry, and all shipping unions plus International Longshoremen's and Warehousemen's Union)	Shipping dispute settled after injunction but prior to last-offer vote except on West Coast. International Longshoremen's and Warehousemen's Union ordered a boycott of vote, and no longshoremen voted. Then a ten-week strike occurred before settlement was reached on the West Coast.
	1948	6. Bituminous coal (industry and United Mine Workers)	Agreement reached by parties prior to strike and prior to report of a board of inquiry.

TABLE 15 (*Continued*)

Administration	Year	Industry, Company, and Union	Results
Truman (continued)	1948	7. Longshore industry (East and Gulf Coast stevedoring firms and International Longshoremen's Association)	Act invoked and injunction issued before strike. Last-offer vote held and rejected. Agreement negotiated but rejected by membership. After two-week strike, improved agreement accepted by membership.
	1949–50	8. Bituminous coal industry (most of industry and United Mine Workers)	Sporadic strikes over four-month period led to board of inquiry appointment. When injunction failed to end strike, government moved for contempt, but court ruled government had failed to produce evidence of contempt. At this point, parties negotiated a new agreement as President Truman was asking Congress for authority to seize mines.
	1951	9. Copper and nonferrous metals industry (Phelps-Dodge, Kennicott, Anaconda, American Smelting and Refining, and smaller companies, and Mine, Mill and Smelter Workers' Union)	After a strike, union declined offer to call it off and submit it to National Wage Stabilization Board; then a board of inquiry was appointed and an injunction issued, ending strike. All major firms settled with the union during the 80-day period, but eight smaller companies did not. Employees in these companies rejected last offer. Record does not indicate terms of settlement in these companies.
	1952	10. Atomic energy (American Locomotive Company, Dunkirk, New York, plant and United Steelworkers)	Strike halted after initial board of inquiry report and injunction. Agreement reached prior to end of 80-day period.

TABLE 15 (*Continued*)

Administration	Year	Industry, Company, and Union	Results
Eisenhower	1953–54	11. Longshore industry (East and Gulf Coast stevedoring companies and two factions of International Longshoremen's Association)	Dispute essentially involved attempt of AFL to replace racket-ridden International Longshoremen's Association, which it disaffiliated, with a new affiliate in port of New York. After two representative elections, several strikes, contempt proceedings, and fines, old ILA group won out by narrow margin, won a contract, and eventual AFL reaffiliation.
	1954	12. Atomic energy (Union Carbide Company, Oak Ridge, Tennessee, and United Gas, Coke and Chemical Workers)	Short strike was followed by board of inquiry report and injunction. "Last" offer rejected, but as in 1948, better offer than "last" one resulted in agreement without strike.
	1954	13. Atomic energy, Oak Ridge, Tennessee (Union Carbide Company and Atomic Trades and Labor Council, a local federation of AFL unions)	Board of inquiry, same as No. 12, reported no threat of stoppage. Issues settled on basis of agreement reached in No. 12.
	1956–57	14. Longshore industry (East and Gulf Coast stevedoring companies and International Longshoremen's Association)	Strike over economic issues and union demand fo industry-wide agreement resulted in board of inquiry, 80-day injunction, considerable litigation, rejection of employers' "last" offer, and another strike of one week in New York and longer in other ports until agreement was reached.
	1957	15. Atomic energy, Portsmouth, Ohio (Goodyear Rubber Company and Oil, Chemical and Atomic Workers)	After short strike, board of inquiry was followed by 80-day injunction and rejection of employers' "last" offer. The day after the injunction was dissolved, the parties reached agreement on a better offer than the "last" one.

TABLE 15 (*Continued*)

Administration	Year	Industry, Company, and Union	Results
Eisenhower (continued).............	1959	16. Longshore industry (East and Gulf Coast stevedoring employees and International Longshoremen's Association)	Strike was followed by board of inquiry, 80-day injunction, and rejection of last offer. Agreement was then reached on new contract.
	1959–60	17. Basic steel industry (major steel producers and United Steelworkers)	Strike began in July. In October, board of inquiry set up, and injunction granted after Arthur Goldberg, then union counsel, contested view that health and safety were involved. Before injunction expired, agreement was reached through pressure and mediation by Vice President Nixon and Secretary of Labor Mitchell. Four small companies did not agree, and their employees rejected "last" offer. A few strikes occurred before eventual settlement.
Kennedy...........................	1961	18. Maritime industry (East and Gulf Coast shipowners, plus a few Pacific Coast ones, and National Maritime Union and other unions)	Strike resulted in board of inquiry and 80-day injunction. Settlement was reached during 80-day period in all disputes, except that of one company, whose employees rejected "last" offer.
	1962	19. Maritime industry (Pacific Coast shipowners and Seafarers' International Union and other unions)	Board of inquiry followed by injunction ended strike. Settlement was reached for new contract during 80-day period.
	1962	20. Aerospace industry (Republic Aviation, Farmingdale, New York, and International Association of Machinists)	Board of inquiry and injunction ended strike. Settlement was reached for a new contract during 80-day period.

TABLE 15 (*Continued*)

Administration	Year	Industry, Company, and Union	Results
Kennedy (continued)	1962	21. Longshore industry (East and Gulf Coast stevedoring employees and International Longshoremen's Association)	Despite "preventive mediation" by federal mediators, strike occurred when contract expired without any change of position by parties on issues involving automation and work crews. After board of inquiry, 80-day injunction, and last-offer vote rejection, strike began again two days before Christmas. After a strike of about one month, President Kennedy appointed an extralegal board headed by Senator Wayne Morse which in effect imposed a settlement too generous for the union to reject and which was reluctantly accepted by the employers.
	1962	22. Aerospace industry (Lockheed Aircraft Company, California, and International Association of Machinists)	After Lockheed refused to permit a vote on union shop, as recommended by an extralegal Presidential board, union struck, and President invoked the Act. Union accepted Lockheed's offer of contract without union shop prior to last offer vote because of indications that employees would vote favorably on company offer.
	1963	23. Aerospace industry (Boeing Aircraft Company, Seattle, Washington, and elsewhere, and International Association of Machinists)	After Boeing refused to accept a union shop recomendation of an extralegal board appointed by President Kennedy, the President invoked the Act to prevent a strike. Dispute settled eventually without union shop after last offer vote rejected.

Source: U.S. Department of Labor, Bureau of Labor Statistics, *National Emergency Disputes under the Labor Management Relations (Taft-Hartley) Act, 1947–October, 1960,* Report No. 169 (Washington, D.C.: U.S. Government Printing Office, 1961); records of National Labor Relations Board and Federal Mediation and Conciliation Service.

those of the Taft-Hartley Act, as will be recounted later in this chapter,[20] one must conclude that these presidents had a greater willingness to invoke emergency procedure, just as they frequently demonstrated a greater willingness to utilize government intervention in other aspects of the economy than did President Eisenhower.

In short, the more "interventionist" the President, the more are parties likely to secure that intervention by pushing their disputes to what are conceived as emergency situations. And as was noticeably true under the Railway Labor Act,[21] the more friendly the administration is to labor, the more unions are likely to push their demands to a stage where intervention by that friendly administration is assured. Thus, despite the abhorrence with which unions have officially regarded the Taft-Hartley Act, certain of them have not hesitated to push for its use where the prospects for satisfactory results appear good.

From an industry analysis, the most invocations have occurred in longshore, atomic energy, and coal. The last all occurred in the early years when coal strikes were both more frequent and more critical than under the conditions of the 1960's. After John L. Lewis and the United Mine Workers were both fined for contempt of an injunction in 1948, the coal operators apparently believed that the Taft-Hartley Act was their "equalizer." When, however, in the 1949–50 case, the courts ruled that the government had to prove its charges by evidence which it had not done, earnest bargaining replaced seeking government intervention. Since then, the parties in this industry have settled their disputes without strikes or fanfare as the market for their product and employment in the industry have continued to plunge downward.

Five disputes in the atomic industry, and three in the aerospace companies, make up a defense industry total of seven. In most of these cases, extralegal procedures, which are discussed later in this chapter, were also utilized. The attitude of the federal government toward strikes and/or labor relations in facilities in which the government is the sole, or almost sole, customer, and in which the products are required for, or utilized in, the nation's defense effort, remains a critical problem of public policy. Analysis of this question is best reserved until our discussion of major issues and problems in Chapter 15.[22]

The East and Gulf Coast longshore industry remains the most persistent utilizer of Taft-Hartley emergency procedure. Faced with serious problems of automation, the racket-ridden International Long-

[20] See below, pages 366–74.

[21] See Chapter 12, pages 322–30.

[22] See pages 434–37.

shoremen's association[23] has countered with a refusal to discuss change intelligently, while the employers have been almost as intransigent in discussing their responsibilities under change. In the 1962–63 dispute the *New York Times* noted that "ever since negotiations began . . . both sides have proceeded with certainty that there would be no real bargaining until after the President had been compelled to invoke his power to order the longshoremen back to work in the public interest."[24] More accurately, there was no bargaining even after the "last" offer was turned down and the strike resumed.

To many observers, it seemed that if the President had not felt "compelled" to invoke the Act's machinery immediately after the strike began in October, the parties might have been stunned into moving toward settlement. Instead, the real "emergency," if it occurred, started when the Act's machinery had been completed. That this union and this industry have created emergency after emergency in order to use the Act's machinery as part of their negotiating tactics appears obvious. The action of President Kennedy in appointing an extralegal board, and that board's most generous award—39 cents in wages and benefits over two years, almost double the employers' last offer—in effect rewarded the union for its intransigeance and irresponsibility and this could be an invitation to more such long strikes.

The Last-Offer Vote

Of all the procedures in the Act, the least successful is the last-offer vote. With few exceptions it has been utilized to gain the unions more. They have simply told their memberships to vote "no" and they will obtain more, *and this has happened in all twelve cases in which a last-offer vote occurred,* more often without a strike than with one. It also happened in eight of the nine cases in which a vote was held under a similar procedure of the Pennsylvania Utility Arbitration Act (see Table 16). The only exception occurred the day before the Korean War wage stabilization program was scheduled to become effective in 1951. The workers voted to accept for fear of having their wages frozen at pre-last-offer levels.

This is to be expected. An offer, once made, is rarely withdrawn, so why not vote "no" and probably get more?

[23] Racket-ridden despite its permitted return to the AFL–CIO, as numerous reports of the New York–New Jersey Waterfront Commission testify. For conditions in the Port of Philadelphia, see Gaeton J. Fonzi, "War on the Waterfront," *Greater Philadelphia,* Vol. LIII (October, 1962), pp. 18–21, 51–61.

[24] *New York Times*, editorial, October 3, 1962.

Actually, there have been two cases in which the last-offer vote served the purpose of inducing agreement. Professor George W. Taylor has noted that the steel industry settled in 1960 partially because the "last" offer was about to be rejected, according to all forecasts.[25] And in the Lockheed case (No. 22, Table 15), the union settled without the union shop because it feared that the employees would not support its insistence on this demand in the last-offer vote. In most cases, however, this provision induces unions not to settle because they might get more after a last-offer vote, or to the extent that it induces employers to hold back until after the last-offer vote, it retards instead of inducing settlement.

TABLE 16

LAST-OFFER VOTES: EXPERIENCE UNDER TAFT-HARTLEY AND PENNSYLVANIA LAWS TO JANUARY 1, 1963

Law	Number of Votes	Last Offer Accepted	Last Offer Rejected
Taft-Hartley Act	12	0*	12
Pennsylvania Utility Arbitration Act	9	1†	8

SOURCE: National Labor Relations Board and Pennsylvania State Labor Relations Board.

* In one case the employees rejected a subsequent and higher offer after the "last" offer had been rejected; in the West Coast longshore case the union asked employees to boycott the vote; no one voted from this group.

† Vote conducted on January 24, 1951, just prior to 1951 Korean War wage freeze. Employees feared that to reject it would mean freezing existing wages.

Other Criticisms Widespread

Criticisms of the Taft-Hartley emergency procedure have not been confined to the last-offer provision, although on that there is probably close to unanimous agreement that it serves little constructive purpose. Presidents Truman, Eisenhower, and Kennedy have all proposed changes in the procedure, as have numerous labor, industry, and public groups. The proposals have run the full gamut from complete repeal of any form of national emergency procedure to the substitution of complete compulsion—for example, compulsory arbitration—for the present procedure.

Before proposals for change in the Taft-Hartley Act are analyzed, an examination of what has already been tried is in order. Actually, few proposals have been made which have not been tested by experience. Therefore, they can be analyzed in terms of experience. This experience

[25] George W. Taylor, "The Adequacy of Taft-Hartley in Public Emergency Disputes," *The Annals*, Vol. CCCXXXIII (January, 1961), p. 79.

on the federal level is discussed in the balance of the chapter, with the varied state experience analyzed in Chapter 14. Then, in Chapter 15, proposals for changing the Taft-Hartley emergency procedures can be evaluated in the light of experience and of the basic issues involved.

AD HOC EXTRALEGAL INTERVENTION

Besides legal procedures for intervention in so-called "emergency strikes," many presidents have acted without benefit of specific legislation, especially to handle singular situations. Thus, in the Pullman strike of 1894, President Grover Cleveland dispatched troops to maintain "law and order," although the governor of Illinois (and most close observers) found no breakdown of law. In the anthracite coal dispute of 1902, President Theodore Roosevelt put heavy pressure on the industry to arbitrate its dispute. And, as noted in Chapter 12, President Franklin D. Roosevelt repeatedly put pressure on railway management to accept settlements beyond the scope of Railway Labor Act fact-finding recommendations.

The establishment of the National Defense Mediation Board and the National War Labor Board by executive orders was also "extralegal," although undoubtedly within the broad framework of Presidential war powers. Following the end of hostilities, as we have already noted, President Truman and his Secretary of Labor followed a policy of appointing fact-finding boards, doing so in about fifteen cases.

When the Taft-Hartley Act was passed, President Truman utilized the emergency procedures of that law seven times in one year—still a record (see Table 15, pages 358–59). After his re-election in 1948 on a program which included repeal of Taft-Hartley, his propensity to invoke it declined sharply. In 1949, he persuaded the steel industry to agree to submit its dispute over pensions and welfare to an extralegal board favored by the United Steelworkers because it did not have the onus which labor attached to Taft-Hartley procedure, *and because such a board could issue recommendations*—which it did, favorable to the union. After a short strike the union won the noncontributory pensions (as well as a contributory welfare plan) which it had requested.

Emergency Disputes and the Korean War

When the Korean War broke out, labor unions proposed that special tripartite emergency machinery be set up to handle both wage stabilization and disputes which interfered with war production. Industry countered by citing the availability of Taft-Hartley machinery to handle labor disputes, but labor wanted no part of Taft-Hartley.

When the Wage Stabilization Board was established in the early fall of 1950, it had no power to intervene in dispute cases but was confined to stabilization matters. In February, 1951, however, labor members of the tripartite Wage Stabilization Board walked out as a result of a dispute over allowable wage adjustments. When the WSB was reconstituted some six weeks later, labor had won its demand that the WSB be given power over emergency disputes as well as over wage stabilization.

The WSB did not become involved in many disputes because labor and industry were in general agreement that labor peace was important to both, and industry offered only token resistance to substantial wage increases. The one big case which was referred to the WSB, the steel case, ended whatever usefulness the WSB had, both as a disputes agency and as a wage stabilizer. The WSB awarded a substantial increase to the CIO Steelworkers, with industry members dissenting; the industry declined to accept the increase without large price increases, which the government at first would not authorize. When the union struck, President Truman blamed the industry and seized it under his "inherent powers." Truman, in a speech to the country, stated that steel production was essential or we would "have to stop making shells and bombs that are going directly to our soldiers . . . in Korea . . . delay our atomic energy program . . . stop making engines for Air Force planes . . . bring our defense production to a halt and throw our domestic economy into chaos."[26]

At this point the industry appealed to the courts. Despite the claim of the government that seizure was "necessary to avert a national catastrophe" and that the President was acting constitutionally to avoid a "grave emergency," the United States Supreme Court ruled that President Truman's seizure was unlawful.[27] The industry was turned back to its private owners, and when they failed to accede to the union demand that the full WSB award be put into effect, the union struck. Public pressure was brought upon President Truman to invoke the Taft-Hartley Act, but he declined to do so on the ground that this would punish the union, which had already postponed a strike longer than the eighty-day Taft-Hartley waiting period, rather than the industry, which President Truman held to be at fault. The strike lasted about three

[26] *New York Times,* April 10, 1952.

[27] *Youngstown Sheet and Tube Co.* v. *Sawyer,* 343 U.S. 579 (1952).

months, when it was settled by granting the WSB award to the workers and by granting substantial price increases to the industry.

The fact that a strike in the basic steel industry could last fifty-five days in the midst of the Korean War without any of the dire consequences predicted by President Truman when he seized the industry, or by numerous commentators before and since in similar or less critical circumstances, is of major importance in any discussion of emergency disputes procedure.

Eisenhower Cabinet Intervention

President Eisenhower eschewed the fact-finding route of his predecessor and repeatedly made public statements emphasizing his desire to keep the government's hands out of key contract settlements. But although intervention by the Eisenhower administration was far less prevalent than that of its two predecessors, it was felt in some key instances, especially in the steel industry. "In 1956, the political architects of the steel settlement were Secretary of the Treasury George M. Humphrey and Secretary of Labor James P. Mitchell. Again the companies were under pressure. They capitulated and improved their offer to the point where an agreement that would quickly end the dispute was possible."[28]

In 1959 the Vice President functioned as the "pressurizer," again with industry as the heavy recipient. "Technically, there was no retreat from this nonintervention position, not, at least, so far as the President himself was concerned. The political pressure emanated from the Vice-president, who happened also to be the Republican heir apparent . . . the man who could be the next occupant of the White House. . . ."[29]

President Eisenhower did appoint one extralegal board—the Presidential Railroad Commission—which, as noted in Chapter 12, was agreed to by the carriers and unions, and made a monumental study of railway labor relations. And as will be discussed below, the Eisenhower administration also kept the atomic energy panel alive.

Kennedy Fact Finding and Defense Contracts

Special boards and commissions again became an important focus of labor relations under the Kennedy administration. Despite the appointment of one extralegal agency—after Railway Labor Act

[28] John Perry Horlacher, "A Political Science View of National Emergency Disputes," *The Annals*, Vol. CCCXXXIII (January, 1961), p. 90. Humphrey, in particular, allegedly pressed his former industry colleagues to end the dispute in order to insure that President Eisenhower could stress peace at home and abroad as his continued theme.

[29] *Ibid.*

procedure had been exhausted—it still required a long strike to break the deadlock involving flight engineers on Eastern Airlines. And in Chapter 8, it was noted that extralegal boards were appointed in the aerospace cases in order to facilitate recommendations involving union security desired by the unions, with Taft-Hartley boards following when the extralegal procedure did not succeed in achieving settlement. In the East Coast longshore case, President Kennedy appointed an extralegal board after Taft-Hartley procedure had run its course.

The most direct—and at the same time undocumentable—type of intervention attributed to the Kennedy administration has been through the use of defense contracts. Government business has become a significant source of work and profit in many industries. In aerospace, it is the bulk of both. When Lockheed Aircraft declined to accept an extralegal board's recommendation for an election to determine the union shop issue, the Defense Department announced, in effect, that its contracts were being especially reviewed and placed on an *ad hoc* basis.[30]

To what extent similar pressures determine contract allocation it is impossible to know. Certainly, however, some officials in the aerospace and other defense industries believe that any opposition to Kennedy administration labor policies threatens government contract possibilities.[31]

PERMANENT EXTRALEGAL AGENCIES

It will be recalled that the first case for which the emergency provisions of the Taft-Hartley Act was invoked, as well as several subse-

[30] See, for example, the Defense Department statements in the *Daily Labor Report,* November 26, 1962. Lockheed, among other things, is the principal contractor in the highly successful Polaris program.

[31] Interviews, November–December, 1962. Needless to note, these accusations are often not precise, but the feeling is certainly almost unanimous among company officials who would talk about it—always with a pledge of secrecy. They point to the Lockheed case, to awards of contracts to one company which agreed to an agency shop, and to the loss of a key contract by another company which rigorously held to its anti-union-shop position. Actually, no one on the outside, as the authors are, is in the position to know the truth or falsity of these whispered charges. They are noted only because of the fact that since many persons in industry believe them to be true, their conduct in key labor relations cases can be affected by this belief. Some of the difficulty lies in the change in Defense Department procurement policies initiated by Secretary of Defense Robert McNamara in which labor relations are not necessarily involved. Nevertheless, the feeling in industry of a relation of labor policies and success in obtaining defense contracts is very strong. (See the editorial in *Fortune,* "What the Hell Do Those Fellows Want?" Vol. LXVII [February, 1963], pp. 81–82.) Senator Lausche (Dem., Ohio) introduced a bill in the Senate on March 4, 1963, barring duress by federal agency officials in labor relations matters pertaining to defense contracts. The Senator stated flatly that this was occurring. (*Daily Labor Report,* March 4, 1963, p. A–2.)

quent cases, involved the atomic energy "industry." Although there is actually no atomic "industry" as such, except for the production of fissionable and special nuclear material, the annual reports of the Atomic Energy Commission show that over 125,000 persons are employed by the AEC and its construction and operations contractors in many locations throughout the country on a great variety of jobs and operations. Particularly in the early days of atomic development, great concern was expressed that there be no interruption in work at vital atomic installations. After the first Taft-Hartley national emergency case in 1948, President Truman appointed a committee headed by William H. Davis, former Chairman of the War Labor Board. From this committee, which reported in 1949, came the creation of what appears to be the first permanent extralegal agency to handle emergency disputes—the Atomic Energy Labor Relations Panel, later reorganized and renamed the Atomic Labor-Management Relations Panel.[32]

Atomic Labor-Management Relations Panel

The original atomic panel was set up by executive order of President Truman in 1949 with Davis as Chairman, and with the panel lodged in the Federal Mediation and Conciliation Service. It attempted to handle disputes which the parties could not settle themselves in an informal manner, and refused a number of cases when advised by the Atomic Energy Commission that national defense was not affected. Often, however, it acted as a fact-finding agency, making recommendations or, if the parties agreed, acting as an arbitration panel. Both the awards and the recommendations of the panel were handled as informally as possible, in line with procedure espoused by Davis. A total of sixty-one cases came before this panel from its inception in 1949 until January, 1953.[33]

When President Eisenhower took office, Davis and the members of his panel resigned, both as a matter of form and as an expression of belief on the part of Davis that the time had come to withdraw special disputes machinery from the atomic labor picture. The President, however, revised and renamed the panel, and transferred it to the Atomic Energy Commission from the FMCS. Cyrus Ching, former head of FMCS, was named Chairman, a post which he still holds.

[32] Also on the basis of this Panel report, certain keystone principles of atomic industry labor relations were agreed to, including making security risks a nonbargainable issue, not subject to the grievance procedure.

[33] See J. J. Bambrick, Jr., and A. A. Blum, *Labor Relations in the Atomic Energy Field,* Studies in Personnel Policy, No. 158 (New York: National Industrial Conference Board, 1957), p. 29.

The procedure under Ching became more formalized. Jurisdiction was not asserted until the FMCS certified the case as being one which could not be resolved by the parties through mediation. The FMCS was required to check beforehand with the Atomic Energy Commission and to verify that a stoppage would vitally harm the atomic energy program. After it takes jurisdiction of a case, the Ching panel usually issues formal recommendations; but unlike fact-finding boards in other jurisdictions, Ching panels never publish the facts as they see them nor do they issue any other bases for their recommendations. This procedure has continued, although some cases since 1957 have been handled informally also.

The elimination of cases not considered harmful to the atomic energy program cut down the jurisdiction of the panel. In its first three years, it handled 27 cases.[34] Its load since then has varied between five and 15 cases per year. In one case a Taft-Hartley emergency board was appointed after the atomic panel recommendation was rejected, a last-offer vote was held, and a settlement was made superior to the "last" offer.[35] In other cases, strikes have been called and occurred without apparent damage to the atomic energy program.[36]

This raises the question of why the Atomic Labor-Management Panel continues to exist. In 1957, that question received a searching answer from the Secretary of Labor's Advisory Committee on Labor-Management Relations in Atomic Energy Installations, under the chairmanship of David L. Cole. It recommended that the panel "taper off" its activities because most of the conditions which induced its creation no longer existed.

The Advisory Committee felt in 1957 that it was then "appropriate to treat labor-management relations at atomic energy installations in the same manner as those in other industries, including those which produce vital military and defense items for the government." Failure to do this, the Advisory Committee noted, would mean a continuation of the tendency on the part of the parties in the industry "to rely more and more" on "alternatives to the pressures of collective

[34] The Ching panel issued annual reports for its first three years, but not thereafter. This estimate of cases is based on a sampling of the *Industrial Relations Newsletter*, published monthly by the Atomic Energy Commission.

[35] This was Case No. 12, Table 15, p. 360, above.

[36] For example, in the 1962 case involving Dow Chemical and the Denver Metal Trades Department, the unions accepted the panel's recommendations, but the company instead requested further negotiations. Whereupon the unions threatened a strike, and the Secretary of Labor requested that the parties meet with him in Washington. There, Dow acceded and agreed to accept the panel's recommendations. Then the membership rejected a settlement. A strike began and lasted for twenty-six days before a settlement was reached.

bargaining . . . provided by the government." For example, "at the installations in which resort to the panel has been most frequent, notably Oak Ridge, Paducah, and Sandia, the ability to reach agreement through negotiations seems to have been weakened, and the panel has considered it necessary to issue detailed recommendations in practically all cases in which it intervenes."

Mediation has likewise suffered from the existence of the panel, according to this Advisory Committee report. "The availability of the panel procedure has impaired the effectiveness of the Federal Mediation and Conciliation Service. The knowledge that the panel can be caused to appear detracts from the continuity and effectiveness of the services of the mediator."[37]

Six years after the issuance of this report, the Atomic Labor-Management Relations Panel had neither tapered off nor showed any signs of so doing. Without specific Congressional sanction, it was continuing to operate, and even showing a tendency to handle an increased case load.

The Missile Sites Labor Commission

In 1960 the United States Senate Committee on Government Operations, under the chairmanship of Senator John L. McClellan, began an investigation of work stoppages, wage practices, and labor conditions at missile sites and bases. The Committee uncovered a situation involving excessive work stoppages, waste, and practices which came very close to outright extortion. Jurisdictional strikes among craft unions and between craft and industrial unions, competition for labor among various governmental procurement agencies, featherbedding work duplication, low productivity and excessive overtime, and a strike record many times worse than the national average were the order of the day at installations, including that at Cape Canaveral, Florida, the most important missile test center. There, man-days lost amounted to 5.5 to 6 per cent of total man-days worked—many times the national average.[38] Meanwhile, it appeared that the missile program was being seriously impeded.

[37] *Report of the Secretary of Labor's Advisory Committee on Labor-Management Relations in Atomic Energy Installations* (Washington, D.C.: U.S. Government Printing Office, 1957). The conclusions and recommendations are reprinted in Bambrick and Blum, *op. cit.*, pp. 45–47.

[38] "Work Stoppages at Missile Bases," *Report of the Committee on Government Operations,* U.S. Senate, 87th Congress, 2d session, Report No. 1312 (Washington, D.C.: U.S. Government Printing Office, 1962), p. 11. Two volumes of Hearings, plus an Index, were also published by the Committee in 1962.

Senator McClellan advocated strong legislative action to bar strikes. To head this off, President Kennedy, in May, 1961, appointed a tripartite Missile Sites Labor Commission, headed by the Secretary of Labor, with the director of the Federal Mediation and Conciliation Service as vice chairman. It appeared quite obvious to the heads of the unions, particularly those in building construction who were especially involved in the repeated work stoppages, that Congress was in a mood to act if the situation did not improve.

Continuing surveillance by the McClellan Senate Committee on Government Operations and the work of the Missile Sites Labor Commission, together with better co-ordination among the government procurement agencies, appear to have brought a semblance of order to labor relations at missile locations, including Cape Canaveral. The FMCS has done outstanding work by assigning key mediators to these areas, and having them work out problems with labor and management at the local level. The national officers of the building trades unions, especially the Structural Iron Workers, the Brotherhood of Electrical Workers, the Plumbers and Steamfitters, the Operating Engineers, and the Carpenters, have exerted more firm control over local business agents, some of whom seemed uninhibited in their desire to achieve the most fantastic wages for the least work.[39] Strikes declined during the first year of the Commission's activity. At Cape Canaveral the strike figure fell below the national average for the construction industry.[40] Orders from national union headquarters for these unions to stay on the job while disputes were being ironed out were a key factor in this reversal of strike incidence.

Another factor which improved the labor situation after the establishment of the Missile Sites Labor Commission was the easement of pressure by government agencies on contractors to settle at all costs in order to avoid stoppages. The knowledge on the part of union business agents and workers that peace at any price was the order of the day was a continuing invitation to the calling of strikes and other harassments.

[39] Consider this testimony relating to Vandenberg Air Force Base: "The lowest paid [plumber earned] . . . $402 and the highest $733. The average weekly earnings . . . was $451. The lowest paid [electrician] received $413 for the week, and the highest $670 . . . the average . . . was $510. . . . The commanding general at Vanderberg . . . is a major general. His total pay and allowances for 25 years' service, including his quarters allowance and his subsistence allowance, amounts to $365 a week. Each and every one of the plumbers and steamfitters and electricians made more than the commanding general." The report, "Work Stoppage at Missile Bases," pp. 7–8, also found that laborers made more than colonels, and semiskilled workers made more than Dr. Wernher von Braun, the missile expert.

[40] Missile Sites Labor Commission, *Report to the President* (Washington, D.C.: U.S. Government Printing Office, 1962).

Moreover, there was evidence that some contractors were purposely overcharging jobs and furthering uneconomic practices, both of which were an invitation to similar practices on the part of unions. With the formation of the Missile Sites Labor Commission came better regulations and control by the government agencies to prevent such practices.[41]

The Missile Sites Labor Commission itself made thirty-two formal decisions during its first year. These directives covered a variety of questions, including jurisdictional disputes and featherbedding.[42] Its decisions were generally adhered to, although some strikes delaying the missile program were not headed off.

The extralegal Missile Sites Labor Commission has been critized by at least two observers for its failure to adhere to national labor policy as expressed in the Taft-Hartley Act. One noted that the Commission had issued directives resolving jurisdictional disputes in situations where "assent of the parties was not obtained," thus "disregarding applicable provisions" of the Taft-Hartley Act and, in effect, overriding "the functions and power entrusted by Congress to the National Labor Relations Board and to the courts. . . ."[43]

Professor John R. Van de Water has called attention to the case of the electronic products subcontractor whose employees voted overwhelmingly in an NLRB election against union affiliation, but were forced off a missile base by a strike because they had so voted. Whereas an NLRB injunction against such a strike and boycott was in order, the Missile Sites Labor Commission intervened and asked the parties to "be mature"—which resulted in the work being done in a manner acceptable to the strikers.[44]

One may well ask whether, even on defense installations, executive improvising should replace action prescribed by duly enacted law.[45] Meanwhile, the extralegal Missile Sites Labor Commission, like its

[41] "Work Stoppages at Missile Bases," pp. 35–36, 39–40.

[42] Missile Sites Labor Commission, *op. cit.*

[43] H. L. Browne, "The Missile Sites Labor Commission and the Derogation of the Taft-Hartley Act," *American Bar Association Journal,* Vol. XLVIII (February, 1962), pp. 121–24.

[44] John R. Van de Water, "Labor Law and National Defense," *Labor Law Journal,* Vol. XIII (August, 1962), pp. 617–18; see also *ibid.,* "Applications of Labor Law to Construction and Equipping of United States Missile Bases," *Labor Law Journal,* Vol. XII (November, 1961), pp. 613–24.

[45] How complicated extralegal intervention may become is illustrated by developments at the Nevada Test Site of the Atomic Energy Commission. Since both a missile test site and atomic energy were involved, the two extralegal agencies avoided a jurisdictional dispute by establishing a third such agency—the Nevada Test and Space Site Construction Labor Board—to look into certain uneconomic and inefficient practices there. See U.S. Atomic Energy Commission, *Industrial Relations Newsletter,* January, 1963, pp. 1–3.

atomic counterpart, appears headed for a long life. However, the business of the Commission is dwindling as sites become completed, so that its jurisdiction may be confined to such large installations as Cape Canaveral and Vandenberg unless it is extended or new installations are created.

Concluding Remarks

Emergency strike control as now practiced on the federal level involves not only the Taft-Hartley machinery, but two apparently permanent extralegal bodies, occasional *ad hoc* extralegal additional groups, plus the machinery of the Railway Labor Act. On the state level an even greater variety of experimentation has existed and will be explored in the next chapter.

QUESTIONS FOR DISCUSSION

1. What do you think the wartime experience of the War Labor Board during World War II taught us about emergency strike controls in war and peace?
2. Why do you think President Truman invoked the emergency procedures of the Taft-Hartley Act so frequently during 1948, and so infrequently thereafter? Explain your answer.
3. Do you think that the Atomic Energy Labor-Management Relations Panel should be discontinued? Give the reasons and the evidence for your view.

SUGGESTIONS FOR FURTHER READING

BAMBRICK, J. J., JR., AND BLUM, A. A. *Labor Relations in the Atomic Energy Field.* Studies in Personnel Policy, No. 158. New York: National Industrial Conference Board, 1957.

A review of the work of the extralegal Atomic Energy Labor-Management Relations Panel, together with the summary and recommendations of the committee which advocated its abolition.

CULLEN, DONALD E. "The Taft-Hartley Act in National Emergency Disputes," *Industrial and Labor Relations Review,* Vol. VI (October, 1953), pp. 15–30.

TAYLOR, GEORGE W. "The Adequacy of Taft-Hartley in Public Emergency Disputes," *The Annals,* Vol. CCCXXXIII (January, 1961), pp. 76–84.

Two analyses of how well the Taft-Hartley Act works in so-called "emergency" disputes.

———. *Government Regulation of Industrial Relations.* New York: Prentice-Hall, Inc., 1948.

Chapters iii–vii are primarily concerned with the governmental control of collective bargaining before, during, and just after World War II, as seen by a Chairman of the National War Labor Board and a frequent appointee to government emergency boards.

STYLES, PAUL L. "Labor Relations in the Space Program," *Labor Law Journal,* Vol. XIV (January, 1963), pp. 91–102.

Problems of labor relations and the space program discussed by the Chief Industrial Relations Officer of the George C. Marshall Space Flight Center.

VAN DE WATER, JOHN R. "Applications of Labor Law to Construction and Equipping of United States Missile Bases," *Labor Law Journal,* Vol. XII (November, 1961), pp. 1003–24.

An analysis of events at missile bases, with emphasis on the failure of the government to make use of existing law to force the end of illegal stoppages.

Chapter 14 STATE STRIKE CONTROL LEGISLATION

The states have experimented with almost every form of government intervention in labor disputes. Besides mediation, they have tried strike notices and strike votes, fact finding, compulsory arbitration, seizure of industrial plants, and choice of procedures.[1] In addition, as on the Presidential level of the federal government, governors or lesser state officials have often intervened in labor disputes without benefit of specific legislation. In this chapter the principal forms of state intervention experience, with emphasis on so-called "emergency strike" controls, are discussed.

STRIKE NOTICES AND VOTES

A number of states have laws on their books which require notice of an intent to strike in industry generally or in specific industries, such as those "affected with a public interest" or those which would affect the survival of an agricultural crop.[2] The objective is to permit the parties to "cool off" before overt action is taken. The theory is that if a notice is given, ample opportunity for collective bargaining or government intervention will occur, and therefore strikes will be prevented.

In practice, however, things have not worked out this way. The most important reason is that the strike notice, like the Taft-Hartley notice of failure to reach agreement, becomes either a perfunctory gesture or an integral part of the bargaining process. The notice is usually given automatically by the unions so as to insure the legality of any action if a strike does occur and, in addition, to increase the union's bargaining power. The union then enters negotiations with the legal technicalities cleared, and with the threat hanging over the employer's head that a strike will take place if a satisfactory agreement is not reached. Failure to give that notice before negotiations would, most union

[1] See Figure 5, p. 274, for definitions.

[2] Colorado, Georgia, Hawaii, Michigan, Minnesota, and Wisconsin.

leaders believe, be looked upon as a sign of weakness. There seems to be no relation between the number of strikes and the existence, or lack thereof, of strike notice provisions.[3]

These laws were never strictly enforced, except possibly in Wisconsin, where failure to give notice is an unfair labor practice.[4] Since the passage of the Taft-Hartley Act in 1947, notices required by it, which must also be sent to state mediation services, have supplanted state requirements, except in purely intrastate commerce; but in any case, such notices also satisfy state requirements, so that state laws are largely dormant.

Strike Votes

Florida, Kansas, Michigan, Minnesota, Missouri, Utah, and Wisconsin,[5] as well as the federal government during the latter part of World War II, have enacted legislation requiring a vote of the membership before a legal strike could occur. The Minnesota law, for example, required the union to take the vote by secret ballot at a meeting after reasonable notice of time and place had been given to affected employees. The Michigan and Missouri laws were more stringent. Both required an affirmative majority of those in the bargaining unit to authorize a strike—which means that those not voting were counted against striking. Michigan modified its law in 1949 to permit strikes if a majority of those voting approved. Both Michigan and Missouri required state agencies to conduct the strike votes.

Whether a government agency or the union itself has conducted the strike votes, the results appear to be the same—an overwhelming vote in favor of a strike. The reason is that the vote becomes one of confidence in the union and of support for the pressure which the union may apply to the employer, who now sees evidence that employees are ready and willing to back up the union demands by walking out. The fact that few actual strikes occur despite the great number of votes in favor of strikes is further proof that these strike vote laws become bargaining tactics, not strike controls.

In Minnesota the law never had a significant effect. The strike vote was usually the most perfunctory procedure conducted by the union and

[3] See, for example, the comparison of the Minnesota and Michigan records, and discussion relating thereto, in B. M. Stewart and W. J. Couper, *Fact Finding in Industrial Disputes* (New York: Industrial Relations Counselors, Inc., 1946), pp. 33–35.

[4] But apparently, no case has been adjudicated under this provision. See Justin C. Smith, "Unfair Labor Practices in Wisconsin," *Marquette Law Review*, Vol. XLV (Fall, 1961), p. 247.

[5] Alabama, Colorado, Delaware, Hawaii, North Dakota, and Oregon also enacted such laws, but they were either repealed or declared invalid before becoming effectively operative.

was challenged by the employers only rarely.[6] Likewise, in Florida and Kansas the law does not seem to have been of much significance.[7]

Table 17 shows the experience under the Missouri law from its enactment in 1947 till its repeal two years later; Table 18 summarizes

TABLE 17

EXPERIENCE UNDER THE MISSOURI STRIKE VOTE LAW, APRIL 12, 1948—OCTOBER 14, 1949

STRIKE VOTES		STRIKES AUTHORIZED				ACTUAL WORK STOPPAGES	
				Employees Voting to Strike			
Number of Elections	Number of Employees Voting	Number	Per Cent	Number	Per Cent	Number	Percentage of Authorized Strikes
475........	49,680	407	85.7	44,144	88.9	20	4.9

SOURCE: National Industrial Conference Board.

TABLE 18

RESULTS OF STRIKE VOTES CONDUCTED BY MICHIGAN LABOR MEDIATION BOARD, 1947–54*

	November, 1947–June, 1950	July, 1950–June, 1954	Total, November, 1947–June, 1954
Number of Elections:	409	138	547
For strike..................	358	89	447
Against strike..............	47	49	96
Tie.........................	4	0	4
Percentage of Elections:			
For strike..................	87.5	64.5	81.7
Against strike..............	11.5	35.5	17.6
Tie.........................	1.0	...	0.7
Number of Workers:			
Eligible to vote............	275,225	6,557	281,782
Voting......................	226,389	5,734	232,123
For strike................	189,906	3,181	193,087
Against strike............	34,730	2,337	37,067
Spoiled or challenged ballots................	1,753	216	1,969
Percentage of:			
Eligible workers voting.....	82.3	87.4	82.4
Voters favoring strike......	83.9	55.5	83.2
Eligible workers voting for strike..................	69.0	48.5	68.5

* Between July, 1954, and June, 1961, 244 strike votes were held in Michigan, in 133 of which the employees voted to strike. The Michigan Labor Mediation Board, which supplied these data, advised the authors that it does not have readily available the number of employees involved.

SOURCE: Adapted from data provided by the Michigan Labor Mediation Board by Herbert S. Parnes, *Union Strike Votes: Current Practice and Proposed Controls* (Princeton: Princeton University, Industrial Relations Section, 1956), p. 125.

[6] Herbert S. Parnes, *Union Strike Votes: Current Practice and Proposed Controls* (Princeton: Princeton University, Industrial Relations Section, 1956), pp. 126–29.

[7] *Ibid.*, pp. 129–33.

the Michigan experience; and Table 19 describes the wartime experience of the federal government in taking strike votes. Even in wartime, em-

TABLE 19

RESULTS OF POLLS UNDER THE WAR LABOR DISPUTES ACT, 1943–45

	Number	Per Cent
Total number of polls*	2,168	100
Voted in favor of interruption of work	1,850	85.3
Voted against interruption of work†	318	14.7
Total number eligible to vote	2,923,655	...
Total valid votes cast	1,926,811	100
Votes in favor of interruption of work	1,593,937	82.7
Votes against interruption of work	332,874	17.3
Number of employers involved	26,630	...

* Polls were conducted in 1,571 separate cases, but involving 2,168 separate voting units.

† Includes 59 polls in which no votes were cast and 28 polls which resulted in a tie vote.

SOURCE: National Labor Relations Board, *Eleventh Annual Report* (Washington, D.C.: U.S. Government Printing Office, 1946), p. 91.

ployees voted "to interrupt war production" in more than 80 per cent of the cases, knowing full well that the chances of an actual strike occurring were very limited, but that to vote against it would lessen their opportunities for economic gain.[8]

In 1950 the United States Supreme Court ruled that state strike vote laws were inoperative in interstate commerce because they conflicted with the notice requirements of the Taft-Hartley Act.[9] The confinement of Michigan votes to intrastate commerce accounts for the sharp drop in votes and voters after 1950, as noted in Table 18.

The Wisconsin and Utah laws remain on the books because they do not forbid strikes, but prohibit picketing, boycotts, and similar secondary support of strikers where the strike is not authorized by a majority of employees in the bargaining unit voting by secret ballot. This restriction has been used to enjoin "quickie" stoppages by a minority, as

[8] Almost the only occasion where employees have failed to give their union a "bargaining club" by voting to strike has been where the employer has a reputation for sticking closely to his position, even if a strike occurs, and where in addition the employer vigorously communicates his position to the employees. This is, of course, the situation in the General Electric Company.

[9] *International Union* v. *O'Brien*, 339 U.S. 454 (1950). Minnesota's courts similarly restricted the Minnesota Act (*Automobile Workers* v. *Finklenburg*, 53 N.W. [2d] 128 [1952]), and it was then repealed.

well as picketing in support of strikes not authorized by a majority.[10]

In the main, however, strike vote laws remain inoperative. How to require that so serious a matter as a strike be passed upon by the majority of those affected in a democratic manner without having the process degenerate into a perfunctory bargaining tactic remains an unsolved problem of public policy.

STATE FACT FINDING

The laws of twenty-eight states (Table 20) provide for some form of official investigation and/or fact finding where labor disputes remain unsettled or threaten to upset, inconvenience, or imperil a community; or where one party to the dispute simply requests "investigation." Under these laws, investigation and fact finding have a variety of interpretations, some narrow, some broad. California, for example, with its well-developed and -manned mediation staff, follows "a narrowly restricted definition of 'investigation' . . . an assignment to develop information as to the nature of a dispute and the possible consequences of a work stoppage. This investigation is made preliminary to a decision to proffer or not to proffer the facilities of the [State Conciliation] Service in a labor dispute."[11]

On the other hand, legislation in Massachusetts and New Hampshire requires their state mediation agencies to investigate a dispute and to issue a public report assigning responsibility for its continuance *after* mediation has not settled the dispute and one or both of the parties have refused the agency's proposal that the case be arbitrated.

In Michigan, Minnesota, and New York, fact finding involves the traditional concept of holding hearings, and writing a report and recommendations. In other states, fact finding is largely mediation in another form, with the "fact finders" actually a mediation panel.

The procedure, the method, and the experiences vary from state to state even where laws are written in similar language. The coverage of the laws also varies. In some states, they may be applied to any dispute. In others, only public utilities are within the jurisdiction of the fact finders. And in still others the jurisdiction covers utilities plus "industries affected with a public interest." Wherever the covered industry lies within the jurisdiction of the Taft-Hartley Act, the constitutionality of

[10] *International Union* v. *Wisconsin Employment Relations Board,* 27 N.W. (2d) 875 (1947); affirmed, 336 U.S. 245 (1947). For a discussion of this approach, see Parnes, *op. cit.,* pp. 113–21, 129–30; and Smith, *op. cit.,* pp. 245–48.

[11] State of California, Department of Industrial Relations, *Third Annual Report of the Conciliation Service* (Sacramento, 1950), p. 5.

TABLE 20

FACT FINDING AND INVESTIGATION BY STATES

State	Summary of Statute	Character of Intervention	Comment
Alabama	Governor may appoint tripartite Board of Mediation.	Fact finding to gather facts and make report and recommendation.	Inactive.
Arkansas	Commissioner of labor may conduct investigations and hearings, publish reports and advertisements, etc.	Investigation and report.	Inactive.
California	Department of Industrial Relations may investigate and mediate labor disputes.	Investigation.	California relies almost exclusively upon mediation. Investigation is used only to develop nature and possible effect of dispute prior to intervention.
Colorado	Industrial commissioner may conduct investigation and hearings, publish reports and advertisements, etc.	Original compulsory investigation law, passed in 1915, provided for notices, cooling-off period, and compulsory investigation and report.	The investigation functions have been infrequently utilized and more recently have rarely been invoked.
Georgia	Commissioner of labor may conduct investigations and hearings, and publish reports and advertisements.	Investigation and report.	Inactive.
Hawaii	Where governor finds mediation has failed, he may appoint an emergency board to investigate and report on controversy.	Fact finding, with recommendations.	Active. (NOTE: A special fact-finding provision for public utilities was ruled inoperative by the United States Attorney General while Hawaii was a territory.)

TABLE 20 (*Continued*)

State	Summary of Statute	Character of Intervention	Comment
Illinois	Department of Labor may investigate dispute and make findings and recommendations public if public utility, food, fuel, or other inconvenience to public is involved.	Investigation and fact finding of emergency disputes.	Inactive.
Indiana	Commissioner of labor may investigate disputes, publish reports, and do other necessary things.	Investigation and report.	Inactive. (NOTE: Indiana also has a compulsory arbitration law which is inactive and inapplicable to utilities in interstate commerce [*Marshall* v. *Schricker*, 20 CCH Labor Cases, 66, 372 (1951)]).
Iowa	Either party to a dispute, or persons affected, may apply to governor for appointment of a Board of Conciliation and Arbitration.	Fact finding. Board of Conciliation and Arbitration's report is not binding unless parties so agree beforehand.	Inactive.
Kentucky	Commissioner of industrial relations may hold hearings to determine the reason for the labor dispute and make public findings of fact.	Investigation and report.	Inactive.
Louisiana	A tripartite Labor Mediation Board may mediate unsettled dispute, and render unenforceable decision and make it public if mediation fails.	Fact finding with recommendations.	Relatively inactive.
Maine	Board of Inquiry may be set up if mediation is declined and if one of parties, or interested persons affected, so request. Report can be made public.	Fact finding and report.	Inactive.

TABLE 20 (*Continued*)

State	Summary of Statute	Character of Intervention	Comment
Maryland	Commissioner of labor may investigate dispute, determine which party is mainly blameworthy or responsible, and publish report in some daily newspaper, assigning responsibility or blame.	Investigation and assignment of responsibility.	Inactive. (NOTE: Maryland also has a seizure law affecting utilities.)
Massachusetts	Tripartite Board of Conciliation and Arbitration, where no settlement is agreeable and parties will not arbitrate, shall investigate dispute and publish a report.	Investigation and assignment of responsibility.	Active until found inapplicable to interstate commerce in *General Electric* v. *Callahan*, 294 F. (2d) 60 (1962). (NOTE: Massachusetts also has a choice-of-procedures law affecting utilities.)
Michigan	Fact finding by board composed of three disinterested persons and two nonvoting members, one from labor and one from industry. Findings not binding, but made public; law applies to public utilities, hospitals, and government employees.	Fact finding with recommendations.	Law extensively used for hospital and government employees. Found inapplicable to utilities in interstate commerce in *Grand Rapids City Coach Lines* v. *Howlett*, 137 F. Supp. 667 (1955).
Minnesota	Fact finding by three-man, tripartite commission where public interest, life, safety, or health are involved.	Fact finding with recommendations.	Most active of state fact-finding agencies. (NOTE: Minnesota also has a compulsory arbitration statute applicable to hospitals only.)
Missouri	Tripartite fact-finding panels may be appointed by parties and State Mediation Board.	Fact finding with recommendations. *But* if parties refuse to accept recommendations and strike threatens public interest, health, and welfare, governor may seize utility—and then strikes are forbidden.	Active. See pages 408–10 for discussion of seizure provisions.

TABLE 20 (*Continued*)

State	Summary of Statute	Character of Intervention	Comment
New Hampshire	If parties refuse to arbitrate, commissioner may investigate and issue a report assigning responsibility.	Investigation with assignment of responsibility.	Fairly active, but future in doubt as result of Massachusetts case.
New York	If Board of Mediation certifies that it cannot settle a dispute by mediation, industrial commissioner may appoint a Board of Inquiry to make report and recommendations.	Fact finding with recommendations.	Active.
North Dakota	Head of State Labor Division may request governor to appoint mediation board, which may issue report and recommendations.	Fact finding with recommendations.	Active.
Ohio	Industrial Commission may investigate dispute, ascertain which party is responsible, and make that fact public. At request of one or both parties, it may make recommendations for settlement and, if not accepted, publish same.	Investigation, with assignment of responsibility; fact finding with recommendations.	Relatively inactive.
Oklahoma	Where a strike or lockout exists which causes injury or inconvenience to the public, the Board of Arbitration and Conciliation may investigate and publish findings and recommendations which will contribute to an equitable settlement.	Fact finding with recommendations.	Inactive.

TABLE 20 (*Continued*)

State	Summary of Statute	Character of Intervention	Comment
Oregon	Facilities of labor conciliator available to public employees and government agencies for "fact-finding purposes only."	Mediation in actual fact.	Public employees only.
Rhode Island	Director of Department of Labor, with approval of governor, may appoint boards of conciliation and mediation to investigate and report on disputes.	Fact finding with recommendations.	Law invoked only twice in forty years, and in neither case was a board actually appointed.
South Carolina	Commissioner of labor may appoint tripartite committee with himself as chairman to make findings of fact designed to induce agreement.	Fact finding with recommendations.	Inactive.
South Dakota	Deputy commissioner of labor may investigate a dispute, make a report of the issues involved, and make recommendations public. He may do this alone, or as chairman of a tripartite panel.	Fact finding with recommendations.	Inactive.
Texas	Governor may appoint a five-man tripartite commission to investigate dispute and make report and public recommendations.	Fact finding with recommendations.	Relatively inactive.
Washington	If the parties to a dispute refuse to arbitrate, director of labor and industries endeavors to have each party state in writing his position and why he refuses to arbitrate.	Investigation by indirection.	Relatively inactive.

SOURCE: State statutes.

state law is in doubt.[12] Besides the fact-finding or investigation provisions of state laws, there are many cases where state governors or mayors of large cities have appointed fact-finding commissions as a means of trying to resolve disputes which have seemed of serious consequence to the local citizenry. Such *ad hoc* fact finding usually has no legal basis, but depends upon the prestige of the public official and the willingness of the parties to co-operate for any success. For example, a citizens' panel appointed by the mayor of Philadelphia in early 1962 resulted, with considerable pressure from both the mayor and the governor of Pennsylvania, in a settlement of the six-month strike between the Yale and Towne Manufacturing Company and the International Association of Machinists. Here, mediation had clearly failed, and no end to the dispute appeared in sight before the special panel led to settlement. On the other hand, too often these *ad hoc* interventions are either politically inspired to bail out a faltering union strike, or they are bumbling efforts on the part of well-meaning but ineffectual citizens who do not understand the issues, and whose efforts may actually prolong the dispute rather than help to solve it.

Many of the state fact-finding and investigation laws are virtually unused in practice, and represent little more than a chance idea which was enacted by the state legislature without consideration of its role in dispute settlement, and is all but forgotten by the state administrator. For example, in Texas, one of the few states which has no mediation law or agency, the governor is authorized, when a labor dispute arises, to appoint an "industrial commission" to hold hearings and to make a public report on the dispute. In Alabama, where the state does virtually no mediation, the governor is authorized to appoint, or even to sit upon, a tripartite fact-finding agency. In neither of these states is there any record of such provisions being utilized.

In Rhode Island the director of the Department of Labor may, subject to the approval of the governor, appoint a board "for the consideration and settlement" of disputes not terminated by mediation. This law was enacted in 1919. It has been invoked only twice, but in neither case was a board actually appointed. In Illinois, state mediation officials interrogated by the writers knew of no use that had ever been made of their fact-finding statute.[13]

Fact Finding in Minnesota

Minnesota has had about as much experience with fact finding as any other state. Under a law enacted in 1939, the state first attempts to

[12] See below, pages 446–48, for a discussion of the constitutionality issue.

[13] Letter, May, 1962.

settle a dispute by mediation. If that fails, the state conciliator suggests that the parties agree to arbitrate. If the parties fail so to agree, and if the dispute is in an industry affected with the public interest, "which includes, but is not restricted to, any industry, business or institution engaged in supplying the necessities of life, safety, or health, so that a temporary suspension of its operation would endanger the life, safety, health or well-being of a substantial number of people of any community," the conciliator must notify the governor, who may appoint a tripartite commission "to conduct a hearing and make a report on the issues involved and the merits of the respective contentions of the parties to the dispute."

The commission's report must be submitted to the governor after twenty-five days, and may be publicized by the governor. Strikes and lockouts are prohibited for 30 days after the governor is notified of the "public interest" dispute, in order to give the commission time to report. If the governor does not appoint a commission, strikes and lockouts are permitted five days after he is notified instead of 30 days thereafter.

This procedure is, of course, very similar to that of the Railway Labor Act, which was enjoying its unearned reputation as a "model law" when the Minnesota legislation was first enacted. An examination of the Minnesota experience indicates some of the same ills which befell its prototype on the railroads—overutilization, inhibition of collective bargaining, lack of the parties' respect for fact-finding recommendations, and lack of public interest in supporting those recommendations.

The Minnesota law began at a difficult time because, soon after its enactment, came the defense program and then World War II. Early in this emergency period the conciliator adopted a policy of considering any industry to be "affected with the public interest" if the employer was materially engaged in the production of defense items. Between 1940 and 1945, 167 commissions were appointed—70 between July 1, 1941, and June 30, 1942. If the commission's recommendations were not accepted, the case might be referred to the National War Labor Board.[14] In any case the war period provides no real guides to the Act's effects.

After World War II an overeagerness to permit Minnesota's unions and employers to utilize the Act persisted for several years. Table 21 shows that an annual average of forty-three commissions was appointed between 1946 and 1949. Hotels and restaurants, manufacturing of every description, laundries, and optical firms were found to be "affected with the public interest." After analyzing the first decade of the Minne-

[14] J. W. Stieber, *Ten Years of the Minnesota Labor Relations Act* (Minneapolis: University of Minnesota, Industrial Relations Center, 1949), p. 23.

sota law (including the war years), Professor Stieber found "considerable evidence . . . to indicate that fact finding procedure, as practiced in Minnesota, has hindered free collective bargaining." He found a

TABLE 21

FACT FINDING IN MINNESOTA, 1946–60

Year	Number of Commissions Appointed	Number of Reports	Dispute Settled on Basis of Commission Recommendation	Dispute Settled by Conciliation or Other Modification of Commission Recommendation	Strike Occurred	No Record of Result
1960–62.....	2	2	2	..	..	..
1958–60.....	1	1*	1*	..	..	..
1956–58.....	5	5	2†	1†	2	..
1954–56.....	2	2	1	..	1	..
1952–54.....	10	..	..	..	..	10
1951–52.....	8	8	6	1	1	..
1950–51.....	10	9	3	5	1	..
1949–50.....	15	13	7	4	2	..
1948–49.....	44	29	7	10	12	..
1947–48.....	52	33	6	16	1	10
1946–47.....	37	34	8	17	..	1

NOTES: Data for 1939–40 not clearly distinguished. Data for 1941–46 not comparable because of war situation and activities of War Labor Board.

* Listed in reports as thirteen disputes—actually one multiemployer dispute.

† Statistics not clearly categorized; distinguished by estimate.

SOURCE: State of Minnesota, Division of Conciliation, annual and biennial reports.

tendency for the same unions and employers to appear before fact-finding commissions each year, for a high percentage of rejection of fact-finding commission reports, and for the conciliator and/or the governor then to step in and usually effectuate a settlement by compromise between what the commission recommended and what the party holding out would take.[15]

Stieber's analysis, of course, is quite consistent with the analysis in this study of the Railway Labor Act.[16] If the parties learn to expect that a fact-finding board or commission will be appointed, they soon toss everything into the commission's lap rather than settle anything in collective bargaining. The fear is that anything conceded in bargaining or mediation will be used as a springboard for further concessions before the commission. If, however, the commission poorly gauges the relative strength of the parties, or turns in a report which either or both parties reject, the real emergency occurs. For here, both collective bargaining and the emergency procedure have been exhausted, and nothing has been settled.

[15] *Ibid.*, pp. 22–23.

[16] See Chapter 12, pages 322–30.

If, at this stage, a conciliator or governor or other public official is available to seek a settlement by putting pressure on one party to make further concessions, the tendency of the party seeking additional concessions to reject a recommendation of a fact-finding commission is further encouraged. Between 1946 and 1949 (Table 21), 45 per cent of the cases for which fact-finding commissions were appointed were settled on the basis of "modification by further conciliation," whereas only 23 per cent were settled on the basis of the commissions' reports.

By 1950 the administrators of the Minnesota law were determined to improve the effectiveness of the fact-finding commission procedure by giving "a more strict interpretation of the legislative intent."[17] The following year the conciliator pointed with pride to the fact that "there has been a continued decrease in the number of disputes referred to fact-finding commissions. This section of the law has been given a more strict interpretation in an attempt to make it more effective."[18]

Table 21 shows that since 1950, there has been a steady reduction in the use of fact-finding commissions. There are several reasons for this; one is the aforenoted new policy of the law's administrators. Certainly, they are correct in stating that the more commissions appointed, the less will be their effectiveness. During the first ten years of the Act, public opinion did not rise to support commission recommendations, nor did strikes decrease relative to other areas or states.[19] If the fact-finding commission is to be of valuable service, it must be utilized most sparingly.

Another reason for the declining use of fact-finding commissions in Minnesota since 1950 has been the general lack of serious strike situations. The most important stoppages in Minnesota since then have been steel or mine strikes under national bargaining, in which the state has been helpless to intervene. The 1950's were a decade of relative labor peace in Minnesota, as in the rest of the United States.

Finally, like most states with strike control laws which have not been ultimately tested in the courts, Minnesota is loath to bring about a final test of constitutionality by forcing the issue through the appointment of fact-finding commissions which are unacceptable to the parties. Most appointments in recent years have not been opposed by the parties. In such instances, of course, with compulsion lacking, fact finding has its greatest opportunity to achieve—actually through a sort of advanced mediation—an acceptable settlement. This is a far cry from the

[17] State of Minnesota, Division of Conciliation, *Annual Report, 1949–50* (St. Paul, 1950), p. 9.

[18] *Ibid., Annual Report, 1950–51* (St. Paul, 1951), p. 27.

[19] Stieber, *op. cit.*, pp. 17–23.

traditional theory of fact finding which assumes that an impartial commission can, by discovering the facts and publicizing them, induce the parties to agree to a rational settlement.

Fact Finding in New York

Fact finding in New York State dates back to 1887 under a law providing for mediation, arbitration, and "investigation" of labor disputes. This authority was later lodged in the jurisdiction of the state industrial commissioner, who has the power to "inquire into and report on the causes of all strikes, lockouts, and other industrial controversies and labor disputes, and may appoint boards of inquiry for that purpose." In 1941 the law was amended to provide that boards of inquiry may be appointed by the industrial commissioner only after the State Board of Mediation certifies "that its efforts to effect a voluntary settlement of the dispute have been unsuccessful."[20]

New York has generally been restrained in the use of fact finding. In most cases, boards have been appointed because of strikes heavily affecting a particular community, or because a strike involved a problem which was especially difficult to resolve. By comparison, Minnesota has appointed more fact-finding commissions in some months than New York has done in twenty-five years.

New York has not had the same experience in having the recommendations of fact finders rejected which has been a recurring problem in Minnesota over the years. There are several reasons for this. In the first place, because New York has appointed so few boards of inquiry, they have not become commonplace; therefore, when they are appointed, their importance and the consequences of rejecting their recommendations have been dramatized quite vividly. An additional result of this infrequent appointment has been that the parties have been unable to feel sufficiently assured that a fact-finding board will be appointed, so that they have not tended to substitute the fact-finding procedure for real collective bargaining.

Another reason why New York boards of inquiry have been relatively successful is that they have usually been appointed at that period of time in a dispute when the parties themselves were looking for a way out. Fact finding in New York has been used in actuality more as a final mediation procedure than as a formal method of investigating and reporting the facts.

With this interesting record, it is unfortunate that New York State

[20] For a good discussion of fact finding in New York State, see Arthur Stark, "Fact Finding in Labor Disputes," *Labor Law Journal,* Vol. III (December, 1952), pp. 859–71.

TABLE 22

Fact Finding in New York, 1937–62

Company	Union	Year	Issues	Settlement
Brooklyn Daily Eagle	Newspaper Guild, CIO	1937	Wages and conditions.	Member of Board of Mediation designated as chairman of panel, but acted as mediator and settled case.
Ludwig Bauman & Co., furniture retailers	Teamsters, AFL; Building Service Employees and Furniture Workers, CIO	1937	Jurisdictional and/or representation disputes.	Furniture workers backed down after strike over validity of arbitration award which fact-finding board sustained.
F. W. Woolworth & Co. (124 stores)	United Retail and Wholesale Workers, CIO	1938	Wages and benefits.	Fact finders mediated dispute and helped to provide data for settlement.
Woodlawn Cemetery	United Cemetery Workers, CIO	1938	Validity of contract.	First case in which a tripartite board was appointed; labor member mediated case by getting union to recognize validity of contract.
Bell Aircraft Corp	United Automobile Workers	1949	Long strike. Back-to-work movement. Contract renewal.	First board of inquiry under 1941 law mediated agreement, which called for arbitration of some issues, negotiation of others.
Realty Advisory Board	Building Service Employees' Union	1950	Wages and conditions.	Parties agreed to a voluntary fact-finding panel to end strike. Report of panel accepted.

TABLE 22 (*Continued*)

Company	Union	Year	Issues	Settlement
Yonkers Bus Co.	Transport Workers' Union	1950	Wages and conditions.	Tripartite fact-finding board set up on urging of chairman of State Mediation Board. Board report not unanimous. Strike continued and was settled by mediation later on somewhat different terms than proposed by fact finders.
New York Shipping Association	International Longshoremen's Association	1951	Rejection of new contract by some locals which staged wildcat strike.	ILA wanted President to set up emergency board, but was refused. Then New York State intervened, and a board of inquiry was appointed. Board mediated between factions to get strike over; then heard case and issued long report on longshore conditions.
Rochester Transportation Co.	Amalgamated Association of Street, Electric and Motor Coach Employees	1952	Wages and conditions.	Dispute settled on basis of board report.
Milk companies	Teamsters	1957	Wages and conditions.	Dispute settled same day board of inquiry appointed.
Long Island Railroad Co.	Brotherhood of Railroad Trainmen	1960	Hours.	Board of inquiry appointed after emergency board under Railway Labor Act had reported, and union struck rather than accept recommendations. Strike finally settled in governor's office after many officials "got into act" over one-month period.

Source: Arthur Stark, "Fact Finding in Labor Disputes," *Labor Law Journal*, Vol. III (December, 1952), pp. 859–68; and files of New York State Board of Mediation.

chose to interfere in the Long Island Railroad case in the summer of 1960, for this intervention raised the question of jurisdiction in a manner which may imperil the future usefulness of the New York procedure. Under long-standing federal law, all railroads are within the sole jurisdiction of the Railway Labor Act. An emergency board had reported on this dispute, after which the Brotherhood of Railroad Trainmen had rejected the report and had instituted a strike which shut down the railroad. The strike had been in effect for several weeks with resulting inconvenience, but surprisingly little difficulty, for the thousands of commuters who seemed somehow to reach their jobs by other means of transportation.

As a tactic the National Mediation Board announced it was discontinuing its efforts to try to settle the strike, undoubtedly in the hope that this would help bring the parties to their senses. Instead, New York State leaped into the fray; the Board of Mediation entered the case and, on the same day, certified that it could not settle the dispute by mediation. The state industrial commissioner then appointed a board of inquiry.

Quite likely, either the railroad or the union could have obtained an injunction precluding the state from proceeding with its inquiry.[21] Instead, they both attempted to co-operate with the state as well as with the federal government, which promptly re-entered the dispute, in which it had never really released and actually could not release jurisdiction. The state fact finders issued a quick report and recommendation which was enthusiastically turned down by the union membershp.

As A. H. Raskin of the *New York Times* pointed out in a cogent analysis, this competitive fact finding served to hinder rather than help settle the dispute:

> In the eight months since the controversy over a shorter workweek began, everyone from President Eisenhower to the Supervisor of the Town of Babylon has tried his hand at settling it. The overlapping peace efforts are suspected of having been a major factor in fortifying the "all-or-nothing" position taken by the two Long Island lodges of the Brotherhood of Railroad Trainmen.
>
> The union based its strategy on an expectation that one politician or another among those who moved into the picture would put sufficient heat on the railroad to force a quick capitulation. However, the relative ease with which subways, buses and car pools swallowed up the displaced commuters was credited with causing a falling-off in the anxiety felt by state, city, and county officials. . . .
>
> The lack of liaison among the would-be peacemakers proved particularly costly in the make-or-break developments of the last two weeks. And the man

[21] For a discussion of this constitutional question, see below, pages 446–48.

both sides considered best qualified to effect an accord [the chairman of the National Mediation Board] found himself repeatedly pushed off-stage by Governor Rockefeller and other officials.[22]

Investigation and Assignment of Responsibility in Massachusetts

Massachusetts typifies a third type of fact finding. When mediation fails and the parties cannot agree on other means of settlement, the mediation agency may make an investigation and may publish a report assigning the blame or the responsibility for the existence or the continuance of the controversy. The theory is that either the threat of such public censure or such censure itself by a governmental agency will have the effect of inducing a recalcitrant party to move toward settlement. The results do not seem to bear out the theory.

Public opinion is difficult to mold to influence a settlement. Experience under the Railway Labor Act, the Taft-Hartley Act, and various state laws would seem to indicate that unless the public is made to feel directly and dramatically involved, appeals to "public opinion" are not likely to produce results. Moreover, frequent use, or use for minor disputes, soon causes the public to lose interest and to regard the whole procedure as commonplace even when a major dispute does occur.

The following is a typical Massachusetts assignment of responsibility notice:

> After a thorough investigation, followed by a public hearing at the Town Hall in Clinton . . . for the purpose of determining which party is to blame for the continuance of the strike at the Colonial Press, Inc., and after listening for three hours to testimony from all persons desiring to be heard, and carefully weighing every bit of evidence that could be deduced from that testimony together with the facts established by our investigation, the Board is forced to place the blame on the Colonial Press, Inc.[23]

It would seem too much to expect the public to become excited over a notice of this character, which tells nothing of the history, the issues, or even the parties involved. As an opinion mobilizer, such an investigation notice is not likely to have much effect.

In addition to its failure effectively to mobilize public opinion in favor of dispute settlement, the administration of the Massachusetts law has raised considerable question as to the general appropriateness of an investigation provision. For by its very nature, such investigation de-

[22] *New York Times,* July 19, 1960.

[23] Quoted by Howard S. Kaltenborn, *Governmental Adjustment of Labor Disputes* (Chicago: Foundation Press, 1943), p. 191.

mands a very high measure of *expertise* and impartiality. To assess responsibility for the continuance of a strike demands that one make a value judgment on a very great number of issues where there is no question of right or wrong, but rather the question of whose views shall prevail. For example, if the union desires to limit the employer's right to subcontract work and the employer feels that to yield would threaten the profit margin he regards as necessary to operate the business, the fact that other labor agreements in the area may or may not have a provision on this subject is a bench mark but no criterion on which one can "blame" either party for not yielding. There are hundreds of such issues involved in labor negotiations. And neither the Massachusetts Board of Arbitration and Conciliation nor any other agency or person has ever defined a "fair wage" satisfactorily to a party who desired to disagree.

The fact of the matter is that investigation and assignment of responsibility open the door to all sorts of partiality and political pressure and chicanery. To avoid such abuse, appointments to an agency of the highest caliber and professionalism are obviously required. Whether Massachusetts meets this qualification is debatable. As a tripartite agency the Massachusetts Board is composed of a majority of partisans, each of whom is very unlikely to blame the group he represents for the continuance of a dispute. As a result, assignment of responsibility has become a tug of pressure on the chairman, with the merits of the case subordinated to union, management, and political pressures. Moreover, the appointment of a number of political personages, not necessarily skilled in industrial relations, to the Massachusetts Board in recent years has not generated confidence in its decisions. It is, therefore, of great interest that a recent court decision will probably have the effect of doing away with the use of the investigation function of the Massachusetts and similar state laws, except in purely local situations.[24]

STATE COMPULSORY ARBITRATION STATUTES

American states have experimented with compulsory arbitration for short periods after both world wars. In each period, state laws banning strikes and providing for compulsory arbitration were enacted following bitter strikes which affected key industries. The post-World War I experiment occurred in Kansas, where a general compulsory arbitration law was enacted in 1920, and rendered inoperative by court

[24] See below, pages 446–48, for a discussion of this decision.

decisions in 1923 and 1925,[25] after an interesting, controversial career.[26]

The year 1946, following World War II, set the record for man-days lost because of strikes. Among the industries affected were a number of public utilities, including electric light and power, and gas operations. As a result, eleven states enacted emergency legislation in 1947. Eight of the laws provided for compulsory arbitration.[27] A majority of these laws became inoperative as a result of a 1951 Supreme Court decision involving the Wisconsin law;[28] but meanwhile, valuable experience was accumulated.

The Indiana Law

A majority of these laws were modeled on the Indiana statute. This law covered privately owned companies supplying electric, power, gas, water, telephone, and transportation (exclusive of railroad and air) services to the public. It exhorted parties to settle their disputes by collective bargaining. In the event a strike was threatened and the governor believed severe hardship to the public would occur, he was required to appoint a conciliator, who attempted to mediate the dispute. If mediation proved unsuccessful within a thirty-day period, the dispute was referred to a Board of Arbitration. No strikes, lockouts, or other use of force was permitted once a conciliator was appointed. The governor could, however, decline to appoint a conciliator if he believed no hardship would occur, and then no prohibition on strikes or lockouts was in force.

The Indiana law featured great care in outlining the duties, functions, and limitations of the Board of Arbitration. It was a public Board, selected from a panel chosen by the governor, and had the power of subpoena and of administering oaths. It was directed, where rates of pay and other conditions of work were in dispute, to establish the same comparable to those established by other public utility employers for workers of the same skills in the area where the dispute existed, or if no comparable public utility employer or employees existed in the area, to make the same comparisons with adjoining labor market areas within the state.

25 *Wolff Packing Co.* v. *Court of Industrial Relations,* 262 U.S. 522 (1923), 267 U.S. 552 (1925).

26 For a careful history of the Kansas law, see D. Gagliardo, *The Kansas Industrial Court* (Lawrence: University of Kansas Publications, 1941).

27 New Jersey, Indiana, Florida, Wisconsin, Pennsylvania, Michigan, Nebraska, and Minnesota.

28 *Amalgamated Association* v. *Wisconsin Employment Relations Board,* 340 U.S. 33 (1951).

Arbitration boards were further required to avoid company-wide determinations but to decide cases by establishing separate labor market areas for each plant, office, or operation of a utility, and, in setting wages, to take into account fringe benefits and the stability of work of public utility employees.

The standards feature of the Indiana law attracted considerable attention, and was the basis for the adoption of similar laws in Florida, Wisconsin, Michigan, Pennsylvania, and Nebraska. As in Indiana, these laws had considerable employer and conservative support, and were opposed by prounion groups.

Although the laws in these other states closely followed the Indiana format, there were differences. For example, Wisconsin vested chief administrative control in its already existing Employment Relations Board instead of the governor. Nebraska established a full-time Court of Industrial Relations which acts in place of arbitration panels and *ad hoc* boards chosen from the panels. Nebraska, a public power state, also provided for jurisdiction by its Court of Industrial Relations over disputes involving government-owned utilities. Pennsylvania excluded communications and transportation from its law and provided for arbitration only after the employees rejected the employer's "last" offer in a vote conducted by the State Labor Relations Board. And Michigan gave control over its law to the judiciary, which the Michigan courts soon found contrary to the state constitution; they therefore voided all sections of the law pertaining to arbitration.[29]

New Jersey Act

New Jersey did not go the "Indiana route." As originally enacted in 1946, the New Jersey law provided for a combination of fact finding and seizure. The statute declared that heat, light, power, sanitation, transportation, communication, and water were essential and that an interruption of these services was a threat to public health and welfare. To avoid such interruption, a panel was set up with labor and industry representatives through the State Board of Mediation. If the parties did not settle their disputes, members of the panel were appointed to hold hearings and make recommendations for settlement to the governor. If a strike still threatened, the governor was empowered to seize the facilities. No penalties before or after seizure were provided.

When this procedure did not stave off a threatened strike of telephone employees, the New Jersey legislature added a compulsory arbitration provision after seizure with severe fines and jail terms for vio-

[29] *Local 170, Transport Workers' Union* v. *Gadola*, 34 N.W. (2d) 71 (1948).

lations. Later the jail terms were eliminated and the fines reduced. Standards were added to the New Jersey law after a court decision requiring such guides as a condition of constitutionality, and the provisions for fact finding before seizure were later eliminated by the legislature as unnecessary. The constitutionality of the New Jersey law was not passed on by the courts after the Wisconsin case was decided by the Supreme Court. The law, however, has not since been invoked.[30]

Minnesota and New York Hospital Acts

Minnesota, as noted earlier in this chapter, had enacted a comprehensive fact-finding law in 1939, which applies to public utilities among other industries. Then, in 1947 the state enacted amendments providing for compulsory arbitration for wage and hour issues in charitable hospitals only. Only hospitals in Minnesota are thus subject to arbitration. This Act will be discussed in Chapter 16, which deals with settlement procedures for public employees. In April, 1963, New York enacted a compulsory arbitration law applicable only to hospitals in New York City.

Effects on Bargaining

All compulsory arbitration statutes contain pronouncements favoring the settlement of disputes by collective bargaining. Most such laws also provide for attempts at settlement by conciliation or mediation, with the express hope that compulsory arbitration will not need to be utilized except rarely and then only for cases in which the disputed issues are exceptionally difficult to resolve.

Does it work out this way, or does compulsory arbitration *compete with* instead of supplementing the bargaining process? The experience of compulsory arbitration in Florida, Wisconsin, Indiana, New Jersey, and Pennsylvania, as set forth in Table 23, provides part of the answer by showing certain state and industry differences in the application of arbitration.

In Wisconsin, Indiana, and New Jersey, for example, the administrators of the laws did not hesitate to use them in disputes in which covered industries were involved, even though the prospective disputes would not have been of major proportions. Disputes sent to arbitration involved small Rural Electrification Administration co-operatives, accounting employees of telephone companies, and bus operators in small cities. Compulsory arbitration was used, as the Supreme Court

[30] A good review of the New Jersey law and its history is found in New Jersey Governor's Committee on Legislation Relating to Public Utility Labor Disputes, *Report to Governor Robert B. Meyner* (Trenton, 1954), pp. 22–25.

stated in the decision invalidating the Wisconsin law, not as "emergency" legislation but as "a comprehensive code for the settlement of labor disputes between public utility employers and employees."

TABLE 23

ARBITRATION CASES BY STATE AND INDUSTRY, 1947*–62

State	Total Cases	Urban Transit	Communication	Electric Light and Power†	Gas	Water Works
Florida	4	3	..	..	1	..
Indiana	29	14	8	6	..	1
New Jersey	25	3	9	3	9	1
Pennsylvania	9	‡	‡	3	6	..
Wisconsin	40	2	10	24	4	..
Total cases	107	22	27	36	20	2

* All laws enacted in 1947; all statistics from dates of enactment.
† Includes gas utilities operated in conjunction with electric light and power.
‡ Jurisdiction of Pennsylvania law does not include these industries.
SOURCE: Data on usage follow those set forth in New Jersey Governor's Committee on Legislation Relating to Public Utility Labor Disputes, *Report to Governor Robert B. Meyner* (Trenton, 1954), pp. 33–40, except for Pennsylvania, where records of the State Labor Relations Board show two additional cases.

Moreover, the willingness of these states to invoke compulsory arbitration encouraged its use. The belief of some unions and employers that they could do better under arbitration than under collective bargaining resulted in perfunctory negotiations and hasty applications for the invocation of arbitration. And the unwillingness of the state administrators to oppose this tide encouraged it.

Wisconsin REA and New Jersey Gas. Special conditions in the electrical industry in Wisconsin and in the gas industry in New Jersey brought increased case loads in those states. By and large, unions and management in the two industries have compiled an excellent record of peaceful settlement without recourse to outside agencies. In Wisconsin, however, a basic dispute over whether Rural Electrification Administration co-operatives should pay rates comparable to private electric utilities accounted for most of the disputes in the electric industry there. And in New Jersey, disputes in the gas industry involving rival AFL, CIO, and independent unions resulted in nine out of the twenty-five arbitration board appointments.

Urban Transit. If a union asks for a 10-cent increase and a company offers 8 cents, the union can refuse the compromise, go to arbitration, and point out that the company has already offered 8 cents. Then the arbitrators are under great pressure to give, instead of 8 cents, a few cents more—in other words, to compromise the company's offer upward. If this happens once, it is most unlikely that the company the following year will make any offer for fear of seeing that offer used as a springboard for further concessions in an arbitration proceeding. The situation may then snowball: Neither party is willing to bargain for fear that any bargaining will be used against it in later arbitration procedure. Such an impasse appears to typify present-day industrial relations in the urban transportation industry in the states surveyed.

The Amalgamated Association of Street, Electric and Motor Coach Employees, the dominant union in urban transportation, has from its inception stated that one of its objectives is "to encourage the settlement of all disputes between employees and employers by arbitration."

> For more than fifty years, this union has made it obligatory for local divisions to offer arbitration to the employer where other means of settlement failed. . . . The International [union] has exercised strict control over the making of collective agreements and has attempted to have incorporated in them all a clause that would provide arbitration not only in case of disputes arising out of the agreement but also in the event that a new agreement could not be negotiated to replace an expiring one. By 1905 . . . arbitration was provided in the majority of . . . agreements then in existence.[31]

Post-World War II strike control legislation, therefore, found this union committed to arbitration as a means of settlement, and, in addition, extremely competent and well staffed to win arbitrations.

Not that the Amalgamated Association welcomed strike control legislation. In 1919, it had emphatically opposed the Kansas compulsory arbitration law;[32] and since 1947, it has led the fight to invalidate state strike control laws. Local divisions of the Amalgamated Association attempted to secure management agreement for voluntary arbitration in those states in which compulsory arbitration existed. In some instances, this occurred; but often, management representatives declined on the ground that management's interests were better protected by arbitrating under state laws which included standards that arbitrators must follow, and which also provide, at least in the minds of managements, preferable methods for selecting arbitrators.[33]

Whether engaged in voluntary or compulsory arbitration, however, it has become fairly common for the parties in the urban transportation industry to prepare for arbitration rather than for collective

[31] E. P. Schmidt, *Industrial Relations in Urban Transportation* (Minneapolis: University of Minnesota Press, 1937), p. 194.

[32] *Ibid.*, p. 195.

[33] See below, pages 446–48.

bargaining. As a result, it is not unusual for the parties in this industry to certify for arbitration, whether voluntary or compulsory, 20 to 40 issues, some of which have obviously been left in by either the Amalgamated Association or the employer in order to improve its chances of winning its really basic demands.

For this industry, it appears that voluntary arbitration has been used as a substitute for collective bargaining. And for a short period, compulsory arbitration replaced voluntary arbitration.

Telephones. Although the history and present situation of labor relations in the telephone industry have been quite different from those in urban transportation, the policies of the Communication Workers of America (CIO), the dominant union in the telephone industry, also contributed to the use of governmental strike control machinery. Perhaps because it was a relatively new organization which did not attain the bargaining power enjoyed by some other large unions, the CWA apparently determined that it could secure more favorable results through fact finding and arbitration than through collective bargaining. Thus, although the CWA maintained official opposition to compulsory arbitration, it actually indicated a preference for such means of settlement.[34]

In recent years, however, technological developments have rendered the telephone industry largely immune to effective strike action. Dialing for both local and long-distance calls, and other automatic mechanisms and controls, permit supervisors to operate struck facilities with little or no loss of service. It is doubtful if, today, a strike of telephone workers could cause an emergency or even significant inconvenience to the public.

The Pennsylvania Situation. The Pennsylvania arbitration law is similar to that of Indiana and Wisconsin, except for (1) a last-offer strike vote provision and (2) its narrow coverage, which excludes transportation and communication. The last-offer strike vote provision was modeled on the provision in the Taft-Hartley Act and has had similar results, as was noted in Chapter 13.[35]

Under the Pennsylvania law, employees send a case to arbitration by refusing the employer's last offer. In theory, this was a tailor-made provision to encourage arbitration because it invited an arbitration

[34] See the report of CWA Vice President A. T. Jones to the 1950 CWA convention, as summarized in *Daily Labor Report,* June 27, 1950, pp. A–6, A–7. Another indication of the desire of CWA officials to use strike control machinery was their unsuccessful attempts to bring Western Electric workers within these laws in Florida and Wisconsin.

[35] See above, page 365.

award above the employer's rejected last offer. Actually, Pennsylvania had fewer arbitrations than Indiana, Wisconsin, and New Jersey. There are several reasons for this:

1. One study found that bargaining relations in most Pennsylvania utilities were sufficiently satisfactory to both labor and management so that neither desired to force invocation of the law.[36] The fact that three of the nine cases involved one gas utility gives some support to this viewpoint.

2. Another reason is that the Pennsylvania Act was apparently administered with a conscious effort to discourage the use of arbitration. As one industrialist put it: "You have to go to Harrisburg and camp on the governor's doorstep for about two weeks, and even then he probably won't invoke the law. By that time, the parties usually get so disgusted that they settle the thing themselves."[37]

3. Probably most important in reducing the number of arbitrations in Pennsylvania is the limited coverage of the statute. The two key industries which are covered in Indiana, New Jersey, and Wisconsin, but excluded in Pennsylvania, are urban transit and telephone. These industries have been involved in almost one half of the state arbitrations. Moreover, in Pennsylvania, there was no problem of rural electrification wage rates, such as existed in Wisconsin, nor interunion competition in gas plants, such as existed in New Jersey. Hence the industrial and union factors in Pennsylvania weighed against utilizing the law instead of collective bargaining.

The Florida Situation. Florida did not utilize its law very much, apparently as much because the opportunity did not arise as for any other reason. The degree of unionism was then lower in Florida, and most disputes which did occur in covered industries did not involve the law. The bitterest strike, that pertaining to the Miami transit industry, occurred after the Wisconsin decision, and caused the Florida law to be struck down by the courts.

The Nebraska Situation. Table 24 summarizes the experience under the Nebraska law. This Act is similar to the Indiana-type legislation, but it is administered by a permanent three-man Court of Industrial Relations, and it covers all local transportation and publicly owned utilities in addition to the coverage of the Indiana-type law. The willingness of Nebraska's Court to invoke its law when local truckers and

[36] Robert R. France and Richard A. Lester, *Compulsory Arbitration of Utility Disputes in New Jersey and Pennsylvania* (Princeton: Princeton University, Industrial Relations Section, 1951), pp. 73–74.

[37] Interview, 1951.

taxicab drivers are involved is difficult to justify on the basis of emergency dispute legislation, although a cessation of local truckers in a food industry could perhaps have serious consequences.

TABLE 24

Arbitration in Nebraska, by Industry, 1947–62

Taxicab companies	5
Power districts	5
Urban transit	3
Motor freight companies	2
Total cases	15

Source: Letter dated March 14, 1962, from Court of Industrial Relations, state of Nebraska.

Nebraska's power industry is entirely owned by the public. The coverage of these government installations by an arbitration law is both unique and interesting in its attempt to provide a means of settlement where employees clearly have no protected right to strike.[38]

STATE SEIZURE LEGISLATION

Five states—New Jersey, Maryland, Massachusetts, Missouri, and Virginia—have utilized seizure in industrial disputes.[39] The New Jersey law, as already noted, provides for seizure as a prelude to compulsory arbitration. The Maryland law has been invoked only once.[40] The laws of Virginia, where seizure stands alone; of Missouri, where seizure may be invoked after fact finding has failed; and of Massachusetts, where seizure is a "choice of procedures," are discussed in the remaining sections of this chapter.

Seizure in Virginia

Virginia adopted seizure in the post-World War II period as a technique to control strikes in industries deemed essential. Laws providing for state seizure and operations to prevent strikes were passed on three occasions, the most significant being the Virginia Public Utility Labor Relations Act, initially passed in 1947, and amended in 1952.[41]

The 1952 Virginia law is written with the clear intent of provid-

[38] Further reference to this law will be made in Chapter 16.

[39] Besides these state laws, North Dakota passed a seizure law in 1919 affecting utilities and coal mines, but never used it. Hawaii passed one in 1949 affecting longshore operators, following a long strike; but again, it was not invoked.

[40] For a careful analysis of the Maryland law, see S. H. Lehrer, "The Maryland Public Utilities Disputes Act," *Labor Law Journal*, Vol. VII (October, 1956), pp. 607–17.

[41] The other Virginia seizure laws are the Ferry Seizure Act of 1946 and the Mine Seizure Act of 1950.

ing for "the continuous, uninterrupted, and proper functioning and operation of public utilities engaged in the business of furnishing water, light, heat, gas, electric power, transportation, or communication, or any one or more of them, to the people of Virginia . . . declared to be essential to their welfare, health, and safety." Although the 1947 law made some attempt at promoting dispute settlement by the parties, with the governor's aid available, the 1952 law makes no mention of the collective bargaining process except as it may affect the parties themselves. The law is not a dispute-settling device. Its only intent is to provide service to the people while the parties attempt to settle their differences.

When there is a threat of a strike or interruption in the operation of any public utility, as mentioned above, the governor makes an investigation to determine whether or not the stoppage "will constitute a serious menace or threat to the public health, safety or welfare." If he determines that such will be the case, he notifies the parties that at the time of stoppage, he will take immediate possession of the utility.

After the governor issues a proclamation of intention to seize the utility, he must ascertain what jobs are essential to operate the utility and whether present jobholders are willing to fill these jobs during government operation. Any employee who is willing to work during state operation must declare that fact and then is entitled to do so; those who do not wish to do so may remain away from their jobs during state operation without penalty. "The status of no person as an employee of the utility shall be affected by either his acceptance of employment by the state or by his refusal of such employment."

If a stoppage occurs and the governor takes possession, strikes, lockouts, picketing, etc., are forbidden and subject to severe penalties. Wages and conditions of employment must be maintained at the levels existing when negotiations were commenced. Seizure remains in effect until the governor is satisfied that the utility is capable of "normal" operaion and "the public interest so requires."

The Virginia law goes beyond the seizure provisions of New Jersey by providing that "after payment of proper operating expenses and reimbursement of the State for all expenses incurred in preparing to operate same . . . eighty-five percentum of . . . net income [see Figure 10] shall be paid to the utility as compensation for the temporary use of its business, facilities and properties." Fifteen per cent of net income is thus retained by the state. In addition to the compensation paid to the state, costs incidental to the operation of the utility which are incurred by the state are charged to the company as part of its operating expenses. In case of a loss the state takes nothing. It neither furnishes money to provide a profit nor assumes any part of the loss as its obligation.

FIGURE 10

DEFINITION OF NET INCOME
IN
VIRGINIA PUBLIC UTILITY LABOR RELATIONS ACT

Net income with respect to operation of a utility by the State shall be construed to mean the gross revenues derived from such operation after deducting therefrom:

(1) the costs of operation and maintenance of the utility;
(2) the amount of depreciation during the time of such operation based on the amount allowed in the utility's federal income tax return;
(3) Federal, State, and local taxes which would be payable by the utility, if the properties were operated by it;
(4) interest on the indebtedness of the utility; and
(5) payments for the cost of insurance.

All of such items shall be prorated on an annual basis in proportion to the time the plant is operated by the State.

The Virginia Public Utility Labor Relations Act was enacted following a threatened strike in an electric utility. Besides electric light and power, however, the law covers water, heat, gas, communication, and transportation not subject to the federal Railway Labor Act. Of the eleven seizures which had occurred as of April, 1962, nine involved urban transit units and the Amalgamated Association of Street, Electric and Motor Coach Employees, and the other two have involved telephone companies and the Communication Workers of America (see Table 25).

Like all innovating legislation, Virginia's seizure law has raised some problems. In the first place, it is conceivable that in time of high employment, it would not be possible to replace personnel who exercised their right not to work for the state during the seizure period. However, in the eleven seizures to date, this problem has not arisen.

A second problem under the Virginia law concerns the role during seizure of the State Corporation Commission, the state public utility regulating body. In one case the Commission was placed in the anomalous position of having before it an application for a rate increase from a utility which had been seized and operated by the Commission. The utility maintained that the increase was needed to pay a wage increase so as to settle the dispute and repossess its properties. The Commission managed to postpone action until after seizure was terminated. Since,

TABLE 25

SEIZURES UNDER VIRGINIA PUBLIC UTILITIES LABOR RELATIONS ACT TO APRIL 1, 1962

Company	Industry	Period of Seizure	State Share of Net Profit (15 per cent*)
Chesapeake & Potomac Telephone Co.	Telephone	May 20, 1947–May 23, 1947	$ 62.76
Citizens Rapid Transit Co.	Urban transit	July 3, 1948–March 28, 1949	245.40
Virginia Transit Co.–Portsmouth Transit Co.	Urban transit	February 3, 1949–March 2, 1949	1,067.16
Alexandria, Barcroft & Washington Transit Co.	Urban transit	July 21, 1949–May 19, 1950	No profit†
Clifton Forge–Waynesboro Telephone Co.	Telephone	August 10, 1949–June 7, 1950	4,071.33
Washington, Virginia & Maryland Coach Co.	Urban transit	November 2, 1949–July 31, 1950	No profit†
Virginia Transit Co.–Portsmouth Transit Co.	Urban transit	February 11, 1950–June 20, 1950	18,052.80
Citizens Rapid Transit Co.	Urban transit	June 25, 1951–June 28, 1951‡	203.11§
Virginia Transit Co.–Portsmouth Transit Co.	Urban transit	January 24, 1952–January 25, 1952	12,925.06§
Washington, Virginia & Maryland Coach Co.	Urban transit	December 10, 1952–February 8, 1953	5,374.92§
Alexandria, Barcroft & Washington Transit Co.	Urban transit	November 1, 1952–November 9, 1952	848.72§

* The expenses incurred in the operations by the state and its agents are charged to the companies as a part of their operating expenses, and are paid the state in addition to the 15 per cent (see note §).

† If, in normal operations, the utility does not earn a profit, the state neither furnishes money to provide a profit nor assumes any percentage of the loss as its obligation.

‡ After two and one-half days of preparation by the State Corporation Commission to take over the Company, the strike was called off.

§ This figure represents the cost to the Company as its part of the expenses of the operation. Section 12 of the Virginia law, pertaining to the sharing of profits, was changed slightly in 1952. The state still turns over 85 per cent of net income to the utility; however, the law provides that this "shall in no wise control the amount of just compensation to be allowed to the utility."

SOURCE: Virginia State Corporation Commission.

however, the Virginia Act does not require that seized utilities be operated by the Commission, this problem is easily avoidable.

Another problem which might arise under the Virginia law is the reaction of a union to a wage-cut request by management during a period of economic depression. A union could refuse to take the cut or to arbitrate the dispute, and threaten to strike. This would involve state seizure with its statutory ban on changes in wages and conditions of work. Utility employees, "as the law now stands . . . could remain employed by the Commonwealth indefinitely. Their wages might be greatly out of line, the utility might be shoved into bankruptcy by the distorted costs of labor, but as long as the workers remained adamant the law could not touch them."[42]

A principal criticism of the administration of the Virginia law is

[42] *Richmond News-Leader*, editorial, August 26, 1949.

that it has been invoked in relatively minor disputes. In a real sense, none of these disputes were actual emergencies. The fact that the law has not been invoked since 1952 may reflect a realization that such minor disputes do not deserve state intervention. Or it may merely be that Virginia desires to avoid litigation over the constitutionality of its law.

Another unusual aspect of the Virginia law is that it could guarantee a minimum increase to employees. If seizure is to cost a public utility 15 per cent of profits, why not give that amount to employees in the form of wages and avoid the problems of a state take-over? Certainly, it would seem that a union which felt seizure was a possibility would not consider settling for less. Of course, the reluctance of the state to invoke the Act in recent years has no doubt curbed any union policy based on this theory.

Strikes, moreover, are more likely to be concerned with so-called "noneconomic" issues, the basic factors involved in control of the shop which are really very economic in effect, and which often mean more to the parties than a few cents in wages. Where such issues are at stake, or where the company is operating at a loss, as some of the urban transit concerns seized in Virginia were, the 15 per cent cost of seizure would not be a deterrent to management action or a spur to union policy.

Despite these problems the Virginia Public Utility Labor Relations Act appears to be carefully considered legislation. Its aim is to afford the public protection but, at the same time, to attempt a minimum interference with collective bargaining by making the parties settle a dispute themselves and by penalizing them during a seizure period.

Seizure in Missouri

Missouri's Public Utility Seizure Act, referred to as the King-Thompson Act, was passed in 1947. The preamble to the Act declares it ". . . to be the policy of the State that heat, light, power, sanitation, transportation, communication, and water are life essentials of the people; . . . and the State's regulation of the labor relations affecting such public utilities is necessary to the public interest."[43] In contrast to similar state laws the Missouri Act does not automatically invoke seizure when the parties are not able to resolve a dispute.

A public hearing panel or fact-finding board is formed when the parties are unable to agree on contract changes or to submit a dispute to arbitration. If either party does not accept the recommendations of the panel or engages in a strike or lockout, the governor is authorized at his

[43] Missouri State Board of Mediation, *Twelve Years under the King-Thompson Act, 1947–1959* (Jefferson City, 1959), p. 3.

discretion to seize the company when he finds that the public interest, health, and welfare may be jeopardized. Since 1947, there have been nine seizure cases of Missouri public utilities and approximately twenty other cases in which fact finding was invoked, but in which no seizure occurred despite strikes. The seizure cases are summarized in Table 26.

TABLE 26

SEIZURES UNDER THE KING-THOMPSON ACT OF MISSOURI*

Company	Industry	Period of Seizure
Kansas City Public Service Co.	Transit	April 29, 1950–December 11, 1950
St. Louis Public Service Co.	Transit	August 10, 1950–October 19, 1950
St. Louis Public Service Co.	Transit	August 11, 1955–December 23, 1955
Laclede Gas Co.	Gas	July 5, 1956–October 31, 1956
Kansas City Power & Light Co.	Electricity	July 6, 1956–July 17, 1956
Kansas City Power & Light Co.	Electricity	August 31, 1957–June 25, 1958
Kansas City Public Service Co.	Transit	November 6, 1957–March 6, 1958
Kansas City Power & Light Co.	Electricity	August 5, 1960–May 31, 1961
Kansas City Transit Co.	Transit	November 13, 1961–†

* About twenty strikes in public utilities have occurred in Missouri since the enactment of the King-Thompson Act in which seizure was not invoked. The governor did not find that these strikes jeopardized the public interest, health, and welfare.

† The Kansas City Transit Company is still under seizure pending a decision in the federal courts to determine constitutionality of the Act.

SOURCE: Missouri State Board of Mediation.

The seizure procedure under the Act is carried out in three steps: (1) The governor issues a proclamation which indicates that an existing or threatened strike jeopardizes the public interest, health, and welfare; (2) Executive Order No. 1 is issued, constituting the official act of seizing the utility; and (3) Executive Order No. 2 establishes the governor's agent and gives him authority to take possession of the utility. Just as it has been shown to be true in Virginia, seizure in Missouri does not serve as a dispute-settling device. But in Missouri, when the state has taken over, it has been pretty much "business as usual." No penalty accompanies the seizure, except the limitations on the right of unions to strike and on employers to lock out. Since the law is silent on the subject, the company is presumably entitled to "just compensation" for the taking of its plant according to a United States Supreme Court decision.[44]

Penalties are provided for in the Act in case of unlawful conduct by either party. If a labor union, labor officer, or public utility calls a strike or work stoppage in violation of the seizure provisions of the Act, a fine of $10,000 per day may be levied against the union or utility and $1,000 against the union official. The penalty was used in the

[44] *United States* v. *Pewee Coal Co.*, 71 S. Ct. 670 (1951).

Laclede Gas Company strike of 1956. Since the employees refused to return to work until a circuit court injunction was issued eight days after seizure, the union and union leaders were subjected to the penalties described above. Another penalty action remains in the courts against the union in the St. Louis Public Service Company seizure of 1955, in which case the union continued the strike three days after seizure.

"CHOICE OF PROCEDURES" IN MASSACHUSETTS

Because of the tendency of emergency laws to become a substitute for collective bargaining, a school of thought has emerged which advocates giving the chief executive a "choice of procedures" to utilize so that those who are pushing an interruption of a vital service are not able to compare settlement by collective bargaining with settlement under governmental direction.[45]

The choice-of-procedures theory has been written into law in Massachusetts, as a result of a report by a tripartite committee, appointed in 1947, by the then Governor, Robert Bradford, to survey the labor legislation of the state. This committee, of which the late Professor Sumner H. Slichter was Chairman, made a unanimous report covering numerous phases of labor law which were almost entirely adopted into law. Among them is included this unique statute governing strikes affecting public health and safety.

The "Slichter law," as it is known, applies to the "production and distribution of food, fuel, water, electric light and power, gas, or hospital or medical services." It provides that in the event of a threatened stoppage in these industries which the governor finds would endanger the health or safety of any community, he may do one of two things:

1. He may require the parties to appear before a governor-appointed moderator, who must be "an impartial person skilled in industrial relations," and show cause why the dispute should not be submitted to voluntary arbitration. The moderator's job is to induce the parties to arbitrate, or to make public the reasons for their refusal to do so. He is forbidden by law to review the merits of the dispute. An arbitration submission or the moderator's report is required within fifteen days of the governor's proclamation of an emergency, during which time no changes in conditions of work and no stoppages are permitted.

2. Or the governor may request the parties to submit the dispute to

[45] W. W. Wirtz, Secretary of Labor in the Kennedy administration, has long been an advocate of this approach. See his article in Irving Bernstein *et al.* (eds.), *Emergency Disputes and National Policy* (New York: Harper & Bros., 1955), pp. 149–65.

a tripartite arbitration board. This board is required not only to decide the issues, but also to "fix in its recommendations the date, prospective or retroactive, as of which its recommendations shall be made effective and in so doing shall consider evidence as to the responsibility of either party for delaying the settlement or rejecting arbitration."

If neither of these methods is successful in avoiding a stoppage, or if the dispute "is of such a nature that these procedures cannot be applied thereto," the governor is required to declare the existence of an emergency during which he may either (1) "enter into arrangements with either or both parties" to continue to produce or to distribute sufficient essential services "to safeguard the public health and safety" or (2) seize the business and operate it "for the account of the person operating it immediately prior to the seizure"; or, if such person elects within ten days after seizure, he may waive the proceeds during seizure and receive instead "fair and reasonable" compensation for the appropriation and use of his property for which he may sue the state. But in determining this compensation, the courts are directed to take into account the fact that a labor dispute existed which interrupted, or threatened to interrupt, private operation of the plant "and the effect of such . . . upon the value to the petitioner of the use" of the facility.

During the emergency seizure, all federal and state labor legislation remains in effect. Conditions of employment, however, may be altered by the governor upon recommendation of a tripartite arbitration board appointed by him. "Such recommendations will be based on the conditions in existence in the industry affected." Strikes, lockouts, or supporting activities to such are forbidden during the emergency period.[46]

An interesting and novel concept in the law is the "show cause" procedure before the moderator as to why the dispute should not be submitted to arbitration. This procedure was designed to encourage voluntary arbitration by the parties themselves, with the idea that no union or company would like to have a finger pointed at it charging that it would rather endanger the community than arbitrate. Moreover, if arbitration is refused, a penalty may be imposed by compulsory arbitration in the form of prospective or retroactive application of the award.

The "show cause" procedure may have another and, paradoxically, contrary merit. A demand, for example, may, in the eyes of one of the parties, be so extreme or so lacking in conformity with existing practices that he feels arbitration involves an impossible risk. But the party refus-

[46] The report on which the Slichter law is based is *Report of the Governor's Labor-Management Committee*, Commonwealth of Massachusetts, House Document No. 1875 (Boston, 1947).

ing to arbitrate has a forum to which he can explain and attempt to justify what the public might otherwise consider as pure disregard of its interests.

The Slichter law attempted to meet all contingencies arising under seizure. Profits and losses go to the private owners unless they elect compensation for use instead. In the latter event, they risk a lesser figure, since their compensation must consider losses which might have occurred if a stoppage were effective. Labor legislation remains in effect. And unlike the Virginia legislation, wages can be raised or lowered by an arbitration board if the governor so desires.

On the other hand, altering conditions of work during seizure has its dangers. Permanent and costly concessions can be made to a union which an employer must accept in order to secure the return of his property. The fact that any contractual changes must be in accord with existing industry conditions does afford protection against startling innovations, but the danger of costly changes is not completely removed.

Another provision in the Slichter law which may prove troublesome is that calling for three-man tripartite arbitration boards. This could result in three-way, no-decision splits in cases where a decision is imperative to maintain peace. Or it could result in the public member being forced to modify his judgment drastically in order to secure a majority report.

Experience with the Slichter Law

As Table 27 indicates, the Slichter law has been invoked six times and has not been invoked since 1953. How has it worked in practice?

A careful study of the law found that the health and safety of any community in Massachusetts had not been imperiled since the passage of the law, but neither had such peril occurred in neighboring states which did not have any emergency legislation.[47] This same study also found indications that the final settlement in four of the cases was about the same as would have occurred under collective bargaining. In two of the cases, however, it noted that the final settlement was probably higher, being more than the unions were willing to accept for settlement at one point.[48]

There seems to be general agreement that the Slichter law has not disrupted collective bargaining. This has been attributed by one author to restraint in administration.[49] *Fortune* magazine noted that the unions

[47] George P. Shultz, "The Massachusetts Choice-of-Procedures Approach to Emergency Disputes," *Industrial and Labor Relations Review,* Vol. X (April, 1957), p. 363.

[48] *Ibid.,* pp. 364–65.

[49] *Ibid.,* pp. 365–70.

TABLE 27

CASES INVOLVING THE SLICHTER LAW

Company	Union	Dates of Initial Proclamation and Final Settlement	Procedures Used	Method of Final Settlement
Truckers Association	Teamsters, Local 25 (AFL)	January 1, 1948 February 4, 1948	Moderator. Mutual agreement for partial operation.	Collective bargaining.
Eastern Gas and Fuel Associates (gas manufacturing plant that serves Boston area and is part of large utility organization)	Gas, Coke and Chemical Workers (CIO)	January 30, 1948 February 17, 1948	Moderator. Seizure.	Collective bargaining.
N.E. Electric System (gas distribution facilities)	United Mine Workers, District No. 50	February 17, 1953 March 3, 1953	Moderator.	Collective bargaining.
Worcester Gas Light Company (subsidiary of New England Gas and Electric Association)	United Mine Workers, District No. 50	March 1, 1953 May 11, 1953	Moderator. Seizure.	Collective bargaining.
Montaup Electric Company (electric power generating and transmitting subsidiary of Eastern Utilities Associates)	Utility Workers of America (CIO)	June 25, 1953 September 9, 1953	Moderator. Emergency arbitration board (held no hearings on merits of dispute).	Voluntary arbitration outside procedures of Slichter law (same arbitration board as appointed by governor but accepted by union only after it became private board).
Association of Milk Dealers (supplying less than half of Greater Boston's needs)	Teamsters, Milk Wagon Drivers Local (AFL)	April 9, 1953 December 23, 1953	Moderator. Emergency arbitration board. Seizure. Special commission for recommendations (never issued recommendations).	Unanimous decision of tripartite voluntary arbitration board (same personnel as special commission).

SOURCE: George P. Shultz, "The Massachusetts Choice-of-Procedures Approach to Emergency Disputes," *Industrial and Labor Relations Review*, Vol. X (April, 1957), p. 364.

were beginning to utilize the law to gain greater benefits when the then Governor Christian Herter was advised by the authors of the law to choose not to invoke the law,[50] even in situations where it previously had been utilized. This seems to have stabilized the situation.

A more practical reason for withholding use of the law has been the political situation in Massachusetts. The Slichter law was enacted by a Republican administration and has been invoked by Republican governors. Although the labor members of the Slichter committee supported it, the law did not have union support and was opposed by the Democratic Party in the state. Professor Slichter told one of the authors several years before he died that the law could always be more successful under governors who were opposed to it, because they would invoke it only reluctantly. The fact that Massachusetts has had few governors favorable to the Slichter law may indeed be a factor explaining its limited encroachment on collective bargaining.

It should also be noted that technical factors have contributed to restraint under the law. Thus, because of automation, supervisors could operate a utility in 1957 that perhaps they could not have operated four years earlier.

The law's coverage, which excluded urban transportation and communication, appears to be wise, although the worst strikes since the passage of the Slichter act have been in transportation industries. In 1954 the coverage of the Slichter law was extended to the ferry which operates between the mainland and the islands of Martha's Vineyard and Nantucket. Nevertheless, a long strike in 1960 involving this ferry did not result in the invocation of the law. Likewise, other transportation strikes have been long and hard in the state. In 1962, however, a special statute was enacted when a strike occurred on the transit system serving metropolitan Boston. Seizure under this statute occurred and lasted one month, although the Slichter law could as easily have been extended.

Whether choice of procedures in fact creates the uncertainty that in theory it is supposed to, so as to discourage its being substituted for collective bargaining, remains a question. Certainly, as administered by Governor Herter in 1953—at least until he stopped invoking the law—it did not. To be sure, the threat of seizure authorities disbursing company cash has given management considerable pause and acts as a spur for management to settle. No such incentive to unions has been demonstrated. One must agree with Professor Shultz that to make this law work, the greatest degree of "administrative finesse and impartiality" is

[50] "Boston Roulette," *Fortune*, February, 1961, pp. 190, 193.

required.[51] In Massachusetts, politics have aided in preventing abuse of the law, but this is an almost accidental advantage which cannot be everywhere present. In 1954, Massachusetts added another facet against hasty invocation—a public hearing unless the governor finds it impractical, "at which the parties to the dispute shall be heard upon the sole question whether an interruption is imminent and would curtail the availability of essential goods or services to such an extent as to endanger the health or safety of any community."

The problem has thus been recognized. Further experience may determine whether choice of procedures is just another form of seizure or whether it can live up to the hope of its proponents as a protector of the public and not as a destroyer of the initiative of the parties to settle disputes themselves.

CONCLUDING REMARKS

The rich and diversified experience of the states adds much to our knowledge as to how strike control legislation actually works. On the basis of the facts developed in this and in the preceding chapters, it is now appropriate to turn to an examination of the key issues involved in and raised by strike control and emergency strike legislation.

QUESTIONS FOR DISCUSSION

1. Do you think that a strike vote law can be developed which will insure that strikes are called after employees have an opportunity to express themselves on the strike issues? Explain your answer.
2. If you were asked what kind of a strike control law—compulsory arbitration or seizure—you would advocate, which would you choose? Which state law of its kind would you advocate, and why?
3. Did the Massachusetts choice-of-procedures law work out as planned?

SUGGESTIONS FOR FURTHER READING

FRANCE, ROBERT R. "Seizure in Emergency Labor Disputes in Virginia," *Industrial and Labor Relations Review,* Vol. VII (April, 1954), pp. 347–56.

A discussion of strike control in Virginia.

FRANCE, ROBERT R., AND LESTER, RICHARD A. *Compulsory Arbitration of Utility Disputes in New Jersey and Pennsylvania.* Princeton: Princeton University, Industrial Relations Section, 1951.

A study of the experiences of New Jersey and Pennsylvania with compulsory arbitration of utility disputes.

[51] Shultz, *op. cit.,* p. 371.

LEHRER, S. H. "The Maryland Public Utilities Disputes Act," *Labor Law Journal,* Vol. VII (October, 1956), pp. 607–17.

A discussion of the experience of Maryland with strike control and emergency legislation.

PARNES, HERBERT S. *Union Strike Votes: Current Practice and Proposed Controls.* Princeton: Princeton University, Industrial Relations Section, 1956.

How strike vote procedures of unions and strike vote laws work in practice.

SHULTZ, GEORGE P. "The Massachusetts Choice-of-Procedures Approach to Emergency Disputes," *Industrial and Labor Relations Review,* Vol. X (April, 1957), pp. 359–74.

A study of strike control in Massachusetts.

Chapter 15 EMERGENCY STRIKE CONTROLS: ANALYSIS AND PROBLEMS

The labor policies of the federal and state governments contain numerous pronouncements in favor of "free collective bargaining," but the strike control laws examined in Chapters 12, 13, and 14 involve clear attempts to limit the workings of such collective bargaining. This raises some key questions of public policy: Is collective bargaining of sufficient importance to protect? Is emergency strike legislation necessary? Can a form of emergency strike legislation be devised which does not inhibit collective bargaining? What are some of the key administrative, practical, and legal problems which have emerged from the workings of federal and state strike control legislation—other than the effects on the bargaining process?

WHY PROTECT COLLECTIVE BARGAINING?

No institution or method of determining conditions of work is, or can be, perfectly satisfactory to everyone. But few things are more important to both the individual and society than the methods of determining the conditions under which individuals buy and sell each other's and their own labor. In the United States the Civil War was fought essentially over this question. Before and since then, numerous controversies have arisen as to what is the best or fairest method of deciding basic industrial relations questions.

Economics and Equities

If any answer has emerged, it is that no objective criterion is, or can be, developed to determine the employment relationship to the satisfaction of everyone. The employment relationship is, and must remain, an economic one. What is economically desirable or even necessary for the good of the business and therefore for the continued employment of the work force may be quite different from what would be personally pleasant or satisfactory to workers or, in the case of unions, helpful to the union as an institution or to the intraunion political fortunes of the union leadership. Likewise, the very existence of the union as a force may make it economically unsound for the employer or corporate manager to operate as he deems most desirable. If the uneconomic is insisted upon by union strength or permitted by employer mismanagement, or furthered by governmental intervention, the net result can well be a decline in the competitive position of the company and a loss of employment to the union members.

When a whole industry embarks upon such an uneconomic course, the results are no different. Competition from other industries—domestic and foreign—makes itself felt. The substitution of oil and gas for coal is a case in point. So is the increasing use of aluminum, prestressed concrete, plastics, and foreign steel, all in place of domestic steel.

Economic conditions change, and economic science is not exact. No one can promise without fear of error that a certain wage will be "proper" to balance income and employment, or wages and profits in a given industry. Moreover, what is "fair" for one is "unfair" for another. There is no objective, exact answer to disputes over wages, working conditions, and other terms of employment, either on the basis of economics or on the basis of equity.[1] "Too high" wages do accelerate or cause unemployment; "too low" ones impede living standards and purchasing power—but between extremes in any given situation, there is likely to be a wide latitude of possibilities and probabilities.

Freedom and Balance

The facts of economics which make it well-nigh impossible to determine a "proper" wage, and the facts of equity which make it equally difficult to determine what is "fair" to all concerned, give added weight to the general premise upon which our society is built—that is, that the freedom to work or withdraw labor, either singly or in concert, is not to be curtailed lightly. Such freedom has never been considered a totally unrestricted one. Nor does it mean a return to eighteenth-century society. It requires balance and, above all, more governmental restraint than interference.

Balancing Liberties—and Strength

The rise of great combinations of capital in this and other countries through the corporate form spurred demands for curbing business free-

[1] This statement is made with full cognizance of the attempts of the Council of Economic Advisors of the Kennedy administration to set "economic guidelines" for wage settlement in line with productivity trends. Besides the fact that the productivity gain is a long-run trend, with wide variations from year to year, the so-called "guidelines" served largely to spur weak unions to push for the magic 3 per cent, and were largely ignored by strong unions—for example, those in the building trades.

dom. In effect, the unrestricted freedom of business was felt to impinge upon the freedom of others. From this developed such regulation as the Sherman Antitrust Act, the Securities Exchange Act, and numerous other federal and state enactments. To protect the individual laborer in his dealings with corporate combinations, social welfare legislation was also passed—minimum wage, protective female and child labor laws, and various social insurances.

Then, in the 1930's, came the enactment of countervailing legislation—laws designed to spur the growth of labor combinations in an attempt to build up the power of labor through unions so that bargaining power in the market place would be equated and reasonably "fair" wages and conditions of work would result. The net effect was also to create a whole set of new problems, and more and more governmental regulation of labor combinations. As in the case of freedom for business combinations, freedom for labor combinations was found to impinge on the freedom of others. The Wagner Act was followed by the Taft-Hartley and Landrum-Griffin laws.

Although these laws regulated union and employer tactics, and certain strikes relating to these tactics,[2] they sought to preserve the basic right to strike. The main exception was the emergency procedures of the Taft-Hartley Act, and this moved into the arena of strike control most gingerly, only as a postponement technique, like its Railway Labor Act counterpart. The laws regulating tactics and the weapons of conflict continue to stress the philosophy that "great restraint should be exercised in interfering with the freedom of the seller and the buyer of labor to participate in determining the conditions of sale. These freedoms can be preserved only under conditions of equitable joint determination of the terms of sale, namely through bona fide collective bargaining. Otherwise they are shrunken or lost to the degree that the terms are fixed unilaterally or imposed from the outside."[3]

Again, it is well to emphasize how this philosophical basis of our society rests on basic economic grounds. Unions and managements have to live with the results of their wage determinations, a fact which is a restraint on both. Such determinations affect the public also—through price movements and distributions of wealth, to name examples. But to permit general wage fixing by government fiat is also to surrender consumer sovereignty. For if wages are fixed, so must prices be determined and resources allocated by the price fixers, not by consumer dictates. That

[2] On this point, see the chapters in Part II, especially Chapter 7.

[3] John Perry Horlacher, "A Political Science View of National Emergency Disputes," *The Annals*, Vol. CCCXXXIII (January, 1961), p. 86. Our debt to Professor Horlacher in this chapter is very great.

such arrangements are not likely to be compatible with a free society is amply demonstrated by contemporary events in other countries.[4]

Therefore, it is difficult to disagree with the succinct summary of Professor John Perry Horlacher:

> Essentially economic disagreements between labor and management are best resolved by the arbitrament of economic facts and forces. To the extent that the disagreements are noneconomic and involve the parties' rights, prerogatives, status, emotions and fetishes—the whole complex of imponderables in their relationship—they are best settled by mutual accommodation. Management and labor ought not to be forced by political pressures or political action to relinquish their sovereignty, their right and power to decide themselves how mutual concerns shall be adjusted between them.[5]

Collective Bargaining and the Function of the Strike

Granted that "free collective bargaining is the best solution we have been able to devise to the employer-employee relationship,"[6] does that mean that any interference with the right to strike means the end of collective bargaining? Assuredly not. But if the strike or lockout are removed from the scene, they cannot perform their essential function. For strikes and lockouts serve "as the motive power which induces a modification of extreme positions and then a meeting of minds. The acceptability of certain terms of employment is determined in relation to the losses of a work stoppage that can be avoided by an agreement. In collective bargaining, economic power provides the final arbitrament."[7]

When the right to strike or to lock out is withdrawn, as through strike control or emergency legislation, the inducement to agree declines sharply. *If the parties are not faced with the consequences of refusing to settle, their desire, determination, or even ability to settle dwindles. This has occurred under each and every law or procedure, federal and state, legal and extralegal, which has been in existence.* No strike control law or extralegal method has succeeded in avoiding this pitfall.[8]

The result is not strike control, but settlement avoidance. Fearing

[4] For an illuminating study of how the combination of economic *and* political power in the single hand of government destroys freedom, see Calvin B. Hoover, *The Economy, Liberty and the State* (New York: Anchor Books, Doubleday & Co., 1961).

[5] Horlacher, *loc. cit.*

[6] *Ibid.*

[7] George W. Taylor, "Is Compulsory Arbitration Inevitable?" *Proceedings of the First Annual Meeting, Industrial Relations Research Association,* 1948, p. 64. Of course, if the company involved has had its business for the strike period made up by stockpiling, as in steel, or if the union pays heavy strike benefits, the strike may not serve this purpose unless it lasts a long time.

[8] See below, pages 427–37, for a discussion of proposals for emergency strike control which have been suggested to avoid this problem.

that to settle will mean a less attractive "package," that it will be a sign of weakness, or that it will involve criticism from rivals or fellow officers or managers, union and companies soon prepare for the emergency procedure instead of for collective bargaining and settlement. The aim is to force intervention—to create the emergency. The more adamant, obdurate, and intransigent the parties, the higher is likely to be the return from public intervenors who see as their principal job the task of ending the strike—or avoiding the emergency. With headlines screaming and merchants complaining about business effects, the pay-off is likely to be greatest to those most willing to fight for more, and most willing to create more and greater emergencies.

Emergency dispute laws thus create their own rationale. Behavior becomes tailored to the laws. The more laws enacted, the more "emergencies" are created, and the more "necessary" become the laws. Even laws which provide no direct settlement procedure—for example, the Virginia Public Utility Labor Relations Act, or a sophisticated statute like the Massachusetts choice-of-procedures (Slichter) law[9]—have followed this pattern. This raises the question whether such laws are more harmful than helpful—indeed, whether emergency legislation is necessary.

ARE EMERGENCY STRIKE LAWS NECESSARY?—AN ECONOMIC VIEW

During wartime, there is little if any disagreement with the proposition that national needs, both physical and political, require a ban on strikes or lockouts. Therefore, a strike of any size during a war period is considered an emergency situation to be stopped as quickly as possible, and not to be permitted to play its collective bargaining role.

It has been suggested that public emergency disputes in peacetime are of a similar nature and that in such disputes the strike cannot "perform its collective bargaining function." Such a stoppage "does not exert pressure primarily upon the disputants to come to terms. The parties can hold out longer than the public or the government. In consequence, a strike which creates a public emergency exerts primary pressure upon the government to intervene and also to specify the terms upon which production is to be resumed."[10]

This analysis is, of course, quite correct. But it does not answer the

[9] See above, pages 404–8 and 410–15, for a discussion of these laws.

[10] Taylor, *op. cit.*, p. 65.

underlying question: To what extent have emergency situations arisen? An analysis of events in key industries sheds light on this question.

Railroads

The closest approximation to a national emergency strike was probably the railroad operating strike of 1946. Although it lasted only two days, it caused severe passenger and freight dislocations throughout the country, as well as threatening the shutdown of numerous industries and the loss of agricultural crops. If the threat of drastic legislation had not ended this strike so quickly, a very grave emergency might have resulted.[11]

Since 1946 the importance of railroads in passenger and freight transportation has declined precipitously. It is quite probable that a nationwide railroad strike today would have a considerably smaller impact.

Bituminous Coal

Nationwide bituminous coal strikes, for a decade a thing of the past, were widely publicized as emergencies. But because of the critical oversupply of coal, a strike was usually "an inescapable layoff by another name."[12] Except for the second strike in 1946, coming after an earlier one occurred, most of these strikes did not involve hardship for many communities.[13] The continued decline of coal as both an industrial and a household fuel, plus the large stockpiles kept by utilities, the major customer of coal, make it unlikely that coal strikes will assume emergency proportions soon again.

Steel

The late Professor Sumner H. Slichter, writing in 1947, believed strongly that "a general steel strike of 100 days would be disastrous."[14] Yet the 1959 steel strike lasted 116 days, "and the brink of disaster was not even then clearly in sight. A critical examination of the evidence and arguments before the courts on whether the national health and safety would be imperiled by continuance of the 1959 strike by no means com-

[11] Irving Bernstein, "The Economic Impact of Strikes," in Bernstein *et al.* (eds.), *Emergency Disputes and National Policy* (New York: Harper & Bros., 1955), pp. 42–44. See also N. W. Chamberlain and J. M. Schilling, *The Impact of Strikes* (New York: Harper & Bros., 1954), pp. 149–59.

[12] Bernstein, *op. cit.*, p. 32.

[13] *Ibid.*, pp. 31–33; Irving Bernstein and H. G. Lovell, "Are Coal Strikes National Emergencies?" *Industrial and Labor Relations Review*, Vol. VI (April, 1953), pp. 352–67; and C. L. Christenson, "The Theory of the Offset Factor: The Impact of Labor Disputes upon Coal Production," *American Economic Review*, Vol. XLIII (September, 1953), pp. 513–47.

[14] *New York Times Magazine*, April 27, 1947.

pels the finding that in another 10 days, or 20 days, or even 50 or 100 days, we would certainly have been over the brink."[15] It will also be recalled that a 55-day strike shutting down the steel industry in 1952 caused neither a civilian catastrophe nor an impediment in the Korean War effort. It was allowed to continue without an invocation of the Taft-Hartley Act because of political considerations, although the evidence does indicate that its economic effects were more severe than any steel strike before or since, including the longer one in 1959.[16]

A very careful study of the impact of steel strikes made after the 1959 stoppage reinforces previous conclusions that the economic impacts of steel strikes

> on the economy are usually seriously exaggerated. Too often the losses of production, employment and wages are evaluated in a context which assumes that there would have been continuous high-level operation had there been no strike. Such losses . . . must be weighed over a time span that encompasses a period prior to the strike, the period of the strike, and a period long enough following the strike to permit restoration of inventory. The secondary effects of strikes must be evaluated in a context which recognizes the extent to which industry is subject to seasoned and cyclical forces, the fact that American industry generally operates well below capacity and the fact of inventory accumulation at several stages beyond basic steel itself. Viewed in this perspective most strikes can last much longer (even in an industry as basic as steel) than is generally believed before the economy will be seriously hurt.[17]

Maritime and Longshore

The main effect of the 1961 strike by the National Maritime Union and others, according to a survey by the *New York Times,* was to have "the minor role of the United States Merchant Marine in the nation's commerce . . . pointed up. The strike . . . had a negligible effect on export and import traffic. . . ."[18] Yet the national emergency provisions of the Taft-Hartley Act were invoked.

Longshore strikes have a greater effect, but increasing mechanization, and lack of skill in the work and therefore ease of strikebreaking, weakens the potential of longshore strikes for damage. A number of such strikes have occurred with no catastrophe or emergency in sight. The existence of separate unions on the East and West coasts also reduces the potential for emergency. There is no evidence that a real emergency was in sight in 1963 after a one-month strike, despite the claims of the parties and of government officials.

15 Horlacher, *op. cit.,* p. 85.

16 H. L. Enarson, "The Politics of an Emergency Dispute: Steel, 1952," in Bernstein *et al.* (eds.), *op. cit.,* pp. 46–74. See also Bernstein, *op. cit.,* pp. 33–42.

17 E. Robert Livernash, *Collective Bargaining in the Basic Steel Industry* (Washington, D.C.: U.S. Department of Labor, 1961), pp. 48–49.

18 *New York Times,* June 28, 1961, p. 15.

Trucking

Trucking strikes have resulted in the invocation of emergency laws in Massachusetts and Nebraska, but not on the national scene. The increased importance of this industry as a freight carrier and the announced intentions of James R. Hoffa, President of the Teamsters' Union, to seek a nationwide over-the-road contract, could result in a serious situation, perhaps in time even comparable to the 1946 railroad strike if local truckers also shut down with their over-the-road counterparts.

Utilities

State strike control legislation has been concerned primarily with strikes in utilities supplying electric light and power, gas, water, telephone, and urban or interurban transportation. A few serious strikes have occurred in these industries, but they are becoming less likely. Automation, plus the use of supervisory help, has about insured the ineffectiveness of telephone strikes, and the same is virtually the case in electric light and power, gas, and water. Strikes in urban transit usually add to already intolerable automobile congestion in our cities and make people later than usual for work (or provide an excuse therefor!), but people seem to get to work without a breakdown of business.

Strikes occurred in public utilities in states which did not have strike control laws during the period 1947–51 while these laws were being most actively invoked in comparable states; and strikes have occurred in utilities since 1951 in a number of states which have laws but which, for constitutional or other reasons, have not invoked them. The impact in both cases has usually been negligible in the case of all utilities except urban transit—and merely troublesome in the case of the latter.[19]

Economic Basis Not Evident

The conclusion appears inescapable that the economic basis in peacetime for emergency strike control legislation does not appear to rest

[19] For cases in point, see the discussion of the Long Island Railroad strike above, pages 391–94, and of Massachusetts strikes, above, pages 412–21. Prior to the 1963 Philadelphia transit strike, newspapers and radio and television commentators referred to the threatened walkout as one which would "paralyze the city." Federal, state, and local mediators, the chairman of the state public utility commission, an extralegal three-judge fact-finding board, and various others all interposed or were interposed as third-party interveners. On the day after the strike began, the *Wall Street Journal* (January 16, 1963) reported that the strike "is putting a heavy burden on other commuter facilities and has slowed downtown store sales, but is having surprisingly little effect on the operations of major companies in the city. The companies in general said they had very few absentees." Reports in Philadelphia papers confirmed this, but as soon as the strike was over, these same Philadelphia papers referred to the "paralyzing" strike, a term never dropped by radio and television commentators despite the clear evidence to the contrary.

upon substantial evidence. This conclusion is reinforced when it is remembered that emergency strike legislation relieves the parties of the incentive to settle. "The freedom to strike is in our society the major deterrent to strikes." As an example, "History in steel indicates that once strikes really begin to be seriously felt over wide segments of the economy, pressure from those affected will in most instances bring about a settlement."[20]

This, however, is not the whole story. Emergency strike control legislation also has a political aspect. And it has also a national defense aspect.

THE POLITICS OF EMERGENCY STRIKE LAWS

Actually, emergency strike laws do not derive from economic fact, but rather from an emotional and political context. Most such legislation dates from the World War II period and its immediate postwar era. During World War II, strikes were not only a potential interference with the war effort; they were also unpatriotic. This feeling carried over during the postwar era, and was furthered by the great strikes of 1945 and 1946.

The fact that strikes have been at a very low level since the late 1940's (see Table 28) does not seem to have eased the public feeling that strikes are a wrong and harmful thing. The closer such strikes come to industries which either touch the public or are reputed to be "essential," the more they seem undesirable, and the more public opinion frowns upon them. Newspaper headlines screaming that a port is "crippled" because longshoremen or seamen strike (even if the seamen man only a small percentage of the ships) add to the uneasiness and fear, and in some cases aggravate the inconvenience. The fact that the health and safety of the community are in no way involved is not remembered until sober afterthought occurs when the strike has long since passed and is no longer food for newspaper sales or television drama.

What happens, therefore, is that a dispute between labor and industry becomes a political issue. To those in power, it seems bad politics to let the parties reach a juncture when the pressures force a settlement. Instead, it seems more heroic (and politically wise) to "save" the public. The appropriate official, with or without appropriate legislation, intervenes and produces a political settlement, which is usually what one or more of the parties want, and which almost always involves a higher economic cost to the public.

[20] Livernash, *op. cit.*, p. 49.

The sources of public opinion creating emotional and political headlines are many and diverse. They include, first of all, one or more of the parties. In past coal industry disputes, for example, John L. Lewis has found great benefits in pushing for emergencies; the coal industry

TABLE 28

STRIKES AND LOCKOUTS IN THE UNITED STATES, SELECTED YEARS, 1917–61

Year	Number of Stoppages	Number of Workers Involved (Thousands)	Man-Days Idle (Millions of Days)	Percentage of Working Time Lost
1917	4,450	1,227	*	*
1919	3,630	4,160	*	*
1921	2,385	1,099	*	*
1925	1,301	428	*	*
1929	921	289	5.4	0.07
1933	1,695	1,168	16.9	0.36
1937	4,740	1,860	28.4	0.43
1941	4,288	2,363	23.0	0.32
1944	4,956	2,116	8.7	0.09
1946	4,985	4,600	116.0	1.43
1947	3,693	2,170	34.6	0.41
1950	4,843	2,410	38.8	0.44
1952	5,117	3,540	59.1	0.57
1956	3,825	1,900	33.1	0.29
1958	3,694	2,060	23.9	0.22
1959	3,900	1,850	69.0	0.61
1961	3,367	1,450	16.3	0.14

*Data unavailable.
SOURCE: U.S. Department of Labor, Bureau of Labor Statistics.

employers tried equally hard to improve their bargaining power by having Lewis encounter court orders head on. In steel, the industry has been accused of failing to bargain in order to justify major price increases; the union has been accused of declining to settle when the White House was in friendly hands and sympathetic intervention was assured.[21] "As recently as the summer of 1961, the government urged subsidized shipowners to give their unions an exceptionally generous settlement. . . . The government's plea amounted to a commitment that bigger subsidies would be forthcoming to cover the increased labor costs. . . . Clearly, the labor-management harmony embodied in the maritime industry is paid for by persistent raids on the public treasury."[22] A dispute

[21] Horlacher, *op. cit.*, p. 89.

[22] Bernard Rossiter, "Some Hidden Costs of Industrial Peace," *The Annals*, Vol. CCCXLIII (September, 1962), p. 106.

involving a fraction of the maritime industry for which the Taft-Hartley emergency procedure was invoked[23] was thus "satisfactorily" settled.

In creating the political emergency, the parties themselves receive powerful assistance. There are, first of all, the indiscriminate news media, more anxious for sensation than fact, blaring out news of grave consequences of things to come, with no note that past promises of disaster in like circumstances were not factual, nor did they actually occur. Businessmen who officially abhor all governmental "interference" deluge a governor or secretary of labor with telegrams "demanding" that this probably all-too-willing official "take action" to stop this "calamity"—which is usually momentary interference with receipt of a product or a part, or other interference with an opportunity for profit. Wives of union members thrown out of work by a strike of their "brother" unionists add their voices to the chorus for action. Other sources creating the climate of public emergency include "the merchant in the strike-bound community who is dissatisfied with his declining trade and his mounting credit transactions as well as the cabinet member who recognizes intervention as an opportunity to increase his political stature and to improve his political fortunes, although he may rationalize his motivation in terms of statesmanship to save the country from the calamity that everybody foresees."[24]

Thus are labor disputes transformed from their economic character into political emergencies "when the disputants themselves seem to want it that way; when public opinion furnishes the appropriate matrix . . . when those who are hurt resort with customary appeals; and when politicians are anxious to make political hay while the emergency sun is bright."[25]

EMERGENCY DISPUTE CRITERIA AND PROPOSALS

The pressures for intervention, which are so formidable, are thus primarily political, not economic. Therefore, if public policy is committed to the maintenance of collective bargaining—as these authors believe is soundly in the public interest—then public policy should be directed toward curbing, not furthering, political intervention. This means that a sound public policy toward emergency disputes must be difficult for the parties to induce and difficult for the politicians to invoke. None of the federal or state laws discussed in the preceding three chapters meet these criteria.

[23] See Case No. 18, Table 15, p. 361.

[24] Horlacher, *op. cit.*, p. 89.

[25] *Ibid.*

If a real emergency occurs, emergency legislation must also be capable of coping with it. This, for example, disqualifies fact finding, which, whenever it is extensively used, has tended to promote political intervention, and therefore political emergencies, but which at the same time creates no substitute method of either maintaining work or providing a settlement once the fact-finding machinery has run its course and the real emergency, if any, has arisen.

This does not mean that fact finding, or any method such as arbitration, seizure, or choice of procedures, is always useless. On the contrary, such procedures have often served a particular purpose. If, however, public policy is to continue to promote settlement by collective bargaining, the problem of politically oriented emergency situations must also be dealt with. The procedures already in effect have not met the criteria set forth to accomplish this problem without seriously affecting the will to settle which is the essential ingredient of collective bargaining, although the seizure provisions of Virginia's Public Utility Labor Relations Act and the Massachusetts "Slichter" choice-of-procedures law are serious attempts in this direction.

Numerous other proposals for emergency disputes settlement have been suggested. They will now be analyzed in terms of the criteria suggested here: relative difficulty of inducement and invocation, and ability to achieve the result of preventing an emergency.

The Advisory Committee Proposal

President Kennedy's Advisory Committee on Labor-Management policy,[26] with several dissents, has suggested a revision of the Taft-Hartley Act procedures. Essentially, the majority of this Committee would empower Taft-Hartley boards of inquiry with authority to make recommendations at the discretion of the President. The name of the board would also be changed from "board of inquiry" to "emergency dispute board," and the conditions of its appointment would be eased to include "any collective bargaining situation in a major or critical industry which may develop into a dispute threatening the national health or safety." Recommendations could also include changes to be put into

[26] The members of the Committee include the Secretaries of Labor and Commerce, and Professors Arthur F. Burns and George W. Taylor, Dr. Clark Kerr, and Messrs. David L. Cole and Ralph E. McGill, representing the public; Messrs. Henry Ford 2d, Joseph L. Block (Inland Steel), Elliot V. Bell (McGraw-Hill), John M. Franklin (United States Lines), Richard S. Reynolds (Reynolds Metals), and Thomas J. Watson, Jr. (IBM), representing industry; and David Dubinsky (Ladies Garment Workers), George M. Harrison (Railway Clerks), J. D. Keenan (Electrical Workers—IBEW), Thomas Kennedy (Mine Workers), D. J. McDonald (Steelworkers), Walter Reuther (Automobile Workers), and George Meany (AFL–CIO), representing labor.

effect during the eighty-day "cooling-off" period. These proposals were prefaced by a plea to "preserve" the "freedom of choice elements in collective bargaining."

In his dissent, Henry Ford 2d commented: "It is difficult to understand how the advocacy of a more dominant government role in the collective bargaining process, by these and other proposals, can make for more freedom in the process."[27]

It would seem that these proposals would create a kind of Railway Labor Act situation for industry generally. One can foresee a gradual atrophy of collective bargaining under this procedure, which would be easily induced and easily invoked, and which would continue Taft-Hartley postponement, instead of settlement. With the potential of recommendations by administrations friendly to one party or the other, "emergencies" would surely magnify; and the potential for real emergencies, once the procedure ran its course, would be great.

On one proposal the Labor-Management Advisory Committee and almost everyone else are unanimous—that is, on abolishing the last-offer vote, which has served little purpose for constructive settlement.

Boards of Accountability

In the 1962–63 Typographical Union strike which shut down all New York City daily newspapers, Secretary of Labor W. W. Wirtz, Governor Rockefeller of New York, and Mayor Wagner of New York City all combined to set up a "Board of Accountability" to determine whether the parties were exercising their collective bargaining functions with due regard for the public interest. Earlier, such a procedure had been urged for emergency disputes by Professor George W. Taylor in one of his provocative discussions of the subject.[28]

Professor Taylor would have such a board clarify the public interest, and "encourage the parties precisely to define the issues and to work at their reconciliation. This is a sort of public mediation as distinct from the traditional private mediation."[29] That such a mediatory role, skillfully handled, might at times be helpful in narrowing differences is indisputable. Like other fact finding, however, the more it is utilized, the less useful it becomes. Moreover, the potential that it might degenerate into complete political determination is very great. The Massachusetts

[27] The proposals of the Committee, and excerpts from the Ford dissent, are found in the *New York Times*, May 2, 1962.

[28] George W. Taylor, "The Adequacy of Taft-Hartley in Public Emergency Disputes," *The Annals*, Vol. CCCXXXIII (January, 1961), pp. 82–83. In the paper case, the union ignored the board which seems to have played no part in the final result.

[29] *Ibid.*, p. 82.

investigation and assignment-of-responsibility procedure is somewhat similar and, as discussed in Chapter 14,[30] was found not very satisfactory as an inducement to settlement.

Public Participation in Negotiations

The use of tripartite committees to work continuously at labor-management problems in special situations, such as those pertaining to automation in the meat-packing industry or the incentive plan at the Kaiser Steel Corporation, has raised the question of whether neutrals can serve as catalysts, protecting the public interest and increasing the possibility of constructive results.[31]

That this can and has been done in special situations is an indication of their limits. The public interest is a vague and nebulous concept. Absence of strife is not per se proof that the public interest is served. It may, for example, indicate collusion at the expense of the public.[32] The interests of the public are not necessarily better protected by the presence of a third party (who owes his place to no public selection), as the analysis in the preceding pages clearly demonstrates. The use of experts, mediators, or any helpful outsiders is commendable when the parties feel that it will aid constructive settlement. This, however, provides no basis to generalize for the handling of emergency disputes.

Statutory Strikes and Semistrikes

A number of proposals for semistrikes or statutory strikes have been put forward,[33] and one was actually tried for three days.[34] Under such a program the company is deprived of all or part of its receipts, the union of dues, and the employees of all or part of wages and benefits. Work goes on, and the public is served, while the parties are put under pressure by loss of income which for the period goes to the federal or state treasuries.

There are many formidable problems in the way of such a procedure. Penalties can vary in effect according to economic conditions: A

[30] See above, pp. 395–96.

[31] See, for example, Taylor, *loc. cit.;* Clark Kerr, "The New Opportunities for Industrial Relations," address before the National Academy of Arbitrators, Santa Monica, California, 1961; and G. H. Hildebrand, "The Use of Tripartite Bodies to Supplement Collective Bargaining," *Labor Law Journal,* Vol. XII (July, 1961), pp. 655–63.

[32] Rossiter, *op. cit.*, pp. 104–8.

[33] See David B. McCalmont, "The Semi-Strike," *Industrial and Labor Relations Review,* Vol. XV (January, 1962), pp. 191–208, and his n. 3, p. 191, for a list of citations on this subject.

[34] It was tried in Miami, Florida, in the urban transit industry. It broke down when the bus drivers were charged with accepting "tips" from riders—a difficult thing to police, indeed!

semistrike would have quite different effects on a company making large profits than on one just breaking even if profits were to be lost during the period. Adjustment of income tax, unemployment compensation, and enforcement all present major difficulties. There is also a real question as to whether the pressures of a semistrike would really approximate those of a real stoppage. For the pressures are not all economic in real life. Yet it would be most salutary if these issues were worked out in a mutual agreement by labor and industry, in an industry such as steel or transportation, and tried. As observed by Professor David B. McCalmont, who has proposed the most detailed plan: "If nothing else, the effort to write a semi-strike contract will serve to refresh the recollection of both sides as to the magnitude of losses which each would suffer if a conventional strike were called. There will be less chance of overlooking one's weaknesses or the strength of one's opponent."[35]

Break Up Unions or Industry-wide Bargaining

One solution, which is frequently put forward in industry or conservative circles, is simply to break up unions. Unions call strikes, so the argument goes; if union power, or union "monopoly power," were reduced, the ability to create emergencies would be equally affected. This argument, of course, rests on the notion that management has nothing to do with causing shutdowns. Actually, strikes are the results of disagreements. Some are caused by management. Even if most strikes are initiated by unions, it is difficult to see why unions should be broken up into local organizations while companies are permitted to operate on a multiplant or even multi-industry basis. If both companies and unions were confined to a local basis, the efficiency of large-scale modern enterprise would disappear (as would America's defense capability). Such proposals are as unrealistic and uneconomic as they are drastic.

Likewise, arguments to solve the problem of emergency disputes by banning multi-employer or industry-wide bargaining would not seem to meet the problem of emergency disputes. As a well-known management consulting organization has noted:

> For one thing, emergency disputes need not necessarily be limited to nation-wide walkouts. Secondly, the law could be made ineffective if unions were to negotiate the terminal dates of many separate agreements to fall at the same time, so that individual employer bargaining still could result in a national strike. Nor would even the breaking-up of national unions necessarily prevent concerted action among their component units. Such a remedy, moreover, is too drastic to command popular support.

[35] McCalmont, *op. cit.*, p. 208.

Finally, such a law could have serious effects upon present collective bargaining relationships and even create chaos in small-scale industries where individual employers might be at the mercy of strong unions, since it is unlikely that union power will be minimized through legislation. Even in larger-scale industries, employers might find themselves the victims of union "whipsawing" tactics.[36]

Choice of Procedures

Although the experience of Massachusetts with the Slichter law has not been as satisfactory in terms of not inviting emergencies as its proponents hoped, many authorities, including the Secretary of Labor and the Solicitor-General in the Kennedy administration,[37] have supported the choice-of-procedures method, with emphasis on the right of the executive *not* to act, as well as to act in a variety of ways. The hope is, of course, that the uncertainty induced by the means available for the government to act (including the right not to act) will result in the parties preferring collective bargaining to an unknown alternative.

Against this is the Massachusetts experience, which resulted in only two alternatives—to seize, or not to act—and the fact that with alternatives the pressure on the President to intervene would be much greater than not to intervene. Moreover, the tremendous power to act adds to the pressure for a political settlement favoring the friends of the administration in power at the time of the dispute. It is difficult to believe that choice of procedures would work in practice much differently elsewhere than it has in Massachusetts, although that may be possible.

Nonsettlement Seizure

Virginia-type seizure, with penalties on the parties during the seizure, has also been proposed as a method of accomplishing the resumption of production without a settlement substitute. The easy availability of seizure, however, remains a drawback. As a careful student of the Virginia law noted: "The attitude of the Virginia Governor has not differed from that of other executives and administrators in invoking statutes dealing with emergency labor disputes. It is safer to use the laws and be criticized by some representatives of labor and management, and a few academicians, than to risk some injury to the public."[38]

[36] Industrial Relations Counselors, Inc., *Emergency Disputes: A National Labor Policy Problem,* Industrial Relations Monograph No. 138 (New York, 1961), p. 29.

[37] See the article by W. W. Wirtz, in Bernstein *et al., op. cit.,* pp. 149–65; and the proposal by Archibald Cox, *Law and the National Labor Policy,* Institute of Industrial Relations Monograph Series, No. 5 (Los Angeles: University of California, 1960), pp. 56–57.

[38] Robert R. France, "Seizure in Emergency Labor Disputes in Virginia," *Industrial and Labor Relations Review,* Vol. VII (April, 1954), pp. 361–62.

Like other well-thought-out laws, such as the Massachusetts Slichter act, Virginia's seizure law was used mainly in disputes not even remotely of an emergency character.[39]

Partial Injunction

An idea which is aimed at restoring needed service, but which makes no attempt to substitute a method of settlement, is the partial injunction.[40] In effect, it would be for the government to prove to the satisfaction of the judiciary explicitly what the emergency was, and therefore what service would have to be restored. For example, a partial resumption of steel production might be ordered for a period necessary to fulfill certain objectives; when these objectives had been met, then the injunction would be lifted. The partial resumption might involve part of the industry only, leaving the other part on strike. The object would be to force the government to pinpoint with some degree of precision what the emergency was, and what would be needed to dissolve it.

This is a difficult and formidable task.

> A vague concept will not do as a basis for saying what steel production is necessary to prevent the threatened emergency from developing. The very necessity, however, for applying a more exact and rigorous concept of national emergency would in itself be a great virtue. That injunctions can now be sustained on the basis of a fairly general and imprecise judgment that an emergency exists has been one of the great shortcomings in the way this problem has been handled.[41]

There are very serious obstacles to be overcome in learning to use such a technique as the partial injunction, but the technique shows enough promise to warrant the most careful study—which should not wait till a problem exists, but should be done in an atmosphere conducive to unemotional responses.

It is possible that the partial injunction could be used as a tactic by either labor or management. For example, under it a union might sustain an "off and on again" strike as a harassment. To prevent this, penalties might be added, such as forcing unions and management to share the government's litigation costs wherever an injunction is granted, plus a sizable assessment of union dues during the period worked under the

[39] See above, pages 404–8, 410–15.

[40] The partial injunction is one of the recommendations of the Independent Study Group established by the Committee on Economic Development. See *The Public Interest in National Labor Policy* (New York: Committee for Economic Development, 1961), pp. 101–3. It has also been proposed by Horlacher, *op. cit.*, pp. 94–95; and by Livernash, *op. cit.*, pp. 48–49, among others.

[41] Horlacher, *op. cit.*, p. 95.

injunction. To prevent management from encouraging work under the injunction, a substantial tax on earnings during that period would be in order.

The partial injunction is no panacea. It does, however, seem to contain the seeds of a program designed to preserve collective bargaining and to protect the national welfare. It seems sufficiently unpleasant to discourage inducement; if rigorous standards can be developed, emergencies will have to approach reality before the injunction can be invoked; and if no settlement procedure is provided, the ability to substitute the injunction for collective bargaining is very limited. If penalties are added, the propensity to maintain the injunction period is also reduced.

There remains the question of whether employees would work under an injunction. They do now under Taft-Hartley, and the penalties for defiance of a court order can be severe, but the conditions of work under an injunction would not be onerous. Any strike control law must rely on compliance. If a group struck in defiance of an injunction, heavy penalties against its union would soon make the strike intolerable. Laws in our society are generally obeyed. Otherwise, our society, not just our economy, is in danger as a result of an emergency dispute.

THE PROBLEM OF NATIONAL DEFENSE

The partial injunction would also be useful in handling national defense issues. Production needed for defense could be resumed under an injunction formula; and at the same time, precise information could be required in court as to what exactly is needed for defense from what plant—not just an assertion by an armed forces spokesman that defense is affected.

The use of the partial injunction, and its rigorous requirement for establishing that an emergency exists, would again be salutary in requiring officials to show factually that a strike is actually a serious deterrent to defense production. Remembering what President Truman stated *would* happen if a steel strike occurred during the Korean War, as compared with what *did* happen when the strike lasted fifty-five days,[42] can demonstrate why a real showing of serious interference with defense requirements is in order.

If production is partially restored in an industry such as steel, it could not be only defense production. Thus, Professor Livernash reports: "In an analysis . . . by the Department of Commerce, the con-

[42] See above, pages 366–68.

clusion was reached that it is technically and economically feasible to meet defense needs through partial operation provided the plants which are kept open are permitted to produce their normal output and are not confined in their operations to producing defense items only."[43]

In most cases, it would also undoubtedly be true that operations restored under a partial injunction technique for defense purposes would also require the complete operation of the plant involved.

The use of the partial injunction technique would surely eliminate any need for such an extralegal function as the Atomic Energy Labor-Management Relations Panel. It would also have been of assistance in curbing work stoppages at missile bases.

The missile base problem could probably also have been aided by a rigorous insistence on the part of the government that existing laws be enforced. According to studies of the Missile Sites Labor Commission,[44] most missile strikes involved jurisdictional or interunion disputes. Such strikes are clear violations of the Taft-Hartley Act, Section 8 (*b*) (4) (*D*).[45]

Also, according to a careful study by Professor John R. Van de Water:

There was also an extensive violation of Section 8 (*b*) (4) (*A*) during the Taft-Hartley era and violation of Section 8 (*b*) (4) (*B*) during the Landrum-Griffin Act era, through secondary labor boycotting. There was repeated coercion of employees who wished to exercise their right under Section 7 of that statute to refrain from unionism, through violation of Section 8 (*b*) (1). And employers violated Section 8 (*a*) (1) and 8 (*a*) (3) in discriminating against employees in their terms and conditions of employment because of their employees' favoring a particular union or no union—often such an employer violation being the result of union pressures engaged in inviolation of Section 8 (*b*) (2).[46]

For such strikes, remedies are available.

In many instances mandatory, temporary restraining orders are available to the injured parties against such conduct, and in all instances permanent injunctions can be gained through Section 10 (*j*) (1) of the amended National Labor Relations Act; there is a work-jurisdiction settlement procedure available, where the parties do not establish their own means of settlement, through Section 10 (*k*); and for the most prominent types of illegal strikes at the missile bases,

[43] Livernash, *op. cit.*, p. 48.

[44] Missile Sites Labor Commission, *Analysis of Work Stoppages on U.S. Missile Sites, June 1961–May 1962* (Washington, D.C.: U.S. Government Printing Office, 1962).

[45] See Chapter 4, above, pages 93–94.

[46] John R. Van de Water, "Labor Law and National Defense," *Labor Law Journal*, Vol. XIII (August, 1962), p. 615.

suits for damages have been available to injured parties all along, through Section 303 of the Labor-Management Relations Act of 1947.[47]

These remedies are not taken advantage of because the Defense Department follows a policy of "neutrality." It will not move to punish violators of the Taft-Hartley Act as a matter of policy.[48] Yet vital defense setbacks occurred, and hundreds of millions of dollars were lost to the taxpayers because of strikes and slowdowns until the McClellan Committee hearings exposed the situation and the Missile Sites Labor Commission was set up. It does seem that when laws are violated and damages occur, and when injunctive relief and damage suits are available, the government has a duty to enforce the law and to collect damages. The present policy of "neutrality" on the part of the Defense Department is actually in favor of conduct ruled unlawful. Professor Van de Water presents convincing evidence that enforcement of the Taft-Hartley and Landrum-Griffin picketing, boycott, and jurisdictional strike provisions, plus a damage suit or two, would have substantially ended the missile sites labor problem without resort to the extralegal procedures of the Missile Sites Labor Commission.

Need for Experimentation

The partial injunction is suggested here as a likely tool, but not as a final answer, because the authors are conscious that in these difficult human and social relationships, final answers may not exist. It is quite possible that scholarly and practical exploration of the issues will uncover either better tools or sufficient flaws in the partial injunction approach so as to reduce its considered potential.

Experience with existing legislation has indicated its basic shortcomings, as discussed in this and the preceding chapters. Such experience has, however, been of great value in permitting a test of the applicability of ideas to factual situations.

In the remainder of this chapter, some practical administrative problems are discussed, particularly as uncovered by the richly varied experiences in the states. A final section points up the constitutional problems which may prohibit a further state role or state experimentation in this field.

ADMINISTRATIVE PROBLEMS

Laws which substitute a procedure for the right to strike have, as has been noted, a profound effect on the willingness and ability of the

[47] *Ibid.*

[48] *Ibid.*, pp. 613–15.

parties to bargain and to settle. The administration of such laws also involves other problems of which the student and practitioner should be aware. The most significant are (1) effect on rate control in regulated utilities, (2) application of standards, (3) effectiveness of sanctions, and (4) legal and constitutional problems.

Strike Controls and Rate Controls

The Railway Labor Act and most state strike control laws cover transportation industries and electric light and power, gas, and water utilities which also are under rate regulation by state or federal administrative bodies. There is considerable feeling in these industries that regulatory bodies are more inclined to grant rate adjustments if emergency procedure is invoked, and results in an increase in labor costs than if such labor costs were freely bargained.[49] Obviously, to the extent that this feeling is warranted by the facts, it will insure that emergency procedure will be invoked whenever the employers desire a compensating rate increase for any wage increase granted.

The same problem complicates labor relations under some defense contracts. The fact that the Atomic Energy Commission must pass upon whether it will reimburse construction and operations contractors for increased labor costs is undoubtedly an inducement to have disputes settled by recommendations of the extralegal Atomic Energy Labor-Management Relations Panel. The fact that AEC is apparently committed to support the existence of the atomic panel rather than to allow collective bargaining to function uninhibited adds emphasis to this view. And the willingness of the Defense Department to assume added, and often unwarranted, additional construction costs, instead of insisting on the protections afforded by the Taft-Hartley Act against jurisdictional and interunion disputes and boycotts, undoubtedly furthered the use of tactics designed to promote such costs in missile sites construction.

Thus, strike control legislation may be both self-defeating and expensive to the consumer if it provides an easy or more certain way of passing on increased costs.

Application of Standards

Earlier in this chapter, it was stressed that reasonable men tend to disagree on what is fair and what is right. Therefore, management and labor risk a great deal when they turn this task over to a person who is unfamiliar with their problems, and who is not required to live with his

[49] See, for example, the discussion in Herbert R. Northrup, *Strike Controls in Essential Industries* (New York: National Industrial Conference Board, 1951), pp. 35–39.

decision. The arbitrator or fact finder may apply, in the absence of specific instructions, any one of many standards in determining a wage dispute: Cost of living, ability to pay, wages in comparable industry plants, wages in the area, and correction of intraplant inequities are among the most popular. Whether any of these standards will favor labor or management depends upon the particular circumstances at the time. But an arbitrator who so desires can pick the formula to rationalize a decision which has already been arrived at.

In order to reduce the arbitrator's discretion, to limit the application of his "social philosophy," and at the same time reduce the hazards in arbitration, particularly to management, the drafters of the pioneer Indiana arbitration law wrote standards into the legislation. These standards, together with those found in the Massachusetts choice-of-procedures law, and those added to the New Jersey legislation after the courts of that state declared them a prerequisite to meet the requirements of the New Jersey constitution, are set forth in Table 29.

The standards in New Jersey and Massachusetts are so broad that they do not effectively limit the arbitrators' discretion. Those in Indiana, Wisconsin, Florida, Pennsylvania, and Nebraska did not work out as planned. Arbitrators found these standards either unworkable or too confining, or interpreted them in a variety of ways.[50] Definitions of labor markets, evaluation of fringe benefits, meaning of "fair," etc., all meant different things to different arbitrators. If standards restrained the discretion of arbitrators, they did not destroy it.

Standards for fact finding are not set forth in any fact-finding laws. This is consistent with the theory of fact finding that if all the facts are known, a dispute will be more easily settled. For the most part, however, the facts are not in dispute; what is usually at issue is what interpretation should be given to these facts, and there are generally as many interpretations as there are interests involved.

In Missouri, where the penalty for refusing fact-finding recommendations may be seizure, the absence of any guides or standards for fact finders has on at least one occasion produced recommendations in similar cases based on precisely opposite criteria (see Figure 11). Under both the Railway Labor Act and the Minnesota Labor Relations Act, fact-finding boards and commissions over the years have utilized a vari-

[50] See, for example, Arthur R. Porter, "Compulsory Arbitration in Indiana," *Labor Law Journal*, Vol. V (November, 1954), pp. 776–78; and Robert R. France and Richard A. Lester, *Compulsory Arbitration of Utility Disputes in New Jersey and Pennsylvania* (Princeton: Princeton University, Industrial Relations Section, 1951), pp. 23–25, 65–70.

TABLE 29

STANDARDS FOR ARBITRATORS IN STATE ARBITRATION LAWS

Criterion	Indiana Type*	New Jersey	Massachusetts
Public interest		1. The interests and welfare of the public.	
Comparative wage rates and conditions of employment	1. Wages paid and conditions of employment maintained for similar work and skills under similar conditions by like public utility employees in same or adjoining labor market areas. 2. Relationship to wages and employment conditions maintained by all other employers in same labor market areas. 3. Labor market and adjoining labor market areas to be defined by boards of arbitration upon evidence presented. 4. If an employer has different plants in different labor market areas, separate rates and conditions shall be established for each labor market area.	2. Comparison of wages, hours, and employment conditions in same or comparable work, with due consideration to factors peculiar to industry. 3. Comparison of wages, hours, and conditions of employment as reflected in industries generally and in public utilities throughout nation and in New Jersey.	1. The conditions in existence in the industry affected. 2. Consistent with existing agreements between the parties.
Fringes and employment security	5. In setting wage rates, over-all compensation, including all fringe benefits, and employment security measures shall be considered.	4. Security and tenure of employment with due consideration of effect of technological development on such security and of any unique skills and attributes developed in industry.	
Other factors		5. Other factors which are traditionally taken into consideration in collective bargaining and arbitration.	

* Indiana, Florida, Pennsylvania, Nebraska, and Wisconsin.

ety of standards and guides—often contradictory—to rationalize recommendations.

FIGURE 11

"ABILITY TO PAY" AS A CRITERION FOR FACT FINDERS
(Two Reports Made by Fact Finders under the Missouri Law on Utility Disputes)

St. Louis Public Service Company versus Amalgamated Association of Street, Electric Railway and Motor Coach Employees, Division 788, July, 1950	"As criteria in *basic* wage determinations, ability to pay *is not,* under any standards, a relative factor to be considered in an arbitration or fact-finding proceeding."
Kansas City Public Service Company versus Amalgamated Association of Street, Electric Railway and Motor Coach Employees, Division 1287, March, 1950	"The union answers that the ability or inability of the company to pay is entirely irrelevant. . . . The union's theory has not received unanimous support and . . . cannot in common sense have such support."

Standards under seizure legislation are sometimes used to govern the administration of properties during the seizure period. Maryland, Massachusetts, and Virginia provide such definite legislative guides (see Table 30). New Jersey and Missouri merely empower the governor to make the necessary rules and regulations.

Seizures in New Jersey and Missouri have not resulted in any legal tangles over the disposition of profits or whether wages should be maintained or altered during the seizure period. Under a Supreme Court decision an employer whose property was seized in these states presumably could sue the state for "just compensation" for the use of his property, or for any increased costs resulting from changes in wages or conditions of employment.[51]

Violations and Sanctions

Emergency strike control legislation, like all laws regulating conduct in a democracy, depends largely upon public support, or at least acquiescence, for its successful operation. If the public were completely antagonistic, the law might fail, as did the Volstead Act and prohibition.

But public support is not enough. Fact-finding legislation depends upon the support of public opinion to secure compliance with the recommendations of fact finders, and the results, as already noted, have not been encouraging. Methods of enforcement and penalties for viola-

[51] *United States* v. *Pewee Coal Co.,* 71 S. Ct. 203 (1951).

TABLE 30

STANDARDS GOVERNING PLANT OPERATION DURING SEIZURE BY STATES

State	Wages and Conditions of Employment	Disposition of Business Profits	Applicability of Labor and Social Legislation during Period of Seizure
Maryland	Seizure authorities shall put into effect recommendations of Board of Arbitration appointed pursuant to statute, and retroactive to date of last agreement where possible, provided that if a valid agreement exists, no action inconsistent with that agreement may be taken.	Plant operated for account of owner; or if owner elects, he may waive same and sue for just compensation, but courts must consider effect on compensation of fact that a labor dispute threatened to cut off production.	No state or federal law affecting health, safety, security, and employment standards shall be affected. All such laws must be complied with during state operation.
Massachusetts	Governor may alter upon recommendation of a tripartite board. All changes must be based on going-industry practice and must be consistent with any existing agreements of parties.	Plant operated for account of owner; or if owner elects, he may waive same and sue for just compensation, but courts must consider effect on compensation of fact that a labor dispute threatened to cut off production.	No state or federal law affecting health, safety, security, and employment standards shall be affected. All such laws must be complied with during state operation.
Virginia	No changes permitted.	Cost to state of operation and 15 per cent of net profit paid to state; rest of profit to owner.	Nothing specific in law.
Missouri	"The Governor is authorized to prescribe the necessary rules and regulations. . . ."	"The Governor is authorized to prescribe the necessary rules and regulations. . . ."	Nothing specific in law.
New Jersey	"The Governor is authorized to prescribe the necessary rules and regulations. . . ."	"The Governor is authorized to prescribe the necessary rules and regulations. . . ."	Nothing specific in law.

tions are, therefore, written into arbitration and seizure statutes in order to deter persons from violating laws and to penalize if they do violate such laws.

These penalties are of three types: criminal, civil, and economic. Criminal penalties are undoubtedly an important influence in restraining possible violations. Once a violation has occurred, however, the effectiveness of criminal penalties may be lessened. Possible political repercussions, the desire to avoid making martyrs out of those who flout the law, and the need to end a stoppage rather than to punish the instigators may all combine to induce a reluctance on the part of public officials to invoke criminal penalties.

Even when public officials are willing to prosecute, the outcome cannot be easily predicted. All strike control legislation specifically safeguards the right of workers to quit as individuals. To secure a conviction, the prosecution must prove willful intent to violate the law—which usually means that workers quit in concert on the instructions of some person. There is no guarantee that individuals may not quit more or less simultaneously "as individuals" and safeguard themselves from prosecution under the law, especially if their leaders ostensibly order them back and they ignore the instructions.

No case was discovered in which the criminal penalties of a strike control law had been successfully invoked—although eight states included such penalties in their legislation (see Table 31).

Some idea of how difficult it may be to enforce criminal penalties may be obtained from the experience of the Railway Labor Act. Since 1934, this statute has provided criminal penalties for unfair labor practices on the part of management. In the years in which this provision has been in effect, only one case has been brought to trial, and in that instance the jury declined to convict.

On the other hand, the provisions for injunctive relief are usually more effective. The injunctive process is more easily initiated. There is no jury to convince or no time-consuming process. Moreover, the courts will hold parties in contempt of court if these restraining orders are not observed. To be sure, an "injunction cannot mine coal" or operate a business. It can, however, make it very costly and unpleasant for those responsible for illegal work stoppages. This was discovered by John L. Lewis and the United Mine Workers in 1948 when they declined to obey a Taft-Hartley order requiring a temporary end to a strike and were heavily fined.[52] An order of a court is thus held

[52] See Table 15, Case No. 3.

in high respect, and rarely is it lightly flouted. Like the Taft-Hartley Act, most strike control laws depend primarily upon this method of enforcement (see Table 31).

The economic sanctions found in the Missouri law are about the most drastic for employees (see Table 31). Being rehired only as a new employee means loss of seniority, pension credits, and all the other perquisites that go with length of service. This penalty was invoked in a case in Missouri in which one union struck a plant in an attempt to upset an order of the National Labor Relations Board. The strike was quickly broken with the assistance of a rival union. Many employees who stayed on strike were forced to rehire as new employees, with the resultant loss of length-of-service benefits, or to seek employment elsewhere.

The other Missouri economic situation—the threat of loss of a certificate of convenience and necessity for a public utility—is likely to be effective only if the state is able and willing to take over the properties and sell them to a new operator, or to force their sale directly. Otherwise, it could take up to several years to put a new utility into operation —a not very practical sanction when the need for continuous operation is the point of the law.

Can Sanctions Prevent Strikes?

Sanctions are designed as both a deterrent and a curative. Certainly, one would think that the prospect of severe fines would prevent rash acts. And even if the rash act be taken, the cumulative effect of sanctions should result in a speedy reconsideration of the desirability of continued defiance of the law. Yet the most drastic sanctions can often fail where more moderate ones can succeed.

For example, Missouri's drastic economic sanctions on individual strikers and equally harsh fines on unions appear capable of breaking any strike in violation of the Missouri law and of discouraging most of them before they commence. If, however, the employees remain on strike and do not break ranks, the public is likely to clamor for resumption of service rather than punishment of strikers. This can induce officials to agree to waive or compromise the law as a condition of settlement. Once this begins, it can "steam-roller," and both the sanctions and the prohibition on strikes can lose their effectiveness.

It is, moreover, very difficult for public officials to enforce sanctions.[53] In the one Missouri case, labor was split, and the strikers were

[53] As we shall see in Chapter 16, this has been the case under New York's Condon-Wadlin Act affecting state employees.

TABLE 31

PENALTIES FOR VIOLATING STATE PUBLIC UTILITY ARBITRATION AND SEIZURE LAWS

State	Criminal	Civil*	Economic
Florida	Violations by groups of employees acting in concert or by any officer acting for employer punishable by fines up to $1,000 and jail up to one year. Unions and companies subject to fines up to $10,000 per day for each day of illegal stoppage.	Person aggrieved by violation of Act may request state court for injunction restraining violation and requiring performance of duty under Act.	....
Indiana	Violations by groups of employees acting in concert or by any officer acting for employer punishable by fines from $500 to $2,500 and maximum of six months in jail.	Person aggrieved by violation of Act may request state court for injunction restraining violation and requiring performance of duty under Act.	....
Maryland	....	State may bring suits to restrain violations of the law.	....
Massachusetts	....	State may bring suits to restrain violations of the law.	....
Minnesota (Hospital Act)	....	Court of equity may enjoin threatened or actual strike or lockout in charitable hospital.	....
Missouri	Union and public utility fined $10,000 per day and union official $1,000 per day for each day of stoppage which they call, incite, or support.	....	No person who incites, supports, or participates in any illegal stoppage may be employed by a utility except as a new employee. Certificate of convenience and necessity of public utility may be revoked if utility is found not bargaining in good faith.

Nebraska	Persons violating subject to fines of $10 to $5,000 and imprisonment from five days to one year.	Failure to obey an order of industrial court is a contempt of district court and punishable thereby.	....
New Jersey	Unions and public utilities subject to fines of $10,000 per day, and union and public utility officers fines of $25 to $250 per day, for each day of illegal stoppage.	Governor or agent may secure injunction to restrain violation and to provide necessary relief.	....
Pennsylvania	Same as Indiana, but with additional provision that penalty of imprisonment may be imposed on representatives or officers of unions and corporations.	Person aggrieved by violation of Act may request state court for injunction restraining violation and requiring performance of duty under Act.	....
Virginia	Persons may be fined $1,000 to $10,000 and jailed not more than one year; unions subject to fines of up to $10,000 for each day of stoppage which causes suspension of a utility in violation of Act.	....	....
Wisconsin	Any violation shall be considered a misdemeanor.	Wisconsin Employment Relations Board may seek court orders restraining violations of, and compelling performance of, duties under Act.	....

* In all arbitration cases the award of the arbitration board is filed in a court and, unless overturned, becomes an award of the court. Violation is then a contempt of court.

clearly in the wrong in their attempt to upset by force a legal ruling of the National Labor Relations Board. If, however, the strike had been a popular one and labor had been united, the problem of enforcement would have been less easy. Statesmen and politicians do not find it easy to invoke sanctions against large numbers of voters or against influential persons or groups.

On the other hand, public clamor against an unpopular strike can force politicians to invoke the sanctions of law. The injunction, with its penalties for contempt of court, appears both the easiest to enforce, the most effective, and the least punitive.

LEGAL AND CONSTITUTIONAL PROBLEMS

Emergency strike control legislation raises many legal problems, but the courts are usually either instructed by the legislation not to, or are loath to, substitute their judgment for the executive. For example, under the Taft-Hartley Act the law provides that "whenever in the opinion of the President of the United States" an emergency situation exists, he may act in accordance with a prescribed procedure. Despite cogent arguments that no emergency exists, courts will not substitute their opinion for that of the President[54] or, in state situations, a governor.

Under compulsory arbitration statutes, appeals to the courts from the decisions of arbitrators are usually limited to consideration of whether due process was observed, whether the decision was based upon the evidence, and whether the arbitration board acted within the scope of its authority. Again, even though a judge may believe that a case should have been decided differently, he cannot overturn an award on that basis.

Seizure legislation usually provides that an owner may petition the courts to secure the return of his property if there is reason to believe that the state is holding the property beyond the duration of the emergency. As noted, owners of property may sue for "just compensation" for the use of their property during seizure.

In Virginia the law would seem to preclude such suits—since just compensation is declared to be 85 per cent of net income during the period of seizure. In Massachusetts and Maryland the owner may elect to waive any suit and permit the state to operate a business for his account, or he may elect to sue for just compensation, but the courts are instructed to take into account in determining just compensation for the

[54] *United Steelworkers* v. *United States*, 361 U.S. 39 (1959).

seizure period the fact that a strike might have occurred if such strike had not been prevented by the seizure.

Fact-finding legislation generally contains no provisions for court appeals, because there is no legal compulsion to abide by recommendations of fact-finding boards, and hence no grievance of which courts generally take cognizance.

Constitutional Questions

The right of the federal government to limit strikes which it deems emergencies is well established, but litigation over state strike control legislation has had a long history and has resulted in a severe limit on such laws. The original Kansas arbitration law was nullified in so far as it applied to the manufacturing industry as an undue violation of due process.[55] The Michigan Act of 1947 was found contrary to the state constitution because of the powers it conferred on state judges,[56] and the original New Jersey Act (later amended to cover this defect) was struck down because of lack of standards.[57]

Most state laws, however, have fallen on the pre-emption issue—the rule that states cannot legislate in areas covered by federal law. Michigan's[58] and Minnesota's[59] strike vote laws, and the Wisconsin,[60] Florida,[61] and Indiana[62] arbitration acts all were declared invalid in so far as they apply to interstate commerce because the rights and duties conferred by these laws were found to conflict with rights and duties conferred by the Taft-Hartley Act. Likewise, the fact-finding statute of Michigan, in so far as it applied to public utilities in interstate commerce,[63] and the investigation and assignment-of-responsibility law of Massachusetts were also found inapplicable to areas covered by the Taft-Hartley Act.[64]

On the other hand, the Minnesota charitable hospital arbitration

[55] *Wolff Packing Company* v. *Court of Industrial Relations,* 262 U.S. 522 (1923); 267 U.S. 552 (1925).

[56] *Local 170, Transport Workers' Union* v. *Gadola,* 34 N.W. (2d) 71 (1948).

[57] *State* v. *Traffic Telephone Workers Federation of New Jersey,* 66 A. (2d) 616 (1949). The New Jersey courts later upheld the revised statute with standards—*New Jersey Bell Telephone Co.* v. *Communication Workers,* 75 A. (2d) 284 (1950)—but this was before the Wisconsin case (note 60 below).

[58] *International Union* v. *O'Brien,* 339 U.S. 454 (1950).

[59] *Automobile Workers* v. *Finklenburg,* 53 N.W. (2d) 128 (1952).

[60] *Amalgamated Association* v. *Wisconsin Employment Relations Board,* 340 U.S. 383 (1951).

[61] *Henderson* v. *Florida ex rel. Lee,* 65 So. (2d) 22 (1953).

[62] *Marshall* v. *Schricker,* Circuit Court, Vanderburgh County, Indiana, May 29, 1951.

[63] *Grand Rapids City Coach Lines* v. *Howlett,* 137 F. Supp. 667 (1956).

[64] *General Electric Company* v. *Callahan,* 294 F. (2d) 60 (1962).

law,[65] and presumably the arbitration act of Nebraska, as it applies to government-owned utilities, and the Michigan fact-finding law, as it applies to hospitals and government employees, are on sound constitutional grounds, since Taft-Hartley coverage excludes these areas of employment.

State seizure laws and the Massachusetts choice-of-procedures legislation have as yet to be tested in the United States Supreme Court. The Massachusetts and Maryland legislation has no court record. The Virginia courts have ruled that state's law a valid exercise of police power;[66] and the United States Supreme Court denied a hearing, but the case involved was moot at the time.[67]

Missouri's law, which is now involved in what may be definitive litigation, has had its constitutionality upheld in a significant state court decision. Said the Missouri Supreme Court:

> The King-Thompson Act is strictly emergency legislation and is not a comprehensive code for the settlement of labor disputes in utilities as the Wisconsin Act appeared to be. Emergency legislation is justified under the police powers. The purpose of seizure is the preservation of community life as encouraged and fostered by the state. The purpose of the Act is to protect its citizens against disaster . . . we deem the strike in the circumstances in this case to be unlawful, and therefore not a peaceful strike. . . .[68]

The Missouri court was impressed by the fact that the State was merely taking possession of the facility to prevent a stoppage which allegedly imperiled the public, and was not attempting to determine terms and conditions of employment which would remain in effect after seizure was terminated. Some writers on the subject believe that this may be the decisive line between constitutionality of a state statute and conflict with the Taft-Hartley law.[69] The United States Supreme Court, however, reversed the Missouri court and invalidated the Missouri law.[70]

[65] *Fairview Hospital Association* v. *Public Board,* 241 Minn. 523 (1954). The newly enacted New York hospital arbitration law is, of course, also not subject to effective challenge on the pre-emption issue, but since it covers only New York City hospitals, some authorities believe it may controvene the state constitution.

[66] *Harris* v. *Battle,* Chancery B–1708, Virginia Circuit Court, City of Richmond, January 2, 1953, and June 12, 1953.

[67] *Harris* v. *Stanley,* 75 S. Ct. 203 (1955).

[68] *State of Missouri* v. *Local No. 8–6, Oil and Chemical Workers,* 317 S.W. (2d) 309 (1958). The United States Supreme Court declined to review this case, not on constitutional grounds, but rather because the case was moot (361 U.S. 363 [1960]).

[69] See, for example, S. H. Lehrer, "The Maryland Public Utilities Disputes Act," *Labor Law Journal,* Vol. VII (October, 1956), pp. 614–17; and Max Rosenn, "State Intervention in Public Utility Disputes," *Labor Law Journal,* Vol. XII (May, 1961), pp. 393–96.

[70] The Missouri Supreme Court reaffirmed its 1960 decision on October 8, 1962, on the case, *Missouri* v. *Division 1287, Amalgamated Association.* On June 10, 1963, the United States Supreme Court reversed the Missouri court.

SHOULD STATE EMERGENCY STRIKE LEGISLATION BE PERMITTED?

Because state emergency strike legislation has been ruled invalid on the pre-emption issue, Congress could, by enacting enabling legislation, permit the states to legislate in this field.

Those who oppose this base their argument on two points: (1) that most so-called emergencies do not actually exist; and (2) that if they should exist, they transcend state lines.

The first point is especially strong. It would be difficult indeed to find a single instance in which a state strike control law has been invoked where great peril actually was threatening a community, although some cases involving gas or electric power could possibly have created such peril if allowed to continue. Moreover, as has already been noted, unlike the situation immediately after World War II, when most of the laws were enacted, a strike today in most utilities—electric power, gas, or telephone—does not involve a shutdown. Automatic equipment, plus use of nonstriking supervisors, permits service to be continued with little or no change to the customer. Only a very long strike in such cases, with a breakdown of maintenance, could involve the type of situation which blacked out Pittsburgh when power employees struck in 1946.

As for urban transit, repeated strikes have served only to prove that people can get to work without public commuter facilities—more harassed, and later than usual—but from experience, we know they get there, and that there is little reason to invoke emergency legislation in most transit strikes.

The second point against emergency legislation is that many of the covered industries are interstate in character. Utilities extend over state lines. Bargaining units are not necessarily geographically oriented. To permit state legislation is often to duplicate, or to subject companies and unions to dual and conflicting regulation. Certainly, if state strike control legislation is validated, Congress must spell out carefully proper areas of state regulation and then leave that jurisdiction solely to the states.

Those who favor permitting state regulation in the strike control areas point out, first of all, that state officials are closest to a situation and know best the needs of communities beset by labor problems. This is undoubtedly correct; but of course, the corollary is that state officials can be more readily "pressured" into premature action precisely because they are so close to a situation. The indiscriminate use of the Wisconsin and Indiana arbitration laws between 1947 and 1951 is a case in point.

The best argument for those who favor permitting state laws to govern strikes deemed to create emergency situations is that the states have been—and, many believe, should be—experimental laboratories for all forms of social legislation and regulation. The ingenuity and variety of laws in just this one area testify to this. Our federal system is based upon the recognition that in this great country, problems of states vary, and solutions to such problems can be met in a variety of ways. Federal pre-emption is often required. Excessive federal pre-emption, however, rules out experimentation, new solutions, and rich experience.

In other areas the courts have recognized that states have a role, at least in limited areas. This is true, for example, in the control of such tactics as jurisdictional disputes, picketing, and boycotts. In the area of union security the Taft-Hartley Act delegates authority to act to the states.

Despite the fact that real emergencies are not likely to occur on the state level as a result of strikes, there is so much to learn, and the area of knowledge is so sparse, that it appears unwise to continue to limit so strictly, or to forbid citizens acting through state legislatures to experiment reasonably with, legislation such as has been discussed in this and the preceding three chapters.

QUESTIONS FOR DISCUSSION

1. The partial injunction has been advocated as a possible means of dealing with emergency strike situations. How do you think it would work out in practice in these industries: steel, railroads, atomic energy, and longshore?
2. The President's Advisory Committee on Labor-Management Policy has proposed certain changes in the emergency procedure of the Taft-Hartley Act. What are these recommendations, and how do you think they would work out in practice?
3. What would you do if you were President of the United States and a steel strike lasted for 50 days, then the steelworkers returned for 80 days under a Taft-Hartley injunction, voted to reject the employers' last offer, and struck the entire basic steel industry once more?

SUGGESTIONS FOR FURTHER READING

BERNSTEIN, IRVING, *et al.* (eds.). *Emergency Disputes and National Policy.* New York: Harper & Bros., 1955.

A series of articles dealing with various experiences and proposals in strikes which tend to create an emergency.

COMMITTEE FOR ECONOMIC DEVELOPMENT. *The Public Interest in National Labor Policy,* especially pp. 86–144. New York, 1961.

A panel of experts examine the emergency strike problem in the context of total labor policy of the country.

HORLACHER, JOHN PERRY. "A Political Science View of National Emergency Disputes," *The Annals,* Vol. CCCXXXIII (January, 1961), pp. 85–95.

An incisive analysis of the issues and the liberties involved in the national emergency strike problem.

LIVERNASH, E. ROBERT. *Collective Bargaining in the Basic Steel Industry.* Washington, D.C.: U.S. Department of Labor, 1961.

An analysis of the effect of government intervention on collective bargaining in the steel industry.

PART IV

The Sovereign Employer

The preceding chapters have been concerned with government direction of private employment relationships. The sovereign power in such instances is used to compel employers and unions in the private domain to conform to the public interest as expressed in laws of the land and their administration.

But the sovereign is also an employer—indeed, the biggest and fastest growing employer. The next chapter is concerned with the policies of the sovereign as employer. It is also concerned with a relationship of increasing importance—that of the nonprofit institution with its employees, using the charitable hospital as an example. This is a gray area, part public and part private, with rights and duties largely not as yet delineated by public policy.

Chapter 16 PUBLIC POLICY AND THE PUBLIC EMPLOYER

The biggest American employer is not General Motors Corporation, or the American Telephone and Telegraph Company, but Uncle Sam. As of January 1, 1963, federal civilian employment was approximately 2.5 million, with the trend moving upward toward the World War II all-time high of 2.8 million.

But even the federal government is dwarfed as a big employer when compared with the burgeoning number of state and local government employees, the total of which exceeds two times that at the federal level. (See Figure 12.) Nor is this all. If military personnel are added, the total federal employment rises to 5.2 million, and the number of government employees mounts to 12 million. In addition, another six million persons are employed at government expense—in civilian jobs, but receiving pay checks which depend directly upon government contracts or grants.[1]

Today, therefore, nine million civilians—one out of every eight persons in the civilian labor force—work for government agencies. An equal number are either in uniform or are supported by government funds—a grand total of nearly one fourth of the labor force. Clearly, therefore, the policies of the government *as employer* are of concern not only to government employees, but to all American citizens concerned with public policy.

In this chapter the major facets of federal and state and local government employee relations policies are reviewed. A final section will be devoted to problems of hospital labor relations as an example of the increased problems coming to the fore in the nonprofit institutional area, where the number of employees is increasing, and where the employer is, in a real sense, both public and private.

The Sovereign Employer and the Right to Strike

Traditionally, the government as employer assumes that since the government represents the sovereign power, it must reserve the sole

[1] Data from *Business Week*, November 3, 1962, based upon governmental statistical sources and a study by the Brookings Institution, with data updated by the authors.

right to determine the terms and conditions of employment under which its employees labor. In actual fact, however, the second premise does not follow the first. The essence of sovereignty includes the right to delegate authority. Hence the sovereign power can delegate or share authority to determine the terms and conditions of employment. To a considerable extent, many governmental agencies actually do this, but many do not.[2]

Probably no government body in the United States concedes the right of its employees to strike. A strike of government employees which results from dissatisfaction over wages, hours, and working conditions becomes, in the light of the principle of sovereignty, an insurrection against public authority. Despite the fact that thousands of government employees have struck at one time or another,[3] a strike of public employees is greeted with extraordinary alarm and concern. If striking government employees are policemen or firemen or equally essential groups, it is easy to understand the public alarm. If these striking employees are truck drivers or street laborers, the situation is a rather anomalous one. For these employees are not only not essential to the conduct of the community's business, but they are, like many government employees, often less essential to the community than are the employees of many private concerns. For example, in most cities, many government employees are less essential than those of private utility companies. Certainly also, the effects of a strike of railroad employees serving Washington, D.C., would cause greater inconvenience than a strike of employees working in the United States Department of Labor.

Moreover, the status of employees can change from private, with the right to strike, to public, with no such right, without their functions or duties being altered. For example, in many cities, like New York, the local government has taken over ownership and operation of the transit facilities, with the work force intact. The former private employees are then advised that as government employees, they have lost the right to strike. But this can work the other way, too. Other municipalities have sold or turned over to private concerns formerly publicly owned power plants. When this is accomplished, the former public employees become private ones, and can assert private rights, including the right to strike.

[2] For an excellent discussion of this subject, see Sterling D. Spero, *Government as Employer* (New York: Remsen Press, 1948).

[3] David Ziskind, *One Thousand Strikes of Government Employees* (New York: Columbia University Press, 1940); and "Strikes of Government Employees, 1942–1961," *Monthly Labor Review*, Vol. LXXXVI (January, 1963), pp. 52–54.

FIGURE 12

BURGEONING BIG GOVERNMENT

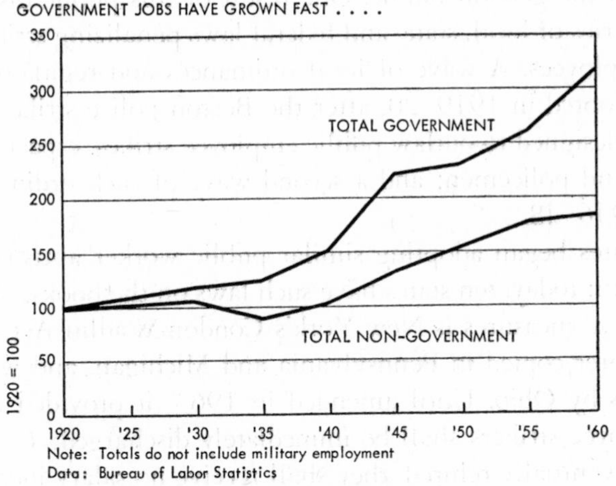

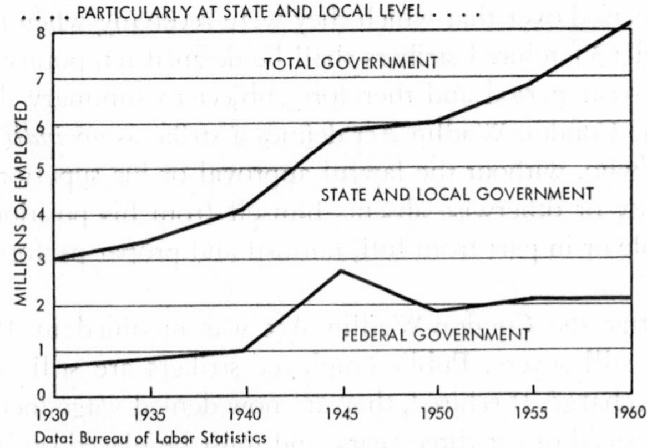

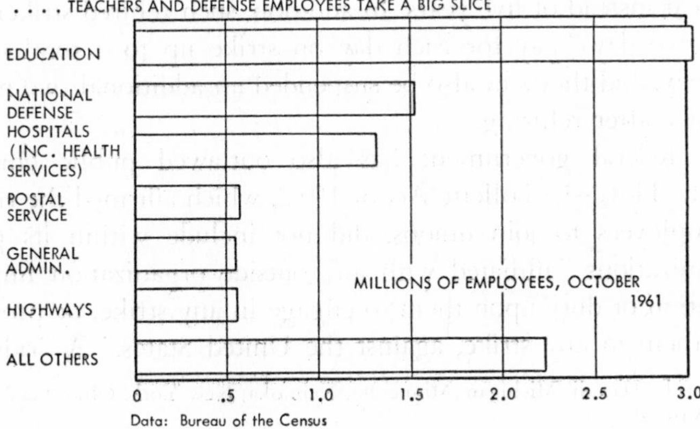

SOURCE: *Business Week*, November 3, 1962.

Despite these anomalies, strikes of public employees both interfere with the efficient operation of government and are extremely unpopular with the general public. One result of this public disapproval has been a series of local, state, and federal laws penalizing striking government employees. A wave of local ordinances and regulatory measures were adopted in 1919–20, after the Boston police strike of 1919, which were designed to outlaw public employee strikes, especially those by firemen and policemen; and a second wave of such ordinances followed in 1946–48.

The states began adopting similar public worker antistrike legislation in 1946; today, ten states have such laws on the books.[4] The most drastic of these measures is New York's Condon-Wadlin Act of 1947, which was later copied in Pennsylvania and Michigan, and with some modifications by Ohio. Until amended in 1963, it provided that (1) public employee strikers shall be immediately discharged; (2) if such strikers are eventually rehired, they shall receive no salary increases for a three-year period over that which they were receiving when the strike occurred; and (3) rehired strikers shall be deemed temporary employees for a five-year period and therefore subject to summary discharge. Moreover, the Condon-Wadlin Act defines a strike as an *individual* act of a person "who, without the lawful approval of his superior, fails to report for duty or otherwise absents himself from his position, or abstains in whole or in part from full, faithful and proper performance of his position."

Even after the Condon-Wadlin Act was modified in 1963, the penalties are still severe. Public employee strikers are still subject to immediate discharge. If rehired, they are now denied wage increases for six months instead of for three years, and must be placed on probation for one year instead of five years. In addition, such rehired strikers may be fined two days' pay for each day on strike up to a total of two months' pay, and they can also be suspended an additional two months without pay after rehiring.

The federal government has also outlawed public employee strikes. The Lloyd–La Follette Act of 1912, which affirmed the right of postal employees to join unions, did not include within its protection organizations "affiliated with any outside organization imposing an obligation or duty upon them to engage in any strike, or proposing to assist them in any strike, against the United States." A "rider" at-

[4] Florida, Hawaii, Michigan, Minnesota, Nebraska, New York, Ohio, Pennsylvania, Texas, and Virginia.

tached to appropriation bills since 1946 forbids payment of salaries to federal employees who are members of an organization "asserting the right to strike against the United States." Then Congress included in the Taft-Hartley Act the following provision modeled upon New York State's Condon-Wadlin Act: "It shall be unlawful for any individual employed by the United States or any agency thereof including wholly owned government corporations to participate in any strike. Any individual employed by the United States or by any such agency, who strikes, shall be discharged immediately from his employment, and shall forfeit his civil service status, if any, and shall not be eligible for reemployment for three years by the United States or any such agency."

Such legislation curbing public employee strikes is not necessary in most jurisdictions. Barring legislation to the contrary, the courts have generally affirmed the right of governmental administrators to penalize or to discharge workers for striking. Most unions in the public service recognize the dominant feelings on this subject by including nonstrike clauses in their constitutions. The main exception (although perhaps not in practice) was the United Public Workers, a now defunct organization which was expelled from the CIO for Communist Party domination. At its 1946 convention, this union adopted a procedure for strike action. This led directly to the 1946 Congressional riders forbidding payment of salaries to members of organizations "asserting the right to strike against the United States."

The Right to Organize and to Bargain Collectively

The federal government concedes the right of its employees to organize and to bargain collectively through unions of the employees' own choosing. The main limitation is that, since 1946, these unions cannot assert "the right to strike against the United States."

Federal employees did not win these rights without a struggle. Commencing in the nineteenth century, but especially in the administrations of Theodore Roosevelt and William Howard Taft, federal employees were generally denied the right to form unions of their own choosing. Moreover, as a result of tenacious attempts by postal employees to form unions and to improve their working conditions, President Theodore Roosevelt issued so-called "gag rules" which forbade all federal employees from seeking to influence legislation either directly or indirectly through associations, or to appear before Congress except through the heads of departments.[5] After a persistent campaign led by

[5] Spero, *op. cit.*, pp. 105–44.

the American Federation of Labor, Congress in 1912 adopted the Lloyd–La Follette Act, which provides:

> That membership in any society, association, club or other form of organization of postal employees not affiliated with any outside organization imposing an obligation or duty upon them to engage in any strike, or proposing to assist them in any strike, against the United States, having for its objects, among other things, improvements in the condition of labor of its members, including hours of labor and compensation therefor and leave of absence, by any person or groups of persons in said postal service, or the presenting by any such person or group of persons of any grievance or grievances to the Congress or any member thereof shall not constitute or be cause for reduction in rank or compensation or removal of such person or groups of persons from said service. The right of persons employed in the civil service of the United States, either individually or collectively, to petition Congress, or any member thereof, or to furnish information to either House of Congress, or to any committee or member thereof, shall not be denied or interfered with.

Although the Lloyd–La Follette Act applies only to postal employees, its principles have been made generally applicable to all federal workers. The Lloyd–La Follette Act, moreover, grants the right of hearing and notice to permanent employees in the civil service, except employees of the State and Defense departments and of the Atomic Energy Commission.

In addition to the protection of the Lloyd–La Follette Act, employees in the federal service are entitled to review of dismissals by the Civil Service Commission. A Presidential directive has instructed department heads to carry out the Civil Service Commission's recommendations. Nevertheless, government employees are excluded from the coverage of the Taft-Hartley Act, and the Lloyd–La Follette Act does not confer rights upon government employees similar to those conferred upon industrial employees by the Taft-Hartley Act. The Lloyd–La Follette Act merely represents Congressional approval of government employee unionization and, in addition, sets forth a procedure which must be followed in instances of employee discharges from the federal service. Once the procedure is followed, discretion to discharge is with the administrator, and the courts will not interfere.

Nor is this fact altered by the provision in the law governing employment in the Post Office which states that "No person in the classified civil service . . . shall be removed therefrom except for cause. . . . Membership in any society . . . or other form of organization of postal employees . . . shall not be the cause for reduction in rank or compensation or removal . . . from said service." According to Dr. Sterling D. Spero:

The net result of these provisions was that the postal authorities gave reasons other than the true ones for their action when seeking to remove or discipline an employee for activity arising out of organization membership. Thus they ordered the removal "for the good of the service," "for bringing the service into disrepute," "for conduct unbecoming a federal employee," "for making false and misleading statements." The postal authorities have found the law no obstacle in their efforts to get rid of troublesome organization members. Postmaster General Burleson, with the law fresh upon the books, discharged the national leaders of every AFL union of postal employees. His successors similarly had no difficulty in dropping workers who had come into conflict with the department during the salary campaign of 1924–25, and Postmaster General Farley's administration under the New Deal made removals for organization activity as readily as its predecessors. So long as the courts refuse to go behind the stated reasons of the authorities in making removals forbidden by law, the guarantees of the law in its present form remain empty.[6]

The Kennedy Administration Program

Prior to the Kennedy administration, the labor policies of the federal government varied considerably. Some agencies, such as the Tennessee Valley Authority, recognized unions and dealt with them as exclusive bargaining agents, even signing contracts with them. Others, which have less discretion in determining conditions of employment, dealt with unions in much the same manner, but did not sign contracts. In such cases, notices were sometimes posted on bulletin boards over the signature of the agency or department manager embodying the substance of what has been agreed to with the government employees' union. Many agencies, however, neither recognized nor dealt with unions.

Outside of the Post Office Department, where union organization in 1961 covered 84 per cent of the employees, government-owned shipyards and arsenals, and special "independent" agencies like the TVA, the extent of organization in the federal government service was estimated at "only a fraction of the norm in private industry . . . about 10 per cent of . . . employees under the Classification Act are affiliated" with unions.[7] Although this comparison is one of a primarily salaried, white-collar civil service group with industry generally including factory workers, and actually illustrates that a *higher* percentage of salaried employees are unionized in federal employment than in business corporations, the Kennedy administration determined to make it easier for unions to operate and to receive recognition in the federal government. After a task force report, the President issued Ex-

[6] *Ibid.*, p. 42.

[7] Wilson R. Hart, "Government Labor's New Frontier through Presidential Directive," *Virginia Law Review*, Vol. XLVIII (June, 1962), p. 910.

ecutive Order 10988 on January 17, 1962, requiring government agencies to recognize unions which, by vote of the employees in an appropriate unit, are shown to represent a majority of the unit, as exclusive bargaining agents. An immediate result has been the recognition of unions as exclusive bargaining agents not only in the Post Office Department, where a form of collective bargaining has long existed, but in such areas as the Military Air Transport Service, the Maritime Administration, and in some more traditional service and white-collar areas; and a substantial growth of union membership in the federal service.

STATE AND LOCAL LEGISLATION

The more favorable attitude of the Kennedy administration toward unions follows a trend at the state and municipal level which developed after the restrictive legislation of the immediate post-World War II period. As state and local governments added services and employees, they commenced finding strong demands for collective bargaining, and occasionally even encountered strikes for which punitive legislative was found either no cure or politically infeasible to enforce. For example, the drastic penalties required by New York's Condon-Wadlin law have been ignored in every major strike of state or local government employees in New York since the passage of the law in 1947, with only a few exceptions.[8] No one was punished, for example, as a result of the New York City teachers' strike of 1962. Moreover, in the few cases in which punishment has been dealt out, it has been uneven, and therefore discriminatory. In November, 1962, drivers attached to several New York City departments struck in defiance of the law, but only those under the jurisdiction of the police commissioner were dismissed.[9]

Experience with the Condon-Wadlin Act has convinced many political leaders that a law is preferable which maintains restrictions on strikes, but provides penalties that are not too drastic to enforce, and also provides methods of dispute settlement through collective bargaining. By 1963, such laws were in effect in a growing number of states.[10] In addition, a large number of cities were dealing with unions and signing collective bargaining contracts. There remained, however, several states and many municipalities which took the position

[8] *New York Times*, November 29, 1962. In only four or five cases have penalties of this Act been invoked, and in no major ones in New York City was it utilized except where an injunction was violated, and where the police commissioner acted (see note 9).

[9] *New York Times*, November 28–30, 1962.

[10] Alaska, California, Florida, Illinois, Massachusetts, Michigan, Minnesota, New Hampshire, New Jersey, Oregon, Rhode Island, and Wisconsin.

that they could not or would not deal with organized groups of employees.[11]

The laws of Michigan, Minnesota, and Wisconsin are of special interest because they indicate a possible trend toward the principle of exclusive representation rights for unions which are designated by a majority of a bargaining unit, and of having the state labor relations agency or agencies conduct representation elections and mediate—or even, as in Michigan, conduct fact-finding hearings on disputes between state and local government agencies and their employees.[12]

In municipal employment the cities of New York and Philadelphia have, by local administrative action and ordinance, established labor relations policies based upon exclusive representation and signed labor agreements.[13] Many smaller communities have done the same thing.[14] In addition, it is becoming increasingly common for municipalities to bargain collectively with a host of specialized employees, such as truck drivers, garbage collectors, and other manual workers. Cities and school districts are becoming more and more accustomed to dealing with their teachers on a group basis, either through a union, such as the American Federation of Teachers in New York City, or through a professional society, the National Education Association, which frequently represents teachers more sedately, but often in a relationship approximating collective bargaining.[15] The interesting questions which are raised by such relationships may be summed up by asking: How should collective bargaining operate in the public service?

COLLECTIVE BARGAINING IN THE PUBLIC SERVICE

More than one million employees in the public services belong to unions, and a majority of these are represented by unions in dealing

[11] The states include Alabama, Arkansas, Georgia, North Carolina, and Virginia, which forbid organization of public employees. Courts in several states still take the view that a division of government cannot bargain collectively. See, for example, "Labor Relations in the Public Service," *Harvard Law Review,* Vol. LXXV (January, 1961), pp. 406–7, for citations and analysis of such decisions.

[12] The Michigan procedure will be discussed below, pages 472–74.

[13] For the New York experience, see Ida Klaus, "Labor Relations in the Public Service: Exploration and Experiment," *Syracuse Law Review,* Vol. X (Spring, 1959), pp. 183–202. For aspects of the Philadelphia experience, see Harriet F. Berger, "The Grievance Process in the Philadelphia Public Service," *Industrial and Labor Relations Review,* Vol. XIII (July, 1960), pp. 568–80.

[14] See, for example, P. A. Brinker, "Recent Trends of Labor Unions in Government," *Labor Law Journal,* Vol. XII (January, 1961), pp. 13–22, 77–87.

[15] For a discussion of collective bargaining by this and other professional groups, see Herbert R. Northrup, "Collective Bargaining by Professional Societies," in Richard A. Lester and J. Shister (eds.), *Insights into Labor Issues* (New York: Macmillan Co., 1948), pp. 134–62.

with government. In most of these bargaining situations, there is no threat of strike, or consideration thereof by the unions. Yet despite the absence of strikes, or the application of force, the will to settle must be present. Obviously, this is a different situation than exists in private industry, in terms of methods and pressures.

Civil Service and Bargaining

Under present legislative practice, basic wages and conditions of employment at the federal level are set by Congress, not by collective bargaining. Specific salaries, salary grades, basic benefits, and time-off practices are thus established for most federal employees before the employee is hired or a union enters the picture. Most federal employees are, moreover, covered by civil service regulations which govern other conditions of employment. This had led many people to question what useful purpose a labor organization of federal government employees can perform. Actually, however, in the federal government, as in any other employment, relations between supervisors and workers result in grievances and other employment problems which are best resolved through collective bargaining. Much discretion is lodged in the administrators of government departments and bureaus to promote, penalize, and otherwise affect the careers of personnel. Only through collective bargaining can grievances of employees be satisfactorily adjusted. This is true for government employees as well as for employees of private concerns.

The general principle followed in collective bargaining in the government service is that administrators may bargain with unions of their employees on matters over which the administrator has authority or discretion. Obviously, if Congress provides by statute that the wage for a certain group of employees shall be a specific amount, the administrator cannot alter that wage. Obviously, also, if employees are hired pursuant to civil service regulations, the closed shop or other forms of union security which make jobs dependent upon union membership are incompatible with civil service regulations and therefore cannot be entered into.[16] On the other hand, in such agencies as the Tennessee Valley Authority, to which Congress has given considerable discretion in handling employee relations, collective bargaining can be more inclusive. The Kennedy administration has sponsored signed agreements covering employees in such departments as Labor and Post Office, but, of course, salary levels remain Congressional prerogatives.

[16] The union security issue is discussed in more detail below, pages 263–66.

On the state and local level the principles are no different; but in practice, civil service regulations are often, especially at the local level, not so widespread. In such cases, collective bargaining can be more flexible and more nearly include the subjects which are bargained about in private industry.

Regardless of the extent of civil service regulations, the tactics of unions in government employment must of necessity be markedly different from those concentrated in private industry.[17] Deprived of effective use of the right to strike—certainly on any protracted or consistent scale—unions of government employees have concentrated their attention on the political side. They operate lobbies, often highly effective, in Congress, in the legislative halls of the states, and before municipal bodies. The Post Office employee unions, for example, with members in every Congressional district, command the respect of members of Congress. Union spokesmen pleading the case of their constitutents are a common sight not only before Congressional committees, but also in the state capitals, the town meetings, and the school board hearings. And of course, the more the terms and conditions of employment are fixed by legislative action, the more must government employee unions concentrate on legislative activity to serve their constituents.

The American Federation of State, County and Municipal Employees, with a membership of over 200,000, is now a fast-growing organization, whereas unions like the Steelworkers and the Automobile Workers are losing ground. Although membership in each of the latter two unions is almost four times that of its fast-growing counterpart in the government service, the potential for the AFSCME is enormous. It could be the country's largest union if it is able to attract members at a growing rate. Among the proposals which this union frequently makes is for contracts that include the union shop and binding arbitration of grievance settlements. Both proposals involve a departure from general practice in government employment.

Union Security and the Government Service

Compulsory unionism has always been considered incompatible with civil service regulations at the federal level of government, as has already been noted. This policy was affirmed by Executive Order 10988,

[17] Many unions have members in both private industry and government employment, especially craft unions which are active in navy shipyards and in arsenals. These unions adapt to their environment, with locals following procedures and policies in accordance with the nature of the employment.

issued by President Kennedy on January 17, 1962, which specifically forbids the negotiation of any contract which contains a union shop clause or any other type of union security agreement.

On the local and state levels the American Federation of State, County and Municipal Employees claims to have signed about seventy-five union shop contracts throughout the country.[18] The largest group covered by an AFSCME compulsory union agreement is in Philadelphia; the agreement was negotiated in August, 1960. It provides that about 12,000 hourly rated and certain lower paid clerical groups must join the union as a condition of employment; that approximately 4,800 clerical, technical, and professional employees may join or not join, as they see fit; and that 1,200 supervisors are barred from union membership. An escape period is provided annually when resignations from the union can occur without loss of jobs.[19]

Other compulsory union agreements in government service are found mainly in manual occupations or groups of employees performing jobs often done by private industry: truckers, garbage collectors, power plant employees, mechanics, etc. Often, the union shop is by unwritten agreement or tacit understanding, instead of by written agreement. Whatever the form of the compulsory membership provision, there are some doubts about whether membership in a private organization should be a requirement for public employment; and in most areas of government employment, these doubts have been controlling.

There are also doubts about the legality of causing the discharge of a government employee because of nonpayment of dues or otherwise not being a union member. Under civil service regulations, this would probably not occur, since the regulations would prescribe no such reason for discharge. The issue, which cannot arise under present federal regulations proscribing the union shop in federal employment, has not been finally passed upon by the courts.[20]

Arbitration of Grievances

A weakness of unions in the government service is the general absence of a clause which submits grievances to binding arbitration, although such agreements are by no means nonexistent.[21] Outside of the

[18] Arnold S. Zander, "Trends in Labor Legislation for Public Employees," *Monthly Labor Review,* Vol. LXXXIII (December, 1960), p. 1295. Zander is President of the AFSCME.

[19] *Business Week,* August 6, 1960, p. 61.

[20] "Labor Relations in the Public Service," *Harvard Law Review,* pp. 402–5.

[21] The TVA is a party to such agreements, and the AFSCME claims to have negotiated more than seventy with various cities. See Brinker, *op. cit.,* p. 21.

minority that provide for binding arbitration, most agreements with grievance machinery provide for a final step by an appeals board, which is usually a permanent agency set up for that purpose, or by the civil service commission of the government involved.

A careful study of the subject concluded that arbitration was inappropriate because of legal barriers in some jurisdictions, lack of authority of administrators to agree to be bound, and lack of authority of administrators over sources of grievances—wages, benefits, etc. Permanent appeal boards, which are used in Massachusetts and Connecticut, this same study found, were often rendered less useful because of the tendency to appoint to these boards "deserving" politicians who were unaware of the basic issues involved, and because they did not have authority over classification or examination issues; while appeal to the civil service commission, the most common method, meant that the agency determining basic conditions of employment would have to pass on some of its own regulations.[22] As a solution, the use of regular arbitrators on an *ad hoc* basis was proposed, with advisory opinions rendered and voluntary compliance with the result.[23] This is the solution which the Kennedy administration has decided to adopt in its program to spur collective bargaining in the federal service.

In its Executive Order providing for increased reliance on collective bargaining in the federal service, the Kennedy administration provided for training of administrators in bargaining. Some such training has occurred, but a check by one of the authors in March, 1963 indicated that many of the administrators in the government service, and many of their union counterparts, had little knowledge of what their responsibilities *vis-à-viz* each other should be. Moreover, the unions were aggressive and the government management representatives afraid to act lest they incur the displeasure of their superiors whom they felt to be politically committed to encourage union growth and activity. The situation was not unlike that which occurred in private industry during the 1930's when unions first became a power in manufacturing. And, as in the private sphere, there will undoubtedly be a period of inefficient management and higher costs until improved relationships are worked out.

The problems of grievance adjustment of mutual accommodation illustrate some of the difficulties of collective bargaining in the public

[22] Charles C. Killingsworth, "Grievance Adjudication in Public Employment," *American Arbitration Journal,* Vol. XIII (1958), pp. 3–15 (reprinted by Michigan State University, Labor and Industrial Relations Center).

[23] *Ibid.*

service. The procedures and practices common in private industry must be modified to meet the requirements of a civil service system and other practices in public employment. A balance is necessary between the rights of the public to obtain service for their tax money and the rights of the employees to receive equitable treatment. In such an environment, collective bargaining requires the thoughtful concern of those who desire to preserve the system of government and the proper balance of freedom and authority. Experiments by several states in the settlement of disputes between employees and their public employers, which will be discussed below, are indications that serious thought is being given to this problem.

Firemen and Policemen: Special Problems

The firemen have long had a union, the International Association of Fire Fighters, which forbids strikes both as a matter of policy and in its constitution, and has for many years been affiliated with the American Federation of Labor, now the AFL–CIO. In recent years, this union has been quite successful in winning recognition as bargaining agent for firemen in many jurisdictions, but its main efforts are directed toward lobbying work designed to secure the passage of legislation improving the working conditions and salaries of firemen.

The International Association of Fire Fighters was not always so well received. The wave of antipolice union feeling which swept through the country following the Boston police strike of 1919 resulted in numerous ordinances and laws aimed at preventing the unionization of firemen as well as policemen, but the tendency is now so much the other way that membership in the Fire Fighters' organization has increased from a World War II period figure of 35,000 to nearly 100,000.[24] Undoubtedly, the emphatic emphasis on strike avoidance has lulled public fears that a union of firemen would mean strikes of a group which is truly essential, and which seems to understand that fact in the conduct of its organizational relationships.[25]

Policemen have no union as such. It is, however, quite common for policemen to be members of associations called "policemen's benevolent associations," which represent policemen in their dealings with community authorities, particularly acting as legislative agents. Occasional efforts to organize policemen have been made by local unions, but this is frowned on by officials of the AFL–CIO in view of the widespread hostility to such a move which both public officials and the com-

[24] Brinker, *op. cit.*, p. 15; and data from U.S. Bureau of Labor Statistics.

[25] Spero, *op. cit.*, pp. 228–44.

munity at large usually display. In New York City, for example, the Police Department is exempt from the city labor relations code, which promotes collective bargaining among city employees. The public scare generated by the Boston police strike destroyed any chance of a police union similar to that of the Fire Fighters.[26]

Policemen are the embodiment of public authority. They are called on to maintain order in strikes and to protect the public from all contingencies. That therefore the one widely publicized strike which ever occurred in an American city involving policemen was, in effect, treated as an insurrection is not hard to understand.[27] It is also not difficult to comprehend why unionization, even with strikes eschewed, is not considered proper for the police, who literally might find themselves in the middle of a strike of fellow unionists.

The other side of the problem is that policemen have grievances over wages, working conditions, unfair treatment by superiors, etc. To provide reasonable mechanisms for handling such grievances, and to permit a benevolent association to assist in such grievance handling, is not to advocate insurrection. On the other hand, the problem of balance remains. The head of a police department must be fully in charge and not "pushed around" by a strong union, which a benevolent association could in fact become. Here again, the rights of the affected policemen, the preservation of public order, and the rights of the public are all entwined.

CHARITABLE HOSPITALS

The institution of prepaid medical and hospital care has resulted in a tremendous expansion of the size and number of American hospitals, and the expansion is likely to continue at a faster rate. As a result, hospitals have become a major employer and institution in our economy. With assets of more than $15 billion, hospitals number nearly seven thousand and employ almost 1.5 million employees. This is a greater number of workers than are attached to the basic steel, the automobile, or the railroad industry. Hospitals may be divided into three types on the basis of control: proprietary, which operate for profit, and comprise about 17 per cent of the total, but only 3 per cent of the beds; governmental, which include those operated by federal agencies, such as the

[26] *Ibid.*, pp. 245–84.

[27] See Spero, *loc. cit.*, for the colorful and tragic story of the Boston police strike, and how it made a hero and Presidential timber out of the Governor of Massachusetts, Calvin Coolidge.

Veterans Administration and Public Health Service, as well as by state and local governments, which together include 31 per cent of the number of hospitals; and the most important group, those operated by nonprofit voluntary organizations.[28]

Employees of hospitals are generally excluded from the coverage of the Taft-Hartley Act. Section 2 (2) specifically excludes nonprofit hospitals from the jurisdiction of the Act; and of course, government-owned hospitals come under the exclusion of all levels of government. In its jurisdictional determinations the National Labor Relations Board has declined jurisdiction over proprietary hospitals unless they are vital to national defense, are located in the District of Columbia where the NLRB acts as a local agency, or are operated in connection with an interstate business over which jurisdiction is or will be asserted.[29]

Hospital employee relations are thus a matter largely for the states. A few have acted, and others may do so. For hospitals have traditionally depended upon low-wage labor for much of their menial work. These employees have indicated by strikes in a number of areas, especially New York City, that they are not too happy with the *status quo.* And their numbers are large enough to attract unions. Since a strike of hospital employees is most upsetting, and potentially dangerous, to a community, substitute methods of settlement have been advocated in many states, and now exist in at least four—Minnesota, Michigan, New York, and Oregon. The remainder of this chapter is devoted to a discussion of these laws and those concerned with the settlement of public employment disputes.

STATE DISPUTE SETTLEMENT: PUBLIC AND HOSPITAL EMPLOYEES

Earlier, it was noted that in Minnesota and Wisconsin the state labor relations agencies conduct elections and determine bargaining units in order to settle representation questions involving public employees. In California the State Conciliation Service has this authority, but only for transit districts. In New York the State Labor Relations Board has jurisdiction over certain types of municipal agencies for representation disputes.

A number of states, including Pennsylvania, Oregon, and North

[28] These and related statistics are based upon the excellent article by Hyman Parker, "The Laws Governing Labor-Management Relations in Michigan Hospitals," *Labor Law Journal*, Vol. XII (October, 1961), especially pp. 974–75.

[29] *Ibid.*, pp. 972–73.

Dakota, provide that the state mediation services shall be available to help to settle disputes between government agencies and bodies and their employees. In a number of other states, mediation is called upon to help solve any such disputes without specific legislation.

Compulsory Arbitration

Three states, as noted in Chapter 14,[30] have adopted compulsory arbitration for public or hospital employees—Nebraska for its publicly owned utilities and Minnesota and New York for charitable hospitals. The Nebraska law is not well regarded by organized labor, and has been used in publicly owned utilities infrequently.[31] In that sense, it might be serving its purpose; for if it induces settlement, but at the same time provides an avenue of redress when settlement by the parties fails, it is achieving its goal.[32]

The Minnesota hospital arbitration law has had most interesting results. It applies only to charitable hospitals and not to those operating for profit. In addition, only "any unsettled issue of maximum hours of work and minimum hourly wage rates" is subject to arbitration, although strikes or lockouts over any issue are forbidden. This latter feature has been strongly criticized by employee groups, who claim that wages won in arbitration can be balanced by unilateral hospital withdrawal of benefits, but this fear has apparently not been realized.

Despite their criticism of the Minnesota arbitration law, hospital employees have not hesitated to use it. The law has been invoked by both professional and nonprofessional hospital workers in Minnesota in recent years in a number of cases. The American Nurses' Association (a professional society which has established a collective bargaining program for its members),[33] as well as unions of nonprofessional hospital workers, realize that they can do better through arbitration than through the use of their limited economic strength. It is noteworthy that surveys have found hospital employees in Minnesota to be more completely unionized than those in most other areas.[34] Organization in Minnesota hospitals is thus being built upon arbitration without collective bargaining over new agreements having previously existed to a significant degree.

[30] See above, pages 399, 403–4.

[31] See Table 24, p. 404.

[32] On the other hand, no compulsory arbitration law has been used in more trivial cases than Nebraska's has in the private sector—for example, in disputes involving taxicabs.

[33] D. H. Kruger, "Bargaining and the Nursing Profession," *Monthly Labor Review*, Vol. LXXXIV (July, 1961), pp. 699–705.

[34] Parker, *op. cit.*, p. 973, n. 9.

In April, 1963, New York State adopted a law guaranteeing the right of collective bargaining to hospital employees in New York City and providing for the compulsory arbitration of disputes which the parties could not themselves dispose of. The law, which also outlawed strikes in covered hospitals, may have constitutional difficulties because it does not apply elsewhere in the state.

Fact Finding in Oregon, North Dakota, and Michigan

In 1961, Oregon passed a special law affecting only "licensed professional and practical nurses employed in health care facilities." The law provides for the determination of representation disputes by the state labor conciliator, proscribes unfair labor practices on the part of employers in health care facilities (which, of course, include hospitals, both public and private), and provides for mediation to settle disputes; and if such disputes are not settled, the law provides that the labor commissioner shall act as a fact-finding body, making recommendations for settlement.

North Dakota's law applies to all public employment under state jurisdiction, including municipal employment. It provides for the appointment of tripartite "mediation boards," whose job it is to find facts and make recommendations for the settlement of such disputes. The law also contains a strong prohibition against public administrators interfering with the right of employees to organize and to bargain collectively.

In both the hospital and the public employment fields, Michigan has had the most interesting fact-finding experience. Under the Michigan statute, nongovernmentally controlled hospitals are handled under one procedure; state or municipally owned hospitals are handled under the procedure established for governmental employees. Hospitals operated by the federal government are, of course, outside the pale of the Michigan law.

In so far as nongovernmental hospitals are concerned, the Michigan law establishes a procedure (similar to that of the Railway Labor Act) which requires due notice of contract changes or threatened strikes, urges the parties to settle disputes by bargaining, provides for mediation by the Michigan Labor Mediation Board or its staff where bargaining does not succeed, and provides that the mediators must urge arbitration if the dispute is not settled by mediation. If either party refuses arbitration, the Michigan Board so reports to the governor, who is required to set up a fact-finding commission composed of three public representatives, and the parties may each add a nonvoting member. No strikes or lockouts are permitted until thirty days after the report and recommendations of the commission.

Table 32 shows that the number of Michigan fact-finding commissions appointed in hospital cases has risen steadily since 1958. This

TABLE 32

FACT FINDING IN MICHIGAN, 1956–61

Year	Public Employee Fact-Finding Reports	Hospital Employee, Governor's Commission Reports and Recommendations
1956	4	...
1957	0	...
1958	3	1
1959	3	2
1960	11	3
1961	17	6
1962	10	5

SOURCE: Michigan Labor Mediation Board.

trend may well continue because hospital employees remain one of the largest and lowest paid groups in the country among which union organization is slight.[35] Moreover, Michigan fact-finding commissions for hospital cases are likely to increase in number because, if the hospital does not consent to a representation election, the only way a union of hospital employees in Michigan may achieve legal recognition as bargaining agent is to threaten to strike, achieve through this means the appointment of a fact-finding commission, and then, if the hospital refuses a representation election, again threaten to strike. At this point the Michigan Board must take a strike vote, which the Michigan courts have construed as a representation election also because the issue on the ballot is stated in terms of desiring a strike because of the hospital's refusal to recognize the union.[36]

Where state or municipally owned hospitals are concerned, the procedure in Michigan follows the general one for state employee relations. The Hutchinson Act of Michigan of 1947 strictly forbids work stoppages for employees of the state or its subdivisions, but provides a means whereby such employees may secure mediation or fact finding of their disputes. Moreover, if the majority of the groups of state government employees petition the Michigan Labor Mediation Board to

[35] Probably less than 5 per cent of the hospitals have union contracts, according to a 1960 survey of the American Hospital Association (Parker, *op. cit.*, p. 973).

[36] *SCME, Local 1644* v. *Oakwood Hospital*, Wayne County Circuit Court, Michigan, 1960, cited in Parker, *op. cit.*, pp. 982–86. Parker's article contains a good account of this case and others involving hospitals under the Michigan law.

mediate their grievances, the public employer must attend the mediation hearing and must discuss the issues with the employees or their representative. The employee representative is, of course, usually a union. The public body, as the employer, need not sign a union contract, although some have done so. Typically, the public body issues a statement embodying the results of the discussion with the union and/or employees.[37]

In 1954 the Michigan Labor Mediation Act was amended to provide a fact-finding procedure for government employees. When mediation fails to resolve a dispute, either the public body or the employees may petition the Labor Mediation Board for fact finding. The Board may then require the parties to present their case to one of its hearing officers in a formal hearing. The hearing officer's report goes to the parties and to the Labor Mediation Board. The parties then have ten days to file written comments with the Board, which reviews the entire record and issues findings of fact and recommendations. Although such recommendations are not binding, the union cannot strike, and the employer is a public body advised by a sister agency as to what it should do to settle its labor problem. Hence, such recommendations are likely to be persuasive.

Since 1956 an amendment provides that public employee disputes may go to tripartite mediation panels instead of to the more formal hearing officer system. However, this procedure requires prior agreement of the public employer, and this has not been usual.

Table 32 shows a marked increase in Michigan fact-finding reports involving public employees for the years 1960 and 1961. The financial crisis in Michigan has perhaps made the settlement of such disputes difficult; but by providing a reasonable nethod for the settlement of such disputes, Michigan has undoubtedly eased a difficult period. It remains to be seen whether fact finding in Michigan will assist hospitals, public bodies, and employees to settle disputes, or whether it will become the method of settlement. If the latter turns out to be the case, would the finality of arbitration be preferable?

Some Policy Issues

The disputes adjustment activities of the states in the hospital and public employee field are likely to increase because unions in these areas either are too weak or are under such legal restraint as to render them dependent upon government machinery for growth or even exist-

[37] See Hyman Parker, "The Role of the Michigan Labor Mediation Board in Public Employee Labor Disputes," *Labor Law Journal*, Vol. X (September, 1959), pp. 633–42.

ence. To what extent the government should foster union growth in these areas remains an unanswered question, which, in turn, begs the question of the extent to which fact finding, as in Michigan, or arbitration, as in Minnesota, aids union growth. Certainly, it does seem that if strikes are banned, as they are by Michigan's Hutchinson Act for public employees, or if they are—at least emotionally—almost intolerable, as they are in hospitals, a substitute method of settling disputes may well be a requirement. In such situations, collective bargaining may become, as it often does, seriously inhibited by the existence of the governmental fact-finding machinery. In such instances, however, there is no reason why we should expect the parties, who, in practical terms, do not have the rights of private parties, to act as we expect labor and management in private industry to behave. In short, the differences of public and hospital employment from private employment may be such that collective bargaining, as we know it in private industry, cannot work in the hospital and public field, anyway. Therefore the Michigan and Minnesota experiences are likely to prove both interesting and helpful.

QUESTIONS FOR DISCUSSION

1. Should the Taft-Hartley Act be applied to federal employment? Explain your answer, emphasizing whether you think that rights of government and private employees should be as nearly alike, or as diverse, as possible.
2. Do you believe that policemen in cities should be treated like other city employees in so far as collective bargaining rights, privileges, and duties are concerned? How about firemen? How about the mayor's secretary?
3. What other nonprofit institutions in your area besides hospitals employ large numbers of people? Does the Taft-Hartley Act apply to them? Should it? Would Michigan's hospital fact-finding procedure be appropriate for these nonprofit institutions also?

SUGGESTIONS FOR FURTHER READING

HART, WILSON R. *Collective Bargaining in the Federal Civil Service.* New York: Harper & Bros., 1961.

The story of labor policies of the federal government and of unions in the federal service by a strong protagonist of unionism in the federal government.

KILLINGSWORTH, CHARLES C. "Grievance Adjudication in Public Employment," *American Arbitration Journal,* Vol. XIII (1958), pp. 3–15. Reprinted by Michigan State University, Labor and Industrial Relations Center.

An account of grievance settlement as practiced by a large sample of government jurisdictions.

PARKER, HYMAN. "The Laws Governing Labor-Management Relations in Michigan Hospitals," *Labor Law Journal,* Vol. XII (October, 1961), pp. 972–90.

———. "The Role of the Michigan Labor Mediation Board in Public Employee Labor Disputes," *Labor Law Journal,* Vol. X (September, 1959), pp. 632–42.

Two excellent articles examining the experience of Michigan in the public and hospital employee relations fields.

SPERO, STERLING D. *Government as Employer.* New York: Remsen Press, 1948.

An outstanding book in the field, despite its age, in terms of balanced treatment and analysis of problems.

WARNER, KENNETH O. (ed.). *Management Relations with Organized Public Employees: Theory, Policies, Programs.* Chicago: Public Personnel Association, 1963.

An up-to-date compendium of excellent articles dealing with many phases of government employees relations in federal, state, and municipal jurisdictions.

PART V

Concluding Observations

Chapter 17 THE FUTURE OF PUBLIC POLICY AND UNION-MANAGEMENT RELATIONS

The labor policy of the United States has developed slowly and haltingly over the years. Each period of history has made some contribution to the present status of labor legislation and governmental action. Much of our present legislation stems from the Roosevelt era during the Great Depression, but even the National Labor Relations Act—the most comprehensive and revolutionary of all our labor laws—had its roots in state and railway labor legislation of the 1890's.

Actually, the United States has no uniform labor policy, but rather a patchwork of policies, comprehensive but not consistent. There is, for example, no uniformity of treatment among the states; and even at the federal level, railway and air-line employees and employers who come under the Railway Labor Act have rights and duties different from those of their fellow employees and employers who come under the National Labor Relations Act.

That this patchwork of policies has developed is not surprising when one considers that labor legislation is enacted in response to the pressure of public opinion and influences exerted by various pressure groups. At various stages of American labor history, different aspects of labor policy have become matters of public concern and have thus gained the ear of Congress. For example, encouragement of collective bargaining by protecting the right of labor to organize was of prime importance in our labor policy during the thirties because the public looked to the strengthening of the position of organized labor as one means of raising wages, income, and employment, and setting the stage for recovery from the depression. Then, in the post-World War II era, restraints on activities of unions were embodied in labor legislation as the public became concerned with certain alleged excesses of unions during the period of relatively unrestricted union organization.

Labor policy is thus continually evolving. The path it may take in the future is difficult to predict and may well depend upon fortuitous events—a war, a major depression, difficulties engendered by the Common Market, etc.—all of which may set the stage for special legislation. While forecasting trends is an interesting pastime, it is perhaps more instructive to analyze our existing national policy and to raise some basic questions about what public policy is really trying to accomplish through the medium of legislation in the field of labor relations.

It may seem odd to end a lengthy text on labor and government with a list of unanswered questions, and yet this is characteristic of the subject matter. There are no definitive answers in labor relations; there is no clearly delineated right or wrong. Basically, labor policy involves a balancing of value judgments which can never be wholly satisfactory and which, depending upon the viewpoint of the observer, will always seem to favor one party and create inequities or hardship for the other.

Our present national labor policy appears to be based upon five major tenets:

1. Collective bargaining should be encouraged as the democratic method of resolving controversy in the field of labor relations.
2. Unions must be uniformly treated by labor legislation regardless of differences in size and strength.[1]
3. The right to strike for lawful objectives such as higher wages, shorter hours, and improvements in working conditions should not be prohibited.
4. Labor should have the right to picket to obtain the above-enumerated goals, subject to limitations where the rights of neutrals are involved.
5. Wages and hours should be determined by collective bargaining between labor and management, rather than by government dictation.

Each of these propositions, while essentially sound, actually hides a host of problems. Let us scrutinize each of these propositions in turn.

Encouragement of Collective Bargaining

Both the Wagner Act and the Taft-Hartley Act state that the national policy is to encourage collective bargaining. If this goal is accepted as a reasonable objective of national labor policy, there are still four important questions about collective bargaining that need to be answered:

[1] To a lesser extent, a similar proposition holds true with respect to government regulation of labor policies of business organizations. However, as a practical matter, many smaller businesses are treated differently than large companies because their activities do not affect interstate commerce and therefore they are not subject to federal regulation under the Taft-Hartley and Landrum-Griffin acts. Unions representing employees in such small companies may nevertheless be subject to federal regulation such as the Landrum-Griffin Act if they have other members in an industry affecting interstate commerce.

1. *How much collective bargaining is good for the economy?* The consequences to the economy of having 50 per cent of the labor force in unions is quite different from having 90 per cent of the labor force in union organizations. It may be argued that this is not a pertinent question today, since less than 25 per cent of the total labor force is organized and this proportion seems to be declining. Nevertheless, the question is a very real one in individual industries. We cannot gloss over the fact that the movement of wages and prices, the repercussions of strikes, and even the influx of new investment will all be significantly affected by the extent of organization in an industry, and *a fortiori* in the economy as a whole. The Wagner Act created the problem of so-called "union monopoly" today because it put the power of the government behind unions without fully appreciating that a consequence of such action would be the creation of organizations which, at the whim of a small group of men, could close down an entire industry and throw hundreds of thousands of workers out of jobs.

2. *What kind of collective bargaining is best for an economy?* Three possible levels of organization can be distinguished. It would theoretically be possible to have all union organization on a local union basis. This is what some legislators have proposed as a cure for the ills of industry-wide bargaining. Obviously, the cure might kill the patient (which may be the objective); and it would, in any case, create many new problems. As has already been pointed out in the discussion in Chapter 2, industry-wide bargaining is not something that unions foisted on an unwilling business community. On the contrary, in many industries, management leaders are staunch proponents of this form of bargaining. Nevertheless, it has been argued that restriction of union organization to a local level would lessen the scope of strike action and thus make government intervention in strike settlement procedure less likely. A second level of organization is what we have at present—with international unions nominally in control of bargaining objectives and tactics, but a good deal of autonomy at the local level. The problems raised by this kind of organization have been fully explored in earlier chapters. In many respects, this level of bargaining combines all the disadvantages of levels one and three as herein outlined. Finally, there is a third alternative—the possibility of true industry-wide bargaining, with a national union council bargaining with a national council representing employers. This is the procedure utilized in Sweden, for example. At this level, at least, it would be possible to map out wage objectives from the point of view of their effect upon the entire economy. In our present setup, no one union

has enough effect upon the total wage picture to do other than take as much as it can get. We shall soon have a practical example of how the organization of collective bargaining affects the achievement of particular goals when the thirty-five-hour week becomes a key issue in negotiations. A few unions have already obtained this objective, and there is pressure upon others to get in step. If the decision had to be made at a national level in a union-management council with the competition of the Common Market, Russia, and other international factors considered, perhaps a more statesmanlike formula could be agreed upon than will result in the free competitive action of our present labor market. But such a national determination would probably insure government dictation to an increasing degree, and in the long run the results might well be considerably less desirable.

3. *Is it really possible to encourage collective bargaining, on the one hand, and, on the other hand, protect the right of those employees who do not wish to join unions?* The Taft-Hartley Act attempts to adopt this ambivalent policy, with the result that it has satisfied neither the exponents of stronger unionism nor the professed defenders of individual employee liberties. The treatment accorded the union shop is a good example of the problems created when the government seeks to encourage two inconsistent policies. The reader will recall from the discussion in Chapter 8 that the Taft-Hartley Act permits the union shop and yet provides that it shall be illegal in those states which adopt right-to-work laws outlawing this type of union security. One may well ask: What is our federal policy toward the union shop? Apparently, we are for it as long as there is not too much opposition against it!

4. *Can collective bargaining settle today's tough bargaining problems?* Experience has demonstrated that collective bargaining is the best method of settling conflicts between management and labor with respect to wage levels, methods of payment, hours of work, and conditions of employment. Settlements in these areas can be properly left to the private parties because to a large extent the means for working out solutions arising from such settlements are within the power of such parties. For example, if a wage increase is agreed upon, the employer can raise the wages, and he is also in a position to adjust prices, utilization of machinery, and other variables of production and sales.

Suppose, however, that the issue between management and labor is manpower utilization, job security, or guaranteed employment. Can the parties really solve it? Can management and union really deal with these problems? Unfortunately, an apparently increasingly large number of major disputes in recent years have pertained to these issues. In noting this to be true, and citing the strikes then in process, or recently concluded, involving flight engineers of air-lines, longshoremen, newspaper printers, steelworkers and railroad employees, Mr. W. Willard Wirtz, Secretary of Labor, declared:

> It is one thing to bargain about terms and conditions of employment, and quite another to bargain about terms of unemployment, about the conditions on which men are to yield their jobs to machines. To the extent that these problems of employee displacement can be met at all in private bargaining, it can be only by a process of accommodation which is almost impossible in the countdown atmosphere of the 30 days before a strike deadline.[2]

Perhaps government or other outside or expert help is needed for labor and management to solve these complex problems. But one may well note that most bargaining is not confined to a 30-day "countdown" period. The parties prepare long in advance and usually know the direction of each other's position and thoughts long before a deadline is reached. Moreover, before turning these issues over to third parties for help or solution, the parties are entitled to ask what magic formula government or third-party experts do indeed have to solve these difficult and pressing problems. The fact of the matter is that no solution has been discovered by anyone in many cases, and especially a solution that would please all parties.

In addition, before we conclude that collective bargaining is not up to the job, perhaps we should give it an opportunity to perform its function. It is worthy of note that all the cases cited by Mr. Wirtz as examples of problems too complex for collective bargaining were complicated by extensive government intervention, which had become, as Mr. Wirtz noted after failing to settle the New York newspaper strike in early 1963, a "dull instrument."[3] In the flight engineers case, four air-lines—Braniff, Delta, Continental, and United—and the unions involved worked out solutions long before the massive intervention affecting other air carriers was inaugurated. Each of these air-lines came up with a different solution, two peacefully, two after short strikes. The differences between the experiences of these air-lines and the ones that went through 39 boards and intervenors and still had more strikes and difficulties may well be explained by the differences in managerial com-

[2] Address before the National Academy of Arbitrators, Chicago, Ill., February 1, 1963; reported in 52 LRR 133 et seq.

[3] The Secretary's exact words were: "There can be no doubt that any repeated resort to extraordinary procedures dulls the instrument." See *Daily Labor Report*, January 9, 1963, p. A–3.

petence rather than by the difficulty of the problem or the ability of collective bargaining to handle such issues.

The Uniform Treatment of Unions

While not too much express reference is made to this aspect of our national labor policy, it is apparent that an implicit element of such policy is the decision that despite the diversity in size, influence, power, and impact of various unions in our economy, they must all be treated the same as far as legislation is concerned. If an organization picket line is illegal after thirty days, this is so whether the picket line is manned by miners who may already have organized 70 per cent of the industry, or by textile workers who may have only a minority of the plants under contract. If there have been abuses in the handling of pension funds, the legislation cuts across all unions, requiring the good and the bad to conform to the same strait jacket of regulation.

The formulation of our national labor policy is made more difficult by the heterogeneous nature of unions in our economy. American unions are much more decentralized than their counterparts in other industrialized countries. In the AFL–CIO, for example, there are only five unions with a membership of over 500,000, and the largest single union has only slightly more than 8 per cent of the total membership.[4] Seventy per cent of the unions in the country have fewer than two hundred members and have gross receipts of less than $20,000 a year.[5] Although it is true that no one union in our country is extremely large, nevertheless one third of all organized workers belong to seven of the country's 186 national unions. If we look at the unions in six major industries—automobile, coal, construction, railroad, steel, and trucking—it is apparent that these unions have achieved a very high degree of organization and that union demands materially determine the trend of wages and employment in these key industries. As a matter of fact, unions are so strong in these industries that the trends which have developed in hourly earnings bear little relation to sales and employment.[6]

[4] P. Henle, "A Union Viewpoint," *The Annals,* Vol. CCCXXXIII (January, 1961), p. 10.

[5] The Kennedy-Ervin bill, as passed by the Senate, would have exempted unions with less than two hundred members and gross annual receipts of less than $20,000 from the obligation to file financial reports; but the Landrum-Griffin Act, in its final form, deleted this exemption.

[6] As Frank C. Pierson puts it: "The most striking conclusion to emerge from the data is that among these six industries, the three which experienced the greatest difficulty in recent years in maintaining sustained expansion in output, that is, sales, and in employment —bituminous coal, railroads and basic steel—also experienced about the greatest relative increase in hourly earnings." See Frank C. Pierson, "The Economic Influence of 'Big Unions,' " *The Annals,* Vol. CCCXXXIII (January, 1961), p. 101.

Should an employer who directs some antiunion remarks to his employees in the trucking industry be held to the same standards of conduct as an employer in a department store where there has been relatively little sustained union activity? Should the same strike settlement procedures be applicable to all industries regardless of the strength of union organization? Americans have a great fear of qualitative action, since it may be discriminatory. But uniform action can also be discriminatory because of the different impact which the same rule or regulation can have upon different labor organizations by reason of diversity in size and economic status. A law aimed at Hoffa can strangle a small union in its formative stage.

Protection of the Right to Strike

The right to strike is not an absolute right. Furthermore, its preservation without restriction is not the *sine qua non* of economic democracy. Experience under both federal and state legislation is testimony to the truth of these propositions, for the right to strike has been subjected to many restrictions. Perhaps a close look is now required to determine whether the present prohibitions make sense. For example, if a group of office workers in the United States Government Printing office were to go on strike, the strike could be enjoined, and the strikers would lose their civil service status. Yet the inconvenience to the public would be *de minimus.* On the other hand, if the longshoremen were to strike and tie up shipping on the entire East Coast of the United States, the Taft-Hartley Act might be invoked to delay the strike action, but at the end of the "cooling-off" period the longshoremen could resume their strike. The reason given for the drastic action in the first case is that this is a strike against the government, which cannot be tolerated. It might be asked: Who is the government? Is not the government really the embodiment of the "public"? Is not a strike against the public interest just as much of an affront to the government even though, technically, it is an action against private employers? Is it fair to penalize government employees in nonessential occupations by depriving them of the right to strike while employees in crucial utilities, defense jobs, etc., can strike? Should the test be the extent to which the public interest is jeopardized rather than whether or not the government or private industry is the immediate employer?

Are we heading into an era of more costly strikes? There is some reason to believe that this may be so. In 1960, fewer man-days were lost through strikes than in any year since 1942. Since 1960, strikes have been on the upturn, but not seriously. However, individual strikes seem to last longer and appear more difficult to settle. This may reflect the basic change which has occurred in the economic environment. Management is very concerned today about the competition of foreign producers and the "squeeze" on profits resulting from overproduction of facilities in this country. Collective bargaining has worked comparatively well during the postwar era of rising wages and rising prices. Can it work as well during a period of price stability when management vigorously fights wage demands which will curtail profits?

What is going to be the attitude of unions toward government intervention in strike settlement? The present administration appears to favor *ad hoc* boards to investigate and settle strikes. May not organized labor secretly welcome this device if its strike attempts fail to obtain desired gains from management? The strike weapon is gradually becoming less effective in manufacturing because the wider application of automation is making it possible for companies to continue to run plants by using supervisory employees. If local police protect the right of employees to work, and if union influence wanes, unions may well turn to the government for assistance to bolster declining strike power.

Protection of the Right to Picket

The right to picket to improve wages and working conditions is jealously guarded by organized labor, and understandably so, for the picket line is a most effective weapon which less than forty years ago was subject to the ever-present curb of the court injunction. After enactment of the Norris–La Guardia Act and the Wagner Act, there followed a period in which the picket line was freely used by unions with little or no statutory prohibition restricting its use. Then came the Taft-Hartley Act and the Landrum-Griffin Act, which imposed limitations, primarily where the picket line was used for organizational purposes and in support of activity deemed contrary to public policy, such as a secondary boycott. It is apparent that our national policy has, in recent years, been moving in the direction of limiting the use of the picket line. The question should therefore be asked whether the present pattern of statutory prohibitions makes sense.

Qualitative judgments have been made by legislators, the NLRB, and the courts as to what is and what is not permissible picketing. These judgments appear to depend not so much on the degree of infringement of the right of free speech as they do on the public policy implications raised by the impact of the particular kind of picketing. For example, NLRB decisions have delineated what can lawfully be stated on a sign carried by a picket and what words may subject the picket line to statutory prohibition. If the sign says that an employer does not pay wages equal to the union standard in the area, this is so-called "union standards" picketing and is lawful; but if the sign says that the employer will not sign a contract with the union and recognize it as bargaining representative, the picket line may be unlawful.

Presumably, the first legend is lawful because it seeks only to improve labor's working conditions, whereas the second seeks to obtain, through the use of economic coercion, recognition of the union which public policy now dictates should be handled peacefully through procedures established by law. Nevertheless, the fact remains that qualitative judgments have been made which attempt to classify lawful and unlawful picket lines, and the distinction between the two is by no means clear. Should similar judgments be attempted in the field of picket lines utilized to obtain purely economic objectives?

Public opinion is undoubtedly sympathetic to a picket line thrown around a plant which pays substandard wages. If there is an inconvenience to the public, most people would agree that it is offset by the advantages the community will gain through elimination of exploitation of labor. But suppose the picket line is put around a plant which pays the highest wages in the industry and the union wants more. Or suppose the picket line is manned by air-line pilots striking because they contend that their salaries of $25,000 a year are inadequate. Should the picket line in such cases be accorded the same degree of protection from employer interference?

In the early days of union organization, nounion plants were frequently the ones which paid substandard wages. Unions therefore needed the weapon of the picket line to bring pressure to bear on these nonunion firms so as to protect the higher standards established in the rest of the industry. Today, in many cases, nonunion firms pay as high or higher rates than union firms. It may be true that they adopt this policy to "keep out the union," but the fact remains that their employees are not usually in the exploited class. Should public policy protect the picket line when used against high-wage-paying nonunion companies?

These questions all lead up to the basic unanswered question which runs through much of our national labor policy: What are we really trying to do? Is union organization an end in itself of sufficient public benefit that the government should actively encourage it? Or are we trying to obtain improvement and greater uniformity in working conditions, with union organization being only a means to this end? Is union organization really a democratic method of determining working conditions in industry which government should foster, or is it a means of enabling a small group of employee representatives and a few key employers in industry to determine working conditions for all?

Market Determination of Wages, Hours, and Working Conditions

If there is one issue on which management and labor agree, it is that wages and prices should be set by the free action of the market place, rather than by government dictate. Government control of wages, perhaps more than any other move, would lead to state socialism, for it would inevitably bring with it control of prices and profits, and a whole heirarchy of regulation. Yet the question must still be asked how, under our present national policy toward wages, we can overcome the enormously complex problems which face our economy. We are faced with a retardation in rate of growth, substantial unemployment, and increasing foreign competition. This foreign competition will become more of a threat with every passing year. Moreover, the Trade Expansion Act of 1962 commits our nation to a very substantial degree of trade liberalization. We are going to have to learn how to compete with foreign nations which not only have lower wage scales than we do, but also frequently have more efficient plant facilities as well. In 1960, while domestic fixed capital formation in the United States amounted to a little over 16 per cent of the gross national product, West Germany was investing 24 per cent, Belgium 27 per cent, France 31 per cent, Italy 29 per cent, and Japan 42 per cent. In the face of this kind of improvement in capital facilities abroad, can American management afford to continue wage increases in excess of the rate of improvement in man-hour productivity?

Despite the seriousness of this situation in the mind of management and the plea for moderation by President Kennedy and other public officials, union leaders continue to seek substantial improvements in wages and hours. The AFL–CIO Executive Council now advocates the thirty-five-hour week as the cure-all for unemployment, with remarkable indifference to its possible effect on costs. Increasing imports and our need to expand exports introduce a new dimension into the American labor relations scene. How can the free market adapt to this situation? Will the government be forced to take a stand in order to prevent a flight from the dollar and increasing unemployment?

The present administration has been attempting to influence the pattern of wage settlements by three different types of approach: (1) by prescribing so-called "guideposts" for noninflationary wage adjustments, (2) by extensive government intervention on an informal basis in key wage situations, and (3) by appointment of special boards to deal with breakdowns in wage negotiations in specific situations. None of these avenues have been particularly productive.

The "guideposts" issued by the President's Council of Economic Advisors indicated that output per man-hour has been increasing at an average of 3 per cent per annum since 1947 and therefore gave rise to the notion that a 3 per cent wage increase had the blessings of the administration. As a practical matter, this figure became a minimum in negotiations; and in situations where unions could obtain more, the criteria were ignored.

It is doubtful whether any general formula can apply to the diversity of economic situations which characterize the multitude of firms and industries in our economy today. Furthermore, there is no general agreement among economists or government officials, or even among union leaders, as to what is the "right" amount of a wage increase. Since government officials are not omniscient and the ability of businesses to make upward adjustments in wages varies widely, it would seem unwise to substitute centralized dictation of wage terms for the decentralized impersonal working of the labor market.

As far as government intervention in wage negotiations is concerned, either informally or through the creation of special boards, the previous discussion in this text has indicated the pitfalls in both approaches. The fundamental difficulty is that government in such situations is interested in ending the strike; management and labor, on the other hand, are primarily interested in reaching an agreement with which they can live. These objectives are not the same. The official who can end a strike becomes a popular hero—the difficulties the terms of settlement engender may not become apparent for years to come. The emergency board will disband once the strike is settled, so it may be inclined to "buy" peace; but management has to consider its ability to compete in both domestic and international markets, and unions should consider the impact of the settlement on employment.

The Future of Government Intervention in Labor Policy

A cornerstone of our democratic form of government has been the use of national policy to control great aggrandizements of power. As a nation, we have long recognized that when particular groups become so powerful that their actions can seriously interfere with market processes and endanger the public interest, government regulation may be required. Thus the Sherman Act recognized the evils inherent in combinations of corporations designed to restrain trade or monopolize an industry. Likewise, our graduated income tax and heavy estate tax were intended, in part, to restrict the concentration of economic and political power which would flow from the amassing of great fortunes passed on from generation to generation without tax.

With this history of the role of governmental regulation in our democratic society, it seems almost inevitable that the extent of regulation of unions will expand in the future. Unions in the past have been accorded many privileges not available to other organizations—such as relative immunity under the antitrust laws. These privileges are likely to be subjected to increasing scrutiny and limitation in the years ahead. To date, the function of government has been primarily to provide the basis for equality of bargaining power between management and labor. The Wagner Act sought to prevent large, strongly entrenched corporations from using their power to throttle unions in their infancy by resort to discriminatory practices. Then, as unions grew in membership and strength, the need for such one-sided intervention in the labor market lessened, and Congress enacted the Taft-Hartley Act in an effort to pare down some of the rights given unions and to equalize bargaining power in the labor market. Finally, Congress enacted the Landrum-Griffin law to protect union members from arbitrary union power.

It might be thought that with the development of strong union organization and the achievement of relative equality in bargaining power between industry and labor in many industries, government could now withdraw to the side lines and let the parties fight it out. Unfortunately, however, the very equality of power between the parties in mass production industries, where strong unions confront large corporations, each with extensive financial resources, increases the possibility of prolonged work stoppages with their attendant inconvenience to the public. Although, as has been pointed out in the earlier discussion in this text, few such stoppages actually create national emergencies, nevertheless the stoppages are serious enough to give rise to a hue and cry that something should be done to prevent such interference with the orderly flow of production.

The struggle between strong unions and large corporations leads to a demand by the public for further government regulation of union activities. One had only to read the editorial columns in newspapers and magazines commenting upon the 1962 newspaper strikes in New York City and Cleveland, and the longshoremen's strike on the East and Gulf coasts, to realize that these influential molders of public opinion are arrayed in favor of increasing use of government power to prevent such stoppages in the future. Indeed, there is increasing reference to compulsory arbitration, applied on some selective basis, as a possible solution for the breakdown of collective bargaining in "essential" industries, although there is little agreement on what is essential.

The cry is frequently heard that union leaders should use "restraint" in wage negotiations. It is to be hoped that government officials will likewise use restraint in bringing the forces of government to bear in labor disputes. Our experience thus far demonstrates that we do not yet know how to use government power to settle labor-management disputes without seriously weakening the entire collective bargaining process. Further experimentation by the states with various types of legislation should be encouraged, for this can teach valuable lessons without committing the entire nation to what may prove to be an unworkable policy.

Labor policy in a democracy should recognize that government regulation is not a panacea. Every walkout which inconveniences the public should not be met with a demand that "there ought to be a law." Free unionism and free collective bargaining are institutions which are worth preserving. By contrast, the growth of government bureaucracy and the intervention of government in the labor market are tendencies which should not lightly be encouraged.

Yet the trends of the last few years all point to increasing government intervention. This pattern may reflect a change in the national mood. The fifties may go down in history as a decade when America slept. Certainly, complacency ruled the roost after the Korean conflict. Today, the American public may want more action-minded leadership. In the field of industrial relations, however, action and leadership involve a concern with basic underlying economics and relationships, and not a requirement that a high government official jump into every labor dispute which might inconvenience a small segment of the population.

There is certainly ample objective evidence that excessive government intervention makes collective bargaining inoperative and tends generally to exert an upward pressure on settlements. This is true simply because the parties fear to bargain if the top of the bargain is only a floor at which the intervening government official begins to operate amid publicity and outside pressure. And furthermore, why should a union not ask for more if the government is going to "get into the act" and put additional pressure on industry to "compromise" at a higher figure? Why should a management not refuse to settle if by so refusing it can gain a higher price for its products?

The economics of the sixties will be the controlling factor shaping the pattern of union-management relations. Assuming, as seems realistic, that chronic unemployment—now five million—will continue as a problem, that creeping inflation will be a danger, and that foreign competition will become more rather than less severe, it is apparent that, for the good of all, labor relations of the sixties should continue to avoid the massive bargains of the early fifties. If the Kennedy administration continues its policy of frequent intervention instead of permitting collective bargaining to run its course, industry will have the hard choice of giving in to combined union and government pressures and settling for unwarranted cost increases, or fighting it out on the picket line.

Either choice may result in higher settlements for unions and also higher unemployment, higher prices, and further loss of business abroad. Like too much complacency, too much assertion of government interest is disquieting. A little moderation instead of a lot of intervention would seem to be called for in the difficult years ahead.

Indexes

INDEX OF AUTHORS CITED

INDEX OF CASES CITED

E

F

G

H

I

J

K

L

T

U

V

W

Y

SUBJECT INDEX

This book has been set on the Linotype in 12 and 10 point Garamond No. 3, leaded one point. Part numbers and chapter titles are in 18 point Spartan Medium; part titles and chapter numbers are in 18 point Spartan Medium italics. The size of the type page is 27 by 46½ picas.